A COLLEGE FORUM

JOSEPH DOGGETT

EVERETT GILLIS

ROSA BLUDWORTH

THE ODYSSEY PRESS, INC. · NEW YORK

PREFACE

In arriving at the special design that characterizes *A College Forum*, the editors have kept in mind a twofold need: the need of the student for readings that will stimulate his own expression; the need of the instructor for a text that is adaptable to either a subject matter or a types approach.

Six broad areas of human experience are dealt with in this text: man in relation to education, the ideal, society, nature, the arts, and the spirit. The selections within each of the six major divisions are arranged chronologically. Ranging from antiquity to the present day, they provide the student with an increased awareness of his cultural and intellectual heritage.

Literary types include fiction, prose narrative, poetry, drama, and essay. Special emphasis is given to the essay—to its various styles and degrees of formality—so that it may more effectively serve as a model for expository writing.

The questions and exercises at the end of each selection are designed to test the student's reading comprehension, promote independent thinking, and develop his writing skills. Notes about the authors and selections provide the student with the information he will need to understand and appreciate each particular selection.

In ancient Rome the term "forum" was used to designate not only a market place but a central meeting place for judicial and public business. Today the word indicates any assembly for the discussion of public affairs or current questions. A student entering the stimulating forum of college will encounter, through books and class lectures, through discussions with teachers and fellow students, new and challenging thoughts. Perhaps he will even discover that some of his old concepts are subject to penetrating and even hostile scrutiny. He will certainly observe a spirit of open inquiry and respect for the ideas of others—both of which are among the most precious of our academic heritages.

CONTENTS

vii

2 BY DREAMS POSSESSED: MAN AND THE IDEAL 153

3 QUEST TO LIVE: MAN AND SOCIETY 233

4 CONSTANT CHALLENGE: MAN AND NATURE 383

5 THE URGE TO CREATE: MAN AND THE ARTS 443

6 NOT BY BREAD ALONE: MAN AND THE SPIRIT   541

LITERARY TYPES

THE STORY

PROSE NARRATIVE

ESSAY

Elegy

Ode

Sonnet

Narrative Verse

Riddle

Dramatic Monologue

DRAMA

SPECIAL FORMS

Scripture · Sermon · Letter · Poetic Essay

A COLLEGE FORUM

1

JOYS OF THE MIND: MAN AND EDUCATION

My mind to me a kingdom is.
Sir Edward Dyer

Though probably few modern men would say, like Sir Edward Dyer, that they are content with what the mind supplies, all would agree that the mind is a kingdom full of present joys. From the beginning of time men have enjoyed inquiring into the unknown, discovering the truth about life and the universe, learning the mysteries of the sun and the stars.

Each individual is born with his mind a virtual *tabula rasa*, a mind before it has received impressions, on which impinges a chaos of sensation and color, and he must learn for himself everything that he will know. Yet no man, during his life span, will have time enough to learn and discover all that he would like to know.

Since the invention of printing from movable type in the fifteenth century, a great body of printed knowledge and belief has accumulated. So that man may learn as much as possible during his relatively short life span, learning has been made easier by the process of formal education, by concentrated study of the great body of knowledge and belief in institutions of learning.

Some of the following selections give insights into the pattern and significance of schooling in its earliest days. Others reflect an awareness of the importance of education in modern times—of the potentialities and the joys of the mind.

PROVERBS 8

Doth not wisdom cry,
And understanding put forth her voice?
In the top of high places by the way,
Where the paths meet, she standeth;
Beside the gates, at the entry of the city,
At the coming in at the doors, she crieth aloud:

"Unto you, O men, I call;
And my voice is to the sons of men.
O ye simple, understand subtilty;
And, ye fools, be ye of an understanding heart.
Hear, for I will speak excellent things;
And the opening of my lips shall be right things.
For my mouth shall utter truth;
And wickedness is an abomination to my lips.
All the words of my mouth are in righteousness;
There is nothing crooked or perverse in them.
They are all plain to him that understandeth,
And right to them that find knowledge.
Receive my instruction, and not silver;
And knowledge rather than choice gold.
For wisdom is better than rubies;
And all the things that may be desired are not to be
    compared unto her.

I wisdom have made subtilty my dwelling,
And find out knowledge and discretion.
The fear of the Lord is to hate evil:
Pride, and arrogancy, and the evil way,
And the froward mouth, do I hate.
Counsel is mine, and sound knowledge:
I am understanding; I have might.
By me kings reign,
And princes decree justice.
By me princes rule,
And nobles, even all the judges of the earth.

I love them that love me;
And those that seek me diligently shall find me.
Riches and honour are with me;
Yea, durable riches and righteousness.
My fruit is better than gold, yea, than fine gold;
And my revenue than choice silver.
I walk in the way of righteousness,
In the midst of the paths of judgment:
That I may cause those that love me to inherit substance,
And that I may fill their treasuries.

The Lord possessed me in the beginning of his way,
Before his works of old.
I was set up from everlasting, from the beginning,
Or ever the earth was.
When there were no depths, I was brought forth;
When there were no fountains abounding with water.
Before the mountains were settled,
Before the hills was I brought forth:
While as yet he had not made the earth, nor the fields,
Nor the beginning of the dust of the world.
When he established the heavens, I was there:
When he set a circle upon the face of the deep:
When he made firm the skies above:
When the fountain of the deep became strong:
When he gave to the sea its bound,
That the waters should not transgress his commandment:
When he marked out the foundations of the earth:
Then I was by him, as a master workman:
And I was daily his delight,
Rejoicing always before him;
Rejoicing in his habitable earth;
And my delight was with the sons of men.

Now therefore, my sons, hearken unto me:
For blessed are they that keep my ways.
Hear instruction, and be wise,
And refuse it not.
Blessed is the man that heareth me,
Watching daily at my gates,
Waiting at the posts of my doors.
For whoso findeth me findeth life,
And shall obtain favour of the Lord.

But he that sinneth against me wrongeth his own soul:
All they that hate me love death."

Author and Selection Notes

Scholars believe that the date of the Book of Proverbs was probably
300-200 B.C. Although authorship of the Book of Proverbs was at one time
ascribed to Israel's King Solomon, who reigned 973-933 B.C., scholars now
believe it had several authors. The entire book is part of the wisdom literature of the Bible. In Hebrew thought, philosophy had a practical turn:
wisdom was pragmatic and also related to God. The Hebrew tendency to
personalize abstract ideas easily led to the personification of wisdom in
Proverbs 8.

Questions and Exercises

1. Sketch the scene where Wisdom first appears to voice her dramatic
appeal.
2. Observe the measured parallelism of Hebrew poetry: the expression of
thought and its echo. Select five choice examples of this repetition.
3. What is the central thought in stanza two? The first five lines might
be written above the door of any university. The last four lines have been
called the highest point of poetry in the Book of Proverbs.
4. In the opinion of Mary Ellen Chase, author and educator, stanza four
comprises one of the noblest poems in all Old Testament literature. Why
do you think she praises stanza four so highly?
5. How does the conclusion give unity to the whole poem?
6. Why is the Bible considered great literature? How many literary types
does the Bible contain?
7. Theme Topics: Joys of the Mind; The Disciplined Mind; What Is
Wisdom? Adult Education; Does a College Degree Complete One's Education? Knowledge Versus Wisdom.

EARLY EDUCATION

Marcus Aurelius Antoninus

1. From my grandfather Verus [I learned] good morals and the
government of my temper.
2. From the reputation and remembrance of my father, modesty
and a manly character.

From *The Meditations of Marcus Aurelius Antoninus,* translated by George
Long, on pages 193-199 of Volume 2 of the Harvard Classics, edited by Charles
W. Eliot. Copyright 1909 by P. F. Collier & Son; copyright 1937 by P. F. Collier &
Son Corporation. Reprinted by permission.

3. From my mother, piety and beneficence, and abstinence, not only from evil deeds, but even from evil thoughts; and further simplicity in my way of living, far removed from the habits of the rich.

4. From my great-grandfather, not to have frequented public schools, and to have had good teachers at home, and to know that on such things a man should spend liberally.

5. From my governor, to be neither of the green nor of the blue party at the games in the Circus, nor a partizan either of the Parmularius or the Scutarius at the gladiators' fights; from him too I learned endurance of labor, and to want little, and to work with my own hands, and not to meddle with other people's affairs, and not to be ready to listen to slander.

6. From Diognetus, not to busy myself about trifling things, and not to give credit to what was said by miracle-workers and jugglers about incantations and the driving away of daemons and such things; and not to breed quails [for fighting], nor to give myself up passionately to such things; and to endure freedom of speech; and to have become intimate with philosophy; and to have been a hearer, first of Bacchius, then of Tandasis and Marcianus; and to have written dialogues in my youth; and to have desired a plank bed and skin, and whatever else of the kind belongs to the Grecian discipline.

7. From Rusticus I received the impression that my character required improvement and discipline; and from him I learned not to be led astray to sophistic emulation, nor to writing on speculative matters, nor to delivering little hortatory orations, nor to showing myself off as a man who practises much discipline, or does benevolent acts in order to make a display; and to abstain from rhetoric, and poetry, and fine writing; and not to walk about in the house in my outdoor dress, nor to do other things of the kind; and to write my letters with simplicity, like the letter which Rusticus wrote from Sinuessa to my mother; and with respect to those who have offended me by words, or done me wrong, to be easily disposed to be pacified and reconciled, as soon as they have shown a readiness to be reconciled; and to read carefully, and not to be satisfied with a superficial understanding of a book; nor hastily to give my assent to those who talk overmuch; and I am indebted to him for being acquainted with the discourses of Epictetus, which he communicated to me out of his own collection.

8. From Apollonius I learned freedom of will and undeviating steadiness of purpose; and to look to nothing else, not even for a moment, except to reason; and to be always the same, in sharp

pains, on the occasion of the loss of a child, and in long illness; and
to see clearly in a living example that the same man can be both
most resolute and yielding, and not peevish in giving his instruction; and to have had before my eyes a man who clearly considered
his experience and his skill in expounding philosophical principles
as the smallest of his merits; and from him I learned how to receive
from friends what are esteemed favors, without being either humbled by them or letting them pass unnoticed.

9. From Sextus, a benevolent disposition, and the example of a
family governed in a fatherly manner, and the idea of living conformably to nature; and gravity without affectation, and to look
carefully after the interests of friends, and to tolerate ignorant
persons, and those who form opinions without consideration: he
had the power of readily accommodating himself to all, so that
intercourse with him was more agreeable than any flattery; and
at the same time he was most highly venerated by those who
associated with him, and he had the faculty both of discovering
and ordering, in an intelligent and methodical way, the principles
necessary for life; and he never showed anger or any other passion,
but was entirely free from passion, and also most affectionate; and
he could express approbation without noisy display, and he possessed much knowledge without ostentation.

10. From Alexander, the grammarian, to refrain from fault-
finding, and not in a reproachful way to chide those who uttered
any barbarous or solecistic or strange-sounding expression; but
dexterously to introduce the very expression which ought to have
been used, and in the way of answer or giving confirmation, or
joining in an inquiry about the thing itself, not about the word,
or by some other fit suggestion.

11. From Fronto I learned to observe what envy and duplicity
and hypocrisy are in a tyrant, and that generally those among us
who are called Patricians are rather deficient in paternal affection.

12. From Alexander the Platonic, not frequently nor without
necessity to say to any one, or to write in a letter, that I have no
leisure; nor continually to excuse the neglect of duties required by
our relation to those with whom we live, by alleging urgent occupations.

13. From Catulus, not to be indifferent when a friend finds fault,
even if he should find fault without reason, but to try to restore
him to his usual disposition; and to be ready to speak well of
teachers, as it is reported of Domitius and Athenodotus; and to
love my children truly.

14. From my brother Severus, to love my kin, and to love truth,

and to love justice; and through him I learned to know Thrasea, Helvidius, Cato, Dion, Brutus; and from him I received the idea of a polity in which there is the same law for all, a polity administered with regard to equal rights and equal freedom of speech, and the idea of a kingly government which respects most of all the freedom of the governed; I learned from him also consistency and undeviating steadiness in my regard for philosophy, and a disposition to do good, and to give to others readily, and to cherish good hopes, and to believe that I am loved by my friends; and in him I observed no concealment of his opinions with respect to those whom he condemned, and that his friends had no need to conjecture what he wished or did not wish, but it was quite plain.

15. From Maximus I learned self-government, and not to be led aside by anything; and cheerfulness in all circumstances, as well as in illness; and a just admixture in the moral character of sweetness and dignity, and to do what was set before me without complaining. I observed that everybody believed that he thought as he spoke, and that in all that he did he never had any bad intention; and he never showed amazement and surprise, and was never in a hurry, and never put off doing a thing, nor was perplexed nor dejected, nor did he ever laugh to disguise his vexation, nor, on the other hand, was he ever passionate or suspicious. He was accustomed to do acts of beneficence, and was ready to forgive, and was free from all falsehood; and he presented the appearance of a man who could not be diverted from right rather than of a man who had been improved. I observed, too, that no man could ever think that he was despised by Maximus, or ever venture to think himself a better man. He had also the art of being humorous in an agreeable way.

16. In my father I observed mildness of temper, and unchangeable resolution in the things which he had determined after due deliberation; and no vainglory in those things which men call honors; and a love of labor and perseverance; and a readiness to listen to those who had anything to propose for the common weal; and undeviating firmness in giving to every man according to his deserts; and a knowledge derived from experience of the occasions for vigorous action and for remission. And I observed that he had overcome all passion for joys; and he considered himself no more than any other citizen, and he released his friends from all obligation to sup with him or to attend him of a necessity when he went abroad, and those who failed to accompany him by reason of any urgent circumstances, always found him the same. I observed, too, his habit of careful inquiry in all matters of deliberation, and his

persistency, and that he never stopped his investigation through being satisfied with appearances which first present themselves; and that his disposition was to keep his friends, and not to be soon tired of them, nor yet to be extravagant in his affection; and to be satisfied on all occasions, and cheerful; and to foresee things a long way off, and to provide for the smallest without display; and to check immediately popular applause and flattery, and to be ever watchful over the things which were necessary for the administration of the empire, and to be a good manager of the expenditure, and patiently to endure the blame which he got for such conduct; and he was neither superstitious with respect to the gods, nor did he court men by gifts or by trying to please them, or by flattering the populace; but he showed sobriety in all things and firmness, and never any mean thoughts or action, nor love of novelty. And the things which conduce in any way to the commodity of life, and of which fortune gives an abundant supply, he used without arrogance and without excusing himself; so that when he had them, he enjoyed them without affectation, and when he had them not he did not want them. No one could ever say of him that he was either a sophist or a [home-bred] flippant slave or a pedant; but every one acknowledged him to be a man ripe, perfect, above flattery, able to manage his own and other men's affairs. Besides this, he honored those who were true philosophers, and he did not reproach those who pretended to be philosophers, nor yet was he easily led by them. He was also easy in conversation, and he made himself agreeable without any offensive affectation. He took a reasonable care of his body's health, not as one who was greatly attached to life, nor out of regard to personal appearance, nor yet in a careless way, but so that, through his own attention, he very seldom stood in need of the physician's art or of medicine or external applications. He was most ready to give way without envy to those who possessed any particular faculty, such as that of eloquence or knowledge of the law or of morals, or of anything else; and he gave them his help, that each might enjoy reputation according to his deserts; and he always acted conformably to the institutions of his country, without showing any affectation of doing so. Further, he was not fond of change, nor unsteady, but he loved to stay in the same places, and to employ himself about the same things; and after his paroxysms of headache he came immediately fresh and vigorous to his usual occupations. His secrets were not many, but very few and very rare, and these only about public matters; and he showed prudence and economy in the exhibition of the public spectacles and the construction of public buildings, his donations to the people, and in such things, for he was a man who looked to what ought to be done, not to the reputation which is got by a man's acts. He did not take the bath at unseasonable hours; he was not fond of building houses, nor curious about what he ate, nor about the texture and colour of his clothes, nor about the beauty of his slaves. His dress came from Lorium, his villa on the coast, and from Lanuvium generally. We know how he behaved to the toll-collector at Tusculum who asked his pardon; and such was all his behaviour. There was in him nothing harsh, nor implacable, nor violent, nor, as one may say, anything carried to the sweating point: but he examined all things severally as if he had abundance of time, and without confusion, in an orderly way, vigorously and consistently. And that might be applied to him which is recorded of Socrates, that he was able both to abstain from, and to enjoy, those things which many are too weak to abstain from, and cannot enjoy without excess. But to be strong enough both to bear the one and to be sober in the other is the mark of a man who has a perfect and invincible soul, such as he showed in the illness of Maximus.

17. To the gods I am indebted for having good grandfathers, good parents, a good sister, good teachers, good associates, good kinsmen and friends, nearly everything good. Further, I owe it to the gods that I was not hurried into any offence against any of them, though I had a disposition which, if opportunity had offered, might have led me to do something of this kind; but, through their favour, there never was such a concurrence of circumstances as put me to the trial. Further, I am thankful to the gods that I was not longer brought up with my grandfather's concubine, and that I preserved the flower of my youth, and that I did not make proof of my virility before the proper season, but even deferred the time; that I was subjected to a ruler and a father who was able to take away all pride from me, and to bring me to the knowledge that it is possible for a man to live in a palace without wanting either guards or embroidered dresses, or torches and statues, and such-like show; but it is in such a man's power to bring himself very near to the fashion of a private person, without being for this reason either meaner in thought, or more remiss in action, with respect to the things which must be done for the public interest in a manner that befits a ruler. I thank the gods for giving me such a brother, who was able by his moral character to rouse me to vigilance over myself, and who, at the same time, pleased me by his respect and affection; that my children have not been stupid nor deformed in body; that I did not make more proficiency in

rhetoric, poetry, and the other studies, in which I should perhaps have been completely engaged, if I had seen that I was making progress in them; that I made haste to place those who brought me up in the station of honour, which they seemed to desire without putting them off with hope of my doing it some time after, because they were then still young; that I knew Apollonius, Rusticus, Maximus; that I received clear and frequent impressions about living according to nature, and what kind of a life that is, so that, so far as depended on the gods, and their gifts and help, and inspirations, nothing hindered me from forthwith living according to nature, though I still fall short of it through my own fault, and though not observing the admonitions of the gods, and, I may almost say, their direct instructions; that my body had held out so long in such a kind of life; that I never touched either Benedicta or Theodotus, and that, after having fallen into amatory passions, I was cured; and, though I was often out of humor with Rusticus, I never did anything of which I had occasion to repent; that, though it was my mother's fate to die young, she spent the last years of her life with me; that whenever I wished to help any man in his need, or on any other occasion, I was never told that I had not the means of doing it; and that to myself the same necessity never happened, to receive any thing from another; that I have such a wife, so obedient, and so affectionate, and so simple; that I had abundance of good masters for my children; and that remedies have been shown to me by dreams, both others, and against blood-spitting and giddiness; . . . and that, when I had an inclination to philosophy I did not fall into the hands of any sophist, and that I did not waste my time on writers [of histories], or in the resolution of syllogisms, or occupy myself about the investigation of appearances in the heavens; for all these things require the help of the gods and fortune.

Author and Selection Notes

From the pen of one of the greatest Roman emperors, Marcus Aurelius Antoninus (121-180), we have an intimate glimpse of the man himself revealed through his *Meditations,* a collection recording his thoughts on various subjects. Between the military and administrative duties of his strenuous life, Marcus Aurelius wrote about one's obligation to duty, his moral responsibility, his debt to others who have enriched his own life. "Early Education" is really an introduction to the *Meditations,* which consists of twelve books.

Questions and Exercises

1. In the section in which he acknowledges his indebtedness to the gods, Marcus Aurelius names three of his teachers: Rusticus, Apollonius, and Maximus. What does he feel he owes to them? (See sections 7, 8, and 15.)

2. Rusticus introduced Marcus Aurelius to the discourses of Epictetus. Who is Epictetus? Why is the author so glad to learn about Epictetus?

3. Marcus Aurelius' education came from contact with both teachers and family. Make a distinction between what he learned from family and from teachers.

4. The father mentioned in section 2 is probably his real father, who died when Marcus Aurelius was a few months old. He was then adopted by his grandfather and later at seventeen years of age by the emperor Antonius Pius. Section 16 is an appreciation of this foster father, whom he calls "ruler" and "father." What did he learn from this father that helped make him the good and generous ruler that he was?

5. Because of his teachers, Marcus Aurelius valued learning, moderation, and self-discipline. Point out passages that stress these virtues.

6. How did Marcus Aurelius' education differ from twentieth-century education in America?

7. Theme Topics: A Great Teacher I Have Known; My Father (or Mother) as Teacher; My Education at Home; What I Owe to Good Teachers.

THE STATE OF LEARNING IN ENGLAND
King Alfred the Great

King Alfred sends his affectionate and friendly greetings to Bishop Werferth;[1] and I make known to thee that I have very often had in mind what learned men there formerly were throughout England both in religious and in secular positions; and what a happy time it was then throughout England; and how the kings who held rule over the people in those days were obedient to God and to his representatives; and how they maintained peace and good morals and order at home and also extended their territory abroad; and how they prospered both in war and in wisdom; and the clerical orders, also, how eager they were both in teaching

From *British Poetry and Prose,* Shorter Edition, eds. Lieder, Lovett, and Root. Copyright 1951 by Houghton Mifflin Company. Reprinted by permission of the publisher.

[1] Bishop of Worcester from 873 till his death in 915.

and in learning and in all the services they owed to God; and how people from abroad came to seek wisdom and instruction in our land, and how we now have to go abroad to get wisdom and instruction, if we are to have them at all. So completely had learning fallen away in England that there were very few south of the River Humber who could understand their church services in English or could translate a letter from Latin into English; and I think that there were not many beyond the Humber. So few there were that I cannot remember a single one south of the Thames at the time I succeeded to the kingdom. Thanks be to almighty God that we now have any supply of teachers! And therefore I command thee to see to it, as I believe thou desirest to do, that thou free thyself from the things of this world as often as possible so as to lay hold on the wisdom that God has given thee. Think what punishments in this world have come upon us because we have neither loved wisdom ourselves nor have allowed other men to seek it. We have loved the bare name of being Christians, but very few of us the Christian virtues.

When I remembered all this, I remembered also how, before the country was all ravaged and burned,[2] I had seen the churches all over England filled with treasures and with books and also a great company of God's ministers. And yet they had very little profit of the books, and could not at all understand them, because they were not written in their own language. It was as though they had said: "Our forefathers who held these places before us loved wisdom, and through wisdom they achieved prosperity and bequeathed it to us. We can still see their path, but we cannot follow after them; and so we have lost both the prosperity and the wisdom, because we would not incline our mind to follow in their footsteps."

When I remembered all this, I wondered greatly why of the good scholars who were formerly to be found throughout England, and who had fully learned all these books, no one translated any part of them into their own language. And I straightway answered myself and said: "They never supposed that men would become so heedless and that learning should so fall away; that is why they did not translate the books. And they thought that the more languages we knew, the greater would be the wisdom of our land."

Then I remembered that the Law was first written in the Hebrew language, and then when the Greeks had learned it they translated it into their own language, and all other books also. And then the Romans did the same; as soon as they had learned it, they trans-

---

[2] i.e., by the Danes.

lated it all by means of wise interpreters into their own language. And all other Christian nations also translated some part of the books into their own language. And so it seems good to me, if it does to you also, that we too should translate into the language that we all can understand such books as it is most needful for all men to know; and that we should make provision, as we very easily may do with God's help if we have a time of peace, that all the young men of England who are sons of free men, and whose parents have the means to provide for them, should be sent to school during the years when they are not fit for other employment, and until they are well able to read English. We may then give further instruction in the Latin language to those whom we wish further to educate and to prepare for one of the higher occupations.

When I remembered how the learning of the Latin language has already fallen off throughout England, and yet many can read English writings, I began, among the many other various and manifold cares of this kingdom, to translate into English the book which in Latin is called *Pastoralis* and in English *Shepherd's Book*, sometimes word by word and sometimes meaning by meaning, as I had learned it from Plegmund my archbishop, and from Asser my bishop, and from Grimbold my mass-priest, and from John my mass-priest. And when I had learned it that I understood it and could interpret its meaning fully, I translated it into English. And I desire to send a copy to every diocese in my kingdom; and in each copy there is a bookmark worth fifty mancuses.[3] And I command in God's name that no one remove the bookmark from the book, nor the book from the cathedral; no one knows how long there will be such learned bishops as now, thank God, are to be found almost everywhere. Therefore I have desired that the books be always in their proper places, unless the bishop wishes to take them with him, or they are on loan somewhere, or someone is making new copies of them.

Author and Selection Notes

King Alfred the Great (849-899), who established the overlordship of the West Saxon royal house, reigned as King of England from 871 to 899. Strong enough as a ruler to halt the invading Danes and fortify the English navy, he was also the intellectual leader of his people and did much to remedy the desolation in learning and education which resulted from the invasion of the Danes. He brought great scholars to England, established schools, encouraged the writing of the *Anglo-Saxon Chronicle*, and through

[3] A mancus was worth one-eighth of a pound.

his own translations became the father of English prose. The preceding selection is his Preface to the translation of Pope Gregory's *Pastoral Care.*

Questions and Exercises

1. Refer to a good encyclopedia for information about the political and social condition of King Alfred's realm. Discuss the significance of his reference to the Humber River. What had caused the low state of learning which Alfred deplores?

2. Why is the title "The Great" reserved for Alfred among all of England's kings? Which of his great contributions are mentioned in this selection?

3. Complete the list of his great contributions to his people.

4. Explain why Alfred ordered that no one remove a book from the cathedral.

5. What purpose is served by the repetition of "When I remembered" and "Then I remembered" as introductory words to the paragraphs?

6. Analyze the organization and the style of writing in "The State of Learning in England." Note how many times the word "and" is repeated.

7. Theme Topics: Johnny Still Can't Read! Federal Aid to Education; A One-Man Campaign for Reform; Care for Public Property; Learning to Capacity.

HOW THE STUDENT SHOULD BEHAVE
John of Garland

Learn how to entertain at table, to provide food and the sauces that go with the various dishes, and to serve seasonable wine in modest quantity. Once again I touch critically on manners in polite society so that my readers may become more genteel. According to good custom you should place the sauce on the right, the service plate on the left; you should have the servant take the first course to him who sits at the head of the table. Take hold of the base of a goblet so that unsightly finger marks may not show on the side. Polite diners pause over their cup, but gluttons, who live like mules and weevils, empty it with one draught. Pour wine properly with both hands so as not to spill any. Always serve two pieces of bread. Have several well-dressed servants in readiness to bring clean towels and to supply the wants of the guests. Lest I should seem to be in

From *Morale Scholarium,* translated by L. J. Paetow. Copyright 1927 by University of California Press. Reprinted by permission.

charge of the cooks like Nebuzaradan, I shall not go into the art of preparing fine dishes. Carve the meats which are not to be served in the broth, and skilfully take off the wings of fowl while they are hot. He who takes a walk or a brief nap after dinner preserves his health. If you wish to regain your strength as a convalescent, and keep your health when you are well, drink moderately. All Epicureans live impure lives; they lose their eyesight; they are rude, unclean, and are doomed to die a sudden death. . . .

The sage of Miletus set down these rules of polite behaviour for which we should be grateful. Regulate your household soberly; do your civic duties cheerfully; have a word of greeting for strangers as for friends; do your utmost to avoid altercations with irate associates; with a smile and a witticism cover up the faults of others; be faultless at table, glad even to entertain your enemies; bear your misfortunes with fortitude and do not let your head be turned by good fortune. Make an effort to follow these seven rules of courtliness. May you be decked out with them, you who declare yourself to be a scholar; unless you have such urbanities you are taken for a rustic. . . .

Even though you be a Socrates, if you have rude manners, you are a ditch-digger. Avoid these seven rusticities which are signalled by Thales, the sage. Light-minded talk is unseemly at table; so is presumption and constant contention. It is rude to be ungrateful or cruel towards the poor. It is reprehensible to be haughty towards your dear friends; if you reject good advice, you are a fool; and you lack the light of reason if you fly in the face of God. These good precepts are not hidden away but are written in the public theatre. Avoid these things lest you be consigned behind the gates of hell. . . .

You will be courteous if you perform the following works of mercy; if at night you give beds to the poor, if you heal the sick, if you clothe the freezing, give food to the beggar, console the afflicted, and offer drink to the thirsty. . . .

Regard as models of deportment the graven images of the churches, which you should carry in your mind as living and indelible pictures. Cherish again the violets of civility without blemish so that, when your blindness has vanished, the eyes of your soul may have no wasting disease. Be not a fornicator, O student, a robber, a murderer, a deceitful merchant, a champion at dice. In the choir-stalls a cleric should chant without noise and commotion. I advocate that the ordinary layman, who does not sing, be kept out of the choir. A student, who is a churchman, is expected to follow good custom, to be willing to serve, to fee the notary who has drawn up a charter for him, to gladden the giver. Do not constantly urge your horse on with the spur, which should be used only on rare occasions. Give your horse the reins when he mounts an incline; fearing a serious accident, avoid crossing swollen rivers, or the Rhine. If a bridge is not safe, you should dismount and let the horse pick his way over the smooth parts. Mount gently on the left stirrup. Select beautiful equestrian trappings suitable to your clerical station. Ride erect unless you are bent by age. If you are of the elect you should have a rich saddle cloth. The cross should be exalted, the voice be raised in prayer, Christ should be worshipped, the foot should be taken out of the stirrup. The horseman will descend from his horse and say his prayers; no matter how far he then will travel, he will ride in safety. He who wishes to serve should be quick, not go to sleep, and not give way to anger against his lord. Avoid drunkards, those who indulge in secret sin, those who like to beat and strike, those who love lewdness, evil games, and quarrels. Passing a cemetery, if you are well-bred, and if you hope for salvation, you pause to pray that the dead may rest in peace. Have nothing to do with the prostitute, but love your wife; all wives should be honoured but especially those who are distinguished by virtue. A person who is well should not recline at table in the fashion of the ancients. When you walk after dinner keep on frequented streets. Avoid insincere speeches. Unless you wish to be considered a fool learn to keep your mouth shut in season. Stand and sit upright, do not scratch yourself. . . .

I must speak about medical matters and drugs, but Phoebus shows that they are harmful if taken too often. In order that a man be kept entirely healthy this chapter is added so that the mind may be purified and the body strengthened. Nutmeg may be taken as well as cloves, musk may be given, fennel may be eaten by anybody; they expel gas from the stomach and thus, along with the triple compartments of the brain, they comfort the cerebellum. By means of cooked pears you can take away fevers with marvellous results. Pliris is good for weak and melancholy men. The thin flux (usia) is cured by means of diapenidia. Ygia is good for rheumatics, athanasia for flux of the bowels. Give diaciminum and sweet wine to those who have indigestion. Justinum and goat's blood dissolve stone in the bladder. Diaprunis makes you immune to fevers; when given to patients who have fasted, a decoction with prunes from Damascus allays fevers. A sane diet is essential to a life of happiness; thus you will be strong and vigorous when health, the aim of the physician, is yours. . . .

Exhibit a good deportment in deeds, and in words; learn the

custom of the country in which you happen to be. Do not be noisy, rash in your actions, odious because of your insulting words, wrathful about little annoyances. You should never despair if you suffer on account of sin; you will bear all the bitterness of poverty, knowing that you are an heir of the eternal Prince. Be peaceful among peaceful citizens, be like a rich patron among the poor. You should disassociate yourself from the rich, for, a celibate on earth, you will dwell with Christ, the celibate, in heaven. Hasten to help a needy friend, give him money if you can. Be a good debtor and hasten to pay your debts lest you be condemned by your burden of sin and by the peasant bewailing his losses. You should take good care of your horse, give him enough water, clean straw when he is worn out, and enough of the kind of food he likes to eat. There are more such precepts for him who wishes to know all the rules of politeness; as such, make it your ambition, by careful study, to learn them.

Author and Selection Notes

Although he was born in England, John of Garland (1202-1252), who was known as Johannes Garlandius, or, more commonly, Johannes de Garlandia, spent most of his life in France, where he was a professor at the University of Paris, one of the oldest universities in Europe. Founded about the middle of the twelfth century, it soon became the chief center of learning in the Western world, excelling especially in theology, "the queen of studies." John of Garland, a Latin grammarian and poet, stresses mundane affairs and discusses religious practices of his time in the preceding essay. Actually he serves as a medieval "Mr. Emily Post."

Questions and Exercises

1. Notice how much besides polite manners John of Garland reveals about medieval life. What do you learn about religious and medical practices, for example?

2. What part of his advice about social behavior still holds good?

3. Find several amusing passages where advice is offered concerning widely different matters all in the same sentence.

4. Analyze John of Garland's writing style and compare it with that of twentieth-century selections which are similar in purpose and content.

5. Theme Topics: Rules for the Polite Driver; Table Manners; Manners at Church; Classroom Manners; Campus Manners and Morals; Who Is a Gentleman (or Lady)?

[handwritten: House of Northumbeland: Henry Percy (HOTSPUR)]

THE FIRST PART OF KING HENRY THE FOURTH

William Shakespeare

DRAMATIS PERSONÆ.

KING HENRY THE FOURTH.
HENRY, *Prince of Wales,* *[handwritten: House of Lancaster]*
JOHN OF LANCASTER, } *Sons to the King.*
EARL OF WESTMORELAND.
SIR WALTER BLUNT.
THOMAS PERCY, *Earl of Worcester.—* *[handwritten: brothers]*
HENRY PERCY, *Earl of Northumberland.—*
HENRY PERCY surnamed HOTSPUR, *his son.*
EDMUND MORTIMER, *Earl of March.* *[handwritten: heir —]*
RICHARD SCROOP, *Archbishop of York.*
ARCHIBALD, *Earl of Douglas.*
OWEN GLENDOWER. *[handwritten: — Welsh chieftain – Magician]*
SIR RICHARD VERNON.
SIR JOHN FALSTAFF.
SIR MICHAEL, *a Friend to the Archbishop of York.*
POINS.
GADSHILL.
PETO.
BARDOLPH.
LADY PERCY, *Wife to Hotspur, and Sister to Mortimer.*
LADY MORTIMER, *Daughter to Glendower, and Wife to Mortimer.*
MISTRESS QUICKLY, *Hostess of a Tavern in Eastcheap.*
Lords, Officers, Sheriff, Vintner, Chamberlain, Drawers, Carriers, Travellers, and Attendants.

[handwritten: Dramatic irony]

SCENE.—*England*

ACT I.

SCENE I.—*London. The Palace.*

Enter KING HENRY, WESTMORELAND, *and Others.*

K. HEN. So shaken as we are, so wan with care,
Find we a time for frighted peace to pant, *[handwritten: uneasy peace]*
And breathe short-winded accents of new broils
To be commenc'd in strands afar remote. *[handwritten: (Referring to France)]*
No more the thirsty entrance of this soil   5
Shall daub her lips with her own children's blood;
No more shall trenching war channel her fields,

*[handwritten left margin: ll. 1-33
1. Shaken & weary from civil war
2. No more Civil War — D't
3. Simile: Meteors in A troubled sky]*

*[handwritten bottom:
3. Crusades planned
5. Levy an army
6. To fight Moslems in Jerusalem
7. Crusades delayed Yr. —
8. Why – in order that Henry could gain throne]*

Nor bruise her flowerets with the armed hoofs　　*trouble forecast*
Of hostile paces: those opposed eyes,
Which, like the (meteors) of a troubled heaven,　　　　　10
All of one nature, of one substance bred, — *common cause*
Did lately meet in the intestine shock　　*internal — Civil War*
And furious close of civil butchery,
Shall now, in mutual well-beseeming ranks, *irony*
March all one way, and be no more oppos'd　　　　　15
Against acquaintance, kindred, and allies: *improperly place —*
The edge of war, like an ill-sheathed knife,
No more shall cut his master. Therefore, friends,
As far as to the sepulchre of Christ, — *Jerusalem*
Whose soldier now, under whose blessed cross　　　20
We are impressed and engag'd to fight,
Forthwith a power of English shall we levy, — *pay some soldiers*
Turkey Whose arms were moulded in their mothers' womb — *predestined*
Moslem To chase these pagans in those holy fields
Sect Over whose acres walk'd those blessed feet　　　25
Which fourteen hundred years ago were nail'd
Salvation For our advantage on the bitter cross.
But this our purpose is a twelvemonth old, — *plans — been fighting*
And bootless 'tis to tell you we will go,　　*Civil War*
recession Therefore we meet not now. Then let me hear　　30
Of you, my gentle cousin Westmoreland,
What yesternight our council did decree — *King's Council*
In forwarding this dear expedience.
　　WEST.   My liege, this haste was hot in question,
And many limits of the charge set down　　　　　35
But yesternight; when all athwart there came
A post from Wales loaden with heavy news;
Whose worst was, that the noble Mortimer,
Leading the men of Herefordshire to fight
Against the irregular and wild Glendower,　　　　40
Was by the rude hands of that Welshman taken,
A thousand of his people butchered;
Upon whose dead corpse there was such misuse,
Such beastly shameless transformation
By those Welshwomen done, as may not be　　　　45
Without much shame re-told or spoken of.
　　K. HEN. It seems then that the tidings of this broil
Brake off our business for the Holy Land.
　　WEST. This match'd with other like, my gracious lord;
For more uneven and unwelcome news　　　　　50

9. Thereby breaking
Chain of being
10. Wants advice on plans for Crusade

Came from the north, and thus it did import:
On Holy-rood day, the gallant Hotspur there,
Young Harry Percy and brave Archibald,
That ever-valiant and approved Scot,
At Holmedon met,   55
Where they did spend a sad and bloody hour;
As by discharge of their artillery,
And shape of likelihood, the news was told;
For he that brought them, in the very heat
And pride of their contention did take horse,   60
Uncertain of the issue any way.
   K. HEN. Here is a dear and true industrious friend,
Sir Walter Blunt, new lighted from his horse,
Stain'd with the variation of each soil
Betwixt that Holmedon and this seat of ours;   65
And he hath brought us smooth and welcome news.
The Earl of Douglas is discomfited;
Ten thousand bold Scots, two-and-twenty knights,
Balk'd in their own blood, did Sir Walter see
On Holmedon's plains: of prisoners Hotspur took   70
Mordake the Earl of Fife, and eldest son
To beaten Douglas, and the Earl of Athol,
Of Murray, Angus, and Menteith.
And is not this an honourable spoil?
A gallant prize? ha, cousin, is it not?   75
   WEST. In faith,
It is a conquest for a prince to boast of.
   K. HEN. Yea, there thou mak'st me sad, and mak'st me sin
In envy that my Lord Northumberland
Should be the father to so blest a son;   80
A son who is the theme of honour's tongue;
Amongst a grove the very straightest plant;
Who is sweet Fortune's minion and her pride:
Whilst I, by looking on the praise of him,
See riot and dishonour stain the brow   85
Of my young Harry. O! that it could be prov'd
That some night-tripping fairy had exchang'd
In cradle-clothes our children where they lay,
And call'd mine Percy, his Plantagenet.
Then would I have his Harry, and he mine.   90
But let him from my thoughts. What think you, coz,
Of this young Percy's pride? the prisoners,
Which he in this adventure hath surpris'd,

To his own use he keeps, and sends me word,
I shall have none but Mordake Earl of Fife.   95

WEST. This is his uncle's teaching, this is Worcester,
Malevolent to you in all aspects;
Which makes him prune himself, and bristle up
The crest of youth against your dignity.

K. HEN. But I have sent for him to answer this;   100
And for this cause awhile we must neglect
Our holy purpose to Jerusalem.
Cousin, on Wednesday next our council we
Will hold at Windsor; so inform the lords:
But come yourself with speed to us again;   105
For more is to be said and to be done
Than out of anger can be uttered.

WEST. I will, my liege.   *Exeunt.*

SCENE II.—*The Same. An Apartment of the*
PRINCE'S.

Enter the PRINCE *and* FALSTAFF.

FAL. Now, Hal, what time of day is it, lad?

PRINCE. Thou are so fat-witted, with drinking of old sack, and
unbuttoning thee after supper, and sleeping upon benches after
noon, that thou hast forgotten to demand that truly which thou
would'st truly know. What a devil has thou to do with the time [5
of the day? Unless hours were cups of sack, and minutes capons, and
clocks the tongues of bawds, and dials the signs of leaping-houses,
and the blessed sun himself a fair hot wench in flame-coloured
taffeta, I see no reason why thou should'st be so superfluous to
demand the time of the day.   10

FAL. Indeed, you come near me now, Hal; for we that take
purses go by the moon and the seven stars, and not by Phœbus, he,
'that wandering knight so fair.' And, I prithee, sweet wag, when
thou art king, as, God save thy grace, majesty, I should say, for
grace thou wilt have none,—   15

PRINCE. What! none?

FAL. No, by my troth; not so much as will serve to be prologue
to an egg and butter.

PRINCE. Well, how then? come roundly, roundly.

FAL. Marry, then, sweet wag, when thou art king, let not us [20
that are squires of the night's body be called thieves of the day's
beauty: let us be Diana's foresters, gentlemen of the shade, minions
of the moon; and let men say we be men of good government, being

governed as the sea is, by our noble and chaste mistress the moon, under whose countenance we steal.   25

PRINCE. Thou sayest well, and it holds well too; for the fortune of us that are the moon's men doth ebb and flow like the sea, being governed as the sea is, by the moon. As for proof now: a purse of gold most resolutely snatched on Monday night and most dissolutely spent on Tuesday morning; got with swearing 'Lay by,' and [30 spent with crying 'Bring in'; now in as low an ebb as the foot of the ladder, and by and by in as high a flow as the ridge of the gallows.

FAL. By the Lord, thou sayest true, lad. And is not my hostess of the tavern a most sweet wench?   35

PRINCE. As the honey of Hybla, my old lad of the castle. And is not a buff jerkin a most sweet robe of durance?

FAL. How now, how now, mad wag? what? in thy quips and thy quiddities? what a plague have I to do with a buff jerkin?

PRINCE. Why, what a pox have I to do with my hostess of [40 the tavern?

FAL. Well, thou hast called her to a reckoning many a time and oft.

PRINCE. Did I ever call for thee to pay thy part?

FAL. No; I'll give thee thy due, thou hast paid all there.   45

PRINCE. Yea, and elsewhere, so far as my coin would stretch; and where it would not, I have used my credit.

FAL. Yea, and so used it that, were it not here apparent that thou art heir apparent,—But, I prithee, sweet wag, shall there be gallows standing in England when thou art king, and resolution thus [50 fobbed as it is with the rusty curb of old father antick the law? Do not thou, when thou art king, hang a thief.

PRINCE. No; thou shalt.

FAL. Shall I? O rare! By the Lord, I'll be a brave judge.

PRINCE. Thou judgest false already; I mean thou shalt have [55 the hanging of the thieves and so become a rare hangman.

FAL. Well, Hal, well; and in some sort it jumps with my humour as well as waiting in the court, I can tell you.

PRINCE. For obtaining of suits?

FAL. Yea, for obtaining of suits, whereof the hangman hath [60 no lean wardrobe. 'Sblood, I am as melancholy as a gib cat, or a lugged bear.

PRINCE. Or an old lion, or a lover's lute.

FAL. Yea, or the drone of a Lincolnshire bagpipe.

PRINCE. What sayest thou to a hare, or the melancholy of [65 Moor-ditch?

FAL. Thou hast the most unsavoury similes, and art indeed the most comparative, rascalliest, sweet young prince. But, Hal, I prithee, trouble me no more with vanity. I would to God thou and I knew where a commodity of good names were to be bought. An old [70 lord of the council rated me the other day in the street about you, sir, but I marked him not; and yet he talked very wisely, but I regarded him not; and yet he talked wisely, and in the street too.

PRINCE. Thou didst well; for wisdom cries out in the streets, and no man regards it. [75

FAL. O! thou hast damnable iteration, and art indeed able to corrupt a saint. Thou hast done much harm upon me, Hal; God forgive thee for it! Before I knew thee, Hal, I knew nothing; and now am I, if a man should speak truly, little better than one of the wicked. I must give over this life, and I will give it over; by the [80 Lord, an I do not, I am a villain: I'll be damned for never a king's son in Christendom.

PRINCE. Where shall we take a purse to-morrow, Jack?

FAL. 'Zounds! where thou wilt, lad, I'll make one; an I do not, call me villain and baffle me. 85

PRINCE. I see a good amendment of life in thee; from praying to purse-taking.

Enter POINS, *at a distance.*

FAL. Why, Hal, 'tis my vocation, Hal; 'tis no sin for a man to labour in his vocation. Poins? Now shall we know if Gadshill have set a match. O! if men were to be saved by merit, what hole in [90 hell were hot enough for him? This is the most omnipotent villain that ever cried 'Stand!' to a true man.

PRINCE. Good morrow, Ned.

POINS. Good morrow, sweet Hal. What says Monsieur Remorse? What says Sir John Sack-and-Sugar? Jack! how agrees the devil [95 and thee about thy soul, that thou soldest him on Good-Friday last for a cup of Madeira and a cold capon's leg?

PRINCE. Sir John stands to his word, the devil shall have his bargain; for he was never yet a breaker of proverbs: he will give the devil his due. 100

POINS. Then art thou damned for keeping thy word with the devil.

PRINCE. Else he had been damned for cozening the devil.

POINS. But, my lads, my lads to-morrow morning, by four o'clock, early at Gadshill! There are pilgrims going to Canterbury with [105 rich offerings, and traders riding to London with fat purses: I have vizards for you all; you have horses for yourselves. Gadshill lies to-night in Rochester; I have bespoke supper to-morrow night in

East-cheap: we may do it as secure as sleep. If you will go I will stuff your purses full of crowns; if you will not, tarry at home [110 and be hanged.

FAL. Hear ye, Yedward: if I tarry at home and go not, I'll hang you for going.

POINS. You will, chops?

FAL. Hal, wilt thou make one?   115

PRINCE. Who, I rob? I a thief? not I, by my faith.

FAL. There's neither honesty, manhood, nor good fellowship in thee, no thou camest not of the blood royal, if thou darest not stand for ten shillings.

PRINCE. Well then, once in my days I'll be a madcap.   120

FAL. Why, that's well said.

PRINCE. Well, come what will, I'll tarry at home.

FAL. By the Lord, I'll be a traitor then, when thou art king.

PRINCE. I care not.

POINS. Sir John, I prithee, leave the prince and me alone: [155 I will lay him down such reasons for this adventure that he shall go.

FAL. Well, God give thee the spirit of persuasion, and him the ears of profiting, that what thou speakest may move, and what he hears may be believed, that the true prince may, for recreation sake, prove a false thief; for the poor abuses of the time want count- [160 enance. Farewell: you shall find me in Eastcheap.

PRINCE. Farewell, thou latter spring! Farewell, all-hallown summer!   *Exit* FALSTAFF.

POINS. Now, my good sweet honey lord, ride with us to-morrow: I have a jest to execute that I cannot manage alone. Falstaff, [165 Bardolph, Peto, and Gadshill shall rob those men that we have already waylaid; yourself and I will not be there; and when they have the booty, if you and I do not rob them, cut this head off from my shoulders.

PRINCE. But how shall we part with them in setting forth?   170

POINS. Why, we will set forth before or after them, and appoint them a place of meeting, wherein it is at our pleasure to fail; and then will they adventure upon the exploit themselves, which they shall have no sooner achieved but we'll set upon them.

PRINCE. Yea, but 'tis like that they will know us by our [175 horses, by our habits, and by every other appointment, to be ourselves.

POINS. Tut! our horses they shall not see, I'll tie them in the wood; our vizards we will change after we leave them; and, sirrah, I have cases of buckram for the nonce, to immask our noted [180 outward garments.

PRINCE. Yea, but I doubt they will be too hard for us.

POINS. Well, for two of them, I know them to be as true-bred cowards as ever turned back; and for the third, if he fight longer than he sees reason, I'll forswear arms. The virtue of this jest [185 will be, the incomprehensible lies that this same fat rogue will tell us when we meet at supper: how thirty, at least, he fought with; what wards, what blows, what extremities he endured; and in the reproof of this lies the jest.

PRINCE. Well, I'll go with thee: provide us all things neces- [190 sary and meet me to-morrow night in Eastcheap; there I'll sup. Farewell.

POINS. Farewell, my lord.   *Exit.*

PRINCE. I know you all, and will awhile uphold
The unyok'd humour of your idleness;   105
Yet herein will I imitate the sun,
Who doth permit the base contagious clouds
To smother up his beauty from the world,
That when he please again to be himself,
Being wanted, he may be more wonder'd at,   200
By breaking through the foul and ugly mists
Of vapours that did seem to strangle him.
If all the year were playing holidays,
To sport would be as tedious as to work;
But when they seldom come, they wish'd for come,   205
And nothing pleaseth but rare accidents.
So, when this loose behaviour I throw off,
And pay the debt I never promised,
By how much better than my word I am
By so much shall I falsify men's hopes;   210
And like bright metal on a sullen ground,
My reformation, glittering o'er my fault,
Shall show more goodly and attract more eyes
Than that which hath no foil to set it off.
I'll so offend to make offence a skill,   215
Redeeming time when men think least I will.

                                                                Exit.

SCENE III.—*The Same.   The Palace.*

Enter KING HENRY, NORTHUMBERLAND, WORCESTER, HOTSPUR,
        SIR WALTER BLUNT, *and Others.*

K. HEN. My blood hath been too cold and temperate,
Unapt to stir at these indignities,
And you have found me; for accordingly

You tread upon my patience: but be sure
I will from henceforth rather be myself,   5
Mighty, and to be fear'd, than my condition,
Which hath been smooth as oil, soft as young down,
And therefore lost that title of respect
Which the proud soul ne'er pays but to the proud.

    Wor. Our house, my sovereign liege, little deserves   10
The scourge of greatness to be used on it;
And that same greatness too which our own hands
Have holp to make so portly.

    North. My lord,—

    K. Hen. Worcester, get thee gone; for I do see   15
Danger and disobedience in thine eye.
O! sir, your presence is too bold and peremptory,
And majesty might never yet endure
The moody frontier of a servant brow.
You have good leave to leave us; when we need   20
Your use and counsel we shall send for you.

                              Exit Worcester

To Northumberland. You were about to speak.

    North.   Yea, my good lord.
Those prisoners in your highness' name demanded,
Which Harry Percy here at Holmedon took,
Were, as he says, not with such strength denied   25
As was deliver'd to your majesty:
Either envy, therefore, or misprision
Is guilty of this fault and not my son.

    Hot. My liege, I did deny no prisoners:
But I remember, when the fight was done,   30
When I was dry with rage and extreme toil,
Breathless and faint, leaning upon my sword,
Came there a certain lord, neat, trimly dress'd,
Fresh as a bridegroom; and his chin, new reap'd,
Show'd like a stubble-land at harvest-home: 35
He was perfumed like a milliner,
And 'twixt his finger and his thumb he held
A pouncet-box, which ever and anon
He gave his nose and took't away again;
Who therewith angry, when it next came there,   40
Took it in snuff: and still he smil'd and talk'd;
And as the soldiers bore dead bodies by,
He call'd them untaught knaves, unmannerly,
To bring a slovenly unhandsome corpse

Betwixt the wind and his nobility.   45
With many holiday and lady terms
He question'd me; among the rest, demanded
My prisoners in your majesty's behalf.
I then, all smarting with my wounds being cold,
To be so pester'd with a popinjay,   50
Out of my grief and my impatience
Answer'd neglectingly, I know not what,
He should, or he should not; for he made me mad
To see him shine so brisk, and smell so sweet,
And talk so like a waiting-gentlewoman   55
Of guns, and drums, and wounds, God save the mark!
And telling me the sovereign'st thing on earth
Was parmaceti for an inward bruise;
And that it was great pity, so it was,
That villanous saltpetre should be digg'd   60
Out of the bowels of the harmless earth,
Which many a good tall fellow had destroy'd
So cowardly; and but for these vile guns
He would himself have been a soldier.
This bald unjointed chat of his, my lord,   65
I answer'd indirectly, as I said;
And I beseech you, let not his report
Come current for an accusation
Betwixt my love and your high majesty.
 BLUNT. The circumstance consider'd, good my lord,   70
Whatever Harry Percy then had said
To such a person, and in such a place,
At such a time, with all the rest re-told,
May reasonably die and never rise
To do him wrong, or any way impeach   75
What then he said, so he unsay it now.
 K. HEN. Why, yet he doth deny his prisoners,
But with proviso and exception,
That we at our own charge shall ransom straight
His brother-in-law, the foolish Mortimer;   80
Who, on my soul, hath wilfully betray'd
The lives of those that he did lead to fight
Against the great magician, damn'd Glendower,
Whose daughter, as we hear, the Earl of March
Hath lately married. Shall our coffers then   85
Be emptied to redeem a traitor home?
Shall we buy treason, and indent with fears,

When they have lost and forfeited themselves?
No, on the barren mountains let him starve;
For I shall never hold that man my friend   90
Whose tongue shall ask me for one penny cost
To ransom home revolted Mortimer.
    HOT. Revolted Mortimer!
He never did fall off, my sovereign liege,
But by the chance of war: to prove that true   95
Needs no more but one tongue for all those wounds,
Those mouthed wounds, which valiantly he took,
When on the gentle Severn's sedgy bank,
In single opposition, hand to hand,
He did confound the best part of an hour   100
In changing hardiment with great Glendower.
Three times they breath'd and three times did they drink,
Upon agreement, of swift Severn's flood,
Who then, affrighted with their bloody looks,
Ran fearfully among the trembling reeds,   105
And hid his crisp head in the hollow bank
Blood-stained with these valiant combatants.
Never did base and rotten policy
Colour her working with such deadly wounds;
Nor never could the noble Mortimer   110
Receive so many, and all willingly:
Then let not him be slander'd with revolt.
    K. HEN. Thou dost belie him, Percy, thou dost belie him:
He never did encounter with Glendower:
I tell thee,
He durst as well have met the devil alone
As Owen Glendower for an enemy.
Art thou not asham'd? But, sirrah, henceforth
Let me not hear you speak of Mortimer:
Send me your prisoners with the speediest means,   120
Or you shall hear in such a kind from me
As will displease you. My Lord Northumberland,
We license your departure with your son.
Send us your prisoners, or you'll hear of it.
                    Exeunt KING HENRY, BLUNT, *and Train.*
    HOT. An if the devil come and roar for them,   125
I will not send them: I will after straight
And tell him so; for I will ease my heart,
Although it be with hazard of my head.

NORTH. What! drunk with choler? stay and pause awhile:
Here comes your uncle.

                    Re-enter WORCESTER.

HOT.   Speak of Mortimer!   130
'Zounds! I will speak of him; and let my soul
Want mercy if I do not join with him:
In his behalf I'll empty all these veins,
And shed my dear blood drop by drop i' the dust,
But I will lift the down-trod Mortimer   135
As high i' the air as this unthankful king,
As this ingrate and canker'd Bolingbroke.

NORTH. Brother, the king hath made your nephew mad.

WOR. Who struck this heat up after I was gone?

HOT. He will, forsooth, have all my prisoners;   140
And when I urg'd the ransom once again
Of my wife's brother, then his cheek look'd pale,
And on my face he turn'd an eye of death,
Trembling even at the name of Mortimer.

WOR. I cannot blame him: was he not proclaim'd   145
By Richard that dead is the next of blood?

NORTH. He was; I heard the proclamation:
And then it was, when the unhappy king,
Whose wrongs in us God pardon! did set forth
Upon his Irish expedition;   150
From whence he, intercepted, did return
To be depos'd, and shortly mudered.

WOR. And for whose death we in the world's wide mouth
Live scandaliz'd and foully spoken of.

HOT. But, soft! I pray you, did King Richard then   155
Proclaim my brother Edmund Mortimer
Heir to the crown?

NORTH.   He did; myself did hear it.

HOT. Nay, then I cannot blame his cousin king,
That wish'd him on the barren mountains starve.
But shall it be that you, that set the crown   160
Upon the head of this forgetful man,
And for his sake wear the detested blot
Of murd'rous subornation, shall it be,
That you a world of curses undergo,
Being the agents, or base second means,   165
The cords, the ladder, or the hangman rather?
O! pardon me that I descend so low,
To show the line and the predicament

Wherein you range under this subtle king.
Shall it for shame be spoken in these days,   170
Or fill up chronicles in time to come,
That men of your nobility and power
Did gage them both in an unjust behalf,
As both of you, God pardon it! have done,
To put down Richard, that sweet lovely rose,   175
And plant this thorn, this canker, Bolingbroke?
And shall it in more shame be further spoken,
That you are fool'd, discarded, and shook off
By him for whom these shames ye underwent?
No; yet time serves wherein you may redeem   180
Your banish'd honours, and restore yourselves
Into the good thoughts of the world again;
Revenge the jeering and disdain'd contempt
Of this proud king, who studies day and night
To answer all the debt he owes to you   185
Even with the bloody payment of your deaths.
Therefore, I say,—
   WOR.   Peace, cousin! say no more.
And now I will unclasp a secret book,
And to your quick-conceiving discontents
I'll read you matter deep and dangerous,   190
As full of peril and adventurous spirit
As to o'er-walk a current, roaring loud,
On the unsteadfast footing of a spear.
   HOT. If he fall in, good night! or sink or swim:
Send danger from the east unto the west,   195
So honour cross it from the north to south,
And let them grapple: O! the blood more stirs
To rouse a lion than to start a hare.
   NORTH. Imagination of some great exploit
Drives him beyond the bounds of patience.   200
   HOT. By heaven methinks it were an easy leap
To pluck bright honour from the pale-fac'd moon,
Or dive into the bottom of the deep,
Where fathom-line could never touch the ground,
And pluck up drowned honour by the locks;   205
So he that doth redeem her thence might wear
Without corrival all her dignities:
But out upon this half-fac'd fellowship!
   WOR. He apprehends a world of figures here,
But not the form of what he should attend.   210

Good cousin, give me audience for a while,
And list to me.
    Hot. I cry you mercy.
    Wor.   Those same noble Scots
That are your prisoners,—
    Hot.   I'll keep them all;
By God, he shall not have a Scot of them: 215
No, if a Scot would save his soul, he shall not:
I'll keep them, by this hand.
    Wor.   You start away,
And lend no ear unto my purposes.
Those prisoners you shall keep.
    Hot.   Nay, I will; that's flat.
He said he would not ransom Mortimer;   220
Forbad my tongue to speak of Mortimer;
But I will find him when he lies asleep,
And in his ear I'll holla 'Mortimer'!
Nay,
I'll have a starling shall be taught to speak   225
Nothing but 'Mortimer,' and give it him,
To keep his anger still in motion.
    Wor. Hear you, cousin; a word.
    Hot. All studies here I solemnly defy,
Save how to gall and pinch this Bolingbroke: 230
And that same sword-and-buckler Prince of Wales,
But that I think his father loves him not,
And would be glad he met with some mischance,
I would have him poison'd with a pot of ale.
    Wor. Farewell, kinsman: I will talk to you   233
When you are better temper'd to attend.
    North. Why, what a wasp-stung and impatient fool
Art thou, to break into this woman's mood,
Tying thine ear to no tongue but thine own!
    Hot. Why, look you, I am whipp'd and scourg'd with rods,   240
Nettled and stung with pismires, when I hear
Of this vile politician, Bolingbroke.
In Richard's time,—what do you call the place?—
A plague upon 't—it is in Gloucestershire;—
'Twas where the madcap duke his uncle kept,   245
His uncle York; where I first bow'd my knee
Unto this king of smiles, this Bolingbroke;
'Sblood!
When you and he came back from Ravenspurgh.

NORTH. At Berkeley castle.   250
HOT. You say true.
Why, what a candy deal of courtesy
This fawning greyhound then did proffer me!
Look, 'when his infant fortune came to age,'
And 'gentle Harry Percy,' and 'kind cousin';   255
O! the devil take such cozeners. God forgive me!
Good uncle, tell your tale, for I have done.
  WOR. Nay, if you have not, to 't again;
We'll stay your leisure.
  HOT.   I have done, i' faith.
  WOR. Then once more to your Scottish prisoners,   260
Deliver them up without their ransom straight,
And make the Douglas' son your only mean
For powers in Scotland; which, for divers reasons
Which I shall send you written, be assur'd,
Will easily be granted.   265
To NORTHUMBERLAND.   You, my lord,
Your son in Scotland being thus employ'd,
Shall secretly into the bosom creep
Of that same noble prelate well belov'd,
The archbishop.   270
  HOT. Of York, is it not?
  WOR. True; who bears hard
His brother's death at Bristol, the lord Scroop.
I speak not this in estimation,
As what I think might be, but what I know   275
Is ruminated, plotted, and set down;
And only stays but to behold the face
Of that occasion that shall bring it on.
  HOT. I smell it:
Upon my life it will do wondrous well.   280
  NORTH. Before the game's afoot thou still lett'st slip.
  HOT. Why, it cannot choose but be a noble plot:
And then the power of Scotland and of York
To join with Mortimer, ha?
  WOR.   And so they shall.
  HOT. In faith, it is exceedingly well aim'd.   285
  WOR. And 'tis no little reason bids us speed,
To save our heads by raising of a head;
For, bear ourselves as even as we can,
The king will always think him in our debt,
And think we think ourselves unsatisfied,   290

Till he hath found a time to pay us home.
And see already how he doth begin
To make us strangers to his looks of love.

HOT. He does, he does: we'll be reveng'd on him.

WOR. Cousin, farewell: no further go in this 295
Than I by letters shall direct your course.
When time is ripe, which will be suddenly,
I'll steal to Glendower and Lord Mortimer;
Where you and Douglas and our powers at once,
As I will fashion it, shall happily meet, 300
To bear our fortunes in our own strong arms,
Which now we hold at much uncertainty.

NORTH. Farewell, good brother: we shall thrive, I trust.

HOT. Uncle, adieu: O! let the hours be short
Till fields and blows and groans applaud our sport. 305

Exeunt.

ACT II.

SCENE I.—*Rochester. An Inn Yard.*

Enter a Carrier, with a lantern in his hand.

FIRST CAR. Heigh-ho! An't be not four by the day I'll be hanged:
Charles' Wain is over the new chimney, and yet our horse not
packed. What, ostler!

OSTLER. *Within.* Anon, anon.

FIRST CAR. I prithee, Tom, beat Cut's saddle, put a few flocks [5
in the point; the poor jade is wrung in the withers out of all cess.

Enter another Carrier.

SECOND CAR. Peas and beans are as dank here as a dog, and that
is the next way to give poor jades the bots: this house is turned
upside down since Robin Ostler died.

FIRST CAR. Poor fellow! never joyed since the price of oats [10
rose; it was the death of him.

SECOND CAR. I think this be the most villanous house in all
London road for fleas: I am stung like a tench.

FIRST CAR. Like a tench! by the mass, there is ne'er a king in
Christendom could be better bit than I have been since the [15
first cock.

SECOND CAR. Why, they will allow us ne'er a jordan, and then we
leak in your chimney; and your chamberlie breeds fleas like a loach.

FIRST CAR. What, ostler! come away and be hanged, come away.

SECOND CAR. I have a gammon of bacon and two races of [20
ginger, to be delivered as far as Charing-cross.

FIRST CAR. God's body! the turkeys in my pannier are quite starved. What, ostler! A plague on thee! hast thou never an eye in thy head? canst not hear? An 'twere not as good a deed as drink to break the pate on thee, I am a very villain. Come, and be   [25 hanged! hast no faith in thee?

Enter GADSHILL.

GADS. Good morrow, carriers. What's o'clock?

FIRST CAR. I think it be two o'clock.

GADS. I prithee, lend me thy lantern, to see my gelding in the stable.   30

FIRST CAR. Nay, by God, soft: I know a trick worth two of that, i' faith.

GADS. I prithee, lend me thine.

SECOND CAR. Ay, when? canst tell? 'Lend me thy lantern,' quoth a'? marry, I'll see thee hanged first.   35

GADS. Sirrah carrier, what time do you mean to come to London?

SECOND CAR. Time enough to go to bed with a candle, I warrant thee. Come, neighbour Mugs, we'll call up the gentlemen: they will along with company, for they have great charge.

Exeunt Carriers.

GADS. What, ho! chamberlain!   40

CHAM. *Within.* 'At hand,' quoth pick-purse.

GADS. That's even as fair as 'at hand,' quoth the chamberlain; for thou variest no more from picking of purses than giving direction doth from labouring; thou layest the plot how.

Enter Chamberlain.

CHAM. Good morrow, Master Gadshill. It holds current that   [45 I told you yesternight: there's a franklin in the wild of Kent hath brought three hundred marks with him in gold: I heard him tell it to one of his company last night at supper; a kind of auditor; one that hath abundance of charge too, God knows what. They are up already and call for eggs and butter: they will away presently.   [50

GADS. Sirrah, if they meet not with Saint Nicholas' clerks, I'll give thee this neck.

CHAM. No, I'll none of it: I prithee, keep that for the hangman; for I know thou worshippest Saint Nicholas as truly as a man of falsehood may.   55

GADS. What talkest thou to me of the hangman? if I hang I'll make a fat pair of gallows; for if I hang old Sir John hangs with me, and thou knowest he's no starveling. Tut! there are other Troyans that thou dreamest not of, the which for sport sake are content to do the profession some grace; that would, if matters should   [60 be looked into, for their own credit sake make all whole. I am

joined with no foot landrakers, no long-staff sixpenny strikers, none
of these mad mustachio purple-hued maltworms; but with nobility
and tranquillity, burgomasters and great oneyers; such as can hold
in, such as will strike sooner than speak, and speak sooner   [65
than drink, and drink sooner than pray: and yet I lie; for they
pray continually to their saint, the commonwealth; or rather, not
pray to her, but prey on her, for they ride up and down on her
and make her their boots.

CHAM. What! the commonwealth their boots? will she hold   [70
out water in foul way?

GADS. She will, she will; justice hath liquored her. We steal as
in a castle, cock-sure; we have the receipt of fern-seed, we walk
invisible.

CHAM. Nay, by my faith, I think you are more beholding to   [75
the night than to fern-seed for your walking invisible.

GADS. Give me thy hand: thou shalt have a share in our purchase,
as I am a true man.

CHAM. Nay, rather let me have it, as you are a false thief.

GADS. Go to; *homo* is a common name to all men. Bid the   [80
ostler bring my gelding out of the stable. Farewell, you muddy knave.

Exeunt.

SCENE II.—*The Road by Gadshill.*

Enter the PRINCE *and* POINS.

POINS. Come, shelter, shelter: I have removed Falstaff's horse,
and he frets like a gummed velvet.

PRINCE. Stand close.

Enter FALSTAFF.

FAL. Poins! Poins, and be hanged! Poins!

PRINCE. Peace, ye fat-kidneyed rascal! What a brawling dost   [5
thou keep!

FAL. Where's Poins, Hal?

PRINCE. He is walked up to the top of the hill: I'll go seek him.

FAL. I am accursed to rob in that thief's company; the rascal hath
removed my horse and tied him I know not where. If I travel   [10
but four foot by the square further afoot I shall break my wind.
Well, I doubt not but to die a fair death for all this, if I 'scape
hanging for killing that rogue. I have forsworn his company hourly
any time this two-and-twenty years, and yet I am bewitched with
the rogue's company. If the rascal have not given me medicines   [15
to make me love him, I'll be hanged; it could not be else: I have
drunk medicines. Poins! Hal! a plague upon you both! Bardolph!
Peto! I'll starve ere I'll rob a foot further. An 'twere not as good

a deed as drink to turn true man and to leave these rogues, I am
the veriest varlet that ever chewed with a tooth. Eight yards of   [20
uneven ground is threescore and ten miles afoot with me, and the
stony-hearted villains know it well enough. A plague upon't when
thieves cannot be true to one another!   *They whistle.*
Whew! a plague upon you all! Give me my horse, you rogues;
give me my horse and be hanged.   25

PRINCE. Peace, ye fat-guts! lie down; lay thine ear close to the
ground and list if thou canst hear the tread of travellers.

FAL. Have you any levers to lift me up again, being down?
'Sblood! I'll not bear mine own flesh so far afoot again for all the
coin in thy father's exchequer. What a plague mean ye to colt   [30
me thus?

PRINCE. Thou liest: thou are not colted; thou art uncolted.

FAL. I prithee, good Prince Hal, help me to my horse, good king's
son.

PRINCE. Out, you rogue! shall I be your ostler?   35

FAL. Go, hang thyself in thine own heir apparent garters! If I
be ta'en I'll peach for this. An I have not ballads made on you all,
and sung to filthy tunes, let a cup of sack be my poison: when a
jest is so forward, and afoot too! I hate it.

Enter GADSHILL.

GADS. Stand.   40

FAL. So I do, against my will.

POINS. O! 'tis our setter: I know his voice.

Enter BARDOLPH *and* PETO.

BARD. What news?

GADS. Case ye, case ye; on with your vizards: there's money of
the king's coming down the hill; 'tis going to the king's ex-   [45
chequer.

FAL. You lie, ye rogue; 'tis going to the king's tavern.

GADS. There's enough to make us all.

FAL. To be hanged.

PRINCE. Sirs, you four shall front them in the narrow lane;   [50
Ned Poins and I will walk lower: if they 'scape from your encounter
then they light on us.

PETO. How many be there of them?

GADS. Some eight or ten.

FAL. 'Zounds! will they not rob us?   55

PRINCE. What! a coward, Sir John Paunch?

FAL. Indeed, I am not John of Gaunt, your grandfather; but yet
no coward, Hal.

PRINCE. Well, we leave that to the proof.

POINS. Sirrah Jack, thy horse stands behind the hedge: when [60 thou needest him there thou shalt find him. Farewell, and stand fast.

FAL. Now cannot I strike him if I should be hanged.

PRINCE. Ned, where are our disguises?

POINS. Here, hard by; stand close. 65

Exeunt PRINCE *and* POINS.

FAL. Now, my masters, happy man be his dole, say I: every man to his business.

Enter Travellers.

FIRST TRAV. Come, neighbour; the boy shall lead our horses down the hill; we'll walk afoot awhile, and ease our legs.

THIEVES. Stand! 70

TRAVELLERS. Jesu bless us!

FAL. Strike; down with them: cut the villains' throats: ah! whoreson caterpillars! bacon-fed knaves! they hate us youth: down with them; fleece them.

TRAVELLERS. O! we are undone, both we and ours for ever. 75

FAL. Hang ye, gorbellied knaves, are ye undone? No, ye fat chuffs; I would your store were here! On, bacons, on! What! ye knaves, young men must live. You are grand-jurors, are ye? we'll jure ye, i' faith. *Here they rob them and bind them. Exeunt.*

Re-enter the PRINCE *and* POINS.

PRINCE. The thieves have bound the true men. Now could [80 thou and I rob the thieves and go merrily to London, it would be argument for a week, laughter for a month, and a good jest for ever.

POINS. Stand close; I hear them coming.

Re-enter Thieves.

FAL. Come, my masters; let us share, and then to horse before day. An the Prince and Poins be not two arrant cowards, [85 there's no equity stirring: there's no more valour in that Poins than in a wild duck.

PRINCE. Your money!

POINS. Villains!

> *As they are sharing, the* PRINCE *and* POINS *set upon them. They all run away, and* FALSTAFF, *after a blow or two, runs away too, leaving the booty behind them.*

PRINCE. Got with much ease. Now merrily to horse: 90
The thieves are scatter'd and possess'd with fear
So strongly that they dare not meet each other;
Each takes his fellow for an officer.
Away, good Ned. Falstaff sweats to death

And lards the lean earth as he walks along: 95
Were't not for laughing I should pity him.
  POINS. How the rogue roar'd!   *Exeunt.*

    SCENE III.—*Warkworth. A Room in the Castle.*
        Enter HOTSPUR, *reading a letter.*
  *But, for mine own part, my lord, I could be well contented to
be there, in respect of the love I bear your house.*
He could be contented; why is he not then? In respect of the love he
bears our house: he shows in this he loves his own barn better than
he loves our house. Let me see some more.   5
  The purpose you undertake is dangerous;—
why, that's certain: 'tis dangerous to take a cold, to sleep, to drink;
but I tell you, my lord fool, out of this nettle, danger, we pluck
this flower, safety.
  The purpose you undertake is dangerous; the friends you   [10
*have named uncertain; the time itself unsorted; and your whole
plot too light for the counterpoise of so great an opposition.*
Say you so, say you so? I say unto you again, you are a shallow
cowardly hind, and you lie. What a lack-brain is this! By the Lord,
our plot is as good a plot as ever was laid; our friends true and   [15
constant: a good plot, good friends, and full of expectation; an
excellent plot, very good friends. What a frosty-spirited rogue is
this! Why, my Lord of York commends the plot and the general
course of the action. 'Zounds! an I were now by this rascal, I could
brain him with his lady's fan. Is there not my father, my uncle,   [20
and myself? Lord Edmund Mortimer, my Lord of York, and Owen
Glendower? Is there not besides the Douglas? Have I not all their
letters to meet me in arms by the ninth of the next month, and
are they not some of them set forward already? What a pagan
rascal is this! an infidel! Ha! you shall see now in very sincerity   [25
of fear and cold heart, will he to the king and lay open all our
proceedings. O! I could divide myself and go to buffets, for moving
such a dish of skimmed milk with so honourable an action. Hang
him! let him tell the king; we are prepared. I will set forward
to-night.   30
          Enter LADY PERCY.
How now, Kate! I must leave you within these two hours.
  LADY P. O! my good lord, why are you thus alone?
For what offence have I this fortnight been
A banish'd woman from my Harry's bed?
Tell me, sweet lord, what is't that takes from thee   35
Thy stomach, pleasure, and thy golden sleep?

Why dost thou bend thine eyes upon the earth,
And start so often when thou sitt'st alone?
Why hast thou lost the fresh blood in thy cheeks,
And given my treasures and my rights of thee   40
To thick-eyed musing and curs'd melancholy?
In thy faint slumbers I by thee have watch'd
And heard thee murmur tales of iron wars,
Speak terms of manage to thy bounding steed,
Cry 'Courage! to the field!' And thou hast talk'd   45
Of sallies and retires, of trenches, tents,
Of palisadoes, frontiers, parapets,
Of basilisks, of cannon, culverin,
Of prisoners' ransom, and of soldiers slain,
And all the currents of a heady fight   50
Thy spirit within thee hath been so at war,
And thus hath so bestirr'd thee in thy sleep,
That beads of sweat have stood upon thy brow,
Like bubbles in a late disturbed stream;
And in thy face strange motions have appear'd,   55
Such as we see when men restrain their breath
On some great sudden hest. O! what portents are these?
Some heavy business hath my lord in hand,
And I must know it, else he loves me not.
    HOT. What, ho!

Enter Servant.

                Is Gilliams with the packet gone?   60
    SERV. He is, my lord, an hour ago.
    HOT. Hath Butler brought those horses from the sheriff?
    SERV. One horse, my lord, he brought even now.
    HOT. What horse? a roan, a crop-ear, is it not?
    SERV. It is, my lord.
    HOT.   That roan shall be my throne.   65
Well, I will back him straight: O *Esperance!*
Bid Butler lead him forth into the park.

                                  Exit Servant.

    LADY P. But hear you, my lord.
    HOT. What say'st thou, my lady?
    LADY P. What is it carries you away?   70
    HOT. Why, my horse, my love, my horse.
    LADY P. Out, you mad-headed ape!
A weasel hath not such a deal of spleen
As you are toss'd with. In faith,
I'll know your business, Harry, that I will.   75

I fear my brother Mortimer doth stir
About his title, and hath sent for you
To line his enterprise. But if you go—
    Hot. So far afoot, I shall be weary, love.
    Lady P. Come, come, you paraquito, answer me   80
Directly unto this question that I ask.
In faith, I'll break thy little finger, Harry,
An if thou wilt not tell me all things true.
   Hot. Away,
Away, you trifler! Love! I love thee not,   85
I care not for thee, Kate: this is no world
To play with mammets and to tilt with lips:
We must have bloody noses and crack'd crowns,
And pass them current too. God's me, my horse!
What say'st thou, Kate? what would'st thou have with me?   90
    Lady P. Do you not love me? do you not indeed?
Well, do not then; for since you love me not,
I will not love myself. Do you not love me?
Nay, tell me if you speak in jest or no.
    Hot. Come, wilt thou see me ride?   95
And when I am o' horseback, I will swear
I love thee infinitely. But hark you, Kate;
I must not have you henceforth question me
Whither I go, nor reason whereabout.
Whither I must, I must; and, to conclude,   100
This evening must I leave you, gentle Kate.
I know you wise; but yet no further wise
Than Harry Percy's wife: constant you are,
But yet a woman: and for secrecy,
No lady closer; for I well believe   105
Thou wilt not utter what thou dost not know;
And so far will I trust thee, gentle Kate.
    Lady P. How! so far?
    Hot. Not an inch further. But hark you, Kate;
Whither I go, thither shall you go too;   110
To-day will I set forth, to-morrow you.
Will this content you, Kate?
    Lady P.   It must, of force.   *Exeunt.*

    Scene IV.—*Eastcheap. A Room in the Boar's Head Tavern.*
Enter the Prince *and* Poins.
    Prince. Ned, prithee, come out of that fat room and lend me thy
hand to laugh a little.

POINS. Where hast been, Hal?

PRINCE. With three or four loggerheads amongst three or four score hogsheads. I have sounded the very base string of humility. [5 Sirrah, I am sworn brother to a leash of drawers, and can call them all by their christen names, as Tom, Dick, and Francis. They take it already upon their salvation, that though I be but Prince of Wales, yet I am the king of courtesy; and tell me flatly I am no proud Jack, like Falstaff, but a Corinthian, a lad of mettle, a [10 good boy, by the Lord, so they call me, and when I am king of England, I shall command all the good lads in Eastcheap. They call drinking deep, dyeing scarlet; and when you breathe in your watering, they cry 'hem!' and bid you play it off. To conclude, I am so good a proficient in one quarter of an hour, that I can drink [15 with any tinker in his own language during my life. I tell thee, Ned, thou hast lost much honour that thou wert not with me in this action. But, sweet Ned,—to sweeten which name of Ned, I give thee this pennyworth of sugar, clapped even now into my hand by an under-skinker, one that never spake other English in his [20 life than 'Eight shillings and sixpence,' and 'You are welcome'; with this shrill addition, 'Anon, anon, sir! Score a pint of bastard in the Half-moon,' or so. But, Ned, to drive away the time till Falstaff come, I prithee do thou stand in some by-room, while I question my puny drawer to what end he gave me the sugar; [25 and do thou never leave calling 'Francis!' that his tale to me may be nothing but 'Anon.' Step aside, and I'll show thee a precedent.

POINS. Francis!

PRINCE. Thou art perfect.

POINS. Francis!   *Exit.* [30

Enter FRANCIS.

FRAN. Anon, anon, sir. Look down into the Pomgarnet, Ralph.

PRINCE. Come hither, Francis.

FRAN. My lord?

PRINCE. How long hast thou to serve, Francis?

FRAN. Forsooth, five years, and as much as to—   35

POINS. *Within.* Francis!

FRAN. Anon, anon, sir.

PRINCE. Five years! by'r lady, a long lease for the clinking of pewter. But, Francis, darest thou be so valiant as to play the coward with thy indenture and show it a fair pair of heels and [40 run from it?

FRAN. O Lord, sir! I'll be sworn upon all the books in England, I could find in my heart—

POINS. *Within.* Francis!

FRAN. Anon, sir.   45

PRINCE. How old art thou, Francis?

FRAN. Let me see—about Michaelmas next I shall be—

POINS. *Within.* Francis!

FRAN. Anon, sir. Pray you, stay a little, my lord.

PRINCE. Nay, but hark you, Francis. For the sugar thou gavest   [50
me, 'twas a pennyworth, was't not?

FRAN. O Lord, sir! I would it had been two.

PRINCE. I will give thee for it a thousand pound: ask me when
thou wilt and thou shalt have it.

POINS. *Within.* Francis!   55

FRAN. Anon, anon.

PRINCE. Anon, Francis? No, Francis; but tomorrow, Francis; or,
Francis, o' Thursday; or, indeed Francis, when thou wilt. But,
Francis!

FRAN. My lord?   60

PRINCE. Wilt thou rob this leathern-jerkin, crystal-button, knot-
pated, agate-ring, puke-stocking, caddis-garter, smooth-tongue, Span-
ish-pouch,—

FRAN. O Lord, sir, who do you mean?

PRINCE. Why then, your brown bastard is your only drink;   [65
for look you, Francis, your white canvas doublet will sully. In
Barbary, sir, it cannot come to so much.

FRAN. What, sir?

POINS. *Within.* Francis!

PRINCE. Away, you rogue! Dost thou not hear them call?   70

> *Here they both call him; the Drawer stands amazed,*
> *not knowing which way to go.*

Enter Vintner

VINT. What! standest thou still, and hearest such a calling? Look
to the guests within.

Exit FRANCIS.

My lord, old Sir John, with half-a-dozen more, are at the door: shall I
let them in?

PRINCE. Let them alone awhile, and then open the door.   [75

Exit Vintner.

Poins!

Re-enter POINS.

POINS. Anon, anon, sir.

PRINCE. Sirrah, Falstaff and the rest of the thieves are at the door:
shall we be merry?

POINS. As merry as crickets, my lad. But hark ye; what cun-   [80 ning match have you made with this jest of the drawer? come, what's the issue?

PRINCE. I am now of all humours that have showed themselves humours since the old days of goodman Adam to the pupil age of this present twelve o'clock at midnight.   85

Re-enter FRANCIS.

What's o'clock, Francis?

FRAN. Anon, anon, sir.   *Exit.*

PRINCE. That ever this fellow should have fewer words than a parrot, and yet the son of a woman! His industry is up-stairs and down-stairs; his eloquence the parcel of a reckoning. I am not   [90 yet of Percy's mind, the Hotspur of the North; he that kills me some six or seven dozen of Scots at a breakfast, washes his hands, and says to his wife 'Fie upon this quiet life! I want work.' 'O my sweet Harry,' says she, 'how many hast thou killed to-day?' 'Give my roan horse a drench,' says he, and answers 'Some fourteen,' an hour   [95 after; 'a trifle, a trifle' I prithee, call in Falstaff: I'll play Percy, and that damned brawn shall play Dame Mortimer his wife. 'Rivo!' says the drunkard. Call in ribs, call in tallow.

Enter FALSTAFF, GADSHILL, BARDOLPH, PETO, *and* FRANCIS.

POINS. Welcome, Jack. Where hast thou been?

FAL. A plague of all cowards, I say, and a vengeance too!   [100 marry, and amen! Give me a cup of sack, boy. Ere I lead this life long, I'll sew nether-stocks and mend them and foot them too. A plague of all cowards! Give me a cup of sack, rogue. Is there no virtue extant?

He drinks.

PRINCE. Didst thou never see Titan kiss a dish of butter,   [105 pitiful-hearted Titan, that melted at the sweet tale of the sun? if thou didst then behold that compound.

FAL. You rogue, here's lime in this sack too: there is nothing but roguery to be found in villanous man: yet a coward is worse than a cup of sack with lime in it. A villanous coward! Go thy ways,   [110 old Jack; die when thou wilt. If manhood, good manhood, be not forgot upon the face of the earth, then am I a shotten herring. There live not three good men unhanged in England, and one of them is fat and grows old: God help the while! a bad world, I say. I would I were a weaver; I could sing psalms or any thing. A   [115 plague of all cowards, I say still.

PRINCE. How now, wool-sack! what mutter you?

FAL. A king's son! If I do not beat thee out of thy kingdom with a dagger of lath, and drive all thy subjects afore thee like a flock of

wild geese, I'll never wear hair on my face more. You Prince of   [120
Wales!

PRINCE. Why, you whoreson round man, what's the matter?

FAL. Are you not a coward? answer me to that; and Poins there?

POINS. 'Zounds! ye fat paunch, an ye call me coward, I'll stab thee.

FAL. I call thee coward! I'll see thee damned ere I call thee   [125
coward; but I would give a thousand pound I could run as fast as
thou canst. You are straight enough in the shoulders; you care not
who sees your back: call you that backing of your friends? A plague
upon such backing! give me them that will face me. Give me a cup
of sack: I am a rogue if I drunk to-day.   130

PRINCE. O villain! thy lips are scarce wiped since thou drunkest
last.

FAL. All's one for that.   *He drinks.*
A plague of all cowards, still say I.

PRINCE. What's the matter?   135

FAL. What's the matter! there be four of us here have ta'en a
thousand pound this day morning.

PRINCE. Where is it, Jack? where is it?

FAL. Where is it! taken from us it is: a hundred upon poor four of
us.   140

PRINCE. What! a hundred, man?

FAL. I am a rogue, if I were not at half-sword with a dozen of them
two hours together. I have 'scaped by miracle. I am eight times
thrust through the doublet, four through the hose; my buckler cut
through and through; my sword hacked like a hand-saw: *ecce*   [145
signum! I never dealt better since I was a man: all would not do. A
plague of all cowards! Let them speak: if they speak more or less
than truth, they are villains and the sons of darkness.

PRINCE. Speak, sirs; how was it?

GADS. We four set upon some dozen,—   150

FAL. Sixteen, at least, my lord.

GADS. And bound them.

PETO. No, no, they were not bound.

FAL. You rogue, they were bound, every man of them; or I am a
Jew else, an Ebrew Jew.   155

GADS. As we were sharing, some six or seven fresh men set upon
us,—

FAL. And unbound the rest, and then come in the other.

PRINCE. What! fought you with them all?

FAL. All! I know not what you call all; but if I fought not   [160
with fifty of them, I am a bunch of radish; if there were not two or
three and fifty upon poor old Jack, then am I no two-legged creature.

PRINCE. Pray God you have not murdered some of them.

FAL. Nay, that's past praying for: I have peppered two of them: two I am sure I have paid, two rogues in buckram suits. I tell [165 thee what, Hal, if I tell thee a lie, spit in my face, call me horse. Thou knowest my old ward; here I lay, and thus I bore my point. Four rogues in buckram let drive at me,—

PRINCE. What! four? thou said'st but two even now.

FAL. Four, Hal; I told thee four.   170

POINS. Ay, ay, he said four.

FAL. These four came all a-front, and mainly thrust at me. I made me no more ado but took all their seven points in my target, thus.

PRINCE. Seven? why, there were but four even now.

FAL. In buckram?   175

POINS. Ay, four, in buckram suits.

FAL. Seven, by these hilts, or I am a villain else.

PRINCE. Prithee, let him alone; we shall have more anon.

FAL. Dost thou hear me, Hal?

PRINCE. Ay, and mark thee too, Jack.   180

FAL. Do so, for it is worth the listening to. These nine in buckram that I told thee of,—

PRINCE. So, two more already.

FAL. Their points being broken,—

POINS. Down fell their hose.   185

FAL. Began to give me ground; but I followed me close, came in foot and hand, and with a thought seven of the eleven I paid.

PRINCE. O monstrous! eleven buckram men grown out of two.

FAL. But, as the devil would have it, three misbegotten knaves in Kendal-green came at my back and let drive at me; for it was so [190 dark, Hal, that thou could'st not see thy hand.

PRINCE. These lies are like their father that begets them; gross as a mountain, open, palpable. Why, thou clay-brained guts, thou knotty-pated fool, thou whoreson, obscene, greasy tallow-ketch,—

FAL. What! art thou mad? art thou mad? is not the truth the [195 truth?

PRINCE. Why, how could'st thou know these men in Kendal-green, when it was so dark thou could'st not see thy hand? come, tell us your reason: what sayest thou to this?

POINS. Come, your reason, Jack, your reason.   200

FAL. What! upon compulsion? 'Zounds! an I were at the strappado, or all the racks in the world, I would not tell you on compulsion. Give you a reason on compulsion! if reasons were as plenty as blackberries I would give no man a reason upon compulsion, I.

PRINCE. I'll be no longer guilty of this sin: this sanguine [205 coward, this bed-presser, this horse-back-breaker, this huge hill of flesh;—

FAL. 'Sblood, you starveling, you elf-skin, you dried neat's-tongue, you bull's-pizzle, you stockfish! O! for breath to utter what is like thee; your tailor's-yard, you sheath, you bow-case, you vile [210 standing tuck;—

PRINCE. Well, breathe awhile, and then to it again; and when thou hast tired thyself in base comparisons, hear me speak but this.

POINS. Mark, Jack.

PRINCE. We two saw you four set on four and bound them, [215 and were masters of their wealth. Mark now, how a plain tale shall put you down. Then did we two set on you four, and, with a word, out-faced you from your prize, and have it; yea, and can show it you here in the house. And, Falstaff, you carried your guts away as nimbly, with as quick dexterity, and roared for mercy, and still [220 ran and roared, as ever I heard bull-calf. What a slave art thou, to hack thy sword as thou hast done, and then say it was in fight! What trick, what device, what starting-hole canst thou now find out to hide thee from this open and apparent shame?

POINS. Come, let's hear, Jack; what trick hast thou now?   225

FAL. By the Lord, I knew ye as well as he that made ye. Why, hear you, my masters: was it for me to kill the heir apparent? should I turn upon the true prince? why, thou knowest I am as valiant as Hercules; but beware instinct: the lion will not touch the true prince. Instinct is a great matter, I was a coward on instinct. I [230 shall think the better of myself and thee during my life; I for a valiant lion, and thou for a true prince. But, by the Lord, lads, I am glad you have the money. Hostess, clap to the doors: watch to-night, pray to-morrow. Gallants, lads, boys, hearts of gold, all the titles of good fellowship come to you! What! shall we be merry? [235 shall we have a play extempore?

PRINCE. Content; and the argument shall be thy running away.

FAL. Ah! no more of that, Hal, and thou lovest me.

Enter MISTRESS QUICKLY.

QUICK. O Jesu! My lord the prince!

PRINCE. How now, my lady the hostess! what sayest thou to [240 me?

QUICK. Marry, my lord, there is a nobleman of the court at door would speak with you: he says he comes from your father.

PRINCE. Give him as much as will make him a royal man, and send him back again to my mother.   245

FAL. What manner of man is he?

QUICK. An old man.

FAL. What doth gravity out of his bed at midnight? Shall I give him his answer?

PRINCE. Prithee, do, Jack. 250

FAL. Faith, and I'll send him packing. *Exit.*

PRINCE. Now, sirs: by'r lady, you fought fair; so did you, Peto; so did you, Bardolph: you are lions too, you ran away upon instinct, you will not touch the true prince, no; fie!

BARD. Faith, I ran when I saw others run. 255

PRINCE. Faith, tell me now in earnest, how came Falstaff's sword so hacked?

PETO. Why, he hacked it with his dagger, and said he would swear truth out of England but he would make you believe it was done in fight, and persuaded us to do the like. 260

BARD. Yea, and to tickle our noses with speargrass to make them bleed, and then to beslubber our garments with it and swear it was the blood of true men. I did that I did not this seven year before; I blushed to hear his monstrous devices.

PRINCE. O villain! thou stolest a cup of sack eighteen years [265 ago, and wert taken with the manner, and ever since thou hast blushed extempore. Thou hadst fire and sword on thy side, and yet thou rannest away. What instinct hadst thou for it?

BARD. My lord, do you see these meteors? do you behold these exhalations? 270

PRINCE. I do.

BARD. What think you they portend?

PRINCE. Hot livers and cold purses.

BARD. Choler, my lord, if rightly taken.

PRINCE. No, if rightly taken, halter. 275

Re-enter FALSTAFF.

Here comes lean Jack, here comes bare-bone. How now, my sweet creature of bombast! How long is 't ago, Jack, since thou sawest thine own knee?

FAL. My own knee! when I was about thy years, Hal, I was not an eagle's talon in the waist; I could have crept into any alder- [280 man's thumb-ring. A plague of sighing and grief! it blows a man up like a bladder. There's villanous news abroad: here was Sir John Bracy from your father: you must to the court in the morning. That same mad fellow of the north, Percy, and he of Wales, that gave Amaimon the bastinado and made Lucifer cuckold, and [285 swore the devil his true liegeman upon the cross of a Welsh hook— what a plague call you him?

POINS. O! Glendower.

FAL. Owen, Owen; the same; and his son-in-law Mortimer, and

old Northumberland; and that sprightly Scot of Scots, Douglas,   [290
that runs o' horseback up a hill perpendicular.

PRINCE. He that rides at high speed and with his pistol kills a
sparrow flying.

FAL. You have hit it.

PRINCE. So did he never the sparrow.   295

FAL. Well, that rascal hath good mettle in him; he will not run.

PRINCE. Why, what a rascal art thou then, to praise him so for
running!

FAL. O' horseback, ye cuckoo! but afoot he will not budge a
foot.   300

PRINCE. Yes, Jack, upon instinct.

FAL. I grant ye, upon instinct. Well, he is there too, and one
Mordake, and a thousand blue-caps more. Worcester is stolen away
tonight; thy father's beard is turned white with the news: you may
buy land now as cheap as stinking mackerel.   305

PRINCE. Why then, it is like, if there come a hot June and this
civil buffeting hold, we shall buy maidenheads as they buy hob-nails,
by the hundreds.

FAL. By the mass, lad, thou sayest true; it is like we shall have good
trading that way. But tell me, Hal, art thou not horrible   [310
afeared? thou being heir apparent, could the world pick thee out
three such enemies again as that fiend Douglas, that spirit Percy,
and that devil Glendower? Art thou not horribly afraid? doth not
thy blood thrill at it?

PRINCE. Not a whit, i' faith; I lack some of thy instinct.   315

FAL. Well, thou wilt be horribly chid to-morrow when thou
comest to thy father: if thou love me, practise an answer.

PRINCE. Do thou stand for my father, and examine me upon the
particulars of my life.

FAL. Shall I? content: this chair shall be my state, this dagger [320
my sceptre, and this cushion my crown.

PRINCE. Thy state is taken for a joint-stool, thy golden sceptre
for a leaden dagger, and thy precious rich crown for a pitiful bald
crown!

FAL. Well, an the fire of grace be not quite out of thee, now [325
shalt thou be moved. Give me a cup of sack to make mine eyes look
red, that it may be thought I have wept; for I must speak in passion,
and I will do it in King Cambyses' vein.

PRINCE. Well, here is my leg.

FAL. And here is my speech. Stand aside, nobility.   330

QUICK. O Jesu! this is excellent sport, i' faith.

FAL. Weep not, sweet queen, for trickling tears are vain.

QUICK. O, the father! how he holds his countenance.

FAL. For God's sake, lords, convey my tristful queen,
For tears do stop the flood-gates of her eyes.   335

QUICK. O Jesu! he doth it as like one of these harlotry players
as ever I see.

FAL. Peace, good pint-pot! peace, good tickle-brain! Harry, I do
not only marvel where thou spendest thy time, but also how thou
art accompanied: for though the camomile, the more it is   [340
trodden on the faster it grows, yet youth, the more it is wasted
the sooner it wears. That thou art my son, I have partly thy mother's
word, partly my own opinion; but chiefly a villanous trick of thine
eye and a foolish hanging of thy nether lip, that doth warrant me.
If then thou be son to me, here lies the point; why, being son   [345
to me, art thou so pointed at? Shall the blessed sun of heaven prove
a micher and eat blackberries? a question not to be asked. Shall
the son of England prove a thief and take purses? a question to be
asked. There is a thing, Harry, which thou hast often heard of, and
it is known to many in our land by the name of pitch: this   [350
pitch, as ancient writers do report, doth defile; so doth the company
thou keepest; for, Harry, now I do not speak to thee in drink but
in tears, not in pleasure but in passion, not in words only, but in
woes also. And yet there is a virtuous man whom I have often noted
in thy company, but I know not his name.   355

PRINCE. What manner of man, an it like your majesty?

FAL. A goodly portly man, i' faith, and a corpulent; of a cheerful
look, a pleasing eye, and a most noble carriage; and, as I think, his
age some fifty, or, by 'r lady, inclining to three-score; and now I remember me, his name is Falstaff: if that man should be lewdly   [360
given, he deceiveth me; for, Harry, I see virtue in his looks. If then
the tree may be known by the fruit, as the fruit by the tree, then,
peremptorily I speak it, there is virtue in that Falstaff: him keep
with, the rest banish. And tell me now, thou naughty varlet, tell
me, where hast thou been this month?   365

PRINCE. Dost thou speak like a king? Do thou stand for me, and
I'll play my father.

FAL. Depose me? if thou dost it half so gravely, so majestically,
both in word and matter, hang me up by the heels for a rabbit-sucker
or a poulter's hare.   370

PRINCE. Well, here I am set.

FAL. And here I stand. Judge, my masters.

PRINCE. Now, Harry! whence come you?

FAL. My noble lord, from Eastcheap.

PRINCE. The complaints I hear of thee are grievous.   375

FAL. 'Sblood, my lord, they are false: nay, I'll tickle ye for a young prince, i' faith.

PRINCE. Swearest thou, ungracious boy? henceforth ne'er look on me. Thou art violently carried away from grace: there is a devil haunts thee in the likeness of an old fat man; a tun of man is [380 thy companion. Why dost thou converse with that trunk of humours, that bolting-hutch of beastliness, that swoln parcel of dropsies, that huge bombard of sack, that stuffed cloak-bag of guts, that roasted Manningtree ox with the pudding in his belly, that reverend vice, that grey iniquity, that father ruffian, that vanity in years? [385 Wherein is he good but to taste sack and drink it? wherein neat and cleanly but to carve a capon and eat it? wherein cunning but in craft? wherein crafty but in villany? wherein villanous but in all things? wherein worthy but in nothing?

FAL. I would your grace would take me with you: whom [390 means your grace?

PRINCE. That villanous abominable misleader of youth, Falstaff, that old white-bearded Satan.

FAL. My lord, the man I know.

PRINCE. I know thou dost.   395

FAL. But to say I know more harm in him than in myself were to say more than I know. That he is old, the more the pity, his white hairs do witness it: but that he is, saving your reverence, a whore-master, that I utterly deny. If sack and sugar be a fault, God help the wicked! If to be old and merry be a sin, then many an old [400 host that I know is damned: if to be fat be to be hated, then Pharaoh's lean kine are to be loved. No, my good lord: banish Peto, banish Bardolph, banish Poins; but for sweet Jack Falstaff, kind Jack Falstaff, true Jack Falstaff, valiant Jack Falstaff, and therefore more valiant, being, as he is, old Jack Falstaff, banish not him [405 thy Harry's company, banish not him thy Harry's company; banish plump Jack, and banish all the world.

PRINCE. I do, I will.   *A knocking heard.*
                                    Exeunt MISTRESS QUICKLY, FRANCIS,
                                                     and BARDOLPH.
                        Re-enter BARDOLPH, *running.*

BARD. O! my lord, my lord, the sheriff with a most monstrous watch is at the door.   410

FAL. Out, ye rogue! Play out the play: I have much to say in the behalf of that Falstaff.

                        Re-enter MISTRESS QUICKLY.

QUICK. O Jesu! my lord, my lord!

PRINCE. Heigh, heigh! the devil rides upon a fiddle-stick: what's
the matter?   415

QUICK. The sheriff and all the watch are at the door: they are
come to search the house. Shall I let them in?

FAL. Dost thou hear, Hal? never call a true piece of gold a counterfeit: thou art essentially mad without seeming so.

PRINCE. An thou a natural coward without instinct.   420

FAL. I deny your major. If you will deny the sheriff, so; if not, let
him enter: if I become not a cart as well as another man, a plague
on my bringing up! I hope I shall as soon be strangled with a halter
as another.

PRINCE. Go, hide thee behind the arras: the rest walk up   [425
above. Now, my masters, for a true face and good conscience.

FAL. Both which I have had: but their date is out, and therefore
I'll hide me.

PRINCE. Call in the sheriff.

Exeunt all but the PRINCE *and* PETO
Enter Sheriff and Carrier.

Now, Master sheriff, what's your will with me!   430

SHER. First, pardon me, my lord. A hue and cry
Hath follow'd certain men unto this house.

PRINCE. What men?

SHER. One of them is well known, my gracious lord;
A gross fat man.

CAR.   As fat as butter.   435

PRINCE. The man, I do assure you, is not here,
For I myself at this time have employ'd him.
And, sheriff, I will engage my word to thee,
That I will, by to-morrow dinner-time,
Send him to answer thee, or any man,   440
For any thing he shall be charg'd withal:
And so let me entreat you leave the house.

SHER. I will, my lord. There are two gentlemen
Have in this robbery lost three hundred marks.

PRINCE. It may be so: if he have robb'd these men,   445
He shall be answerable; and so farewell.

SHER. Good night, my noble lord.

PRINCE. I think it is good morrow, is it not?

SHER. Indeed, my lord, I think it be two o'clock.

Exeunt Sheriff and Carrier.

PRINCE. This oily rascal is known as well as Paul's. Go, call [450
him forth.

PETO. Falstaff! Fast asleep behind the arras, and snorting like a horse.

PRINCE. Hark, how hard he fetches breath. Search his pockets.

He searcheth his pockets, and findeth
certain papers.

What hast thou found?   455

PETO. Nothing but papers, my lord.

PRINCE. Let's see what they be: read them.

PETO. *Item, A capon* .... 2s. 2d.

      Item, Sauce .... 4d.

      Item, Sack, two gallons .... 5s. 8d. [460

      Item, Anchovies and sack after supper ..... 2s. 6d.

      Item, Bread .... ob.

PRINCE. O monstrous! but one half-penny-worth of bread to this intolerable deal of sack! What there is else, keep close; we'll read it at more advantage. There let him sleep till day. I'll to the court   [465 in the morning. We must all to the wars, and thy place shall be honourable. I'll procure this fat rogue a charge of foot; and I know his death will be a march of twelve-score. The money shall be paid back again with advantage. Be with me betimes in the morning; and so, good morrow, Peto.   470

PETO. Good morrow, good my lord.   *Exeunt.*

ACT III.
SCENE I.—*Bangor. A Room in the Archdeacon's House.*

Enter HOTSPUR, WORCESTER, MORTIMER, *and* GLENDOWER.

MORT. These promises are fair, the parties sure,
And our induction full of prosperous hope.

HOT. Lord Mortimer, and cousin Glendower,
Will you sit down?
And uncle Worcester: a plague upon it!   5
I have forgot the map.

GLEND.   No, here it is.
Sit, cousin Percy; sit, good cousin Hotspur;
For by that name as oft as Lancaster
Doth speak of you, his cheek looks pale and with
A rising sigh he wisheth you in heaven.   10

HOT. And you in hell, as oft as he hears Owen Glendower spoke of.

GLEND. I cannot blame him: at my nativity
The front of heaven was full of fiery shapes,
Of burning cressets; and at my birth
The frame and huge foundation of the earth   15
Shak'd like a coward.

HOT. Why, so it would have done at the same season, if your
mother's cat had but kittened, though yourself had never been born.

GLEND. I say the earth did shake when I was born.

HOT. And I say the earth was not of my mind,   20
If you suppose as fearing you it shook.

GLEND. The heavens were all on fire, the earth did tremble.

HOT. O! then the earth shook to see the heavens on fire,
And not in fear of your nativity.
Diseased nature oftentimes breaks forth   25
In strange eruptions; oft the teeming earth
Is with a kind of colic pinch'd and vex'd
By the imprisoning of unruly wind
Within her womb; which, for enlargement striving,
Shakes the old beldam earth, and topples down   30
Steeples and moss-grown towers. At your birth
Our grandam earth, having this distemperature,
In passion shook.

GLEND.   Cousin, of many men
I do not bear these crossings. Give me leave
To tell you once again that at my birth   35
The front of heaven was full of fiery shapes,
The goats ran from the mountains, and the herds
Were strangely clamorous to the frighted fields.
These signs have mark'd me extraordinary;
And all the courses of my life do show   40
I am not in the roll of common men.
Where is he living, clipp'd in with the sea
That chides the banks of England, Scotland, Wales,
Which calls me pupil, or hath read to me?
And bring him out that is but woman's son   45
Can trace me in the tedious ways of art
And hold me pace in deep experiments.

HOT. I think there's no man speaks better Welsh.
I'll to dinner.

MORT. Peace, cousin Percy! you will make him mad.   50

GLEND. I can call spirits from the vasty deep.

HOT. Why, so can I, or so can any man;
But will they come when you do call for them?

GLEND. Why, I can teach you, cousin, to command
The devil.   55

HOT. And I can teach thee, coz, to shame the devil
By telling truth: tell truth and shame the devil.

If thou have power to raise him, bring him hither,
And I'll be sworn I have power to shame him hence.
O! while you live, tell truth and shame the devil.   60
   MORT. Come, come;
No more of this unprofitable chat.
   GLEND. Three times hath Henry Bolingbroke made head
Against my power; thrice from the banks of Wye
And sandy-bottom'd Severn have I sent him   65
Bootless home and weather beaten back.
   HOT. Home without boots, and in foul weather too!
How 'scapes he agues, in the devil's name?
   GLEND. Come, here's the map: shall we divide our right
According to our threefold order ta'en?   70
   MORT. The archdeacon hath divided it
Into three limits very equally.
England, from Trent and Severn hitherto,
By south and east, is to my part assign'd:
All westward, Wales beyond the Severn shore,   75
And all the fertile land within that bound,
To Owen Glendower: and, dear coz, to you
The remnant northward, lying off from Trent.
And our indentures tripartite are drawn,
Which being sealed interchangeably,   80
A business that this night may execute,
To-morrow, cousin Percy, you and I
And my good Lord of Worcester will set forth
To meet your father and the Scottish power,
As is appointed us, at Shrewsbury.   85
My father Glendower is not ready yet,
Nor shall we need his help these fourteen days.
Within that space you may have drawn together
Your tenants, friends, and neighbouring gentlemen.
   GLEND. A shorter time shall send me to you, lords;   90
And in my conduct shall your ladies come,
From whom you now must steal and take no leave;
For there will be a world of water shed
Upon the parting of your wives and you.
   MORT. Methinks my moiety, north from Burton here,   95
In quantity equals not one of yours:
See how this river comes cranking in,
And cuts me from the best of all my land
A huge half-moon, a monstrous cantle out.
I'll have the current in this place damn'd up,   100

And here the smug and silver Trent shall run
In a new channel, fair and evenly:
It shall not wind with such a deep indent,
To rob me of so rich a bottom here.
 Glend. Not wind! it shall, it must; you see it doth.   105
 Mort. Yea, but
Mark how he bears his course, and runs me up
With like advantage on the other side;
Gelding the opposed continent as much
As on the other side it takes from you.   110
 Wor. Yea, but a little charge will trench him here,
And on this north side win this cape of land;
And then he runs straight and even.
 Hot. I'll have it so; a little charge will do it.
 Glend. I will not have it alter'd.
 Hot.   Will not you?   115
 Glend. No, nor you shall not.
 Hot.   Who shall say me nay?
 Glend. Why, that will I.
 Hot. Let me not understand you then: speak it in Welsh.
 Glend. I can speak English, lord, as well as you,
For I was train'd up in the English court;   120
Where, being but young, I framed to the harp
Many an English ditty lovely well,
And gave the tongue a helpful ornament;
A virtue that was never seen in you.
 Hot. Marry, and I'm glad of it with all my heart.   125
I had rather be a kitten, and cry mew
Than one of these same metre ballad-mongers;
I had rather hear a brazen canstick turn'd,
Or a dry wheel grate on the axle-tree;
And that would set my teeth nothing on edge,   130
Nothing so much as mincing poetry:
'Tis like the forc'd gait of a shuffling nag.
 Glend. Come, you shall have Trent turn'd.
 Hot. I do not care: I'll give thrice so much land
To any well-deserving friend;   135
But in the way of bargain, mark ye me,
I'll cavil on the ninth part of a hair.
Are the indentures drawn? Shall we be gone?
 Glend. The moon shines fair, you may away by night:
I'll haste the writer and withal   140
Break with your wives of your departure hence:

I am afraid my daughter will run mad,
So much she doteth on her Mortimer.   *Exit.*

   MORT. Fie, cousin Percy! how you cross my father!

   HOT. I cannot choose: sometime he angers me   145
With telling me of the moldwarp and the ant,
Of the dreamer Merlin and his prophecies,
And of a dragon, and a finless fish,
A clip-wing'd griffin, and moulten raven,
A couching lion, and a ramping cat,   150
And such a deal of skimble-skamble stuff
As puts me from my faith. I tell you what;
He held me last night at least nine hours
In reckoning up the several devils' names
That were his lackeys: I cried 'hum,' and 'well go to,' 155
But mark'd him not a word. O! he's as tedious
As a tired horse, a railing wife;
Worse than a smoky house. I had rather live
With cheese and garlic in a windmill, far,
Than feed on cates and have him talk to me   160
In any summer-house in Christendom.

   MORT. In faith, he is a worthy gentleman,
Exceedingly well read, and profited
In strange concealments, valiant as a lion
And wondrous affable, and as bountiful   165
As mines of India, Shall I tell you, cousin?
He holds your temper in high respect,
And curbs himself even of his natural scope
When you do cross his humour; faith, he does.
I warrant you, that man is not alive   170
Might so have tempted him as you have done,
Without the taste of danger and reproof:
But do not use it oft, let me entreat you.

   WOR. In faith, my lord, you are too wilful-blame;
And since your coming hither have done enough   175
to put him quite beside his patience.
You must needs learn, lord, to amend this fault:
Though sometimes it show greatness, courage, blood,
And that's the dearest grace it renders you,
Yet oftentimes it doth present harsh rage,   180
Defect of manners, want of government,
Pride, haughtiness, opinion, and disdain:
The least of which haunting a nobleman
Loseth men's hearts and leaves behind a stain

Upon the beauty of all parts besides, 185
Beguiling them of commendation.
 Hot. Well, I am school'd; good manners be your speed!
Here come our wives, and let us take our leave.
                Re-enter Glendower *with the Ladies*
 Mort. This is the deadly spite that angers me;
My wife can speak no English, I no Welsh. 190
 Glend. My daughter weeps; she will not part with you:
She'll be a soldier too: she'll to the wars.
 Mort. Good father, tell her that she and my aunt Percy
Shall follow in your conduct speedily.
                                Glendower *speaks to her in Welsh, and*
                                        she answers him in the same.
 Glend. She is desperate here; a peevish self-willed harlotry, [195
one that no persuasion can do good upon.
                                She speaks to Mortimer *in Welsh.*
 Mort. I understand thy looks: that pretty Welsh
Which thou down pourest from these swelling heavens
I am too perfect in; and, but for shame,
In such a parley should I answer thee. 200
                                She speaks again.

I understand thy kisses and thou mine,
And that's a feeling disputation:
But I will never be a truant, love,
Till I have learn'd thy language; for thy tongue
Makes Welsh as sweet as ditties highly penn'd, 205
Sung by a fair queen in a summer's bower,
With ravishing division, to her lute
 Glend. Nay, if you melt, then will she run mad.
                                She speaks again.
 Mort. O! I am ignorance itself in this.
 Glend. She bids you on the wanton rushes lay you down 210
And rest your gentle head upon her lap,
And she will sing the song that pleaseth you,
And on your eyelids crown the god of sleep,
Charming your blood with pleasing heaviness,
Making such difference 'twixt wake and sleep 215
As is the difference betwixt day and night
The hour before the heavenly-harness'd team
Begins his golden progress in the east.
 Mort. With all my heart I'll sit and hear her sing:
By that time will our book, I think, be drawn. 220
 Glend. Do so;

And those musicians that shall play to you
Hang in the air a thousand leagues from hence,
An straight they shall be here: sit, and attend.

HOT. Come, Kate, thou are perfect in lying down: come,   225
quick, quick, that I may lay my head in thy lap.

LADY P. Go, ye giddy goose.

The music plays.

HOT. Now I perceive the devil understands Welsh;
And 'tis no marvel he is so humorous.
By'r lady, he's a good musician.   230

LADY P. Then should you be nothing but musical, for you are
altogether governed by humours. Lie still, ye thief, and hear the lady
sing in Welsh.

HOT. I had rather hear Lady, my brach, howl in Irish.

LADY P. Would'st have thy head broken?   235

HOT. No.

LADY P. Then be still.

HOT. Neither; 'tis a woman's fault.

LADY P. Now God help thee!

HOT. To the Welsh lady's bed.   240

LADY P. What's that?

HOT. Peace! she sings.

A Welsh song sung by LADY MORTIMER.

HOT. Come, Kate, I'll have your song too.

LADY P. Not mine, in good sooth.

HOT. Not yours, 'in good sooth!' Heart! you swear like a   [245
comfit-maker's wife. Not you, 'in good sooth'; and 'as true as I live';
and 'as God shall mend me'; and 'as sure as day':
And giv'st such sarcenet surety for thy oaths,
As if thou never walk'dst further than Finsbury.
Swear me, Kate, like a lady as thou art,   250
A good mouth-filling oath; and leave 'in sooth,'
And such protest of pepper-gingerbread,
To velvet-guards and Sunday-citizens.
Come, sing.

LADY P. I will not sing.   255

HOT. 'Tis the next way to turn tailor or be red-breast teacher.
An the indentures be drawn, I'll away within these two hours; and
so come in when ye will.   *Exit.*

GLEND. Come, come, Lord Mortimer; you are as slow
As hot Lord Percy is on fire to go.   260
By this our book is drawn; we will but seal,

And then to horse immediately.
MORT. With all my heart.   *Exeunt.*

SCENE *II—London. A Room in the Palace.*

Enter KING HENRY, *the* PRINCE, *and Lords.*

K. HEN. Lords, give us leave; the Prince of Wales and I
Must have some private conference: but be near at hand,
For we shall presently have need of you.   *Exeunt Lords.*
I know not whether God will have it so,
For some displeasing service I have done,   5
That, in his secret doom, out of my blood
He'll breed revengement and a scourge for me;
But thou dost in thy passages of life
Make me believe that thou art only mark'd
For the hot vengeance and the rod of heaven   10
To punish my mistreadings. Tell me else,
Could such inordinate and low desires,
Such poor, such bare, such lewd, such mean attempts,
Such barren pleasures, rude society,
As thou art match'd withal and grafted to,   15
Accompany the greatness of thy blood
And hold their level with thy princely heart?
    PRINCE. So please your majesty, I would I could
Quit all offences with as clear excuse
As well as I am doubtless I can purge   20
Myself of many I am charged withal:
Yet such extenuation let me beg,
As, in reproof of many tales devis'd,
Which oft the ear of greatness needs must hear,
By smiling pick-thanks and base newsmongers,   25
I may, for some things true, wherein my youth
Hath faulty wander'd and irregular,
Find pardon on my true submission.
    K. HEN. God pardon thee! Yet let me wonder, Harry,
At thy affections, which do hold a wing   30
Quite from the flight of all thy ancestors.
Thy place in council thou hast rudely lost,
Which by thy younger brother is supplied,
And art almost an alien to the hearts
Of all the court and princes of my blood.   35
The hope and expectation of thy time
Is ruin'd, and the soul of every man
Prophetically does forethink thy fall.

Had I so lavish of my presence been,
So common-hackney'd in the eyes of men,   40
So stale and cheap to vulgar company,
Opinion, that did help me to the crown,
Had still kept loyal to possession
And left me in reputeless banishment,
A fellow of no mark nor likelihood.   45
By being seldom seen, I could not stir
But like a comet I was wonder'd at;
That men would tell their children 'This is he';
Others would say 'Where? Which is Bolingbroke?'
And then I stole all courtesy from heaven,   50
And dress'd myself in such humility
That I did pluck allegiance from men's hearts,
Loud shouts and salutations from their mouths,
Even in the presence of the crowned king.
Thus did I keep my person fresh and new;   55
My presence, like a robe pontifical,
Ne'er seen but wonder'd at: and so my state,
Seldom but sumptuous, showed like a feast,
And won by rareness such solemnity.
The skipping king, he ambled up and down   60
With shallow jesters and rash bavin wits,
Soon kindled and soon burnt; carded his state,
Mingled his royalty with capering fools,
Had his great name profaned with their scorns,
And gave his countenance, against his name,   65
To laugh at gibing boys and stand the push
Of every beardless vain comparative;
Grew a companion to the common streets,
Enfeoff'd himself to popularity;
That, being daily swallow'd by men's eyes,   70
They surfeited with honey and began
To loathe the taste of sweetness, whereof a little
More than a little is by much too much.
So when he had occasion to be seen,
He was but as the cuckoo is in June,   75
Heard, not regarded; seen, but with such eyes
As, sick and blunted with community,
Afford no extraordinary gaze,
Such as is bent on sun-like majesty
When it shines seldom in admiring eyes;   80
But rather drows'd and hung their eyelids down,

Slept in his face, and render'd such aspect
As cloudy men use to their adversaries,
Being with his presence glutted, gorg'd, and full.
And in that very line, Harry, stand'st thou;   85
For thou hast lost thy princely privilege
With vile participation: not an eye
But is aweary of thy common sight,
Save mine, which hath desir'd to see thee more;
Which now doth that I would not have it do,   90
Make blind itself with foolish tenderness.
   PRINCE. I shall hereafter, my thrice gracious lord,
Be more myself.
   K. HEN.   For all the world
As thou art to this hour was Richard then
When I from France set foot at Ravenspurgh;   95
And even as I was then is Percy now.
Now, by my sceptre and my soul to boot,
He hath more worthy interest to the state
Than thou the shadow of succession;
For of no right, nor colour like to right,   100
He doth fill fields with harness in the realm,
Turns head against the lion's armed jaws,
And, being no more in debt to years than thou,
Leads ancient lords and reverend bishops on
To bloody battles and to bruising arms.   105
What never-dying honour hath he got
Against renowned Douglas! whose high deeds,
Whose hot incursions and great name in arms
Holds from all soldiers chief majority,
And military title capital,   110
Through all the kingdoms that acknowledge Christ.
Thrice hath this Hotspur, Mars in swathling clothes,
This infant warrior, in his enterprises
Discomfited great Douglas; ta'en him once,
Enlarged him and made a friend of him,   115
To fill the mouth of deep defiance up
And shake the peace and safety of our throne.
And what say you to this? Percy, Northumberland,
The Archbishop's grace of York, Douglas, Mortimer,
Capitulate against us and are up.   120
But wherefore do I tell these news to thee?
Why, Harry, do I tell thee of my foes,
Which art my near'st and dearest enemy?

Thou that art like enough, through vassal fear,
Base inclination, and the start of spleen,   125
To fight against me under Percy's pay
To dog his heels, and court'sy at his frowns,
To show how much thou art degenerate.
 PRINCE. Do not think so; you shall not find it so:
And God forgive them that so much have sway'd   130
Your majesty's good thoughts away from me!
I will redeem all this on Percy's head,
And in the closing of some glorious day
Be bold to tell you that I am your son;
When I will wear a garment all of blood   135
And stain my favours in a bloody mask,
Which, wash'd away, shall scour my shame with it:
And that shall be the day, whene'er it lights,
That this same child of honour and renown,
This gallant Hotspur, this all-praised knight,   140
And your unthought-of Harry chance to meet.
For every honour sitting on his helm,
Would they were multitudes, and on my head
My shames redoubled! for the time will come
That I shall make this northern youth exchange   145
His glorious deeds for my indignities.
Percy is but my factor, good my lord,
To engross up glorious deeds on my behalf;
And I will call him to so strict account
That he shall render every glory up,   150
Yea, even the slightest worship of his time,
Or I will tear the reckoning from his heart.
This, in the name of God, I promise here:
The which if he be pleas'd I shall perform,
I do beseech your majesty may salve   155
The long-grown wounds of my intemperance:
If not, the end of life cancels all bands,
And I will die a hundred thousand deaths
Ere break the smallest parcel of this vow.
 K. HEN. A hundred thousand rebels die in this: 160
Thou shalt have charge and sovereign trust herein.
Enter BLUNT.
How now, good Blunt! thy looks are full of speed.
 BLUNT. So hath the business that I come to speak of.
Lord Mortimer of Scotland hath sent word
That Douglas and the English rebels met   165

The eleventh of this month at Shrewsbury.
A mighty and a fearful head they are,
If promises be kept on every hand,
As ever offer'd foul play in a state.

K. HEN. The Earl of Westmoreland set forth to-day, 170
With him my son, Lord John of Lancaster;
For this advertisement is five days old.
On Wednesday next, Harry, you shall set forward;
On Thursday we ourselves will march: our meeting
Is Bridgenorth; and, Harry, you shall march 175
Through Gloucestershire; by which account,
Our business valued, some twelve days hence
Our general forces at Bridgenorth shall meet.
Our hands are full of business: let's away;
Advantage feeds him fat while men delay. 180

Exeunt.

SCENE III.—*Eastcheap. A Room in the Boar's Head Tavern.*

Enter FALSTAFF *and* BARDOLPH.

FAL. Bardolph, am I not fallen away vilely since this last action?
do I not bate? do I not dwindle? Why, my skin hangs about me like
an old lady's loose gown; I am withered like an old apple-john.
Well, I'll repent, and that suddenly, while I am in some liking; I
shall be out of heart shortly, and then I shall have no strength [5
to repent. An I have not forgotten what the inside of a church is
made of, I am a peppercorn, a brewer's horse: the inside of a church!
Company, villanous company, hath been the spoil of me.

BARD. Sir John, you are so fretful, you cannot live long.

FAL. Why, there is it: come, sing me a bawdy song; make me [10
merry. I was as virtuously given as a gentleman need to be; virtuous
enough: swore little; diced not above seven times a week; went to
a bawdy-house not above once in a quarter—of an hour; paid money
that I borrowed three or four times; lived well and in good compass;
and now I live out of all order, out of all compass. 15

BARD. Why, you are so fat, Sir John, that you must needs be out
of all compass, out of all reasonable compass, Sir John.

FAL. Do thou amend thy face, and I'll amend my life: thou art
our admiral, thou bearest the lantern in the poop, but 'tis in the
nose of thee: thou art the Knight of the Burning Lamp. 20

BARD. Why, Sir John, my face does you no harm.

FAL. No, I'll be sworn; I make as good use of it as many a man
doth of a Death's-head or a *memento mori*. I never see thy face but
I think upon hell-fire and Dives that lived in purple; for there

he is in his robes, burning, burning. If thou wert any way given [25 to virtue, I would swear by thy face; my oath should be, 'By this fire, that's God's angel.' But thou art altogether given over, and wert indeed, but for the light in thy face, the son of utter darkness. When thou rannest up Gadshill in the night to catch my horse, if I did not think thou hadst been an *ignis fatuus* or a ball of [30 wildfire, there's no purchase in money. O! thou art a perpetual triumph, an everlasting bonfire-light. Thou. hast saved me a thousand marks in links and torches, walking with thee in the night betwixt tavern and tavern: but the sack that thou hast drunk me would have bought me lights as good cheap at the dearest [35 chandler's in Europe. I have maintained that salamander of yours with fire any time this two-and-thirty years; God reward me for it!

BARD. 'Sblood! I would my face were in your belly.

FAL. God-a-mercy! so should I be sure to be heart-burned.

Enter MISTRESS QUICKLY.

How now, Dame Partlet the hen! have you inquired yet who [40 picked my pocket?

QUICK. Why, Sir John, what do you think, Sir John? Do you think I keep thieves in my house? I have searched, I have inquired, so has my husband, man by man, boy by boy, servant by servant: the tithe of a hair was never lost in my house before. 45

FAL. Ye lie, hostess; Bardolph was shaved and lost many a hair; and I'll be sworn my pocket was picked. Go to, you are a woman; go.

QUICK. Who, I? No; I defy thee: God's light! I was never called so in mine own house before.

FAL. Go to, I know you well enough. 50

QUICK. No, Sir John; you do not know me, Sir John: I know you, Sir John: you owe me money, Sir John, and now you pick a quarrel to beguile me of it: I bought you a dozen of shirts to your back.

FAL. Dowlas, filthy dowlas: I have given them away to bakers' wives, and they have made bolters of them. 55

QUICK. Now, as I am a true woman, holland of eight shillings an ell. You owe money here besides, Sir John, for your diet and by-drinkings, and money lent you, four-and-twenty pound.

FAL. He had his part of it; let him pay.

QUICK. He! alas! he is poor: he hath nothing. 60

FAL. How! poor? look upon his face; what call you rich? let them coin his nose, let them coin his cheeks. I'll not pay a denier. What! will you make a younker of me? shall I not take mine ease in mine inn but I shall have my pocket picked? I have lost a seal-ring of my grandfather's worth forty mark. 65

QUICK. O Jesu! I have heard the prince tell him, I know not how oft, that that ring was copper.

FAL. How! the prince is a Jack, a sneak-cup; 'sblood! an he were here, I would cudgel him like a dog, if he would say so.

Enter the PRINCE *and* POINS, *marching.* FALSTAFF *meets them, playing on his truncheon like a fife.*

How now, lad! is the wind in that door, i'faith? must we all [70 march?

BARD. Yea, two and two, Newgate fashion.

QUICK. My lord, I pray you, hear me.

PRINCE. What sayest thou, Mistress Quickly? How does thy husband? I love him well, he is an honest man.   75

QUICK. Good my lord, hear me.

FAL. Prithee, let her alone, and list to me.

PRINCE. What sayest thou, Jack?

FAL. The other night I fell asleep here behind the arras and had my pocket picked: this house is turned bawdy-house; they pick [80 pockets.

PRINCE. What didst thou lose, Jack?

FAL. Wilt thou believe me, Hal? three or four bonds of forty pound a-piece, and a seal-ring of my grandfather's.

PRINCE. A trifle; some eight-penny matter.   85

QUICK. So I told him, my lord; and I said I heard your grace say so: and, my lord, he speaks most vilely of you, like a foul-mouthed man as he is, and said he would cudgel you.

PRINCE. What! he did not?

QUICK. There's neither faith, truth, nor womanhood in me [90 else.

FAL. There's no more faith in thee than in a stewed prune; nor no more truth in thee than in a drawn fox; and for womanhood, Maid Marian may be the deputy's wife of the ward to thee. Go, you thing, go.   95

QUICK. Say, what thing? what thing?

FAL. What thing! why, a thing to thank God on.

QUICK. I am no thing to thank God on, I would thou should'st know it; I am an honest man's wife; and, setting thy knighthood aside, thou art a knave to call me so.   100

FAL. Setting thy womanhood aside, thou art a beast to say otherwise.

QUICK. Say, what beast, thou knave thou?

FAL. What beast! why, an otter.

PRINCE. An otter, Sir John! why an otter?   105

FAL. Why, she's neither fish nor flesh; a man knows not where to have her.

QUICK. Thou are an unjust man in saying so: thou or any man knows where to have me, thou knave thou!

PRINCE. Thou sayest true, hostess; and he slanders thee most [110 grossly.

QUICK. So he doth you, my lord; and said this other day you ought him a thousand pound.

PRINCE. Sirrah! do I owe you a thousand pound?

FAL. A thousand pound, Hal! a million: thy love is worth a [115 million; thou owest me thy love.

QUICK. Nay, my lord, he called you Jack, and said he would cudgel you.

FAL. Did I, Bardolph?

BARD. Indeed, Sir John, you said so.   [120

FAL. Yea; if he said my ring was copper.

PRINCE. I say 'tis copper: darest thou be as good as thy word now?

FAL. Why, Hal, thou knowest, as thou art but man, I dare; but as thou art a prince, I fear thee as I fear the roaring of the lion's whelp.   [125

PRINCE. And why not as the lion?

FAL. The king himself is to be feared as the lion: dost thou think I'll fear thee as I fear thy father? nay, an I do, I pray God my girdle break!

PRINCE. O! if it should, how would thy guts fall about thy [130 knees. But, sirrah, there's no room for faith, truth, nor honesty in this bosom of thine; it is all filled up with guts and midriff. Charge an honest woman with picking thy pocket! Why, thou whoreson, impudent, embossed rascal, if there were any thing in thy pocket but tavern reckonings, memorandums of bawdy-houses, and one [135 poor pennyworth of sugar-candy to make thee long-winded; if thy pocket were enriched with any other injuries but these, I am a villain. And yet you will stand to it, you will not pocket up wrong. Art thou not ashamed?

FAL. Dost thou hear, Hal? thou knowest in the state of inno-[140 cency Adam fell; and what should poor Jack Falstaff do in the days of villany? Thou seest I have more flesh than another man, and therefore more frailty. You confess then, you picked my pocket?

PRINCE. It appears so by the story.

FAL. Hostess, I forgive thee. Go, make ready breakfast; love [145 thy husband, look to thy servants, cherish thy guests: thou shalt find me tractable to any honest reason: thou seest I am pacified. Still! Nay prithee, be gone.

Exit MISTRESS QUICKLY.

Now, Hal, to the news at court: for the robbery, lad, how is that answered?   150

PRINCE. O! my sweet beef, I must still be good angel to thee: the money is paid back again.

FAL. O! I do not like that paying back; 'tis a double labour.

PRINCE. I am good friends with my father and may do any thing.

FAL. Rob me the exchequer the first thing thou dost, and do it [155 with unwashed hands too.

BARD. Do, my lord.

PRINCE. I have procured thee, Jack, a charge of foot.

FAL. I would it had been of horse. Where shall I find one that can steal well? O! for a fine thief, of the age of two-and-twenty or [160 thereabouts; I am heinously unprovided. Well, God be thanked for these rebels; they offend none but the virtuous: I laud them, I praise them.

PRINCE. Bardolph!

BARD. My lord?   165

PRINCE. Go bear this letter to Lord John of Lancaster, to my brother John; this to my lord of Westmoreland. Go, Poins, to horse, to horse! for thou and I have thirty miles to ride yet ere dinner-time. Jack, meet me to-morrow in the Temple-Hall at two o'clock in the afternoon: 170
There shalt thou know thy charge, and there receive
Money and order for their furniture.
The land is burning; Percy stands on high;
And either we or they must lower lie.

Exeunt the PRINCE, POINS, *and* BARDOLPH.

FAL. Rare words! brave world! Hostess, my breakfast; come!   175
O! I could wish this tavern were my drum.

Exit.

ACT IV.

SCENE I.—*The Rebel Camp near Shrewsbury.*

Enter HOTSPUR, WORCESTER, *and* DOUGLAS.

HOT. Well said, my noble Scot: if speaking truth
In this fine age were not thought flattery,
Such attribution should the Douglas have,
As not a soldier of this season's stamp

Should go so general current through the world.   5
By God, I cannot flatter; do defy
The tongues of soothers; but a braver place
In my heart's love hath no man than yourself.
Nay, task me to my word; approve me, lord.
　　Doug. Thou art the king of honour: 10
No man so potent breathes upon the ground
But I will beard him.
　　Hot.　　　　　Do so, and 'tis well.
　　　　　　　Enter a Messenger, with letters.
What letters hast thou there? I can but thank you.
　　Mess. These letters come from your father.
　　Hot. Letters from him! why comes he not himself?   15
　　Mess. He cannot come, my lord: he's grievous sick.
　　Hot. 'Zounds! how has he the leisure to be sick
In such a justling time? Who leads his power?
Under whose government come they along?
　　Mess. His letters bear his mind, not I, my lord.   20
　　Wor. I prithee, tell me, doth he keep his bed?
　　Mess. He did, my lord, four days ere I set forth:
And at the time of my departure thence
He was much fear'd by his physicians.
　　Wor. I would the state of time had first been whole   25
Ere he by sickness had been visited:
His health was never better worth than now.
　　Hot. Sick now! droop now! this sickness doth infect
The very life-blood of our enterprise;
'Tis catching hither, even to our camp.   30
He writes me here, that inward sickness—
And that his friends by deputation could not
So soon be drawn; nor did he think it meet
To lay so dangerous and dear a trust
On any soul remov'd but on his own.   35
Yet doth he give us bold advertisement,
That with our small conjunction we should on,
To see how fortune is dispos'd to us;
For, as he writes, there is no quailing now,
Because the king is certainly possess'd   40
Of all our purposes. What say you to it?
　　Wor. Your father's sickness is a maim to us.
　　Hot. A perilous gash, a very limb lopp'd off:
And yet, in faith, 'tis not; his present want
Seems more than we shall find it. Were it good   45

To set the exact wealth of all our states
All at one cast? to set so rich a main
On the nice hazard of one doubtful hour?
It were not good; for therein should we read
The very bottom and the soul of hope,   50
The very list, the very utmost bound
Of all our fortunes.
    Doug.   Faith, and so we should;
Where now remains a sweet reversion:
We may boldy spend upon the hope of what
Is to come in: 55
A comfort of retirement lives in this.
    Hot. A rendezvous, a home to fly unto,
If that the devil and mischance look big
Upon the maidenhead of our affairs.
    Wor. But yet, I would your father had been here.   60
The quality and hair of our attempt
Brooks no division. It will be thought
By some that know not why he is away,
That wisdom, loyalty and mere dislike
Of our proceedings, kept the earl from hence.   65
And think how such an apprehension
May turn the tide of fearful faction
And breed a kind of question in our cause;
For well you know we of the offering side
Must keep aloof from strict arbitrement,   70
And stop all sight-holes, every loop from whence
The eye of reason may pry in upon us:
This absence of your father's draws a curtain,
That shows the ignorant a kind of fear
Before not dreamt of.
    Hot.   You strain too far.   75
I rather of his absence make this use:
It lends a lustre and more great opinion,
A larger dare to our great enterprise,
Than if the earl were here; for men must think,
If we without his help can make a head   80
To push against a kingdom, with his help
We shall o'erturn it topsy-turvy down.
Yet all goes well, yet all our joints are whole.
    Doug. As heart can think: there is not such a word
Spoke of in Scotland as this term of fear.   85
                Enter SIR RICHARD VERNON.

Hot. My cousin Vernon! welcome, by my soul.

Ver. Pray God my news be worth a welcome, lord.
The Earl of Westmoreland, seven thousand strong,
Is marching hitherwards; with him Prince John.

Hot. No harm: what more?

Ver.   And further, I have learn'd,   90
The king himself in person is set forth,
Or hitherwards intended speedily,
With strong and mighty preparation.

Hot. He shall be welcome too. Where is his son,
The nimble-footed madcap Prince of Wales,   95
And his comrades, that daff'd the world aside,
And bid it pass?

Ver.   All furnish'd, all in arms,
All plum'd like estridges that wing the wind,
Baited like eagles having lately bath'd,
Glittering in golden coats, like images,   100
As full of spirit as the month of May,
And gorgeous as the sun at midsummer,
Wanton as youthful goats, wild as young bulls.
I saw young Harry, with his beaver on,
His cuisses on his thighs, gallantly arm'd,   105
Rise from the ground like feather'd Mercury,
And vaulted with such ease into his seat,
As if an angel dropp'd down from the clouds,
To turn and wind a fiery Pegasus
And witch the world with noble horsemanship.   110

Hot. No more, no more: worse than the sun in March
This praise doth nourish agues. Let them come;
They come like sacrifices in their trim,
And to the fire-eyed maid of smoky war
All hot and bleeding will we offer them: 115
The mailed Mars shall on his altar sit
Up to the ears in blood. I am on fire
To hear this rich reprisal is so nigh
And yet not ours. Come, let me taste my horse,
Who is to bear me like a thunderbolt   120
Against the bosom of the Prince of Wales:
Harry to Harry shall, hot horse to horse,
Meet and ne'er part till one drop down a corse.
O! that Glendower were come.

Ver.   There is more news:
I learn'd in Worcester, as I rode along,   125

He cannot draw his power this fourteen days.
DOUG. That's the worst tidings that I hear of yet.
WOR. Ay, by my faith, that bears a frosty sound.
HOT. What may the king's whole battle reach unto?
VER. To thirty thousand.
HOT.   Forty let it be: 130
My father and Glendower being both away,
The powers of us may serve so great a day.
Come, let us take a muster speedily:
Doomsday is near; die all, die merrily.
DOUG. Talk not of dying: I am out of fear   135
Of death or death's hand for this one half year.

Exeunt.

SCENE II.—*A public Road near Coventry*

Enter FALSTAFF *and* BARDOLPH.

FAL. Bardolph, get thee before to Coventry; fill me a bottle of
sack: our soldiers shall march through; we'll to Sutton Co'fil'
to-night.
BARD. Will you give me money, captain?
FAL. Lay out, lay out.   5
BARD. This bottle makes an angel.
FAL. An if it do, take it for thy labour; and if it make twenty,
take them all, I'll answer the coinage. Bid my lieutenant Peto meet
me at the town's end.
BARD. I will, captain: farewell.   *Exit.* [10
FAL. If I be not ashamed of my soldiers, I am a soused gurnet.
I have misused the king's press damnably. I have got, in exchange
of a hundred and fifty soldiers, three hundred and odd pounds. I
press me none but good householders, yeomen's sons; inquire me
out contracted bachelors, such as had been asked twice on the [15
banns; such a commodity of warm slaves, as had as lief hear the
devil as a drum; such as fear the report of a caliver worse than a
struck fowl or a hurt wild-duck. I pressed me none but such toasts-
and-butter, with hearts in their bellies no bigger than pins' heads,
and they have bought out their services; and now my whole [20
charge consists of ancients, corporals, lieutenants, gentlemen of
companies, slaves as ragged as Lazarus in the painted cloth, where
the glutton's dogs licked his sores; and such as indeed were never
soldiers, but discarded unjust servingmen, younger sons to younger
brothers, revolted tapsters and ostlers trade-fallen, the cankers [25
of a calm world and a long peace; ten times more dishonourable
ragged than an old faced ancient: and such have I, to fill up the

rooms of them that have bought out their services, that you would think that I had a hundred and fifty tattered prodigals, lately come from swine-keeping, from eating draff and husks. A mad fellow [30 met me on the way and told me I had unloaded all the gibbets and pressed the dead bodies. No eye hath seen such scarecrows. I'll not march through Coventry with them, that's flat: nay, and the villains march wide betwixt the legs, as if they had gyves on; for indeed I had the most of them out of prison. There's but a shirt and a [35 half in all my company; and the half shirt is two napkins tacked together and thrown over the shoulders like an herald's coat without sleeves; and the shirt, to say the truth, stolen from my host at Saint Alban's, or the red-nose innkeeper of Daventry. But that's all one; they'll find linen enough on every hedge.   40

Enter the PRINCE *and* WESTMORELAND.

PRINCE. How now, blown Jack! how now, quilt!

FAL. What, Hal! how now, mad wag! what a devil dost thou in Warwickshire? My good Lord of Westmoreland, I cry you mercy: I thought your honour had already been at Shrewsbury.

WEST. Faith, Sir John, 'tis more than time that I were there, [45 and you too; but my powers are there already. The king, I can tell you, looks for us all: we must away all night.

FAL. Tut, never fear me: I am as vigilant as a cat to steal cream.

PRINCE. I think to steal cream indeed, for thy theft hath already made thee butter. But tell me, Jack, whose fellows are these [50 that come after?

FAL. Mine, Hal, mine.

PRINCE. I did never see such pitiful rascals.

FAL. Tut, tut; good enough to toss; food for powder, food for powder; they'll fill a pit as well as better: tush, man, mortal [55 men, mortal men.

WEST. Ay, but, Sir John, methinks they are exceeding poor and bare; too beggarly.

FAL. Faith, for their poverty, I know not where they had that; and for their bareness, I am sure they never learned that of me. [60

PRINCE. No, I'll be sworn; unless you call three fingers on the ribs bare. But, sirrah, make haste: Percy is already in the field.

FAL. What! is the king encamped?

WEST. He is, Sir John: I fear we shall stay too long.

FAL. Well,   65
To the latter end of a fray and the beginning of a feast
Fits a dull fighter and a keen guest.   *Exeunt.*

Scene III.—*The Rebel Camp near Shrewsbury.*

Enter Hotspur, Worcester, Douglas, *and* Vernon.

Hot. We'll fight with him to-night.
Wor.   It may not be.
Doug. You give him then advantage.
Ver.   Not a whit.
Hot. Why say you so? looks he not for supply?
Ver. So do we.
Hot.   His is certain, ours is doubtful.
Wor. Good cousin, be advis'd: stir not to-night.   5
Ver. Do not, my lord.
Doug.   You do not counsel well:
You speak it out of fear and cold heart.
Ver. Do me no slander, Douglas: by my life,
And I dare well maintain it with my life,
If well-respected honour bid me on,   10
I hold as little counsel with weak fear
As you, my lord, or any Scot that this day lives:
Let it be seen to-morrow in the battle
Which of us fears.
Doug.   Yea, or to-night.
Ver.   Content.
Hot. To-night, say I.   15
Ver. Come, come, it may not be. I wonder much,
Being men of such great leading as you are,
That you foresee not what impediments
Drag back our expedition: certain horse
Of my cousin Vernon's are not yet come up: 20
Your uncle Worcester's horse came but to-day;
And now their pride and mettle is asleep,
Their courage with hard labour tame and dull,
That not a horse is half the half of himself.
Hot. So are the horses of the enemy   25
In general, journey-bated and brought low:
The better part of ours are full of rest.
Wor. The number of the king exceedeth ours:
For God's sake, cousin, stay till all come in.
                    The trumpet sounds a parley.
            Enter Sir Walter Blunt.
Blunt. I come with gracious offers from the king,   30
If you vouchsafe me hearing and respect.

Hot. Welcome, Sir Walter Blunt; and would to God
You were of our determination!
Some of us love you well; and even those some
Envy your great deservings and good name,   35
Because you are not of our quality,
But stand against us like an enemy.
  Blunt. And God defend but still I should stand so,
So long as out of limit and true rule
You stand against anointed majesty.   40
But to my charge. The king hath sent to know
The nature of your griefs, and whereupon
You conjure from the breast of civil peace
Such bold hostility, teaching his duteous land
Audacious cruelty. If that the king   45
Have any way your good deserts forgot,
Which he confesseth to be manifold,
He bids you name your griefs; and with all speed
You shall have your desires with interest,
And pardon absolute for yourself and these   50
Herein misled by your suggestion.
  Hot. The king is kind; and well we know the king
Knows at what time to promise, when to pay.
My father and my uncle and myself
Did give him that same royalty he wears;   55
And when he was not six-and-twenty strong,
Sick in the world's regard, wretched and low,
A poor unminded outlaw sneaking home,
My father gave him welcome to the shore;
And when he heard him swear and vow to God   60
He came but to be Duke of Lancaster,
To sue his livery and beg his peace,
With tears of innocency and terms of zeal,
My father, in kind heart and pity mov'd,
Swore him assistance and perform'd it too.   65
Now when the lords and barons of the realm
Perceiv'd Northumberland did lean to him,
The more and less came in with cap and knee;
Met him in boroughs, cities, villages,
Attended him on bridges, stood in lanes,   70
Laid gifts before him, proffer'd him their oaths,
Gave him their heirs as pages, follow'd him
Even at the heels in golden multitudes.
He presently, as greatness knows itself,

Steps me a little higher than his vow   75
Made to my father, while his blood was poor,
Upon the naked shore at Ravenspurgh;
And now, forsooth, takes on him to reform
Some certain edicts and some strait decrees
That lie too heavy on the commonwealth,   80
Cries out upon abuses, seems to weep
Over his country's wrongs; and by this face,
This seeming brow of justice, did he win
The hearts of all that he did angle for;
Proceeded further; cut me off the heads   85
Of all the favourites that the absent king
In deputation left behind him here,
When he was personal in the Irish war.
    BLUNT. Tut, I came not to hear this.
    HOT.   Then to the point.
In short time after, he depos'd the king;   90
Soon after that, depriv'd him of his life;
And in the neck of that, task'd the whole state;
To make that worse, suffer'd his kinsman March—
Who is, if every owner were well plac'd,
Indeed his king—to be engag'd in Wales,   95
There without ransom to lie forfeited;
Disgrac'd me in my happy victories;
Sought to entrap me by intelligence;
Rated mine uncle from the council-board;
In rage dismiss'd my father from the court;   100
Broke oath on oath, committed wrong on wrong;
And in conclusion drove us to seek out
This head of safety; and withal to pry
Into his title, the which we find
Too indirect for long continuance.   105
    BLUNT. Shall I return this answer to the king?
    HOT. Not so, Sir Walter: we'll withdraw awhile.
Go to the king; and let there be impawn'd
Some surety for a safe return again,
And in the morning early shall my uncle   110
Bring him our purposes; and so farewell.
    BLUNT. I would you would accept of grace and love.
    HOT. And may be so we shall.
    BLUNT.   Pray God, you do!
                                          Exeunt.

SCENE IV.—*York. A Room in the Archbishop's Palace.*

Enter the Archbishop of YORK *and* SIR MICHAEL.

ARCH. Hie, good Sir Michael; bear this sealed brief
With winged haste to the lord marshal;
This to my cousin Scroop, and all the rest
To whom they are directed. If you knew
How much they do import, you would make haste.   5
SIR M. My good lord,
I guess their tenour.
ARCH.   Like enough you do.
To-morrow, good Sir Michael, is a day
Wherein the fortune of ten thousand men
Must bide the touch; for, sir, at Shrewsbury,   10
As I am truly given to understand,
The king with mighty and quick-raised power
Meets with Lord Harry: and I fear, Sir Michael,
What with the sickness of Northumberland,
Whose power was in the first proportion,   15
And what with Owen Glendower's absence thence,
Who with them was a rated sinew too,
And comes not in, o'er-rul'd by prophecies,
I fear the power of Percy is too weak
To wage an instant trial with the king.   20
SIR M. Why, my good lord, you need not fear:
There is Douglas and Lord Mortimer.
ARCH. No, Mortimer is not there.
SIR M. But there is Mordake, Vernon, Lord Harry Percy,
And there's my Lord of Worcester, and a head   25
Of gallant warriors, noble gentlemen.
ARCH. And so there is; but yet the king hath drawn
The special head of all the land together:
The Prince of Wales, Lord John of Lancaster,
The noble Westmoreland, and war-like Blunt,   30
And many more corrivals and dear men
Of estimation and command in arms.
SIR M. Doubt not, my lord, they shall be well oppos'd.
ARCH. I hope no less, yet needful 'tis to fear;
And, to prevent the worst, Sir Michael, speed: 35
For if Lord Percy thrive not, ere the king
Dismiss his power, he means to visit us,
For he hath heard of our confederacy,
And 'tis but wisdom to make strong against him:

Therefore make haste. I must go write again   40
To other friends: and so farewell, Sir Michael.

                                        Exeunt.

ACT V.

SCENE I.—*The King's Camp near Shrewsbury.*

Enter KING HENRY, *the* PRINCE, JOHN OF LANCASTER, SIR WALTER
        BLUNT, *and* SIR JOHN FALSTAFF.

K. HEN. How bloodily the sun begins to peer
Above you busky hill! the day looks pale
At his distemperature.
PRINCE.   The southern wind
Doth play the trumpet to his purposes,
And by his hollow whistling in the leaves   5
Foretells a tempest and a blustering day.
K. HEN. Then with the losers let it sympathize,
For nothing can seem foul to those that win.

                                Trumpet sounds.
        Enter WORCESTER *and* VERNON

How now, my Lord of Worcester! 'tis not well
That you and I should meet upon such terms   10
As now we meet. You have deceiv'd our trust,
And made us doff our easy robes of peace,
To crush our old limbs in ungentle steel:
This is not well, my lord; this is not well.
What say you to it? will you again unknit   15
This churlish knot of all-abhorred war,
And move in that obedient orb again
Where you did give a fair and natural light,
And be no more an exhal'd meteor,
A prodigy of fear and a portent   20
Of broached mischief to the unborn times?
WOR. Hear me, my liege.
For mine own part, I could be well content
To entertain the lag-end of my life
With quiet hours; for I do protest,   25
I have not sought the day of this dislike.
K. HEN. You have not sought it! how comes it then?
FAL. Rebellion lay in his way, and he found it.
PRINCE. Peace, chewet, peace!
WOR. It pleas'd your majesty to turn your looks   30
Of favour from myself and all our house;

And yet I must remember you, my lord,
We were the first and dearest of your friends.
For you my staff of office did I break
In Richard's time; and posted day and night   35
To meet you on the way, and kiss your hand,
When yet you were in place and in account
Nothing so strong and fortunate as I.
It may myself, my brother, and his son,
That brought you home and boldly did out-dare   40
The dangers of the time. You swore to us,
And you did swear that oath at Doncaster,
That you did nothing purpose 'gainst the state,
Nor claim no further than your new-fall'n right,
The seat of Gaunt, dukedom of Lancaster.   45
To this we swore our aid: but in short space
It rain'd down fortune showering on your head,
And such a flood of greatness fell on you,
What with our help, what with the absent king,
What with the injuries of a wanton time,   50
The seeming sufferances that you had borne,
And the contrarious winds that held the king
So long in his unlucky Irish wars,
That all in England did repute him dead:
And from this swarm of fair advantages   55
You took occasion to be quickly woo'd
To gripe the general sway into your hand;
Forgot your oath to us at Doncaster;
And being fed by us you us'd us so
As that ungentle gull, the cuckoo's bird,   60
Useth the sparrow: did oppress our nest,
Grew by our feeding to so great a bulk
That even our love durst not come near your sight
For fear of swallowing; but with nimble wing
We were enforc'd, for safety sake, to fly   65
Out of your sight and raise this present head;
Whereby we stand opposed by such means
As you yourself have forg'd against yourself
By unkind usage, dangerous countenance,
And violation of all faith and troth   70
Sworn to us in your younger enterprise.
    K. HEN. These things indeed you have articulate,
Proclaim'd at market-crosses, read in churches,
To face the garment of rebellion

With some fine colour that may please the eye   75
Of fickle changelings and poor discontents,
Which gape and rub the elbow at the news
Of hurlyburly innovation:
And never yet did insurrection want
Such water-colours to impaint his cause;   80
Nor moody beggars, starving for a time
Of pell-mell havoc and confusion.
    PRINCE. In both our armies there is many a soul
Shall pay full dearly for this encounter,
If once they join in trial. Tell your nephew,   85
The Prince of Wales doth join with all the world
In praise of Henry Percy: by my hopes,
This present enterprise set off his head,
I do not think a braver gentleman,
More active-valiant or more valiant-young,   90
More daring or more bold, is now alive
To grace this latter age with noble deeds.
For my part, I may speak it to my shame,
I have a truant been to chivalry;
And so I hear he doth account me too;   95
Yet this before my father's majesty—
I am content that he shall take the odds
Of his great name and estimation,
And will, to save the blood on either side,
Try fortune with him in a single fight.   100
    K. HEN. And, Prince of Wales, so dare we venture thee,
Albeit considerations infinite
Do make against it. No, good Worcester, no,
We love our people well, even those we love
That are misled upon your cousin's part;   105
And, will they take the offer of our grace,
Both he and they and you, yea, every man
Shall be my friend again, and I'll be his.
So tell your cousin, and bring me word
What he will do; but if he will not yield,   110
Rebuke and dread correction wait on us,
And they shall do their office. So, be gone:
We will not now be troubled with reply;
We offer fair, take it advisedly.
                    Exeunt WORCESTER *and* VERNON.
    PRINCE. It will not be accepted, on my life.   115
The Douglas and the Hotspur both together

Are confident against the world in arms.

K. HEN. Hence, therefore, every leader to his charge;
For, on their answer, will we set on them;
And God befriend us, as our cause is just!   120

Exeunt KING HENRY, BLUNT, *and*
JOHN OF LANCASTER.

FAL. Hal, if thou see me down in the battle, and bestride me, so;
'tis a point of friendship.

PRINCE. Nothing but a colossus can do thee that friendship. Say
thy prayers, and farewell.

FAL. I would it were bed-time, Hal, and all well.   125

PRINCE. Why, thou owest God a death.   *Exit.*

FAL. 'Tis not due yet: I would be loath to pay him before his
day. What need I be so forward with him that calls not on me? Well,
'tis no matter; honour pricks me on. Yea, but how if honour prick
me off when I come on? how then? Can honour set to a leg? No. [130
Or an arm? No. Or take away the grief of a wound? No. Honour
hath no skill in surgery then? No. What is honour? A word. What is
that word honour? Air. A trim reckoning! Who hath it? He that died
o' Wednesday. Doth he feel it? No. Doth he hear it? No. Is it insensible then? Yea, to the dead. But will it not live with the living? [135
No. Why? Detraction will not suffer it. Therefore I'll none of it.
Honour is a mere scutcheon; and so ends my catechism.   *Exit.*

SCENE II.—*The Rebel Camp near Shrewsbury.*

Enter WORCESTER *and* VERNON.

WOR. O! no, my nephew must not know, Sir Richard,
The liberal kind offer of the king.

VER. 'Twere best he did.

WOR.   Then are we all undone.
It is not possible, it cannot be,
The king should keep his word in loving us;   5
He will suspect us still, and find a time
To punish this offence in other faults:
Suspicion all our lives shall be stuck full of eyes;
For treason is but trusted like the fox,
Who, ne'er so tame, so cherish'd, and lock'd up,   10
Will have a wild trick of his ancestors.
Look how we can, or sad or merrily,
Interpretation will misquote our looks,
And we shall feed like oxen at a stall,
The better cherish'd, still the nearer death.   15
My nephew's trespass may be well forgot,

It hath the excuse of youth and heat of blood;
And an adopted name of privilege,
A hare-brain'd Hotspur, govern'd by a spleen.
All his offences live upon my head   20
And on his father's: we did train him on;
And, his corruption being ta'en from us,
We, as the spring of all, shall pay for all.
Therefore, good cousin, let not Harry know
In any case the offer of the king.   25
    VER. Deliver what you will, I'll say 'tis so.
Here comes your cousin.
      Enter HOTSPUR *and* DOUGLAS; *Officers and Soldiers behind.*
    HOT. My uncle is return'd: deliver up
My Lord of Westmoreland, Uncle, what news?
    WOR. The king will bid you battle presently.   30
    DOUG. Defy him by the Lord of Westmoreland.
    HOT. Lord Douglas, go you and tell him so.
    DOUG. Marry, and shall, and very willingly.
                                Exit.

    WOR. There is no seeming mercy in the king.
    HOT. Did you beg any? God forbid!   35
    WOR. I told him gently of our grievances,
Of his oath-breaking; which he mended thus,
By now forswearing that he is forsworn:
He calls us rebels, traitors; and will scourge
With haughty arms this hateful name in us.   40
           Re-enter DOUGLAS.
    DOUG. Arm, gentlemen! to arms! for I have thrown
A brave defiance in King Henry's teeth,
And Westmoreland, that was engag'd, did bear it;
Which cannot choose but bring him quickly on.
    WOR. The Prince of Wales stepp'd forth before the king,   45
And, nephew, challeng'd you to single fight.
    HOT. O! would the quarrel lay upon our heads,
And that no man might draw short breath to-day
But I and Harry Monmouth. Tell me, tell me,
How show'd his tasking? seem'd it in contempt?   50
    VER. No, by my soul; I never in my life
Did hear a challenge urg'd more modestly,
Unless a brother should a brother dare
To gentle exercise and proof of arms.
He gave you all the duties of a man,   55
Trimm'd up your praises with a princely tongue,

Spoke your deservings like a chronicle,
Making you ever better than his praise
By still dispraising praise valu'd with you;
And, which became him like a prince indeed,   60
He made a blushing cital of himself,
And chid his truant youth with such a grace
As if he master'd there a double spirit
Of teaching and of learning instantly.
There did he pause.   But let me tell the world,   65
If he outlive the envy of this day,
England did never owe so sweet a hope,
So much misconstru'd in his wantonness.
  HOT. Cousin, I think thou art enamoured
Upon his follies: never did I hear   70
Of any prince so wild a libertine.
But be he as he will, yet once ere night
I will embrace him with a soldier's arm,
That he shall shrink under my courtesy.
Arm, arm with speed! and, fellows, soldiers, friends,   75
Better consider what you have to do,
Than I, that have not well the gift of tongue,
Can lift your blood up with persuasion.
              Enter a Messenger.
  MESS. My lord, here are letters for you.
  HOT. I cannot read them now.   80
O gentlemen! the time of life is short;
To spend that shortness basely were too long,
If life did ride upon a dial's point,
Still ending at the arrival of an hour.
An if we live, we live to tread on kings;   85
If die, brave death, when princes die with us!
Now, for our consciences, the arms are fair,
When the intent of bearing them is just.
              Enter another Messenger.
  MESS. My lord, prepare; the king comes on apace.
  HOT. I thank him that he cuts me from my tale,   90
For I profess not talking.   Only this,—
Let each man do his best: and here draw I
A sword, whose temper I intend to stain
With the best blood that I can meet withal
In the adventure of this perilous day.   95
Now, *Esperance!* Percy! and set on.
Sound all the lofty instruments of war,

And by that music let us all embrace;
For, heaven to earth, some of us never shall
A second time do such a courtesy.   100
    The trumpets sound.   They embrace, and exeunt.

SCENE III.—*Between the Camps.*

*Excursions, and Parties fighting. Alarum to the battle. Then
enter* DOUGLAS *and* SIR WALTER BLUNT, *meeting.*

BLUNT. What is thy name, that in the battle thus
Thou crossest me? what honour dost thou seek
Upon my head?
    DOUG.   Know then, my name is Douglas;
And I do haunt thee in the battle thus
Because some tell me that thou art a king.   5
    BLUNT. They tell thee true.
    DOUG. The Lord of Stafford dear to-day hath bought
Thy likeness; for instead of thee, King Harry,
This sword hath ended him: so shall it thee,
Unless thou yield thee as my prisoner.   10
    BLUNT. I was not born a yielder, thou proud Scot;
And thou shalt find a king that will revenge
Lord Stafford's death.

They fight, and BLUNT *is slain.*

Enter HOTSPUR

HOT. O Douglas! hadst thou fought at Holmedon thus,
I never had triumph'd upon a Scot.   15
    DOUG. All's done, all's won: here breathless lies the king.
    HOT. Where?
    DOUG. Here.
    HOT. This, Douglas? no: I know this face full well;
A gallant knight he was, his name was Blunt;   20
Semblably furnish'd like the king himself.
    DOUG. A fool go with thy soul, whither it goes!
A borrow'd title hast thou bought too dear:
Why didst thou tell me that thou wert a king?
    HOT. The king hath many marching in his coats.   25
    DOUG. Now, by my sword, I will kill all his coats;
I'll murder all his wardrobe, piece by piece,
Until I meet the king.
    HOT.   Up, and away!
Our soldiers stand full fairly for the day.   *Exeunt.*

Alarums.   Enter FALSTAFF.

FAL. Though I could 'scape shot-free at London, I fear the shot [30

here; here's no scoring but upon the pate. Soft! who art thou? Sir
Walter Blunt: there's honour for you! here's no vanity! I am as hot
as molten lead, and as heavy too: God keep lead out of me! I need
no more weight than mine own bowels. I have led my ragamuffins where they are peppered: there's not three of my hundred [35
and fifty left alive, and they are for the town's end, to beg during
life. But who comes here?

Enter the PRINCE.

PRINCE. What! stand'st thou idle here? lend me thy sword:
Many a nobleman lies stark and stiff
Under the hoofs of vaunting enemies,   40
Whose deaths are unreveng'd: prithee, lend me thy sword.

FAL. O Hal! I prithee, give me leave to breathe awhile. Turk
Gregory never did such deeds in arms as I have done this day. I have
paid Percy, I have made him sure.

PRINCE. He is indeed; and living to kill thee. I prithee, lend me [45
thy sword.

FAL. Nay, before God, Hal, if Percy be alive, thou gettest not my
sword; but take my pistol, if thou wilt.

PRINCE. Give it me. What! is it in the case?

FAL. Ay, Hal; 'tis hot, 'tis hot: there's that will sack a city.   50

The PRINCE *draws out a bottle of sack.*

PRINCE. What! is 't a time to jest and dally now?

Throws it at him, and exit.

FAL. Well, if Percy be alive, I'll pierce him. If he do come in my
way, so: if he do not, if I come in his willingly, let him make a
carbonado of me. I like not such grinning honour as Sir Walter
hath: give me life; which if I can save, so; if not, honour comes [55
unlooked for, and there's an end.   *Exit.*

SCENE IV.—*Another Part of the Field.*

Alarums. Excursions. Enter KING HENRY, *the* PRINCE, JOHN OF
LANCASTER, *and* WESTMORELAND.

K. HEN. I prithee,
Harry, withdraw thyself; thou bleed'st too much.
Lord John of Lancaster, go you with him.

LANC. Not I, my lord, unless I did bleed too.

PRINCE. I beseech your majesty, make up,   5
Lest your retirement do amaze your friends.

K. HEN. I will do so.
My Lord of Westmoreland, lead him to his tent.

WEST. Come, my lord, I'll lead you to your tent.

PRINCE. Lead me, my lord! I do not need your help: 10

And God forbid a shallow scratch should drive
The Prince of Wales from such a field as this,
Where stain'd nobility lies trodden on,
And rebels' arms triumph in massacres!

LANC. We breathe too long: come, cousin Westmoreland,   15
Our duty this way lies: for God's sake, come.

Exeunt JOHN OF LANCASTER *and* WESTMORELAND.

PRINCE. By God, thou hast deceiv'd me, Lancaster;
I did not think thee lord of such a spirit:
Before, I lov'd thee as a brother, John;
But now, I do respect thee as my soul.   20

K. HEN. I saw him hold Lord Percy at the point
With lustier maintenance than I did look for
Of such an ungrown warrior.

PRINCE.   O! this boy
Lends mettle to us all.   *Exit.*

Alarums.   Enter DOUGLAS.

DOUG. Another king! they grow like Hydra's heads: 25
I am the Douglas, fatal to all those
That wear those colours on them: what art thou,
That counterfeit'st the person of a king?

K. HEN. The king himself; who, Douglas, grieves at heart
So many of his shadows thou hast met   30
And not the very king. I have two boys
Seek Percy and thyself about the field:
But, seeing thou fall'st on me so luckily,
I will assay thee; so defend thyself.

DOUG. I fear thou art another counterfeit;   35
And yet, in faith, thou bear'st thee like a king:
But mine I am sure thou art, whoe'er thou be,
And thus I win thee.

They fight: KING HENRY *being in danger,*
re-enter the PRINCE.

PRINCE. Hold up thy head, vile Scot, or thou art like
Never to hold it up again; the spirits   40
Of valiant Shirley, Stafford, Blunt, are in my arms:
It is the Prince of Wales that threatens thee,
Who never promiseth but he means to pay.

They fight: DOUGLAS *flies.*

Cheerly, my lord: how fares your grace?
Sir Nicholas Gawsey hath for succour sent,   45
And so hath Clifton: I'll to Clifton straight.

K. HEN. Stay, and breathe awhile.

Thou hast redeem'd thy lost opinion,
And show'd thou mak'st some tender of my life,
In this fair rescue thou hast brought to me.   50
   PRINCE. O God! they did me too much injury
That ever said I hearken'd for your death.
If it were so, I might have let alone
The insulting hand of Douglas over you;
Which would have been as speedy in your end   55
As all the poisonous potions in the world,
And sav'd the treacherous labour of your son.
   K. HEN. Make up to Clifton: I'll to Sir Nicholas Gawsey. *Exit.*
           Enter HOTSPUR.
   HOT. If I mistake not, thou art Harry Monmouth.
   PRINCE. Thou speak'st as if I would deny my name.   60
   HOT. My name is Harry Percy.
   PRINCE.   Why, then I see
A very valiant rebel of that name.
I am the Prince of Wales; and think not, Percy,
To share with me in glory any more:
Two stars keep not their motion in one sphere;   65
Nor can one England brook a double reign,
Of Harry Percy and the Prince of Wales.
   HOT. Nor shall it, Harry; for the hour is come
To end the one of us; and would to God
Thy name in arms were now as great as mine!   70
   PRINCE. I'll make it greater ere I part from thee;
And all the budding honours on thy crest
I'll crop, to make a garland for my head.
   HOT. I can no longer brook thy vanities.
                             They fight.
          Enter FALSTAFF.
   FAL. Well said, Hal! to it, Hal! Nay, you shall find no boy's   [75
play here, I can tell you.
Re-enter DOUGLAS; *he fights with* FALSTAFF, *who falls down as if he
   were dead, and exit* DOUGLAS. HOTSPUR *is wounded, and falls.*
   HOT. O Harry! thou hast robb'd me of my youth.
I better brook the loss of brittle life
Than those proud titles thou hast won of me;
They wound my thoughts worse than thy sword my flesh: 80
But thought's the slave of life, and life time's fool:
And time, that takes survey of all the world,
Must have a stop. O! I could prophesy,
But that the earthy and cold hand of death

Lies on my tongue. No, Percy, thou art dust, 85
And food for— *Dies.*

PRINCE. For worms, brave Percy. Fare thee well, great heart!
Ill-weav'd ambition, how much art thou shrunk!
When that this body did contain a spirit,
A kindom for it was too small a bound; 90
But now two paces of the vilest earth
Is room enough: this earth, that bears thee dead,
Bears not alive so stout a gentleman.
If thou wert sensible of courtesy,
I should not make so dear a show of zeal: 95
But let my favours hide thy mangled face,
And, even in thy behalf, I'll thank myself
For doing these fair rites of tenderness.
Adieu! and take thy praise with thee to heaven,
Thy ignomy sleep with thee in the grave, 100
But not remember'd in thy epitaph!

He spies FALSTAFF *on the ground.*

What! old acquaintance! could not all this flesh
Keep in a little life? Poor Jack, farewell!
I could have better spar'd a better man.
O! I should have a heavy miss of thee 105
If I were much in love with vanity.
Death hath not struck so fat a deer to-day,
Though many dearer, in this bloody fray.
Embowell'd will I see thee by and by:
Till then in blood by noble Percy lie. *Exit.* [110

FAL. *Rising.* Embowelled! if thou embowel me to-day, I'll give you
leave to powder me and eat me too to-morrow. 'Sblood! 'twas time to
counterfeit, or that hot termagant Scot had paid me scot and lot
too. Counterfeit? I lie, I am no counterfeit: to die is to be a counterfeit; for he is but the counterfeit of a man, who hath not the [115
life of a man; but to counterfeit dying, when a man thereby
liveth, is to be no counterfeit, but the true and perfect image of
life indeed. The better part of valour is discretion; in the which
better part I have saved my life. 'Zounds! I am afraid of this gun-
powder Percy though he be dead. How if he should counter- [120
feit too and rise? By my faith I am afraid he would prove the better
counterfeit. Therefore I'll make him sure; yea, and I'll swear I
killed him. Why may not he rise as well as I? Nothing confutes
me but eyes, and nobody sees me: therefore, sirrah. *Stabbing him.*
with a new wound in your thigh come you along with me. [125

He takes HOTSPUR *on his back.*

Re-enter the PRINCE *and* JOHN OF LANCASTER.

PRINCE. Come, brother John; full bravely hast thou flesh'd
Thy maiden sword.

LANC.   But, soft! whom have we here?
Did you not tell me this fat man was dead?

PRINCE. I did; I saw him dead,
Breathless and bleeding on the ground.   130
Art thou alive? or is it fantasy
That plays upon our eyesight? I prithee, speak;
We will not trust our eyes without our ears:
Thou are not what thou seem'st.

FAL. No, that's certain; I am not a double man: but if I be not ⌈135
Jack Falstaff, then am I a Jack. There is Percy: *Throwing down the
body*. If your father will do me any honour, so; if not, let him
kill the next Percy himself. I look to be either earl or duke, I can
assure you.

PRINCE. Why, Percy I killed myself, and saw thee dead.   ⌈140

FAL. Didst thou? Lord, Lord! how this world is given to lying.
I grant you I was down and out of breath, and so was he; but we
rose both at an instant, and fought a long hour by Shrewsbury
clock. If I may be believed, so; if not, let them that should reward
valour bear the sin upon their own heads. I'll take it upon my ⌈145
death, I gave him this wound in the thigh: if the man were alive
and would deny it, 'zounds! I would make him eat a piece of my
sword.

LANC. This is the strangest tale that e'er I heard.

PRINCE. This is the strangest fellow, brother John.   150
Come, bring your luggage nobly on your back:
For my part, if a lie may do thee grace,
I'll gild it with the happiest terms I have.

A retreat is sounded.

The trumpet sounds retreat; the day is ours.
Come, brother, let us to the highest of the field,   155
To see what friends are living, who are dead.

Exeunt the PRINCE *and* JOHN OF LANCASTER.

FAL. I'll follow, as they say, for reward. He that rewards me, God
reward him! If I do grow great, I'll grow less; for I'll purge, and
leave sack, and live cleanly, as a nobleman should do.

Exit.

SCENE V.—*Another Part of the Field.*

The trumpets sound. Enter KING HENRY, *the* PRINCE, JOHN OF
LANCASTER, WESTMORELAND, *and Others, with* WORCESTER
and VERNON, *prisoners.*

K. HEN. Thus ever did rebellion find rebuke.
Ill-spirited Worcester! did we not send grace,
Pardon, and terms of love to all of you?
And would'st thou turn our offers contrary?
Misuse the tenour of thy kinsman's trust?   5
Three knights upon our party slain to-day,
A noble earl and many a creature else
Had been alive this hour,
If like a Christian thou hadst truly borne
Betwixt our armies true intelligence.   10
    WOR. What I have done my safety urg'd me to;
And I embrace this fortune patiently,
Since not to be avoided it falls on me.
    K. HEN. Bear Worcester to the death and Vernon too:
Other offenders we will pause upon.   15
        Exeunt WORCESTER *and* VERNON, *guarded.*
How goes the field?
    PRINCE. The noble Scot, Lord Douglas, when he saw
The fortune of the day quite turn'd from him,
The noble Percy slain, and all his men
Upon the foot of fear, fled with the rest;   20
And falling from a hill he was so bruis'd
That the pursuers took him. At my tent
The Douglas is, and I beseech your grace
I may dispose of him.
    K. HEN.   With all my heart.
    PRINCE. Then, brother John of Lancaster, to you   25
This honourable bounty shall belong.
Go to the Douglas, and deliver him
Up to his pleasure, ransomless, and free:
His valour shown upon our crests to-day
Hath taught us how to cherish such high deeds,   30
Even in the bosom of our adversaries.
    LANC. I thank your grace for this high courtesy,
Which I shall give away immediately.
    K. HEN. Then this remains, that we divide our power.
You, son John, and my cousin Westmoreland   35
Towards York shall bend you, with your dearest speed,
To meet Northumberland and the prelate Scroop,
Who, as we hear, are busily in arms:
Myself and you, son Harry, will towards Wales,
To fight with Glendower and the Earl of March.   40
Rebellion in this land shall lose his sway,

Meeting the check of such another day:
And since this business so fair is done,
Let us not leave till all our own be won.

Exeunt.

Author and Selection Notes

English drama came into full flower with the plays of William Shakespeare (1564-1616), and down through the ages praise of the bard has hardly stopped short of idolatry. Even in Shakespeare's own day, Ben Jonson foresaw that he was "not of an age but for all time." In writing *The First Part of King Henry the Fourth,* as in many of his other historical plays, Shakespeare drew his materials from Holinshed's *Chronicles* and freely changed situations to heighten the drama. He makes King Henry IV older than he actually was at the Battle of Shrewsbury and Hotspur younger; he also arranges the meeting of Hotspur and Prince Hal in single combat.

Questions and Exercises

1. Briefly sketch the two plots within the play: The Hotspur Plot; The Falstaff Plot.

2. How does the king solve his two problems: the defection of his nobles; the dissoluteness of his heir?

3. Why does the king's conscience hurt him? What connection is there between his conscience and the pilgrimage, and his conscience and Hal's wildness?

4. In what way can Falstaff be called "a Puritan fallen from grace"?

5. How is the play a defeat of two rebellious men? In what ways is Hal constantly measured against these two men?

6. Explain the significance of the battlefield scene (V, iv).

7. By extension could the term "courtesy book" be applied to this selection in relation to Prince Hal's education? For a definition of "courtesy book" refer to *A Handbook to Literature* by Thrall, Hibbard, and Holman, or some other reliable source.

8. Theme Topics: The Concepts of Honor in *The First Part of King Henry the Fourth;* The Education of a Prince; The Parallelism of the Plots Hatched by the Percys and by Falstaff; Hal and Hotspur: A Contrast; Hal and Falstaff: A Contrast; Falstaff the Inexhaustible Merrymaker.

OF STUDIES

Francis Bacon

Studies serve for delight, for ornament, and for ability. Their chief use for delight is in privateness and retiring; for ornament, is in discourse; and for ability, is in the judgment and disposition of business. For expert men can execute, and perhaps judge of particulars, one by one; but the general counsels, and the plots and marshaling of affairs come best from those that are learned. To spend too much time in studies is sloth; to use them too much for ornament is affectation; to make judgment wholly by their rules is the humor of a scholar. They perfect nature, and are perfected by experience; for natural abilities are like natural plants, that need pruning by study; and studies themselves do give forth directions too much at large, except they be bounded in by experience. Crafty men contemn studies; simple men admire them; and wise men use them: for they teach not their own use; but that is a wisdom without them and above them, won by observation. Read not to contradict and confute; nor to believe and take for granted; nor to find talk and discourse; but to weigh and consider. Some books are to be tasted, others to be swallowed, and some few to be chewed and digested: that is, some books are to be read only in parts; others to be read, but not curiously; and some few to be read wholly, and with diligence and attention. Some books also may be read by deputy, and extracts made of them by others; but that would be only in the less important arguments, and the meaner sort of books; else distilled books are like common distilled waters, flashy[1] things. Reading maketh a full man; conference a ready man; and writing an exact man. And therefore, if a man write little, he had need have a great memory; if he confer little, he had need have a present wit; and if he read little, he had need have much cunning, to seem to know that he doth not. Histories make men wise; poets witty; the mathematics subtle; natural philosophy deep; moral grave; logic and rhetoric able to contend. *Abeunt studia in mores.*[2] Nay, there is no stond[3] or impediment in the wit, but may be wrought out by fit studies, like as diseases of the body may have appropriate exercises. Bowling is good for the stone and reins;[4] shooting for the lungs and breast; gentle walking for the stomach; riding for the head; and the like. So if a man's wit be wandering, let him study the mathematics; for in demonstrations, if his wit be called away never so little, he must begin again: if his wit be not apt to distinguish or find differences, let him study the schoolmen; for they are *cymini sectores:*[5] if he be not apt to beat over matters, and to

[1] insipid.
[2] studies develop into manners (Ovid, *Heroides,* XV, 83).
[3] hindrance.
[4] kidneys.
[5] splitters of cumin, i.e., hair-splitters.

call one thing to prove and illustrate another, let him study the lawyers' cases: so every defect of the mind may have a special receipt.

Author and Selection Notes

Sir Francis Bacon (1561-1626) —English essayist, philosopher, and states-man—climbed high in political life to positions such as Solicitor General, Attorney General, and then Lord Chancellor. Finally convicted of bribery, he suffered public disgrace; yet, ironically, he possessed a remarkable intellectual integrity that is evident in his famous *Advancement of Learning* and *The New Atlantis* as well as in the *Essays.*

Questions and Exercises

1. Notice how long Bacon's "paragraph" is. What kind of paragraph development is used? Make an outline showing how this essay might be broken down into paragraphs.

2. Select six quotable sentences that would make excellent thesis sentences for themes.

3. Bacon would probably call our century an age of "distilled books." Make a list of current "distilled" books and periodicals. Build a case for or against them.

4. Point out all words or expressions which remind us that Bacon was writing in the sixteenth century.

5. Bacon writes: "Some books are to be tasted, others to be swallowed, and some few to be chewed and digested. . . ." From your own reading cite examples for each category.

THE EDUCATION OF A QUAKER
John Woolman

I have often felt a motion of love to leave some hints in writing of my experience of the goodness of God; and now, in the thirty-sixth year of my age, I begin this work.

I was born in Northampton, in Burlington county, West-Jersey, in the year 1720; and before I was seven years old I began to be acquainted with the operations of divine love. Through the care of my parents, I was taught to read nearly as soon as I was capable of it; and, as I went from school one seventh day, I remember, while my companions went to play by the way, I went forward out of sight, and, sitting down, I read the 22nd chapter of the Revelations. "He shewed me a pure river of water of life, clear as crystal, proceeding out of the throne of God and of the lamb, &c." and, in reading it, my mind was drawn to seek after that pure habitation, which, I then believed, God had prepared for his servants. The place where I sat, and the sweetness that attended my mind, remain fresh in my memory.

This, and the like gracious visitations, had that effect upon me, that when boys used ill language it troubled me; and, through the continued mercies of God, I was preserved from it.

The pious instructions of my parents were often fresh in my mind when I happened to be among wicked children, and were of use to me. My parents, having a large family of children, used frequently, on first days after meeting, to put us to read in the holy scriptures, or some religious books, one after another, the rest sitting by without much conversation; which, I have since often thought, was a good practice. From what I had read and heard, I believed there had been, in past ages, people who walked in uprightness before God, in a degree exceeding any that I knew, or heard of, now living: and the apprehension of there being less steadiness and firmness, amongst people in this age than in past ages, often troubled me while I was a child.

A thing remarkable in my childhood was, that once, going to a neighbour's house, I saw, on the way, a robin sitting on her nest, and as I came near she went off, but, having young ones, flew about, and with many cries expressed her concern for them; I stood and threw stones at her, till, one striking her, she fell down dead: at first I was pleased with the exploit, but after a few minutes was seized with horror, as having, in a sportive way, killed an innocent creature while she was careful for her young: I beheld her lying dead, and thought those young ones, for which she was so careful, must now perish for want of their dam to nourish them; and, after some painful considerations on the subject, I climbed up the tree, took all the young birds, and killed them; supposing that better than to leave them to pine away and die miserably: and believed, in this case, that scripture-proverb was fulfilled, "The tender mercies of the wicked are cruel." I then went on my errand, but, for some hours, could think of little else but the cruelties I had committed, and was much troubled. Thus He, whose tender mercies are over all his works, hath placed a principle in the human mind, which incites to exercise goodness towards every living creature; and this being singly attended to, people become tenderhearted and sympathising; but, being frequently and totally rejected, the mind becomes shut up in a contrary disposition.

About the twelfth year of my age, my father being abroad, my mother reproved me for some misconduct, to which I made an un-dutiful reply; and, the next first day, as I was with my father re-turning from meeting, he told me he understood I had behaved amiss to my mother, and advised me to be more careful in future. I knew myself blameable, and in shame and confusion remained silent. Being thus awakened to a sense of my wickedness, I felt re-morse in my mind, and getting home, I retired and prayed to the Lord to forgive me; and do not remember that I ever, after that, spoke unhandsomely to either of my parents, however foolish in some other things.

Having attained the age of sixteen years, I began to love wanton company; and though I was preserved from profane language, or scandalous conduct, still I perceived a plant in me which produced much wild grapes; yet my merciful Father forsook me not utterly, but, at times, through his grace, I was brought seriously to consider my ways; and the sight of my backslidings affected me with sorrow; but, for want of rightly attending to the reproofs of instruction, vanity was added to vanity, and repentance to repentance: upon the whole, my mind was more and more alienated from the truth, and I hastened toward destruction. While I meditate on the gulph towards which I travelled, and reflect on my youthful disobedience, for these things I weep, mine eyes run down with water.

Advancing in age, the number of my acquaintances increased, and thereby my way grew more difficult; though I had found com-fort in reading the holy scriptures, and thinking on heavenly things, I was now estranged therefrom; hence serious reflections were uneasy to me, and youthful vanities and diversions my great-est pleasure. Running in this road I found many like myself; and we associated in that which is the reverse to true friendship.

But in this swift race it pleased God to visit me with sickness, so that I doubted of recovering; and then did darkness, horror, and amazement, with full force, seize me, even when my pain and dis-tress of body was very great. I thought it would have been better for me never to have had a being, than to see the day which I now saw. I was filled with confusion; and in great affliction, both of mind and body, I lay and bewailed myself. I had not confidence to lift up my cries to God, whom I had thus offended; but, in a deep sense of my great folly, I was humbled before him; and, at length, that word which is as a fire and a hammer, broke and dissolved my rebellious heart, and then my cries were put up in contrition; and in the multitude of his mercies I found inward relief, and felt a close engagement, that, if he was pleased to restore my health, I might walk humbly before him.

After my recovery, this exercise remained with me a considerable time; but, by degrees, giving way to youthful vanities, they gained strength, and, getting with wanton young people, I lost ground. The Lord had been very gracious, and spoke peace to me in the time of my distress; and I now most ungratefully turned again to folly; on which account, at times, I felt sharp reproof. I was not so hardy as to commit things scandalous; but to exceed in vanity, and promote mirth, was my chief study. Still I retained a love for pious people, and their company brought an awe upon me. My dear parents, several times, admonished me in the fear of the Lord, and their admonition entered into my heart, and had a good effect for a season; but, not getting deep enough to pray rightly, the tempter, when he came, found entrance. I remember once, having spent a part of the day in wantonness, as I went to bed at night, there lay in a window, near my bed, a Bible, which I opened, and first cast my eye on this text, "We lie down in our shame, and our confusion covers us": this I knew to be my case: and, meeting with so unexpected a reproof, I was somewhat affected with it, and went to bed under remorse of conscience; which I soon cast off again.

Thus time passed on: my heart was replenished with mirth and wantonness, and pleasing scenes of vanity were presented to my imagination, till I attained the age of eighteen years; near which time I felt the judgements of God, in my soul, like a consuming fire; and, looking over my past life, the prospect was moving.—I was often sad, and longed to be delivered from those vanities; then again, my heart was strongly inclined to them, and there was in me a sore conflict; at times I turned to folly, and then again, sorrow and confusion took hold of me. In a while, I resolved totally to leave off some of my vanities; but there was a secret reserve, in my heart, of the more refined part of them, and I was not low enough to find true peace. Thus, for some months, I had great troubles; there remaining in me an unsubjected will, which rendered my labours fruitless, till at length, through the merciful continuance of heavenly visitations, I was made to bow down in spirit before the Lord. I remember one evening I had spent some time in reading a pious author; and walking out alone, I humbly prayed to the Lord for his help, that I might be delivered from all those vanities which so ensnared me. Thus, being brought low, he helped me; and, as I learned to bear the cross, I felt refreshment to come from his presence; but, not keeping in that strength which gave victory, I lost ground again; the sense of which greatly affected me: and I sought deserts and lonely places, and there, with tears, did confess my sins to God, and humbly craved help of him. And

I may say, with reverence, he was near to me in my troubles, and in those times of humiliation opened my ear to discipline. I was now led to look seriously at the means by which I was drawn from the pure truth, and learned this, that, if I would live in the life which the faithful servants of God lived in, I must not go into company as heretofore in my own will; but all the cravings of sense must be governed by a divine principle. In times of sorrow and abasement these instructions were sealed upon me, and I felt the power of Christ prevail over selfish desires, so that I was preserved in a good degree of steadiness; and, being young, and believing at that time that a single life was best for me, I was strengthened to keep from such company as had often been a snare to me.

I kept steadily to meetings; spent first day afternoons chiefly in reading the scriptures and other good books; and was early convinced, in my mind, that true religion consisted in an inward life, wherein the heart doth love and reverence God the Creator, and learns to exercise true justice and goodness, not only toward all men, but also toward the brute creatures.—That as the mind was moved, by an inward principle, to love God as an invisible incomprehensible Being, by the same principle it was moved to love him in all his manifestations in the visible world.—That, as by his breath the flame of life was kindled in all animal sensible creatures, to say we love God, and, at the same time exercise cruelty toward the least creature, is a contradiction in itself.

I found no narrowness respecting sects and opinions; but believed, that sincere upright-hearted people, in every society who truly love God, were accepted of him.

As I lived under the cross, and simply followed the openings of truth, my mind, from day to day, was more enlightened; my former acquaintances were left to judge of me as they would, for I found it safest for me to live in private, and keep these things sealed up in my own breast. While I silently ponder on that change wrought in me, I find no language equal to it, nor any means to convey to another a clear idea of it. I looked upon the works of God in this visible creation, and an awfulness covered me; my heart was tender and often contrite, and universal love to my fellow-creatures increased in me: this will be understood by such as have trodden the same path. Some glances of real beauty may be seen in their faces, who dwell in true meekness.

There is a harmony in the sound of that voice to which divine love gives utterance, and some appearance of right order in their temper and conduct, whose passions are regulated; yet all these do not fully shew forth that inward life to such as have not felt it: But this white stone and new name is known rightly to such only as have it.

Though I have been thus strengthened to bear the cross, I still found myself in great danger, having many weaknesses attending me, and strong temptations to wrestle with; in the feeling whereof I frequently withdrew into private places, and often with tears besought the Lord to help me, whose gracious ear was open to my cry.

All this time I lived with my parents, and wrought on the plantation; and, having had schooling pretty well for a planter, I used to improve it in winter-evenings, and other leisure times; and, being now in the twenty-first year of my age, a man, in much business at shop-keeping and baking, asked me, if I would hire with him to tend shop and keep books. I acquainted my father with the proposal; and, after some deliberation, it was agreed for me to go.

At home I had lived retired; and now, having a prospect of being much in the way of company, I felt frequent and fervent cries in my heart to God, the father of mercies, that he would preserve me from all corruption; that in this more publick employment, I might serve him, my gracious Redeemer, in that humility and self-denial, with which I had been, in a small degree, exercised in a more private life. The man, who employed me, furnished a shop in Mount-Holly, about five miles from my father's house, and six from his own; and there I lived alone, and tended his shop. Shortly after my settlement here I was visited by several young people, my former acquaintance, who knew not but vanities would be as agreeable to me now as ever; and, at these times, I cried to the Lord, in secret, for wisdom and strength; for I felt myself encompassed with difficulties, and had fresh occasion to bewail the follies of time past, in contracting a familiarity with libertine people: and, as I had now left my father's house outwardly, I found my heavenly Father to be merciful to me beyond what I can express.

By day I was much amongst people, and had many trials to go through; but, in the evenings, I was mostly alone, and may with thankfulness acknowledge, that, in those times, the spirit of supplication was often poured upon me; under which I was frequently exercised, and felt my strength renewed.

In a few months after I came here, my master bought several Scotchmen, servants from on-board a vessel, and brought them to Mount-Holly to sell; one of which was taken sick, and died.

In the latter part of his sickness, he, being delirious, used to

curse and swear most sorrowfully; and, the next night after his
burial, I was left to sleep alone in the same chamber where he died;
I perceived in me a timorousness; I knew, however, I had not injured the man, but assisted in taking care of him according to my
capacity; and was not free to ask any one, on that occasion, to sleep
with me: nature was feeble; but every trial was a fresh incitement
to give myself up wholly to the service of God, for I found no
helper like him in times of trouble. After a while, my former acquaintance gave over expecting me as one of their company; and
I began to be known to some whose conversation was helpful to me:
and now, as I had experienced the love of God, through Jesus
Christ, to redeem me from many pollutions, and to be a succour
to me through a sea of conflicts, with which no person was fully
acquainted; and as my heart was often enlarged in this heavenly
principle, I felt a tender compassion for the youth, who remained
entangled in snares, like those which had entangled me from one
time to another: this love and tenderness increased; and my mind
was more strongly engaged for the good of my fellow-creatures. I
went to meetings in an awful frame of mind, and endeavoured to
be inwardly acquainted with the language of the true Shepherd;
and, one day, being under a strong exercise of spirit, I stood up,
and said some words in a meeting; but, not keeping close to the
divine opening, I said more than was required of me; and being
soon sensible of my error, I was afflicted in mind some weeks,
without any light or comfort, even to that degree that I could not
take satisfaction in any thing: I remembered God, and was troubled,
and, in the depth of my distress, he had pity upon me, and sent the
Comforter: I then felt forgiveness for my offence, and my mind
became calm and quiet, being truly thankful to my gracious Redeemer for his mercies; and, after this, feeling the spring of divine
love opened, and a concern to speak, I said a few words in a meeting,
in which I found peace; this, I believe, was about six weeks from
the first time: and, as I was thus humbled and disciplined under
the cross, my understanding became more strengthened to distinguish the pure spirit which inwardly moves upon the heart, and
taught me to wait in silence sometime many weeks together, until
I felt that rise which prepares the creature.

From an inward purifying, and stedfast abiding under it, springs
a lively operative desire for the good of others: all the faithful
are not called to the public ministry; but whoever are, are called
to minister of that which they have tasted and handled spiritually.
The outward modes of worship are various; but, wherever any are
true ministers of Jesus Christ, it is from the operation of his spirit

upon their hearts, first purifying them, and thus giving them a just sense of the conditions of others.

This truth was clearly fixed in my mind; and I was taught to watch the pure opening, and to take heed, lest, while I was standing to speak, my own will should get uppermost, and cause me to utter words from worldly wisdom, and depart from the channel of the true gospel-ministry.

In the management of my outward affairs, I may say, with thankfulness, I found truth to be my support; and I was respected in my master's family, who came to live in Mount-Holly within two years after my going there.

About the twenty-third year of my age, I had many fresh and heavenly openings, in respect to the care and providence of the Almighty over his creatures in general, and over man as the most noble amongst those which are visible. And being clearly convinced in my judgement, that to place my whole trust in God was best for me, I felt renewed engagements, that in all things I might act on an inward principle of virtue, and pursue worldly business no farther, than as truth opened my way therein.

About the time called Christmas, I observed many people from the country, and dwellers in town, who, resorting to public-houses, spent their time in drinking and vain sports, tending to corrupt one another; on which account I was much troubled. At one house, in particular, there was much disorder; and I believed it was a duty incumbent on me to go and speak to the master of that house. I considered I was young, and that several elderly friends in town had opportunity to see these things; but though I would gladly have been excused, yet I could not feel my mind clear.

The exercise has heavy: and as I was reading what the Almighty said to Ezekiel, respecting his duty as a watchman, the matter was set home more clearly; and then, with prayers and tears, I besought the Lord for his assistance, who in loving-kindness, gave me a resigned heart: then, at a suitable opportunity, I went to the public-house; and seeing the man amongst much company, I went to him, and told him, I wanted to speak with him; so we went aside, and there, in the fear of the Almighty, I expressed to him what rested on my mind; which he took kindly, and afterward shewed more regard to me than before. In a few years afterwards he died, middle-aged; and I often thought that, had I neglected my duty in that case, it would have given me great trouble; and I was humbly thankful to my gracious Father, who had supported me herein.

My employer having a negro woman, sold her, and desired me

to write a bill of sale, the man being waiting who bought her: the thing was sudden; and though the thoughts of writing an instrument of slavery for one of my fellow-creatures felt uneasy, yet I remembered I was hired by the year, that it was my master who directed me to do it, and that it was an elderly man, a member of our society, who bought her; so, through weakness, I gave way, and wrote; but, at the executing it, I was so afflicted in my mind, that I said, before my master and the friend, that I believed slave-keeping to be a practice inconsistent with the Christian religion: this in some degree abated my uneasiness; yet, as often as I reflected seriously upon it, I thought I should have been clearer, if I had desired to have been excused from it, as a thing against my conscience; for such it was. And, some time after this, a young man, of our society, spoke to me to write a conveyance of a slave to him, he having lately taken a negro into his house: I told him I was not easy to write it; for, though many of our meeting and in other places kept slaves, I still believed the practice was not right, and desired to be excused from writing. I spoke to him in good will; and he told me that keeping slaves was not altogether agreeable to his mind; but that the slave being a gift to his wife, he had accepted of her.

Author and Selection Notes

Although we remember John Woolman (1720-1772) as a New Jersey Quaker preacher, he made his living as a teacher, tailor, and tradesman. In his *Journal* he records in simple sincerity the progress of a soul. This practical mystic has been called "as saintly as a man can be," and his writings were highly praised by literary men. Ralph Waldo Emerson, for instance, inscribed the following comment in the back of his copy of Woolman's *Journal*: "I find more wisdom in these pages than in any other book written since the days of the apostles."

Questions and Exercises

1. Cite experiences from Woolman's early childhood which reflect his sensitive conscience.

2. Discuss Woolman's effective use of concrete details and examples.

3. Was his conduct as "wanton" as he claims it was?

4. Read portions of either *Grace Abounding for the Chief of Sinners* by John Bunyan or *Confessions* by Saint Augustine and compare them with this selection from Woolman's *Journal*. Read especially those sections describing Bunyan's or Saint Augustine's early life.

5. It is evident that Woolman's education is not based primarily on books and schools. How, then, does the Quaker become "educated"?

6. Theme Topics: An Educated Conscience; A Profile in Courage; My Childhood Conscience; The Quakers and Slavery; The Social Conscience of the Quakers; The Quaker's "Inner Light."

THE BRAIN IS WIDER THAN THE SKY
Emily Dickinson

The brain is wider than the sky,
    For, put them side by side,
The one the other will include
    With ease, and you beside.

The brain is deeper than the sea,
    For, hold them, blue to blue,
The one the other will absorb,
    As sponges, buckets do.

The brain is just the weight of God,
    For, lift them, pound for pound,
And they will differ, if they do,
    As syllable from sound.

Author and Selection Notes

When Emily Dickinson (1830-1886) died, her sister Lavinia found hundreds of poems in manuscript form and decided that they ought to be published, although the poet herself had said, "How can you print a piece of your soul!" Thus through Emily, "the shy New England Bluebird" who lived the latter part of her life as a recluse, America made a significant addition to the literature of the world.

Questions and Exercises

1. State in your own words what Emily Dickinson is saying about the brain.
2. How can you account for this keen challenge to the intellect being couched in such simple form and diction?

From *The Poems of Emily Dickinson,* edited by Bianchi and Hampson, copyright 1932, Little, Brown and Company.

3. Why did Dickinson compare the brain to the weight of God last? Would the poem have been more effective or less effective if the last comparison had been placed first?

4. Theme Topics: The Capacity of the Human Brain; The Power of Thought; "As He Thinketh in His Heart, So Is He"; "There Is Nothing Either Good or Bad, But Thinking Makes It So"; Failure to Utilize Our Intellectual Capacities.

THERE IS NO FRIGATE LIKE A BOOK
Emily Dickinson

There is no frigate like a book
To take us lands away,
Nor any coursers like a page
Of prancing poetry.

This traverse may the poorest take
Without oppress of toll;
How frugal is the chariot
That bears a human soul!

Author and Selection Notes

See page 101.

Questions and Exercises

1. Name the sustaining idea that gives unity to this poem.

2. Point out words that convey unusual color and meaning.

3. Find evidence of Dickinson's "impossible rhyme," as it has been called. William Dean Howells declares, "The artist meant just this harsh exterior to remain." Refute or defend her imperfect rhyme.

4. What does the "chariot" symbolize?

5. Theme Topics: Books as Substitutes for Travel; If Printing Presses Had Never Been Invented; The Progress of Science Without Books; What Books Mean to Me.

THE LAST LESSON
Alphonse Daudet

That morning I was very late in going to school, and was much afraid of being scolded; all the more so, as M. Hamel had told us he would question us upon the participles, and I did not know the first word. For a moment I thought of playing truant and setting off across the country.

The weather was so warm and clear!

One heard the blackbirds whistling at the edge of the wood, and in the Rippert meadow, behind the saw mill, the Prussians who were drilling. All that tempted me much more than the rule of participles; but I had the strength to resist and I ran fast to school.

In passing by the mayor's office, I saw that a group of people had stopped at the little bulletin board. For two years all the bad news had come to us from there, lost battles, requisitions, orders from headquarters; and without pausing I said:

"What is it this time?"

Then, as I crossed the square on the run, the blacksmith Wachter, who was there with his apprentice engaged in reading the notice, cried out to me:

"Do not hurry so, youngster; you will arrive soon enough at your school!"

I thought he was making fun of me, and out of breath I went into M. Hamel's little yard.

Usually, at the beginning of a class, there was a great uproar which could be heard in the street,—desks opening and closing, lessons being repeated all together at the top of the voice, the pupils stopping their ears with their fingers, the better to learn them, and the big rule of the master tapping upon the table,

"A little silence!"

I counted on all this din to reach my seat without notice, but as luck would have it, on this day everything was quiet, as on Sunday morning. Through the open window I saw my schoolmates already in their places, and M. Hamel pacing back and forth with the terrible iron-tipped rule under his arm. I had to open the door

From *A Book of Short Stories*, edited and translated by Blanche Colton Williams. Copyright, 1918, D. Appleton & Company. Reprinted by permission of Appleton-Century-Crofts.

and enter in the midst of the great stillness. Well you may think I blushed and was afraid.

But nothing happened. M. Hamel looked at me without anger and said to me very gently:

"Go quickly to your place, my little Franz; we were going to begin without you."

I stepped over the bench and sat down at once at my desk. Then only, a little recovered from my fright, I noticed that our master had on his beautiful green frock coat, his carefully plaited shirt-frill, and the skull-cap of embroidered black silk which he wore only on the days of inspection and distribution of prizes. Besides, there was something unusual and solemn about the whole class. But what surprised me most was to see at the end of the room, on the benches that were usually vacant, the men of the village seated and silent like us; old Hauser with his three-cornered hat, the ex-mayor, the former postman, and others. They all seemed sad; and Hauser had brought an old dog-eared spelling book, which he held wide open on his knees, with his big spectacles placed across the pages.

While I was marveling at all this, M. Hamel had gone up into his chair, and in the same gentle and serious voice with which he had greeted me, he said to us:

"My children, it is the last time I take the class. The order has come from Berlin to teach only German in the schools of Alsace and Lorraine. . . . The new teacher comes to-morrow. To-day's is your last French lesson. I beg you to be very attentive."

These few words overwhelmed me. Ah, the villains, that was what they had posted at the *mairie!*

My last lesson in French!

And I who hardly knew how to write. . . . I should never learn. I should have to stop there! How I blamed myself for the time lost, for cutting classes, to hunt bird's eggs or to practice sliding on the Saar. My books, which only a moment ago I had found so tiresome, so heavy to carry, my Grammar, my Scripture History, seemed to me old friends from whom I should find it hard to part. It was the same with M. Hamel. The idea that he was going to leave, that I should never see him again, made me forget punishments, blows from the ruler.

Poor man!

It was in honor of this last lesson that he had put on his handsome Sunday clothes; and now I understood why the old men of the village had come to sit at the end of the room. It was as if to say they were sorry they had not come more often to this school of theirs. It was also a way of thanking our master for his forty years of good service, and of paying their respects to the departing fatherland.

Such was the course of my thoughts, when I heard my name called. It was my turn to recite. What would I not have given to be able to say from beginning to end the famous rule of the participles, in a loud, clear voice, without a mistake! But I got tangled up in the first words, and I stood swaying against my bench, with a bursting heart, not daring to raise my head. I heard M. Hamel speaking to me:

"I shall not scold you, little Franz; you should be punished enough. That's the way of it. Every day one says to oneself, 'Bah! I have time enough. I will learn to-morrow.' And then you see what happens. . . . Ah, it has been the great misfortune of our Alsace always to put off learning until to-morrow. Now these people have the right to say to us: 'What! you pretend to be French, and you do not know how to speak or write your own language?' In all that, my poor Franz, it is not you who are most guilty. We have all a good share of reproaches for ourselves.

"Your parents have not sufficiently cared to see you instructed. They liked better to send you to till the fields or to work at the spinning mills, for the sake of a few extra sous. Have I not often made you water my garden instead of working? And when I wished to go fishing for trout, did I hesitate to give you a holiday? . . ."

Then, from one thing to another, M. Hamel began to talk to us about the French language, saying that it was the most beautiful language in the world, the clearest, the most solid, that it should be kept among us and never forgotten; because when a people falls into slavery, so long as it holds fast its language it holds the key of its prison. Then he took a grammar and read us our lesson. I was astonished to see how well I understood. Everything he said seemed to me easy, easy. I believe also that I had never listened so well, and that as for him he had never put so much patience into his explanations. One would have said that before going away the poor man wished to give us all his knowledge, to make it enter our heads at a single blow.

When the lesson was over, we went on to writing. For that day M. Hamel had prepared for us entirely new examples, on which he had written in a beautiful round hand: *France, Alsace, France, Alsace*. They looked like little flags waving all round the class, hung to the rods of our desks. It was something to see how each one applied himself, and in what silence. There was nothing to be heard but the scratching of the pens on the paper. Once some beetles flew in, but nobody paid any attention, not even the very little ones, who were busy tracing their strokes with a courage and conscience, as if even the pot-hooks were in French. Upon the roof of the school-house pigeons cooed low, and listening, I said to myself:

"Will they not make them sing in German, too?"

From time to time when I lifted my eyes from my page, I saw M. Hamel motionless in his chair, taking a long look at the objects around him, as if he wished to carry off in his mind's eye all the little school-house. . . . Think! For forty years he had been there in the same place, with his yard in front of him and his class just the same. Only the seats and the desks had been polished, rubbed by use, the walnut trees in the yard had grown taller, and the hop-vine which he had himself planted wreathed about the windows and up to the roof. What a heart-break it must have been to the poor man to leave these things, and to hear his sister as she went and came in the room overhead packing their trunks. For they were to go on the morrow, to leave the country forever.

All the same he had the courage to go on with the recitation to the end. After the writing, we had our history lesson; and then the little ones sang the BA, BE, BI, BO, BU. Away at the end of the room old Hauser had put on his spectacles, and holding his A, B, C book in both hands, he spelled out the letters with them. He, too, was visibly applying himself. His voice trembled with emotion, and it was so funny to hear him that we all wanted to laugh and to cry. Ah, I shall remember that last lesson!

Suddenly the church clock struck noon, then the Angelus. At the same moment the trumpets of the Prussians who were returning from drill blared under our windows. . . . M. Hamel rose, very pale, from his chair. Never had he appeared to me so tall.

"My friends," he said, "My friends, I . . . I. . . ."

But something stifled him. He could not finish his sentence.

Then he turned to the black-board, took a piece of chalk, and bearing on it with all his strength, he wrote as large as he could:

"VIVE LA FRANCE!"

Then he came to a stop; his head pressed against the wall, and without speaking he signed to us with his hand:

"That is all . . . Go."

Author and Selection Notes

The early teaching experience of Alphonse Daudet (1840-1897) and his military service during the Franco-Prussian War are both reflected in "The

Last Lesson." This famous French novelist's career as a journalist helped sharpen his powers of observation and enabled him to write realistic stories of human interest.

Questions and Exercises

1. What effect is achieved by having the reader see everything through the eyes of the child?

2. How do we learn to know the teacher? What is your opinion of his teaching methods?

3. Explain the significance of the title. Comment on the behavior of teacher, children, and adult visitors on this last day of school. Is it psychologically sound? Why or why not?

4. How does Daudet create suspense at the beginning of his story? After the suspense subsides, why does the story continue to hold your interest?

5. Theme Topics: Plenty of Time; A Lost Opportunity; My Last Day in High School; Sudden Maturity; If I Had the Time.

LAUSANNE

Thomas Hardy

In Gibbon's Old Garden:
11-12 P.M.
June 27, 1897
(The 110th anniversary of the completion of the "Decline and Fall"
at the same hour and place)

A spirit seems to pass,
Formal in pose, but grave withal and grand:
He contemplates a volume in his hand,
And far lamps fleck him through the thin acacias.

Anon the book is closed,
With "It is finished!" And at the alley's end
He turns, and when on me his glances bend
As from the Past comes speech—small, muted, yet composed.

"How fares the Truth now?—Ill?
—Do pens but slily further her advance?

May one not speed her but in phrase askance?
Do scribes aver the Comic to be Reverend still?

"Still rule those minds on earth
At whom sage Milton's wormwood words were hurled:
'Truth like a bastard comes into the world
Never without ill-fame to him who gives her birth'?"

Author and Selection Notes

An unsuccessful poet as a young man, Thomas Hardy (1840-1928) began writing prose fiction in his mid-twenties and was considered a successful novelist by the time he was thirty-two. However, in the middle of his career he returned to writing poetry, and today he is acclaimed in English literature as both poet and novelist. Although often considered a pessimist, Hardy considered himself a realist and believed that human effort could make the world better. He considered his writings to be an appeal against "man's inhumanity to man." Edward Gibbon, the subject of "Lausanne," was, like Hardy, a fighter for truth against superstition and prejudice.

Questions and Exercises

1. What does Gibbon mean by man's unwillingness to face the truth? Is he referring to the censuring of his own frequent anti-Christian remarks, or is there a more universal application?
2. What effect does Hardy gain by including a quote from Milton's *Areopagitica* in his poem? Is he able to blend it harmoniously within the framework of the poem?
3. Cite modern applications of Milton's words.
4. Theme Topics: A Definition of Truth; Truth Is Absolute; Truth Is Relative; A Case of Pure Prejudice; Should We Always Tell the Truth? The Relationship of Truth and Education.

THE LEARNED MEN

Archibald MacLeish

Whose minds like horse or ox,
Dispassionate in the stall,
Grow great in girth and wax
Beyond the animal,

While mine, like country hog,
Grows leaner as I age,
Chivvied by flea and dog,
Bated by love and rage.

If mind by God was meant
To grow and gain in girth,
Swelling in sweet content,
I cease I have no worth:

But if it was God's will
That mind, no wish refused
Should waste by wanting still
By God I am well used!

Author and Selection Notes

Archibald MacLeish (1892-   ), a Pulitzer Prize poet, has served prominently in public life, both as Librarian of Congress and Assistant Secretary of State. He has also experimented in radio and ballet, and his verse play, *J. B.*, was widely acclaimed. His ability to use ordinary language effectively is reflected in "The Learned Men."

Questions and Exercises

1. Within a simple, regular verse pattern this poem houses thoughts which will require more than casual reading. Describe the growth of the two different types of minds; then explain the meaning of this growth.

2. Why does the poet refer to such creatures as horse, ox, hog, flea, and dog? What modifiers are especially fitting, and what effect do they have on you as you read the poem?

3. What examples of "forced rhyme" do you find?

4. Identify the verse pattern of the poem.

5. Theme Topics: The Self-Satisfied Scholar; The True Scholar; The Pedant; The Humbling Effect of Knowledge.

THE MARKS OF AN EDUCATED MAN

Alan Simpson

Any education that matters is *liberal*. All the saving truths and healing graces that distinguish a good education from a bad one

From *Context*, I, No. 1, Spring, 1961, copyright by the author. Reprinted by permission of the author.

or a full education from a half-empty one are contained in that word. Whatever ups and downs the term "liberal" suffers in the political vocabulary, it soars above all controversy in the educational world. In the blackest pits of pedagogy the squirming victim has only to ask, "What's liberal about this?" to shame his persecutors. In times past a liberal education set off a free man from a slave or a gentleman from laborers and artisans. It now distinguishes whatever nourishes the mind and spirit from the training which is merely practical or professional or from the trivialities which are no training at all. Such an education involves a combination of knowledge, skills, and standards.

So far as knowledge is concerned, the record is ambiguous. It is sufficiently confused for the fact-filled freak who excels in quiz shows to have passed himself off in some company as an educated man. More respectable is the notion that there are some things which every educated man ought to know; but many highly educated men would cheerfully admit to a vast ignorance, and the framers of curriculums have differed greatly in the knowledge they prescribe. If there have been times when all the students at school or college studied the same things, as if it were obvious that without exposure to a common body of knowledge they would not be educated at all, there have been other times when specialization ran so wild that it might almost seem as if educated men had abandoned the thought of ever talking to each other once their education was completed.

If knowledge is one of our marks, we can hardly be dogmatic about the kind or the amount. A single fertile field tilled with care and imagination can probably develop all the instincts of an educated man. However, if the framer of a curriculum wants to minimize his risks, he can invoke an ancient doctrine which holds that an educated man ought to know a little about everything and a lot about something.

The "little about everything" is best interpreted these days by those who have given most thought to the sort of general education an informed individual ought to have. More is required than a sampling of the introductory courses which specialists offer in their own disciplines. Courses are needed in each of the major divisions of knowledge—the humanities, the natural sciences, and social sciences—which are organized with the breadth of view and the imaginative power of competent staffs who understand the needs of interested amateurs. But, over and above this exciting smattering of knowledge, students should bite deeply into at least one subject and taste its full flavor. It is not enough to be dilettantes in everything without striving also to be craftsmen in something.

If there is some ambiguity about the knowledge an educated man should have, there is none at all about the skills. The first is simply the training of the mind in the capacity to think clearly. This has always been the business of education, but the way it is done varies enormously. Marshalling the notes of a lecture is one experience; the opportunity to argue with a teacher is another. Thinking within an accepted tradition is one thing; to challenge the tradition itself is another. The best results are achieved when the idea of the examined life is held firmly before the mind and when the examination is conducted with the zest, rigor, and freedom which really stretches everyone's capacities.

The vital aid to clear thought is the habit of approaching everything we hear and everything we are taught to believe with a certain skepticism. The method of using doubt as an examiner is a familiar one among scholars and scientists, but it is also the best protection which a citizen has against the cant and humbug that surround us.

To be able to listen to a phony argument and to see its dishonesty is surely one of the marks of an educated man. We may not need to be educated to possess some of this quality. A shrewd peasant was always well enough protected against impostors in the market place, and we have all sorts of businessmen who have made themselves excellent judges of phoniness without the benefit of a high-school diploma; but this kind of shrewdness goes along with a great deal of credulity. Outside the limited field within which experience has taught the peasant or the illiterate businessman his lessons, he is often hopelessly gullible. The educated man, by contrast, has tried to develop a critical faculty for general use, and he likes to think that he is fortified against imposture in all its forms.

It does not matter for our purposes whether the impostor is a deliberate liar or not. Some are, but the commonest enemies of mankind are the unconscious frauds. Most salesmen under the intoxication of their own exuberance seem to believe in what they say. Most experts whose *expertise* is only a pretentious sham behave as if they had been solemnly inducted into some kind of priesthood. Very few demagogues are so cynical as to remain undeceived by their own rhetoric, and some of the worst tyrants in history have been fatally sincere. We can leave the disentanglement of motives to the students of fraud and error, but we cannot afford to be taken in by the shams.

We are, of course, surrounded by shams. Until recently the schools were full of them—the notion that education can be had without tears, that puffed rice is a better intellectual diet than oatmeal, that adjustment to the group is more important than knowing where the group is going, and that democracy has made it a sin to separate the sheep from the goats. Mercifully, these are much less evident now than they were before Sputnik startled us into our wits.

If this is true of universities with their solemn vows and limited temptations, how much truer is it of the naughty world outside, where the prizes are far more dazzling and the only protection against humbug is the skepticism of the ordinary voter, customer, reader, listener, and viewer? Of course, the follies of human nature are not going to be exorcised by anything that the educator can do, and I am not sure that he would want to exorcise them if he could. There is something irresistibly funny about the old Adam, and life would be duller without his antics. But they ought to be kept within bounds. We are none the better for not recognizing a clown when we see one.

The other basic skill is simply the art of self-expression in speech and on paper. A man is uneducated who has not mastered the elements of clean forcible prose and picked up some relish for style.

It is a curious fact that we style everything in this country—our cars, our homes, our clothes—except our minds. They still chug along like a Model T—rugged, persevering, but far from graceful.

No doubt this appeal for style, like the appeal for clear thinking, can be carried too far. There was once an American who said that the only important thing in life was "to set a chime of words ringing in a few fastidious minds." As far as can be learned, he left this country in a huff to tinkle his little bell in a foreign land. Most of us would think that he lacked a sense of proportion. After all, the political history of this country is full of good judgment expressed in bad prose, and the business history has smashed through to some of its grandest triumphs across acres of broken syntax. But we can discard some of these frontier manners without becoming absurdly precious.

The road ahead bristles with obstacles. There is the reluctance of many people to use one word where they can get away with a half-dozen or a word of one syllable if they can find a longer one. No one has ever told them about the first rule in English composition: every slaughtered syllable is a good deed. The most persuasive teachers of this maxim are undoubtedly the commercial firms that offer a thousand dollars for the completion of a slogan in twenty-five words. They are the only people who are putting a handsome premium on economy of statement.

There is the decay of the habit of memorizing good prose and good poetry in the years when tastes are being formed. It is very difficult to write a bad sentence if the Bible has been a steady companion and very easy to imagine a well-turned phrase if the ear has been tuned on enough poetry.

There is the monstrous proliferation of gobbledy-gook in government, business, and the professions. Take this horrible example of verbal smog.

It is inherent to motivational phenomena that there is a drive for more gratification than is realistically possible, on any level or in any type of personality organization. Likewise it is inherent to the world of objects that not all potentially desirable opportunities can be realized within a human life span. Therefore, any personality must involve an organization that allocates opportunities for gratifications, that systematizes precedence relative to the limited possibilities. The possibilities of gratification, simultaneously or sequentially, of all need-dispositions are severely limited by the structure of the object system and by the intra-systemic incompatibility of the consequences of gratifying them all.

What this smothered soul is trying to say is simply, "We must pick and choose, because we cannot have everything we want."

Finally, there is the universal employment of the objective test as part of the price which has to be paid for mass education. Nothing but the difficulty of finding enough readers to mark essays can condone a system which reduces a literate student to the ignoble necessity of "blackening the answer space" when he might be giving his mind and pen free play. Though we have managed to get some benefits from these examinations, the simple fact remains that the shapely prose of the Declaration of Independence or the "Gettysburg Address" was never learned under an educational system which employed objective tests. It was mastered by people who took writing seriously, who had good models in front of them, good critics to judge them, and an endless capacity for taking pains. Without that sort of discipline, the arts of self-expression will remain as mutilated as they are now.

The standards which mark an educated man can be expressed in terms of three tests.

The first is a matter of sophistication. Emerson put it nicely when he talked about getting rid of "the nonsense of our wigwams." The wigwam may be an uncultivated home, a suburban conformity, a crass patriotism, or a cramped dogma. Some of this nonsense withers in the classroom. More of it rubs off by simply mixing with people, provided they are drawn from a wide range of backgrounds and exposed within a good college to a civilized tradition. An educated man can be judged by the quality of his prejudices. There is a refined nonsense which survives the raw nonsense which Emerson was talking about.

The second test is a matter of moral values. Though we all know individuals who have contrived to be both highly educated and highly immoral, and though we have all heard of periods in history when the subtlest resources of wit and sophistication were employed to make a mockery of simple values, we do not really believe that a college is doing its job when it is simply multiplying the number of educated scoundrels, hucksters, and triflers.

The health of society depends on simple virtues like honesty, decency, courage, and public spirit. There are forces in human nature which constantly tend to corrupt them, and every age has its own vices. The worst features of ours is probably the obsession with violence. Up to some such time as 1914, it was possible to believe in a kind of moral progress. The quality which distinguished the Victorian from the Elizabethan was a sensitivity to suffering and a revulsion from cruelty which greatly enlarged the idea of human dignity. Since 1914 we have steadily brutalized ourselves. The horrors of modern war, the bestialities of modern political creeds, the uncontrollable vices of modern cities, the favorite themes of modern novelists—all have conspired to degrade us. Some of the corruption is blatant. The authors of the best sellers, after exhausting all the possibilities of sex in its normal and abnormal forms and all the variations of alcoholism and drug addiction, are about to invade the recesses of hospitals. A clinical study of a hero undergoing the irrigation of his colon is about all there is left to gratify a morbid appetite.

Some of the corruption is insidious. A national columnist recently wrote an article in praise of cockfighting. He had visited a cockfight in the company of Ernest Hemingway. After pointing out that Hemingway had made bullfighting respectable, he proceeded to describe the terrible beauty of fierce indomitable birds trained to kill each other for the excitement of the spectators. Needless to say, there used to be a terrible beauty about Christians defending themselves against lions or about heretics being burned at the stake, and there are still parts of the world where a public execution is regarded as a richly satisfying feast. But for three or four centuries the West taught itself to resist these excitements in the interest of a moral idea.

Educators are needlessly squeamish about their duty to uphold moral values and needlessly perplexed about how to implant them. The corruptions of our times are a sufficient warning that we cannot afford to abandon the duty to the homes and the churches, and the capacity which many institutions have shown to do their duty in a liberal spirit is a sufficient guaranty against bigotry.

Finally, there is the test imposed by the unique challenge of our own times. We are not unique in suffering from moral confusion—these crises are a familiar story—but we are unique in the tremendous acceleration of the rate of social change and in the tremendous risk of a catastrophic end to all our hopes. We cannot afford educated men who have every grace except the gift for survival. An indispensable mark of the modern educated man is the kind of versatile, flexible mind that can deal with new and explosive conditions.

With this reserve, there is little in this profile which has not been familiar for centuries. Unfortunately, the description which once sufficed to suggest its personality has been debased in journalistic currency. The "well-rounded man" has become the organization man, or the man who is so well rounded that he rolls wherever he is pushed. The humanists who invented the idea and preached it for centuries would recoil in contempt for any such notion. They understood the possibilities of the whole man and wanted an educational system which would give the many sides of his nature some chance to develop in harmony. They thought it a good idea to mix the wisdom of the world with the learning of the cloister, to develop the body as well as the mind, to pay a great deal of attention to character, and to neglect no art which could add to the enjoyment of living. It was a spacious idea which offered every hospitality to creative energy. Anyone who is seriously interested in a liberal education must begin by rediscovering it.

Author and Selection Notes

Born in England and educated at Oxford, Alan Simpson (1912-   ) joined the University of Chicago as professor of history in 1946 and rose to become dean of the college in 1959. He held this position until 1963, when he was appointed president of Vassar College.

Questions and Exercises

1. Analyze the organization and development of the first paragraph.
2. Notice how often Simpson clarifies a general statement by use of examples. Point out three such instances.
3. Find examples of good transition between paragraphs.

4. Twice the author indicates what is to follow in succeeding paragraphs before he carefully guides the reader through the development of his thought. Trace the transitions between paragraphs as they guide the reader through the explanation of the skills of an educated man, and the tests which indicate the standards of an educated man.

5. Theme Topics: The Well-Rounded Man; The Truly Educated Man; Liberal Education Before Specialization; All Learning Is (Is Not) of Equal Value; What I Want from College.

SO WE SENT OUR SON TO COLLEGE

Sally and James Reston

Helping your eldest son pick a college is one of the great educational experiences of life—for the parents. Next to trying to pick his bride, it's the best way to learn that your authority, if not entirely gone, is slipping fast. Age seventeen is the point in the journey when the parents retire to the observation car; it is the time when you stop being critical of your eldest son and he starts being critical of you.

We didn't know that at the time of the big college decision because, as all mothers and some fathers eventually realize, parents are always at least a little behind the eldest child. He is always a new experience. You are always practicing on him. Just when you get used to him at five, he's suddenly turned into something totally different at eight. When you've figured out the mysteries of age nine, all at once he's an adolescent. And when he gets through *that*—and if you get through it—there's the problem of college.

There are three ways for parents to go about this problem. The best way is to skip it and let him do it, no matter how long that school form lies unanswered on the hall table. Another good way is to have a brilliant, foresighted son who knows exactly what he wants to study and where. The worst way is to make a solemn project out of it and get caught between what you think he should do and what he thinks he should do.

We chose the third way. We started out with the old Middle Western parental attitude: "We'll learn 'em, durn 'em." We analyzed; we researched; we argued. We got ourselves every college guide in the library. We collected more college catalogues than the Ford Foundation. We listened attentively to every sentimental old grad in town. And, of course, we discussed the problem with the boy in five-minute snatches while he was running in or out of the house.

"I want to go to the University of North Carolina," he said, never having seen North Carolina.

"Why?" we asked.

"Because I hear it's a nice place. And besides Pete's going there."

"If you don't go to North Carolina, where will you go?"

"Anywhere I don't have to take math!"

So we fell back on the Guide, which was our first mistake. There were others, as you'll see. "Going to college," said Clarence E. Lovejoy, the College Guide man, "is a family affair. . . . It is a joint operation. It must be done carefully and earnestly."

Carefully and earnestly, we started with the experts. Robert Frost, the poet, was encouraging. "Education," he said, "is hanging around the right places and the right people until you get an idea." The boy liked that.

"I'll hang around North Carolina," Dick said. "Besides I've already got an idea. At least I know what I don't want. I don't want to try to make myself into a great brain, because I'm not. I don't want to go to a small New England men's college. I've been to a boys' school all my life and liked it, but now I'm ready for something else—something more like real life."

"H'm'm," we said. "Such as what?"

"Well, a fairly big place, but not too big."

The thing to do, we decided, was to go see for ourselves. We started first with the great state universities and the smaller land-grant colleges of the Middle West. These are what Henry Morton Robinson, the author and poet, calls "those educational rabbit warrens . . . whose inmates, I hear from reliable sources, gradually learn the use of commas and can be trained to perform simple feats of logic connected with chain-store management, ethical embalming and other disciplines much revered by the American demos."

Undismayed by this Menckenish spoofing, we sent our rabbit first to reconnoiter Miami University in Oxford, Ohio. This is a new college by Mr. Robinson's standard—didn't get going until 1809—but it is populated by American demos of both the male and the female sexes, has quite a number of two-story thinkers, is situated in a lovely town in Southern Ohio and has standards of education at least as good as the institutions that turned out most members of President Eisenhower's Cabinet.

It is true that the son of an Ohio taxpayer has little more trouble getting into Miami, a state-supported institution, than he would getting into the United States Army, but some do not stay so long. For example, a farmer sent his daughter there several years ago and was dismayed when the authorities flunked her out. He demanded her readmission. He won an order of reinstatement in the lower courts. He argued, when the university carried the case to the Court of Appeals, that he was a taxpayer of the state, whose duty it was, therefore, to educate his child. The girl had a high-school diploma, went to classes and tried the best she could. If she had been smart, he argued, he wouldn't have sent her to college! The Court of Appeals ruled against the farmer's daughter.

We would have been glad to see our boy go to Miami. It just didn't work out, like most of the other things we considered, because our son, like most sons, while no genius, was smarter and more stubborn than his parents. Besides, his experience at Miami was a little unexpected.

Father and son bivouacked in Cincinnati for the descent on the university on a Saturday morning. It was a golden day. There was a football game that afternoon, Miami vs. Xavier. Oxford doesn't have as much atmosphere as its English namesake, but it is full of ivy and pretty girls.

Father and son toured the campus, visited the classrooms and laboratories, had lunch at the pregame faculty feed and talked to the dean of men, an attractive and able educator. Passing one building, they saw a plaque on the wall announcing this as the spot where Phi Delta Theta fraternity was founded.

"Your Grandfather Fulton was a Phi Delt," said father. "And so were your Uncle Bill and your Uncle Bob."

"Can we see the fraternity house?" Dick asked.

"Well, that's a little difficult," said the dean. "It's closed now."

"Closed?" asked Dick.

"Yes, they had a little trouble last year and we had to close them up."

"H'm'm," said the boy, suddenly interested. "What happened?"

"Well, they had a picnic last spring, out in the woods south of here, and I'm afraid some of them had too much to drink."

"So you closed the house for that?"

"Not exactly. There were some Boy Scouts in the same woods, also having a picnic."

"Yes?"

"And some of the Phi Delts spiked the Boy Scouts' lemonade."

"Oh!" said Dick.

"I believe," said the dean, "the sheriff found some of the Scouts in bad shape later on, and there was an investigation—but I think we'd better be getting over to the Faculty Club."

"Yes," said Dad.

"Boy!" said Dick.

Miami won the football game, but we're afraid it didn't win Dick. He talked about it on the train going back, but he wasn't very responsive. Next night we discovered why: the doctor came in the middle of the night and removed a ruptured appendix. Things like this interfere with planned college picking.

While he was recuperating, we asked the advice of the experts. The headmaster of his school thought Dartmouth just the place: the director of studies recommended Bowdoin. An English teacher said family background was important. Where did his father go?

"The University of Illinois," Dick replied.

"Well, it doesn't matter," the English teacher remarked. "I think every boy should go to college where his father went."

This was appealing. We would give the theory a try.

"It's important," said his father, "to know where your roots are. We know the Middle West. Our families are out there. The area around the Great Lakes and the Northwest are the coming part of the country. In your generation the St. Lawrence Seaway will be carrying ocean vessels from Europe to Chicago and Cleveland. And these are fine schools."

"You're talking about your families and where you came from," said the boy. "I'm not from the Middle West. I've lived in Washington most of my life. I like it around here."

"Why not go and see?" we asked. And he agreed.

So the next stop was Urbana, Illinois. Just to show the growth of such universities, Dick's grandmother and grandfather were in the Class of 1898 at the same university. There were 1824 students there then. When his mother graduated from Illinois in 1934, the total in all colleges was 10,747 including the enrollment in the branch colleges outside Urbana. Now it has reached 25,159.

Since Dick was cocaptain of his school football team, his father took him to the university football practice. He was impressed—too impressed. The squad looked as big as an army, and the men were giants. He was very quiet.

We went to a freshman-survey history course and met one of the faculty members in history. Yes, the classes were much bigger, he conceded. In fact, in this class, a student didn't even put his name on examination papers. He merely put down his seat number, and the paper was graded, not by his instructor, but by some graduate assistant, who hadn't the slightest notion whose paper he was grading.

"Is that a good idea?" Dick asked.

"No," we answered. And that was that.

We then approached the Ivy League colleges with what we hoped was the proper reverence. The aforementioned Mr. Robinson has explained why this is necessary.

"Despite the leveling influences that would 'democratize' the A.B. degree—that is, bring it down to the level of a vaccination certificate"—he said, "the Ivy colleges cling to the somewhat mystical notion that a candidate for the eight-hundred-year-old degree of *Baccalaureus in Artibus* shall be, among other things, a person of marked intellectual promise.

"They hold, further, that he shall be capable of achieving a rigorous kind of excellence, not limited to mind, manners—or even muscles—but penetrating into the very marrow and matrix of life itself."

This was not promising. We are going to admit that "marked intellectual promise" and "a rigorous kind of excellence" are not the outstanding traits in our family. Besides, of the 400,000 students who applied for entrance into all American colleges only 7500, or about two per cent, were accepted by the Ivy League. Nevertheless, they let us look—first at Harvard.

We didn't take Dick there to a football game. We went on a Tuesday morning and attended a course in American history. Everybody was pleasant. The lecture was superb. There were several nice Radcliffe girls in the class, and we carried away packets of information.

"Harvard exists," said dean McGeorge Bundy, "for the student who wants to become a liberally educated man. It is a broad development of their powers . . . and for an enriched cultural life."

We discussed this with Dick on the journey home.

"Do you feel the need for broad development of your powers and an enriched cultural life?"

"Who, me?" he asked. "Harvard's a wonderful school for the 'brains,' " he went on, "but somewhere I've heard that a 'high-brow's a person who's educated beyond his own intelligence.' And that's not for me!"

On our way home we came to another Ivy college, which, for the purposes of this story, had better be nameless. It was the weekend and the day of the last football game of the year. We stopped to have a look, and learned something new about the business of college picking.

After dinner on Saturday night we were invited by a faculty member to a party given by one of the minor football coaches for the football squad. This was held at a house out in the country a few miles from the campus. When we got there, we drove to a large cinder-block house apart from the main dwelling—sort of a grown-up playhouse. This was something new in our experience.

The house itself was original. It was rectangular in shape, two stories high. On the lower floor was a basketball court. The second story was a balcony, running along the length and one side of the basketball floor, and on the long side of the balcony was a fixed bar in the shape of an O, with about ninety feet of drinking space.

When we arrived fairly late in the evening the place was in an uproar. The bar was crowded with old grads and students, faculty members and coaches, squad members and their dates though some of the last had been abandoned by this hour and looked slightly bewildered.

On the basketball court below a scrub game was in progress. The players were dressed in their street clothes, a couple of them in Tuxedos, some with their hats on, one in an overcoat, and all with their shoes off.

Looking over the balcony, we watched until one of the gladiators finally passed out and had to be carted off to the showers by the others. It was, to put it mildly, quite a party, and made us feel slightly out of date.

This, however, is one of the flaws in the theory that you can make judgments about a university during a weekend visit. You get an impression, but it may be a totally false impression. Yet the impression, whatever it is, sticks, and may lead you and the boy elsewhere.

So there are some limitations to the "We'll learn 'em, durn 'em" attitude. All our travels didn't settle anything, but there are consolations. Time passes, even for a seventeen-year-old, and the day comes when he has to pick up that entrance blank off the hall table, fill in the three colleges of his choice and take the documents back to school. Otherwise, his grades aren't sent to the colleges and he gets squeezed out by what the professors call the "new barbarian invasion" now descending on the nation's campuses.

This is one of the few occasions when time is on your side. Under the head-master's prodding, the young man comes to you and asks what he should put down. Of course, you have been struggling with this, at great cost, for months, but he suddenly focuses on imminent disaster and needs help.

"What do I say?" he asks.

"Harvard, Yale and Princeton," says father.

"Come on, I'm serious. I have to hand this thing in tomorrow," he explains.

"How about Cornell?" mother asks.

"O.K., North Carolina, Cornell and—What about Dartmouth?"

Then, of course, there are other questions; course of study, honors in high school, rooming plans, educational objectives.

"What am I studying?" he asks.

"Nuclear physics," says dad. "You don't have to have math for that."

"Put down liberal arts," mother suggests.

"Good. And what about 'high-school honors and activities'? Can I say football, basketball and baseball?"

"Sure," says brother, "and don't forget 'flag raiser, senior year,' and 'dance committee.'"

"I think I'll just add: 'Trophies to come,'" says Dick, and eventually the form was complete.

When the long ordeal was all over we decided to establish a Society for the Prevention of Cruelty to Parents, and we have been working on it quietly ever since.

Our view is that in a way it's a pity to waste college on children. Obviously, it's the parents who should go to college and the kids who should stay home and manage the house.

Pending the arrival of this great day, however, we have put down a few tips to remember when the time comes for Dick's two brothers to go to college, and meanwhile these may be of some use to other parents:

1. Don't grieve over your eldest boy going to college. Console yourself with the thought that you're not losing a son, but gaining a bathroom.

2. See that he goes *away* to college. This makes you appreciate him and vice versa.

3. Suggest, as deftly as you can, that co-educational colleges have one advantage which will be apparent to him. Remember what Edgar Wallace says: "A high-brow is a man who has found something more interesting than women."

4. Don't take him to college. Let him go on his own. He learns more. He makes a better impression and has a better chance to get in. Besides, it's cheaper.

5. Don't worry if he doesn't get into the college you want or even into the one he wants; the funny thing about these kids is that they love it wherever they go.

6. Let him go into "Outer Mediocrity." The main thing is not

what the college gives him, but what you gave him before he ever thought of college.

Finally, it is not a bad idea to think a little about what college is for. Unless you have a resident genius in your family, and even if you have, the intellect is only part of what you're trying to develop. After all, the brain is only muscle.

We went to a big conference at Princeton recently about how to get the best men in the country to run the Government. After a whole weekend of debates by some of the loftiest brains in the country, including quite a few double-domes from Princeton itself, the conclusion was that the qualities they were looking for were first, vitality; second, courage; third, sensitivity; and fourth, intelligence.

Lord Russell, who is an expert in these matters, came to the same conclusion long ago. After all, the big question, to which no college has found the answer, is still the mystery of "What makes Sammy run?" And the chances are that he can develop that in one good university as well as another.

By the way, Dick went to North Carolina. He loves it, and so do we. Also, he joined Phi Delta Theta, in spite of those Boy Scouts at Miami.

Author and Selection Notes

James Reston (1909-   ), born in Scotland and brought to the United States one year later, has become an outstanding newspaper correspondent. The winner of many awards as national correspondent and reporter, he counts among his honors the Pulitzer Prize in Journalism. In 1935 he married "Sally" (Sarah Jane Fulton), who is co-author of the preceding article.

Questions and Exercises

1. James Reston and his wife Sally make a hilarious family project out of choosing a college for their son. How do they set the tone of the essay in the opening paragraph?
2. Throughout the essay how do they produce humorous effects? What is gained by the light touch?
3. Do they ever strike a serious note? What would be gained or lost by writing the essay in a serious mood?
4. What sort of boy is Dick? Do you think you would enjoy visiting in the Reston home? Why or why not?
5. Theme Topics: Choosing a College; My First Impressions of College; A Visit to Another Campus; Getting Ready for College; My First Week in the Dormitory; My Advice to High-School Seniors.

THE TERRIBLE MISS DOVE

Frances Gray Patton

Miss Dove was waiting for the sixth grade to file in for its geography lesson. She stood behind her desk, straight as the long map pointer in her hand. And suddenly she had the feeling of not being really alone. Someone or something was moving about the room. Over there, near the sand table where the first grade's herd of rickety clay caribou grazed at the edge of the second grade's plateau, it paused and looked at her. But even when the presence glided, like the shadow of a drifting cloud, along the wall behind her; even when she heard—or almost heard—a new stick of chalk squeaking on the blackboard, Miss Dove did not turn around. She knew, of course, that nobody was there. Her imagination was playing tricks again. It was something, she had to admit, humiliatingly close to nerves. Miss Dove did not believe in nerves.

Through the open door she watched the sixth graders come out of the music room down the hall. They came out with a rush, as if for two minutes of freedom between classroom and classroom they were borne along upon some mass exhilaration. They always left the music room in that fashion, but this morning they managed to be noisier than usual. It was the season, she supposed. The spring day was warm, and the children were restless as the weather. There was a sharp sound among them, as of a plump posterior being spanked with a book; there was a voice saying, "Double dare, Watty!"; there was a breathless giggling.

But as they approached Miss Dove's room their disorder began to vanish. They pulled their excitement in, like a proud but well-broken pony. One by one they stepped sedately across her doorsill. "Good morning, Miss Dove," they said, one by one, with the same proper lack of voice inflection, and went demurely to their places. At a nod from her they took their seats. Hands folded, eyes to the front, posture correct—they were ready for direction.

Jincey Webb, Miss Dove noticed without enthusiasm, had a permanent wave. Yesterday her carrot-colored mane had been neatly braided and pulled back from her serious, freckled face. Now it hung to her shoulders, a bushy mop of undulations and frizzy ringlets. It hung on her mind, too; that was plain to see. For Jincey's expression was one of utter and enviable complacency. It seemed doubtful that a long lifetime of repeated triumphs could again offer her an achievement so sublime with self-satisfaction.

Watty Baker, a pink boy of exceptional daring, wiggled his ears at Jincey. Miss Dove looked at him. Watty's pinkness paled. A glaze of innocence came over his round eyes. His ears grew very still.

Miss Dove kept looking at him, but she had stopped seeing him. Instead, she was seeing his brother Thomas, who had sat there at Watty's desk seven years before, with the same glaze over the mischief in his eyes. And then she saw Thomas on a raft in the Pacific. She did not see him as they had described him in the papers—skin and bones and haggard young face overgrown with a rough, wild beard. The Thomas she saw looked like Watty. He had braces on his teeth and a dimple in his chin. And he was all alone in the dismal gray mountains of the sea.

A wave of giddiness swept over her, but she did not sit down. It was nothing. It had been happening to her off and on all year, and it always passed. Miss Dove had a poor opinion of teachers who could not practice self-control.

For thirty years Miss Dove had taught geography in Cedar Grove Elementary School. She had been there before the brooding cedars had been chopped down by a city council that believed in progress and level playgrounds. She had seen principals and fads and theories come and go. But the school still squatted there, red brick, ugly, impervious. Inside it still smelled of wet raincoats and pickle sandwiches. Galahad still petted his charger on the left wall of the vestibule, and Washington still crossed the Delaware on the right. Every fall nervous six-year-olds had to be sent home in tears to put on dry drawers. Every spring there occurred the scandal of cigarette butts in the boy's basement. The same deplorable, old-fashioned words sprang up overnight like mushrooms on the cement walk. And now and then some hitherto graceless child could still surprise you with an act of loyalty or understanding. The school had not changed much. Neither had human nature. Neither had Miss Dove. Each June some forty-odd little girls and boys—transformed by the magic of organdy ruffles and white duck pants into a group picture of purity—were graduated from Cedar Grove. They went on to the wider world of junior high and, beyond that, to further realms of pleasure and pain. In the course of time they forgot much. They forgot dates and decimals and how to write business letters.

But they never forgot Miss Dove.

Years afterward the mention of the Euphrates River or the Arctic

Circle or the Argentinian pampas would put them right back in the geography room. They would see again the big map with its flat blue ocean and its many-colored countries. (India was pink, they would recall, and China was orange, and the Italian boot was purple.) They would see Miss Dove lifting her long stick to point out the location of strange mountains and valleys. And they would feel again the wonder of a world far-flung and various and, like themselves, entirely under control. They would also feel a little thirsty.

"Remember Miss Dove?" they would smile.

But this green remembrance and the accident of her name's rhyming with a tender word should not deceive anybody about Miss Dove. She was no valentine. Miss Dove was a terror.

She had been young when she first started teaching. Her pupils would have hooted at the notion; they would have felt it more reasonable to believe Miss Dove had been born middle-aged with her mousy hair screwed into a knot at the back of her head and a white handkerchief pinned to her dark, bony bosom. Nevertheless, it is true. She had once been quite young.

Her father had died, leaving her little besides a library of travel books, an anemic violet-scented mother, and two young sisters in school. It had been up to Miss Dove. Older people had pitied her. She seemed too thin and pale and untried, they thought, to carry the burden alone. But Miss Dove never pitied herself. Responsibility was the climate of her soul.

The children of each grade came to her forty-five minutes a day, five days a week, six years of their lives. She saw them as a challenge. Their babyish shyness, their lisping pronunciation, their reckless forgetfulness—these evoked no compassion from Miss Dove. They were qualities to be nipped and pruned. Her classes were like a body of raw recruits that she was to toughen and charge with purpose. Miss Dove was the stuff that commanders are made of.

Other teachers had trouble keeping order, but not Miss Dove. Other teachers tried to make a game of their work—they played store and pasted gold stars on foreheads. They threatened and cajoled. Miss Dove never raised her voice. She rarely smiled. She laid before the children the roster of her unalterable laws. And the laws were obeyed. Work was to be done on time. There was to be no whispering, no hair chewing, no wriggling. Coughing, if indulged in at all, was to be covered with a clean handkerchief. When one of these laws was chipped, Miss Dove merely looked at the offender. That was all. If a child felt obliged to disturb the class routine by leaving the room for a drink of water (Miss Dove loftily ignored any other necessity), he did so to the accompaniment of dead silence.

The whole class would sit, idle and motionless, until he had returned. It was easier—even if you had eaten salt fish for breakfast —to remain and suffer.

Miss Dove managed to introduce a moral quality into the very subject she taught. The first graders, who studied the animals of different lands, repeated after her, "The yak is a very helpful animal." And they knew she expected them all to be yaks. Later they learned a more complicated sentence. "The camel," they recited in perfect unison, "is not a pretty beast, either in looks or disposition, but he is able to go many days without water." And they knew what was meant. "Above the fiftieth parallel," sixth graders wrote in their notebooks (keeping the margins even), "life requires hardihood."

Occasionally a group of progressive mothers would nearly rebel. "She's been teaching too long," they would cry. "Her pedagogy hasn't changed since we were in the third grade. She rules the children through fear." They would turn to the boldest one among them. "*You go*," they would say. "You go talk to her."

The bold one would go, but somehow she never did much talking. For under the level gaze of Miss Dove she would begin to feel— though she wore her handsomest tweeds and perhaps a gardenia for courage—that she was about ten years old and her petticoat was showing. Her throat would tickle. She would wonder desperately if she had a clean handkerchief to cough into.

And then there was the little matter of the state achievement tests. Cedar Grove always placed first in geography.

Occasionally, too, there would be an independent child who did not yield readily to group discipline. Miss Dove knew how to deal with him.

Once she had overheard two small boys talking about her at the drinking fountain. (They had no business at the fountain; it was their library period. But the librarian was lax.)

"I bet Miss Dove could lick Joe Louis," one of them had said.

"Who? That ole stick?" the other one had jeered. "I could beat her with my little finger."

He had glanced up then to see Miss Dove looking down at him. She had looked at him for a long time. Her light gray eyes were expressionless. Her long nose was pink at the tip, but no pinker than usual. At last she had spoken.

"Thomas Baker," she had said in the tone of one making a pure observation, "you talk too much, don't you?"

"Yes, ma'am," Thomas had said in a tiny voice. He went off without getting any water. Seven years later he sweated when he thought of it. He could not know that Miss Dove also remembered. But she did.

Ever since Pearl Harbor Miss Dove had been troubled. She lived quite alone, for her sisters had married and her mother had departed for a place not on the map. (But decently, with every possible comfort. Miss Dove liked to remind herself of that.) And one evening while she was correcting papers she sensed, with that uncanny perception of the teacher, that something intruded upon her solitude. She turned quickly and looked about the room. A starched white curtain rustled in a puff of wind; her grandmother's rosewood whatnot cast a curious shadow on the polished floor; a finger of lamplight picked out the gilt titles of her father's old brown travel books. There was nothing else. But the red correction pencil was shaking in her fingers; for a moment her throat ached with a spasm of desolate, unaccountable grief, and—less familiar still—with a feeling of her own unworthiness. Miss Dove had never felt unworthy before in her life.

After that the thing happened frequently, until at last she saw who the intruders were. They were the children she had taught long ago.

War had scattered those children. There was a girl—a vain, silly little piece she had been—who was a nurse on Corregidor. At least, when last heard of she had been on Corregidor. One of the boys was dead in Tunisia. Others were on the Anzio beachhead, or in the jungles of New Guinea, or in the flak-brightened skies over Germany. But they came back to Miss Dove. She saw them as they had been at seven, at ten, at twelve. Only they had a beauty she had never seen in them then. They lifted their faces like starry morning flowers. Their limbs quivered with the unreasonable joy of childhood. And as Miss Dove looked at them they grew still. Their faces paled. Their eyes stopped dancing. They folded their little hands. They faded and were gone.

The child who came oftenest was Thomas Baker. The town paper had been full of Thomas. His ship had been bombed, his officers killed, and Thomas had taken over. A hundred men owed their lives to his presence of mind. For days he had floated on a raft with no food and only the water in his canteen. When they picked him up his tongue had protruded from his mouth, black and swollen with thirst. That was what got Miss Dove—he had run out of water.

The Thomas who came to stand before her now was a sturdy boy in knickers. He held his chin at a cocky angle, but the dimple in it trembled. He ran the tip of his tongue over his lips. He looked thirsty.

But they came only at night. When daylight returned Miss Dove could believe she had been imagining things. She would eat her customary boiled egg and her wholewheat toast; she would take an extra vitamin pill with her orange juice; she would walk forth at her usual measured pace and assume her usual role of unshakable authority. The children at the school would seem plain and ordinary. They would have little in common with those graceful and evanescent figures that haunted her. And no intruders dared come into the geography room. Or they never had until this morning.

A boy on the back row cleared his throat. One by the window followed suit. Soon the whole room was dotted with the sound, a rough "h-hrmph," like frogs in a distant marsh. Miss Dove knew what the sound meant. It was the school's traditional signal—a kind of dare. She had heard other teachers speak of it in exasperation. It had never happened in her room before.

Slowly Watty Baker raised his hand. The sounds stopped. Silence like a caught breath hung on the room. Miss Dove could see a fine dew pop out on Watty's brow; his open palm was damp and gleaming.

"Yes, Watson?" she said.

Watty stood up. Miss Dove's pupils always stood when they addressed her. He smoothed his round stomach with his hand. "I got a letter from Tom yestiddy," he said.

"*Received,* Watson," said Miss Dove. "You received a letter from your brother *yesterday.* That was nice."

"Yes, ma'am," said Watty. He paused. He was clearly floundering. "He sent me a dollar he won playing poker in the convalescent hospital."

"I am sorry to hear that Thomas gambles," said Miss Dove, "but we are all proud of his war record. If you have nothing more interesting to tell us you may take your seat, Watson."

"H-hr-rmpth!" went the boy behind Watty.

"He's been decorated," said Watty, "for bravery beyond the call of duty." The high words seemed to inspirit him. "He sent a message to the class."

"Did you bring the letter?" asked Miss Dove. "If so, you may read that part aloud."

Watty took an air-mail envelope from his hip pocket. Miss Dove noticed that Thomas' handwriting was as sprawling and untidy as ever. Somehow the observation pleased her.

The class stirred. The ghost of a titter rippled the air.

"Attention, please," said Miss Dove.

Watty opened the letter. The paper was smudged and crumpled.

Obviously it had suffered many readings and many hands. Watty cleared his throat. The sound was not a link in the chain signal. Miss Dove could tell the difference. "It's sort of long," Watty demurred hopefully.

Miss Dove knew there was naughtiness afoot. The frog noises as well at Watty's hesitation had told her that. But she did not believe in avoiding an issue. She made a practice of facing impudence in the open—and facing down.

"We can spare the time," she said.

Watty began to read. His voice was high and clear; it had the girlish sweetness that comes just before the breaking point.

"The funny thing about the world," Watty read, "is that it looks just like you think it does. When they flew me back to Cal. in a hospital plane I looked down and, heck, I might as well have been looking at those diagrams on the geography board back in dear (ha, ha!) ole Cedar Grove. I spotted a peninsula just as plain. A body of land almost entirely surrounded by water. I saw some atolls too. And they really are made in rings like doughnuts, with palm trees sprouting out of the cake part and blue water in the hole in the middle. The water is the color of that blue chalk I swiped once and drew the picture of Miss Dove on the sidewalk with. Remember?"

So it *was* Thomas who had drawn that caricature. She had always suspected him. "Proceed, Watson," she said.

"You want to know if I was scared when the little yellow insects from"—Watty swallowed and went on—"from hell"—in his embarrassment he brought out the word with unnecessary force—"dive-dombed us. The answer is, you bet. But it came to me in a flash that I wasn't much scareder than I was that time old lady Dove caught me bragging about how I could beat her up at the drinking fountain. 'I didn't run that time,' I told myself, 'so I won't run now.' Besides, there wasn't any place to run to."

The class laughed nervously.

"And later," read Watty, "when I was bobbing up and down like Crusoe on my raft, what do you guess I thought about? Well, it wasn't any pin-up girl. It was Miss Dove. I thought about that fishy stare she used to give us when we needed a drink of water. So to make my supply hold out I played I was back in the geography room. And even after the water was all gone I kept playing that. I'd think, 'The bell is bound to ring in a few minutes. You can last a little longer.' It took the same kind of guts in the Pacific it did in school. Tell that to the kids in Cedar Grove." Watty stopped abruptly.

"Is that the end?" asked Miss Dove.

Watty looked directly at her. For a fleeting moment she thought he was going to say yes. If he did, the incident would be closed, of course, for Miss Dove never questioned a child's word. That was why they generally told her the truth. He shook his head.

"No, ma'am," he said. "There's a little more." His face turned the color of a nearly ripe tomato. "He says here"—Watty gulped— "he says"—Watty took a deep breath—"he says: 'Give the terrible Miss Dove a kiss for me.' "

"Well, Waston," said Miss Dove, "I am waiting."

There was an electric stillness that was followed, as the full meaning of her words penetrated the children's consciousness, by a gasp. Watty folded the letter and put it back into his pocket. Then he began to walk toward her. He walked with the deliberate stoicism of a martyr going to the chopping block. Miss Dove inclined her head and turned her cheek in his direction. He did not come any closer than he had to. He leaned forward stiffly from the waist and placed his puckered lips against her cheek. (*He smells like a last year's bird's nest,* thought Miss Dove. It was strange. However frequently a twelve-year-old boy was washed, he always smelled like a bird's nest.) Watty smacked. His kiss resounded, a small explosion in the room.

"Thank you, Watson," said Miss Dove. "You may give Thomas my regards." She straightened up and faced the class. To her surprise, nobody was grinning.

Jincey Webb spoke. She did not raise her hand first for permission. She just spoke out. "It's like a medal," said Jincey softly. "It's like a medal on Miss Dove."

For a moment a lamp seemed to burn behind her face. Then over the light swept a shadow, a look of awe. It was as if Jincey had glimpsed some universal beauty—of sorrow, perhaps, or of nobility —too poignant for her youth to bear. She began to cry. She flopped her head down on her desk with her red hair falling forward and spreading out like a crinkly fan.

All the other girls were weeping too. All the boys were trying not to.

For the first time in her teaching career, Miss Dove was at a loss. She wanted to make a speech. She wanted to say something beautiful and grateful about what life really meant to her, about the overwhelming generosity of children. No, not generosity. It was something better than that, something much harder to come by. It was justice. And Miss Dove did not know how to say what she felt. She had never thought it dignified to express emotion.

But as she stood there waiting for the words to form in her mind, she realized that she was neglecting her duty. The first duty of a teacher was to preserve order.

She fished a piece of string from a receptacle on her desk. She walked down the aisle to Jincey Webb. She took Jincey's hair, that marvel of art and nature, and bunched it in her hand. She tied it securely at the nape of Jincey's neck with the little bit of grocery string.

"Now it will be out of your way," she said.

At the sound of her voice, cool, precise and natural, the children rallied. They sat erect. They blew their noses on clean handkerchiefs. They folded their hands on their desks.

"Get out your notebooks, class," she said.

A transient mist came over her eyes. Through it, as through a prism, the children glowed. Freckles, cowlicks, pinafores and polo shirts seemed bathed in a rainbow iridescence. Her love flowed out to her children—to those opening their notebooks before her, and to those in the far places she had once helped them locate on the map. It did not flow tenderly like a mother's coddling love. It flowed on a fierce rush of pride and hope, as an old general's heart might follow his men into battle.

She went to the blackboard and picked up a piece of chalk. "Above the fiftieth parallel—" wrote the terrible Miss Dove.

Author and Selection Notes

Frances Gray Patton (1906-   ) has written for *The New Yorker* many short stories, which in 1950 were published in a collection called *The Finer Things of Life*. In 1954 she published a novel entitled *Good Morning, Miss Dove*.

Questions and Exercises

1. Miss Dove is well known to us by the author's comments about her, by what she says and does, by the reactions of others to her. Write a one-page character sketch of this remarkable woman and state her philosophy of life.

2. Analyze her teaching methods: their merits, their faults, their results.

3. Cite several witty sentences which are examples of "understatement" and "overstatement."

4. How does the author build and maintain suspense?

5. State the theme of this story.

6. Find examples of Patton's fresh, apt comparisons.

7. Theme Topics: One Teacher I Will Never Forget; A Strict Discipli-

narian; Miss Dove Was (Was Not) Too Strict; Impartial Justice in School; Do We Have Enough Discipline in Our Schools?

THE NATURE OF COMMUNICATION
Robert C. Pooley

THE FUNCTION OF LANGUAGE

Languages evolved in the history of man's development as the means by which an individual can convey information, thoughts, and ideas to one or many of his associates, and also as the means by which he can in turn receive information, thoughts, and ideas from others. Thus the nature of language is strictly functional and its purpose is to promote communication. Whatever forms of language facilitate clear, concise, and accurate communication may be defined as good language; whatever forms of language fail to communicate clearly, or lead to ambiguity and obscurity may, for practical purposes, be defined as bad language. This is an important principle whose significance will be developed in this chapter.

Communication occurs when a meaningful signal passes from a sender, who originates it, to a receiver, who understands it. In ordinary communication the sender transmits his message by signs, by speech, or by writing. To accomplish his end, the sender must have, of necessity, something to communicate and a medium of transmission. The medium is, for all but the most elementary types of communication, spoken and written language. The sender becomes increasingly effective as he develops through experience new material to communicate and advances his skill in the use of the medium. The receiver, too, must be responsive to the means of communication; he develops as he increases his powers to recognize and interpret the signals which come to him through the medium of language.

In communication, therefore, there are two elements always present—the material to be communicated and the medium (usually language) by which it is transmitted. It is a peculiar fallacy of language teaching in American schools and colleges that in teaching the use of language enormous stress is laid on the language itself, which is only the medium, to the great neglect of the material to be communicated, which after all is the more essential part of the communication. In the typical English classroom countless hours are spent on the analysis and classification of language forms, with drill and practice in their use, *in isolation from the specific needs of communication*. The number of moments given to the analysis and clarification of meaning in communication are all too few.

This overemphasis on language for its own sake is nowhere more clearly seen than in the common attitudes toward usage and in the teaching of correctness. Indeed, the primary force behind nearly all efforts to correct and "purify" the English language has been the distrust of change, the desire to conserve and perpetuate what is considered the tradition. The relationship of meaning to form or the relative clarity of two alternate forms, rarely enters discussions of usage. Yet our language is not a static medium, nor can it be made static. Words change, grammatical forms change, there are styles in syntax which vary from decade to decade. The teaching of English and correct usage must never lose sight of the fluid nature of language. Decisions in usage must be reached in terms of the efficiency of communication rather than in terms of preserving what has been or "improving" the language by appeals to logic, reason, etymology, or any other factor not consistent with communication.

The common attitude toward English usage and correctness is that some forms of English are "right" and some forms are "wrong." Such decisions are made in the absolute and are applied indiscriminately to all linguistic situations. From this practice arises the absurdities which were referred to in Chapter I. Actually any English is "right" which enables the speaker or writer to communicate clearly, efficiently, and accurately what he wants to say. The usage decisions affecting his employment of language for any specific purpose must be arrived at in the light of the communication itself and its purposes, and not from any external, arbitrary standards. Thus the factors governing communication in each specific instance set the standards of correctness for that communication; usage conceived of in this light is relative rather than positive, fluid rather than static, psychological rather than logical. In teaching usage the emphasis will have to turn from the indoctrination of absolute rules to the development of sensitivity to and appreciation of the factors governing communication.

THE FACTORS INFLUENCING COMMUNICATION

In every situation calling for speech or writing there are three factors influencing the form of the communication, or in other words, determining the nature of the language usage. These factors are: (1) the meaning to be commumicated; (2) the intention or purpose of the communication; and (3) the tone or effect desired in the communication.

First in importance is the matter to be conveyed, which may be a warning, a fact, an observation, a decision, or a judgment. The communication may vary in complexity from a monosyllabic cry of warning or expression of momentary emotion, as in "ouch!" "ugh!" "quick!" to an elaborately constructed sequence of sentences as in a legal decision, a literary evaluation, or a philosophical argument. In every case, whether simple or involved, the motivating force for the commumication is the need to convey an idea to someone else. Therefore, the first factor determining the choice of words and their order in any linguistic situation is the desire to convey meaning from oneself to another in the most efficient way.

But the transfer of meaning is only one factor in communication. The second controlling factor influencing usage is the intent or purpose of the communication. In the following examples note how the same fact is expressed in word usage voicing widely differing intentions: (1) Pick up your gloves! (2) Pardon me, I believe you have dropped your gloves. (3) You've shed your mittens, old dear. (4) Can't you go anywhere without leaving those gloves behind? In each of these sentences the same meaning is expressed—someone has dropped or left behind a pair of gloves. But the intention of the different speakers is made clear by the words they have chosen to call attention to the same fact. The first speaker assumes an attitude of responsibility toward the owner of the gloves and reveals a relationship permitting the use of the imperative mood. This speaker might be a parent, a husband or wife, or a close associate. The second speaker, although he refers to the same circumstance as the first, reveals an intention of conventionalized courtesy. His word choice is typical of a stranger addressing another over a trifling circumstance. The same words spoken by an intimate of the glove-dropper would convey in most circumstances an intention of irony or sarcasm. The third speaker reveals an intention of affectionate reminder or mild remonstrance. The fourth speaker, however, reveals by his choice of words both a relationship of intimacy and unconcealed irritation or annoyance. The intent of his speech is not only to call attention to the gloves but also to give voice to remonstrance and exasperation.

Closely related to the second factor, the intent of the communication, is the third, the tone of the communication. Tone may be defined as the appropriateness of the word choice to the meaning and intention of the speaker. In the four sentences listed above, three of the speakers used the word *gloves* while the other substituted *mittens*. The tone of the third speaker was clearly playful and affectionate. Therefore, the word *mittens,* suggesting little gloves as an affectionate diminutive, was appropriate to the intention and set the desired tone.

There are clearly recognized gradations of tone in the expression of any idea. Take for example the commonplace circumstance of going to bed. At least five gradations of tone may be employed in expressing this idea, each one appropriate to a particular situation.

1. I think I'll hit the hay.
2. It's time for me to turn in.
3. I believe I'll go to bed.
4. I think it is time to retire.
5. I shall withdraw to seek repose.

What tone is conveyed by each of these usages to express the same meaning? Sentence 1. is intentionally slangy, appropriate only to intimate circumstances when humor is the intent. Sentence 2. is still intimate, but less slangy; it would pass as appropriate usage in the close family circle. Sentence 3. is the simplest and most direct of the five forms; it is acceptable usage in almost any circumstance. Sentence 4. implies less intimate circumstances; the word *retire* is a polite substitute for the blunt "go to bed." This form would be appropriate to a guest in the home of relative strangers. Sentence 5. is stilted and artificial. The simple act of going to bed makes such elaborate wording slightly ridiculous. Yet there are people with a mistaken idea of elegance who would approve sentence 5.

Almost innumerable examples of such gradations of tone can be found. As another example, consider the idea expressed by the verb *to go.*

1. You'd better scram!
2. Get out fast!
3. You ought to go.
4. It is necessary to depart.
5. Get thee hence!

IMPLICATIONS FOR TEACHING USAGE

It is hoped that three significant principles regarding English usage have emerged from this chapter. These principles are: (1) the correct usage of contemporary English cannot be determined by appeals to logic, etymology, or the traditions of former days. It cannot be determined by rules of "right" and "wrong." It must be determined by the needs of communication in every situation in which language is used.

(2) Since correctness is a relative matter, derived from the needs of communication, the teaching of correct English requires the development of sensitivity to the factors influencing communication: meaning, intention, and tone. Attention to these factors develops the art of appropriateness in language, which is the foundation of correct usage.

(3) The teaching of correctness in school and college courses must shift in emphasis from the laying down of negative rules to the development of positive insights. The correction of errors is less than half the teaching of good usage. Far more important is the awakening in pupils' minds of a recognition of the nature of communication, a recognition of how communication determines usage, and the development of a sensitivity to the gradations of intent and tone in every communication created by the selection of appropriate words, idioms, and constructions.

Author and Selection Notes

Robert C. Pooley (1898-   ), English professor and author of *Teaching English Usage* and *Teaching English Grammar,* has long been associated with the University of Wisconsin. He has served as editor of *America Reads* and as president of the National Council of Teachers of English. "The Nature of Communication" is a chapter from his *Teaching English Usage,* endorsed by the NCTE as a basic tool for English teachers everywhere.

Questions and Exercises

1. What does the author mean by "the fluid nature of language"?

2. Using the words "Let us end the discussion," give variations of meaning as Pooley does with "Pick up your gloves."

3. In your own words explain the basis of correct English usage set forth by Pooley.

4. Write a conversation for one of the following: a father and his hot-rod son; a dignified adult and any slangy adolescent; an English teacher at a hamburger stand; a parent and a Little League star; a landlubber on board ship; a raw recruit at boot camp.

5. Defend or refute the following statement by Pooley: "Decisions in usage must be reached in terms of the efficiency of communication rather than in terms of preserving what has been or 'improving' the language by appeals to logic, reason, etymology, or any other factor not consistent with communication."

6. Write a theme comparing and contrasting Pooley's theory of language with the theory set forth in the following article, "The Dictionary as a Battlefront," by Mario Pei. With which author do you agree and why?

THE DICTIONARY AS A BATTLEFRONT
Mario Pei

For some years, there have been more and more insistent rumblings from all sorts of quarters concerning the quality of the English imparted in our schools and colleges. Graduates of our educational institutions, the critics have charged, do not know how to spell, punctuate, or capitalize; to divide a thought concept into phrases, sentences, and paragraphs; or to express themselves, either in speech or writing, in the sort of English that is meaningful and acceptable. As a single sample of the many complaints that have been voiced, I may cite a friend who is a high official in WNBC-TV: "Recently we interviewed over a hundred college graduates to fill a post calling for a knowledge of good English. Not one of them made the grade. None of them knew the rules of good writing, and none of them could express himself or herself in clear, simple, forthright English sentences."

The blame for this state of affairs has consistently been put upon two branches of the educational world: the teachers of English and the progressive educationists. Books such as "Why Johnny Can't Read" are indictments of modern educational practice. A cultured lay writer, J. Donald Adams of the New York *Times Book Review,* said in his column of December 20, 1959:

If more parents who were themselves the recipients of a decent education could be made aware of the asinine statements about the teaching of the English language which are being spewed forth by today's educational theorists, there would be an armed uprising among the Parent-Teacher Associations all over the United States. It would be an uprising armed by common sense and hot indignation, and it would demand and get the scalps of those so-called educators whose indefensible doctrines are rapidly producing a generation of American illiterates. . . . The root responsibility for the decline in standards of English rests, I think, with the teachers of English in our primary and secondary schools, and even more so, with the teachers of education who produced them. . . . There is an organization called the National Council of Teachers of English, whose attitudes and activities constitute one of the chief threats to the cultivation of good English in our schools.

Reprinted from the *Saturday Review Education Supplement,* July 21, 1962. Reprinted by permission.

What critics of present-day methods of teaching English have in the past failed to realize is that the responsibility for the situation lies deeper than the departments of English and the teachers colleges. The practices of both are merely a reflection of the philosophy and theories of a school of linguistics that is in turn linked with a school of cultural anthropology of the equalitarian persuasion whose views color far more than the teaching of languages in general or English in particular.

As far back as 1948, in a New York *Herald Tribune* book review, Bernard De Voto came out with a blast at the cultural anthropologists for assuming that methods that seem to work with the Ubangi and the Trobriand Islanders will produce dependable results when applied to the English or Americans. But his was a voice crying in the wilderness. Few people were sufficiently specialized, or interested, to perceive the link between theories presented in scholarly books on anthropology or linguistics and practices that affect the daily lives of all of us.

It was only with the appearance of the new third edition of "Webster's Unabridged International Dictionary" late in 1961 that the issues at stake, at least for what concerns language, became clear to the cultured, educated layman of America. For this there was a deep, underlying reason that reaches down to the grass roots of our mores.

The English language, as is well known, has no set standard and no accepted authority, in the sense that countries such as France, Italy, and Spain have language academies that undertake to tell the speakers what is and what is not good standard practice. Since the days of Dr. Johnson, who refused to embalm the language and thereby destroy liberty, English speakers have submitted to the Doctrine of Usage rather than to the Voice of Authority. But usage has its own canons. In Britain, something called the King's (or Queen's) English has been enshrined over and above local dialects that range from London's Cockney to super-cultivated Oxford, and from the harsh speech of the North Country to the mellifluous accents of Kent. In America there is no President's American, but there is the Dictionary. From the time of Noah Webster, Americans have been wont to dip into a dictionary, the more unabridged the better, to settle questions of usage and proper practice.

It may be stressed at this point that at no time did the compilers of the various editions of the Merriam Webster, the most comprehensive dictionary of America, set themselves up as authorities or arrogate the right to tell the people what was right and what was wrong in the matter of language. All they did was to record prevailing usage among the more educated classes. They listed and described plenty of variant regional pronunciations and words. They recorded, too, speech-forms of the lower classes, carefully labeling them "colloquial," "substandard," "vulgar," or "slang." This was not meant to prescribe or proscribe the use of certain forms, but merely to inform the reader as to the distribution of their occurrence. The attitude of the earlier lexicographers seemed to be: "Go ahead and use this form if you want to; but if you do, don't complain if someone says you are using a slang term."

The new 1961 edition of the Merriam-Webster has many features to commend it. Not only does it list the multitude of new terms, technological and otherwise, that have entered the language in recent years; it also has the merit of listing, with full definitions and examples, word combinations that have acquired special connotations not inherent in their component parts. The older Webster's defines both "guilt" and "association"; but the new Webster's also gives you "guilt by association." This means that the new edition is a handier tool than the older.

But the new edition makes one startling innovation which has recommended itself to the attention of all reviewers and of the general public as well. It blurs to the point of obliteration the older distinction between standard, substandard, colloquial, vulgar, and slang. "Ain't," it says, is now used by many cultivated speakers; "who" in the accusative function and "me" after a copulative verb are of far more frequent occurrence than "whom" and "I," and, by implication, should be preferred. This viewpoint goes right down the line. It led the editor of the New York *Times* to compose a passage that starts:

A passel of double-dones at the G. & C. Merriam Company joint in Springfield, Mass., have been confabbing and yakking for twenty-seven years—which is not intended to infer that they have not been doing plenty work—and now they have finalized Webster's Third New International Dictionary, Unabridged, a new edition of that swell and esteemed word book.

Those who regard the foregoing paragraph as acceptable English prose will find that the new Webster's is just the dictionary for them.

There is more: the older Webster's, insofar as it gave citations, used only established authors, recognized masters of the language. The new Webster's cites profusely from people who are in the public eye, but who can hardly be said to qualify as shining examples of fine speaking or writing. This leads another critic to complain that Churchill, Maritain, Oppenheimer, and Schweitzer are ranged as language sources side by side with Billy Rose, Ethel Merman, James Cagney, and Ted Williams; Shakespeare and Milton with Polly Adler and Mickey Mantle.

Dr. Gove's defense, fully presented in the pages of the same New York *Times* that had thundered editorially against his product, is both able and forthright: a dictionary's function, he said in substance, is to record the language, not to judge or prescribe it. Language, like practically everything else, is in a state of constant flux. It is not responsible to expect it to remain static, to retain unchanged forms that were current at one period but are no longer current today. We have changed our point of view in many fields; why not language? His defense is, in a sense, a counterattack against the forces of purism, conservatism, and reaction. Why disguise the true function of a dictionary by turning it into a tool of prescriptivism, a fortress of a language traditionalism that no one today really wants? Language, after all, is what people speak, not what someone, be it even Webster, thinks they ought to speak.

This both clarifies and restricts the issue. But an issue still remains. Should a dictionary be merely a record of what goes on in language (all language, both high and low), or should it also be not so much a prescriptive tool as a guide for the layman, to not merely what *is* usage, but what is the *best* usage?

A speaking community that has been accustomed for the better part of two centuries to rely upon the dictionary to settle questions of usage balks at finding all usage now set on an identical plane. The contention of the objectors is that there are different, clearly identifiable levels of usage, which it is the duty of the dictionary to define. Without necessarily using the terms "correct" and "incorrect," they still would like to see a distinction made between what is better and what is worse.

In opposition to their stand, the new philosophy, linguistic and otherwise, seems to be summed up in this formula: "What is is good, simply because it is." Good and bad, right and wrong, correct and incorrect no longer exist. Any reference to any of these descriptive adjectives is a value judgment, and unworthy of the scientific attitude, which prescribes that we merely observe and catalogue the facts, carefully refraining from expressing either judgment or preference.

This relativistic philosophy, fully divorced from both ethics and esthetics, is said to be modern, sophisticated, and scientific. Perhaps it is. Some claim that its fruits are to be seen in present-day moral standards, national, international, and personal, as well as in modern so-called art, music, literature, and permissive education.

But we are concerned here only with its reflections on the language. The appearance of the new Webster's International has had several major effects. It has brought the question of permissiveness in language squarely to the attention of millions of educated laymen, who use the dictionary and refer to it for guidance. Without forcing a renunciation of Anglo-American reliance on usage rather than on the Voice of Authority, it has brought into focus the paramount question: "Whose usage? That of the cultivated speakers, or that of the semi-literates?" Finally, it has for the first time brought forth, into the view of the general public, those who are primarily responsible for the shift in attitude and point of view in matters of language—not the ordinary classroom teachers of English, not the educationists of the teachers colleges, but the followers of the American, anthropological, descriptive, structuralistic school of linguistics, a school which for decades has been preaching that one form of language is as good as another; that there is no such thing as correct or incorrect so far as native speakers of the language are concerned; that at the age of five anyone who is not deaf or idiotic has gained a full mastery of his language; that we must not try to correct or improve language, but must leave it alone; that the only language activity worthy of the name is speech on the colloquial, slangy, even illiterate plane; that writing is a secondary, unimportant activity which cannot be dignified with the name of language; that systems of writing serve only to disguise the true nature of language; and that it would be well if we completely refrained from teaching spelling for a number of years.

If these pronouncements come as a novelty to some of my readers, it is the readers themselves who are at fault. The proponents of these language theories certainly have made no mystery about them; they have been openly, even vociferously advancing them for years, and this can easily be documented from their voluminous writings.

The real novelty of the situation lies in the fact that, through the publication of the new Webster's—compiled in accordance with these principles—the principles themselves and their original formulators, rather than their effects upon the younger generations, now come to the attention of the general public. Lay reviewers generally display their complete awareness.

Dwight MacDonald, reviewing the new Webster extensively in the March 10, 1962 *New Yorker,* after claiming that the "scientific" revolution in linguistics has meshed gears with a trend toward permissiveness, in the name of democracy, that is debasing our language by rendering it less precise and thus less effective as communication, goes on to say:

Dr. Gove and the other makers of 3 are sympathetic to the school of language study that has become dominant since 1934. It is sometimes called Structural Linguistics and sometimes, rather magnificently, just Modern Linguistic Science. . . . Dr. Gove and his editors are part of the dominant movement in the professional study of language—one that has in the last few years established strong beachheads in the National Council of Teachers of English and the College English Association. . . . As a scientific discipline, Structural Linguistics can have no truck with values or standards. Its job is to deal only with The Facts.

Max S. Marshall, Professor of Microbiology at the University of California, writing in *Science*, March 2, 1962, says in part:

Opposed to [believers in a standard of quality in English] with several ringleaders at the head, is a group which goes back some thirty years, but has been actively proselytizing only in relatively recent years. These are the advocates of 'observing precisely what happens when native speakers speak.' These are the self-styled structural linguists, presenting language in a way so foreign that it might be imposed before users of the language discover its existence. . . . Gove declares himself flatly on the side of the structural linguists, calmly assuming, as do their ringleaders, that they are about to take over.

The principles of the American school of linguistics described above may come as a shock to some, but there is no need to be shocked. They are based upon definitely observable historical facts. Language invariably changes. Within our own personal experience we have noticed certain forms and expressions once considered slangy turning into regularly accepted parts of the standard language.

All that the American school of linguistics advocates is that we accept the process of change in language and submit gracefully to its inevitability. If we persist in hanging on to language forms and concepts that are antiquated and superceded [sic], then we are merely subscribing to what they call "the superstitions of the past." We should be forward-looking, and progressive-minded. We renounce imperialism and colonialism in international relations, and admit nations like Ghana and the Congo to full equality with the established countries of Europe; by the same token, we should view the languages of the Arapahoes and the Zulus as being of equal importance with Latin and French. We believe in democracy and majority rule in political elections. Then, if a majority of the speakers of American English use "ain't," "knowed," "I'll learn you," "I laid on the bed," "who did you see," "between you and I," "like a cigarette should," these forms are by definition standard usage, and the corresponding minority forms, though sanctioned by traditional grammars, are, if not incorrect, at least obsolescent.

It may be argued, as does our Professor of Microbiology in *Science,* that "weighing the speech of casual speakers with no pretense of expertness on the same IBM card as usages of topnotch writers of past and present is an example of what the modern linguist calls 'science.' Tabulation is not science. Public opinion polls do not settle questions of science, or even of right and wrong. . . . If the guttersnipes of language do more talking than professors of English they get proportionally more votes."

But the structuralistic linguists can easily reply that language is a matter of habit and convention, not of dogma or esthetics, and that if the basic purpose of semantic communication is achieved, it matters little what linguistic form is used. In engineering, calculations as to stresses and structures must be precise and correct, under penalty of seeing the bridge collapse. In medicine, correct dosage is essential, under penalty of seeing your patient die. But in language, the use of a substandard for a standard form seldom leads to irreparable consequences; at the most, as picturesquely stated by a leader of the school, you may not be invited to tea again.

On the other hand, members of the American school of linguistics are not always consistent in the application of their democratic and equalitarian principles. In reply to his critics, Dr. Gove remarked that while comments in lay newspapers and magazines had generally been unfavorable, the learned journals had not yet reviewed the new edition. The implication seemed to be that favorable reviews from a few members of his own clique, read and approved by a small circle of professional structuralistic linguists, would more than offset the generally unfavorable reaction of newspapers like the New York *Times* and magazines like the *New Yorker,* which appeal to large audiences of cultivated laymen. This not only puts the process of democracy into reverse; it comes close to setting up a hierarchy of professional linguists acting as the Voice of Authority for a recalcitrant majority of educated people.

There is no doubt in my mind that widespread localisms, slang, vulgarisms, colloquialisms, even obscenities and improprieties, should be duly noted in a comprehensive dictionary, whose first duty is to record what goes on in the field of language. Should such forms be labeled and described for what they are, not in a spirit of condemnation, but merely for the guidance of the reader? That, too, seems reasonable. If this procedure helps to slow up the inevitable process of language change by encouraging the speakers to use what the older dictionaries call standard forms, and discouraging them from using substandard, this impresses me as a distinct advantage. Too rapid and too widespread language change is a hindrance to communications. It lends itself to confusion and misunderstanding. The use of a more or less uniform standard by all members of the speaking community is desirable in the interests of efficiency rather than of esthetics. There is no question that within the next 500 years the English language, along with all other languages spoken today, will be so changed as to be practically unrecognizable. This will happen, whether we like it or not. But need we deliberately hasten and amplify the process? Between sudden revolution and stolid reaction there is a middle ground of sound conservatism and orderly change.

Also, without being puristic to the point of ejecting "ain't" and kindred forms from a dictionary of recorded usage, it might be worth while to recognize the existence of a standard language, neither literary nor slangy, which has acceptance and is understood practically everywhere in the country, even if everybody does not use it. Such phrases as "Them dogs is us'uns" and "I'll call you up without I can't," which an American structural linguist claims are good, meaningful language to him, merely because they are uttered by some native American speakers, definitely do not form part of that standard language. By all means let us record them for our own information and amusement, but let us not try to palm them off on the public on the general ground that the native speaker can do no wrong, and that "correct" and "incorrect" are terms that can be legitimately applied only to the speech of foreigners attempting to use English.

Language is something more than a heritage of sentimental value. It is an indispensable tool of communication and exchange of ideas. The more standardized and universal it is, the more effective it is. The more it is allowed to degenerate into local and class forms, the less effective it becomes. It may be perfectly true that in the past language has been allowed to run its own sweet, unbridled course, with the chips falling where they might. We are now in an age where we no longer believe in letting diseases and epidemics run their natural course, but take active, artificial means to control them. In fact, we endeavor to control natural, physical, and sociological phenomena of all descriptions, from floods to business cycles, from weather to diet, from the monetary system to racial relations. Is it unreasonable for us, far from leaving our language alone, as advocated by the American school of linguistics, to wish to channel it in the directions where it will prove of maximum efficiency for its avowed function, which is that of semantic transfer?

For the concern of that other burning question, standards of writing, as apart from standards of speech, ought we not to recognize that until such a time as tapes, recordings, dictaphones and spoken films altogether replace our system of written communications, the latter should be viewed and treated with respect? Again, we need not let ourselves be led too far afield by purely literary or esthetic considerations. The written language, in a modern civilization, is practically on a par with speech as a communications tool. It is incongruous to see our American structuralistic linguists devote so much painstaking attention to phonetic phenomena like pitch, stress, intonation, and juncture, to the fine distinctions between "a light housekeeper" and "a lighthouse keeper," "an iceman" and "a nice man," and yet shrug their shoulders at correct spelling, punctuation, and capitalization. More misunderstandings have occurred over misplaced commas than over misplaced junctures, and a wrong spelling can be just as fatal as a wrong intonation.

Perhaps the time has come, in language as in other fields, for the return of reason, and its ascendancy over dogma, whether the latter be of the puristic or of the structuralistic variety.

Above all, there is need for sound, scientific consideration of *all* the facts of language, not merely that portion which happens to suit the tastes and inclinations of a small group. Language is more than a set of phonemes, morphemes, junctures, and stresses. It also happens to be our most important instrument of semantic transfer, and the common possession of all of us. If democracy means anything, we, the speakers, have the right to have our say as to how it shall be viewed and used, and not to be forced to subscribe to the prescriptive excesses of what the European professor of linguistics describes as "the God's Truth School."

Author and Selection Notes

Born in Rome, Italy, Dr. Mario Pei (1901-   ) came to the United States as a child. He is now a noted philologist who has a fluent command of English, Italian, French, and Spanish; a working knowledge of German, Portuguese, Russian, Dutch, and Rumanian—also of Arabic, Slavic, Gothic, Umbrian, and Sanscrit. The author also of several books on language, he is well qualified to examine the new Webster's "3."

Questions and Exercises

1. Explain how Mario Pei and Robert Pooley, author of "The Nature of Communication," differ on the subject of correct English usage. With

which man have most of your English teachers agreed? With which do you agree?

2. On what occasions would you consider it good taste to use formal English, informal or colloquial speech, slang? What degree of formality should you use in writing class themes?

3. Explain the difference between the older editions of Webster's Unabridged Dictionary and the new "3." On the basis of "The Nature of Communication," what would Pooley's judgment of the new edition be?

4. Compare three college-level dictionaries to find what information is given concerning the usage levels of words.

5. What information about usage do you think a dictionary should give?

6. Do you agree that the fruits of relativistic philosophy "are to be seen in present-day moral standards, national, international, and personal, as well as in modern so-called art, music, literature, and permissive education"? If you agree, state what you think the results are and will be in relation to the individual and the country as a whole.

7. Defend or refute the following statement: "Too rapid and too widespread language change is a hindrance to communications."

8. Theme Topics: The Dictionary Habit; Good English Opens Doors; Good Writing Means Clear Thinking; Words Are Tools.

PLEASURES OF READING
Clifton Fadiman

We Americans are on the threshold of a society in which everyone will belong to what used to be called "the leisure class." Whether we step across the threshold into Utopia or into a pit of "play," passive entertainment and relentlessly organized sport, is up to us. Great forces are urging us toward Utopia, luring us on to the most worth-while uses of leisure. One of the greatest is the revolution in the printing and distribution of good books at a price well within the range of the great majority of American adult citizens. There has been nothing like it in the history of the world. The publishers have no more idea of what they have started than did Gutenberg.

Potentially the effects for good of the cheap reprint can overshadow all that the television and radio industries as at present constituted can possibly effect as rival media. The reason is simple.

Reprinted from *Holiday,* March, 1956, Volume 19, by special permission from *Holiday,* copyright 1956 by The Curtis Publishing Company, and by permission of the author.

Good books have an editor. TV and radio have none. The editor is the judgment of three thousand years of civilization which tells us what ideas are worth preserving. This judgment TV and radio, by their very structure, geared to the temporary and the contemporary, cannot for the most part make any use of.

Two staggering facts are involved in this revolution. The first is that for less than a thousand dollars an American citizen can at once place on his shelves, for the first time in recorded or unrecorded history, what Matthew Arnold called "the best that has been known and said in the world." The second fact is that we Americans have been conditioned to buy and use in quantity any product that is both cheap and demonstrably good. That we also buy things that are demonstrably silly does not affect the truth of this statement. We are not yet wise. But we are already curious—and curiosity is the beginning of wisdom.

The whole wonderful point was put better than I could ever express it by an American who wrote in a letter to the publisher of a thirty-five-cent edition of *The Odyssey:* "Just read *The Odyssey!* Boy, that guy Homer sure can write! Do you have any more books by him?"

This reader has grasped the nature of the most satisfying leisure. He is engaged in a self-rewarding activity which has nothing to do with academic compulsions, degrees, social prestige. Briefly, he has discovered that he has a mind which will start working enjoyably as soon as it is put in touch with a better one. That's all there is to it. From now on the direction is irreversible and the movement capable of continuous acceleration.

I am no longer as impressed as I once was by lugubrious statistics showing that we are not a book-reading people. A recent survey shows that 59 per cent of the people of England read books, as against 17 per cent in the United States. What of it? That means merely that we have not yet started to read, that we have still ahead of us the pleasure of forming a new good habit. There is a weakness of infancy, as well as of senility.

In 1939 Pocket Books experimented successfully with twenty-five-cent reprints. Today, only seventeen years later, you can get reprints at well over 100,000 outlets, of which only about 1500 unfortunately are bookstores. Homer has sold in the millions, which means that after three thousand years he's back just where he started, when everybody within reach of his voice listened to him. A recognized superior modern novel, James T. Farrell's *Young Lonigan,* sold six hundred copies in the regular edition during its first year of publication in 1932. At twenty-five cents it has sold well over a *million* copies. Last year about one thousand titles, both of new and re-printed books, were released in cheap, paperbound editions, total-ing about 300,000,000 copies. In the past sixteen years we have con-sumed approximately two *billion* copies of about twelve thousand titles.

What is more important, the books themselves are constantly improving in quality. Gresham's Law isn't working. The type of book that depends almost entirely on the pictorial depiction of the mammary gland is being displaced by literature that ranges from the harmlessly entertaining to the absolutely magnificent. The same publisher whose list a few years ago showed a high percentage of tripe will probably make a killing out of his new fifty-cent edition of Dostoevski's *Crime and Punishment,* illustrated by a leading woodcut artist and featuring statements by famous writers. This reprint of a great classic was published in the same week that also saw (I am merely selecting at random) the appearance in paperback reprints of such absolutely first-rate stuff as a selection from the works of Diderot, Tobias Dantzig's fascinating *Number: The Lan-guage of Science,* and Jacob Burckhardt's *Age of Constantine the Great;* of such fine reference books as Richard Morris' edition of *Basic Documents in American History;* of such provocative con-temporary studies as Samuel Lubell's *Future of American Politics* and Peter Viereck's *Conservatism: From John Adams to Churchill.*

Are you game to shell out four bits for Thomas Mann's *Budden-brooks* or Melville's *Moby Dick* or John Hersey's *The Wall* or D. H. Lawrence's *Women in Love?* Care for a magnificent new translation of Rabelais at ninety cents? Robert Graves' marvelous retelling of the Greek myths in two volumes at $1.95? Interested in starting or adding to your library at painless prices by purchasing interesting books by J. D. Salinger, Faulkner, Joyce, Hemingway, Henry James, Brooks Adams, Balzac, Lewis Mumford?

Let me put it another way. There used to be a phrase, the "gentle-man's library." It had two meanings. It meant that the library con-sisted of the best books that a cultivated mind would want to have around the house. It also meant that only a gentleman of some fortune could afford them. During the last seventeen years and particularly during the last five years the phrase has been rendered meaningless. Few 19th Century English or American gentlemen could have afforded the books now readily available to us; and in any case not one of them would have had the choice of titles now on hand in bookstore, drugstore, cigar store, subway newsstand and even through a recently organized Paper Editions Book Club.

I'll put it still another way. Any five-thousand-dollar-a-year family that is willing to refrain from a few dubious expenditures a year can in a short time (I should say three years) build up and house in even a very small home most of the finest books, including the best ones of the last twenty years, that have been written by the best writers here and abroad.

It's worth doing this even if the heads of the family are them-selves non-readers. We're a queer people. Just *because* our cultural traditions are shallowly rooted (which means also that they are not deeply rutted), non-reading parents are quite apt to produce an odd child or two who will go for books in a big way. But—only if they're available, lying all over the house like ash trays. The habit may skip a generation or even two. It doesn't matter. Most of these books will last; covers may tatter, but not words. There's no harm in leav-ing a magnificent library costing very little to your great-grandson whom you may never see. Such accidents often determine part of the future of a country: think of the boy Lincoln reading by his log fire.

Do you think I am crazily optimistic? I would have thought so myself five years ago. But weird things are happening. Recent re-searches reveal that reading of *all* sorts (of magazines like this one, for example) is increasing; that TV and radio and movies are being absorbed without danger to the habit of reading. Miss Evelyn Peer-less of the Elmhurst branch of the Queens (New York City) Public Library marks out a whole trend in her conclusion: "Once the novelty [of TV] wears off there is a return to books— better books than had been read previously." Maybe the mass-communications boys, who are smart, are just *too* smart. By trying to appeal to every-body they may be losing lots of somebodies. The book publisher, by the nature of his business, cannot, even if he wanted to, make this mistake. Sooner or later every one of his varied products will find its public—if the product is cheap, which it is, and sound, which it increasingly is.

In ten years there will be on the average two and a half more hours of leisure time per day than at present. The thirty-hour week is around the corner; the twenty-hour week may be around the next corner. It doesn't take a psychologist to predict that if we try to fill this time by putting a small white ball into a slightly larger hole or by gawking at television crooners, we will as a people go quietly or noisily nuts. It is my hunch that we will turn to reading partly because, for the first time, like Mallory's mountain, it's *there;* and partly because mental novocain will sooner or later become a bore. "Constructive leisure," to use the excellent phrase of *Holiday's* editor, will prove attractive, not because we're filled with any desire to become highbrows but simply because we're bound to find out that a healthy mind, like a healthy body, is far more interesting than a sick one and infinitely more interesting than a dead one.

Finally, the more thoughtful among us—and there are plenty—will also discover that such a mind, nourished on the best that has been known and said in the world, forms part of the bulwark of our beloved country, without which we are as nothing. Ponder these words: "The condition of success, your sole safeguard, is the moral worth and intellectual clearness of the individual citizen." Paste that sentence in your hat, right next to your forehead. It was addressed to the American public by Thomas Henry Huxley. That was in 1876.

I would not want anything I have said to be construed as discouraging the buying of new books or hard-cover books. No old book can substitute exactly for a good new book. It is part of our nature to want to know what our contemporaries are saying. The point is that now, for the first time, nothing prevents us from reading both kinds, and I hope we will do so. But the habit of "keeping up" stands in less need of stimulus than the habit of building a library of good books of the remote and immediate past.

How do we tie a lifeline between our selves and our shelves? The first thing to do is not to buy individual titles at all but, like any good businessman, to research the field. Buy or borrow a few good books *about* books, including books listing books. Use a sharp pencil to tick off titles that seem interesting. Let the general information you absorb stew and simmer in your mind for a few weeks. There's no hurry: building a library is a lifetime occupation.

Author and Selection Notes

Clifton Fadiman (1904-   ) is well known as writer, editor, literary critic, and entertainer. For ten years he was master of ceremonies for the popular radio program "Information Please." He is a member of the selection committee of the Book-of-the-Month Club, book editor for *The New Yorker,* and regular essayist for *Holiday,* in which the preceding essay first appeared.

Questions and Exercises

1. How important is the paperback innovation in comparison to Gutenberg's invention of printing from movable type in the fifteenth century?

2. State Fadiman's case for and against the paperback in twentieth-century America.

3. State his case for and against statistics.

4. Point out the means of transition between paragraphs from paragraph seven through paragraph twelve.

5. In "the battle of the books" between old and modern offerings, which side do you choose? Why?

6. Theme Topics: How to Build a New Library; Book Influence on Children; A Plan for Unrequired Reading; My Childhood Reading; My Observation of Home Libraries.

2

BY DREAMS POSSESSED: MAN AND THE IDEAL

He whom a dream hath possessed.
·Shaemas O'Sheel

A modern fable tells of the farmer who lived all his life in the midst of acres of diamonds, never realizing the precious jewels were anything but worthless gravel. Just so, all about us lie the raw materials of great ideas or great deeds. But most of us, like the farmer, are content to spend our time as comfortably and effortlessly as our daily jobs or our bank accounts will permit; and civilization rests, curiously enough, on relatively few great ideas and relatively few great deeds. For more than two thousand years mankind has been influenced by the teachings of Plato; and modern history is dated from the birth of Christ.

Man always has admired the explorer, whether a traveler lured beyond the horizons into the far, mysterious corners of the earth or the quester enlarging the boundaries of intellectual frontiers. And even as men in the past thrilled to Marco Polo's accounts of the fabulous kingdoms of Cathay and to those of Columbus and Cabot about the brave new worlds lying beyond the numberless leagues of the Atlantic, so we today read avidly of the conquest of Mt. Everest or Antarctica, of man's dream of pioneering into the limitless realms of space. Our even greater interest, however, may lie in those trails blazed by the intrepid dreamer into man's intellectual realms. It is with such travels that this section deals.

THE ALLEGORY OF THE CAVE
Plato

Next, said I, here is a parable to illustrate the degrees in which our nature may be enlightened or unenlightened. Imagine the condition of men living in a sort of cavernous chamber underground, with an entrance open to the light and a long passage all down the cave. Here they have been from childhood, chained by the leg and also by the neck, so that they cannot move and can see only what is in front of them, because the chains will not let them turn their heads. At some distance higher up is the light of a fire burning behind them; and between the prisoners and the fire is a track with a parapet built along it, like the screen at a puppet-show, which hides the performers while they show their puppets over the top.

I see, said he.

Now behind this parapet imagine persons carrying along various artificial objects, including figures of men and animals in wood or stone or other materials, which project above the parapet. Naturally, some of these persons will be talking, others silent.

It is a strange picture, he said, and a strange sort of prisoners.

Like ourselves, I replied; for in the first place prisoners so confined would have seen nothing of themselves or of one another, except the shadows thrown by the fire-light on the wall of the cave facing them, would they?

Not if all their lives they had been prevented from moving their heads.

And they would have seen as little of the objects carried past.

Of course.

Now, if they could talk to one another, would they not suppose that their words referred only to those passing shadows which they saw?

Necessarily.

And suppose their prison had an echo from the wall facing them? When one of the people crossing behind them spoke, they could only suppose that the sound came from the shadow passing before their eyes.

No doubt.

In every way, then, such prisoners would recognize as reality nothing but the shadows of those artificial objects.

Inevitably.

Now consider what would happen if their release from the chains and the healing of their unwisdom should come about in this way. Suppose one of them were set free and forced suddenly to stand up, turn his head, and walk with eyes lifted to the light; all these movements would be painful, and he would be too dazzled to make out the objects whose shadows he had been used to seeing. What do you think he would say, if someone told him that what he had formerly seen was meaningless illusion, but now, being somewhat nearer to reality and turned towards more real objects, he was getting a truer view? Suppose further that he were shown the various objects being carried by and were made to say, in reply to questions, what each of them was. Would he not be perplexed and believe the objects now shown him to be not so real as what he formerly saw?

Yes, not nearly so real.

And if he were forced to look at the fire-light itself, would not his eyes ache, so that he would try to escape and turn back to the things which he could see distinctly, convinced that they really were clearer than these other objects now being shown to him?

Yes.

And suppose someone were to drag him away forcibly up the steep and rugged ascent and not let him go until he had hauled him out into the sunlight, would he not suffer pain and vexation at such treatment, and, when he had come out into the light, find his eyes so full of its radiance that he could not see a single one of the things that he was now told were real?

Certainly he would not see them all at once.

He would need, then, to grow accustomed before he could see things in that upper world. At first it would be easiest to make out shadows, and then the images of men and things reflected in water, and later on the things themselves. After that, it would be easier to watch the heavenly bodies and the sky itself by night, looking at the light of the moon and stars rather than the Sun and the Sun's light in the day-time.

Yes, surely.

Last of all, he would be able to look at the Sun and contemplate its nature, not as it appears when reflected in water or any alien medium, but as it is in itself in its own domain.

No doubt.

And now he would begin to draw the conclusion that it is the

Sun that produces the seasons and the course of the year and controls everything in the visible world, and moreover is in a way the
cause of all that he and his companions used to see.

Clearly he would come at last to that conclusion.

Then if he called to mind his fellow prisoners and what passed
for wisdom in his former dwelling-place, he would surely think
himself happy in the change and be sorry for them. They may have
had a practice of honoring and commending one another, with prizes
for the man who had the keenest eye for the passing shadows and the
best memory for the order in which they followed or accompanied
one another, so that he could make a good guess as to which was
going to come next. Would our released prisoner be likely to covet
those prizes or to envy the men exalted to honour and power in
the Cave? Would he not feel like Homer's Achilles, that he would
far sooner "be on earth as a hired servant in the house of a landless
man" or endure anything rather than go back to his old beliefs
and live in the old way?

Yes, he would prefer any fate to such a life.

Now imagine what would happen if he went down again to take
his former seat in the Cave. Coming suddenly out of the sunlight,
his eyes would be filled with darkness. He might be required once
more to deliver his opinion on those shadows, in competition with
the prisoners who had never been released, while his eyesight was
still dim and unsteady; and it might take some time to become used
to the darkness. They would laugh at him and say that he had gone
up only to come back with his sight ruined; it was worth no one's
while even to attempt the ascent. If they could lay hands on the
man who was trying to set them free and lead them up, they would
kill him.

Yes, they would.

Every feature in this parable, my dear Glaucon, is meant to fit
our earlier analysis. The prison dwelling corresponds to the region
revealed to us through the sense of sight, and the firelight within it to
the power of the Sun. The ascent to see the things in the upper world
you may take as standing for the upward journey of the soul into the
region of the intelligible; then you will be in possession of what
I surmise, since that is what you wish to be told. Heaven knows
whether it is true; but this, at any rate, is how it appears to me. In
the world of knowledge, the last thing to be perceived and only
with great difficulty is the essential Form of Goodness. Once it is perceived, the conclusion must follow that, for all things, this is the
cause of whatever is right and good; in the visible world it gives
birth to light and to the lord of light, while it is itself sovereign in

the intelligible world and the parent of intelligence and truth. Without having had a vision of this Form no one can act with wisdom, either in his own life or in matters of state.

Author and Selection Notes

The student of Socrates and the teacher of Aristotle, Plato (c. 427-347 B.C.) was one of the Greek philosophers who formed the basis of much of our thinking. While he was a professor of philosophy at the court at Syracuse, this man, sometimes called "the world's richest personality," wrote his *Dialogues,* which have a range so great that all of modern philosophy and science bears their influence. Seeking to explain the true meaning of the universe, Plato wove "the loveliest of allegories," as they are named, the most famous of which is "The Allegory of the Cave."

Questions and Exercises

1. Refer to a good encyclopedia for information concerning the popularity of allegory during the Middle Ages. Why do you think allegory was more popular then than it is now?

2. Define the Socratic method of questioning and explain its use in this selection.

3. Draw a diagram showing the fire, the parapet, the chained figures, the shadows on the wall.

4. In what way could the modern cinema be a substitute for the shadows on the wall?

5. Have you ever had a long-standing and much-cherished prejudice literally "torn" away by the truth? What was your reaction at first and how were you able to adjust to the truth?

6. Why do people resist the truth when it threatens their prejudices?

7. How do prejudices become established?

8. Theme Topics: Sudden Knowledge; What You Don't Know Can Hurt You; Blind Spots; Willingness to Face the Truth; The Effects of Self-Deceit.

MESSIANIC ECLOGUE
Virgil

Muses to whom Sicilian shepherds sang,
Teach me a loftier strain. The hazel copse
And lowly tamarisk will not always please.

From *Virgil's Messianic Eclogue,* by Joseph B. Mayor, W. Warde Fowler, and R. S. Conway. Copyright 1907 by John Murray, Ltd.

If still the wild, free woodland note be heard,
Our woodland song must suit a consul's ear.   5

Lo, the last age of Cumae's seer[1] has come!
Again the great millennial aeon dawns.
Once more the hallowed Maid appears, once more
Kind Saturn reigns, and from high heaven descends
The firstborn child of promise. Do but thou,   10
Pure Goddess,[2] by whose grace on infant eyes
Daylight first breaks, smile softly on this babe;
The age of iron in his time shall cease
And golden generations fill the world.
E'en now thy brother, Lord of Light and Healing,   15
Apollo,[3] rules and ends the older day.

Thy office, Pollio,[4] thine, shall mark the year
Wherein this star begins his glorious course.
Under thy banner all the stains of ill,
That shame us yet, shall melt away and break   20
The long, long night of universal dread.
For the child's birthright is the life of gods,
Heroes and gods together he shall know,
And rule a world his sire has blessed with peace.

For thee, fair child, the lavish Earth shall spread   25
Thy earliest playthings, trailing ivy-wreaths
And foxgloves red and cups of water-lilies,
And wild acanthus leaves with sunshine stored.
The goats shall come uncalled, weighed down with milk,
Nor lions' roar affright the labouring kine.   30
Thy very cradle, blossoming for joy,
Shall with soft buds caress thy baby face;
The treacherous snake and deadly herb shall die,
And Syrian spikenard blow on every bank.

[1] Sybil of Cumae, who foretold by her sacred rhymes that the golden age of
Saturn was about to begin again.
[2] Lucina, the goddess of birth.
[3] Beautiful young god of light, healing, music, poetry, and prophecy. The last
month of the year was under his lordship. Thus the father has chosen him for
special protector of the child who is to be born.
[4] Gaius Asinius Pollio—soldier, statesman, and poet—was consul at this time,
near the end of 40 B.C. He was one of Virgil's friends who had helped restore to
Virgil his father's farm, which was bestowed for a while upon one of Octavian's
soldiers.

But when thy boyish eyes begin to read   35
Rome's ancient prowess and thy sire's great story,
Gaining the power to know what manhood is,
Then, league by league, the plain without a sower
Shall ripen into waves of yellow corn;
On every wild-thorn purple grapes shall cluster,   40
And stubborn oaks yield honey clear as dew.
But in men's hearts some lingering seed of ill
E'en yet shall bid them launch adventurous keels,
And brave the inviolate sea, and wall their towns,
And cut earth's face with furrows. Then behold   45
Another Tiphys[5] take the helm and steer
Another Argo,[6] manned by chosen souls
Seeking the golden, undiscovered East.
New wars shall rise, and Troy[7] renewed shall see
Another great Achilles[8] leap to land.   50

At last, when stronger years have made thee man,
The voyager will cease to vex the sea
Nor ships of pinewood longer serve in traffic,
For every fruit shall grow in every land.
The field shall thrive unharrowed, vines unpruned,   55
And stalwart ploughmen leave their oxen free.
Wool shall not learn the dyer's cozening art,
But in the meadow, on the ram's own back,
Nature shall give new colours to the fleece,
Soft blushing glow of crimson, gold of crocus,   60
And lambs be clothed in scarlet as they feed.
"Run, run, ye spindles! On to this fulfilment
Speed the world's fortune, draw the living thread."
So heaven's unshaken ordinance declaring
The Sister Fates[9] enthroned together sang.   65

Come then, dear child of gods, Jove's mighty heir,
Begin thy high career; the hour is sounding.
See how it shakes the vaulted firmament,

[5] steersman for the *Argo*.
[6] the ship in which Jason sailed in quest of the Golden Fleece.
[7] besieged by the Greeks for ten years.
[8] the greatest Greek warrior in the Trojan War, who came to be the ideal of Greek manhood.
[9] the three goddesses of destiny: Clotho spins the thread of life, Lachesis measures it, and Atropos cuts it.

Earth and the spreading seas and depth of sky!
See, in the dawning of a new creation   70
The heart of all things living throbs with joy!
Oh, if but life would bring me days enough
And breath not all too scant to sing thy deeds,
Not Thracian Orpheus[10] should outdo the strain,
Nor Linus,[11] though his mother aid the one,   75
His sire the other, sweet Calliope[12]
And beautiful Apollo, Lord of Song.
Nay, even Pan,[13] his own Arcadia[14] judging,
Should, by Arcadia's judgment, own defeat.

Come, child, and greet thy mother with a smile!   80
Ten weary waiting months her love has known.
Come little Child! Whoso is born in sorrow
Jove ne'er hath bidden join the immortal banquet,
Nor deathless Hebe[15] deigned to be his bride.

Author and Selection Notes

Publius Virgilius Maro (70-19 B.C.) is perhaps best known as author of
The Aeneid. Living in Rome in a time of civil wars and legalized massacres, brutal slaughter and crucifixion of prisoners, and a major expan-
sion of slavery, he must indeed have dreamed of a Deliverer who would
bring peace and mercy to a sin-weary world.

For fourteen centuries men believed that Virgil was prophesying in this
poem the birth of Christ. The Emperor Constantine first advanced the
interpretation; Dante's similar belief led him to give Virgil a place of
honor in *The Divine Comedy*. Some modern scholars still think Virgil
was voicing man's mystical yearning for a Deliverer or for a reincarnation
of the new Golden Age under Augustus. Others dismiss that idea as
ridiculous, saying that the poet had in mind Pollio's expected child or
perhaps the one expected by Octavian and Scribonia late in 40 B.C.—the
expected boy that turned out to be "Julia."

The "Messianic Eclogue" is often called "The Fourth Eclogue" or
"The Messiah."

[10] son of Apollo and Calliope, a Thracian singer and player of the lyre.
[11] another son of Apollo and Calliope.
[12] the Muse of heroic poetry.
[13] the god of forests, pastures, flocks, and shepherds. He is represented as having
the upper body of a man and the legs of a goat—sometimes he also has the ears
and horns of a goat.
[14] a mountainous district in ancient Greece, noted for its contented pastoral
people.
[15] the goddess of youth and spring.

Questions and Exercises

1. Check the encyclopedia for further information about the Augustan Golden Age and the Golden Age of Saturn.

2. What is an "eclogue"? Look in *A Handbook to Literature* by Thrall, Hibbard, and Holman or some similar source.

3. According to Virgil's poem, what blessings will be ushered in with the Golden Age? Will men find perfection on earth?

4. Outline the three stages in the unfolding of the new era.

5. Which do you think Virgil was prophesying: the birth of Christ; the advent of the new Golden Age; or the birth of Pollio's or Octavian and Scribonia's child? Defend your answer.

6. Theme or Discussion Topics: The World Is Going to the Dogs; The World Is Growing Better; What One Man Can Do; The Potent Minority; Training for Leadership.

SERMON CALLING FOR THE FIRST CRUSADE

Pope Urban II*

"A station of perpetual safety will be awarded you, for the exertion of a trifling labor against the Turks."

You recollect, my dearest brethren, many things that have been decreed for you at this time: some matters in our council have been commanded, others inhibited. A rude and confused chaos of crimes required the deliberation of many days; an inveterate malady demanded a sharp remedy. For while we give unbounded scope to our clemency, our papal office finds numberless matters to proscribe, none to spare. But it has hitherto arisen from human frailty that you have erred, and that, deceived by the speciousness of vice, you have exasperated the long suffering of God, by too lightly regarding His forbearance. It has arisen, too, from human wantonness that, disregarding lawful wedlock, you have not duly considered the heinousness of adultery. From too great covetousness, also, it has arisen that, as opportunity offered, by making captive your brethren,

From *A Treasury of the World's Great Speeches*, edited by Houston Peterson. Copyright 1954 by Simon and Schuster, Inc. Reprinted by permission of the publisher.

* Thirty years after Pope Urban preached this sermon in 1095, William of Malmesbury wrote this plausible version of it.

who were bought by the same great price, you have outrageously extorted from them their wealth.

To you, however, now suffering this perilous shipwreck of sin, a secure haven of rest is offered, unless you neglect it. A station of perpetual safety will be awarded you, for the exertion of a trifling labor against the Turks. Compare now the labors you underwent in the practice of wickedness and those you will encounter in the undertaking I advise. The intention of committing adultery or murder begets many fears, for, as Solomon says, "There is nothing more timid than guilt"; many labors, for what is more toilsome than wickedness? But "He who walks uprightly walks securely." Of these labors, of these fears, the end was sin; the wages of sin is death; the death of sinners is most dreadful. Now the same labors and apprehensions are required from you for a better consideration. The cause of these labors will be charity, if, thus warned by the command of God, you lay down your lives for the brethren; the wages of charity will be the grace of God; the grace of God is followed by eternal life.

Go then prosperously; go then with confidence to attack the enemies of God. For they long since, O sad reproach to Christians! have seized Syria, Armenia, and, lastly, all Asia Minor, the provinces of which are Bithynia, Phrygia, Galatia, Lydia, Caria, Pamphylia, Isauria, Lycia, Cilicia; and now they insolently domineer over Illyricum and all the hither countries, even to the sea that is called the Straits of St. George. Nay, they usurp even the sepulcher of our Lord, that singular assurance of our faith, and sell to our pilgrims admission to that city, which ought, if Christians had a trace of their ancient courage left, to be open to Christians only. This alone might be enough to cloud our brows; but now who, except the most abandoned or the most hostile to the reputation of Christians, can endure that we do not divide the world equally with them?

They inhabit Asia, the third portion of the world, as their native soil, which was justly esteemed by our ancestors equal, by the extent of its tracts and greatness of its provinces, to the two remaining parts. There, formerly, sprang up the first germs of our faith; there, all the Apostles, except two, glorified God by their deaths; there, at the present day, the Christians, if any survive, sustain life by a wretched kind of agriculture, and pay these miscreants tribute. Even with stifled sighs, they long for participation in your liberty, since they have lost their own. They hold Africa also, another portion of the world, already possessed by their arms for more than two hundred years; which I declare to be derogatory to Christian honor, because that country was anciently the nurse of celebrated geniuses, who by their divine writings will mock the rust of antiquity as long as there shall be a person who can relish Roman literature: the learned know the truth of what I say. Europe, the third portion of the world, remains; of which how small a part do we Christians inhabit! for who can call all those barbarians who dwell in remote islands of the frozen ocean Christians, since they live after a savage manner? Even this small portion of the world belonging to us is oppressed by the Turks and Saracens. Thus, for three hundred years, Spain and the Balearic Isles have been subjugated by them, and the possession of the remainder is eagerly anticipated by feeble men, who, not having courage to engage in close encounter, love a flying mode of warfare. The Turk never ventures upon close fight; but, when driven from his station, he bends his bow at a distance, and trusts the winds to cause the wound he intends. As he has poisoned arrows, venom, and not valor, inflicts death on the man he strikes. Whatever he effects, then, I attribute to fortune, not to courage, because he wars by flight and by poison. It is apparent, too, that every race born in that region, being scorched with the intense heat of the sun, abounds more in reflection than in blood; and, therefore, they avoid coming to close quarters, because they are aware how little blood they possess. Whereas the people who are born amid the polar frosts, and distant from the sun's heat, are less cautious indeed, but, animated by their copious and rich flow of blood, they fight with the greatest alacrity. You are a nation born in the more temperate regions of the world, who may be both prodigal of blood in defiance of death and wounds; and you are not deficient in prudence. For you equally preserve good conduct in camp and are considerate in battle. Thus endued with skill and with valor, you undertake a memorable expedition.

You will be extolled throughout all ages if you rescue your brethren from danger. To those present, in God's name, I command this; to the absent I enjoin it. Let such as are going to fight for Christianity put the form of the cross upon their garments, that they may outwardly demonstrate the love arising from their inward faith. Let them enjoy, by the gift of God and the privilege of St. Peter, absolution from all their crimes. Put an end, then, to your crimes, that Christians may at least live peaceably in these countries. Go, and employ in noble warfare that valor and that sagacity which you used to waste in civil broils. Go, soldiers, everywhere renowned in fame, go, and subdue these dastardly nations. Let the noted valor of the French advance, which, accompanied by its adjoining nations, shall affright the whole world by the single terror of its name.

But why do I delay you longer by detracting from the courage of the Gentiles? Rather bring to your recollection the saying of God: "Narrow is the way that leadeth to life." Be it so then; the track to be followed is narrow, replete with death, and terrible with dangers; still this path will lead to your lost country. No doubt you must "by much tribulation enter into the kingdom of God." Place, then, before your imagination, if you shall be made captive, torments and chains; nay, every possible suffering that can be inflicted. Expect, for the firmness of your faith, even horrible punishments; that so, if it be necessary, you may redeem your souls at the expense of your bodies. Do you fear death, you men of exemplary courage and intrepidity? Surely human wickedness can devise nothing against you worthy to be put in competition with heavenly glory; for "the sufferings of the present time are not worthy to be compared to the glory which shall be revealed in us." Know ye not "that for men to live is wretchedness, and to die is happiness"? This doctrine, if you remember, you imbibed with your mother's milk, through the preaching of the clergy; and this doctrine your ancestors, the martyrs, held out by example. Death sets free from its earthy prison the human soul, which then takes flight for the mansions fitted to its virtues. Death brings near their country to the good; death cuts short the wickedness of the ungodly. By means of death, then, the soul, made free, is either soothed with joyful hope or is punished without further apprehension of worse. So long as it is fettered to the body, it derives from it earthly contagion; or, to say more truly, is dead. For earthly with heavenly, and divine with mortal, ill agree. The soul, indeed, even now, in its state of union with the body, is capable of great efforts; it gives life to its instrument, secretly moving and animating it to exertions almost beyond mortal nature. But when freed from the clog that drags it to the earth, it regains its proper station, it partakes of a blessed and perfect energy, communicating after some fashion with the invisibility of the divine nature. Discharging a double office, therefore, it ministers life to the body when it is present, and is the cause of its change when it departs. You must observe how pleasantly the soul wakes in the sleeping body, and apart from the senses sees many future events, from the principle of its relationship to the Deity. Why, then, do ye fear death, who love the repose of sleep, which resembles death? Surely it must be madness, through lust of a transitory life, to deny yourselves that which is eternal.

Rather, my dearest brethren, should it so happen, lay down your lives for the brotherhood.

Rid God's sanctuary of the wicked; expel the robbers; bring in the pious. Let no love of relations detain you; for man's chiefest love is toward God. Let no attachment to your native soil be an impediment; because all the world is exile to the Christian, but from another point of view all the world is his country. Thus exile is his country, and his country exile. Let none be restrained from going by the largeness of his patrimony, for a still larger patrimony is promised him: not of such things as soothe the miserable with vain expectation, or flatter the indolent disposition with the mean advantages of wealth, but of such as are shown by perpetual example and approved by daily experience. Yet these too are pleasant, but vain, and, to such as despise them, produce reward a hundredfold.

These things I publish, these I command: and for their execution I fix the end of the ensuing spring. God will be gracious to those who undertake this expedition, that they may have a favorable year, both in abundance of produce and in serenity of season. Those who may die will enter the mansions of heaven; while the living shall behold the sepulcher of the Lord. And what can be greater happiness than for a man, in his lifetime, to see those places where the Lord of heaven lived as a man? Blessed are they who, called to these occupations, shall inherit such a recompense; fortunate are those who are led to such a conflict, that they may partake of such rewards.

Before the Pope had finished, the crowd cried out again and again, "God wills it! God wills it!" And thousands took the cross at once.

Author and Selection Notes

Pope Urban II (c. 1042-1099) carried on his pontificate from 1088 to 1099 with shrewd and realistic statesmanship. When the Saracens, who had terrorized Western Europe for centuries, began a fresh attack, he launched the First Crusade by preaching a sermon. For centuries men believed that an itinerant monk called Peter the Hermit incited the movement. Actually, during the Council of Clermont in France, Pope Urban II announced an open-air meeting at which he called on his hearers to rescue Eastern Christendom.

Questions and Exercises

1. How does Pope Urban II prepare his audience to heed his call?
2. Notice the Pope's emotional appeal. List his main arguments for the Crusade.

3. How does he finally stir the people to action? Read aloud the moving oratory of the last paragraph.

4. Would Pope Urban II's sermon be good preliminary reading for a modern-day army officer preparing to send his men into battle? Why or why not?

5. Imagine that you are a commanding officer in the armed services and are preparing to send your men into battle. Write a speech encouraging your men to be brave in the battle, in which many lives may be lost.

6. Theme Topics: Wake Up and Read! (an appeal during National Library Week); Campaign Against Litterbugs; Community Chest Drive; Join the Navy! Help the College of Your Choice.

TRAVELS

Marco Polo

PROLOGUE

Great princes, emperors and kings, dukes and marquises, counts, knights, and burgesses! and people of all degrees who desire to get knowledge of the various races of mankind and of the diversities of the sundry regions of the World, take this book and cause it to be read to you. For you shall find therein all kinds of wonderful things, and the divers histories of the great Armenia, and of Persia, and of the Land of the Tartar, and of India, and of many another country of which our book does speak particularly and in regular succession, according to the description of Messer Marco Polo, a wise and noble citizen of Venice, as he saw them with his own eyes. Some things indeed there be therein which he beheld not; but these he heard from men of credit and veracity. And we shall set down things seen as seen, and things heard as heard only, so that no jot of falsehood may mar the truth of our book, and that all who shall read it or hear it may put full faith in the truth of all its contents.

For let me tell you that since our Lord God did mold with His hands our first Father Adam, even until this day, never has there been Christian, or Pagan, or Tartar, or Indian, or any man of any nation, who in his own person has had so much knowledge and experience of the divers parts of the World and its Wonders as hath had this Messer Marco! And for that reason he bethought himself that it would be a very great pity did he not cause to be put in writing all the great marvels that he had seen, or on sure information heard of, so that other people who had not these ad-

This is an excerpt from *The Travels of Marco Polo*.

vantages might, by his Book, get such knowledge. And I may tell you that in acquiring this knowledge he spent in those various parts of the World good twenty-six years. Now, being thereafter an inmate of the Prison at Genoa, he caused Messer Rusticiano of Pisa, who was in the said Prison likewise, to reduce the whole to writing; and this befell in the year 1298 from the birth of Jesus.

CHAPTER I

HOW THE TWO BROTHERS POLO SET FORTH FROM CONSTANTINOPLE TO TRAVERSE THE WORLD

It came to pass in the year of Christ 1260, when Baldwin was reigning at Constantinople, that Messer Nicolas Polo, the father of my lord Mark, and Messer Maffeo Polo, the brother of Messer Nicolas, were at the said city of Constantinople, whither they had gone from Venice with their merchants' wares. Now these two brothers, men singularly noble, wise, and provident, took counsel together to cross the Greater Sea on a venture of trade; so they laid in a store of jewels and set forth from Constantinople, crossing the Sea to Soldaia.

CHAPTER II

HOW THE TWO BROTHERS WENT ON BEYOND SOLDAIA

Having stayed a while at Soldaia, they considered the matter, and thought it well to extend their journey further. So they set forth from Soldaia and traveled till they came to the court of a certain Tartar prince, Barka Khan by name, whose residences were at Sarai and at Bolgara and who was esteemed one of the most liberal and courteous princes that ever was among the Tartars. This Barka was delighted at the arrival of the two brothers, and treated them with great honor; so they presented to him the whole of the jewels that they had brought with them. The prince was highly pleased with these, and accepted the offering most graciously, causing the brothers to receive at least twice its value.

After they had spent a twelvemonth at the court of this prince there broke out a great war between Barka and Hulagu, the lord of Tartars of the Levant, and great hosts were mustered on either side.

But in the end Barka, the lord of the Tartars of the Ponent, was defeated, though on both sides there was great slaughter. And by reason of this war no one could travel without peril of being taken; thus it was at least on the road by which the brothers had come, though there was no obstacle to their traveling forward. So the brothers, finding they could not retrace their steps, determined to go forward. Quitting Bolgara, therefore, they proceeded to a city called Ukek, which was at the extremity of the kingdom of the lord of the Ponent; and thence departing again, and passing the great River Tigris, they traveled across a desert which extended for seventeen days' journey, and wherein they found neither town nor village, falling in only with the tents of Tartars occupied with their cattle at pasture.

CHAPTER III

HOW THE TWO BROTHERS, AFTER CROSSING A DESERT, CAME TO THE CITY OF BOKHARA, AND FELL IN WITH CERTAIN ENVOYS THERE

After they had passed the desert, they arrived at a very great and noble city called Bokhara, the territory of which belonged to a king whose name was Borrak, and is also called Bokhara. The city is the best in all Persia. And when they had got thither, they found they could neither proceed further forward nor yet turn back again; wherefore they abode in that city of Bokhara for three years. And whilst they were sojourning in that city, there came from Hulagu, lord of the Levant, envoys on their way to the court of the Great Khan, the lord of all the Tartars in the world. And when the envoys beheld the two brothers they were amazed, for they had never before seen Latins in that part of the world. And they said to the brothers: "Gentlemen, if ye will take our counsel, ye will find great honor and profit shall come thereof." So they replied that they would be right glad to learn how. "In truth," said the envoys, "the Great Khan hath never seen any Latins, and he hath a great desire so to do. Wherefore, if you will keep us company to his court, you may depend upon it that he will be right glad to see you, and will treat you with great honor and liberality; while in our company you shall travel with perfect security, and need fear to be molested by nobody."

CHAPTER IV

HOW THE TWO BROTHERS TOOK THE ENVOY'S COUNSEL, AND WENT TO THE COURT OF THE GREAT KHAN

So when the two brothers had made their arrangements, they set out on their travels, in company with the envoys, and journeyed for a whole year, going northward and north-eastward, before they reached the court of that prince. And on their journey they saw many marvels of divers and sundry kinds, but of these we shall say nothing at present, because Messer Mark, who has likewise seen them all, will give you a full account of them in the book which follows.

CHAPTER V

HOW THE TWO BROTHERS ARRIVED AT THE COURT
OF THE GREAT KHAN

When the two brothers got to the Great Khan, he received them with great honor and hospitality, and showed much pleasure at their visit, asking them a great number of questions. First, he asked about the emperors, how they maintained their dignity, and administered justice in their dominions; and how they went forth to battle, and so forth. And then he asked the like questions about the kings and princes and other potentates.

CHAPTER VI

HOW THE GREAT KHAN ASKED ALL ABOUT THE MANNERS
OF THE CHRISTIANS, AND PARTICULARLY
ABOUT THE POPE OF ROME

And then he inquired about the Pope and the Church, and about all that is done at Rome, and all the customs of the Latins. And the two brothers told him the truth in all its particulars, with order and good sense, like sensible men as they were; and this they were able to do as they knew the Tartar language well.

CHAPTER VII

HOW THE GREAT KHAN SENT THE TWO BROTHERS AS HIS
ENVOYS TO THE POPE

When that prince, whose name was Kublai Khan, lord of the Tartars all over the earth, and of all the kingdoms and provinces and territories of that vast quarter of the world, had heard all that the brothers had to tell him about the ways of the Latins, he was greatly pleased, and he took it into his head that he would send them on an embassy to the Pope. So he urgently desired them to undertake this mission along with one of his barons; and they replied that they would gladly execute all his commands as those of their sovereign lord. Then the prince sent to summon to his presence one of his barons whose name was Cogatal, and desired him to get ready, for it was proposed to send him to the Pope along with the two brothers. The baron replied that he would execute the lord's commands to the best of his ability.

After this the prince caused letters from himself to the Pope to be indited in the Tartar tongue, and committed them to the two brothers and to that baron of his own, and charged them with what he wished them to say to the Pope. Now the contents of the letters were to this purport: He begged that the Pope would send as many as a hundred persons of our Christian faith; intelligent men, acquainted with the seven arts, well qualified to enter into controversy, and able clearly to prove by force of argument to idolaters and other kinds of folk, that the law of Christ was best, and that all other religions were false and naught; and that if they would prove this, he and all under him would become Christians and the Church's liegemen. Finally he charged his envoys to bring back to him some oil of the lamp which burns on the sepulchre of our Lord at Jerusalem.

[Upon their return home, the two brothers found the pope had just died; thus they were delayed over two years until the new pope was chosen and their request could be granted. Two friars were to accompany them to the Khan—not the hundred asked for. And these two, frightened at the dangers on the way, turned back home. Only the two brothers and young Mark arrived before the Khan.]

CHAPTER XIV

HOW MESSER NICOLO AND MESSER MAFFEO POLO AND MARCO PRESENTED THEMSELVES BEFORE THE GREAT KHAN

And what shall I tell you? When the two brothers and Mark had arrived at that great city, they went to the imperial palace, and there they found the sovereign attended by a great company of barons. So they bent the knee before him, and paid their respects to him, with all possible reverence prostrating themselves on the ground. Then the lord bade them stand up, and treated them with great honor, showing great pleasure at their coming, and asked many questions as to their welfare, and how they had sped. They replied that they had in verity sped well, seeing that they found the Khan well and safe. Then they presented the credentials and letters which they had received from the Pope, which pleased him right well; and after that they produced the oil from the sepulchre, and at that also he was very glad, for he set great store thereby. And next, spying Mark, who was then a young gallant, he asked who was that in their company? "Sir," said his father, Messer Nicolo, " 'tis my son and your liegeman." "Welcome is he too," said the emperor. And why should I make a long story? There was great rejoicing at the court because of their arrival; and they met with attention and honor from everybody.

So there they abode at the court with the other barons.

BOOK SECOND
PART I—THE KHAN, HIS COURT AND CAPITAL

CHAPTER I

OF KUBLAI KHAN, THE GREAT KHAN NOW REIGNING, AND OF HIS GREAT PUISSANCE

Now am I come to the part of our book in which I shall tell you of the great and wonderful magnificence of the great Khan now reigning, by name Kublai Khan; *Khan* being a title which signifies "The Great Lord of Lords," or emperor. And of a surety he hath good right to such a title, for all men know for a certain truth that he is the most potent man, as regards forces and lands and treasure, that existeth in the world, or ever hath existed from the time of our first father Adam until this day. All this I will make clear to you for truth, in this book of ours, so that every one shall be fain to acknowledge that he is the greatest lord that is now in the world, or ever hath been. And now ye shall hear how and wherefore.

CHAPTER XXVIII

HOW THE GREAT KHAN CAUSES TREES TO BE PLANTED BY THE HIGHWAYS

The emperor moreover has taken order that all the highways traveled by his messengers and the people generally should be planted with rows of great trees a few paces apart; and thus these trees are visible a long way off, and no one can miss the way by day or night. Even the roads through uninhabited tracts are thus planted, and it is the greatest possible solace to travelers. And this is done on all the ways, where it can be of service. The great Khan plants these trees all the more readily, because his astrologers and diviners tell him that he who plants trees lives long.

But where the ground is so sandy and desert that trees will not grow, he causes other landmarks, pillars or stones, to be set up to show the way.

CHAPTER XXX

CONCERNING THE STONES THAT ARE DUG IN CATHAY, AND ARE BURNED FOR FUEL

It is a fact that all over the country of Cathay there is a kind of black stones existing in beds in the mountains, which they dig out and burn like firewood. If you supply the fire with them at night, and see that they are well kindled, you will find them still alight in the morning; and they make such capital fuel that no other is used throughout the country. It is true that they have plenty of wood also, but they do not burn it, because those stones burn better and cost less.

Moreover with that vast number of people, and the number of hot baths that they maintain—for every one has such a bath at least three times a week, and in the winter if possible every day while every nobleman and man of wealth has a private bath for his own use—the wood would not suffice for the purpose.

CHAPTER XXXI

HOW THE GREAT KHAN CAUSES STORES OF GRAIN TO BE MADE, TO HELP HIS PEOPLE WITHAL IN TIME OF DEARTH

You must know that when the emperor sees that grain is cheap and abundant, he buys up large quantities, and has it stored in all his provinces in great granaries, where it is so well looked after that it will keep for three or four years.

And this applies, let me tell you, to all kinds of grain, whether wheat, barley, millet, rice, panic, or what not, and when there is any scarcity of a particular kind of grain, he causes that to be issued. And if the price of the grain is at one bezant the measure, he lets them have it at a bezant for four measures, or at whatever price will produce general cheapness; and everyone can have food in this way. And by this providence of the emperor's, his people can never suffer from dearth. He does the same over his whole empire; causing these supplies to be stored everywhere, according to calculation of the wants and necessities of the people.

. . . .

Author and Selection Notes

Marco Polo (c. 1254-1324) traveled with his father and his uncle Maffeo throughout the East. The three were courteously received by Kublai Khan, whose service Marco entered for several years. Later while in prison Marco dictated his *Travels,* which influenced the geographic outlook of the day.

Questions and Exercises

1. The incredulous Venetians called Marco Polo's tales "a fabrication of wonders." Why do we reverse their judgment and name Polo the first modern explorer? Why is the plural "we" used in the prologue, and why is much of the story told in third person?

2. Observe Polo's use of accurate detail to substantiate his narrative. Trace the journey of the two brothers on a map.

3. Compare our American highways with those of the Great Khan. Compare the Khan's storage of grain with Joseph's fortification against famine in ancient Egypt (see Genesis).

4. What were the black stones found in the mountains of Cathay?

5. Why did Polo think the bathing habits of the people of Cathay were significant enough to be described in his *Travels?*

6. Theme Topics: My First Flight (or Ocean Voyage) ; Sojourn in a Big City: An American Abroad; Travel by Bus; Guided Tour; Visit to Disneyland.

FREEDOM OF THE PRESS

John Milton

I deny not but that it is of greatest concernment in the church and commonwealth to have a vigilant eye how books demean themselves as well as men; and thereafter to confine, imprison, and do sharpest justice on them as malefactors. For books are not absolutely dead things, but do contain a potency of life in them to be as active as that soul was whose progeny they are; nay, they do preserve as in a vial the purest efficacy and extraction of that living intellect that bred them. I know they are as lively and as vigorously productive as those fabulous dragon's teeth; and being sown up and down, may chance to spring up armed men.[1] And yet, on the other hand, unless wariness be used, as good almost kill a man as kill a good book: who kills a man kills a reasonable creature, God's image; but he who destroys a good book, kills reason itself, kills the image of God, as it were, in the eye. Many a man lives a burden to the earth; but a good book is the precious lifeblood of a master spirit, embalmed and treasured up on purpose to a life beyond life. 'Tis true, no age can restore a life, whereof perhaps there is no great loss; and revolutions of ages do not oft recover the loss of a rejected truth, for the want of which whole nations fare the worse. We should be wary, therefore, what persecution we raise against the living labors of public men, how we spill that seasoned life of man preserved and stored up in books; since we see a kind of homi-

---

From "Areopagitica" in *John Milton: Complete Poems and Major Prose* by Merritt Y. Hughes; copyright 1957 by The Odyssey Press. Some footnotes have been omitted, and others have been shortened.

[1] Milton had in mind the almost complete mutual slaughter of the warriors who sprang from the teeth of the dragon which Ovid says (*Met.* III, 95-126) were sown by its slayer, Cadmus, King of Thebes in Boeotia.

cide may be thus committed, sometimes a martyrdom; and if it extend to the whole impression, a kind of massacre, whereof the execution ends not in the slaying of an elemental life, but strikes at that ethereal and fifth essence, the breath of reason itself, slays an immortality rather than a life. But lest I should be condemned of introducing license, while I oppose licensing, I refuse not the pains to be so much historical as will serve to show what hath been done by ancient and famous commonwealths against this disorder, till the very time that this project of licensing crept out of the Inquisition, was caught up by our prelates, and hath caught some of our presbyters.

In Athens, where books and wits were ever busier than in any other part of Greece, I find but only two sorts of writings which the magistrate cared to take notice of; those either blasphemous and atheistical, or libellous. Thus the books of Protagoras[2] were by the judges of Areopagus commanded to be burnt, and himself banished the territory for a discourse begun with his confessing not to know whether there were gods, or whether not. And against defaming, it was decreed that none should be traduced by name, as was the manner of Vetus Comœdia,[3] whereby we may guess how they censured libelling; and this course was quick enough, as Cicero[4] writes, to quell both the desperate wits of other atheists and the open way of defaming, as the event showed. Of other sects and opinions, though tending to voluptuousness and the denying of divine providence, they took no heed. Therefore we do not read that either Epicurus,[5] or that libertine school of Cyrene,[6] or what

[2] *Protagoras* (? 480-411 B.C.) of Abdera, in Thrace, was the first of the great sophists or professional teachers of rhetoric. In 411 he was impeached for a theological treatise which began by disclaiming all knowledge on his part as to whether or not the gods existed. The book was burned and Protagoras is said to have been banished from Athens.

[3] *Vetus Comoedia:* in the Old Comedy of Athens, says Gilbert Norwood in *Greek Comedy* (1931), p. 28, "we know certainly of but one law restraining" comic freedom of personal reference, and that "endured from 440-39 till 438-7, less than three years."

[4] The reference is to *Cicero's* treatise *On the Nature of the Gods* I, xxiii, where the punishment of Protagoras is regarded as having done much to repress open atheism, "inasmuch as even doubt" of the existence of the gods "was punished."

[5] "Who can but pity the virtuous Epicurus," asked Thomas Browne in *Vulgar Errors* VII, xvii, "who is commonly conceived to have placed his chief felicity in pleasure and sensual delights, and hath therefore left an infamous name behind him? . . . The ground hereof seems a misapprehension of his opinion, who placed his felicity not in the pleasures of the body, but the mind, and tranquility thereof, obtained by wisdom and virtue."

[6] The life of the founder of the Cyrenaic school, Aristippus, as told by Diogenes Laertius, contains many scandalous stories of his libertinism.

the Cynic impudence uttered,[7] was ever questioned by the laws. Neither is it recorded that the writings of those old comedians were suppressed, though the acting of them were forbid; and that Plato commended the reading of Aristophanes, the loosest of them all, to his royal scholar Dionysius, is commonly known and may be excused, if holy Chrysostom,[8] as is reported, nightly studied so much the same author and had the art to cleanse a scurrilous vehemence into the style of a rousing sermon.

That other leading city of Greece, Lacedæmon, considering that Lycurgus[9] their lawgiver was so addicted to elegant learning as to have been the first that brought out of Ionia the scattered works of Homer, and sent the poet Thales[10] from Crete to prepare and mollify the Spartan surliness with his smooth songs and odes, the better to plant among them law and civility, it is to be wondered how museless[11] and unbookish they were, minding nought but the feats of war. There needed no licensing of books among them, for they disliked all but their own laconic apothegms and took a slight occasion to chase Archilochus[12] out of their city, perhaps for composing in a higher strain than their own soldierly ballads and roundels could reach to; or if it were for his broad verses, they were not therein so cautious, but they were as dissolute in their promiscuous conversing; whence Euripides affirms in *Andromache* that their

[7] The stories of Diogenes' search in open daylight with a lantern for an honest man, and of his contempt for Alexander's invitation to live at court in preference to his tub or shack, illustrate the severity and unconventionality of the *Cynics,* whose famous representative he was.

[8] An interest in Aristophanes on the part of John Chrysostom (347-407 A.D.) would seem noteworthy to Puritans who honored him most because (according to Socrates Scholasticus, *Ecclesiastical History* VI, xvi) he was banished from his see for opposing the idolatrous honor paid to the empress Eudoxia and the "common playes and showes" that she approved.

[9] Although Plutarch declared in his Life of *Lycurgus* that the Spartan law-giver forbade any of his laws to be put into written form, he makes it clear that they were designed to prevent tyranny from developing.

[10] *Thales,* one of the earliest Ionian poets, is mentioned in Plutarch's *Life of Lycurgus* (IV, v) as having been persuaded by Lycurgus to leave his home in Crete and settle in Sparta. "His odes," says Plutarch, "were so many persuasives to obedience and unanimity, and . . . they softened insensibly the manners of the audience, drew them often from the animosities which then prevailed, and united them in zeal for . . . virtue."

[11] *museless:* unfamiliar with the Muses, goddesses of poetry and the other arts.

[12] *Archilochus* (early seventh century B.C.) "took delight in flouting the conventions of the aristocracy" (H. J. Rose, *A Handbook of Greek Literature,* p. 89) and may have earned his traditional banishment from Sparta for his supposedly licentious verses or for his poem boasting of his own cowardice in throwing away his shield in a retreat.

women were all unchaste. Thus much may give us light after what sort books were prohibited among the Greeks.

The Romans also, for many ages trained up only to a military roughness, resembling most the Lacedæmonian guise, knew of learning little but what their twelve tables[13] and the Pontific College with their augers and flamens[14] taught them in religion and law, so unacquainted with other learning that when Carneades[15] and Critolaus,[16] with the Stoic Diogenes[17] coming ambassadors to Rome, took thereby occasion to give the city a taste of their philosophy, they were suspected for seducers by no less a man than Cato[18] the Censor, who moved it in the senate to dismiss them speedily, and to banish all such Attic babblers out of Italy. But Scipio[19] and others of the noblest senators withstood him and his old Sabine austerity; honored and admired the men; and the censor himself at last, in his old age, fell to the study of that whereof before he

[13] The Twelve Tables were the earliest statement of Roman law and were understood to have been engraved on bronze about 450 B.C.

[14] The *Pontific College* went back to the most revered of the half-legendary Roman kings, Numa, and its president, the Pontifex Maximus, was the greatest religious dignitary in republican Rome. The *flamens* were priests subordinate to the *pontifices*, and the *augurs*, whose business it was to consult the omens before public acts such as battles, treaties and holidays, composed another priestly college.

[15] *Carneades* (?213-129 B.C.), the founder of the Third or New Academy at Athens, was a sceptic and an opponent of Stoicism. In 155 B.C. he was sent from Athens to Rome with Diogenes and Critolaus to protest against a fine which had been assessed against the Athenians for destroying Oropus. In Rome he shocked public opinion by first defending and then attacking the principle of justice in two formal addresses.

[16] *Critolaus* was the head of the Peripatetic or Aristotelian School of philosophy in Athens in the middle of the second century B.C.

[17] *Diogenes* succeeded Zeno as head of the Stoic School at Athens. He must not be confused with Diogenes the Cynic, to whom n. 7 above refers.

[18] One of Plutarch's final anecdotes in his life of *Cato the Censor* (Marcus Porcius Cato, 234?-149 B.C.) is the story of Cato's gruff scepticism about the influence of Carneades and even of the Socratic philosophical tradition upon the young men of Rome. "For his blasphemy against learning," said Bacon in the *Advancement* I, ii, 9; p. 17, ". . . he was well punished, . . . for when he was past threescore years old, he was taken with an extreme desire to go to school again, and to learn the Greek tongue, to the end to peruse the Greek authors, which doth well demonstrate that his former censure of the Grecian learning was rather an affected gravity than according to the inward sense of his own opinion."

[19] *Scipio* the Younger (?185-129 B.C.), who captured Carthage in 146, was friendly with Terence and Polybius and other writers. In Cicero's dialogue *On Friendship* his geniality and his esteem for the virtues that Cato practised on his Sabine farm were familiar to every schoolboy.

was so scrupulous. And yet at the same time, Nævius[20] and Plautus,[21] the first Latin comedians, had filled the city with all the borrowed scenes of Menander[22] and Philemon.[23]

Then began to be considered there also what was to be done to libellous books and authors; for Nævius was quickly cast into prison for his unbridled pen and released by the tribunes upon his recantation; we read also that libels were burnt, and the makers punished by Augustus.[24] The like severity, no doubt, was used, if aught were impiously written against their esteemed gods. Except in these two points, how the world went in books, the magistrate kept on reckoning. And therefore Lucretius[25] without impeachment versifies his Epicurism to Memmius, and had the honor to be set forth the second time by Cicero, so great a father of the commonwealth; although himself disputes against that opinion in his own writings. Nor was the satirical sharpness or naked plainness of Lucilius,[26] or Catullus,[27] or Flaccus,[28] by any order prohibited.

And for matters of state, the story of Titus Livius[29] though it extolled that part which Pompey held, was not therefore suppressed

[20] *Naevius* produced the first of his satiric plays about 235 B.C. He was imprisoned for attacking Scipio the younger and the aristocratic party in his plays and obliged to recant. He died in exile in Utica ?202 B.C.

[21] *Plautus* (?254-184 B.C.) was the most popular of Roman writers of comedy.

[22] *Menander* (342-291 B.C.) wrote over one hundred comedies, the surviving portions of seven of which are almost our only representation of the Athenian New Comedy, upon which Plautus' plays were modelled.

[23] *Philemon* (?361-263 B.C.) was a rival of Menander. Only a few short fragments of his plays survive, but two of them are suggested as sources which Plautus followed closely in his *Mercator* and *Trinummus*.

[24] Tacitus declared (*Annals* I, lxxii) that *Augustus* so resented the damage done to the best people in Rome by the insolent libels of Cassius Severus that he urged the passage of a law against libel.

[25] Lucretius' *De rerum natura,* a frank defense of Epicurean views about the gods and the human soul, was dedicated to Gaius Memmius Gemellus (Praetor in 58 B.C.). The belief that Cicero edited Lucretius rests upon a vague statement of St. Jerome in his additions to Eusebius' *Chronicon* and is hardly consistent with Cicero's attacks on Epicureanism in the *Tusculan Disputations* II and III, and in the *De finibus* I and II.

[26] *Lucilius* (148-103 B.C.) is usually recognized as the founder of Roman satire.

[27] Among the vivid lyrics of *Catullus* (87-47? B.C.) were some lampoons of Caesar and his partisans.

[28] Quintus Horatius *Flaccus* (Horace, 65-8 B.C.) hardly challenged censorship of any kind by his *Satires.*

[29] In his *History of Rome* Livy (*Titus Livius,* 59 B.C.-17 A.D.) is said by Tacitus (*Annals* IV, 34) to have praised Augustus' great rival for power, Pompey, very highly, and to have had Augustus' approval for so doing.

by Octavius Cæsar of the other faction. But that Naso[30] was by him banished in his old age for the wanton poems of his youth, was but a mere covert of state over some secret cause: and besides, the books were neither banished nor called in. From hence we shall meet with little else but tyranny in the Roman empire,[31] that we may not marvel, if not so often bad as good books were silenced. I shall therefore deem to have been large enough in producing what among the ancients was punishable to write, save only which, all other arguments were free to treat on.

By this time the emperors were become Christians, whose discipline in this point I do not find to have been more severe than what was formerly in practice. The books of those whom they took to be grand heretics were examined, refuted, and condemned in the general councils,[32] and not till then were prohibited, or burnt, by authority of the emperor. As for the writings of heathen authors, unless they were plain invectives against Christianity, as those of Porphyrius[33] and Proclus,[34] they met with no interdict that can be cited till about the year 400 in a Carthaginian Council[35] wherein bishops themselves were forbid to read the books of Gentiles, but heresies they might read: while others long before them, on the contrary, scrupled more the books of heretics than of Gentiles. And that the primitive councils and bishops were wont only to declare what books were not commendable, passing no further, but leaving it to each one's conscience to read or to lay by, till after the year 800, is observed already by Padre Paolo, the great unmasker

[30] *Naso:* Ovid (Publius Ovidius Naso) was banished to Tomi near the mouth of the Danube; tradition says less on account of his licentious poems than for an intrigue with the granddaughter of the Emperor Augustus, Julia. He died at Tomi in 18 A.D.

[31] So in the Epistle Dedicatory to *The Liberty of Prophecying* Jeremy Taylor quoted Tacitus' *Agricola* to prove that under the more tyrannous Roman emperors books were suppressed by "an illiterate policy" which supposed that "such indirect and uningenuous proceedings can, among wise and free men, disgrace the authors and disrepute their discourses."

[32] In the following survey of the attempts of some of the *general councils* and popes to suppress heresy Milton is mainly following Padre Paolo Sarpi's *Historie of the Council of Trent* (as it was entitled in Nathaniel Brent's translation, 1620).

[33] *Prophyry* (233-305? A.D.) is said to have been a pupil of Origen and to have apostatized under the influence of Plotinus in Rome. His book against Christianity was publicly destroyed by order of the emperor Theodosius.

[34] *Proclus* (412-485 A.D.) was a lifelong enemy of Christianity.

[35] Sirluck observes that Milton follows Sarpi's statement that a council at Cathage burned heretical books "about the year 400," without identifying any of the four councils held there between 397 and 412 as the responsible one.

of the Trentine Council.[36] After which time the Popes of Rome, engrossing what they pleased of political rule into their own hands, extended their dominion over men's eyes as they had before over their judgments, burning and prohibiting to be read what they fancied not; yet sparing in their censures, and the books not many which they so dealt with; till Martin V,[37] by his bull, not only prohibited, but was the first that excommunicated the reading of heretical books; for about that time Wycliffe and Huss,[38] growing terrible, were they who first drove the papal court to a stricter policy of prohibiting. Which course Leo X[39] and his successors followed, until the Council of Trent and the Spanish Inquisition,[40] engendering together, brought forth, or perfected those catalogs and expurging indexes[41] that rake through the entrails of many an old good author with a violation worse than any could be offered to his tomb.

Nor did they stay in matters heretical, but any subject that was not to their palate they either condemned in a prohibition, or had it straight into the new purgatory of an Index. To fill up the measure of encroachment, their last invention was to ordain that no book, pamphlet, or paper should be printed (as if St. Peter had bequeathed them the keys of the press also out of paradise) unless it were approved and licensed under the hands of two or three glutton friars. For example:

[36] The Council of Trent (in the Tyrol) met frequently between Dec. 13, 1545, and Dec. 4, 1563, and ended its efforts to reconcile Protestant with Catholic Europe by reaffirming most of the great doctrines of Roman Catholicism, and by affirming that in matters of faith and morals the tradition of the Church ranked with the Bible as an authority. In describing Sarpi (1552-1623) as its "unmasker," Milton does not misrepresent the spirit of his *History,* which was first published in 1619. He wrote as a Catholic, but also from the point of view of a supporter of the Venetian Republic in its struggle with the popes.

[37] *Martin* V (Otto Colonna) was Pope from 1417 to 1431. Sirluck notes that Milton wrote from knowledge of the full text of Martin's bull of 1418, *Inter cunctas,* when he declared that the bull definitely excommunicated contumacious heretics. Sarpi, knowing the bull only in an abridged form, was unaware of its full severity. Cf. n. 32 above.

[38] *Lollards* was the name given to the followers of the fourteenth-century reformer, John Wycliff, possession of whose books was forbidden by a bull of Pope Alexander V in 1409. The spread of Wycliffite doctrines on the Continent owed much to the Bohemian, John Huss, who was burned in 1415.

[39] *Leo X* (Giovanni dei Medici) was Pope from 1513 to 1521.

[40] Sirluck notes that the *Inquisition* was reorganized by a bull of Paul III on July 21, 1542.

[41] The first *Index Expurgatorius* was issued by Paul IV in 1559.

Let the Chancellor Cini be pleased to see if in this present work
  be contained aught that may withstand the printing.

Vincent Rabbatta, Vicar of Florence.

I have seen this present work, and find nothing athwart the
  Catholic faith and good manners: in witness whereof I have
  given, &c.

Nicolo Cini, Chancellor of Florence.

Attending the precedent relation, it is allowed that this present
  work of Davanzati[42] may be printed.

Vincent Rabatta, &c.

It may be printed, July 15.

Friar Simon Mompei d'Amelia,
Chancellor of the holy office in Florence.

Sure they have a conceit, if he of the bottomless pit had not
long since broke prison, that this quadruple exorcism would bar
him down. I fear their next design will be to get into their custody
the licensing of that which they say Claudius intended but went
not through with. Vouchsafe to see another of their forms, the
Roman stamp:

Imprimatur, If it seem good to the reverend Master of the holy
  Palace,

Belcastro, Vicegerent.

Imprimatur,

Friar Nicolo Rodolphi,
Master of the holy Palace.

Sometimes five Imprimaturs are seen together, dialoguewise, in
the piazza of one titlepage, complimenting and ducking each to
other with their shaven reverences, whether the author, who stands
by in perplexity at the foot of his epistle, shall to the press or to
the sponge. These are the pretty responsories,[43] these are the dear
antiphonies[44] that so bewitched of late our prelates and their
chaplains with the goodly echo they made; and besotted us to the
gay imitation of a lordly Imprimatur,[45] one from Lambeth House,[46]

---

[42] The little book *On the English Schism (Lo Scisma d'Inghilterra)* by Bernardo
Davanzati (1529-1606) was reissued in Florence in 1638 in an edition which may
have been published while Milton was there, and which has been identified by
A. Allodoli in *Giovanni Milton e l'Italia*, p. 82, as having been used by him in
writing *Areop.*

[43] *responsories:* sections of the Psalms sung interspersed between readings from
the missal in the mass.

[44] *antiphonies:* hymns or anthems sung in responsive parts by two choirs.

[45] *Imprimatur:* "let it be printed," the order stamped on manuscripts which
are permitted by ecclesiastical authority to be sent to the press. "To the sponge"

another from the west end of Paul's,[47] so apishly Romanizing that the word of command still was set down in Latin; as if the learned grammatical pen that wrote it would cast no ink without Latin; or perhaps, as they thought, because no vulgar tongue was worthy to express the pure conceit of an Imprimatur; but rather, as I hope, for that our English, the language of men ever famous and foremost in the achievements of liberty, will not easily find servile letters enough to spell such a dictatory presumption English.

And thus ye have the inventors and the original of book-licensing ripped up and drawn as lineally as any pedigree. We have it not, that can be heard of, from any ancient state, or polity, or church, nor by any statute left us by our ancestors elder or later; nor from the modern custom of any reformed city or church abroad; but from the most antichristian council and the most tyrannous inquisition that ever inquired.

Till then books were ever as freely admitted into the world as any other birth; the issue of the brain was no more stifled than the issue of the womb; no envious Juno[48] sat cross legged over the nativity of any man's intellectual offspring; but if it proved a monster, who denies but that it was justly burnt, or sunk into the sea? But that a book in worse condition than a peccant soul, should be to stand before a jury ere it be born to the world and undergo yet in darkness the judgment of Rhadamanth[49] and his colleagues, ere it can pass the ferry backward into light, was never heard before, till that mysterious iniquity, provoked and troubled at the first entrance of reformation, sought out new limbos[50] and new hells wherein they might include our books also within the number of their damned. And this was the rare morsel so officiously snatched

---

—meaning, to have the contents wiped off—has been applied to manuscripts unworthy of publication since Suetonius helped to popularize the expression in the *Life of Augustus*, 85.

[46] *Lambeth* Palace is still the residence of the Archbishop of Canterbury, on the south bank of the Thames.

[47] *St. Paul's* is the cathedral church of the Bishop of London.

[48] In *Metamorphoses* IX, 285-319, Ovid tells the story of *Juno's* cruelty to Alcmena in placing the goddess of childbirth cross-legged beside her, muttering charms to prevent her delivery of the infant Hercules. On the seventh night of labor the wit of Alcmena's maid tricked the cross-legged goddess into rising and so breaking the charm that closed her mistress's womb.

[49] According to Plato in *Gorgias*, 524a, the Cretan king *Rhadamanthus*, together with Minos and Aeacus, was made a judge of the dead by Zeus, and had power to strip every soul naked of its body for examination.

[50] purlieus of hell, such as the *limbus puerorum* or limbo of babes, and *limbus patrum* or limbo of the patriarchs, who were delivered in Christ's harrowing of hell.

up, and so ill-favoredly imitated by our inquisiturient bishops and the attendant minorities,[51] their chaplains. That ye like not now these most certain authors of this licensing order, and that all sinister intention was far distant from your thoughts, when ye were importuned the passing it, all men who know the integrity of your actions, and how ye honor truth, will clear ye readily.

But some will say, what though the inventors were bad, the thing for all that may be good. It may so; yet if that thing be no such deep invention, but obvious and easy for any man to light on, and yet best and wisest commonwealths through all ages and occasions have forborne to use it, and falsest seducers and oppressors of men were the first who took it up, and to no other purpose but to obstruct and hinder the first approach of reformation; I am of those who believe it will be a harder alchemy than Lullius[52] ever knew to sublimate[53] any good use out of such an invention. Yet this only is what I request to gain from this reason, that it may be held a dangerous and suspicious fruit, as certainly it deserves, for the tree that bore it, until I can dissect one by one the properties it has. But I have first to finish, as was propounded, what is to be thought in general of reading books, whatever sort they be, and whether be more the benefit or the harm that thence proceeds?

Not to insist upon the examples of Moses, Daniel,[54] and Paul,[55] who were skilful in all the learning of the Egyptians, Chaldeans, and Greeks, which could not probably be without reading their books of all sorts; in Paul especially, who thought it no defilement to insert into holy scripture the sentences of three Greek poets, and one of them a tragedian; the question was notwithstanding sometimes controverted among the primitive doctors, but with great odds on that side which affirmed it both lawful and profitable, as

[51] the Franciscans, traditionally the humblest of the monastic orders.

[52] Raymond Lully (1234?-1315) was traditionally better known for his writings on alchemy and medicine than for the missionary ardor that took him to north Africa three times and finally ended his life by martyrdom in Mauretania.

[53] in alchemy, to transform a base into a precious metal.

[54] In Acts vii, 22, *Moses* is called "learned in all the wisdom of the Egyptians," and in Dan. i, 17, *Daniel* is described as seemingly more learned than any of the other Hebrew princes who were educated in the wisdom of Chaldea. St. Paul's learning was got partly under the great Hebrew teacher Gamaliel (Acts xxii, 3), but it also included knowledge of Greek literature.

[55] Acts xvii, 28, represents *Paul* as quoting Aratus. I Cor. xv, 33, "evil communications corrupt good manners" translates a fragment of Euripides or Menander. The saying in Titus i, 12—"the Cretans are always liars"—is attributed to the Cretan poet, Epimenides.

was then evidently perceived when Julian the Apostate[56] and subtlest enemy to our faith, made a decree forbidding Christians the study of heathen learning; for, said he, they wound us with our own weapons, and with our own arts and sciences they overcome us. And indeed the Christians were put so to their shifts by this crafty means, and so much in danger to decline into all ignorance, that the two Apollinarii[57] were fain, as a man may say, to coin all the seven liberal sciences[58] out of the Bible, reducing it into divers forms of orations, poems, dialogues, even to the calculating of a new Christian grammar. But, saith the historian Socrates, the providence of God provided better than the industry of Apollinarius and his son, by taking away that illiterate law with the life of him who devised it.[59]

So great an injury they then held it to be deprived of Hellenic learning; and thought it a persecution more undermining, and secretly decaying the Church, than the open cruelty of Decius[60] or Diocletian.[61] And perhaps it was the same politic drift that the devil whipped St. Jerome[62] in a Lenten dream, for reading Cicero; or else it was a phantasm bred by the fever which had then seized

[56] *Julian the Apostate* (Flavius Claudius Julianus, 331-363 A.D.) became emperor in 361 and was killed by the Persians two years later. Though trained as a Christian, he seems to have been attracted early by pagan thought, and he publicly apostatized and made his famous decree against *teaching* pagan literature by the Christians when he became emperor.

[57] The *Ecclesiastical History* of Socrates Scholasticus (385?-440? A.D.), Book III, chapter xiv, recounts that when "the Emperour Julian forbad the Christians the studie of Prophane literature, both the Apollinariuses, the father, and the sonne, fell a writing. . . . For the father . . . turned the five bookes of *Moses* into Heroicall verse, together with other bookes of the old Testament, which contained Histories: partly in Hexameter verse, & partly after the forme of comedies and tragedies. . . . The son (who became bishop of Alexandria), an eloquent Rhetorician, brought the writings of the Euangelistes, and works of the Apostles, into Dialogues, as *Plato* used among the Heathens."

[58] The traditional Seven Liberal Arts were Grammar, Logic, Rhetoric, Arithmetic, Geometry, Astronomy, and Music, which presupposed proficiency in Latin, if not in Greek.

[59] Socrates' eighteenth chapter tells the story of Julian's perhaps providential taking-off in battle with the Persians, and chapter nineteen celebrates the restoration of full cultural rights to the Christians by his Christian successor, Jovian.

[60] *Decius* was emperor from 249 until 251.

[61] The persecutions under Decius and *Diocletian,* who reigned from 284 to 305, were particularly severe.

[62] The story of St. *Jerome's* dream of being brought by an angel before a tribunal in heaven and accused of being a Ciceronian because he had Cicero's works by heart, goes back to Jerome's *Epistle* XVIII, "To Eustochius on Virginity." Milton's interpretation of it goes back as far as Gratian's *Decretum,* Prima

him. For had an angel been his discipliner, unless it were for dwelling too much upon Ciceronianisms, and had chastised the reading, not the vanity, it had been plainly partial; first to correct him for grave Cicero, and not for scurril Plautus, whom he confesses to have been reading not long before; next to correct him only, and let so many more ancient fathers wax old in those pleasant and florid studies without the lash of such a tutoring apparition; insomuch that Basil[63] teaches how some good use may be made of *Margites,* a sportful poem not now extant writ by Homer; and why not then of *Morgante,*[64] an Italian romance much to the same purpose?

But if it be agreed we shall be tried by visions, there is a vision recorded by Eusebius,[65] far ancienter than this tale of Jerome to the nun Eustochium, and, besides, has nothing of a fever in it. Dionysius Alexandrinus was, about the year 240, a person of great name in the church for piety and learning, who had wont to avail himself much against heretics by being conversant in their books; until a certain presbyter laid it scrupulously to his conscience, how he durst venture himself among those defiling volumes. The worthy man, loth to give offense, fell into a new debate with himself what was to be thought; when suddenly a vision sent from God (it is his own *Epistle* that so avers it) confirmed him in these words: "Read any books whatever come to thy hands, for thou art sufficient both to judge aright and to examine each matter." To this revelation he assented the sooner, as he confesses, because it was answerable to

---

Pars. Distinctio, XXXVII, vii, where the saint is said to have replied to his heavenly judge by asking whether clergymen ought not to have skill in secular literature.

[63] *Basil* the Great, Bishop of Cappodocia, 370-379 A.D., is described in the *Ecclesiastical History* (IV, xxi) of Socrates Scholasticus as preparing for a career as a Christian apologist by reading pagan philosophy in Athens in his youth. Milton is quoting Basil's *The Right to Use Greek Literature* (Padelford's Ed, p. 102).

[64] The mock-heroic romance of Luigi Pulci (1431-1487), the *Morgante Maggiore* (published in 1488), was coarser than Ariosto's *Orlando Furioso,* of which it was one of the main sources of inspiration. As Homer's *Margites* was traditionally regarded as the first great humorous poem in the ancient world, the *Morgante* was accepted as having founded its type in Renaissance Europe.

[65] Milton quoted loosely from the summary of Dionysius' (Bishop of Alexandria, 247-65) letter to Philemon in Eusebius' *Ecclesiastical History* VII, vi, confessing that he had "read over the traditions and commentaries of the heretickes" because a vision had commanded him to "Reade all whatsoever come into thy handes; thou shalt be able to weye, to prove, and trye all" (Meredith Hanmer's translation, p. 127).

that of the apostle to the Thessalonians: "Prove all things, hold fast that which is good."[66]

And he might have added another remarkable saying of the same author: "To the pure, all things are pure";[67] not only meats and drinks, but all kind of knowledge whether of good or evil; the knowledge cannot defile, nor consequently the books, if the will and conscience be not defiled. For books are as meats and viands are—some of good, some of evil substance, and yet God in that unapocryphal vision said without exception, "Rise, Peter, kill and eat,"[68] leaving the choice to each man's discretion. Wholesome meats to a vitiated stomach differ little or nothing from unwholesome, and best books to a naughty mind are not unappliable to occasions of evil. Bad meats will scarce breed good nourishment in the healthiest concoction; but herein the difference is of bad books, that they to a discreet and judicious reader serve in many respects to discover, to confute, to forewarn, and to illustrate.

Whereof what better witness can ye expect I should produce than one of your own now sitting in parliament, the chief of learned men reputed in this land, Mr. Selden;[69] whose volume of natural and national laws proves, not only by great authorities brought together, but by exquisite reasons and theorems almost mathematically demonstrative, that all opinions, yea errors, known, read, and collated, are of main service and assistance toward the speedy attainment of what is truest.

I conceive, therefore, that when God did enlarge the universal dict of man's body, saving ever the rules of temperance, he then also, as before, left arbitrary the dieting and repasting of our minds; as wherein every mature man might have to exercise his own leading capacity. How great a virtue is temperance, how much of moment through the whole life of man! Yet God commits the managing so great a trust, without particular law or prescription, wholly to the demeanor of every grown man. And therefore, when he himself

[66] I Thess. v, 21.

[67] Titus i, 15.

[68] In a vision teaching that the Jewish ceremonial law which stigmatized the gentiles as *unclean* had been abrogated, St. Peter saw "four-footed beasts of the earth, and wild beasts, and creeping things, and fowls of the air"; and he heard "a voice saying, Arise, Peter; slay and eat." To his objection that the beasts were unclean the voice answered "from heaven, What God hath cleansed, that call not thou common" (Acts xi, 5-10).

[69] John *Selden* (1584-1654) published his *De Jure Naturali et Gentium iuxta Disciplinam Hebraeorum* in 1640.

tabled the Jews from heaven, that omer[70] which was every man's daily portion of manna, is computed to have been more than might have well sufficed the heartiest feeder thrice as many meals. For those actions which enter into a man, rather than issue out of him, and therefore defile not, God uses not to captivate under a perpetual childhood of prescription, but trusts him with the gift of reason to be his own chooser; there were but little work left for preaching, if law and compulsion should grow so fast upon those things which heretofore were governed only by exhortation. Solomon[71] informs us that much reading is a weariness to the flesh; but neither he nor other inspired author tells us that such or such reading is unlawful; yet certainly had God thought good to limit us herein, it had been much more expedient to have told us what was unlawful than what was wearisome.

As for the burning of those Ephesian books by St. Paul's converts;[72] 'tis replied the books were magic, the Syriac so renders them. It was a private act, a voluntary act, and leaves us to a voluntary imitation: the men in remorse burnt those books which were their own; the magistrate by this example is not appointed; these men practised the books, another might perhaps have read them in some sort usefully.

Good and evil we know in the field of this world grow up together almost inseparably; and the knowledge of good is so involved and interwoven with the knowledge of evil, and in so many cunning resemblances hardly to be discerned, that those confused seeds which were imposed on Psyche[73] as an incessant labor to cull out and sort asunder, were not more intermixed. It was from out the rind of one apple tasted, that the knowledge of good and evil, as two twins cleaving together, leaped forth into the world. And perhaps this is that doom which Adam fell into of knowing good and evil, that is to say, of knowing good by evil.[74]

[70] The *omer* was the measure of manna which Moses was commanded in Exod. xvi, 16, to ration to the Israelites daily. The account lays stress on the abundance of the supply.

[71] Eccles. xii, 12. Mark vii, 15: "There is nothing from without a man, that entering into him can defile him: but the things which come out of him, those are they that defile the man."

[72] The story is found in Acts xix, 19.

[73] Milton would know the story of *Psyche* best in *The Golden Ass* of Apuleius IV-VI. Anger because Psyche has won Cupid's love makes Venus doom her to sort the various kinds of grain out of a vast, mixed pile, but the work is done for her by the sympathetic ants.

[74] Milton reaffirms this interpretation of the meaning of the fall of man in Gen. iii.

As therefore the state of man now is, what wisdom can there be to choose, what continence to forbear without the knowledge of evil? He that can apprehend and consider vice with all her baits and seeming pleasures, and yet abstain, and yet distinguish, and yet prefer that which is truly better, he is the true warfaring[75] Christian. I cannot praise a fugitive and cloistered virtue, unexercised and unbreathed, that never sallies out and sees her adversary, but slinks out of the race where that immortal garland[76] is to be run for, not without dust and heat. Assuredly we bring not innocence into the world, we bring impurity much rather: that which purifies us is trial, and trial is by what is contrary. That virtue therefore which is but a youngling in the contemplation of evil, and knows not the utmost that vice promises to her followers, and rejects it, is but a blank[77] virtue, not a pure; her whiteness is but an excremental[78] whiteness; which was the reason why our sage and serious poet Spenser,[79] whom I dare be known to think a better teacher than Scotus[80] or Aquinas,[81] describing true temperance under the person of Guyon, brings him in with his palmer through

---

[75] *wayfaring*, the reading of the first edition, has the weight of priority, but in three extant copies of the first edition of *Areopagitica* the "y" in *Wayfaring* is changed to "r" in a hand that may be Milton's.

[76] *that:* like the Latin *ille*, the word is used to refer to something well known. Milton is perhaps thinking of that prize for which St. Paul described himself as pressing forward in Philippians iii, 14, or of the crown of righteousness in II Timothy iv, 8, or of the crown of life that is promised in James i, 12, to him "that endureth temptation" and "is tried."

[77] *blank:* pale or colorless.

[78] *excremental:* excrescential, external.

[79] In the account of Guyon's temptation in *F.Q.* II, viii, as E. Sirluck observes in *MP*, XLVIII (1950), 90-96, the Palmer does not accompany Guyon into the Cave of Mammon. In Spenser's Aristotelian allegory the Knight of Temperance represents the "firm and unchangeable character" of Aristotle's truly temperate man, and in the cave of Mammon he does not need the support of the Palmer who, in Spenser's allegory, objectifies the "rational principle" which restrains passion when the settled habits of character fail to do so. But in many passages Milton disapproves of virtue which is a matter of settled habit, or at least reserves his admiration for the kind that is constantly won "with dust and heat."

[80] John Duns *Scotus* (1265?-1308), the Subtle Doctor in the Scholastic tradition, was born in Scotland but taught at Paris and Oxford and died in Cologne. He was a Franciscan, and in several important ways his teaching was opposed to that of his great Dominican predecessor, St. Thomas. The prejudice against Scholastic logic which Milton illustrates here was responsible for the quite unfair development of the word *dunce* from Duns Scotus' name.

[81] St. Thomas *Aquinas* (1225?-1274), the Seraphic Doctor, in his *Summa Theologica* left the greatest monument of Scholastic thought, and in his *Summa contra Gentiles,* the greatest medieval compendium of Christian doctrine.

the cave of Mammon and the bower of earthly bliss, that he might see and know, and yet abstain.

Since therefore, the knowledge and survey of vice is in this world so necessary to the constituting of human virtue, and the scanning of error to the confirmation of truth, how can we more safely and with less danger scout into the regions of sin and falsity than by reading all manner of tractates and hearing all manner of reason? And this is the benefit which may be had of books promiscuously read.

Author and Selection Notes

Besides being one of the greatest English poets, John Milton (1608-1674) was also a master of prose. Much of his prose was written as a public duty when he was Foreign Secretary under Cromwell. His *Areopagitica,* unsurpassed as a defense of liberty of the press, is an example of the classic oration. Following Quintilian's principles of oratory, as did Cicero and Demosthenes, Milton even used the title of a speech which Isocrates delivered to the Athenian Court of the Areopagus.

Questions and Exercises

1. Review English history of 1664 to understand the licensing act of Parliament that provoked Milton's defense of the freedom of the press.

2. Trace in paragraph one Milton's comparison of a man with a book. Point out several powerful sentences.

3. Explain how the history of licensing from ancient times has always been concurrent with tyranny.

4. How does Milton apply his argument against "cloistered virtue" and external restraint to the reading of books? Do you agree or disagree with him?

5. In outline form list the major points of this essay. Does Milton proceed logically from the initial presentation of the problem of censorship to a valid solution or conclusion?

6. Theme Topics: Free Public Libraries; Book Censorship by the Government (or the Church or Various Self-Appointed Groups); Each Man's Discretion in Reading; Cloistered Virtue; Guidance in Reading.

THE STORY OF ALEXANDER SELKIRK

Richard Steele

Talia monstrabat relegens errata retrorsum. Virg.

Under the Title of this Paper, I do not think it foreign to my Design, to speak of a Man born in Her Majesty's Dominions, and relate an Adventure in his Life so uncommon, that it's doubtful whether the like has happen'd to any other of human Race. The Person I speak of is *Alexander Selkirk,* whose Name is familiar to Men of Curiosity, from the Fame of his having lived four Years and four Months alone in the Island of *Juan Fernandez.* I had the pleasure frequently to converse with the Man soon after his Arrival in *England,* in the Year 1711. It was matter of great Curiosity to hear him, as he is a Man of good Sense, give an Account of the different Revolutions in his own Mind in that long Solitude. When we consider how painful Absence from Company for the space of but one Evening, is to the generality of Mankind, we may have a sense how painful this necessary and constant Solitude was to a Man bred a Sailor, and ever accustomed to enjoy and suffer, eat, drink, and sleep, and perform all Offices of Life, in Fellowship and Company. He was put ashore from a leaky Vessel, with the Captain of which he had had an irreconcileable difference; and he chose rather to take his Fate in this place, than in a crazy Vessel, under a disagreeable Commander. His Portion were a Sea-Chest, his wearing Cloaths and Bedding, a Fire-lock, a Pound of Gun-powder, a large quantity of Bullets, a Flint and Steel, a few Pounds of Tobacco, an Hatchet, a Knife, a Kettle, a Bible, and other Books of Devotion, together with Pieces that concerned Navigation, and his Mathematical Instruments. Resentment against his Officer, who had ill used him, made him look forward on this Change of Life, as the more eligible one, till the Instant in which he saw the Vessel put off; at which moment, his Heart yearned within him, and melted at the parting with his Comrades and all Human Society at once. He had in Provisions for the Sustenance of Life but the quantity of two Meals, the Island abounding only with wild Goats, Cats and Rats. He judged it most probable that he should find more immediate and easy Relief, by finding Shell-fish on the Shore, than seeking Game with his Gun. He accordingly found great quantities of Turtles, whose Flesh is extreamly delicious, and of which he frequently eat very plentifully on his first Arrival, till it grew disagreeable to his Stomach, except in Jellies. The Necessities of Hunger and Thirst, were his greatest Diversions from the Reflection on his lonely Condition. When those Appetites were satisfied, the Desire of Society was as strong a Call upon him, and he appeared to himself least necessitous when he wanted every thing; for the Supports of his Body were easily attained, but the eager Longings for seeing again the Face of Man during the Interval of craving bodily Appetites, were hardly supportable. He grew dejected, languid, and melancholy, scarce able to refrain from doing himself Violence, till by Degrees, by the Force of Reason, and frequent reading of the Scriptures, and turning his Thoughts upon the Study of Navigation, after the Space of eighteen Months, he grew thoroughly reconciled to his Condition. When he had made this Conquest, the Vigour of his Health, Disengagement from the World, a constant, chearful, serene Sky, and a temperate Air, made his Life one continual Feast, and his Being much more joyful than it had before been irksome. He now taking Delight in every thing, made the Hutt in which he lay, by Ornaments which he cut down from a spacious Wood, on the side of which it was situated, the most delicious Bower, fann'd with continual Breezes, and gentle Aspirations of Wind, that made his Repose after the Chase equal to the most sensual Pleasures.

I forgot to observe, that during the Time of his Dissatisfaction, Monsters of the Deep, which frequently lay on the Shore, added to the terrors of his Solitude; the dreadful Howlings and Voices seemed too terrible to be made for human Ears; but upon the Recovery of his Temper, he could with Pleasure not only hear their Voices, but approach the Monsters themselves with great Intrepidity. He speaks of Sea-Lions, whose jaws and Tails were capable of seizing or breaking the Limbs of a Man, if he approached them: But at that Time his Spirits and Life were so high, and he could act so regularly and unconcerned, that meerly from being unruffled in himself, he killed them with the greatest Ease imaginable: For observing, that though their Jaws and Tails were so terrible, yet the Animals being mighty slow in working themselves round, he had nothing to do but place himself exactly opposite to their Middle, and as close to them as possible, and he dispatched them with his Hatchet at Will.

The Precaution which he took against Want, in case of Sickness, was to lame Kids when very young, so as that they might recover their Health, but never be capable of Speed. These he had in great Numbers about his Hutt; and when he was himself in full Vigour,

he could take at full Speed the swiftest Goat running up a Promon-
tory, and never failed of catching them but on a Descent.

His Habitation was extreamly pester'd with Rats, which gnaw'd
his Cloaths and Feet when sleeping. To defend him against them,
he fed and tamed Numbers of young Kitlings, who lay about his
Bed, and preserved him from the Enemy. When his Cloaths were
quite worn out, he dried and tacked together the Skins of Goats,
with which he cloathed himself, and was enured to pass through
Woods, Bushes, and Brambles with as much Carelessness and Pre-
cipitance as any other Animal. It happened once to him, that running on the Summit of a Hill, he made a Stretch to seize a Goat,
with which under him, he fell down a Precipice, and lay senseless
for the Space of three Days, the Length of which Time he Measured
by the Moon's Growth since his last Observation. This manner of
Life grew so exquisitely pleasant, that he never had a Moment
heavy upon his Hands; his Nights were untroubled, and his Days
joyous, from the Practice of Temperance and Exercise. It was his
Manner to use stated Hours and Places for Exercises of Devotion,
which he performed aloud, in order to keep up the Faculties of
Speech, and to utter himself with greater Energy.

When I first saw him, I thought, if I had not been let into his
Character and Story, I could have discerned that he had been much
separated from Company, from his Aspect and Gesture; there was a
strong but chearful Seriousness in his Look, and a certain Disregard
to the ordinary things about him, as if he had been sunk in
Thought. When the Ship which brought him off the Island came
in, he received them with the greatest Indifference, with relation
to the Prospect of going off with them, but with great Satisfaction
in an Opportunity to refresh and help them. The Man frequently
bewailed his Return to the World, which could not, he said, with
all its Enjoyments, restore him to the Tranquility of his Solitude.
Though I had frequently conversed with him, after a few Months
Absence he met me in the Street, and though he spoke to me, I
could not recollect that I had seen him; familiar Converse in this
Town had taken off the Loneliness of his Aspect, and quite altered
the Air of his Face.

This plain Man's Story is a memorable Example, that he is
happiest who confines his Wants to natural Necessities; and he
that goes further in his Desires, increases his Wants in Proportion
to his Acquisitions; or to use his own Expression, *I am now worth
800 Pounds, but shall never be so happy, as when I was not worth
a Farthing.*

Author and Selection Notes

Among the "twins" of literature we find the names of Richard Steele (1672-1729) and Joseph Addison, whose best work was done jointly in their essays written for the *Spectator,* a famous eighteenth-century periodical. Steele's story about Selkirk, which appeared in *The Englishman,* is the true relation of a sailor deserted on the island of Juan Fernandez from 1704-1709. One of the thousands who read this headline news from the pen of England's popular essayist was Daniel Defoe, who saw within it the germ for his masterpiece, *Robinson Crusoe.*

Questions and Exercises

1. Notice the author's spelling, punctuation, and capitalization. List the first dozen variations from our present rules for correct English usage.

2. Give evidence to prove that Steele did or did not hear this adventure from Selkirk's own lips.

3. What portions of the first paragraph would you consider valuable for Defoe's use in fiction? If you have read Defoe's *Robinson Crusoe,* tell how he expanded the account into book length.

4. How does Selkirk show the effects of his island solitude?

5. Theme Topics: The Bliss of Solitude; Loneliness in a Crowd; Human Ingenuity in Extremity; Our Increased Wants; Inner Resources.

THE DECLARATION OF INDEPENDENCE

Thomas Jefferson

In Congress, July 4, 1776

A declaration by the representatives of the
United States of America, in Congress Assembled

When, in the course of human events, it becomes necessary for one people to dissolve the political bands which have connected them with another, and to assume, among the powers of the earth, the separate and equal station to which the laws of nature and of nature's God entitle them, a decent respect to the opinions of mankind requires that they should declare the causes which impel them to the separation.

We hold these truths to be self-evident:—That all men are created equal; that they are endowed by their Creator with certain unalienable rights; that among these are life, liberty, and the pursuit of happiness. That, to secure these rights, governments are instituted among men, deriving their just powers from the consent of the governed; that, whenever any form of government becomes destructive of these ends, it is the right of the people to alter or to abolish it, and to institute a new government, laying its foundation on such principles, and organizing its powers in such form, as to them shall seem most likely to effect their safety and happiness. Prudence, indeed, will dictate, that governments long established should not be changed for light and transient causes; and accordingly all experience hath shown that mankind are more disposed to suffer while evils are sufferable, than to right themselves by abolishing the forms to which they are accustomed. But when a long train of abuses and usurpations, pursuing invariably the same object, evinces a design to reduce them under absolute despotism, it is their right, it is their duty, to throw off such government, and to provide new guards for their future security.

Such has been the patient sufferance of these colonies; and such is now the necessity which constrains them to alter their former systems of government. The history of the present King of Great Britain is a history of repeated injuries and usurpations, all having in direct object the establishment of an absolute tyranny over these states. To prove this, let facts be submitted to a candid world.

He has refused his assent to laws the most wholesome and necessary for the public good.

He has forbidden his governors to pass laws of immediate and pressing importance, unless suspended in their operation till his assent should be obtained; and when so suspended, he has utterly neglected to attend to them.

He has refused to pass other laws for the accommodation of large districts of people, unless those people would relinquish the right of representation in the legislature—a right inestimable to them, and formidable to tyrants only.

He has called together legislative bodies at places unusual, uncomfortable, and distant from the depository of their public records, for the sole purpose of fatiguing them into compliance with his measure.

He has dissolved representative houses repeatedly, for opposing, with manly firmness, his invasions on the rights of the people.

He has refused, for a long time after such dissolutions, to cause others to be elected, whereby the legislative powers, incapable of annihilation, have returned to the people at large for their exercise;

the State remaining, in the mean time, exposed to all the dangers of invasions from without, and convulsions within.

He has endeavored to prevent the population of these States; for that purpose obstructing the laws for the naturalization of foreigners; refusing to pass others to encourage their migration hither, and raising the conditions of new appropriations of lands.

He has obstructed the administration of justice, by refusing his assent to laws for establishing judiciary powers.

He has made judges dependent on his will alone for the tenure of their offices, and the amount and payment of their salaries.

He has erected a multitude of new offices, and sent hither swarms of officers to harass our people and eat out their substance.

He has kept among us in times of peace, standing armies, without the consent of our legislatures.

He has affected to render the military independent of, and superior to, the civil power.

He has combined with others to subject us to a jurisdiction foreign to our constitutions, and unacknowledged by our laws; giving his assent to their acts of pretended legislation:

For quartering large bodies of armed troops among us;

For protecting them, by a mock trial, from punishment for any murders which they should commit on the inhabitants of these States;

For cutting off our trade with all parts of the world;

For imposing taxes on us without our consent;

For depriving us, in many cases, of the benefits of trial by jury;

For transporting us beyond seas, to be tried for pretended offences;

For abolishing the free system of English laws in a neighboring province, establishing therein an arbitrary government, and enlarging its boundaries, so as to render it at once an example and fit instrument for introducing the same absolute rule into these colonies;

For taking away our charters, abolishing our most valuable laws, and altering, fundamentally, the forms of our governments;

For suspending our own legislatures, and declaring themselves invested with power to legislate for us in all cases whatsoever.

He has abdicated government here, by declaring us out of his protection, and waging war against us.

He has plundered our seas, ravaged our coasts, burned our towns, and destroyed the lives of our people.

He is at this time transporting large armies of foreign mercenaries to complete the works of death, desolation and tyranny, already begun with circumstances of cruelty and perfidy scarcely paralleled in the most barbarous ages, and totally unworthy the head of a civilized nation.

He has constrained our fellow-citizens, taken captive on the high seas, to bear arms against their country, to become the executioners of their friends and brethren; or to fall themselves by their hands.

He has excited domestic insurrection among us, and has endeavored to bring on the inhabitants of our frontiers the merciless Indian savages, whose known rule of warfare is an undistinguished destruction of all ages, sexes, and conditions.

In every stage of these oppressions we have petitioned for redress in the most humble terms; our repeated petitions have been answered only by repeated injury. A prince whose character is thus marked by every act which may define a tyrant, is unfit to be the ruler of a free people.

Nor have we been wanting in our attentions to our British brethren. We have warned them, from time to time, of attempts by their legislature to extend an unwarrantable jurisdiction over us. We have reminded them of the circumstances of our emigration and settlement here. We have appealed to their native justice and magnanimity; and we have conjured them, by the ties of our common kindred, to disavow these usurpations, which would inevitably interrupt our connections and correspondence. They, too, have been deaf to the voice of justice and consanguinity. We must, therefore, acquiesce in the necessity which denounces our separation, and hold them, as we hold the rest of mankind, enemies in war, in peace friends.

We, therefore, the Representatives of the United States of America, in General Congress assembled, appealing to the Supreme Judge of the world for the rectitude of our intentions, do, in the name and by the authority of the good people of these colonies, solemnly publish and declare, That these united Colonies are, and of right ought to be, free and independent states; that they are absolved from all allegiance to the British crown, and that all political connection between them and the state of Great Britain is, and ought to be, totally dissolved; and that, as free and independent states, they have full power to levy war, conclude peace, contract alliances, establish commerce, and do all other acts and things which independent states may of right do. And, for the support of this declaration, with a firm reliance on the protection of Divine Providence, we mutually pledge to each other our lives, our fortunes, and our sacred honor.

Author and Selection Notes

Thomas Jefferson (1743-1826) is known to every American school child as the third President of the United States and author of the Declaration of Independence. His intellectual curiosity was insatiable. He was an excellent architect; he helped plan the national capital, founded the University of Virginia, encouraged religious freedom, and generally influenced the development of American political thought.

Questions and Exercises

1. In its final form the Declaration stands as the preamble to democratic America. Explain in 100 words what Jefferson meant when he told Lee that the Declaration was intended to be an expression of the American mind.

2. The Declaration has sometimes been designated as a "ceremonial essay." Explain this term. What is the over-all tone of the essay?

3. Notice the length of the opening sentence. Restate the central thought in ten words.

4. Make an outline, grouping all the grievances against the King under one heading and tell whether or not the essay is logically developed.

5. John Adams claimed that Jefferson had "a reputation for literature, science, and a happy talent for composition." Point out sentences which reflect this "happy talent."

6. Theme Topics: The Pursuit of Happiness; How Democratic Are We? What Freedom Costs; Created Unequal; A Declaration for Change (some major change needed in community or school policies).

A MAN'S A MAN FOR A' THAT
Robert Burns

Is there, for honest poverty,
   That hangs his head, and a' that?
The coward-slave, we pass him by,
   We dare be poor for a' that!
For a' that, and a' that,
   Our toil's obscure, and a' that;
The rank is but the guinea's[1] stamp;
   The man's the gowd[2] for a' that.

[1] British gold coin.   [2] gold.

What though on hamely fare we dine,
   Wear hodden gray,[3] and a' that;
Gie fools their silks, and knaves their wine,
   A man's a man for a' that.
For a' that, and a' that,
   Their tinsel show, and a' that;
The honest man, though e'er sae poor,
   Is king o' men for a' that.

Ye see yon birkie,[4] ca'd a lord,
   Wha struts, and stares, and a' that;
Though hundreds worship at his word,
   He's but a coof[5] for a' that:
For a' that, and a' that,
   His riband, star, and a' that,
The man of independent mind,
   He looks and laughs at a' that.

A prince can mak' a belted knight,
   A marquis, duke, and a' that;
But an honest man's aboon his might,
   Guid faith he mauna fa' that![6]
For a' that, and a' that,
   Their dignities, and a' that,
The pith o' sense and pride o' worth
   Are higher ranks than a' that.

Then let us pray that come it may,
   As come it will for a' that,
That sense and worth, o'er a' the earth,
   May bear the gree,[7] and a' that;
For a' that, and a' that,
   It's coming yet, for a' that,
That man to man, the warld o'er,
   Shall brothers be for a' that.

---

[3] coarse woolen cloth, undyed.
[4] fine fellow.
[5] stupid lout.

[6] cannot accomplish that.
[7] prize.

Author and Selection Notes

A much-loved poet, Robert Burns (1759-1796) wrote in his own Scottish dialect about love and nature and the dignity of man. Reared in poverty, he wanted to shelter the poor and helpless; he had no patience with hypocrisy or cant and dreamed of a world where all men shall brothers be. While America was declaring herself an independent nation, Burns was giving poetic expression to the same democratic plea for man's intrinsic worth.

Questions and Exercises

1. Give a prose summary of Burns' defense of genuine manliness. How highly is such manliness valued in this country today?

2. Although Burns could write well in formal English, he deliberately chose to speak Scots. What effect is achieved by his use of the native dialect? Read the poem aloud and if possible listen to a recording of it by a good reader.

3. Has Burns' prayer in the last stanza come true? Why or why not?

4. Theme Topics: "Plain Living and High Thinking"; An Argument for (Against) Class Distinction; the Brotherhood of Man; Values and Characteristics of the Democratic Man.

THE GETTYSBURG ADDRESS

Abraham Lincoln

Delivered at the Dedication of the
National Cemetery, November 19, 1863

Fourscore and seven years ago our fathers brought forth on this continent a new nation, conceived in liberty, and dedicated to the proposition that all men are created equal.

Now we are engaged in a great civil war, testing whether that nation, or any nation so conceived and so dedicated, can long endure. We are met on a great battle-field of that war. We have come to dedicate a portion of that field as a final resting-place for those who here gave their lives that that nation might live. It is altogether fitting and proper that we should do this.

But, in a larger sense, we cannot dedicate—we cannot consecrate—we cannot hallow—this ground. The brave men, living and dead, who struggled here, have consecrated it far above our poor power to add or detract. The world will little note nor long remember what we say here, but it can never forget what they did here. It is for us, the living, rather, to be dedicated here to the unfinished work which they who fought here have thus far so nobly advanced. It is rather for us to be here dedicated to the great task remaining before us—that from these honored dead we take increased devotion to that cause for which they gave the last full measure of devotion; that we here highly resolve that these dead shall not have died in vain; that this nation, under God, shall have a new birth of freedom; and that government of the people, by the people, for the people, shall not perish from the earth.

Author and Selection Notes

We sometimes forget that the Abraham Lincoln (1809-1865) of history made a valuable contribution to American prose literature. The lengthy speech of Edward Everett, the principal orator at the dedication of the national cemetery at Gettysburg, has long been superseded by Lincoln's ten short sentences, described by Carl Sandburg as "one of the supreme utterances of democratic peoples of the world."

Questions and Exercises

1. Read the address aloud and explain why, contrary to Lincoln's statement, this speech has been long remembered.

2. Point out the chronological sequence of ideas; the subtle reference to birth, death, and rebirth; the spatial order from continent to battlefield—from large to small area, from great accomplishment to small. Explain how Lincoln has made preparation for the triumphant conclusion.

3. Can you think of any twentieth-century presidential speech which is equal in literary quality, seriousness of purpose, and expression of American ideals to this speech?

4. Compare this address with Jefferson's Declaration of Independence in length, loftiness of tone, simplicity of diction, seriousness of purpose, expression of American ideals.

5. Theme Topics: Our National Debt in Human Terms; How Wise Are "The People"? The Torch They Threw; Still Fighting the Civil War; How Much Federal Control?

OUR LADY'S JUGGLER
Anatole France

In the days of King Louis, there was a poor juggler in France, a native of Compiègne, Barnaby by name, who went about from town to town performing feats of skill and strength.

On fair days he would unfold an old worn-out carpet in the public square, and when by means of a jovial address, which he had learned of a very ancient juggler, and which he never varied in the least, he had drawn together the children and loafers, he assumed extraordinary attitudes, and balanced a tin plate on the tip of his nose. At first the crowd would feign indifference.

But when, supporting himself on his hands face downwards, he threw into the air six copper balls, which glittered in the sunshine, and caught them again with his feet; or when throwing himself backwards until his heels and the nape of the neck met, giving his body the form of a perfect wheel, he would juggle in this posture with a dozen knives, a murmur of admiration would escape the spectators, and pieces of money rain down upon the carpet.

Nevertheless, like the majority of these who live by their wits, Barnaby of Compiègne had a great struggle to make a living.

Earning his bread in the sweat of his brow, he bore rather more than his share of the penalties consequent upon the misdoings of our father Adam.

Again, he was unable to work as constantly as he would have been willing to do. The warmth of the sun and the broad daylight were as necessary to enable him to display his brilliant parts as to the trees if flower and fruit should be expected of them. In winter time he was nothing more than a tree stripped of its leaves, and as it were dead. The frozen ground was hard to the juggler, and, like the grasshopper of which Marie de France tells us, the inclement season caused him to suffer both cold and hunger. But as he was simple-natured he bore his ills patiently.

He had never meditated on the origin of wealth, nor upon the inequality of human conditions. He believed firmly that if this life should prove hard, the life to come could not fail to redress the balance, and this hope upheld him. He did not resemble those

Reprinted by permission of Dodd, Mead & Company from *Mother of Pearl* by Anatole France.

thievish and miscreant Merry Andrews who sell their souls to the
devil. He never blasphemed God's name; he lived uprightly, and
although he had no wife of his own, he did not covet his neighbour's, since woman is ever the enemy of the strong man, as it
appears by the history of Samson recorded in the Scriptures.

In truth, his was not a nature much disposed to carnal delights,
and it was a greater deprivation to him to forsake the tankard than
the Hebe who bore it. For whilst not wanting in sobriety, he was
fond of a drink when the weather waxed hot. He was a worthy
man who feared God, and was very devoted to the Blessed Virgin.

Never did he fail on entering a church to fall upon his knees
before the image of the Mother of God, and offer up this prayer
to her:

"Blessed Lady, keep watch over my life until it shall please God
that I die, and when I am dead, ensure to me the possession of the
joys of paradise."

Now on a certain evening after a dreary wet day, as Barnaby
pursued his road, sad and bent, carrying under his arm his balls
and knives wrapped up in his old carpet, on the watch for some
barn where, though he might not sup, he might sleep, he perceived on the road, going in the same direction as himself, a monk,
whom he saluted courteously. And as they walked at the same rate
they fell into conversation with one another.

"Fellow traveller," said the monk, "how comes it about that you
are clothed all in green? Is it perhaps in order to take the part of
a jester in some mystery play?"

"Not at all, good father," replied Barnaby. "Such as you see me,
I am called Barnaby, and for my calling I am a juggler. There
would be no pleasanter calling in the world if it would always
provide one with daily bread."

"Friend Barnaby," returned the monk, "be careful what you
say. There is no calling more pleasant than the monastic life. Those
who lead it are occupied with the praises of God, the Blessed Virgin,
and the saints; and, indeed, the religious life is one ceaseless hymn
to the Lord."

Barnaby replied—

"Good father, I own that I spoke like an ignorant man. Your
calling cannot be in any respect compared to mine, and although
there may be some merit in dancing with a penny balanced on a
stick on the tip of one's nose, it is not a merit which comes within
hail of your own. Gladly would I, like you, good father, singing
my office day by day, and specially the office of the most Holy Virgin,

to whom I have vowed a singular devotion. In order to embrace the monastic life I would willingly abandon the art by which from Soissons to Beauvais I am well known in upwards of six hundred towns and villages."

The monk was touched by the juggler's simplicity, and as he was not lacking in discernment, he at once recognized in Barnaby one of those men of whom it is said in the Scriptures: Peace on earth to men of good will. And for this reason he replied—

"Friend Barnaby, come with me, and I will have you admitted into the monastry of which I am Prior. He who guided St. Mary of Egypt in the desert set me upon your path to lead you into the way of salvation."

It was in this manner, then, that Barnaby became a monk. In the monastery into which he was received the religious vied with one another in the worship of the Blessed Virgin, and in her honor each employed all the knowledge and all the skill which God had given him.

The prior on his part wrote books dealing according to the rules of scholarship with the virtues of the Mother of God.

Brother Maurice, with a deft hand copied out these treatises upon sheets of vellum.

Brother Alexander adorned the leaves with delicate miniature paintings. Here were displayed the Queen of Heaven seated upon Solomon's throne, and while four lions were on guard at her feet, around the nimbus which encircled her head hovered seven doves, which are the seven gifts of the Holy Spirit, the gifts, namely, of Fear, Piety, Knowledge, Strength, Counsel, Understanding, and Wisdom. For her companions she had six virgins with hair of gold, namely, Humility, Prudence, Seclusion, Submission, Virginity, and Obedience.

At her feet were two little naked figures, perfectly white, in an attitude of supplication. These were souls imploring her all-powerful intercession for their soul's health, and we may be sure not imploring in vain.

Upon another page facing this, Brother Alexander represented Eve, so that the Fall and the Redemption could be perceived at one and the same time—Eve the Wife abased, and Mary the Virgin exalted.

Furthermore, to the marvel of the beholder, this book contained presentments of the Well of Living Waters, the Fountain, the Lily, the Moon, the Sun, and the Garden Enclosed of which the Song of Songs tells us, the Gate of Heaven and the City of God, and all these things were symbols of the Blessed Virgin.

Brother Marbode was likewise one of the most loving children of Mary.

He spent all his days carving images in stone, so that his beard, his eyebrows, and his hair were white with dust, and his eyes continually swollen and weeping; but his strength and cheerfulness were not diminished, although he was now well gone in years, and it was clear that the Queen of Paradise still cherished her servant in his old age. Marbode represented her seated upon a throne, her brow encircled with an orb-shaped nimbus set with pearls. And he took care that the folds of her dress should cover the feet of her, concerning whom the prophet declared: My beloved is as a garden enclosed.

Some times, too, he depicted her in the semblance of a child full of grace, and appearing to say, "Thou art my God, even from my mother's womb."

In the priory, moreover, were poets who composed hymns in Latin, both in prose and verse, in honour of the Blessed Virgin Mary, and amongst the company was even a brother from Picardy who sang the miracles of Our Lady in rhymed verse and in the vulgar tongue.

Being a witness of this emulation in praise and the glorious harvest of their labors, Barnaby mourned his own ignorance and simplicity.

"Alas!" he sighed, as he took his solitary walk in the little shelterless garden of the monastery, "wretched wight that I am, to be unable, like my brothers, worthily to praise the Holy Mother of God, to whom I have vowed my whole heart's affection. Alas! Alas! I am but a rough man and unskilled in the arts, and I can render you in service, blessed Lady, neither edifying sermons, nor treatises set out in order according to rule, nor ingenious paintings, nor statues truthfully sculptured, nor verses whose march is measured to the beat of feet. No gift have I, alas!"

After this fashion he groaned and gave himself up to sorrow. But one evening, when the monks were spending their hour of liberty in conversation, he heard one of them tell the tale of a religious man who could repeat nothing other than the Ave Maria. This poor man was despised for his ignorance; but after his death there issued forth from his mouth five roses in honor of the five letters of the name Mary (Marie), and thus his sanctity was made manifest.

Whilst he listened to this narrative Barnaby marvelled yet once again at the loving kindness of the Virgin; but the lesson of that blessed death did not avail to console him, for his heart overflowed with zeal, and he longed to advance the glory of his Lady, who is in heaven.

How to compass this he sought but could find no way, and day by day he became the more cast down, when one morning he awakened filled full with joy, hastened to the chapel, and remained there alone for more than an hour. After dinner he returned to the chapel once more.

And, starting from that moment, he repaired daily to the chapel at such hours as it was deserted, and spent within it a good part of the time which the other monks devoted to the liberal and mechanical arts. His sadness vanished, nor did he any longer groan.

A demeanour so strange awakened the curiosity of the monks. These began to ask one another for what purpose Brother Barnaby could be indulging so persistently in retreat.

The prior, whose duty it is to let nothing escape him in the behaviour of his children in religion, resolved to keep a watch over Barnaby during his withdrawals to the chapel. One day, then, when he was shut up there after his custom, the prior, accompanied by two of the older monks, went to discover through the chinks in the door what was going on within the chapel.

They saw Barnaby before the altar of the Blessed Virgin, head downwards, with his feet in the air, and he was juggling with six balls of copper and a dozen knives. In honour of the Holy Mother of God he was performing those feats, which aforetime had won him most renown. Not recognizing that the simple fellow was thus placing at the service of the Blessed Virgin his knowledge and skill, the two old monks exclaimed against the sacrilege.

The prior was aware how stainless was Barnaby's soul, but he concluded that he had been seized with madness. They were all three preparing to lead him swiftly from the chapel, when they saw the Blessed Virgin descend the steps of the altar and advance to wipe away with a fold of her azure robe the sweat which was dropping from her juggler's forehead.

Then the prior, falling upon his face upon the pavement, uttered these words—

"Blessed are the simple-hearted, for they shall see God."

"Amen!" responded the old brethren, and kissed the ground.

Author and Selection Notes

Jacques Anatole François Thibault (1844-1924), commonly known by his pseudonym of Anatole France, was one of the most prominent and honored writers of his day. In 1921 he won the Nobel Prize in literature.

Keenly aware of any hypocrisy in Church or State or society, he was quick to point out human imperfections, and his works often evince a special sympathy for the popular legends of the Middle Ages. "Our Lady's Juggler" is based on an old story that is part of a large body of medieval literature devoted to the service of the Blessed Virgin. France was called "the stylist par excellence," but he disclaimed such praise, saying rather, "I have passed my life twisting dynamite into curlpapers."

Questions and Exercises

1. Suggest headings for the three parts of the story.
2. From whose viewpoint is the story told? Which method does the author use most to describe Barnaby—dialogue or exposition? Would the story have been more effective if the author had relied more on the other method?
3. In Part Two the author dispenses with direct description. By what means do we learn more about Barnaby's character? What do we learn about life within the monastery?
4. In Part Three how does the Virgin's blessing resolve the plot and further reveal the characters?
5. Theme Topics: The One-Talent Man; Unworthy Suspicions; The Bottom of the Barrel; My Inferiority Complex; A Curious Old Character I Know.

THE GIFT OUTRIGHT

Robert Frost

The land was ours before we were the land's.
She was our land more than a hundred years
Before we were her people. She was ours
In Massachusetts, in Virginia;
But we were England's, still colonials,
Possessing what we still were unpossessed by,
Possessed by what we now no more possessed,
Something we were withholding made us weak
Until we found out that it was ourselves
We were withholding from our land of living,
And forthwith found salvation in surrender.
Such as we were we gave ourselves outright

(The deed of gift was many deeds of war)
To the land vaguely realizing westward,
But still unstoried, artless, unenhanced,
Such as she was, such as she would become.

Author and Selection Notes

Robert Frost (1874-1963) won innumerable awards, including the Pulitzer Prize four times. Though he wrote usually with the flavor of New England, he interpreted all of America. John Ciardi, well-known poet and critic, calls the preceding poem "the noblest utterance yet to be spoken of the American continent." Jointly selected by Frost and President Kennedy for the 1962 inauguration, "The Gift Outright" is an expression of our national dream.

Questions and Exercises

1. Explain what Frost means by "The land was ours before we were the land's."
2. What influence has the Westward movement, the moving frontier, had upon American democracy?
3. What verb tense does the poet choose in speaking of the dream's realization?
4. What is the tone of this poem? Why is it appropriate to the theme of the poem?
5. Theme Topics: England the Mother, America the Child; The Maturing of a Country; Early America—"Unstoried, Artless, Unenhanced"; Ruggedness—the Foundation Stone for Democracy; America's Future.

FOUR YEARS IN A SHED

Eve Curie

A man chosen at random from a crowd to read an account of the discovery of radium would not have doubted for one moment that radium existed: beings whose critical sense has not been sharpened and simultaneously deformed by specialized culture keep their imaginations fresh. They are ready to accept an unexpected fact, however extraordinary it may appear, and to wonder at it.

The physicist colleagues of the Curies received the news in

From *Madame Curie* by Eve Curie. Copyright 1937 by Doubleday & Company, Inc. Reprinted by permission.

slightly different fashion. The special properties of polonium and radium upset fundamental theories in which scientists had believed for centuries. How was one to explain the spontaneous radiation of the radioactive bodies? The discovery upset a world of acquired knowledge and contradicted the most firmly established ideas on the composition of matter. Thus the physicist kept on the reserve. He was violently interested in Pierre and Marie's work, he could perceive its infinite developments, but before being convinced he awaited the acquisition of decisive results. The attitude of the chemist was even more downright. By definition, a chemist only believes in the existence of a new substance when he has seen the substance, touched it, weighed and examined it, confronted it with acids, bottled it, and when he has determined its "atomic weight."

Now, up to the present, nobody had seen radium. Nobody knew the weight of radium. And the chemists, faithful to their principles, concluded: "No atomic weight, no radium. Show us some radium and we will believe you."

To show polonium and radium to the incredulous, to prove to the world the existence of their "children," and to complete their own conviction, M. and Mme Curie were now to labor for four years.

The aim was to obtain pure radium and polonium. In the most strongly radioactive products the scientists had prepared, these substances figured only in imperceptible traces. Pierre and Marie already knew the method by which they could hope to isolate the new metals, but the separation could not be made except by treating very large quantities of crude material.

Here arose three agonizing questions:

How were they to get a sufficient quantity of ore? What premises could they use to effect their treatment? What money was there to pay the inevitable cost of the work?

Pitchblende, in which polonium and radium were hidden, was a costly ore, treated at the St Joachimsthal mines in Bohemia for the extraction of uranium salts used in the manufacture of glass. Tons of pitchblende would cost a great deal: a great deal too much for the Curie household.

Ingenuity was to make up for wealth. According to the expectation of the two scientists, the extraction of uranium should leave, intact in the ore, such traces of polonium and radium as the ore contains. There was no reason why these traces should not be found in the residue. And, whereas crude pitchblende was costly, its residue after treatment had very slight value. By asking an

Austrian colleague for a recommendation to the directors of the mine of St Joachimsthal would it not be possible to obtain a considerable quantity of such residue for a reasonable price?

It was simple enough: but somebody had to think of it.

It was necessary, of course, to buy this crude material and pay for its transportation to Paris. Pierre and Marie appropriated the required sum from their very slight savings. They were not so foolish as to ask for official credits. . . . If two physicists on the scent of an immense discovery had asked the University of Paris or the French government for a grant to buy pitchblende residue they would have been laughed at. In any case their letter would have been lost in the files of some office, and they would have had to wait months for a reply, probably unfavorable in the end. Out of the traditions and principles of the French Revolution, which had created the metric system, founded the Normal School, and encouraged science in many circumstances, the State seemed to have retained, after more than a century, only the deplorable words pronounced by Fouquier-Tinville at the trial in which Lavoisier was condemned to the guillotine: "The Republic has no need for scientists."

But at least could there not be found, in the numerous buildings attached to the Sorbonne, some kind of suitable workroom to lend to the Curie couple? Apparently not. After vain attempts, Pierre and Marie staggered back to their point of departure, which is to say the School of Physics where Pierre taught, to the little room where Marie had done her first experiments. The room gave on a courtyard, and on the other side of the yard there was a wooden shack, an abandoned shed, with a skylight roof in such bad condition that it admitted the rain. The Faculty of Medicine had formerly used the place as a dissecting room, but for a long time now it had not even been considered fit to house the cadavers. No floor: an uncertain layer of bitumen covered the earth. It was furnished with some worn kitchen tables, a blackboard which had landed there for no known reason, and an old cast-iron stove with a rusty pipe.

A workman would not willingly have worked in such a place: Marie and Pierre, nevertheless, resigned themselves to it. The shed had one advantage: it was so untempting, so miserable, that nobody thought of refusing them the use of it. Schutzenberger, the director of the school, had always been very kind to Pierre Curie and no doubt regretted that he had nothing better to offer. However that may be, he offered nothing else; and the couple, very pleased at not being put out into the street with their material, thanked him, saying that "this would do" and that they would "make the best of it."

As they were taking possession of the shed, a reply arrived from Austria. Good news! By extraordinary luck, the residue of recent extraction of uranium had not been scattered. The useless material had been piled up in a no-man's-land planted with pine trees, near the mine of St Joachimsthal. Thanks to the intercession of Professor Suess and the Academy of Science of Vienna, the Austrian government, which was the proprietor of the State factory there, decided to present a ton of residue to the two French lunatics who thought they needed it. If, later on, they wished to be sent a greater quantity of the material, they could obtain it at the mine on the best terms. For the moment the Curies had to pay only the transportation charges on a ton of ore.

One morning a heavy wagon, like those which deliver coal, drew up in the Rue Lhomond before the School of Physics. Pierre and Marie were notified. They hurried bareheaded into the street in their laboratory gowns. Pierre, who was never agitated, kept his calm; but the more exuberant Marie could not contain her joy at the sight of the sacks that were being unloaded. It was pitchblende, *her* pitchblende, for which she had received a notice some days before from the freight station. Full of curiosity and impatience, she wanted to open one of the sacks and contemplate her treasure without further waiting. She cut the strings, undid the coarse sackcloth and plunged her two hands into the dull brown ore, still mixed with pine needles from Bohemia.

There was where radium was hidden. It was from there that Marie must extract it, even if she had to treat a mountain of this inert stuff like dust on the road.

Marya Sklodovska had lived through the most intoxicating moments of her student life in a garret; Marie Curie was to know wonderful joys again in a dilapidated shed. It was a strange sort of beginning over again, in which a sharp subtle happiness (which probably no woman before Marie had ever experienced) twice elected the most miserable setting.

The shed in the Rue Lhomond surpassed the most pessimistic expectations of discomfort. In summer, because of its skylights, it was as stifling as a hothouse. In winter one did not know whether to wish for rain or frost; if it rained, the water fell drop by drop, with a soft, nerve-racking noise, on the ground or on the worktables, in places which the physicists had to mark in order to avoid putting apparatus there. If it froze, one froze. There was no recourse. The stove, even when it was stoked white, was a complete disappointment. If one went near enough to touch it one received a little heat, but two steps away and one was back in the zone of ice.

It was almost better for Marie and Pierre to get used to the cruelty of the outside temperature, since their technical installation—hardly existent—possessed no chimneys to carry off noxious gases, and the greater part of their treatment had to be made in the open air, in the courtyard. When a shower came the physicists hastily moved their apparatus inside: to keep on working without being suffocated they set up draughts between the opened door and windows.

Marie probably did not boast to Dr Vauthier of this very peculiar cure for attacks of tuberculosis.

We had no money, no laboratory and no help in the conduct of this important and difficult task [she was to write later]. It was like creating something out of nothing, and if Casimir Dluski once called my student years "the heroic years of my sister-in-law's life," I may say without exaggeration that this period was, for my husband and myself, the heroic period of our common existence.

. . . And yet it was in this miserable old shed that the best and happiest years of our life were spent, entirely consecrated to work. I sometimes passed the whole day stirring a mass in ebullition, with an iron rod nearly as big as myself. In the evening I was broken with fatigue.

In such conditions M. and Mme Curie worked for four years from 1898 to 1902.

During the first year they busied themselves with the chemical separation of radium and polonium and they studied the radiation of the products (more and more active) thus obtained. Before long they considered it more practical to separate their efforts. Pierre Curie tried to determine the properties of radium, and to know the new metal better. Marie continued those chemical treatments which would permit her to obtain salts of pure radium.

In this division of labor Marie had chosen the "man's job." She accomplished the toil of a day laborer. Inside the shed her husband was absorbed by delicate experiments. In the courtyard, dressed in her old dust-covered and acid-stained smock, her hair blown by the wind, surrounded by smoke which stung her eyes and throat, Marie was a sort of factory all by herself.

I came to treat as many as twenty kilograms of matter at a time [she writes], which had the effect of filling the shed with great jars full of precipitates and liquids. It was killing work to carry the receivers, to pour off the liquids and to stir, for hours at a stretch, the boiling matter in a smelting basin.

Radium showed no intention of allowing itself to be known by human creatures. Where were the days when Marie naively expected the radium content of pitchblende to be *one per cent*? The radiation of the new substance was so powerful that a tiny quantity of radium, disseminated through the ore, was the source of striking phenomena which could be easily observed and measured. The difficult, the impossible thing, was to isolate this minute quantity, to separate it from the gangue in which it was so intimately mixed.

The days of work became months and years: Pierre and Marie were not discouraged. This material which resisted them, which defended its secrets, fascinated them. United by their tenderness, united by their intellectual passions, they had, in a wooden shack, the "anti-natural" existence for which they had both been made, she as well as he.

At this period we were entirely absorbed by the new realm that was, thanks to an unhoped-for discovery, opening before us [Marie was to write]. In spite of the difficulties of our working conditions, we felt very happy. Our days were spent at the laboratory. In our poor shed there reigned a great tranquility: sometimes, as we watched over some operation, we would walk up and down, talking about work in the present and in the future: when we were cold a cup of hot tea taken near the stove comforted us. We lived in our single preoccupation as if in a dream.

... We saw only very few persons at the laboratory; among the physicists and chemists there were a few who came from time to time, either to see our experiments or to ask for advice from Pierre Curie, whose competence in several branches of physics was well-known. Then took place some conversations before the blackboard—the sort of conversation one remembers well because it acts as a stimulant for scientific interest and the ardor for work without interrupting the course of reflection and without troubling that atmosphere of peace and meditation which is the true atmosphere of a laboratory.

Whenever Pierre and Marie, alone in this poor place, left their apparatus for a moment and quietly let their tongues run on, their talk about their beloved radium passed from the transcendent to the childish.

"I wonder what *It* will be like, what *It* will look like," Marie said one day with the feverish curiosity of a child who has been promised a toy. "Pierre, what form do you imagine *It* will take?"

"I don't know," the physicist answered gently. "I should like it to have a very beautiful color. . . ."

It is odd to observe that in Marie Curie's correspondence we find, upon this prodigious effort, none of the sensitive comments, decked out with imagery, which used to flash suddenly amid the familiarity of her letters. Was it because the years of exile had somewhat relaxed the young woman's intimacy with her people? Was she too pressed by work to find time?

The essential reason for this reserve is perhaps to be sought elsewhere. It was not by chance that Mme Curie's letters ceased to be original at the exact moment when the story of her life became exceptional. As student, teacher or young wife, Marie could tell her story. . . . But now she was isolated by all that was secret and inexpressible in her scientific vocation. Among those she loved there was no longer anybody able to understand, to realize her worries and her difficult design. She could share her obsessions with only one person, Pierre Curie, companion. To him alone could she confide rare thoughts and dreams. Marie, from now on, was to present to all others, however near they might be to her heart, an almost commonplace picture of herself. She was to paint for them only the bourgeois side of her life. She was to find sometimes accents full of contained emotion to express her happiness as a woman. But of her work she was to speak only in laconic, inexpressive little phrases: news in three lines, without even attempting to suggest the wonders that work meant to her.

Here we feel an absolute determination not to illustrate the singular profession she had chosen by literature. Through subtle modesty, and also through horror of vain talk and everything super-fluous, Marie concealed herself, dug herself in; or rather, she offered only one of her profiles. Shyness, boredom, or reason, whatever it may have been, the scientist of genius effaced and dissimulated herself behind "a woman like all others."

Marie to Bronya, 1899:

Our life is always the same. We work a lot but we sleep well, so our health does not suffer. The evenings are taken up by caring for the child. In the morning I dress her and give her her food, then I can generally go out at about nine. During the whole of this year we have not been either to the theater or a concert, and we have not paid one visit. For that matter, we feel very well. . . . I miss my family enormously, above all you, my dears, and Father. I often think of my isolation with grief. I cannot complain of anything else, for our health is not bad, the child is growing well, and I have the best husband one could dream of; I could never have imagined finding one like him. He is a true gift of heaven, and the more we live together the more we love each other.

Our work is progressing. I shall soon have a lecture to deliver on the subject. It should have been last Saturday but I was prevented from giving it, so it will no doubt be this Saturday, or else in a fortnight.

This work, which is so dryly mentioned in passing, was in fact progressing magnificently. In the course of the years 1899 and 1900 Pierre and Marie Curie published a report on the discovery of "induced radioactivity" due to radium, another on the effects of radioactivity, and another on the electric charge carried by the rays. And at last they drew up, for the Congress of Physics of 1900, a general report on the radioactive substances, which aroused immense interest among the scientists of Europe.

The development of the new science of radioactivity was rapid, overwhelming—the Curies needed fellow workers. Up to now they had had only the intermittent help of a laboratory assistant named Petit, an honest man who came to work for them outside his hours of service—working out of personal enthusiasm, almost in secret. But they now required technicians of the first order. Their discovery had important extensions in the domain of chemistry, which demanded attentive study. They wished to associate competent research workers with them.

Our work on radioactivity began in solitude [Marie was to write]. But before the breadth of the task it became more and more evident that collaboration would be useful. Already in 1898 one of the laboratory chiefs of the school, G. Bemont, had given us some passing help. Toward 1900 Pierre Curie entered into relations with a young chemist, André Debierne, assistant in the laboratory of Professor Friedel, who esteemed him highly. André Debierne willingly accepted work on radioactivity. He undertook especially the research of a new radio element, the existence of which was suspected in the group of iron and rare clays. He discovered this element, named "actinium." Even though he worked in the physico-chemical laboratory at the Sorbonne directed by Jean Perrin, he frequently came to see us in our shed and soon became a very close friend to us, to Dr Curie and later on to our children.

Thus, even before radium and polonium were isolated, a French scientist, André Debierne, had discovered a "brother," *actinium*.

At about the same period [Marie tells us], a young physicist, Georges Sagnac, engaged in studying X rays, came frequently to talk to Pierre Curie about the analogies that might exist between these rays, their secondary rays, and the radiation of radioactive bodies. Together they performed a work on the electric charge carried by these secondary rays.

Marie continued to treat, kilogram by kilogram, the tons of pitchblende residue which were sent her on several occasions from St Joachimsthal. With her terrible patience, she was able to be, every day for four years, a physicist, a chemist, a specialized worker, an engineer and a laboring man all at once. Thanks to her brain and muscle, the old tables in the shed held more and more concentrated products—products more and more rich in radium. Mme Curie was approaching the end: she no longer stood in the courtyard, enveloped in bitter smoke, to watch the heavy basins of material in fusion. She was now at the stage of purification and of the "fractional crystallization" of strongly radioactive solutions. But the poverty of her haphazard equipment hindered her work more than ever. It was now that she needed a spotlessly clean workroom and apparatus perfectly protected against cold, heat and dirt. In this shed, open to every wind, iron and coal dust was afloat which, to Marie's despair, mixed itself into the products purified with so much care. Her heart sometimes constricted before these little daily accidents, which took so much of her time and strength.

Pierre was so tired of the interminable struggle that he would have been quite ready to abandon it. Of course, he did not dream of dropping the study of radium and of radioactivity. But he would willingly have renounced, for the time being, the special operation of preparing pure radium. The obstacles seemed insurmountable. Could they not resume this work later on, under better conditions? More attached to the meaning of natural phenomena than to their material reality, Pierre Curie was exasperated to see the paltry results to which Marie's exhausting effort had led. He advised an armistice.

He counted without his wife's character. Marie wanted to isolate radium and she would isolate it. She scorned fatigue and difficulties, and even the gaps in her own knowledge which complicated her task. After all, she was only a very young scientist: she still had not the certainty and great culture Pierre had acquired by twenty years' work, and sometimes she stumbled across phenomena or methods of calculation of which she knew very little, and for which she had to make hasty studies.

So much the worse! With stubborn eyes under her great brow, she clung to her apparatus and her test tubes.

In 1902, forty-five months after the day on which the Curies announced the probable existence of radium, Marie finally carried off the victory in this war of attrition: she succeeded in preparing a decigram of pure radium, and made a first determination of the atomic weight of the new substance, which was 225.

The incredulous chemists—of whom there were still a few—could only bow before the facts, before the superhuman obstinacy of a woman.

Radium officially existed.

It was nine o'clock at night. Pierre and Marie Curie were in their little house at 108 Boulevard Kellermann, where they had been living since 1900. The house suited them well. From the boulevard, where three rows of trees half hid the fortifications, could be seen only a dull wall and a tiny door. But behind the one-story house, hidden from all eyes, there was a narrow provincial garden, rather pretty and very quiet. And from the "barrier" of Gentilly they could escape on their bicycles toward the suburbs and the woods. . . .

Old Dr Curie, who lived with the couple, had retired to his room. Marie had bathed her child and put it to bed, and had stayed for a long time beside the cot. This was a rite. When Irène did not feel her mother near her at night she would call out for her incessantly, with that "Mé!" which was to be our substitute for "Mamma" always. And Marie, yielding to the implacability of the four-year-old baby, climbed the stairs, seated herself beside the child and stayed there in the darkness until the young voice gave way to light, regular breathing. Only then would she go down again to Pierre, who was growing impatient. In spite of his kindness, he was the most possessive and jealous of husbands. He was so used to the constant presence of his wife that her least eclipse kept him from thinking freely. If Marie delayed too long near her daughter, he received her on her return with a reproach so unjust as to be comic:

"You never think of anything but that child!"

Pierre walked slowly about the room. Marie sat down and made some stitches on the hem of Irène's new apron. One of her principles was never to buy ready-made clothes for the child: she thought them too fancy and impractical. In the days when Bronya was in Paris the two sisters cut out their children's dresses together, according to patterns of their own invention. These patterns still served for Marie.

But this evening she could not fix her attention. Nervous, she got up; then, suddenly:

"Suppose we go down there for a moment?"

There was a note of supplication in her voice—altogether superfluous, for Pierre, like herself, longed to go back to the shed they had left two hours before. Radium, fanciful as a living creature, endearing as a love, called them back to its dwelling, to the wretched laboratory.

The day's work had been hard, and it would have been more reasonable for the couple to rest. But Pierre and Marie were not always reasonable. As soon as they had put on their coats and told Dr Curie of their flight, they were in the street. They went on foot, arm in arm, exchanging few words. After the crowded streets of this queer district, with its factory buildings, wastelands and poor tenements, they arrived in the Rue Lhomond and crossed the little courtyard. Pierre put the key in the lock. The door squeaked, as it had squeaked thousands of times, and admitted them to their realm, to their dream.

"Don't light the lamps!" Marie said in the darkness. Then she added with a little laugh:

"Do you remember the day when you said to me 'I should like radium to have a beautiful color'?"

The reality was more entrancing than the simple wish of long ago. Radium had something better than "a beautiful color": it was spontaneously luminous. And in the somber shed where, in the absence of cupboards, the precious particles in their tiny glass receivers were placed on tables or on shelves nailed to the wall, their phosphorescent bluish outlines gleamed, suspended in the night.

"Look . . . Look!" the young woman murmured.

She went forward cautiously, looked for and found a straw-bottomed chair. She sat down in the darkness and silence. Their two faces turned toward the pale glimmering, the mysterious sources of radiation, toward radium—their radium. Her body leaning forward, her head eager, Marie took up again the attitude which had been hers an hour earlier at the bedside of her sleeping child.

Her companion's hand lightly touched her hair.

She was to remember forever this evening of glowworms, this magic.

Author and Selection Notes

Eve Curie (1904-   ), daughter of the famous Pierre and Marie Curie who discovered radium, is a talented writer in her own right, also a concert pianist, musical critic, and public lecturer.

Questions and Exercises

1. In presenting the discoverer of radium, Eve Curie gives an intimate portrayal of the woman who was wife and mother as well as dedicated scientist. Compare and contrast Pierre and Marie as scientists and parents.

2. Find the paragraph beginning: "Ingenuity was to make up for wealth." Point out the topic sentence and analyze the development of this paragraph. Continue a similar analysis of the following paragraphs until the good news arrived from Austria.

3. How does the author make radium seem almost a human being?

4. As she interprets her mother's human side, what does the author mean by Marie's "terrible patience," her "character," and her "stubborn eyes"?

5. Theme Topics: The Curie Marriage as a Working Partnership; Marie Curie as a Mother; Elements of Greatness in Madame Curie; Resistance to New Ideas; The Lean Years; The Woman with Brains.

CHOOSE SOMETHING LIKE A STAR

Robert Frost

O Star (the fairest one in sight),
We grant your loftiness the right
To some obscurity of cloud—
It will not do to say of night,
Since dark is what brings out your light.
Some mystery becomes the proud.
But to be wholly taciturn
In your reserve is not allowed.
Say something to us we can learn
By heart and when alone repeat.
Say something! And it says "I burn."
But say with what degree of heat.
Talk Fahrenheit, talk Centigrade.
Use language we can comprehend.
Tell us what elements you blend.
It gives us strangely little aid,
But does tell something in the end.
And steadfast as Keats' Eremite,
Not even stooping from its sphere,
It asks a little of us here.
It asks of us a certain height,
So when at times the mob is swayed
To carry praise or blame too far,
We may choose something like a star
To stay our minds on and be staid.

Author and Selection Notes

See page 206.

Questions and Exercises

1. Notice the tone of elevation and grace as Frost speaks from his deep religious nature. How does he say we may escape from the restless business about us?

2. Explain the plural "we." Is its use effective here?

3. The star is used as a symbol of what?

4. Discuss any of Frost's other poems reflecting his religion which you have read.

5. Theme Topics: Robert Frost's Religion; When Times Are Tough; The Necessity of an Unshakeable God; My Defense Against the Mob.

OUT OF EVIL, GOOD
Dorothy Thompson

"I am the spirit who willing Evil forever creates Good."

This cryptic remark is uttered by Mephistopheles in Goethe's *Faust,* to illustrate the paradoxical nature of good and evil. And one might, with equal truth, put it the other way. Many acts aimed at the creation of good bring unforeseen evils in their train.

For centuries mankind has recognized war to be evil and waged it (or believed it was waging it) only as a last resort for the attainment of what it considered to be just or even benevolent aims, or conditions of survival, or defense against aggression and the greed and domination of others. By another paradox, as war has become ever more total, unlimited and destructive, involving whole populations, societies and economies, along with, and as a consequence of, the disposition to regard the enemy as the embodiment of all evil, the will to end war forever has likewise increased. So that no matter what policies are pursued by states, likely to lead to war, they must, if they are to win popular support, be advocated in the name of peace.

Reprinted from *Ladies' Home Journal,* November, 1955, Volume 72. Reprinted by special permission of the *Ladies' Home Journal.* Copyright by The Curtis Publishing Company.

Men have believed, even, that the instruments that would make war more destructive would restrain it.

When Alfred Nobel, himself a pacifist, invented dynamite he was aware that it would vastly increase the explosive power of weapons, knew that there was no secret about it, and was convinced that when nations realized what they could do to each other, they would abandon war. But they did not.

I recall hearing my elders discuss the earliest airplanes, predicting then that when armies could bomb civilians and cities from the air, war would stop. But airplanes piloted by all belligerents became war's most terrifying instruments.

The German scientists Bosch and Haber, who discovered a process for extracting nitrates from air, had worked for that end only to solve a pressing need of their own and other economies for a cheap, universally available, agricultural fertilizer. But it was used almost immediately in the First World War as a chief ingredient of poison gas. Gas was not used in World War II, not because it had proved a "deterrent to war," and not even because of fear of reprisals, but because, with rapidly moving armies (as contrasted with trench warfare), it was no longer a very efficient weapon.

So far, therefore, the accelerating invention of more and more destructive weapons has not abolished war, nor have solemn international conventions entered upon during peace restrained their use if war came. Armies demobilized in peace are quickly remobilized under threat of war; swords beaten into plowshares are reforged; and we may assume that if every stockpile of atomic bombs and weapons were destroyed tomorrow morning they would be reconstituted in war, since the knowledge of how to make them would continue to exist. Though fear of atomic war may be—and indeed is—a deterrent, it is no cure. And fear can itself contribute to precipitating atomic war, since the overwhelming advantage in thermonuclear weapons is with those who use them by surprise attack.

Atomic fission was achieved, probably a generation earlier than it otherwise would have been, purely for war purposes. Its first demonstration was at Hiroshima and Nagasaki. The face it presented to the world was the face of doom. It has been associated in men's minds with evil and terror. The fact that America used it—and in the way we did—lost us the confidence of people all over the globe. It was not condoned by this writer then or now.

And yet by the paradox between evil and good discerned by Goethe, atomic fission has opened the prospect of a world in which the most basic and perennial cause of war *and* violent revolution may be abolished once and for all, in the course of a few generations.

The most enlightened and imaginative act of President Eisenhower (whose Administration has been marked by a number of such acts) was not the meeting at the "summit" in Geneva last July, but the meeting of world atomic scientists, including Soviet Academicians, that immediately followed it. The papers they read, the reports they gave, the discussions they held, and the exhibits to which they all contributed, announced the dawn of the greatest industrial revolution in history, engendering justified hope that it may be that "revolution for civilization" predicted for the twentieth century by Victor Hugo.

The basic causes of armed conquests and of what is called imperialism have been economic—the pressure of population on land and land resources.

Nature has not distributed these resources equally among nations and peoples. Always there have been have and have-not nations; and, always, vigorous, industrious and inventive peoples, aspiring to create and maintain prosperous, flourishing cultures and societies, have sought abroad what did not exist at home. When they could not get it by peaceful trade, they got it by war. When they found it among peoples unable or unwilling to develop or use it, they staked out development claims, legalized them by treaties with local rulers, and prepared to defend them by war.

When their populations became too dense to be sustained on the food and mineral resources available at home, they colonized them among primitive tribes abroad, to turn hunting grounds into pastures and fields to produce their own nourishment and a surplus for the home country; to plant cotton for homeland factories and to open mines and dredge rivers for necessary industrial raw materials. Eventually, colonists and/or natives revolted, to build their own economies, the revolts often leading to wars.

If guilt be attached to this, who can plead innocence? Every great civilization and culture of which history has a record has been driven by economic necessity to expansionism. Will any American plead that it would have been better for mankind as a whole to have left this vast continent to its few primitive native inhabitants, instead of making it, in two centuries, into a beautiful and prosperous home for a large part of the world's population—and without "wiping out the Indians," who are more numerous now than in the days of George Washington?

Wars have been fought to get, or to keep, gold and silver, copper and tin, coal and iron, agricultural land and oil. Desert tribes have fought one another for access to water wells for their flocks and themselves. And this has happened because there never have been sufficient food and resources—yes, even water—existing or adequately developed to permit all peoples to attain, even were their abilities equal, a satisfactory standard of living.

The element most essential to life is air. People can live for weeks without food and days without water, but not for five minutes without air. But nations have never fought for air, for the simple reason that it is a universal and inexhaustible commodity.

The prospect that opened up last August, in Geneva, was of a commodity, inexhaustible because capable of re-creating and even increasing itself, which could eventually fuel every factory, turn every wheel, light every building and propel every engine everywhere. The mind finds it difficult first to believe it is true, and even harder to envisage the social and political consequences. But it *is* true, though it is not yet a factual reality. And the time lag between theoretical knowledge and practical realization becomes ever shorter.

Great Britain, for instance, with her greatly diminished and everywhere threatened empire, is today a have-not nation. Her only source of power energy is coal, now rapidly dwindling. Her scientists are, therefore, concentrating on the development of energy from atomic fission, fully confident that within a generation British industry will be totally atomic.

By reason of the self-reproducing nature of the energy itself, monopoly, as with air, offers no advantages. The more all knowledge is shared, the more rapidly will all peoples reap the results. And, following the reports from Geneva, it was fascinating to learn that all the participating countries, even under cover of secrecy, had made nearly identical progress—some more in one direction, all in fundamental knowledge.

Transportation enters an entirely new era. Coal and oil present an immense haulage problem, even within large countries. But a child can carry in a little bundle the atomic-energy equivalent of 3000 tons of coal.

Nor, say the scientists, will the cost be prohibitive. Eventually it will be the cheapest form of energy.

Meanwhile, and simultaneously, enormous advances are being made in the field of food chemistry—advances that promise to find, from sources never before dreamed of, the proteins, carbohydrates and fats with which we fuel our bodies.

Violent social revolutions are the results of revolutions in modes of life produced by changes in the production system. The French

Revolution was induced by the industrial revolution that preceded it and pronounced the death of feudalism, which was based on land. The Russian Revolution, in fact if not in theory, was impelled by the drive rapidly to industrialize a semifeudal agricultural country without adequate private capital or the desire to invite foreign capital. The mode of life foreshadowed by the atomic revolution is hardly predictable. But if we can assume that food and energy will become present in inexhaustible abundance within, say, the next hundred years, the basic causes of international war will have been removed—and a basic cause of the class struggle. The day there is enough for all—enough, at least, to satisfy the basic needs of man and his societies; the day when all, and not merely some, can survive, and not at the expense of others—will culminate the greatest revolution in human history. Of course men may cut off this prospect by blowing up a large part of the planet first. If so, one can attribute it only to original sin.

Atomic energy can perform the greatest evil or the greatest good. What it cannot do, of itself, is to choose which. The choice is not even in the hands of the scientists who released and are releasing this power. It lies with political leaders everywhere.

Author and Selection Notes

Dorothy Thompson (1894-1961) was a leading American newspaper columnist, lecturer, and radio commentator. For many years she was editorial writer for *The Ladies' Home Journal,* in which "Out of Evil, Good" was published.

Questions and Exercises

1. In what ways does Dorothy Thompson use the title to give direction and unity to the essay?

2. Find the transitional sentence that turns from the subject of war to that of economic resources. How are the two subjects inseparable?

3. Air is called an "inexhaustible commodity." In the light of recent scientific experimentation is the term still applicable?

4. How may atomic power lessen the threat of Thomas Robert Malthus' theory that the population, if unchecked, will increase beyond the food supply?

5. Compare the attitude toward war in Thompson's "Out of Evil, Good" with that in Pope Urban II's "Sermon Calling for a Crusade."

6. Theme Topics: Out of Weakness, Strength; Out of Failure, Progress; Out of Ugliness, Beauty; Out of Defeat, Victory; Out of Cowardice, Courage; Out of Hate, Forgiveness.

REVERENCE FOR LIFE

Albert Schweitzer

Two perceptions cast their shadows over my existence. One consists in my realization that the world is inexplicably mysterious and full of suffering; the other in the fact that I have been born into a period of spiritual decadence in mankind. I have become familiar with and ready to deal with each, through the thinking which has led me to the ethical and affirmative position of Reverence for Life. In that principle my life has found a firm footing and a clear path to follow.

I therefore stand and work in the world as one who aims at making men less shallow and morally better by making them think.

With the spirit of the age I am in complete disagreement, because it is filled with disdain for thinking. That such is its attitude is, to some extent, to be explained by the fact that thought has never yet reached the goal which it must set before itself. Time after time it was convinced that it had clearly established an attitude toward life which was in accordance with knowledge and ethically satisfactory. But time after time the truth came out that it had not succeeded.

Doubts, therefore, could well arise as to whether thinking would ever be capable of answering current questions about the world and our relation to it in such a way that we could give a meaning and a content to our lives.

But today in addition to that neglect of thought there is also prevalent a mistrust of it. The organized political, social, and religious associations of our time are at work to induce the individual man not to arrive at his convictions by his own thinking but to make his own such convictions as they keep ready-made for him. Any man who thinks for himself and at the same time is spiritually free, is to them something inconvenient and even uncanny. He does not offer sufficient guarantee that he will merge himself in their organization in the way they wish. All corporate bodies look today for their strength not so much to the spiritual worth of the ideas which they represent and to that of the people who belong to them, as to the attainment of the highest possible degree of unity and exclusiveness. It is in this that they expect to find their strongest power for offense and defense.

Hence the spirit of the age rejoices, instead of lamenting, that thinking seems to be unequal to its task, and gives it no credit for what, in spite of imperfections, it has already accomplished. It refuses to admit, what is nevertheless the fact, that all spiritual progress up to today has come about through the achievement of thought, or to reflect that thinking may still be able in the future to accomplish what it has not succeeded in accomplishing as yet. Of such considerations the spirit of the age takes no account. Its only concern is to discredit individual thinking in every possible way, and it deals with that on the lines of the saying: "Whosoever hath not, from him shall be taken away that which he hath."

Thus, his whole life long, the man of today is exposed to influences which are bent on robbing him of all confidence in his own thinking. The spirit of spiritual dependence to which he is called on to surrender is in everything that he hears or reads; it is in the people whom he meets every day; it is in the parties and associations which have claimed him as their own; it pervades all the circumstances of his life.

From every side and in the most varied ways it is dinned into him that the truths and convictions which he needs for life must be taken by him from the associations which have rights over him. The spirit of the age never lets him come to himself. Over and over again convictions are forced upon him in the same way as, by means of the electric advertisements which flare in the streets of every large town, any company which has sufficient capital to get itself securely established, exercises pressure on him at every step he takes to induce him to buy their boot polish or their soup tablets.

By the spirit of the age, then, the man of today is forced into skepticism about his own thinking, in order to make him receptive to truth which comes to him from authority. To all this constant influence he cannot make the resistance that is desirable because he is an overworked and distracted being without power to concentrate. Moreover, the manifold material trammels which are his lot work upon his mentality in such a way that he comes at last to believe himself unqualified even to make any claim to thoughts of his own.

His self-confidence is also diminished through the pressure exercised upon him by the huge and daily increasing mass of knowledge. He is no longer in a position to take in as something which he has grasped all the new discoveries that are constantly announced; he has to accept them as fact although he does not understand them. This being his relation to scientific truth he is tempted to acquiesce in the idea that in matters of thought also his judgment cannot be trusted.

Thus do the circumstances of the age do their best to deliver us up to the spirit of the age.

The seed of skepticism has germinated. In fact, the modern man has no longer any spiritual self-confidence at all. Behind a self-confident exterior he conceals a great inward lack of confidence. In spite of his great capacity in material matters he is an altogether stunted being, because he makes no use of his capacity for thinking. It will ever remain incomprehensible that our generation, which has shown itself so great by its achievements in discovery and invention, could fall so low spiritually as to give up thinking.

In a period which regards as absurd and little worth, as antiquated and long ago left far behind, whatever it feels to be in any way akin to rationalism or free thought, and which even mocks at the vindication of unalienable human rights which was secured in the eighteenth century, I acknowledge myself to be one who places all his confidence in rational thinking. I venture to say to our generation that it must not think it has done with rationalism because the rationalism of the past had to give first place to romanticism, and then to a *Realpolitik* which is coming to dominate the spiritual sphere as well as the material. When it has run the gauntlet of the follies of this universal *Realpolitik* and has thereby got itself into deeper and deeper misery, both spiritual and material, it will discover at last that there is nothing for it to do but trust itself to a new rationalism, deeper and more efficient than the old, and in that seek its salvation.

Renunciation of thinking is a declaration of spiritual bankruptcy. Where there is no longer a conviction that men can get to know the truth by their own thinking, skepticism begins. Those who work to make our age skeptical in this way, do so in the expectation that, as a result of denouncing all hope of self-discovered truth, men will end by accepting as truth what is forced upon them with authority and by propaganda.

But their calculations are wrong. No one who opens the sluices to let a flood of skepticism pour itself over the land must expect to be able to bring it back within its proper bounds. Of those who let themselves get too disheartened to try any longer to discover truth by their own thinking, only a few find a substitute for it in truth taken from others. The mass of people remain skeptical.

They lose all feeling for truth, and all sense of need for it as well, finding themselves quite comfortable in a life without thought driven now here, now there, from one opinion to another.

But the acceptance of authoritative truth, even if that truth has both spiritual and ethical content, does not bring skepticism to an end; it merely covers it up. Man's unnatural condition of not believing that any truth is discoverable by himself, continues, and produces its natural results. The city of truth cannot be built on the swampy ground of skepticism. Our spiritual life is rotten throughout because it is permeated through and through with skepticism, and we live in consequence in a world which in every respect is full of falsehood. We are not far from shipwreck on the rock of wanting to have even truth organized.

Truth taken over by skepticism which has become believing has not the spiritual qualities of that which originated in thinking. It has been externalized and rendered torpid. It does obtain influence over a man, but it is not capable of uniting itself with him to the very marrow of his being. Living truth is that alone which has its origin in thinking.

Just as a tree bears year after year the same fruit and yet fruit which is each year new, so must all permanently valuable ideas be continually born again in thought. But our age is bent on trying to make the barren tree of skepticism fruitful by tying fruits of truth on its branches.

It is only by confidence in our ability to reach truth by our own individual thinking, that we are capable of accepting truth from outside. Unfettered thought, provided it be deep, never degenerates into subjectivity. With its own ideas it stirs those within itself which enjoy any traditional credit for being true, and exerts itself to be able to possess them as knowledge.

Not less strong than the will to truth must be the will to sincerity. Only an age which can show the courage of sincerity can possess truth which works as a spiritual force within it.

Sincerity is the foundation of the spiritual life.

With its depreciation of thinking our generation has lost its feeling for sincerity and with it that for truth as well. It can therefore be helped only by its being brought once more on to the road of thinking.

Because I have this certainty I oppose the spirit of the age, and take upon myself with confidence the responsibility of taking my part in the rekindling of the fire of thought.

Thought on the lines of Reverence for Life is by its very nature peculiarly qualified to take up the struggle against skepticism. It is elemental.

Elemental thinking is that which starts from the fundamental questions about the relations of man to the universe, about the meaning of life, and about the nature of goodness. It stands in the most immediate connection with the thinking which impulse stirs in everyone. It enters into that thinking, widening and deepening it. . . .

The belief that elemental thinking is now arriving at an ethical and affirmative attitude toward the world and life, which it has hitherto vainly striven to reach, is no self-deception, but is connected with the fact that thinking has become thoroughly realistic.

It used to deal with the world as being only a totality of happenings. With this totality of happenings the only spiritual relation which man can reach is one in which, acknowledging his own natural subordination to it, he secures a spiritual position under it by resignation. To attribute any meaning and purpose to his own activities is impossible with such a conception of the world. He cannot possibly place himself at the service of this totality of happenings which crushes him. His way to acceptance of the world and to ethics is barred.

It thereupon attempts, but in vain, to grasp by means of some sort of explanation of the world what elemental thinking, hindered by this lifeless and incomplete representation of the world, cannot reach in the natural way. This thinking is like a river which on its way to the sea is held up by a range of mountains. Its waters try to find a passage to the sea by roundabout ways. In vain. They only pour themselves into other valleys and fill them. Then, centuries later, the dammed up waters manage to break through.

The world does not consist of happenings only; it contains life as well, and to the life in the world, so far as it comes within my reach, I have to be in a relation which is not only passive but active. By placing myself in the service of that which lives I reach an activity, exerted, upon the world which has meaning and purpose.

However simple and obvious a proceeding it may seem to be when once accomplished, to replace that lifeless idea of the world by a real world which is full of life, a long period of evolution was needed, nevertheless, before it became possible. Just as the solid rock of a mountain range which has risen from the sea first becomes visible when the layers of chalk which covered it have been eroded and washed away by the rain, so, in questions of philosophy, is realistic thinking overlaid by unrealistic.

The idea of Reverence for Life offers itself as the realistic answer to the realistic question of how man and the world are related to each other. Of the world man knows only that everything which exists is, like himself, a manifestation of the Will-to-Live. With this world he stands in a relation of passivity and of activity. On the one hand he is subordinate to the course of events which is given in this totality of life; on the other hand he is capable of affecting the life which comes within his reach by hampering or promoting it, by destroying or maintaining it.

The one possible way of giving meaning to his existence is that of raising his natural relation to the world to a spiritual one. As a being in a passive relation to the world he comes into a spiritual relation to it by resignation. True resignation consists in this: that man, feeling his subordination to the course of world happenings, wins his way to inward freedom from the fortunes which shape the outside of his existence. Inward freedom means that he finds strength to deal with everything that is hard in his lot, in such a way that it all helps to make him a deeper and more inward person, to purify him, and to keep him calm and peaceful. Resignation, therefore, is the spiritual and ethical affirmation of one's own existence. Only he who has gone through the stage of resignation is capable of accepting the world.

As a being in an active relation to the world he comes into a spiritual relation with it by not living for himself alone, but feeling himself one with all life that comes within his reach. He will feel all that life's experiences as his own, he will give it all the help that he possibly can, and will feel all the saving and promotion of life that he has been able to effect as the deepest happiness that can ever fall to his lot.

Let a man once begin to think about the mystery of his life and the links which connect him with the life that fills the world, and he cannot but bring to bear upon his own life and all other life that comes within his reach the principle of Reverence for Life, and manifest this principle by ethical affirmation of life. Existence will thereby become harder for him in every respect than it would be if he lived for himself, but at the same time it will be richer, more beautiful, and happier. It will become, instead of mere living, a real experience of life.

Beginning to think about life and the world leads a man directly and almost irresistibly to Reverence for Life. Such thinking leads to no conclusions which could point in any other direction.

If the man who has once begun to think wishes to persist in his mere living he can do so only by surrendering himself, whenever this idea takes possession of him, to thoughtlessness, and stupefying himself therein. If he perseveres with thinking he can come to no other result than Reverence for Life.

Any thinking by which men assert that they are reaching skepticism or life without ethical ideals, is not thinking but thoughtlessness which poses as thinking, and it proves itself to be such by the fact that it is unconcerned about the mystery of life and the world.

Reverence for Life contains in itself resignation, an affirmative attitude toward the world, and ethics—the three essential elements in a philosophy of life, as mutually interrelated results of thinking.

Up to now there have been systems of thought based on resignation, others based on an affirmative view of the world and still others that sought to satisfy ethics. Not one has there been, however, which has been able to combine the three elements. That is possible only on condition that all three are conceived as essentially products of the universal conviction of Reverence for Life, and are recognized as being one and all contained in it. Resignation and an affirmative view of the world have no separate existence of their own by the side of ethics; they are its lower octaves.

Having its origin in realistic thinking, the ethic of Reverence for life is realistic, and brings man to a realistic and steady facing of reality.

It may seem, at first glance, as if Reverence for Life were something too general and too lifeless to provide the content of a living ethic. But thinking has no need to trouble as to whether its expressions sound living enough, so long as they hit the mark and have life in them. Anyone who comes under the influence of the ethic of Reverence for Life will very soon be able to detect, thanks to what that ethic demands from him, what fire glows in the lifeless expression. The ethic of Reverence for Life is the ethic of Love widened into universality. It is the ethic of Jesus, now recognized as a logical consequence of thought.

Objection is made to this ethic that it sets too high a value on natural life. To this it can retort that the mistake made by all previous systems of ethics has been the failure to recognize that life as such is the mysterious value with which they have to deal. All spiritual life meets us within natural life. Reverence for Life, therefore, is applied to natural life and spiritual life alike. In the parable of Jesus, the shepherd saves not merely the soul of the lost sheep but the whole animal. The stronger the reverence for natural life, the stronger grows also that for spiritual life.

The ethic of Reverence for Life is found particularly strange because it establishes no dividing line between higher and lower, between more valuable and less valuable life. For this omission it has its reasons.

To undertake to lay down universally valid distinctions of value between different kinds of life will end in judging them by the greater or lesser distance at which they seem to stand from us human beings—as we ourselves judge. But that is a purely subjective criterion. Who among us knows what significance any other kind of life has in itself, and as a part of the universe?

Following on such a distinction there comes next the view that there can be life which is worthless, injury to which or destruction of which does not matter. Then in the category of worthless life we come to include, according to circumstances, different kinds of insects, or primitive peoples.

To the man who is truly ethical all life is sacred, including that which from the human point of view seems lower in the scale. He makes distinctions only as each case comes before him, and under the pressure of necessity, as, for example, when it falls to him to decide which of two lives he must sacrifice in order to preserve the other. But all through this series of decisions he is conscious of acting on subjective grounds and arbitrarily, and knows that he bears the responsibility for the life which is sacrificed.

I rejoice over the new remedies for sleeping sickness, which enable me to preserve life, whereas I had previously to watch a painful disease. But every time I have under the microscope the germs which cause the disease, I cannot but reflect that I have to sacrifice this life in order to save other life.

I buy from natives a young fish eagle, which they have caught on a sandbank, in order to rescue it from their cruel hands. But now I have to decide whether I shall let it starve, or kill every day a number of small fishes, in order to keep it alive. I decide on the latter course, but every day I feel it hard that this life must be sacrificed for the other on my responsibility.

Standing, as he does, with the whole body of living creatures under the law of this dilemma (*Selbstentzweiung*) in the will-to-live, man comes again and again into the position of being able to preserve his own life and life generally only at the cost of other life. If he has been touched by the ethic of Reverence for Life, he injures and destroys life only under a necessity which he cannot avoid, and never from thoughtlessness. So far as he is a free man he uses every opportunity of tasting the blessedness of being able to assist life and avert from it suffering and destruction.

Devoted as I was from boyhood to the cause of the protection of animal life, it is a special joy to me that the universal ethic

of Reverence for Life shows the sympathy with animals which
is so often represented as sentimentality, to be a duty which no
thinking man can escape. Hitherto ethics have faced the problem
of man and beast either uncomprehending or helpless. Even when
sympathy with the animal creation was felt to be right, it could
not be brought within the scope of ethics, because ethics were
really focused only on the behavior of man to man.

When will the time come when public opinion will tolerate
no longer any popular amusements which depend on the ill-
treatment of animals?

The ethic, then, which originates in thinking is not "according
to reason," but nonrational and enthusiastic. It marks off no skillfully defined circle of duties, but lays upon each individual the
responsibility for all life within his reach, and compels him to devote
himself to helping it.

Any profound view of the world is mysticism, in that it brings
men into a spiritual relation with the Infinite. The view of Reverence for Life is ethical mysticism. It allows union with the Infinite
to be realized by ethical action. This ethical Mysticism originates in
logical thinking. If our will-to-live begins to think about itself and
the world, we come to experience the life of the world, so far as
it comes within our reach, in our own life, and to devote our will-
to-live to the infinite will-to-live through the deeds we do. Rational
thinking, if it goes deep, ends of necessity in the nonrational of
mysticism. It has, of course, to deal with life and the world, both
of which are nonrational entities.

In the world the infinite will-to-live reveals itself to us as will-
to-create, and this is full of dark and painful riddles for us; in
ourselves it is revealed as will-to-love, which will through us remove
the dilemma (Selbstentzweiung) of the will-to-live.

The concept of Reverence for Life has, therefore, a religious
character. The man who avows his belief in it, and acts upon the
belief, shows a piety which is elemental.

Author and Selection Notes

Often called "the modern Saint Francis" and the greatest humanitarian
of our day, Albert Schweitzer (1875-   ) of Alsace—eminent theologian,
musician, philosopher, and authority on tropical diseases—became a
medical doctor after the age of thirty in order to minister to the suffering people of the world. With his own hands he helped build his hospital
in French Equatorial Africa, where he still labors. The whole world now
honors him upon his birthday.

Questions and Exercises

1. It is characteristic of Albert Schweitzer to place the thinking mind at the center of his philosophy. How does he link it with the solution of the two major problems that cast their shadows over our existence?

2. How can man cure his inability to think clearly? What element in our spiritual foundation does Schweitzer feel we have lost? Notice his use of analogy.

3. Explain Schweitzer's formula for giving meaning to life. How is this connected with a sense of mystery, with reverence for life?

4. Compare Schweitzer's religious views with John Woolman's in "The Education of a Quaker."

5. Do you agree with Schweitzer that this is a period of spiritual decadence in mankind and that the spirit of the age is filled with disdain for thinking? Discuss.

6. Theme Topics: Reference for Life; Kindness to Animals; Loving the Unlovely; Students Are (Are Not) Bores; The Challenge of the Curious Mind; The Effect of Competition for Grades on Thought; Nobody Wants Me to Think for Myself; No Time for Thought.

3

QUEST TO LIVE:
MAN AND SOCIETY

No man is an island, entire of itself; every man is a piece of the continent, a part of the main. . . .

John Donne

Man is by nature gregarious. His records as a social being, whether in an ancient city or in a modern industrialized one, whether in savage combat for survival or in civilized pursuits, reveal that his ultimate well-being depends upon the inclusion of others in his compelling quest to live. Fortunately, the instinct to herd together tends in the long run to promote an atmosphere of mutual sharing and achieving. When man respects the welfare of others, he is usually rewarded with the same tolerance and respect.

The selections chosen for this portion of the text are reflections of man in his society: the relative claims of agrarian and urban life, the impact of such disruptive influences as global conflicts or major population shifts, the factors that stratify society into various levels. The selections deal with man's individual responsibility and are concerned equally with the role of the hero offering his life for others and the part played by the common man in the normal routine of daily affairs.

TO ARISTIUS FUSCUS

Greetings from the Country
Epistles I, 10

Horace

Health, from the lover of the Country me,
Health, to the lover of the City thee,
A difference in our souls, this only proves,
In all things else, w' agree like married doves.
But the warm nest, and crowded dove-house thou   5
Dost like; I loosely fly from bough to bough,
And Rivers drink, and all the shining day,
Upon fair Trees, or mossy Rocks I play;
In fine, I live and reign when I retire
From all that you equal with Heaven admire.   10
Like one at last from the Priests' service fled,
Loathing the honie'd Cakes, I long for Bread.
Would I a house for happiness erect,
Nature alone should be the Architect.
She'd build it more convenient, then great,   15
And doubtless in the Country choose her seat.
Is there a place, doth better helps supply,
Against the wounds of Winter's cruelty?
Is there an Ayr that gentl'er does assuage
The mad Celestial Dogs, or Lyons rage?   20
Is it not there that sleep (and only there)
Nor noise without, nor cares within does fear?
Does art through pipes, a purer water bring,
Then that which nature straines into a spring?
Can all your Tap'stries, or your Pictures show   25
More beauties than in herbs and flowers do grow?
Fountains and trees our wearied Pride do please,
Even in the midst of gilded Palaces.
And in your townes that prospect gives delight,
Which opens round the country to our sight.   30
Men to the good, from which they rashly fly,
Return at last, and their wild Luxury
Does but in vain with those true joyes contend,
Which Nature did to mankind recommend.

The man who changes gold for burnisht Brass,   35
Or small right Gems, for larger ones of glass:
Is not, at length, more certain to be made
Ridiculous, and wretched by the trade,
Than he, who sells a solid good, to buy
The painted goods of Pride and Vanity.   40
If thou be wise, no glorious fortune choose,
Which 'tis but pain to keep, yet grief to lose,
For, when we place even trifles, in the heart,
With trifles too, unwillingly we part.
An humble Room, plain bed, and homely board,   45
More clear, untainted pleasures to afford,
Then all the Tumult of vain greatness brings
To Kings, or to the favorites of Kings
The horned Deer by Nature arm'd so well,
Did with the Horse in common pasture dwell;   50
And when they fought, the field is always wan,
Till the ambitious Horse begg'd help of Man,
And took the bridle, and henceforth did reign
Bravely alone, as Lord of all the plain:
But never after could the Rider get   55
From off his back, or from the mouth his bit.
So they, who poverty too much do fear,
T' avoid that weight, a greater burden bear;
That they might Pow'r above their equals have,
To cruel Masters they themselves enslave.   60
For Gold, their Liberty exchang'd we see,
That fairest flow'r, which crowns Humanity.
And all this mischief does upon them light,
Only, because they know now how, aright.
That great, but secret, happiness to prize,   65
That's laid up in a Little, for the Wise:
That is the best, and easiest Estate,
Which to man sits close, but not too strait;
'Tis like a shooe; it pinches, and it burns,
Too narrow; and too large it overturns.   70
My dearest friend, stop thy desires at last,
And cheerfully enjoy the wealth thou hast.
And, if me still seeking for more you see,
Chide, and reproach, despise and laugh at me.
Money was made not to command our will,   75
But all our lawful pleasures to fulfil.

Shame and woe to us, if we our wealth obey;
The Horse doth with the Horse-Man run away.

Author and Selection Notes

The poet Horace (Quintus Horatius Flaccus) was born in Venusia, in southern Italy, in 65 B.C. His father, a former slave who had earned his freedom, saw to it that his son received the best in schooling, both in Rome and in Athens. As a young man Horace served as a junior officer under Brutus and fought in the Battle of Philippi. Upon his return to Rome, through his friend Virgil he met Maecenas, a literary patron, who shortly afterwards presented the young poet with the Sabine farm, made famous in his verses.

Horace is remembered for his *Satires, Odes, Epodes,* and *Epistles,* the latter containing the well-known "Ars Poetica." His lines, graceful and polished, reflect a consuming interest in the world about him.

Questions and Exercises

1. In the poem "To Aristius Fuscus" Horace writes to a city friend of the joys of living in the country. Do you agree with the sentiments of the poet or would you refute his position?

2. What is the meaning of "loathing the honie'd Cakes, I long for Bread"?

3. The praise of nature sounds much like the English poet Wordsworth. Can you cite lines from Wordsworth that are similar?

4. To what do "Celestial Dogs" refer?

5. Theme Topics: What I Enjoy About a Visit to the Country; One Can Enjoy a Better Way of Life in the Country; The Country in Winter; A Slave to Wealth; The Ideal Way of Life.

THE CITY FARMER

Epode 2

Horace

How happy in his low degree,
How rich in humble Poverty, is he,
Who leads a quiet country life!
Discharg'd of business, void of strife,
And from the gripeing Scrivener free.
(Thus, e're the Seeds of Vice were sown,
Liv'd Men in better Ages born,

5

Who Plow'd, with Oxen of their own,
Their small paternal field of Corn.)
Nor Trumpets summon him to War 10
Nor drums disturb his morning Sleep,
Nor knows he Merchants' gainful care,
Nor fears the dangers of the deep.
The clamours of contentious Law,
And Court and state, he wisely shuns, 15
Nor brib'd with hopes, nor dar'd with awe,
To servile Salutations runs;
But either to the clasping Vine
Does the supporting Poplar Wed,
Or with his pruning hook disjoyn 20
Unbearing Branches from their Head.
And grafts more happy in their stead;
Or climbing to a hilly steep,
He views his Herds in Vales afar,
Or Sheers his overburden'd Sheep, 25
Or mead for cooling drink prepares
Of Virgin honey in the Jars.
Or in the now declining year,
When bounteous *Autumn* rears his head,
He joyes to pull the ripen'd Pear, 30
And clustering Grapes with purple spread.
The fairest of his fruit he serves,
Priapus thy rewards:
Sylvanus too his part deserves,
Whose care the fences guards. 35
Sometimes beneath an ancient Oak,
Or on the matted grass he lies:
No God of Sleep he need invoke;
The stream, that o're the pebbles flies,
With gentle slumber crowns his Eyes. 40
The Wind, that Whistles through the sprays,
Maintains the consort of the Song;
And hidden Birds, with native layes,
The golden sleep prolong.
But when the blast of Winter blows, 45
And hoary frost inverts the year,
Into the naked Woods he goes,
And seeks the tusky Boar to rear,
With well mouth'd hounds and pointed Spear.
Or spreads his subtle Nets from sight 50

With twinckling glasses to betray
The Larkes that in the Meshes light,
Or makes the fearful Hare his prey.
Amidst his harmless easie joys
No anxious care invades his health,   55
Nor Love his peace of mind destroys,
Nor wicked avarice of Wealth.
But if a chast and pleasing Wife,
To ease the business of his Life,
Divides with him his household care,   60
Such as the Sabine *Matrons* were,
Such as the swift *Apulians* Bride.
Sunburnt and Swarthy tho' she be,
Will fire for Winter Nights provide,
And without noise will oversee   65
His Children and his Family,
And order all things till he come,
Sweaty and overlabour'd, home;
If she in pens his Flocks will fold,
And then produce her Dairy store,   70
With Wine to drive away the cold,
And unbought dainties of the poor;
Not Oysters of the *Lucrine* Lake
My sober appetite wou'd wish,
Nor *Turbet*, or the Foreign Fish   75
That rowling Tempests overtake,
And hither waft the costly dish.
Not *Heathpout*, or the rarer Bird,
Which *Phasis*, or *Ionia* yields,
More pleasing morsels wou'd afford   80
Than the fat Olives of my fields;
Than Shards or Mallows for the pot,
That keep the loosen'd Body sound
Or than the Lamb, that falls by Lot,
To the just Guardian of my ground.   85
Amidst these feasts of happy Swains,
The jolly Shepherd smiles to see
His flock returning from the Plains;
The farmer is as pleas'd as he,
To view his Oxen, sweating smoak,   90
Bear on their Necks the loosen'd Yoke:
To look upon his menial Crew,
That sits around his cheerful hearth,

And bodies spent in toil renew
With wholesome Food and Country Mirth.   95

This *Morecraft* said within himself;
Resolv'd to leave the wicked Town;
And live retir'd upon his own;
He call'd his Mony in:
But the prevailing love of pelf   100
Soon split him on the former shelf,
And put it out again.

Author and Selection Notes

See page 236.

Questions and Exercises

1. Do you think the city farmer is assured of further gain, and what do you think of his sense of values?

2. Discuss the poet's picture of rusticity as imagined by the city farmer.

3. Is the picture realistic or romanticized to extreme?

4. For additional literature descriptive of country life, you may want to read Goldsmith's "The Deserted Village" or Robert Burns' "The Cotter's Saturday Night."

5. You may also want to compare Thomson's "The Seasons" with "The City Farmer."

6. Compare and contrast the attitude toward city and country life in "To Aristius Fuscus" and "The City Farmer." Also compare the attitude toward wealth held by the speakers of the two poems.

7. Theme Topics: The Evil of Good Intentions; Letting Life Pass You By; The Force of Custom in Daily Life; Money and Unhappiness; The Sweet Uses of Adversity.

BEOWULF

The Myth of the Sheaf-Child

List to an old-time lay of the Spear-Danes,
Full of the prowess of famous kings,
Deeds of renown that were done by the heroes;

From *Old English Poetry,* translated by J. Duncan Spaeth. Copyright 1922 by Princeton University Press.

Scyld the Sheaf-Child[1] from scourging foemen,
From raiders a-many their mead-halls wrested.   5
He lived to be feared, though first as a waif,
Puny and frail he was found on the shore.
He grew to be great, and was girt with power
Till the border-tribes all obeyed his rule,
And sea-folk hardy that sit by the whale-path   10
Gave him tribute, a good king was he.
Many years after, an heir was born to him,
A goodly youth, whom God had sent
To stay and support his people in need.
(Long time leaderless living in woe,   15
The sorrow they suffered He saw full well.)
The Lord of Glory did lend him honor,
Beowulf's[2] fame afar was borne,
Son of old Scyld in the Scandian lands.
A youthful heir must be open-handed,   20
Furnish the friends of his father with plenty,
That thus in his age, in the hour of battle,
Willing comrades may crowd around him
Eager and true. In every tribe
Honorable deeds shall adorn an earl.   25
The aged Scyld, when his hour had come,
Famous and praised, departed to God.
His faithful comrades carried him down
To the brink of the sea, as himself had bidden,
The Scyldings' friend, before he fell silent,   30
Their lord beloved who long had ruled them.
Out in the bay a boat was waiting
Coated with ice, 'twas the king's own barge.
They lifted aboard their bracelet-bestower,
And down on the deck their dear lord laid,   35
Hard by the mast. Heaped-up treasure
Gathered from far they gave him along.
Never was ship more nobly laden
With wondrous weapons and warlike gear.
Swords and corslets covered his breast,   40
Floating riches to ride afar with him
Out o'er the waves at the will of the sea.
No less they dowered their lord with treasure,

[1] The Sheaf-Child, Scyld, is the mythical ancestor of Hrothgar, King of the
Spear-Danes.
[2] not the Beowulf of this poem, but another of the same name.

Things of price, than those who at first
Had launched him forth as a little child   45
Alone on the deep to drift o'er the billows.
They gave him to boot a gilded banner,
High o'er his head they hung it aloft.
Then set him adrift, let the surges bear him.
Sad were their hearts, their spirits mournful;   50
Man hath not heard, no mortal can say
Who found that barge's floating burden.

I

The Line of the Danish Kings and the Building of Heorot

Now Beowulf was king in the burgs of the Scyldings,
Famed among folk. (His father had left
The land of the living.) From his loins was sprung
Healfdene the royal, who ruled to old age,
Gray and battlegrim, the bold-hearted Scyldings.   5
Children four to this chief of the people
Woke unto life, one after another;
Heorogar and Hrothgar, and Halga the brave,
And winsome Sigeneow, a Scylfing she wedded;
Saewela's queen they say she became.   10
To Hrothgar was given such glory in battle,
Such fame he won, that his faithful band
Of youthful warriors waxed amain.
So great had grown his guard of kinsmen,
That it came in his mind to call on his people   15
To build a mead-hall, mightier far
Than any e'er seen by the sons of men,
Wherein to bestow upon old and young,
Gifts and rewards, as God vouchsafed them,
Save folk-share lands and freemen's lives.   20
Far and wide the work was published;
Many a tribe, the mid-earth round,
Helped to fashion the folk-stead fair.
With speed they built it, and soon 'twas finished,
Greatest of halls. Heorot[3] he named it,   25
Whose word was law o'er lands afar;
Nor failed in his promise, but freely dealt
Gifts at the feast. The fair hall towered

[2] not the Beowulf of this poem, but another of the same name.

Wide-gabled and high, awaiting its doom,
The sweep of fire; not far was the time   30
That ancient feuds should open afresh,
And sword-hate sunder sons from fathers.
In the darkness dwelt a demon-sprite,
Whose heart was filled with fury and hate,
When he heard each night the noise of revel   35
Loud in the hall, laughter and song,
To the sound of the harp the singer chanted
Lays he had learned, of long ago;
How the Almighty had made the earth,
Wonder-bright lands, washed by the ocean;   40
How he set triumphant, sun and moon
To lighten all men that live on the earth.
He brightened the land with leaves and branches;
Life he created for every being,
Each in its kind, that moves upon earth.   45
So, happy in hall, the heroes lived,
Wanting naught, till one began
To work them woe, a wicked fiend.
The demon grim was Grendel called,
March-stalker huge, the moors he roamed.   50
The joyless creature had kept long time
The lonely fen, the lairs of monsters,
Cast out from men, an exile accurst.
The killing of Abel, on offspring of Cain
Was justly avenged by the Judge Eternal.   55
Nought gained by the feud the faithless murderer;
He was banished unblest from abode of men.
And hence arose the host of miscreants,
Monsters and elves and eldritch sprites,
Warlocks and giants, that warred against God;   60
Jotuns and goblins; He gave them their due.

II

The Ravaging of Heorot Hall by the Monster Grendel

When night had fallen, the fiend crept near
To the lofty hall, to learn how the Danes
In Heorot fared, when the feasting was done.
The aethelings all within he saw
Asleep after revel, not recking of danger,   5
And free from care. The fiend accurst,

Grim and greedy, his grip made ready;
Snatched in their sleep, with savage fury,
Thirty warriors; away he sprang
Proud of his prey, to repair to his home,　　　　　10
His blood-dripping booty to bring to his lair.
At early dawn, when day-break came,
The vengeance of Grendel was revealed to all,
Their wails after wassail were widely heard,
Their morning-woe. The mighty ruler,　　　　　15
The aetheling brave, sat bowed with grief.
The fate of his followers filled him with sorrow,
When they traced the tracks of the treacherous foe,
Fiend accurst. Too fierce was that onset,
Too loathsome and long, nor left them respite.　　20
The very next night, anew he began
To maim and to murder, nor was minded to slacken
His fury of hate, too hardened in crime.
'Twas easy to find then carls who preferred
A room elsewhere, for rest at night,　　　　　25
A bed in the bowers, when they brought this news
Of the hall foe's hate; and henceforth all
Who escaped the demon, kept distance safe.

So Grendel wrongfully ruled the hall,
One against all till empty stood　　　　　30
That lordly mansion, and long remained so.
For the space of twelve winters the Scyldings' Friend[4]
Bore in his breast the brunt of this sorrow,
Measureless woe. In mournful lays
The tale became known; 'twas told abroad　　　35
In gleemen's songs, how Grendel had warred
Long against Hrothgar, and wreaked his hate
With murderous fury through many a year,
Refusing to end the feud perpetual,
Or decently deal with the Danes in parley,　　　40
Take their tribute for treaty of peace;
Nor could their leaders look to receive
Pay from his hands for the harm that he wrought.
The fell destroyer kept feeding his rage
On young and old. So all night long　　　　　45
He prowled o'er the fen and surprised his victims,

[4] Hrothgar.

Death-shadow dark. (The dusky realms
Where the hell-runes haunt are hidden from men.)
So the exiled roamer his raids continued;
Wrong upon wrong in his wrath he heaped.   50
In midnights dark he dwelt alone
'Mongst Heorot's trophies and treasures rich.
Great was the grief of the gold-friend of Scyldings,
Vexed was his mood that he might not visit
His goodly throne, his gift-seat proud,   55
Deprived of joy by the judgment of God.
Many the wise men that met to discover
Ways of escape from the scourge of affliction.
Often they came for counsel together;
Often at heathen altars they made   60
Sacrifice-offerings, beseeching their idols
To send them deliverance from assault of the foe.
Such was their practice, they prayed to the Devil;
The hope of the heathen on hell was fixed,
The mood of their mind. Their Maker they knew not,   65
The righteous Judge and Ruler on high.
The Wielder of Glory they worshipped not,
The Warden of Heaven. Woe be to him
Whose soul is doomed through spite and envy,
In utter despair and agony hopeless   70
Forever to burn. But blessed is he
Who, after this life, the Lord shall seek,
Eager for peace in the arms of the Father.

III

The Voyage of Beowulf to the
Hall of Hrothgar

Thus boiled with care the breast of Hrothgar;
Ceaselessly sorrowed the son of Healfdene,
None of his chieftains might change his lot.
Too fell was the foe that afflicted the people
With wrongs unnumbered, and nightly horrors.   5
Then heard in his home king Hygelac's thane,[5]
The dauntless Jute,[6] of the doings of Grendel.
In strength he outstripped the strongest of men
That dwell in the earth in the days of this life.

[5] Beowulf.
[6] The people are called Geats in the original; the translator assumes that they are Jutes from Jutland on the Baltic.

Gallant and bold, he gave command   10
To get him a boat, a good wave-skimmer.
O'er the swan-road, he said, he would seek the king
Noble and famous, who needed men.
Though dear to his kin, they discouraged him not;
The prudent in counsel praised the adventure,   15

Whetted his valor, awaiting good omens.
So Beowulf chose from the band of the Jutes
Heroes brave, the best he could find;
He with fourteen followers hardy,
Went to embark; he was wise in seamanship,   20
Showed them the landmarks, leading the way.
Soon they descried their craft in the water,
At the foot of the cliff. Then climbed aboard
The chosen troop; the tide was churning
Sea against sand; they stowed away   25
In the hold of the ship their shining armor,
War-gear and weapons; the warriors launched
Their well-braced boat on her welcome voyage.

Swift o'er the waves with a wind that favored,
Foam on her breast, like a bird she flew.   30
A day and a night they drove to seaward,
Cut the waves with the curving prow,
Till the seamen that sailed her sighted the land,
Shining cliffs and coast-wise hills,
Headlands bold. The harbor opened,   35
Their cruise was ended. Then quickly the sailors,
The crew of Weder-folk clambered ashore,
Moored their craft with clank of chain-mail,
And goodly war-gear. God they thanked
That their way was smooth o'er the surging waves.   40

High on the shore, the Scylding coast-guard
Saw from the cliff where he kept his watch,
Glittering shields o'er the gang-plank carried,
Polished weapons. It puzzled him sore,
He wondered in mind who the men might be.   45
Down to the strand on his steed came riding
Hrothgar's thane, with threatening arm
Shook his war-spear and shouted this challenge:
"Who are ye, men, all mailed and harnessed,

That brought yon ship o'er the broad sea-ways,   50
And hither have come across the water,
To land on our shores? Long have I stood
As coast-guard here, and kept my sea-watch,
Lest harrying foe with hostile fleet
Should dare to damage our Danish land.   55
Armed men never from overseas came
More openly hither. But how do ye know
That law of the land doth give ye leave
To come thus near. I never have seen
Statelier earl upon earth than him,—   60
Yon hero in harness. No house-carl he,
In lordly array, if looks speak true,
And noble bearing. But now I must learn
Your names and country, ere nearer ye come,
Underhand spies, for aught I know,   65
In Danish land. Now listen ye strangers,
In from the sea, to my open challenge:
Heed ye my words and haste me to know
What your errand and whence ye have come."

IV

Beowulf's Words with the Coast-Guard

Him the hero hailed with an answer,
The war-troop's leader, his word-hoard unlocked:
"In truth we belong to the tribe of the Jutes;
We are Hygelac's own hearth-companions.
Far among folk my father was known,   5
A noble chieftain; his name was Ecgtheow.
Honored by all, he ended his days
Full of winters and famed in the land.
Wise men everywhere well remember him.
Hither we fare with friendly purpose   10
To seek thy lord, the son of Healfdene,
The land-protector. Instruct us kindly.
Bound on adventure we visit thy lord,
The prince of the Danes. Our purpose is open;
Nought keep we secret; thou surely wilt know   15
If the tale we were told is true or not:
That among the Scyldings a monster strange,
A nameless demon, when nights are dark,
With cruel cunning, for cause unknown,
Works havoc and slaughter. I have in mind   20

A way to help your wise king Hrothgar,
Your ruler to rid of the ravening foe,
If ever his tide of troubles shall turn,
The billows of care that boil in his breast
Shall cool and subside, and his sorrow be cured;   25
Else, failing my purpose, forever hereafter
He shall suffer distress, while stands on its hill,
Mounting on high, his matchless hall."
Straight answered the coast-guard, astride his horse,
The warrior brave: "Twixt words and deeds   30
A keen-witted thane, if he thinks aright,
Must well distinguish and weigh the difference.
Your words I believe, that you wish no evil
To the Scylding lord. I will let you bring
Your shields ashore and show you the way.   35
My comrades here shall keep the watch,
From meddling foe defend your craft,
Your fresh-tarred boat, fast by the beach,
And faithfully guard her till again she bear
With curving bow, o'er the bounding main,   40
Her master well-loved to the Wedermark.
Fortune oft favors the fighter who yields not;
Hero unflinching comes unhurt from the fray."
Landward they hastened, leaving behind them
Fast at her moorings the full-bosomed boat,   45
The ship at anchor. Shone the boar-heads,
Gleaming with gold, o'er the guards of their helmets;
Bright and fire-forged the beast kept watch.
Forward they pressed, proud and adventurous,
Fit for the fight, till afar they descried   50
The high-peaked radiant roof of the hall.
Of houses far-praised 'neath heaven by the people
That inhabit the earth, this house was most famous,
The seat of King Hrothgar; its splendor gleamed bright
O'er many a land. Their leader well-armed   55
Showed them the shining shield-burg of heroes,
And set them right on the road to their goal.
Then, wheeling his steed, he wished them farewell:

" 'Tis time that I leave you; the Lord of Heaven,
The Father Almighty in mercy keep you   60
Safe on your journey; seaward I turn,
Watch to keep and ward against foe."

V

Beowulf's Arrival at the Hall and the
Manner of His Reception

The street was stone-paved; straight it led
To the goal of their journey. Glistened their byrnies
Stout and strong-linked; sang the rings
Of their iron mail as they marched along,
In armor and helmet right up to the hall.   5
Sea-voyage-sated, they set their shields,
Their linden-woods broad, along the wall.
As they bent to the bench, their byrnies clattered.
They stacked their spears that stood in a row,
Ashwood tipped with iron above;   10
Well-equipped was the warlike band.
A stately Dane the strangers addressed,
Asked who they were and whence they had come:
"Whence do ye bear your burnished shields,
Your visored helmets and harness gray   15
Your heap of spear-shafts? A servant of Hrothgar's,
His herald, am I. Hardier strangers,
Nobler in mien, have I never seen.
'Tis clear you come to the court of Hrothgar,
Not outlaws and beggars, but bent on adventure."   20
To him gave answer the hero brave,
The lord of the Weders these words returned,
Bold 'neath his helmet: "We are Hygelac's men,
His board-companions. I am Beowulf called.
Ready am I the ruler to answer,   25
To say to thy lord, the son of Healfdene,
Why we have come his court to seek,
If he will graciously grant us a hearing."
Wulfgar replied (he was prince of the Wendlcs,
His noble renown was known to many,   30
His courage in war, and wisdom in counsel):
"I will carry thy quest to the king of the Danes,
And ask him whether he wishes to grant
The boon thou dost ask of the breaker-of-rings,
To speak to himself concerning thy journey;   35
And straight will I bring thee the answer he sends."
Swiftly he hied him where Hrothgar sat,
White-haired and old, his earls around him.
Stately he strode, till he stood in the presence

Of the king of the Danes,—in courtly ways   40
Was Wulfgar skilled; he spoke to his lord:
"Hither have fared from a far country,
A band of Jutes o'er the bounding sea.
Their leader and chief by his chosen comrades
Is Beowulf called; this boon they ask: 45
That they may find with thee, my lord,
Favor of speech; refuse them not,
But grant them, Hrothgar, gracious hearing.
In armor clad, they claim respect
Of choicest earls; but chiefly their lord   50
Who lately hither hath led his comrades."

VI

Hrothgar's Welcome to Beowulf

Hrothgar spoke, the Scyldings' protector:
"Beowulf I knew in his boyhood days;
His aged father was Ecgtheow named.
To him, to take home, did Hrethel give
His only daughter. Their dauntless son   5
Now comes to my court in quest of a friend.
My sea-faring men whom I sent afar
To the land of the Jutes, with generous gifts,
In token of friendship, have told me this,
That the power of his grip was so great it equalled   10
The strength of thirty stout-armed thanes.
Him bold in battle, the blessed God
Hath sent in his mercy, to save our people
—So I hope in my heart—from the horror of Grendel.
I shall offer him gold for his gallant spirit.   15
Go now in haste, and greet the strangers;
Bid to the hall the whole of the company;
Welcome with words the warrior band,
To the home of the Danes." To the hall door went
Wulfgar the courtly, and called them in: 20
"My master commands me this message to give you,
The lord of the Danes your lineage knows;
Bids me to welcome you, brave-hearted warriors,
Bound on adventure o'er the billowy main.
Ye may rise now and enter, arrayed in your armor,   25
Covered with helmets, the king to greet.
But leave your shields, and your shafts of slaughter,
Here by the wall to await the issue."

Then rose the leader, around him his comrades,
Sturdy war-band; some waited without,   30
Bid by the bold one their battle-gear to guard.
Together they hastened where the herald led them,
Under Heorot's roof. The hero went first,
Strode under helmet, till he stood by the hearth.
Beowulf spoke, his byrnie glistened,   35
His corslet chain-linked by cunning of smithcraft:
"Hail, king Hrothgar! Hygelac's thane
And kinsman am I. Known is the record
Of deeds of renown I have done in my youth.
Far in my home, I heard of this Grendel;   40
Sea-farers tell the tale of the hall:
How bare of warriors, this best of buildings
Deserted stands, when the sun goes down
And twilight deepens to dark in the sky.
By comrades encouraged, I come on this journey.   45
The best of them bade me, the bravest and wisest,
To go to thy succor, O good king Hrothgar;
For well they approved my prowess in battle,
They saw me themselves come safe from the conflict
When five of my foes I defeated and bound,   50
Beating in battle the brood of the monsters.
At night on the sea with nicors I wrestled,
Avenging the Weders, survived the sea-peril,
And crushed in my grip the grim sea-monsters
That harried my neighbors. Now I am come   55
To cope with Grendel in combat single,
And match my might against the monster, alone.
I pray thee therefore, prince of the Scyldings,
Not to refuse the favor I ask,
Having come so far, O friend of the Shield-Danes,   60
That I alone with my loyal comrades,
My hardy companions, may Heorot purge.
Moreover they say that the slaughterous fiend
In wanton mood all weapons despises.
Hence,—as I hope that Hygelac may,   65
My lord and king, be kind to me,—
Sword and buckler I scorn to bear,
Gold-adorned shield, as I go to the conflict.
With my grip will I grapple the gruesome fiend,
Foe against foe, to fight for our life.   70
And he that shall fall his faith must put

In the judgment of God. If Grendel wins
He is minded to make his meal in the hall
Untroubled by fear, on the folk of the Jutes,
As often before he fed on the Danes.   75
No need for thee then to think of my burial.
If I lose my life, the lonely prowler
My blood-stained body will bear to his den,
Swallow me greedily, and splash with my gore
His lair in the marsh; no longer wilt then   80
Have need to find me food and sustenance.
To Hygelac send, if I sink in the battle,
This best of corslets that covers my breast,
Heirloom of Hrethel, rarest of byrnies,
The work of Weland.[7] So Wyrd[8] will be done."   85

VII

The Feasting in Heorot and the Customs of the Hall

Hrothgar spoke, the Scyldings' defender:
"Thou hast come, dear Beowulf, to bring us help,
For the sake of friendship to fight our battles.

Fifteen lines are omitted, in which Hrothgar recounts the exploits of
Beowulf's father.

Sad is my spirit and sore it grieves me
To tell to any the trouble and shame   5
That Grendel hath brought me with bitter hate,
The havoc he wrought in my ranks in the hall.
My war-band dwindles, driven by Wyrd
Into Grendel's grasp; but God may easily
End this monster's mad career.   10
Full often they boasted, my beer-bold warriors,
Brave o'er their ale-cups, the best of my fighters,
They'd meet in the mead-hall the mighty Grendel,
End his orgies with edge of the sword.
But always the mead-hall, the morning after,   15
The splendid building, was blood-bespattered;
Daylight dawned on the drippings of swords,
Soiled with slaughter were sills and benches.
My liegemen perished, and left me poor.
Sit down to the board; unbend thy thoughts;   20
Speak to my men as thy mood shall prompt."

---

[7] the smith of Norse legend.   [8] fate.

For the band of the Jutes a bench was cleared;
Room in the mead-hall was made for them all.
Then strode to their seats the strong-hearted heroes.
The warriors' wants a waiting-thane served;   25
Held in his hand the highly-wrought ale-cup,
Poured sparkling mead, while the minstrel sang
Gaily in Heorot. There was gladness of heroes,
A joyous company of Jutes and of Danes.

VIII

Unferth Taunts Beowulf

Then up spoke Unferth, Ecglaf's son,
Who sat at the feet of the Scylding ruler;
He vented his jealousy.   The journey of Beowulf,
His sea-adventure, sorely displeased him.
It filled him with envy that any other   5
Should win among men more war-like glory,
More fame under heaven than he himself:
"Art thou the Beowulf that battled with Brecca,
Far out at sea, when ye swam together,
What time you two made trial of the billows,   10
Risking your lives in reckless folly,
On the open sea? None might dissuade you,
Friend nor foe, from the fool-hardy venture,
When straight from the shore you struck for the open,
Breasted the waves and beat with your arms   15
The mounting billows, measured the sea-paths
With lusty strokes. Stirred was the ocean
By wintry storms. Seven days and nights
Your sea-strife lasted; at length he beat you,
His strength was the better; at break of day   20
He made the beach where the Battle-Reamas
Dwell by the shore; and straightway returned
To his people beloved in the land of the Brondings,
Where liegemen and towns and treasure were his.
In sooth I say, the son of Beanstan   25
His boast against thee made good to the full.
But now I ween a worse fate awaits thee
Though thy mettle be proved in many a battle
And grim encounter, if the coming of Grendel
Thou darest abide, in the dead of the night."   30
Beowulf spoke, the son of Ecgtheow:
"What a deal of stuff thou hast talked about Brecca,

Garrulous with drink, my good friend Unferth.
Thou hast lauded his deeds. Now listen to me!
More sea-strength had I, more ocean-endurance,   35
Than any man else, the wide earth round.
'Tis true we planned in the pride of our youth
This ocean-adventure, and vowed we would risk
Our lives in the deep, each daring the other.
We were both of us boys, but our boast we fulfilled.   40
Our naked swords as we swam from the land,
We held in our grasp, to guard against whales.
Not a stroke could he gain on me, strive as he would,
Make swifter speed through the swelling waves,
Nor could I in swimming o'ercome him at sea.   45
Side by side in the surge we labored
Five nights long. At last we were parted
By furious seas and a freezing gale.
Night fell black; the norther wild
Rushed on us ruthless and roughened the sea.   50
Now was aroused the wrath of the monsters,
But my war-proof ring-mail, woven and hand-locked,
Served me well 'gainst the sea-beasts' fury;
The close-linked battle-net covered my breast.
I was dragged to the bottom by a blood-thirsty monster,   55
Firm in his clutch the furious sea-beast
Helpless held me. But my hand came free,
And my foe I pierced with point of my sword.
With my battle-blade good 'twas given me to kill
The dragon of the deep, by dint of my blow."   60

IX

Beowulf Completes the Story of His Swimming
Adventure with Brecca. Hrothgar's
Departure from the Hall

"Thus sore beset me sea-beasts thronging,
Murderous man-eaters. I met their charges,
Gave them their due with my goodly blade.
They failed of their fill, the feast they expected
In circle sitting on the sea-floor together   5
With me for their meal. I marred their pleasure.
When morning came, they were cast ashore
By the wash of the waves; their wounds proved fatal;
Bloated and dead on the beach they lay.
No more would they cross the course of the ships,   10

In the chop of the channel charge the sailors.
Day broke in the east, bright beacon of God;
The sea fell smooth. I saw bold headlands,
Windy walls; for Wyrd oft saveth
A man not doomed, if he dauntless prove.   15
My luck did not fail me, my long sword finished
Nine of the nicors. Ne'er have I heard
Of fiercer battle fought in the night,
Of hero more harried by horrors at sea.
Yet I saved my life from the sea-beasts' clutch.   20
Worn with the struggle, I was washed ashore
In the realm of the Finns by the run of the tide,
The heave of the flood. I have failed to hear
Of like adventure laid to thee,
Battle so bitter. Brecca did never,—   25
Neither of you was known to achieve
Deed so valiant, adventure so daring,
Sword-play so nimble; not that I boast of it,
But mark me Unferth, you murdered your brothers,
Your closest of kin. The curse of hell   30
For this you will suffer, though sharp be your wit.
In sooth I say to you, son of Ecglaf,
Never had Grendel such grim deeds wrought,
Such havoc in Heorot, so harried your king
With bestial fury, if your boasted courage   35
In deeds as well as in words you had proved.
But now he has found he need not fear
Vengeance fierce from the Victory-Scyldings,
Ruthless attack in return for his raids.
He takes his toll of your tribe as he pleases,   40
Sparing none of your spearmen proud.
He ravens and rages and recks not the Dane folk,
Safe from their sword-play. But soon I will teach him
How the Jute-folk fight. Then freely may go
To the mead-hall who likes, when the light of morning,   45
The next day's dawn, the dark shall dispel,
And the heaven-bright sun from the south shall shine."

Glad in his heart was the giver of rings,
Hoped to have help, the hoar-headed king;
The Shield-Danes' shepherd was sure of relief,   50
When he found in Beowulf so firm a resolve.
There was laughter of heroes. Loud was their revelry,

Words were winsome as Wealhtheow rose,
Queen of Hrothgar, heedful of courtesy,
Gold-adorned greeted the guests in the hall.   55
First to her lord, the land-defender,
The high-born lady handed the cup;
Bade him be gleeful and gay at the board,
And good to his people. Gladly he took it,
Quaffed from the beaker, the battle-famed king.   60
Then leaving her lord, the lady of the Helmings
Passed among her people in each part of the hall,
Offered the ale-cup to old and young,
Till she came to the bench where Beowulf sat.
The jewel-laden queen in courteous manner   65
Beowulf greeted; to God gave thanks,
Wise in her words, that her wish was granted,
That at last in her trouble a trusted hero
Had come for comfort. The cup received
From Wealhtheow's hand the hardy warrior,   70
And made this reply, his mind on the battle;
Beowulf spoke, the son of Ecgtheow:
"I made up my mind when my mates and I
Embarked in our boat, outbound on the sea,
That fully I'd work the will of thy people,   75
Or fall in the fight, in the clutch of the fiend.
I surely shall do a deed of glory,
Worthy an earl, or end my days,
My morning of life, in the mead-hall here."
His words pleased well the wife of Hrothgar,   80
The Jutish lord's boast. The jewelled queen
Went to sit by the side of her lord.
Renewed was the sound of noisy revel,
Wassail of warriors. Brave words were spoken.
Mirth in the mead-hall mounted high,   85
Till Healfdene's son[9] the sign did give
That he wished to retire. Full well he knew
The fiend would find a fight awaiting him,
When the light of the sun had left the hall,
And creeping night should close upon them,   90
And shadowy shapes come striding on
Dim through the dark. The Danes arose.
Hrothgar again gave greeting to Beowulf,

[9] Hrothgar.

Wished him farewell; the wine-hall lofty
He left in his charge. These last words spoke he: 95
"Never before have I fully entrusted
To mortal man this mighty hall,
Since arm and shield I was able to lift.
To thee alone I leave it now,
To have and to hold it. Thy hardihood prove!   100
Be mindful of glory; keep watch for the foe!
No reward shalt thou lack if thou live through this fight."

X

Beowulf's Watch in Heorot

Then Hrothgar went with his warrior-band,
The Arm-of-the-Scyldings, out of the hall.
Would the war-lord Wealhtheow seek,
The queen for his bed-mate. The best of kings
Had placed in the hall, so heroes report,   5
A watch against Grendel, to guard his house,
Deliverance bring to the land of the Danes.
But the lord of the Jutes joyfully trusted
In the might of his arm and the mercy of God.
Off he stripped his iron byrnie,   10
Helmet from head, and handed his sword,
Choicest of blades, to his body-thane,
And bade him keep the battle armor.
Then made his boast once more the warrior,
Beowulf the bold, ere his bed he sought,   15
Summoned his spirit; "Not second to Grendel
In combat I count me and courage of war.
But not with the sword will I slay this foeman,
Though light were the task to take his life.
Nothing at all does he know of such fighting,   20
Of hewing of shields, though shrewd be his malice
Ill deeds to contrive. We two in the night
Shall do without swords, if he dare to meet me
In hand to hand battle. May the holy Lord
To one or the other award the victory,   25
As it seems to Him right, Ruler all-wise."
Then he sought his bed. The bolster received
The head of the hero. In the hall about him,
Stretched in sleep, his sailormen lay.
Not one of them thought he would ever return   30
Home to his country, nor hoped to see

His people again, and the place of his birth.
They had heard of too many men of the Danes
O'ertaken suddenly, slain without warning,
In the royal hall. But the Ruler on High   35
Through the woof of fate to the Wederfolk gave
Friendship and help, their foes to o'ercome,
By a single man's strength to slay the destroyer.
Thus all may learn that the Lord Almighty
Wields for aye the Wyrds of men. . . .   40

XI

Beowulf's Fight with Grendel

Now Grendel came, from his crags of mist
Across the moor; he was curst of God.
The murderous prowler meant to surprise
In the high-built hall his human prey.
He stalked 'neath the clouds, till steep before him   5
The house of revelry rose in his path,
The gold-hall of heroes, the gaily adorned.
Hrothgar's home he had hunted full often,
But never before had he found to receive him
So hardy a hero, such hall-guards there.   10
Close to the building crept the slayer,
Doomed to misery. The door gave way,
Though fastened with bolts, when his fist fell on it.
Maddened he broke through the breach he had made;
Swoln with anger and eager to slay,   15
The ravening fiend o'er the bright-paved floor
Furious ran, while flashed from his eyes
An ugly glare like embers aglow.
He saw in the hall, all huddled together,
The heroes asleep. Then laughed in his heart   20
The hideous fiend; he hoped ere dawn
To sunder body from soul of each;
He looked to appease his lust of blood,
Glut his maw with the men he would slay.
But Wyrd had otherwise willed his doom;   25
Never again should he get a victim
After that night. Narrowly watched
Hygelac's thane how the horrible slayer
Forward should charge in fierce attack.
Nor was the monster minded to wait: 30
Sudden he sprang on a sleeping thane,

Ere he could stir, he slit him open;
Bit through the bone-joints, gulped the blood,
Greedily bolted the body piecemeal.
Soon he had swallowed the slain man wholly,   35
Hands and feet. Then forward he hastened,
Sprang at the hero, and seized him at rest;
Fiercely clutched him with fiendish claw.
But quickly Beowulf caught his forearm,
And threw himself on it with all his weight.   40
Straight discovered that crafty plotter,
That never in all midearth had he met
In any man a mightier grip.
Gone was his courage, and craven fear
Sat in his heart, yet helped him no sooner.   45
Fain would he hide in his hole in the fenland,
His devil's den. A different welcome
From former days he found that night!
Now Hygelac's thane, the hardy, remembered
His evening's boast, and bounding up,   50
Grendel he clenched, and cracked his fingers;
The monster tried flight, but the man pursued;
The ravager hoped to wrench himself free,
And gain the fen, for he felt his fingers
Helpless and limp in the hold of his foe.   55
'Twas a sorry visit the man-devourer
Made to the Hall of the Hart that night.
Dread was the din, the Danes were frighted
By the uproar wild of the ale-spilling fray.
The hardiest blenched as the hall-foes wrestled   60
In terrible rage. The rafters groaned;
'Twas wonder great that the wine-hall stood,
Firm 'gainst the fighters' furious onslaught,
Nor fell to the ground, that glorious building.
With bands of iron 'twas braced and stiffened   65
Within and without. But off from the sill
Many a mead-bench mounted with gold
Was wrung where they wrestled in wrath together.
The Scylding nobles never imagined
That open attack, or treacherous cunning,   70
Could wreck or ruin their royal hall,
The lofty and antlered, unless the flames
Should some day swallow it up in smoke.
The din was renewed, the noise redoubled;

Each man of the Danes was mute with dread,   75
That heard from the wall the horrible wail,
The gruesome song of the godless foe,
His howl of defeat, as the fiend of hell
Bemoaned his hurt. The man held fast;
Greatest he was in grip of strength,   80
Of all that dwelt upon earth that day.

XII

The Defeat of Grendel

Loath in his heart was the hero-deliverer
To let escape his slaughterous guest.
Of little use that life he deemed
To human kind. The comrades of Beowulf
Unsheathed their weapons to ward their leader,   5
Eagerly brandished their ancient blades,
The life of their peerless lord to defend.
Little they deemed, those dauntless warriors,
As they leaped to the fray, those lusty fighters,
Laying on boldly to left and to right,   10
Eager to slay, that no sword upon earth,
No keenest weapon, could wound that monster:
Point would not pierce, he was proof against iron;
'Gainst victory-blades the devourer was charmed.
But a woful end awaited the wretch,   15
That very day he was doomed to depart,
And fare afar to the fiends' domain.

Now Grendel found, who in former days
So many a warrior had wantonly slain,
In brutish lust, abandoned of God,   20
That the frame of his body was breaking at last.
Keen of courage, the kinsman of Hygelac
Held him grimly gripped in his hands.
Loath was each to the other alive.
The grisly monster got his death-wound: 25
A huge split opened under his shoulder;
Crunched the socket, cracked the sinews.
Glory great was given to Beowulf.
But Grendel escaped with his gaping wound,
O'er the dreary moor his dark den sought,   30
Crawled to his lair. 'Twas clear to him then,
The count of his hours to end had come,

Done were his days. The Danes were glad,
The hard fight was over, they had their desire.
Cleared was the hall, 'twas cleansed by the hero   35
With keen heart and courage, who came from afar.
The lord of the Jutes rejoiced in his work,
The deed of renown he had done that night.
His boast to the Danes he bravely fulfilled;
From lingering woe delivered them all;   40
From heavy sorrow they suffered in heart;
From dire distress they endured so long;
From toil and from trouble. This token they saw:
The hero had laid the hand of Grendel
Both arm and claws, the whole forequarter   45
With clutches huge, 'neath the high-peaked roof.

XIII

The Celebration of the Victory and the Song
of the Gleeman

When morning arrived, so runs the report,
Around the gift-hall gathered the warriors;
The folk-leaders fared from far and near,
The wide ways o'er, the wonder to view,
The wild beast's foot-prints. Not one of them felt   5
Regret that the creature had come to grief,
When they traced his retreat by the tracks on the moor;
Marked where he wearily made his way,
Harried and beaten, to the haunt of the nicors,
Slunk to the water, to save his life.   10
There they beheld the heaving surges,
Billows abrim with bloody froth,
Dyed with gore, where the gruesome fiend,
Stricken and doomed, in the struggle of death
Gave up his ghost in the gloom of the mere,   15
His heathen soul for hell to receive it.
Then from the mere the thanes turned back,
Men and youths from the merry hunt,
Home they rode on their horses gray,
Proudly sitting their prancing steeds.   20
Beowulf's prowess was praised by all.
They all agreed that go where you will,
'Twixt sea and sea, at the south or the north,
None better than he, no braver hero,

None worthier honor could ever be found, 25
(They meant no slight to their master and lord
The good king Hrothgar, their ruler kind.)
Now and again the noble chiefs
Gave rein to their steeds, and spurred them to race,
Galloped their grays where the ground was smooth. 30
Now and again a gallant thane,
Whose mind was stored with many a lay,
With songs of battle and sagas old,
Bound new words in well-knit bars,
Told in verse the valor of Beowulf,
Matched his lines and moulded his lay.

Here is introduced an episode of the Nibelungen Legend. The gleeman
tells how Sigmund the Volsung, with his son and nephew Fitela, ranged
the forests and slew wild beasts. Later, when Fitela was no longer with
him, Sigmund killed a dragon and won a great treasure. [44 lines are
omitted.]

When the lay was ended they urged once more
Their racers fleet to fly o'er the plain.
As the morning sped, and the sun climbed higher,
Many went in, the marvellous sight 40
More closely to scan. The king himself
With a troop of trusty retainers about him
Strode from his bower; the bestower-of-rings
Came, and with him the queen, in state,
The meadow-path trod, by her maidens attended. 45

XIV

Hrothgar's Praise of Beowulf, and Beowulf's Reply

Hrothgar spoke when he reached the hall,
Stood on the step, and stared at the roof
Adorned with gold, and Grendel's hand:
"Prompt be my heart to praise the Almighty
For the sight I behold. Much harm have I suffered, 5
And grief from Grendel, but God still works
Wonder on wonder, the Warden of Glory.
But a little while since, I scarcely dared,
As long as I lived, to look for escape
From my burden of sorrow, when blood-stained stood 10
And dripping with slaughter, this stately hall.
Wide-spread woe my warriors scattered;

They never hoped this house to rid,
While life should last, this land-mark of people,
Of demons and devils. 'Tis done by the hero.   15
By the might of the Lord this man has finished
The feat that all of us failed to achieve
By wit or by war. And well may she say,
—Whoever she be,—that bore this son,
That the Ancient of Days dealt with her graciously,   20
And blest her in child-birth. Now Beowulf, hear!
I shall henceforth hold thee, hero beloved,
As child of my own, and cherish thee fondly
In kinship new. Thou shalt never lack
Meed of reward that is mine to give.   25
For deeds less mighty have I many times granted
Fullest reward to warriors feebler,
In battle less brave. Thy boldness and valor
Afar shall be known; thy fame shall live
To be great among men. Now God the Almighty   30
With honor reward thee, as ever he doth."

Beowulf spoke, the son of Ecgtheow:
"Gladly we fought this good fight through,
Fearlessly faced the foe inhuman,
Grappled him gruesome; it grieves me sore   35
That the man-beast himself you may not see,
Dead in the hall, fordone in the fray.
I meant to master the monster quickly,
To his death-bed pin him by power of my grip,
Hold him hard till my hand could strangle him,   40
Bringing him low, but he broke away.
In vain I tried to prevent his escape.
The Lord was unwilling; I lost my hold
On the man-destroyer; too strong was the monster,
Too swift on his feet. But to save his life   45
He left behind him the whole of his fore-paw,
Arm and shoulder. 'Twas a useless shift,
Profiting nothing. He ne'er will prolong
His life by the loss, the loathly slayer,
Sunk in sin; but sorrow holds him,   50
Caught in the grasp of its grip relentless,
In woful bonds to await in anguish,
Guilty wretch, the rest of his doom,
As the Lord Almighty shall mete it to him."

More silent seemed the son of Ecglaf,[10]   55
Less boastful in bragging of brave deeds done,
When all of them, looking aloft, beheld
The hand on high, where it hung 'neath the roof,
The claw of the fiend; each finger was armed
With a steel-like spur instead of a nail,   60
The heathen's handspikes, the horrible paw
Of the evil fiend. They all declared
No iron blade could e'er have bit
On the monstrous bulk of the man-beast's hide,
Or hewn away that woful talon.   65

XV

The Feasting and Giving of Treasure in the Hall

Now orders were given the guest-hall to cleanse,
And furnish it fresh. Forth went hurrying
Men and maids. To the mead-hall they went
And busily worked. Woven tapestries,
Glinting with gold, hung gay on the walls,   5
Marvellous wonders for men to look upon.
Ruin and wreck had been wrought in the building,
Though braced within by iron bands,
The hinges were wrenched, the roof alone stood
Undamaged and sound, when the sin-spotted wretch,   10
The demon destroyer, in despair of his life,
Turned and made off,—not easy it is
To escape from death, essay it who will
(So each of us all to his end must come,
Forced by fate to his final abode   15
Where his body, stretched on the bier of death,
Shall rest after revel.) Now right was the hour
For Healfdene's heir to enter the hall;
The king himself would come to the feast.
I never have heard of nobler bearing   20
'Mongst ranks of liegemen surrounding their lord
As they took their seats, the trusty comrades,
And fell to feasting. Freely quaffed
Many a mead-cup the mighty kinsmen,
Hrothgar and Hrothulf, the high hall within.   25
Heorot was filled with a friendly host.
(Far was the day when the Scylding host

[10] Unferth.

Should treachery plot, betraying each other.)
Then Healfdene's son bestowed on Beowulf
A gold-adorned banner for battle-reward,   30
A rich-broidered standard, breast-plate and helmet.
The swordmen assembled saw the treasures
Borne before the hero. Beowulf drank
The health of Hrothgar, nor had reason to feel
Ashamed before shieldmen to show his reward   35
Never were offered by earls that I heard of,
In token of friendship four such treasures,
Never was equalled such ale-bench bounty.
Round the ridge of the helmet a rim of iron,
Wound with wire, warded the head,   40
That the offspring of files, with fearful stroke,
The hard-tempered sword-blade, might harm it not,
When fierce in the battle the foemen should join.
At a sign from the king, eight stallions proud,
Bitted and bridled, were brought into hall.   45
On the back of one was a wondrous saddle,
Bravely wrought and bordered with jewels,
The battle-seat bold of the best of kings
When Hrothgar himself would ride to the sword-play.
(Nor flinched from the foe the famous warrior   50
In the front of the fight where fell the slain.)
To the hero delivered the lord of the Scyldings,
The heir of Ing, both armor and horses,
Gave them to Beowulf, and bade him enjoy them.
Thus royally, the ruler famous,   55
The heroes' hoard-guard, heaped his bounty;
Repaid the struggle with steeds and trophies,
Praised by all singers who speak the truth.

XVI

The King's Gifts to Beowulf's Men, and the Gleeman's Lay of Finn

The Lord of the earls then added gifts,
At the mead-bench remembered the men, each one,
That Beowulf brought o'er the briny deep,
With ancient heirlooms and offered to pay
In gold for the man that Grendel had slain,   5
As more of them surely the monster had killed
Had not holy God and the hero's courage
Averted their doom. (So daily o'errules

The Father Almighty the fortunes of men.
Therefore is insight ever the best,   10
And prudence of mind; for much shall suffer
Of lief and of loath who long endures
The days of his life in labor and toil.)
Now music and song were mingled together,
In the presence of Hrothgar, ruler in war.   15
Harp was struck and hero-lays told.
Along the mead-bench the minstrel spread
Cheer in hall when he chanted the lay
Of the sudden assault on the sons of Finn.

The episode which follows alludes obscurely to details of a feud between Frisians and Danes. The Finnsburg fragment contains a portion of the same story; and one of the heroes, Hnaef, is also mentioned in Widsith. [91 lines are here omitted.]

XVII

The Lay of Finn Ended. The Speech of the Queen

The lay was ended,
The gleeman's song. Sound of revelry
Rose again. Gladness spread
Along bench and board. Beer-thanes poured
From flagons old the flowing wine.   5
Wealhtheow the queen walked in state,
Under her crown, where uncle and nephew
Together sat,—they still were friends.
There too sat Unferth, trusted counsellor,
At Hrothgar's feet; though faith he had broken   10
With his kinsmen in battle, his courage was proved.
Then the queen of the Scyldings spoke these words:
"Quaff of this cup my king and my lord,
Gold-friend of men. To thy guests be kind,
To the men of the Jutes be generous with gifts.   15
Far and near thou now hast peace.
I have heard thou dost wish the hero for son
To hold as thy own, now Heorot is cleansed,
The jewel-bright hall. Enjoy while thou mayest,
Allotment of wealth, and leave to thy heirs   20
Kingdom and rule when arrives the hour
That hence thou shalt pass to thy place appointed.
Well I know that my nephew Hrothulf

Will cherish in honor our children dear
If thou leavest before him this life upon earth;   25
He will surely requite the kindness we showed him,
Faithfully tend our two young sons,
When to mind he recalls our care and affection,
How we helped him and housed him when *he* was a child."
She turned to the bench where her two boys sat,   30
Hrethric and Hrothmund, and the rest of the youth.
A riotous band, and right in their midst,
Between the two brothers, Beowulf sat.

XVIII

The Queen's Gifts to Beowulf

With courteous bow the cup she offered,
Greeted him graciously and gave him to boot
Two armlets rare of twisted gold,
A robe and rings, and the rarest collar;
A better was never known among men,   5
Since Hama brought to his bright-built hall
The jewelled necklace, the gem of the Brisings.

The 15 lines omitted here interrupt the narrative to tell of the subse-
quent history of Wealhtheow's gift; how Beowulf gave it to Hygelac, who
wore it on his famous raid against the Frisians, in which he was slain by
the Franks.

Before the warriors Wealhtheow spoke:
"Accept, dear Beowulf, this bright-gemmed collar;
Make happy use of this heirloom jewelled,   10
This ring and robe and royal treasure;
Be brave and bold. My boys instruct
In gentle manners; mine be the praise.
Thou hast done such a deed that in days to come
Men will proclaim thy might and valor   15
To the ends of the earth, where the ocean-wave
Washes the windy walls of the land.
I wish thee joy of thy jewelled treasure,
Long be thy life; enlarge thy prosperity,
Show thee a friend to my sons in deed.   20
Here each earl to the other is faithful,
True to his liege-lord, loyal and kind.
My warriors obey me, willing and prompt.
The Danes carousing, do as I bid."

She went to her seat, the wine flowed free; 25
'Twas a glorious feast. The fate that impended,
None of them knew, though near to them all.

When darkness came, the king of the Danes
Went to his rest in the royal bower;
But a throng of his kinsmen kept the hall 30
As they used to do in the days of old.
They cleared the boards and covered the floor
With beds and bolsters. One beer-thane there
Lay down to sleep with his doom upon him.
They placed by their heads their polished shields, 35
Their battle-boards bright, on the bench nearby.
Above each earl, within easy reach,
Was his helmet high and his harness of mail
And the spear-shaft keen. 'Twas their custom so,
That always at rest they were ready for war 40
At home or abroad, where'er they might be,
At what hour soever for aid might call
Their lord and king; they were comrades true.

END OF THE FIRST ADVENTURE

XIX

The Coming of Grendel's Dam to Avenge Her Son

Then sank they to sleep, but sorely paid
One poor wretch for his sleep that night.
The same thing fell, as in former days
When Grendel his raids on the gold-hall made,
Before the fiend had found his match, 5
Caught in his sins. 'Twas seen that night
An avenger survived the villainous fiend,
Although they had ceased from their sorrow and care.
'Twas Grendel's mother, a monstrous hag.
She remembered her loss. She had lived in the deep, 10
In a water-hell cold, since Cain had become
The evil slayer of his only brother,
His king by blood; accursed he fled,
Marked by murder, from men's delights,
Haunted the wilds; from him there sprung 15
Ghastly demon-shapes, Grendel was one.

The 10 lines omitted here break the narrative to turn back to the Grendel fight.

Now grim and vengeful
His mother set out on her errand of woe,
Damage to wreak for the death of her son.
Arrived at Heorot, the Ring-Danes she found   20
Asleep in the hall. Soon was to come
Surprise to the earls when into the hall
Burst Grendel's dam. (Less grim was the terror,
As terror of woman in war is less,
—The fury of maidens, than full-armed men's,   25
When the blood-stained war-blade with wire-bound hilt,
Hard and hammer-forged, hurtling through air,
Hews the boar from the helmet's crest.)
Many the swords that were suddenly drawn,
Blades from the benches; buckler and shield   30
Were tightly grasped; no time for the helmet,
For harness of mail, when the horror was on them.
The monster was minded to make for the open;
Soon as discovered, she sought to escape.
Quickly she seized a sleeping warrior,   35
Fast in her clutch to the fens she dragged him.
He was to Hrothgar of heroes the dearest,
Most trusted of liegemen between the two seas,
Comrade the nearest, killed in his sleep,
The bravest in battle. Nor was Beowulf there,   40
They had elsewhere quartered the earl that night,
After the giving of gifts in the hall.
There was shouting in Heorot; the hand she seized,
The bloody talon, she took away.
Sorrow was renewed in the nearby dwellings,   45
Bad was the bargain that both had made
To pay for their friends with further lives lost.
With grief overcome was the gray-haired king,
When he learned that his thane was alive no more,
His dearest comrade by death o'ertaken;   50
Quick from his bower was Beowulf fetched,
The hero brave. At break of dawn
He with his comrades came to the place
Where the king in sorrow was waiting to see
Whether God the Wielder of All would grant him   55
A turn in his tide of trouble and woe.

Then entered the room the ready hero;
With his band of brave men the boards resounded.
He eagerly greeted the aged ruler,
Delayed not to ask the lord of the Ingwines 60
If his night had passed in peace and quiet.

XX

Hrothgar Describes the Haunt of the Monster
and Asks Beowulf to Undertake
a Second Adventure

Hrothgar spoke, the Scylding defender:
"Speak not of peace for pain is renewed
'Mongst all the Danes. Dead is Æschere,
Elder brother of Irmenlaf,
My comrade true and counsellor trusted, 5
My right-hand friend when in front of the combat
We stood shoulder to shoulder, when shieldburg broke,
And boar-crests crashed in battle together.
Earls should ever like Æschere be.
On Heorot's floor he was foully slain 10
By warlock wild. I wot not whither
The prey-proud fury hath fled to cover,
Glutted and gorged. With gruesome claws
And violence fierce she avenged thy deed,
The slaying of Grendel her son last night, 15
Because too long my loyal thanes
He had hunted and hurt. In the hall he fell,
His life was forfeit. To the fray returned
Another as cruel, her kin to avenge;
Faring from far, the feud re-opened. 20
Hence many a thane shall mourn and think
Of the giver of gifts with grief renewed
And heart-woe heavy. The hand lies low
That fain would have helped and defended you all.
I have heard my people, the peasant folk 25
Who house by the border and hold the fens,
Say they have seen two creatures strange,
Huge march-stalkers, haunting the moorland,
Wanderers outcast. One of the two
Seemed to their sight to resemble a woman; 30
The other manlike, a monster misshapen,
But huger in bulk than human kind,

Trod an exile's track of woe.
The folk of the fen in former days
Named him Grendel. Unknown his father,   35
Or what his descent from demons obscure.
Lonely and waste is the land they inhabit,
Wolf-cliffs wild and windy headlands,
Ledges of mist, where mountain torrents
Downward plunge to dark abysses,   40
And flow unseen. Not far from here
O'er the moorland in miles, a mere expands:
Spray-frosted trees o'erspread it, and hang
O'er the water with roots fast wedged in the rocks.
There nightly is seen, beneath the flood,   45
A marvellous light. There lives not the man
Has fathomed the depth of the dismal mere.
Though the heather-stepper, the strong-horned stag,
Seek this cover, forspent with the chase,
Tracked by the hounds, he will turn at bay,   50
To die on the brink ere he brave the plunge,
Hide his head in the haunted pool.
Wan from its depths the waves are dashed,
When wicked storms are stirred by the wind,
And from sullen skies descends the rain.   55
In thee is our hope of help once more.
Not yet thou hast learned where leads the way
To the lurking-hole of this hatcher of outrage.
Seek, if thou dare, the dreaded spot!
Richly I pay thee for risking this fight,   60
With heirlooms golden and ancient rings,
As I paid thee before, if thou come back alive."

XXI

The Arrival of Hrothgar and Beowulf at
Grendel's Mere

Beowulf spoke, the son of Ecgtheow:
"Sorrow not, gray-beard, nor grieve o'er thy friend!
Vengeance is better than bootless mourning.
To each of us here the end must come
Of life upon earth: let him who may   5
Win glory ere death. I deem that best,
The lot of the brave, when life is over.
Rise, O realm-ward, ride we in haste,
To track the hag that whelped this Grendel.

I tell thee in truth, she may turn where she will,   10
No cave of ocean nor cover of wood,
No hole in the ground shall hide her from me.
But one day more thy woe endure,
And nurse thy hope as I know thou wilt."
Sprang to his feet the sage old king,   15
Gave praise to God for the promise spoken.
And now for Hrothgar a horse was bridled,
A curly-maned steed. The king rode on,
Bold on his charger. A band of shield-men
Followed on foot. Afar they saw   20
Footprints leading along the forest.
They followed the tracks, and found she had crossed
Over the dark moor, dragging the body
Of the goodliest thane that guarded with Hrothgar
Heorot Hall, and the home of the king.   25
The well-born hero held the trail;
Up rugged paths, o'er perilous ridges,
Through passes narrow, an unknown way,
By beetling crags, and caves of the nicors.
With a chosen few he forged ahead,   30
Warriors skilled, to scan the way.
Sudden they came on a cluster of trees
Overhanging a hoary rock,
A gloomy grove; and gurgling below,
A stir of waters all stained with blood.   35
Sick at heart were the Scylding chiefs,
Many a thane was thrilled with woe,
For there they beheld the head of Æschere
Far beneath at the foot of the cliff.
They leaned and watched the waters boil   40
With bloody froth. The band sat down,
While the war-horn sang its summons to battle.
They saw in the water sea-snakes a many,
Wave-monsters weird, that wallowed about.
At the base of the cliff lay basking the nicors,   45
Who oft at sunrise ply seaward their journey,
To hunt on the ship-trails and scour the main,
Sea-beasts and serpents. Sudden they fled,
Wrathful and grim, aroused by the hail
Of the battle-horn shrill. The chief of the Jutes,   50
With a bolt from his bow a beast did sunder
From life and sea-frolic; sent the keen shaft

Straight to his vitals. Slow he floated,
Upturned and dead at the top of the waves.
Eager they boarded their ocean-quarry;   55
With barb-hooked boar-spears the beast they gaffed,
Savagely broached him and brought him to shore,
Wave-plunger weird. The warriors viewed
The grisly stranger. But straightway Beowulf
Donned his corslet nor cared for his life. . . .   60

  The 30 lines here omitted break the narrative with a description of
Beowulf's armor and the sword Hrunting, lent him by Unferth.

XXII
Beowulf's Fight with Grendel's Dam

To Hrothgar spoke the son of Ecgtheow:
"Remember O honored heir of Healfdene,
Now that I go, thou noble king,
Warriors' gold-friend, what we agreed on,
If I my life should lose in thy cause,   5
That thou wouldst stand in stead of my father,
Fulfil his office when I was gone.
Be guardian, thou, to my thanes and kinsmen,
My faithful friends, if I fail to return.
To Hygelac send, Hrothgar beloved,   10
The goodly gifts thou gavest to me.
May the lord of the Jutes, when he looks on this treasure,
May Hrethel's son, when he sees these gifts,
Know that I found a noble giver,
And joyed, while I lived, in a generous lord.   15
This ancient heirloom to Unferth give,
To the far-famed warrior, my wondrous sword
Of matchless metal, I must with Hrunting
Glory gain, or go to my death."

After these words the Weder-Jute lord   20
Sprang to his task, nor staid for an answer.
Swiftly he sank 'neath the swirling flood;
'Twas an hour's time ere he touched the bottom.
Soon the sea-hag, savage and wild,
Who had roamed through her watery realms at will,   25
For winters a hundred, was 'ware from below,
An earthling had entered her ocean domain.
Quickly she reached and caught the hero;

Grappled him grimly with gruesome claws.
Yet he got no scratch, his skin was whole;   30
His battle-sark shielded his body from harm.
In vain she tried, with her crooked fingers,
To tear the links of his close-locked mail.
Away to her den the wolf-slut dragged
Beowulf the bold, o'er the bottom ooze.   35
Though eager to smite her, his arm was helpless.
Swimming monsters swarmed about him,
Dented his mail with dreadful tusks.
Sudden the warrior was 'ware they had come
To a sea-hall strange and seeming hostile,   40
Where water was not nor waves oppressed,
For the caverned rock all round kept back
The swallowing sea.[11] He saw a light,
A flicker of flame that flashed and shone.
Now first he discerned the sea-hag monstrous.   45
The water wife wolfish. His weapon he raised,
And struck with his sword a swinging blow.
Sang on her head the hard-forged blade
Its war song wild. But the warrior found
That his battle-flasher refused to bite,   50
Or maim the foe. It failed its master
In the hour of need, though oft it had cloven
Helmets, and carved the casques of the doomed
In combats fierce. For the first time now
That treasure failed him, fallen from honor.   55
But Hygelac's earl took heart of courage;
In mood defiant he fronted his foe.
The angry hero hurled to the ground,
In high disdain, the hilt of the sword,
The gaudy and jewelled; rejoiced in the strength   00
Of his arm unaided. So all should do
Who glory would find and fame abiding,
In the crash of conflict, nor care for their lives.
The Lord of the Battle-Jutes braved the encounter;
The murderous hag by the hair he caught;   65
Down he dragged the dam of Grendel
In his swelling rage, till she sprawled on the floor.
Quick to repay in kind what she got,
On her foe she fastened her fearful clutches;

[11] perhaps a cave behind a waterfall.

Enfolded the warrior weary with fighting;   70
The sure-footed hero stumbled and fell.
As helpless he lay, she lept on him fiercely;
Unsheathed her hip-knife, shining and broad,
Her son to avenge, her offspring sole.
But the close-linked corselet covered his breast,   75
Foiled the stroke and saved his life.
All had been over with Ecgtheow's son,
Under the depths of the ocean vast,
Had not his harness availed to help him,
His battle-net stiff, and the strength of God.   80
The Ruler of battles aright decided it;
The Wielder all-wise awarded the victory:
Lightly the hero leaped to his feet.

XXIII

Beowulf's Victory and Return to Heorot

He spied 'mongst the arms a sword surpassing,
Huge and ancient, a hard-forged slayer,
Weapon matchless and warriors' delight,
Save that its weight was more than another
Might bear into battle or brandish in war;   5
Giants had forged that finest of blades.
Then seized its chain-hilt the chief of the Scyldings;
His wrath was aroused, reckless his mood,
As he brandished the sword for a savage blow.
Bit the blade in the back of her neck,   10
Cut the neck-bone, and cleft its way
Clean through her flesh; to the floor she sank;
The sword was gory; glad was the hero.
A light flashed out from the inmost den,
Like heaven's candle, when clear it shines   15
From cloudless skies. He scanned the cave,
Walked by the wall, his weapon upraised.
Grim in his hand the hilt he gripped.
Well that sword had served him in battle.
Steadily onward he strode through the cave,   20
Ready to wreak the wrongs untold,
That the man-beast had wrought in the realm of Danes.

[Here are omitted 6 lines.]

He gave him his due when Grendel he found
Stretched as in sleep, and spent with the battle.

But dead was the fiend, the fight at Heorot   25
Had laid him low. The lifeless body
Sprang from the blows of Beowulf's sword,
As fiercely he hacked the head from the carcass.
But the men who were watching the water with Hrothgar
Suddenly saw a stir in the waves,   30
The chop of the sea all churned up with blood
And bubbling gore. The gray-haired chiefs
For Beowulf grieved, agreeing together
That hope there was none of his home-returning,
With victory crowned, to revisit his lord.   35
Most of them feared he had fallen prey
To the mere-wolf dread in the depths of the sea.
When evening came, the Scyldings all
Forsook the headland, and Hrothgar himself
Turned homeward his steps. But sick at heart   40
The strangers sat and stared at the sea,
Hoped against hope to behold their comrade
And leader again.
                          Now that goodly sword
Began to melt with the gore of the monster;
In bloody drippings it dwindled away   45
'Twas a marvellous sight: it melted like ice,
When fetters of frost the Father unlocks,
Unravels the ropes of the wrinkled ice,
Lord and Master of months and seasons.
Beheld in the hall the hero from Juteland   50
Treasures unnumbered, but naught he took,
Save Grendel's head, and the hilt of the sword,
Bright and jewelled,—the blade had melted,
Its metal had vanished, so venomous hot
Was the blood of the demon-brute dead in the cave.   55

Soon was in the sea the slayer of monsters;
Upward he shot through the shimmer of waves;
Cleared was the ocean, cleansed were its waters,
The wolfish water-hag wallowed no more;
The mere-wife had yielded her miserable life.   60
Swift to the shore the sailors' deliverer
Came lustily swimming, with sea-spoil laden;
Rejoiced in the burden he bore to the land.
Ran to meet him his mailéd comrades,
With thanks to God who gave them their leader   65

Safe again back and sound from the deep.
Quickly their hero's helmet they loosened,
Unbuckled his breastplate. The bloodstained waves
Fell to a calm 'neath the quiet sky.
Back they returned o'er the tracks with the footprints,   70
Merrily measured the miles o'er the fen,
Way they knew well, those warriors brave;
Brought from the holm-cliff the head of the monster;
'Twas toil and labor to lift the burden,
Four of their stoutest scarce could carry it   75
Swung from a spear-pole, a staggering load.

[Here are omitted 3 lines.]

Thus the fourteen of them, thanes adventurous,
Marched o'er the moor to the mead-hall of Hrothgar.
Tall in the midst of them towered the hero;
Strode among his comrades, till they came to the hall.   80
In went Beowulf, the brave and victorious,
Battle-beast hardy, Hrothgar to greet.
Lifting by the hair the head of Grendel,
They laid it in the hall, where the heroes were carousing,
Right before the king, and right before the queen;   85
Gruesome was the sight that greeted the Danes.

XXIV, XXV

Beowulf's Story of His Fight, and
Hrothgar's Counsel

Beowulf spoke, the son of Ecgtheow:
"Gladly we offer this ocean-booty,
That here thou lookest on, lord of the Scyldings,
For sign of victory, son of Healfdene.
Hard was the fight I fought under water;   5
That combat nearly cost me my life.
Soon had been ended the ocean-encounter,
Had God in his mercy not given me aid.
No help I got from the good blade Hrunting;
The well-tried weapon worthless proved.   10
By the grace of God, who guided me friendless,
A splendid old sword I spied on the wall,
Hanging there, huge; by the hilt I grasped it,
And seeing my chance, I struck amain
At the sea-cave's wardens, when sudden the blade   15
Melted and burned, as the blood gushed out,

The battle-gore hot. The hilt I saved
From the villainous fiends, and avenged their crimes,
The murder of the Danes, as was meet and due.
I promise thee now, in peace thou shalt sleep   20
In Heorot hall, with the whole of thy band.
Thou and thy thanes may throng within
As ye used of yore, both young and old.
Thou need'st not fear renewal of strife,
Harm to thy folk at the hands of the fiends."   25
The golden hilt was given to the king;
The jewelled work of the giants of old
Came into hand of the hoary warrior.
On the death of the demons, the Danish lord kept it,
Wondersmiths' work. When the world was rid   30
Of the evil fiend, the enemy of God,
Guilty of murder, and his mother too,
The trophy passed to the peerless lord,
The goodliest king, that gave out treasure
Between the two seas on Scandia's isle.   35
Hrothgar gazed on the golden hilt,
Relic of old, where was writ the tale
Of a far-off fight, when the flood o'erwhelmed,
The raging sea, the race of the giants
(They wantonly dared to war against God;   40
Then rose in his wrath the Ruler Eternal,
'Neath the heaving billows buried them all.)
On the polished gold of the guard of the hilt,
Runes were writ that rightly told,
To him that read them, for whom that weapon,   45
Finest of sword-blades, first was made,
The splendid hilt with serpents entwined.
All were silent, when the son of Healfdene,
The wise king spoke: "Well may he say,
The aged ruler, who aye upholds   50
Truth and right, 'mid the ranks of his people,
Whose mind runs back to by-gone days,
This guest is born of a goodly breed.
Thy fame shall fly afar among men,
Beowulf my friend, firmly thou holdest   55
Both wisdom and might. My word will I keep,
The love that I proffered. Thou shalt prove a deliverer
To thy folk and followers in far-off years,
A help to the heroes. Not Heremod thus,

Ecgwela's heir, did offer at need   60
His strength to the Scyldings; instead, he brought
Slaughter and death on the sons of the Danes.
Swoln with wrath he slew his comrades,
His friends at the board and fled alone,
Ill-famed earl, an outcast from men.   65
Though God endowed him with gifts of strength,
With boldness and might above all men,
And prospered him greatly, yet he grew to be
Blood-thirsty and cruel. No bracelets he gave
To the Danes as was due, but dwelt in gloom,   70
Reaped the reward of the woful strife,
And wearisome feud. Take warning from him."

  Hrothgar now delivers a long sermon to Beowulf on the dangers of
pride, the fickleness of fortune, and the brevity of life, and ends by asking
him to sit down to the feast, promising more gifts on the morrow. [43 lines
are omitted.]

Beowulf hastened, happy in mood,
To seek his bench as bid by the king.
Once more, as of old, for the earls in hall,   75
The famous in battle, the board was set
For feasting anew. When night with its shadows
O'erwhelmed the world, the heroes arose.
The gray-haired ruler his rest would seek,
The Scylding his bed; and Beowulf too,   80
The lusty warrior, longed for his sleep.
Soon an attendant showed the way
To the stranger from far, spent with his faring.
With courtly custom, he cared for his needs.
All that to warriors, overseas wandering,   85
Was due in those days, he did for the guest.
High-gabled and gold-decked, the gift-hall towered;
The stout-hearted hero slept soundly within,
Till the raven black, with blithe heart hailed
The bliss of heaven, and bright the sun   90
Came gliding o'er earth. Then, eager to start,
The warriors wakened; they wished to set out
On their homeward journey. The hero brave
Would board his ship, and back again sail.
The hardy one bade that Hrunting be brought   95
To the son of Ecglaf:[12] the sword he offered him;

[12] Unferth.

Thanked him for lending the lovely weapon;
Called it a war-friend, keen in the battle;
Not a word in blame of the blade he uttered,
Great-hearted hero. Now hastened the guests,   100
Eager to part, and armed for their voyage.
Their dauntless leader, beloved of the Danes.
Came to the high-seat, and to Hrothgar the king
The bold-in-battle now bade farewell.

XXVI
Beowulf's Leave-Taking of Hrothgar

Beowulf spoke, the son of Ecgtheow:
"Now we sea-farers would make known our desire;
Far-travelled wanderers, we wish to return
To Hygelac now. A hearty welcome
We here have found, thou hast harbored us well.   5
If ever on earth I may anywise win,
Master of men, more of thy love
Than now I have won, for another adventure
Of arms and war I am eager and willing.
If ever I hear, o'er the ocean-ways   10
That neighbor-tribes threaten annoyance or war,
As feud-seeking foemen aforetime assailed thee,
A thousand thanes to thee will I bring,
Heroes to help thee. For Hygelac, I know,
Though young in years will yield me aid;   15
The people's Shepherd will surely help me
By word and deed to do thee service,
And bring thee spear-shafts to speed thee in battle,
Thy might to strengthen when men thou needest.
If ever Hrethric, heir of thy line,   20
Should come to sojourn at the court of the Jutes,
A host of friends he will find awaiting him.
Who boasts himself brave, abroad should travel."
The aged Hrothgar answering spoke:
"To utter these words, the All-wise Lord   25
Hath prompted thy heart; more prudent counsel
From one in years so young as thou,
I never have heard. Thou art hardy in strength,
And sage in spirit, and speakest well.
If ever it happen that Hrethel's heir   30
Be stricken by spear and slain in battle,

If sickness or sword assail thy lord,
And thou survive him, I think it likely
The Sea-Jutes in vain will seek for a better
As choice for their king, their chief to become   35
And rule o'er the thanes, if thou be willing
The lordship to hold. The longer I know thee
The better I like thee, Beowulf my friend.
Thou hast brought it about that both our peoples,
Jutes and the Spear-Danes, shall be joined in peace.   40
They shall cease from war, the strife shall be ended,
The feuds of aforetime, so fiercely waged.
While I rule this realm, our riches we share;
Many shall travel with treasure laden,
Each other to greet, o'er the gannet's bath;   45
O'er the rolling waves the ringéd prow
Tokens of friendship shall freely bring
And bind our people in peace together,
Toward friend and foe, in faith as of old."

Still other treasures, twelve in all,   50
Healfdene's heir in the hall bestowed
On Beowulf brave, and bade him take them
And seek his people, and soon return.
Then kissed the king, of kin renowned,
The thane beloved. The lord of the Scyldings   55
Fell on his neck. Fast flowed the tears
Of the warrior gray; he weighed both chances,
But held to the hope, though hoary with years,
That each should see the other again,
And meet in the mead-hall. The man was so dear   60
That he could not restrain the storm in his breast.
Locked in his heart, a hidden longing
For the man he loved so, left him no peace,
And burnt in his blood. But Beowulf went;
The gold-decked hero the grass-way trod,   65
Proud of his booty. The boat awaited
Its owner and master, where at anchor it rode.
As they went on their way, the warriors praised
The bounty of Hrothgar, the blameless king.
None was his equal till age snatched away   70
The joy of his manhood,—no mortal it spares.

XXVII

Beowulf's Return Voyage to Hygelac

Then came to the coast the comrades brave,
The lusty warriors, wearing their ring-nets,
Their chain-linked corslets. The coast-guard saw them,
The same that at first had spied them coming;
This time he chose not to challenge them harshly,   5
But gave them his greeting, galloping toward them.
Said the Weder-folk would welcome the sight of them,
Boarding their ship in shining armor.
Then by the sands, the seaworthy craft,
The iron-ringed keel, with arms was laden,   10
With horses and treasure. On high the mast
Towered above the treasures of Hrothgar.
To the man who had waited as watchman aboard,
Beowulf gave a gold-bound sword.
(Oft on the mead-bench that heirloom precious   15
Its owner would honor.) When all had embarked,
They drove for the deep, from Daneland's shore.
Then soon did the mast its sea suit wear,
A sail was unfurled, made fast with ropes,
The sea-wood sang as she sped o'er the ocean,   20
No baffling head-wind hindered her course;
The foamy-necked floater flew o'er the billows,
The sea-craft staunch o'er the salt-sea waves,
Till they came in sight of the cliffs of Jutland
The well known capes, and the wind-driven keel,   25
Grating the sand, stood still on the shore.
Soon was at hand the harbor-watch eager.
Long had he looked for his loved companions,
Scanning the sea for their safe return.
The broad-bosomed boat to the beach he moored   30
With anchor-ropes fast, lest the force of the waves
That comely craft should cast adrift.
Then Beowulf bade them bring ashore
His treasure-cargo of costly gold
And weapons fine; not far was the way   35
To Hygelac's hall, where at home he dwelt,
The king and his comrades, close by the sea.

END OF THE SECOND ADVENTURE

After the death of Hygelac and his son, Beowulf became king of the Jutes, and ruled over them fifty years. In his old age his people were harried by a fire-dragon, whom the hero went out to fight. It seems that an outlaw, banished and flying for shelter, had come upon a treasure hid in a deep cave or barrow, guarded by a dragon. Long years before, an earl, the last of his race, had buried the treasure. After his death the dragon, sniffing about the stones, had found it and guarded it three hundred years, until the banished man discovered the place, and carried off one of the golden goblets. In revenge the dragon made nightly raids on Beowulf's realm, flying through the air, spitting fire, burning houses and villages, even Beowulf's hall, the "gift-stool" of the Jutes. Beowulf had an iron shield made against the dragon's fiery breath, and with eleven companions, sought out the hill-vault near the sea. These events are related in Sections XXVIII—XXXV of the *Beowulf* MS.

Author and Selection Notes

The heroic poem *Beowulf* stands at the beginning of English literature. It is also the earliest important poem of the modern languages of Europe. In all probability it was composed immediately after 700 A.D. somewhere in the north of England. The identity of its author is lost, but he would seem to have been a poet in the household of a tribal ruler, no doubt a courtly person of aristocratic understanding. In all probability he was acquainted with Virgil's great epic, *The Aeneid*. Although the atmosphere of the poem is from the ancient past and far away regions of the Baltic, the manners and customs portrayed seem to be those of the poet's own time.

The poem itself falls into three main adventures, two of which appear in this text. The first two adventures constitute a continuous narrative.

Questions and Exercises

1. Discuss the customs, war, and comradeship of Beowulf's time as they are revealed in the narrative.

2. What do you think of the characters? Do they seem like real people?

3. Can you find Biblical references or allusions? Discuss the religious elements of both a Christian and a heathen nature found in this narrative. What does Beowulf's religion seem to be?

4. Can you imagine the narrative without Grendel? Explain.

5. Write a character sketch of Beowulf.

6. What do you think about Beowulf's boasting before going into battle? Is this description of his boasting before meeting Grendel psychologically sound?

7. Analyze section III, lines 22-36, in relation to assonance, consonance, alliteration, simile, and rhythm. If you are not familiar with these terms,

refer to *A Handbook to Literature* by Thrall, Hibbard, and Holman or some other good reference book.

8. Look up the definition of "kenning" in *A Handbook to Literature* and list six kennings from *Beowulf*.

9. Theme Topics: An Old Story or Legend I Once Heard; Grendel's Mother; The Vivid Descriptions in *Beowulf*.

THE WIFE'S LAMENT

A song I sing of sorrow unceasing,
The tale of my trouble, the weight of my woe,
Woe of the present, and woe of the past,
Woe never-ending of exile and grief,
But never since girlhood greater than now.   5
First, the pang when my lord departed,
Far from his people, beyond the sea;
Bitter the heartache at break of dawn,
The longing for rumor in what far land
So weary a time my loved one tarried.   10
Far I wandered then, friendless and homeless,
Seeking for help in my heavy need.
With secret plotting his kinsman purposed
To wedge us apart, wide worlds between,
And bitter hate. I was sick at heart.   15
Harshly my lord bade lodge me here.
In all this land I had few to love me,
Few that were loyal, few that were friends.
Wherefore my spirit is heavy with sorrow
To learn my beloved, my dear man and mate,   20
Bowed by ill-fortune and bitter in heart,
Is masking his purpose and planning a wrong.
With blithe hearts often of old we boasted
That nought should part us save death alone;
All that has failed and our former love   25
Is now as if it had never been!
Far or near where I fly there follows
The hate of him who was once so dear.
In this forest-grove they have fixed my abode

From *An Anthology of Old English Poetry*, translated by Charles W. Kennedy, copyright 1960 by Oxford University Press, Inc. Reprinted by permission.

Under an oak in a cavern of earth,   30
An old cave-dwelling of ancient days,
Where my heart is crushed by the weight of my woe.
Gloomy its depths and the cliffs that o'er hang it,
Grim are its confines with thorns overgrown—
A joyless dwelling where daily the longing   35
For an absent loved one brings anguish of heart.
Lovers there are who may live their love,
Joyously keeping the couch of bliss,
While I in my earth-cave under the oak
Pace to and fro in the lonely dawn.   40
Here must I sit through the summer-long day,
Here must I weep in affliction and woe;
Yet never, indeed, shall my heart know rest
From all its anguish, and all its ache,
Wherewith life's burdens have brought me low.   45
Ever man's years are subject to sorrow,
His heart's thoughts bitter, though his bearing be blithe;
Troubled his spirit, beset with distress—
Whether all wealth of the world be his lot,
Or haunted by Fate in a far country   50
My beloved is sitting soul-weary and sad,
Swept by the storm, and stiff with the frost,
In a wretched cell under rocky cliffs
By severing waters encircled about—
Sharpest of sorrow my lover must suffer   55
Remembering always a happier home.
Woeful his fate whose doom is to wait
With longing heart for an absent love.

Author and Selection Notes

In the Exeter Book are two short poems to which the titles "The Wife's
Lament" and "The Husband's Message" have been given. These, though
perhaps not written consecutively, are quite similar in theme. The fact
that each deals with the tragic separation of a man and woman seems to
identify them with each other. In "The Wife's Lament" a woman speaks
of her exiled husband, who, before his departure, commanded his kinsmen to condemn her to living in a dreary cave. Unfortunately, no reason
is given for his command. The wife, nonetheless, loves the husband and
with great feeling longs for his return to her.

In "The Husband's Message" the speaker is in reality a letter carved on
a sapling. The husband, in exile and living overseas, chiseled a message
asking his wife to take a ship and join him in his distant world.

The two poems are of interest in that they express universal feelings and sentiments. They were probably composed in the ninth century.

Questions and Exercises

1. Can you decide from the content of the poem why the husband is in a far country and why "his kinsmen purposed to wedge" the couple apart?

2. Why is the husband "masking his purpose and planning a wrong"? Can you identify the wrong?

3. Why does her husband's family hide the wife "under an oak in a cavern of earth"? How does this line reflect the general feeling of the poem?

4. Near the end of "The Wife's Lament" the wife seems inconsistent; that is, she no longer speaks of an unfaithful, deserting husband, but a beloved "sitting soul-weary and sad, swept by the storm . . . remembering always a happier home." Write your explanation of this apparent inconsistency.

5. Theme Topics: Inlaws, an Age-Old Problem; Unforeseen Problems in Marriage; Marriage and Separation; Absence Makes (Does Not Make) the Heart Grow Fonder.

THE HUSBAND'S MESSAGE

In the sand I grew, by the rocky sea-wall
Near the surf firm rooted in fixed abode.
Few were the men who beheld my refuge
In the lonely reaches beside the sea;
Only the dark wave at the day's dawning   5
Sportively bound me in flowing embrace.
Little I weened that I, who was voiceless,
Should ever hold speech, or discourse at the feast.
That is a marvel amazing the mind
Of those who know little of such-like things   10
How a knife's sharp edge, and a strong hand's skill,
Steel's keen point, and man's cunning craft,
Purposely planned me, assigned me my part
To give thee a message that we two may grasp,
To utter it boldly, yet so that no other   15
May publish abroad the words I report.

From *An Anthology of Old English Poetry,* translated by Charles W. Kennedy, copyright 1960 by Oxford University Press, Inc. Reprinted by permission.

To thine ear only I tell the tale
How first as a sapling I flourished and grew.

*   *   *   *

In the hold of a ship, o'er the salt sea-streams,
Where my liege lord sent me oft I have sailed.   20
Now in a bark's bosom here am I borne.
Now shalt thou learn of my lord's loyal love;
His enduring affection I dare to affirm.
Lady ring-laden, he bade me implore thee,
Who carved this wood, that thou call to mind   25
The pledges ye plighted before ye were parted,
While still in the same land together ye shared
A lordly home and the rapture of love,
Before a feud drove him far from his folk.
He it is bids me eagerly urge   30
When from the hill slope, out of the wood,
Thou hearest the cuckoo plaintively calling,
Haste thee to ship on the tossing sea.
Let no living man, then, delay thee in sailing,
Stay thee in leaving or stop thee in flight.   35
Spread thy sail on the home of the sea-mew,
Take seat in thy galley, and steer away south
To where o'er the sea-lane thy lover awaits.
No greater bliss could his heart engage
In all the world—'twas his word to me—   40
If God the Almighty would grant you two
To dwell together and deal out gifts,
To tired retainers, of treasure and rings.
He hath abundance of beaten gold. . . .

*   *   *   *

Now in a far land my lord holds in fee   45
Home and fair fields . . . though here once of old,
Fated and lonely, need forced him to flight,
Launching his ship on the lanes of the deep,
Churning the sea-streams in haste to escape.
Now his troubles are over and all distress,   50
He lacks no wealth that the heart may wish,
Jewels and horses and joys of the hall,
Now any fair treasure that earth can afford.
O Prince's daughter! If he may possess thee,

To add to the pledges ye plighted of old,   55
Here S and R together I set,
EA, W, and D, by oath to declare
That while life lasts so long he'll be faithful
To lover's vow and to true love's pledge
Which often ye plighted in days of old.   60

Author and Selection Notes

See page 284.

Questions and Exercises

1. Does the poem give a clue as to why the husband and wife were separated?

2. In what season does the message ask the wife to join her husband?

3. Would you say that "none but the lonely heart" could express the husband's sentiment? Do you feel that the expression of the husband's loneliness is genuine?

4. The author (or authors) of "The Wife's Lament" and "The Husband's Message" is unknown. What kind of person would you imagine him to be?

5. Analyze "The Wife's Lament" and "The Husband's Message" and write a complete love story based on the events and comments in the two poems.

HOW SIEGFRIED WAS SLAIN

Gunther and Hagen, the passing bold knights, faithlessly let cry a-hunting in the woods, that with sharp spears they would hunt boars and bears and bison. What might be braver? With them rode Siegfried in lordly guise; many kinds of victual did they take along. At a cool spring he later lost his life, the which Brunhild, King Gunther's wife, had counseled. The bold knight then went to where he found Kriemhild. His costly hunting garb and those of his fellowship were already bound upon the sumpters, for they would cross the Rhine. Never could Kriemhild have been more sorrowful. He kissed his love upon her mouth. "God let me see thee, lady, still in

From *The Nibelungenlied*, translated by G. H. Needler. Reprinted by permission of Holt, Rinehart and Winston, Inc.

health and grant that thine eyes may see me too. Thou shalt have pastime with thy loving kinsmen. I may not stay at home."

Then she thought of the tale she had told to Hagen, though she durst not say a whit. The noble queen began to rue that she was ever born. Lord Siegfried's wife wept out of measure. She spake to the knight: "Let be your hunting. I had an evil dream last night, how two wild boars did chase you across the heath; then flowers grew red. I have in truth great cause to weep so sore. I be much adread of sundry plans and whether we have not misserved some who might bear us hostile hate. Tarry here, dear my lord, that I counsel by my troth."

He spake: "Dear love, I'll come back in a few short days. I wot not here of people who bear me aught of hate. Each and all of thy kinsmen be my friends, nor have I deserved it other of the knights."

"No, no, Sir Siegfried, in truth I fear thy fall. I had last night an evil dream, how two mountains fell upon thee. I saw thee nevermore. It doth cut me to the heart, that thou wilt part from me."

In his arms he clasped his courteous wife and kissed her tenderly. Then in a short space he took his leave and parted hence. Alas, she never saw him in health again.

Then they rode from thence into a deep wood for pastime's sake. Many bold knights did follow Gunther and his men, but Gernot and Giselher stayed at home. Many laden sumpters were sent before them across the Rhine, the which bare for the hunting fellowship bread and wine, meat and fish, and great store of other things, which so mighty a king might rightly have. They bade the proud huntsmen and bold halt before a green wood over against the courses of the game, upon a passing broad glade where they should hunt. The king was told that Siegfried, too, was come. The hunting fellowship now took their stand on every side. Then the bold knight, the sturdy Siegfried, asked: "Ye heroes bold and brave, who shall lead us to the game within the wood?"

"Let us part," spake Hagen, "ere we begin the chase. Thereby my lords and I may know who be the best hunter on this woodland journey. Let us divide the folk and hounds and let each turn whithersoever he list. He who doth hunt the best shall have our thanks." Short time the huntsmen bided by another after that.

Then spake Lord Siegfried: "I need no dogs save one brach that hath been trained that he can tell the track of the beasts through the pine woods." Quoth Kriemhild's husband: "We'll find the game."

Then an old huntsman took a good sleuthhound and in a short space brought the lord to where many beasts were found. Whatso rose from its lair the comrades hunted as good hunters still are wont to do. Whatever the brach started, bold Siegfried, the hero of Netherland, slew with his hand. His horse did run so hard that none escaped him. In the chase he gained the prize above them all. Doughty enow he was in all things. The beast which he slew with his hands was the first, a mighty boar; after which he found full soon a monstrous lion. When the brach started this from its lair, he shot it with his bow, in which he had placed a full sharp arrow. After the shot the lion ran the space of but three bounds. The hunting fellowship gave Siegfried thanks. Thereafter he speedily slew a bison and an elk, four strong ure-oxen, and a savage shelk. His horse bare him so swiftly that naught escaped him, nor could hart or hind avoid him. Then the sleuth-hound found a mighty boar, when he began to flee, at once there came the master of the hunt and encountered him upon his path. Wrathfully the boar did run against the valiant hero, but Kriemhild's husband slew him with his sword. Another huntsmen might not have done this deed so lightly. When he had felled him, they leashed the sleuth-hound; his rich booty was soon well known to the Burgundian men.

Then spake his huntsmen: "Sir Siegfried, if might so be, let us leave a deal of the beasts alive. Ye'll empty both our hill and woods to-day."

At this the brave knight and a bold gan smile. Then the calls of men and the baying of hounds were heard on every side; so great was the noise that both hill and pine woods echoed with the sound. The huntsmen had let loose full four and twenty packs. Then passing many beasts must needs lose their lives. Each man weened to bring it to pass that men should give him the prize of the hunt, that might not be, for the stalwart Siegfried was already standing by the fire. The chase was over, and yet not quite. Those who would to the camp-fire brought with them thither hides of many beasts and game in plenty. Ho, how much the king's meiny bare them to the kitchen!

Then bade the king announce to the huntsmen that he would dismount. A horn was blown full loud just once, that all might know that one might find the noble prince in camp. Spake then one of Siegfried's huntsmen: "My lord, I heard by the blast of a horn that we must now hie us to the quarters; I'll now give answer."

Thus by many blasts of horns they asked about the hunters. Then spake Sir Siegfried: "Now let us leave the pine wood!" His steed bare him smoothly and with him they hasted hence. With their rout they started up a savage beast; a wild bear it was. Quoth then the knight to those behind: "I'll give our fellowship a little pastime. Let loose the brach. Forsooth I spy a bear which shall journey with us to the camp. Flee he never so fast, he shall not escape us."

The brach was loosed, the bear sprang hence: Kriemhild's husband would fain overtake him. He reached a thicket, where none could follow. The mighty beast weened now to escape from the hunter with his life, but the proud knight and a good leaped from his steed and began to chase him. The bear was helpless and could not flee away. At once the hero caught it and bound it quickly with not a wound, so that it might neither scratch nor bite the men. The doughty knight then tied it to his saddle and horsed him quickly. Through his overweening mood the bold warrior and a good brought it to the camp-fire as a pastime. In what lordly wise he rode to the quarters! Mickle was his boar-spear, strong and broad. A dainty sword hung downward to his spurs. The lord bare also a fair horn of ruddy gold. Never heard I tale of better hunting weeds. One saw him wear a coat of black and silky cloth and a hat of sable: rich enow it was. Ho, what costly bands he wore upon his quiver! A panther's skin was drawn over it for its sweet fragrance sake. He bare a bow, which any but the hero must needs draw back with a windlass, and he would bend it. His vesture was befurred with otter skin from head to toe. From the bright fur shone out on both sides of the bold master of the hunt many a bar of gold. Balmung he also bare, a good broad sword, that was so sharp that it never failed when 'twas wielded 'gainst a helmet; its edge was good. In high spirits was the lordly huntsman. Sith I must tell you all the tale, his costly quiver was full of goodly darts, the heads a full hand's breadth, on golden shafts. What he pierced therewith must needs die soon.

Thus the noble knight rode hence in hunter's garb. Gunther's men espied him coming and ran out to meet him and took his horse in charge. On his saddle he carried a large bear and a strong. When he had dismounted, he loosed the bonds from feet and snout. Those of the pack bayed loudly, that spied the bear. The beast would to the woods; the serving folk had fear. Dazed by the din, the bear made for the kitchen. Ho, how he drove the scullions from the fire! Many a kettle was upset and many a firebrand scattered. Ho, what good victual men found lying in the ashes! Then the lordings and their liegemen sprang from their seats. The bear grew furious and the king bade loose the pack that lay enleashed. Had all sped well, they would have had a merry day. No longer the doughty men delayed, but ran for the bear with bows and pikes. There was such press of dogs that none might shoot, but from the people's shouts the whole hill rang. The bear began to flee before the dogs; none could follow him but Kriemhild's husband, who caught and slew him with his sword. Then they bore the bear again to the fire. Those that saw it, averred he was a mighty man.

Men bade now the proud hunting fellowship seat them at the tables. Upon a fair mead there sate a goodly company. Ho, what rich viands they bare them to the noble huntsmen! The butlers who should bring the wine delayed; else might never heroes have been better served. Had they not been so falsely minded, then had the knights been free of every blame.

Now the Lord Siegfried spake: "Me-wondereth, since men do give us such great store from the kitchen, why the butlers bring us not the wine. Unless men purvey the hunters better, I'll be no more your hunting-fellow. I have well deserved that they regard me, too."

The king addressed him from his seat with guile: "We fain would do you remedy of what we lack. It is Hagen's fault, who is willed to let us die of thirst."

Then spake Hagen: "Dear my lord, I weened that the hunt should be in the Spessart wood, therefore sent I thither the wine. Though we may not drink today, how well will I avoid this in the future!"

At this Lord Siegfried spake: "Small thanks ye'll get for that. One should have brought me hither seven sumpter loads of mead and mulled wine. If that might not be, then men should have placed our benches nearer to the Rhine."

Then spake Hagen of Troneg: "Ye noble knights and bold, I wot near by a good cold spring. Let us go thither, that ye wax not wroth."

To the danger of many a knight was this counsel given. The pangs of thirst now plagued the warrior Siegfried. He bade the tables be borne away the sooner, for he would go to the spring in the mountains. With false intent the counsel was then given by the knights. They bade the game which Siegfried's hand had slain, be carried home on wains. Whoever saw it gave him great laud. Hagen of Troneg now foully broke his troth to Siegfried. When they would hence to the broad linden, he spake: "It hath oft been told me, that none can keep pace with Kriemhild's husband when he be minded for to race. Ho, if he would only let us see it here!"

Bold Siegfried from Netherland then answered: "Ye can well test that, and ye will run a race with me to the spring. When that is done, we can give the prize to him who winneth."

"So let us try it then," quoth Hagen, the knight.

Spake the sturdy Siegfried: "Then will I lay me down on the green sward at your feet."

How lief it was to Gunther, when he heard these words! Then the bold knight spake again: "I'll tell you more. I'll take with me all my trappings, my spear and shield and all my hunting garb." Around him he quickly girded his quiver and his sword.

Then they drew the clothes from off their limbs; men saw them stand in two white shifts. Like two wild panthers through the clover they ran, but men spied bold Siegfried first at the spring. In all things he bare away the prize from many a man. Quickly he ungirt his sword and laid aside his quiver and leaned the stout spear against a linden bough. The lordly stranger stood now by the flowing spring. Passing great was Siegfried's courtesie. He laid down his shield where the spring gushed forth, but the hero drank not, albeit he thirsted sore, until the king had drunk, who gave him evil thanks. Cool, clear, and good was the spring. Gunther stooped down then to the flowing stream, and when he had drunken straightened up again. Bold Siegfried would fain also have done the same, but now he paid for his courtesie. Hagen bare quite away from him both bow and sword and bounded then to where he found the spear; then he looked for the mark on bold Siegfried's coat. As Lord Siegfried drank above the spring, he pierced him through the cross, so that his heart's blood spurted from the wounds almost on Hagen's clothes. Nevermore will hero do so foul a deed. Hagen left the spear a-sticking in his heart and fled more madly than he ever in the world had run from any man.

When Lord Siegfried felt the mighty wound, up from the spring he started in a rage. From betwixt his shoulder blades a long spear-shaft towered. He weened to find his bow or his sword, and then had Hagen been repaid as he deserved. But when the sorely wounded hero found no trace of his sword, then had he naught else but his shield. This he snatched from the spring and ran at Hagen; nor could King Gunther's man escape him. Albeit he was wounded unto death, yet he smote so mightily that a plenty of precious stones were shaken from the shield. The shield itself burst quite apart. Fain would the lordly stranger have avenged him. Now was Hagen fallen to the ground at his hands, and from the force of the blow the glade rang loudly. Had he had a sword in hand, then had it been Hagen's death, so sore enraged was the wounded man. Forsooth he had good cause thereof. His hue grew pale, he could not stand; his strength of body melted quite away, for in bright colors he bore the signs of death. Thereafter he was bewailed by fair dames enow.

Kriemhild's husband fell now among the flowers. Fast from his wounds his blood was seen to gush. He began to rail, as indeed he had great cause, at those who had planned this treacherous death. The deadly wounded spake: "Forsooth, ye evil cowards, what avail my services now that ye have slain me? This is my reward that I was always faithful to you. Alas, ye have acted ill against your kinsmen. Those of them who are born in after days will be disgraced. Ye have avenged your wrath too sore upon me. With shame shall ye be parted from all good warriors."

The knights all ran to where he lay slain. For enow of them it was a hapless day. He was bewailed by those who had aught of loyalty, and this the brave and lusty knight had well deserved. The king of the Burgundians bemoaned his death. Quoth the deadly wounded: "There is no need that he should weep who hath done the damage; he doth merit mickle blame. It had been better left undone."

Then spake the fierce Hagen: "Forsooth I wot not what ye now bewail. All our fear and all our woe have now an end. We shall find scant few who dare withstand us now. Well is me, that to his rule I have put an end."

"Ye may lightly boast you," Siegfried then replied. "Had I wist your murderous bent, I had well guarded my life against you. None doth rue me so sore as Lady Kriemhild, my wife. Now may God have pity that I ever had a son to whom the reproach will be made in after days, that his kindred have slain a man with murderous intent. If I might," so spake Siegfried, "I should rightly make complaint of this." Piteously the deadly wounded spake again: "Noble king, if ye will keep your troth to any in the world, then let my dear love be commended to your grace and let it avail her that she be your sister. For the sake of your princely courtesie protect her faithfully. My father and my men must wait long time for me. Never was woman sorer wounded in a loving friend."

The flowers on every side were wet with blood. With death he struggled, but not for long, sith the sword of death had cut him all too sorely. Then the lusty warrior and a brave could speak no more.

When the lordings saw that the knight was dead, they laid him on a shield of ruddy gold and took counsel how they might conceal that Hagen had done the deed. Enow of them spake: "Ill hath it gone with us. Ye must all hide it and aver alike that robbers slew Kriemhild's husband as he rode alone a-hunting through the pine wood."

Then Hagen of Troneg spake: "I'll bring him home; I care not if it be known to her, for she hath saddened Brunhild's heart. Little doth it trouble me however much she weep."

Author and Selection Notes

The selection "How Siegfried was Slain" is taken from *The Nibelungenlied* (c. 1200), an epic, by an unknown poet, reflecting the days of chivalry in early German life and lore.

Gunther, king of the Burgundians and brother of Kriemhild, promised his sister in marriage to Siegfried, a prince of the Netherlands, if the hero would help him secure the powerful Brunhild as his queen. Brunhild discovered that Gunther lacked the strength which had been displayed in wooing her, and on the bridal night tied him in her girdle and suspended him from her window. Gunther reported the intimidation to Siegfried, who donned his magic cloak, which made him invisible, and overcame Brunhild in a wrestling match; she then submitted to Gunther, her king and husband.

Unfortunately Kriemhild knew that twice before Siegfried, while disguised as Gunther, had conquered Brunhild in contests. When Kriemhild told Brunhild of the trickery, jealousy was immediately aroused, and Gunther and his favorite knight, Hagen, plotted the death of Siegfried.

Questions and Exercises

1. This selection opens with an ominous note—a foretelling by dreams of trouble and death. Can you recall similar forecasts in other selections you have read?

2. Do you believe that man's thought and action today are influenced to some degree by premonition, hunch, foretelling, and the like? Discuss.

3. Are there character descriptions in the account that remind you of Chaucer's descriptions of his characters in the *Prologue to the Canterbury Tales?* Identify.

4. Compare and contrast the customs and dress of the characters in this excerpt with those in *Beowulf*.

5. Write a theme comparing and contrasting the characters of Siegfried and Beowulf.

FEDERIGO'S FALCON

Giovanni Boccaccio

Federigo degli Alberighi loves and is not loved in return; he wastes his substance by lavishness until nought is left but a single falcon, which, his lady being come to see him at his house, he gives her to eat: she, knowing his case, changes her mind, takes him to husband and makes him rich.

So ended Filomena; and the queen, being ware that besides herself only Dioneo (by virtue of his privilege) was left to speak, said with gladsome mien:—'Tis now for me to take up my parable; which, dearest ladies, I will do with a story like in some degree to the foregoing, and that, not only that you may know how potent are your charms to sway the gentle heart, but that you may also learn how upon fitting occasions to make bestowal of your guerdons of your own accord, instead of always waiting for the guidance of Fortune, which most times, not wisely, but without rule or measure, scatters her gifts.

You are then to know, that Coppo di Borghese Domenichi, a man that in our day was, and perchance still is, had in respect and great reverence in our city, being not only by reason of his noble lineage, but, and yet more, for manners and merit most illustrious and worthy of eternal renown, was in his old age not seldom wont to amuse himself by discoursing of things past with his neighbors and other folk; wherein he had not his match for accuracy and compass of memory and concinnity of speech. Among other good stories, he would tell, how that there was of yore in Florence a gallant named Federigo di Messer Filippo Alberighi, who for feats of arms and courtesy had not his peer in Tuscany; who, as is the common lot of gentlemen, became enamored of a lady named Monna Giovanna, who in her day held rank among the fairest and most elegant ladies of Florence; to gain whose love he jousted, tilted, gave entertainments, scattered largess, and in short set no bounds to his expenditure. However the lady, no less virtuous than fair, cared not a jot for what he did for her sake, nor yet for him.

Spending thus greatly beyond his means, and making nothing, Federigo could hardly fail to come to lack, and was at length re-

From *The Decameron* by Giovanni Boccaccio. Translated by J. M. Rigg. Everyman's Library Edition. Reprinted by permission of E. P. Dutton & Co., Inc.

duced to such poverty that he had nothing left but a little estate, on the rents of which he lived very straitly, and a single falcon, the best in the world. The estate was at Campi, and thither, deeming it no longer possible for him to live in the city as he desired, he repaired, more in love than ever before; and there, in complete seclusion, diverting himself with hawking, he bore his poverty as patiently as he might.

Now, Federigo being thus reduced to extreme poverty, it so happened that one day Monna Giovanna's husband, who was very rich, fell ill, and, seeing that he was nearing his end, made his will, whereby he left his estate to his son, who was now growing up, and in the event of his death without lawful heir named Monna Giovanna, whom he dearly loved, heir in his stead; and having made these dispositions he died.

Monna Giovanna, being thus left a widow, did as our ladies are wont, and repaired in the summer to one of her estates in the country which lay very near to that of Federigo. And so it befell that the urchin began to make friends with Federigo, and to shew a fondness for hawks and dogs, and having seen Federigo's falcon fly not a few times, took a singular fancy to him, and greatly longed to have him for his own, but still did not dare to ask him of Federigo, knowing that Federigo prized him so much. So the matter stood when by chance the boy fell sick; whereby the mother was sore distressed, for he was her only son, and she loved him as much as might be, insomuch that all day long she was beside him, and ceased not to comfort him, and again and again asked him if there were aught that he wished for, imploring him to say the word, and, if it might by any means be had, she would assuredly do her utmost to procure it for him. Thus repeatedly exhorted, the boy said:— "Mother mine, do but get me Federigo's falcon, and I doubt not I shall soon be well." Whereupon the lady was silent a while, bethinking her what she should do. She knew that Federigo had long loved her, and had never had so much as a single kind look from her: wherefore she said to herself:—How can I send or go to beg of him this falcon, which by what I hear is the best that ever flew, and moreover is his sole comfort? And how could I be so unfeeling as to seek to deprive a gentleman of the one solace that is now left him? And so, albeit she very well knew that she might have the falcon for the asking, she was perplexed, and knew not what to say, and gave her son no answer. At length, however, the love she bore the boy carried the day, and she made up her mind, for his contentment, come what might, not to send, but to go herself and fetch him the falcon. So:—"Be of good cheer, my son," she said, "and doubt not thou wilt soon be well; for I promise thee that the very first thing that I shall do to-morrow morning will be to go and fetch thee the falcon." Whereat the child was so pleased that he began to mend that very day.

On the morrow the lady, as if for pleasure, hied her with another lady to Federigo's little house, and asked to see him. 'Twas still, as for some days past, no weather for hawking, and Federigo was in his garden, busy about some small matters which needed to be set right there. When he heard that Monna Giovanna was at the door, asking to see him, he was not a little surprised and pleased, and hied him to her with all speed. As soon as she saw him, she came forward to meet him with womanly grace, and having received his respectful salutation, said to him:—"Good morrow, Federigo," and continued:—"I am come to requite thee for what thou hast lost by loving me more than thou shouldst: which compensation is this, that I and this lady that accompanies me will breakfast with thee without ceremony this morning." "Madam," Federigo replied with all humility, "I mind not ever to have lost aught by loving you, but rather to have been so much profited that, if I ever deserved well in aught, 'twas to your merit that I owed it, and to the love that I bore you. And of a surety had I still as much to spend as I have spent in the past, I should not prize it so much as this visit you so frankly pay me, come as you are to one who can afford you but a sorry sort of hospitality." Which said, with some confusion, he bade her welcome to his house, and then led her into his garden, where, having none else to present to her by way of companion, he said:—"Madam, as there is none other here, this good woman, wife of this husbandman, will bear you company, while I go to have the table set." Now, albeit his poverty was extreme, yet he had not known as yet how sore was the need to which his extravagance had reduced him, but this morning 'twas brought home to him, for that he could find nought wherewith to do honor to the lady, for love of whom he had done the honors of his house to men without number; wherefore, distressed beyond measure, and inwardly cursing his evil fortune, he sped hither and thither like one beside himself, but never a coin found he, nor yet aught to pledge. Meanwhile it grew late, and sorely he longed that the lady might not leave his house altogether unhonored and yet to crave help of his own husbandman was more than his pride could brook. In these desperate straits his glance happened to fall on his brave falcon on his perch in his little parlor. And so, as a last resource, he took him, and finding him plump, deemed that he would make a dish meet for such a lady. Wherefore, without thinking twice about it, he wrung the bird's neck, and caused his maid forthwith pluck him and set him on a spit, and roast him carefully; and having still some spotless table-linen, he had the table laid therewith, and with a cheerful countenance hied him back to his lady in the garden, and told her that such breakfast as he could give her was ready. So the lady and her companion rose and came to table, and there, with Federigo, who waited on them most faithfully, ate the brave falcon, knowing not what they ate.

When they were risen from table, and had dallied a while in gay converse with him, the lady deemed it time to tell the reason of her visit: wherefore, graciously addressing Federigo, thus began she:—"Federigo, by what thou rememberest of thy past life and my virtue, which, perchance, thou has deemed harshness and cruelty, I doubt not thou must marvel at my presumption, when thou hearest the main purpose of my visit; but if thou hadst sons, or hadst had them, so that thou mightest know the full force of the love that is borne them, I should make no doubt that thou wouldst hold me in part excused. Nor, having a son, may I, for that thou hast none, claim exemption from the laws to which all other mothers are subject, and, being thus bound to own their sway, I must, though fain were I not, and though 'tis neither meet nor right, crave of thee that which I know thou dost of all things and with justice prize most highly, seeing that this extremity of thy adverse fortune has left thee nought else wherewith to delight, divert and console thee; which gift is no other than thy falcon, on which my boy has so set his heart that, if I bring him it not, I fear lest he grow so much worse of the maladay that he has, that thereby it may come to pass that I lose him. And so, not for the love which thou dost bear me, and which may nowise bind thee, but for that nobleness of temper, whereof in courtesy more conspicuously than in aught else thou hast given proof, I implore thee that thou be pleased to give me the bird, that thereby I may say that I have kept my son alive, and thus made him for aye thy debtor."

No sooner had Federigo apprehended what the lady wanted, than, for grief that 'twas not in his power to serve her, because he had given her the falcon to eat, he fell a-weeping in her presence, before he could so much as utter a word. At first the lady supposed that 'twas only because he was loath to part with the brave falcon that he wept, and as good as made up her mind that he would refuse her: however, she awaited with patience Federigo's answer, which was on this wise:—"Madam, since it pleased God that I should set my affections upon you there have been matters not a few, in which to my sorrow I have deemed Fortune adverse to me; but they have all been trifles in comparison of the trick that she

now plays me: the which I shall never forgive her, seeing that you
are come here to my poor house, where while I was rich, you deigned
not to come, and ask a trifling favor of me, which she has put it
out of my power to grant: how 'tis so, I will briefly tell you. When
I learned that you, of your grace, were minded to breakfast with
me, having respect to your high dignity and desert, I deemed it
due and seemly that in your honor I should regale you, to the best
of my power, with fare of a more excellent quality than is commonly set before others; and, calling to mind the falcon which you
now ask of me, and his excellence, I judged him meet food for
you, and so you have had him roasted on the trencher this morning;
and well indeed I thought I had bestowed him; but, as now I see
that you would fain have had him in another guise, so mortified
am I that I am not able to serve you, that I doubt I shall never
know peace of mind more." In witness whereof he had the feathers
and feet and beak of the bird brought in and laid before her.

The first thing the lady did, when she had heard Federigo's story,
and seen the relics of the bird, was to chide him that he had killed
so fine a falcon to furnish a woman with a breakfast; after which
the magnanimity of her host, which poverty had been and was
powerless to impair, elicited no small share of inward commendation. Then, frustrate of her hope of possessing the falcon, and
doubting of her son's recovery, she took her leave with the heaviest
of hearts, and hied her back to the boy: who, whether for fretting,
that he might not have the falcon, or by the unaided energy of
his disorder, departed this life not many days after, to the exceeding
great grief of his mother. For a while she would do nought but
weep and bitterly bewail herself; but being still young, and left
very wealthy, she was often urged by her brothers to marry again,
and though she would rather have not done so, yet being importuned, and remembering Federigo's high desert, and the magnificent
generosity with which he had finally killed his falcon to do her
honor, she said to her brothers:—"Gladly, with your consent,
would I remain a widow, but if you will not be satisfied except
I take a husband, rest assured that none other will I ever take
save Federigo degli Alberighi." Whereupon her brothers derided
her, saying:—"Foolish woman, what is't thou sayst? How shouldst
thou want Federigo, who has not a thing in the world?" To whom
she answered:—"My brothers, well wot I that 'tis as you say; but
I had rather have a man without wealth than wealth without a
man." The brothers, perceiving that her mind was made up, and
knowing Federigo for a good man and true, poor though he was,
gave her to him with all her wealth. And so Federigo, being mated

with such a wife, and one that he had so much loved, and being very wealthy to boot, lived happily, keeping more exact accounts, to the end of his days.

Author and Selection Notes

Giovanni Boccaccio (1313-1375), born in Paris of an Italian banker father, lived in Italy at a time when it was torn by political intrigue and struggle. Civil war was common. Soon after young Giovanni's birth, the father returned to Italy, and the boy resided in France. Giovanni's father wanted him to enter business, or at least study law. The young Giovanni, however, would have none of it, and, when at the age of twenty-three he met Maria d'Aquino, the daughter of King Robert of Naples, any plans he may have had for his career were lost in the pursuit of her. But such intrigues did not last, and Boccaccio was left only a memory. It was from this memory, however, that much of his later literature grew, and the Princess Maria became well known as Fiammetta in his later stories.

Giovanni Boccaccio is one of the great story tellers of the world. His narrative power lies chiefly in his capacity for retelling effectively the old stories of Italy, France, Persia, and India in a style often witty and ironical. Many of the stories and tales of Chaucer, Shakespeare, Dryden, Keats, and Molière take their themes from Boccaccian tales.

Questions and Exercises

1. Discuss the plausibility of Federigo's devotion to Monna Giovanna. Is this story a modification of the courtly love tradition which began in Europe in chivalric times?

2. Account for the renewal of friendship between the two characters in the story.

3. Would one act today as unselfishly as Federigo in a similar instance if faced with the possibility of renewal of a faded romance?

4. Describe the emotional situation which exists between the two characters just after Federigo's breakfast.

5. Discuss the ending of the story. Does each character deserve the apparent mutual blessing each received?

6. Is contemporary society so constituted that men and women suffer the same caprices and benefits as did Federigo and Monna Giovanna? Discuss this issue in writing as extensively as you can.

7. You may also find it worthwhile to discuss the widow's statement that she "had rather have a man without wealth than wealth without a man."

8. Give your opinion of Monna Giovanna's character. Did she grow in wisdom and devotion or is her marriage to Federigo one of duty without love?

9. Theme Topics: The Characteristics of Courtly Love; The Origin of Courtly Love; Federigo—a Courtly Lover; Love in the Twentieth Century Compared with Love in the Fourteenth Century; A Definition of Love.

NOAH'S FLOOD

First GOD, *sitting in some high place, or in clouds, if it can be done,*
  speaks to NOAH, *standing with all his family outside the ark.*

GOD. I, God, that all the world have wrought,
Heaven and earth, and all of nought,
I see my people in deed and thought
  Are foully set in sin.
My spirit shall not remain in any man   5
That through fleshly liking is my fone,[1]
But till six score years be gone,
  To look if they will blynne.[2]

Man that I made I will destroy,
Beast, man, and fowl that fly,   10
For on earth they do me annoy,
  The folk that are thereon;
It harms me so hurtfully,
The malice now that does multiply,
That sore it grieveth me inwardly   15
  That ever I made man.

Therefore, Noah, my servant free,
That righteous man art, as I see,
A ship soon thou shalt make thee
  Of trees dry and light;   20
Little chambers therein do thou make,
And binding pitch also do thou take:
Within and without do thou not slake[3]
  To anoint it with all thy might.

Reprinted from *A Book of English Literature*, Vol. I (4th ed., 1942), eds. Franklin Bliss Snyder and Robert Grant Martin, pp. 179-185, and, with the permission of the Council of the Early English Text Society, based on the medieval version printed in *The Chester Plays*, Part I, ed H. Deimling (E.E.T.S., Extra Series 62, 1892), slightly modernized as to vocabulary and punctuation.
  [1] foe.   [3] be not slack.
  [2] cease.

Three hundred cubits it shall be long,   25
And fifty of breadth, to make it strong,
Of height fifty, the measure do thou fonge:[4]
   Thus measure it about.
One window work by thy wit,
One cubit of length and breadth make it;   30
Upon the side a door shall sit,
   For to come in and out.

Eating places do thou make also,
Three roofed chambers, one or two,
For with water I think to flow[5]   35
   Man that I did make;
Destroyed all the world shall be,
Save thou, thy wife, thy sons three,
And all their wives also with thee,
   Shall saved be for their sake.   40

   NOAH, Ah, Lord I thank thee loud and still,
That to me art in such will,
And sparest me and my house to spill,[6]
   As now I soothly find;
Thy bidding, Lord, I shall fulfil,   45
And never more thee grieve nor grill,[7]
That such grace hast sent me till,
   Among all mankind.

                [NOAH *calls to his family.*

Have done, you men and women all!
Help, for aught that may befall,   50
To make this ship, chamber and hall,
   As God hath bidden us do.
   SHEM. Father, I am already bowne:[8]
An axe I have, by my crown,
As sharp as any in all this town,   55
   For to go thereto.

   HAM. I have a hatchet wonder keen
To bite well, as may be seen;

---

[4] take.   [7] vex.
[5] flood.   [8] prepared.
[6] destroy.

A better ground, as I ween,
　Is not in all this town.　　　　　　　　　　　　60
　JAPHET. And I can well make a pin,
And with this hammer knock it in;
Go and work without more din,
　And I am ready bowne.

　NOAH'S WIFE. And we shall bring timber too,　　　65
For we may nothing else do:
Women be weak to undergo
　Any great travail.
　SHEM'S WIFE. Here is a good hackstock,[9]
On this you may hew and knock;　　　　　　　　70
Shall none be idle in this flock,
　Nor now may no man fail.

　HAM'S WIFE. And I will go to gather slich[10]
The ship for to clean and pitch:
Annointed it must be every stitch,[11]　　　　　　75
　Board, tree and pin.
　JAPHET'S WIFE. And I will gather chips here
To make a fire for you in fere [12]
And for to dight[13] your dinner
　Against you come in.　　　　　　　　　　　80

*Then they make signs as though they were working with various
implements.*

　NOAH. Now in the name of God I will begin
To make the ship that we shall go in,
That we be ready for a swim
　At the coming of the flood:
These boards I join here together　　　　　　　　85
To keep us safe from the weather,
That we may row both hither and thither,
　And safe be from this flood.

Of this tree will I make the mast,
Tied with cables that will last,　　　　　　　　90

---

[9] chopping-block.　　　　　　[12] all together.
[10] pitch.　　　　　　　　　　　[13] prepare.
[11] stick.

With a sailyard for each blast,
   And each thing in their kind;
With topcastle and bowsprit,
With cords and ropes I have all meet
To sail forth at the next weete:[14]   95
   This ship is at an end.

Then NOAH *and all his family again make signs of working with various implements.*

Wife, in this castle we shall be kept;
My children and thou I would in leapt.
   NOAH's WIFE. In faith, Noah, I had as lief thou slept
   For all thy frankish fare,   100
I will not do after thy rede.[15]
   NOAH. Good wife, do now as I thee bid.
   NOAH's WIFE. By Christ! not ere I see more need,
   Though thou stand all the day and stare.

   NOAH. Lord, that women be crabbed aye,   105
And never are meek, that dare I say;
This is well seen by me today
   In witness of you each one.
Good wife, let be all this bere[16]
That thou makest in this place here,   110
For al-they ween thou art master—
   And so thou art, by St. John!

                              [GOD *speaks above.*

   GOD. Noah, take thou thy company,
And in the ship hie that you be,
For none so righteous man to me   115
   Is now on earth living.
Of clean beasts do thou with thee take
Seven and seven, ere thou slake,
He and she, make to make,[17]
   Quickly in do thou bring.   120

---

[14] wet weather.   [16] noise.
[15] counsel.   [17] mate.

Of beasts unclean, two and two,
Male and female, without mo; [18]
Of clean fowls seven also,
   The he and she together;
Of fowls unclean, two and no more,   125
As I of beasts said before,
That shall be saved through my lore,
   Against I send the weather.

Of all meats that must be eaten
Into the ship look there be getten,   130
For that no way may be forgotten,
   And do all this bydene,[19]
To sustain man and beast therein,
Aye till this water cease and blynne.[20]
This world is filled full of sin,   135
   And that is now well seen.

Seven days be yet coming,
You shall have space them in to bring;
After that is my liking
   Mankind for to annoy: 140
Forty days and forty nights
Rain shall fall for their unrights,
And what I have made through my mights,
   Now think I to destroy.

   NOAH. Lord, at your bidding I am bayne;[21]   145
Since none other your grace will gain,
It will I fulfil fain,
   For gracious I thee find.
A hundred winters and twenty
This ship making tarried have I,   150
If through amendment any mercy
   Would fall unto mankind.

                [NOAH *calls to his family.*

Have done, you men and women all!
Hie you, lest this water fall.

[18] more.   [20] disappear.
[19] quickly.   [21] ready.

That each beast were in his stall,   155
   And unto the ship be brought!
Of clean beasts seven shall be,
Of unclean two, this God bade me.
This flood is nigh, well may we see;
   Therefore tarry you not.   160

Then NOAH *shall enter the ark, and his family shall exhibit and
name all the animals depicted on sheets of parchment, and after
each one has spoken his part, he shall go into the ark, except*
NOAH'S WIFE. *The animals depicted ought to correspond to the
descriptions; and thus let the first son begin*:

SHEM. Sir, here are lions, leopards in,
Horses, mares, oxen, and swine,
Goats, calves, sheep, and kine,
   Here sitting thou mayst see.
HAM. Camels, asses, men may find,   165
Buck, doe, hart, and hind,
And beasts of all manner of kind
   Here be, as thinks me.

   JAPHET. Take here cats, and dogs too,
Otter, fox, fulmart,[22] also,   170
Hares hopping gaily can go,
   Have cowle[23] here for to eat.
   NOAH'S WIFE. And here are bears, wolves set,
Apes, owls, marmoset,
Weasels, squirrels, and ferret;   175
   Here they eat their meat.

   SHEM'S WIFE. Yet more beasts are in this house:
Here cats make it full crowse,[24]
Here a rat, here a mouse,
   They stand nigh together.   180
   HAM'S WIFE. And here are fowls, less and more:
Herons, cranes, and bittour,[25]
Swans, peacocks; and them before
   Meat for this weather.

---

[22] skunk.   [24] jolly.
[23] a cruciferous plant, probably the turnip.   [25] bittern.

JAPHET'S WIFE. Here are cocks, kites, crows,   185
Rooks, ravens, many rows;
Ducks, curlews: whoever knows
   Each one in his kind?
And here are doves, ducks, drakes,
Redshanks, running through the lakes;   190
And each fowl that language makes
   In this ship men may find.

[NOAH *approaches his wife, who has joined her gossips at the other*
end of the pageant.

NOAH. Wife, come in! why standest thou here?
Thou art ever froward, that dare I swear.
Come in, on God's half![26] time it were,   195
   For fear lest that we drown.
   NOAH'S WIFE. Yea, sir, set up your sail,
And row forth with evil hail!
For without any fail
   I will not out of this town.   200

Unless I have my gossips every one
One foot further I will not gone;[27]
They shall not drown, by St. John!
   If I may save their life!
They loved me full well, by Christ!   205
Unless thou wilt let them in thy chest,
Row forth, Noah, whither thou list,
   And get thee a new wife.

[NOAH *returns to the Ark.*

NOAH. Shem, son, lo! thy mother is wraw:[28]
Forsooth, such another I do not know!   210
   SHEM. Father, I shall fetch her in, I trow,
   Without any fail.
Mother, my father after thee sent,
And bids thee into yonder ship wend.
Look up and see the wind,   215
   For we be ready to sail.

[26] for God's sake.   [28] angry.
[27] go—an infinitive.

NOAH'S WIFE. Son, go again to him and say
I will not come therein today.

> [NOAH *and his sons go to her.*

NOAH. Come in, wife, in twenty devils' way!
Or else stand there without.   220
HAM. Shall we all fetch her in?
NOAH. Yea, sons, in Christ's blessing and mine!
I would you hied you betime,
  For of this flood I am in doubt.[29]

[NOAH *returns to the Ark. The* WIFE'S *"Good Gossips" enter with
a pottle of malmsey.*

THE GOOD GOSSIPS. *They sing.*
The flood comes in full fleeting fast,   225
On every side it spreadeth full far;
For fear of drowning I am aghast,
Good gossip, let us draw near.
And let us drink ere we depart,
For oftentimes we have done so;   230
For at a draught thou drink'st a quart,
And so will I do, ere I go.[30]

JAPHET. Mother, we pray you altogether,
For we are here, your own children,
Come into the ship for fear of the weather,   235
  For his love that you bought.[31]
NOAH'S WIFE. That will I not for all your call,
Unless I have my gossips all.
  SHEM. In faith, mother, yet you shall,
  Whether you will or not!   340

> [*Then she will go.*

NOAH. Welcome, wife, into this boat!
NOAH'S WIFE. And have thou that for thy mote![32]

[29] fear.

[30] At this point in other MSS they sing the following song:
  Here is a pottell of malmesy, good and stronge,
  It will reioyce both hart and tong;
  Though Noy thinke us neuer so long
  Yet wee will drinke alyke.

[31] for the love of Christ who redeemed you. The many anachronistic references
to Christ are quite characteristic of the miracle plays.

[32] chatter.

[She deals NOAH *a blow.*

  NOAH. Aha, marry, this is hot!
    It is good to be still.
Ah, children, methinks my boat removes!   245
Our tarrying here hugely me grieves;
Over the land the water spreads—
    God do as he will!

Ah, great God that are so good,
He that works not thy will is wood.[33]   250
Now all this world is in a flood,
    As I see well in sight;
This window I will shut anon,
And into my chamber will I gone,
Till this water, so great one,   255
    Be slaked through thy might.

Then let NOAH *shut the window of the ark, and let them, remaining
within for a short time, sing the psalm "Save me, O God"; then
let* NOAH *open the window and look around.*

Now forty days are fully gone.
Send a raven I will anon,
To see if anywhere, earth, tree, or stone,
    Be dry in any place;   260
And if this fowl come not again,
It is a sign, sooth to sayne,[34]
That dry it is on hill or plain,
    And God hath done some grace.

*Then let him send out the raven, and taking a dove in his hands,
let him speak.*

Ah, Lord, wherever this raven be,   265
Somewhere is dry, well I see.
But yet a dove, by my loyalty,
    After I will send.
Thou wilt turn again to me,
For of all fowls that may fly,   270
    Thou art most meek and hend.[35]

[33] mad.   [35] gentle.
[34] say.

Then he shall put forth the dove, and there shall be on the ship
another dove bearing an olive branch in her mouth, which some-
one shall let down from the mast by a cord into NOAH's *hand,*
and afterwards let NOAH *speak.*

Ah, Lord, blessed be thou aye,
That me hast comforted thus today!
By this sight I may well say
   This flood begins to cease: 275
My sweet dove to me brought has
A branch of olive from some place;
This betokeneth God has done us some grace,
   And is a sign of peace.

Ah, Lord, honored may thou be!   280
All earth dries now, I see,
But yet till thou commandest me,
   Hence will I not hie.
All this water is away;
Therefore as soon as I may,   285
Sacrifice I shall do in fay[36]
   To thee devoutly.

                             [GOD *speaks above.*

   GOD. Noah, take thy wife anon,
And thy children every one;
Out of the ship thou shalt gone   290
   And they all with thee;
Beasts and all that can fly
Out anon they shall hie,
On earth to grow and multiply;
   I will that it so be.   295

   NOAH. Lord, I thank thee, through thy might,
Thy bidding shall be done in hight,[37]
And as fast as I may dight
   I will do thee honor,
And to thee offer sacrifice.   300
Therefore comes in all wise,

---

[36] faith.   [37] haste.

For of these beasts that be his
    Offer I will this store.

Then coming out of the ark with all his family NOAH *shall take his
animals and fowls and make an offering, and sacrifice.*

Lord God in majesty,
That such grace hast granted me   305
Where all was lost, safe to be,
    Therefore now I am bowne,
My wife, my children, my company,
With sacrifice to honor thee,
With beasts, fowls, as thou mayst see,   310
    Which I offer here right soon.

                              [GOD *speaks above.*

    GOD. Noah, to me thou art full able,[38]
And thy sacrifice acceptable,
For I have found thee true and stable;
    On thee must I now mind.[39]   315
Curse earth will I no more
For man's sin that grieves me sore,
For of youth man full yore
    Has been inclined to sin.

You shall now grow and multiply,   320
And earth again you shall edify;
Each beast and fowl that may fly
    Shall be afraid of you;
And fish in sea that may flytte[40]
Shall sustain you, I you behite;[41]   325
To eat of them do not let,[42]
    That clean be you may know.

Whereas you have eaten before
Grass and roots since you were born,
Of clean beasts, less and more,   330
    I give you leave to eat;

[38] pleasing.   [41] promise.
[39] think.   [42] hesitate.
[40] swim.

Save blood and flesh both in fere[43]
Of wrong dead carrion that is here:
Eat not of that in no manner,
   For that aye shall you let.[44]   335

Manslaughter also you shall flee,
For that is not pleasant to me.
That sheds blood, he or she,
   Anywhere amongst mankind,
That blood foully shed shall be,   340
And vengeance have that men shall see.
Therefore beware now all ye,
   You fall not in that sin.

A foreward[45] now with thee I make,
And all thy seed for thy sake,   345
From such vengeance for to slake,
   For now I have my will;
Here I promise thee a hest:[46]
That man, woman, fowl nor beast
With water, while the world shall last,   350
   I will no more spill.[47]

My bow between you and me
In the firmament shall be
For every token that you may see
   That such vengeance shall cease;   355
That man nor woman shall never more
Be wasted by water, as before;
But for sin, that grieveth me sore,
   Therefore this vengeance was.

Where clouds in the welkin been[48]   360
That same bow shall be seen,
In token that my wrath and teen[49]
   Shall never thus wreaked be;
The string is turned toward you,
And toward me is bent the bow,   365

[43] together.
[44] leave alone.
[45] convenant.
[46] assurance.

[47] destroy.
[48] be.
[49] anger.

That such weather shall never show,
  And this promise I thee.

My blessing now I give thee here,
To thee, Noah, my servant dear,
For vengeance shall no more appear.   370
And now, farewell, my darling dear.

Author and Selection Notes

The Chester Cycle of religious plays mixes simple animal lore with humorous character interpretation and religious history. The plays were acted in Whitsun Week by the Guilds of Chester; each Guild acted one episode in the Cycle. The Guild of Watermen performed "Noah's Flood." The Cycle plays, performed in the thirteenth to sixteenth centuries, serve as precursors to later drama and are a major step in dramatic development.

Questions and Exercises

1. Does "Noah's Flood" vary noticeably from the Biblical account found in the book of Genesis? Read the Genesis account and make comparisons.
2. Discuss the simplicity of character delineation, plot and setting, situation.
3. Do you think this type of drama effective in its purpose to entertain and inform? Why or why not?
4. Discuss the humor of the play.
5. Theme Topics: Why I Like (Dislike) Drama; On Seeing Shakespeare Acted; The Lesson of the Stage; What I Think Would Make a Good Play; The Best Play I've Ever Seen; The Cycle Plays.

HOW A MONK OF SEVILLE SAVED THE ABBEY
François Rabelais

So much they did, and so far they went pillaging and stealing, that at last they came to Seville, where they robbed both men and women, and took all they could catch: nothing was either too hot or too heavy for them. Although the plague was there in the most part of all the houses, they nevertheless entered everywhere, then plundered and carried away all that was within, and yet for all this not one of them took any hurt, which is a most wonderful case. For the curates, vicars, preachers, physicians, chirurgeons, and apothecaries, who went to visit, to dress, to cure, to heal, to preach unto and admonish those that were sick, were all dead of the infection, and these devilish robbers and murderers caught never any harm at all. Whence comes this to pass, my masters? I beseech you think upon it. The town being thus pillaged, they went unto the abbey with a horrible noise and tumult, but they found it shut and made fast against them. Whereupon the body of the army marched forward towards a pass or ford called the Gué de Vède, except seven companies of foot and two hundred lancers, who, staying there, broke down the walls of the close, to waste, spoil, and make havoc of all the vines and vintage within that place. The monks (poor devils) knew not in that extremity to which of all their sancts they should vow themselves. Nevertheless, at all adventures, they rang the bells *ad capitulum capitulantes.* There it was decreed that they should make a fair procession, stuffed with good lectures, prayers, and litanies *contra hostium insidias,* and jolly responses *pro pace.*

There was then in the abbey a claustral monk, called Friar John of the funnels and gobbets, in French *des entoumeures,* young, gallant, frisk, lusty, nimble, quick, active, bold, adventurous, resolute, tall, lean, wide-mouthed, long-nosed, a fair despatcher of morning prayers, unbridler of masses, and runner over of vigils; and, to conclude summarily in a word, a right monk, if ever there was any, since the monking world monked a monkery; for the rest, a clerk even to the teeth in matter of breviary. This monk, hearing the noise that the enemy made within the enclosure of the vineyard, went out to see what they were doing; and perceiving that they were cutting and gathering the grapes, whereon was grounded the foundation of all their next year's wine, returned unto the choir of the church where the other monks were, all amazed and astonished like so many bell-melters. Whom when he heard sing, ini, nim, pe, ne, ne, ne, ne, nene, tum ne, num, num, im, i, mi, co, o, no, o, o, neno, ne, no, no, no, rum, nenum, num: It is well . . . sung, said he. By the virtue of God, why do not you sing, Panniers, farewell, vintage is done? The devil snatch me, if they be not already within the middle of our close, and cut so well both vines and grapes, that, by Cod's body, there will not be found for these four years to come so much as a gleaning in it. By the belly of Sanct James, what shall we poor devils drink the while? Lord God, *do mihi potum.* Then said the prior of the convent: What should this drunken fellow do here? Let him be carried to prison for troubling the divine service. Nay, said the monk, the wine service, let us behave ourselves so that it be not troubled; for you yourself, my lord prior, love to drink of the best, and so doth every honest man. Never yet did a man of worth dislike good wine; it is a monastical apophthegm. But these responses that you chant here, by G—, are not in season. Wherefore is it, that our devotions were instituted to be short in the time of harvest and vintage, and long in the advent, and all the winter? The late friar, Massepelosse, of good memory, a true zealous man, or else I give myself to the devil, of our religion, told me, and I remember it well, how the reason was, that in this season we might press and make the wine, and in winter whiff it up. Hark you, my masters, you that love the wine, Cod's body, follow me; for Sanct Anthony burn me as freely as a faggot, if they get leave to taste one drop of the liquor that will not now come and fight for relief of the wine. Hog's belly, the goods of the church! Ha, no, no. What the devil, Sanct Thomas of England was well content to die for them; if I died in the same cause, should not I be a sanct likewise? Yes. Yet shall not I die there for all this, for it is I that must do it to others and send them a-packing.

As he spake this he threw off his great monk's habit, and laid hold upon the staff of the cross, which was made of the heart of a sorbapple-tree, it being of the length of a lance, round, of a full grip and a little powdered with lilies called flower de luce, the workmanship whereof was almost all defaced and worn out. Thus went he out in a fair long skirted jacket, putting his frock scarfwise athwart his breast, and in this equipage, with his staff, shaft or truncheon of the cross, laid on so lustily, brisk, and freely upon his enemies, who, without any order, or ensign, or trumpet, or drum, were busied in gathering the grapes of the vineyard. For the cornets, guidons, and ensign-bearers had laid down their standards, banners, and colors by the wall sides; the drummers had knocked out the heads of their drums on one end to fill them with grapes; the trumpeters were loaded with great bundles of bunches and huge knots of clusters; in sum, everyone of them was out of array, and all in disorder. He hurried therefore, upon them so rudely, without crying gare or beware, that he overthrew them like hogs, tumbled them over like swine, striking athwart and alongst, and by one means or other laid so about him, after the old fashion of fencing, that to some he beat out their brains, to others he crushed their arms, battered their legs, and bethwacked their sides till their ribs cracked with it. To others again he unjointed the spondyles or knuckles of the neck, disfigured their chaps, gashed their faces, made their cheeks hang flapping on their chin, and so swinged and belammed them that they fell down before him like hay before a mower. To some others he spoiled the frame of their kidneys, marred their backs, broke their thigh-bones, pashed in their noses, poached out their eyes, cleft their mandibles, tore their jaws, dung in their teeth into their throat, shook asunder their omoplates or shoulder blades, sphacelated their shins, mortified their shanks, inflamed their ankles, heaved off the hinges their ishies, their sciatica or hip-gout, dislocated the joints of their knees, squattered into pieces the boughts or pestles of their thighs, and so thumped, mauled and belabored them everywhere, that never was corn so thick and threefold threshed upon by ploughmen's flails as were the pitifully disjointed members of their mangled bodies under the merciless baton of the cross. If any offered to hide himself amongst the thickest of the vines, he laid him squat as a flounder, bruised the ridge of his back, and dashed his reins like a dog. If any thought by flight to escape, he made his head to fly in pieces by the lamdoidal commissure, which is a seam in the hinder part of the skull. If anyone did scramble up into a tree, thinking there to be safe, he rent up his perinee, and impaled him in the fundament. If any of his old acquaintance happened to cry out, Ha, Friar John, my friend Friar John, quarter, quarter, I yield myself to you, to you I render myself! So thou shalt, said he, and must, whether thou wouldst or no, and withal render and yield up thy soul to all the devils in hell; then suddenly gave them dronos, that is, so many knocks, thumps, raps, dints, thwacks, and bangs, as sufficed to warn Pluto of their coming and despatch them a-going. If any was so rash and full of temerity as to resist him to his face, then was it he did show the strength of his muscles, for without more ado he did transpierce him, by running him in at the breast, through the mediastine and the heart. Others, again, he so quashed and bethumped, that, with a sound bounce under the hollow of their short ribs, he overturned their stomachs so that they died immediately. To some, with a smart souse on the epigaster, he would make their midriff swag, then, redoubling the blow, gave them such a homepush on the navel that he made their puddings to gush out. To others through their ballocks he pierced their bum-gut, and left not bowel, tripe, nor entrail in their body that had not felt the impetuosity, fierceness, and fury of his violence. Believe, that it was the most horrible spectacle that ever one saw. Some cried unto Sanct Barbe, others to St. George. O the holy Lady Nytouch, said one, the good Sanctess; O our Lady of Succours, said another, help, help! Others cried, Our Lady of Cunaut, of Loretto, of Good Tidings, on the other side of the water St. Mary Over. Some vowed a pilgrimage of St. James, and others to the holy handkerchief of Chamberry, which three months after that burnt so well in the fire that they could not get one thread of it saved. Others sent up their vows to St. Cadouin, others to St. John d'Angely, and to St. Eutropiius of Xaintes. Others again invoked St. Mesmes of Cinon, St. Martin of Candes, St. Clouaud of Sinays, the holy relics of Laurezay, with a thousand other jolly little sancts and santrels. Some died without speaking, others spoke in dying. Others shouted as loud as they could Confession, Confession, *Confiteor, Miserere, In manus!* So great was the cry of the wounded, that the prior of the abbey with all his monks came forth, who, when they saw these poor wretches so slain amongst the vines, and wounded to death, confessed some of them. But whilst the priests were busied in confessing them, the little monkics ran all to the place where Friar John was, and asked him wherein he would be pleased to require their assistance. To which he answered that they should cut the throats of those he had thrown down upon the ground. They presently, leaving their outer habits and cowls upon the rails, begin to throttle and make an end of those whom he had already crushed. Can you tell with what instruments they did it? With fair gullies, which are little hulch-backed demi-knives, the iron tool whereof is two inches long, and the wooden handle one inch thick, and three inches in length, wherewith the little boys in our country cut ripe walnuts in two while they are yet in the shell, and pick out the kernel, and they found them very fit for the expediting of that weasand-slitting exploit. In the meantime Friar John, with his formidable baton of the cross, got to the breach which the enemies had made, and there stood to snatch up those that endeavored to escape. Some of the monkitos carried the standards, banners, ensigns, guidons, and colours into their cells and chambers to make garters of them. But when those that had been shriven would have gone out at the gap of the said breach, the sturdy monk quashed and felled them down with blows, saying, These men have had confession and are penitent souls; they have got their absolution and gained the pardons: they go into paradise as straight as a sickle, or as the way is to Faye (like Crooked-Lane at Eastcheap). Thus by his prowess and valor were discomfited all those of the army that entered into the close of the abbey, unto the number of thirteen thousand, six hundred, twenty and two, besides the

women and little children, which is always to be understood.
Never did Maugis the Hermit bear himself more valiantly with
his bourbon or pilgrim's staff against the Saracens, of whom it is
written in the Acts of the four sons of Aymon, than did this monk
against his enemies with the staff of the cross.

Author and Selection Notes

François Rabelais (1495-1553) combines much of the old medievalism
with the elements of the new spirit of the Renaissance. One finds in his
writing much exuberance and enthusiasm for a hearty laugh at the
pedantry of the old learning, contemporary religion, politics, and social
institutions. Satire, exaggeration, and disregard for conventional literary
form are present in his works and might well account for what could be
termed "romantic."

Rabelais was born at Chinon in the province of Touraine in France
and went to the monastery schools. He later entered the Order of the
Franciscans and subsequently the Benedictines. When the monastic life
proved unhappy, he pursued the study of medicine, rapidly earned his
degrees, and practiced in France and Italy.

The selection in this text is taken from *Gargantua* (1535), one of Rabelais' two great books. The church was involved in strife at this time,
and when Martin Luther appeared before the Diet of Worms, the
Reformation got underway. Rabelais drew from the confusion of his day
his expressions on war, education, and monastic life.

Questions and Exercises

1. Write a character sketch of Friar John. Did Rabelais admire Friar
John or was he poking fun at him?

2. Do you feel that Rabelais in any way is censoring generally the
ecclesiastical orders of his day? What do you think of the routine of the
religious orders mentioned in the story?

3. Cite passages which reveal Rabelais' medical background.

4. Cite several passages or sentences which exemplify Rabelais' talent
for writing satire.

5. Which do you think Rabelais appreciated most—Friar John's action
or his fellow monks' passivity?

6. What are the major characteristics of Rabelais' style of writing?
Explain what is meant by "Rabelaisian," a term identifying a particular
literary style.

7. Theme Topics: The Purpose of Satire; Rabelais' Exaggerated Style of
Writing; A Satirical Sketch (of either an event or a person); Rabelais,
the Rebel.

OF THE INCONVENIENCE OF GREATNESS
Michel de Montaigne

Since we cannot attain unto it, let us revenge ourselves by railing at it; and yet it is not absolutely railing against anything, to proclaim its defects, because they are in all things to be found, how beautiful or how much to be coveted soever. Greatness has, in general, this manifest advantage, that it can lower itself when it pleases, and has, very near, the choice of both the one and the other condition; for a man does not fall from all heights; there are several from which one may descend without falling down. It does, indeed, appear to me that we value it at too high a rate, and also overvalue the resolution of those whom we have either seen, or heard, contemned it, or displaced themselves of their own accord: its essence is not so evidently commodious that a man may not, without a miracle, refuse it. I find it a very hard thing to undergo misfortunes, but to be content with a moderate measure of fortune, and to avoid greatness I think a very easy matter. 'Tis, methinks, a virtue to which I, who am no conjuror, could without any great endeavor arrive. What, then, is to be expected from them that would yet put into consideration the glory attending this refusal, wherein there may lurk worse ambition than even in the desire itself, and fruition of greatness? For as much as ambition never comports itself better, according to itself, than when it proceeds by obscure and unfrequented ways.

I incite my courage to patience, but I rein it as much as I can towards desire. I have as much to wish for as another, and allow my wishes as much liberty and indiscretion; but, yet it never befel me to wish for either empire or royalty, or the eminency of those high and commanding fortunes: I do not aim that way; I love myself too well. When I think to grow greater 'tis but very moderately, and by a compelled and timorous advancement, such as is proper for me in resolution, in prudence, in health, in beauty, and even in riches too; but this supreme reputation, this mighty authority, oppress my imagination; and, quite contrary to that other, I should, peradventure, rather choose to be the second or third in Perigord, than the first in Paris: at least, without lying, rather the third at Paris than the first. I would neither dispute, a miserable unknown, with a nobleman's porter, nor make crowds open in adoration as I pass. I am trained up to a moderate condition, as well as by my choice as fortune; and have made it appear, in the whole conduct of my life and enterprises, that I have rather avoided than otherwise the climbing above the degree of fortune wherein God has placed me by my birth: all natural constitution is equally just and easy. My soul is so sneaking that I measure not good fortune by the height, but by the facility.

But if my heart be not great enough, 'tis open enough to make amends, at any one's request, freely to lay open its weakness. Should any one put me upon comparing the life of L. Thorius Balbus, a brave man, handsome, learned, healthful, understanding, and abounding in all sorts of conveniences and pleasures, leading a quiet life, and all his own, his mind well prepared against death, superstition, pain, and other incumbrances of human necessity, dying, at last, in battle, with his sword in his hand, for the defence of his country, on the one past; and on the other past, the life of M. Regulus, so great and high as is known to every one, and his end admirable; the one without name and without dignity, the other exemplary, and glorious to wonder, I should doubtless say as Cicero did, could I speak as well as he. But if I was to compare them with my own, I should then also say that the first is as much according to my capacity, and from desire, which I conform to my capacity, as the second is far beyond it; that I could not approach the last but with veneration, the other I could readily attain by use.

But let us return to our temporal greatness, from which we are digressed. I disrelish all dominion, whether active or passive. Otanes, one of the seven who had right to pretend to the kingdom of Persia, did, as I should willingly have done, which was, that he gave up to his concurrents his right of being promoted to it, either by election or by lot, provided that he and his might live in the empire out of all authority and subjection, those of the ancient laws excepted, and might enjoy all liberty that was not prejudicial to these, being as impatient of commanding as of being commanded.

The most painful and difficult employment in the world, in my opinion, is worthily to discharge the office of a king. I excuse more of their mistakes than men commonly do, in consideration of the intolerable weight of their function, which astounds me. 'Tis hard to keep measure in so immeasurable a power; yet so it is, that it is, even to those who are not of the best nature, a singular incitement to virtue, to be seated in a place where you cannot do the least good that shall not be put upon record; and where the least benefit redounds to so many men, and where your talent of administration, like that of preachers, principally addresses itself to the people, no very exact judge, easy to deceive, and easily content. There are few things wherein we can give a sincere judgment, by reason that there are few wherein we have not, in some sort, a private interest. Superiority and inferiority, dominion and subjection, are bound to a natural envy and contest, and must of necessity perpetually intrench upon one another. I believe neither the one nor the other touching the rights of the other party; let reason therefore, which is inflexible and without passion, determine when we can avail ourselves of it. 'Tis not above a month ago that I read over two Scotch authors contending upon this subject, of whom he who stands for the people makes kings to be in a worse condition than a carter; and he who writes for monarchy places them some degrees above God Almighty in power and sovereignty.

Now, the inconveniency of greatness that I have made choice of to consider in this place, upon some occasion that has lately put it into my head, is this: there is not, peradventure, anything more pleasant in the commerce of men than the trials that we make against one another, out of emulation of honor and worth, whether in the exercises of the body or in those of the mind, wherein sovereign greatness can have no true part. And, in earnest, I have often thought that by force of respect itself men use princes disdainfully and injuriously in that particular; for the thing I was infinitely offended at in my childhood, that they who exercised with me forbore to do their best because they found me unworthy of their utmost endeavor, is what we see happen to them daily, every one finding himself unworthy to contend with them. If we discover that they have the least desire to get the better of us, there is no one who will not make it his business to give it them, and who will not rather betray his won glory than offend theirs; and will, therein, employ so much force only as is necessary to save their honor. What share have they, then, in the engagement, where every one is on their side? Methinks I see those Paladins of ancient times presenting themselves to jousts and battle with enchanted arms and bodies. Brisson, running against Alexander, purposely missed his blow and made a fault in his career; Alexander chid him for it, but he ought to have had him whipped. Upon this consideration Carneades said that "the sons of princes learned nothing right but to ride; by reason that, in all their other exercises, every one bends and yields to them; but a horse, that is neither a flatterer nor a courtier, throws the son of a king with no more ceremony than he would throw that of a porter."

Homer was fain to consent that Venus, so sweet and delicate a goddess as she was, should be wounded at the battle of Troy, thereby to ascribe courage and boldness to her, qualities that cannot possibly be in those who are exempt from danger. The gods are made to be angry, to fear, to run away, to be jealous, to grieve, to be transported with passions, to honor them with the virtues that, amongst us, are built upon these imperfections. Who does not participate in the hazard and difficulty can claim no interest in the honor and pleasure that are the consequents of hazardous actions. 'Tis pity a man should be so potent that all things must give way to him; fortune therein sets you too remote from society, and places you in too great a solitude. This easiness and mean facility of making all things bow under you is an enemy to all sorts of pleasure: 'tis to slide, not to go; 'tis to sleep, and not to live. Conceive man accompanied with omnipotence: you overwhelm him; he must beg disturbances and opposition as an alms; his being and his good are in indigence.

Their good qualities are dead and lost; for they can only be perceived by comparison, and we put them out of this: they have little knowledge of true praise, having their ears deafened with so continual and uniform an approbation. Have they to do with the stupidest of all their subjects? They have no means to take advantage of him; if he but say: "'Tis because he is my king," he thinks he has said enough to express, that he, therefore, suffered himself to be overcome. This quality stifles and consumes the other true and essential qualities: they are sunk in the royalty; and leave them nothing to recommend themselves with but actions that directly concern and serve the function of their place; 'tis so much to be a king, that this alone remains to them. The outer glare that environs him conceals and shrouds him from us; our sight is there repelled and dissipated, being filled and stopped by this prevailing light. The senate awarded the prize of eloquence to Tiberius; he refused it, esteeming that though it had been just, he could derive no advantage from a judgment so partial, and that was so little free to judge.

As we give them all advantages of honor, so do we soothe and authorize all their vices and defects, not only by approbation, but by imitation also. Every one of Alexander's followers carried his head on one side, as he did; and the flatterers of Dionysius ran against one another in his presence, and stumbled at and overturned whatever was under foot, to show they were as purblind as he. Hernia itself has also served to recommend a man to favor; I have seen deafness affected; and because the master hated his wife, Plutarch has seen his courtiers repudiate theirs, whom they loved: and, which is yet more, uncleanliness and all manner of dissolution have so been in fashion; as also disloyalty, blasphemy, cruelty, heresy, superstition, irreligion, effeminacy, and worse there be; and by an example yet more dangerous than that of Mithridates' flatterers who, as their master pretended to the honor of a good physician, came to him to have incisions and cauteries made in their limbs; for these others suffered the soul, a more delicate and noble part, to be cauterised.

But to end where I began: the Emperor Adrian, disputing with the philosopher Favorinus about the interpretation of some word, Favorinus soon yielded him the victory; for which his friends rebuking him; "You talk simply," said he, "would you not have him wiser than I who commands thirty legions?" Augustus wrote verses against Asinius Pollio, and "I," said Pollio, "say nothing, for it is not prudence to write in contest with him who has power to prescribe"; and he had reason; for Dionysius, because he could not equal Philoxenus in poesy, and Plato in discourse, condemned the one to the quarries, and sent the other to be sold for a slave into the island of Aegina.

Author and Selection Notes

Michel Eyquem de Montaigne (1533-1592) was born on the family estate near Bordeaux, France, and was educated in an unconventional fashion in simple surroundings by servants who spoke no French and yet orally taught their charge Latin. At thirteen, he began the study of law, and in 1571, when he was still a young man, he retired to his country estate and devoted himself to reading, study, and meditation. Nine years later, the first edition of his famous essays was issued. Montaigne's essays are not about philosophic systems, but rather reveal his personal observations on almost all phases of life.

Questions and Exercises

1. What do you think the author means when he says greatness "can lower itself when it pleases"?

2. Why might one value greatness "at too high a rate"?

3. Can you reason why the author loves himself too well to aim at greatness?

4. Discuss the statement "To grow greater, 'tis but very moderately, and by a compelled and timorous advancement."

5. What is your attitude toward veneration of the great? Would you feel humble if in the presence of a truly great person? What is your opinion of "yes" men? Of flatterers?

6. Is true greatness the result of experience which includes suffering?

Must we know the hazards and difficulties of life before we approach greatness?

7. What are the advantages and disadvantages of being great?

8. Theme Topics: Greatness Is as Greatness Does; What Makes a Person Great? A Great Person Whom I Know; The Relationship of Greatness to Responsibility.

LUBBERLAND

William Byrd

[March 24, 1728] This being Sunday, we had a Numerous congregation, which flockt to our Quarters from all the adjacent Country. The News that our Surveyors were come out of the Dismal, increas'd the Number very much, because it wou'd give them an Opportunity of guessing, at least, whereabouts the Line wou'd cut, whereby they might form Some Judgment whether they belong'd to Virginia or Carolina. Those who had taken up Land within the Disputed Bounds were in great pain lest it should be found to ly in Virginia; because this being done contrary to an Express Order of that government, the Patentees had great reason to fear they should in that case have lost their land. But their Apprehensions were now at an end, when they understood that all the Territory which had been controverted was like to be left in Carolina.

In the afternoon, those who were to re-enter the Dismal were furnisht with the Necessary Provisions, and Order'd to repair the Over-Night to their Landlord, Peter Brinkley's, that they might be ready to begin their Business early on Monday Morning. Mr. Irvin was excus'd from the Fatigue, in complement to his Lungs; but Mr. Mayo and Mr. Swan were Robust enough to return upon that painful Service, and, to do them Justice, they went with great Alacrity. The Truth was, they now knew the worst of it; and cou'd guess pretty near at the time when they might hope to return to Land again.

[March] 25. The air was chill'd this Morning with a Smart Northwest Wind, which favour'd the Dismalites in their Dirty March. They return'd by the Path they had made in coming out, and with great Industry arriv'd in the Evening at the Spot where the Line had been discontinued.

From *The History of the Dividing Line.*

After so long and laborious a Journey, they were glad to repose themselves on their couches of Cypress-bark, where their sleep was as sweet as it wou'd have been on a Bed of Finland Down.

In the mean time, we who stay'd behind had nothing to do, but to make the best observations we cou'd upon that Part of the Country. The Soil of our Landlord's Plantation, tho' none of the best, seem'd more fertile than any thereabouts, where the Ground is near as Sandy as the Desarts of Affrica, and consequently barren. The Road leading from thence to Edenton, being in distance about 27 Miles, lies upon a Ridge call'd Sandy-Ridge, which is so wretchedly Poor that it will not bring Potatoes.

The Pines in this Part of the country are of a different Species from those that grow in Virginia; their bearded Leaves are much longer and their Cones much larger. Each Cell contains a Seed of the Size and Figure of a black ey'd Pea, which, Shedding in November, is very good Mast for Hogs, and fattens them in a Short time.

The Smallest of these Pines are full of Cones, which are 8 or 9 Inches long, and each affords commonly 60 or 70 Seeds. This Kind of Mast has the Advantage of all other, by being more constant, and less liable to be nippt by the Frost, or Eaten by the Caterpillars. The Trees also abound more with Turpentine, and consequently yield more Tarr, than either the Yellow or the White Pine; And for the same reason make more durable Timber for building. The Inhabitants hereabouts pick up Knots of Lightwood in Abundance, which they burn into tar, and then carry it to Norfolk or Nansimond for a Market. The Tar made in this method is the less Valuable, because it is said to burn the Cordage, tho' it is full as good for all other uses, as that made in Sweden and Muscovy.

Surely there is no place in the World where the Inhabitants live with less Labour than in N Carolina. It approaches nearer to the Description of Lubberland than any other, by the great felicity of the Climate, the easiness of raising Provisions, and the Slothfulness of the People.

Indian Corn is of so great increase, that a little Pains will Subsist a very large Family with Bread, and then they may have meat without any pains at all, by the Help of the Low Grounds, and the great Variety of Mast that grows on the High-land. The Men, for their Parts, just like the Indians, impose all the Work upon the poor Women. They make their Wives rise out of their Beds early in the Morning, at the same time that they lye and Snore, till the Sun has run one third of his course, and disperst all the unwholesome Damps. Then, after Stretching and Yawning for half an Hour, they light their Pipes, and under the Protection of a cloud of Smoak, venture out into the open Air; tho', if it happens to be never so little cold, they quickly return Shivering into the Chimney corner. When the Weather is mild, they stand leaning with both their arms upon the corn-field fence, and gravely consider whether they had best go and take a Small Heat at the Hough; but generally find reasons to put it off till another time.

Thus they loiter away their Lives, like Solomon's Sluggard, with their Arms across, and at the Winding up of the Year Scarcely have Bread to Eat.

To speak the Truth, tis a thorough Aversion to Labor that makes People file off to N Carolina, where Plenty and a Warm Sun confirm them in their Disposition to Laziness for their whole Lives.

[March] 26. Since we were like to be confin'd to this place, till the People return'd out of the Dismal, twas agreed that our Chaplain might Safely take a turn to Edenton, to preach the Gospel to the Infidels there, and Christen their Children. He was accompany'd thither by Mr. Little, One of the Carolina Commissioners, who, to shew his regard for the Church, offer'd to treat Him on the Road with a Fricassee of Rum. They fry'd half a Dozen Rashers of very fat Bacon in a Pint of Rum, both which being disht up together, serv'd the Company at once both for meat and Drink.

Most of the Rum they get in this Country comes from New England, and is so bad and unwholesome, that it is not improperly call'd "Kill-Devil". It is distill'd there from forreign molosses, which, if Skillfully manag'd, yields near Gallon for Gallon. Their molosses comes from the same country and has the name of "Long Sugar" in Carolina, I suppose from the Ropiness of it, and Serves all the purposes of Sugar, both in their Eating and Drinking.

When they entertain their Friends bountifully, they fail not to set before them a Capacious Bowl of Bombo, so call'd from the Admiral of that name. This is a Compound of Rum and Water in Equal Parts, made palatable with the said long Sugar. As good Humour begins to flow, and the Bowl to Ebb, they take Care to replenish it with Shear Rum, of which there always is a Reserve under the Table. But such Generous doings happen only when that Balsam of life is plenty; for they have often such Melancholy times, that neither Land-graves nor Cassicks can procure one drop for their Wives, when they ly in, or are troubled with the Colick or Vapours. Very few in this Country have the Industry to plant Orchards, which, in a Dearth of Rum, might supply them with much better Liquor.

The Truth is, there is one Inconvenience that easily discourages lazy People from making This improvement: very often, in Autumn, when the Apples begin to ripen, they are visited with Numerous

Flights of paraqueets, that bite all the Fruit to Pieces in a moment, for the sake of the Kernels. The Havock they make is Sometimes so great, that whole Orchards are laid waste in Spite of all the Noises that can be made, or Mawkins that can be dresst up, to fright 'em away. These Ravenous Birds visit North Carolina only during the warm Season, and so soon as the Cold begins to come on, retire back towards the Sun. They rarely Venture so far North as Virginia, except in a very hot Summer, when they visit the most Southern Parts of it. They are very Beautiful; but like some other pretty Creatures, are apt to be loud and mischievous.

[March] 27. Betwixt this and Edenton there are many thuckle-berry Slashes, which afford a convenient Harbour for Wolves and Foxes. The first of these wild Beasts is not so large and fierce as they are in other countries more Northerly. He will not attack a Man in the Keenest of his Hunger, but run away from him, as from an Animal more mischievous than himself.

The Foxes are much bolder, and will Sometimes not only make a Stand, but likewise assault any one that would balk them of their Prey. The Inhabitants hereabouts take the trouble to dig abundance of Wolf-Pits, so deep and perpendicular, that when a Wolf is once tempted into them, he can no more Scramble out again, than a Husband who has taken the Leap can Scramble out of Matrimony.

Most of the Houses in this Part of the Country are Log-houses, covered with Pine or Cypress Shingles, 3 feet long, and one broad. They are hung upon Laths with Peggs, and their doors too turn upon Wooden Hinges, and have wood Locks to Secure them, so that the Building is finisht without Nails or other Iron-Work. They also set up their Pales without any Nails at all, and indeed more Securely than those that are nail'd. There are 3 Rails mortised into the Posts, the lowest of which serves as a Sill with a Groove in the Middle, big enough to receive the End of the Pales: the middle Part of the Pale rests against the Inside of the Next Rail, and the Top of it is brought forward to the outside of the uppermost. Such Wreathing of the Pales in and out makes them stand firm, and much harder to unfix than when nail'd in the Ordinary way.

Within 3 or 4 Miles of Edenton, the Soil appears to be a little more fertile, tho' it is much cut with Slashes, which seem all to have a tendency towards the Dismal.

This Towne is Situate on the North side of Albemarle Sound, which is there about five miles over. A Dirty Slash runs all along the Back of it, which in the Summer is a foul annoyance, and furnishes abundance of the Carolina plague, musquetas. There may be 40 or 50 Houses, most of them Small, and built without Expense.

A Citizen here is counted extravagant, if he has Ambition enough to aspire to a Brick-chimney. Justice herself is but indifferently Lodged, the Court-House having much the Air of a Common To-bacco-House. I believe this is the only Metropolis in the Christian or Mahometan World, where there is neither Church, Chappel, Mosque, Synagogue, or any other Place of Publick Worship of any Sect or Religion whatsoever.

What little Devotion there may happen to be is much more pri-vate than their vices. The People seem easy without a Minister, as long as they are exempted from paying Him. Some times the Society for propagating the Gospel has had the Charity to send over Missionaries to this Country; but unfortunately the Priest has been too Lewd for the people, or, which oftener happens, they too lewd for the Priest. For these Reasons these Reverend Gentlemen have always left their Flocks as arrant Heathen as they found them. Thus much however may be said for the Inhabitants of Edenton, that not a Soul has the least taint of Hypocrisy, or Superstition, acting very Frankly and above-board in all their Excesses.

Provisions here are extremely cheap, and extremely good, so that People may live plentifully at a triffleing expense. Nothing is dear but Law, Physick, and Strong Drink, which are all bad in their Kind, and the last they get with so much Difficulty, that they are never guilty of the Sin of Suffering it to Sour upon their Hands. Their Vanity generally lies not so much in having a handsome Dining-Room, as a Handsome House of Office: in this Kind of Structure they are really extravagant.

They are rarely guilty of Flattering or making any Court to their governors, but treat them with all the Excesses of Freedom and Familiarity. They are of Opinion their rulers wou'd be apt to grow insolent, if they grew Rich, and for that reason take care to keep them poorer, and more dependent, if possible, than the Saints in New England used to do their Governors. They have very little coin, so they are forced to carry on their Home-Triffick with Paper-Money. This is the only Cash that will tarry in the Country, and for that reason the Discount goes on increasing between that and real Money, and will do so to the End of the Chapter.

[March] 28. Our Time passt heavily in our Quarters, where we were quite cloy'd with the Carolina Felicity of having nothing to do. It was really more insupportable than the greatest Fatigue, and made us even envy the Drudgery of our Friends in the Dismal. Besides, tho' the Men we had with us were kept in Exact Discipline, and behav'd without Reproach, yet our Landlord began to be tired of them, fearing they would breed a Famine in his Family.

Indeed, so many keen Stomachs made great Havock amongst the Beef and Bacon, which he had laid in for his Summer Provision, nor cou'd he easily purchase More at that time of the Year, with the Money we paid him, because the People having no certain Market seldom provide any more of these Commodities than will barely supply their own Occasions. Besides the Weather was now grown too warm to lay in a fresh Stock so late in the Spring. These Considerations abated somewhat of that chearfulness with which he bidd us Welcome in the Beginning, and made him think the time quite as long as we did till the Surveyors return'd.

While we were thus all Hands uneasy, we were comforted with the News that this Afternoon the Line was finisht through the Dismal. The Messenger told us it had been the hard work of three days to measure the Length of only 5 Miles, and mark the Trees as they past along, and by the most exact Survey they found the Breadth of the Dismal in this Place to be completely 15 miles.

How wide it may be in other Parts, we can give no Account, but believe it grows narrower towards the North; possibly towards Albemarle Sound it may be something broader, where so many Rivers issue out of it. All we know for certain is, that from the Place where the Line enter'd the Dismal, to where it came out, we found the Road round that Portion of it which belongs to Virginia to be about 65 Miles. How great the Distance may be from Each of those Points, round that Part that falls within the Bounds of Carolina, we had no certain Information: tho' tis conjectur'd it cannot be so little as 30 miles. At which rate the whole Circuit must be about an Hundred. What a Mass of Mud and Dirt is treasur'd up within this filthy circumference, and what a Quantity of Water must perpetually drain into it from the riseing ground that Surrounds it on every Side?

Without taking the Exact level of the Dismal, we may be sure that it declines towards the Places where the Several Rivers take their Rise, in order to carrying off the constant Supplies of Water. Were it not for such Discharges, the whole Swamp would long Since have been converted into a Lake. On the other Side this Declension must be very gentle, else it would be laid perfectly dry by so many continual drains; Whereas, on the contrary, the Ground seems every where to be thoroughly drencht even in the dryest Season of the Year.

The Surveyors concluded this day's Work with running 25 chains up into the Firm Land, where they waited further Orders from the Commissioners.

Author and Selection Notes

Virginia-born William Byrd (1674-1744) was educated in England and on the Continent as was the custom of early Southern aristocracy. When he returned to Virginia, he managed his large plantation and served in the Virginia House of Burgesses. He entertained with lavishness and devoted himself to studying the classics from his large library of 3,500 volumes. Byrd was a man of wide interests; he furnished his mansion, Westover, with the costliest objects of art and planned the city of Richmond on his own lands. He was a member of the Royal Society.

Byrd's Journals, published long after his death, reveal a literary style of wit and sophistication similar to that of Swift and Pope, his English contemporaries. *The History of the Dividing Line* tells of a surveying trip he directed to identify the Virgina-North Carolina boundary. The selection in this text is a record of observations during one period of the expedition.

Questions and Exercises

1. What is your general appraisal of the account of Lubberland?
2. Discuss the living conditions of the Lubberland dwellers—habits, food, and drink.
3. What kind of citizen was the Lubberland dweller?
4. Can you account for the attitudes of the natives?
5. What are the major differences between Byrd's style of writing and twentieth-century writing?
6. Theme Topics: An Expedition into New Territory; My Journey into the Dismal Swamp (imaginary); Description of a Typical Present-Day "Dweller"; Life in a Simple Society; William Byrd.

AN ESSAY ON MAN

Epistle III

Alexander Pope

Here then we rest: "The Universal Cause
Acts to one end, but acts by various laws."
In all the madness of superfluous health,
The trim of pride, the impudence of wealth,
Let this great truth be present night and day;   5
But most be present, if we preach or pray.
  I. Look round our world; behold the chain of love

Combining all below and all above.
See plastic nature working to this end,
The single atoms each to other tend,   10
Attract, attracted to, the next in place
Formed and impelled its neighbour to embrace.
See matter next, with various life endued,
Press to one centre still, the general good.
See dying vegetables life sustain,   15
See life dissolving vegetate again:
All forms that perish other forms supply,
(By turns we catch the vital breath, and die)
Like bubbles on the sea of matter born,
They rise, they break, and to that sea return.   20
Nothing is foreign: parts relate to whole;
One all-extending, all-preserving soul
Connects each being, greatest with the least;
Made beast in aid of man, and man of beast;
All served, all serving: nothing stands alone;   25
The chain holds on, and where it ends, unknown.
    Has God, thou fool! worked solely for thy good,
Thy joy, thy pastime, thy attire, thy food?
Who for thy table feeds the wanton fawn,
For him as kindly spread the flowery lawn.   30
Is it for thee the lark ascends and sings?
Joy tunes his voice, joy elevates his wings.
Is it for thee the linnet pours his throat?
Loves of his own and raptures swell the note.
The bounding steed you pompously bestride,   35
Shares with the lord the pleasure and the pride.
Is thine alone the seed that strews the plain?
The birds of heaven shall vindicate their grain.
Thine the full harvest of the golden year?
Part pays, and justly, the deserving steer: 40
The hog, that ploughs not nor obeys thy call,
Lives on the labours of this lord of all.
    Know, nature's children all divide her care.
The fur that warms a monarch, warmed a bear.
While man exclaims, "See all things for my use!"   45
"See man for mine!" replies a pampered goose;
And just as short of reason he must fall
Who thinks all made for one, not one for all.
    Grant that the powerful still the weak control;
Be man the wit and tyrant of the whole: 50

Nature that tyrant checks; he only knows,
And helps, another creature's wants and woes.
Say, will the falcon, stooping from above,
Smit with her varying plumage, spare the dove?
Admires the jay the insect's gilded wings?   55
Or hears the hawk when Philomela sings?
Man cares for all: to birds he gives his woods,
To beasts his pastures, and to fish his floods;
For some his interest prompts him to provide,
For more his pleasure, yet for more his pride: 60
All feed on one vain patron, and enjoy
The extensive blessing of his luxury.
That very life his learnèd hunger craves,
He saves from famine, from the savage saves;
Nay, feasts the animal he dooms his feast,   65
And, till he ends the being, makes it blessed;
Which sees no more the stroke, or feels the pain,
Than favoured man by touch ethereal slain.
The creature had his feast of life before,
Thou too must perish, when thy feast is o'er!   70
    To each unthinking being, Heaven, a friend,
Gives not the useless knowledge of its end:
To man imparts it; but with such a view
As, while he dreads it, makes him hope it too:
The hour concealed, and so remote the fear,   75
Death still draws nearer, never seeming near.
Great standing miracle! that Heaven assigned
Its only thinking thing this turn of mind.
    II. Whether with reason or with instinct blessed,
Know, all enjoy that power which suits them best;   80
To bliss alike by that direction tend,
And find the means proportioned to their end.
Say, where full instinct is the unerring guide,
What pope or council can they need beside?
Reason, however able, cool at best,   85
Cares not for service, or but serves when pressed,
Stays till we call, and then not often near;
But honest instinct comes a volunteer,
Sure never to o'ershoot, but just to hit;
While still too wide or short is human wit;   90
Sure by quick nature happiness to gain,
Which heavier reason labours at in vain,
This too serves always, reason never long;

One must go right, the other may go wrong.
See then the acting and comparing powers   95
One in their nature, which are two in ours;
And reason raise o'er instinct as you can,
In this 'tis God directs, in that 'tis man.
   Who taught the nations of the field and wood
To shun their poison, and to choose their food?   100
Prescient, the tides or tempests to withstand,
Build on the wave, or arch beneath the sand?
Who made the spider parallels design,
Sure as Demoivre, without rule or line?
Who bid the stork, Columbus-like, explore   105
Heavens not his own, and worlds unknown before?
Who calls the council, states the certain day,
Who forms the phalanx, and who points the way?
   III. God in the nature of each being founds
Its proper bliss, and sets its proper bounds;   110
But as he framed a whole, the whole to bless,
On mutual wants built mutual happiness:
So from the first, eternal order ran,
And creature linked to creature, man to man.
Whate'er of life all-quickening ether keeps,   115
Or breathes through air, or shoots beneath the deeps
Or pours profuse on earth, one nature feeds
The vital flame, and swells the genial seeds.
Not man alone, but all that roam the wood,
Or wing the sky, or roll along the flood,   120
Each loves itself, but not itself alone,
Each sex desires alike, till two are one.
Nor ends the pleasure with the fierce embrace;
They love themselves a third time in their race.
Thus beast and bird their common charge attend,   125
The mothers nurse it, and the sires defend;
The young dismissed to wander earth or air,
There stops the instinct, and there ends the care;
The link dissolves, each seeks a fresh embrace,
Another love succeeds, another race.   130
A longer care man's helpless kind demands;
That longer care contracts more lasting bands;
Reflection, reason, still the ties improve,
At once extend the interest, and the love;
With choice we fix, with sympathy we burn;   135
Each virtue in each passion takes its turn:

And still new needs, new helps, new habits rise,
That graft benevolence on charities.
Still as one brood, and as another rose,
These natural love maintained, habitual those: 140
The last, scarce ripened into perfect man,
Saw helpless him from whom their life began:
Memory and forecast just returns engage,
That pointed back to youth, this on to age;
While pleasure, gratitude, and hope, combined,   145
Still spread the interest, and preserved the kind.
    IV. Nor think, in nature's state they blindly trod;
The state of nature was the reign of God:
Self-love and social at her birth began,
Union the bond of all things, and of man.   150
Pride then was not; nor arts, that pride to aid;
Man walked with beast, joint tenant of the shade;
The same his table, and the same his bed;
No murder clothed him, and no murder fed.
In the same temple, the resounding wood,   155
All vocal beings hymned their equal God:
The shrine with gore unstained, with gold undressed,
Unbribed, unbloody, stood the blameless priest:
Heaven's attribute was universal care,
And man's prerogative to rule, but spare.   160
Ah! how unlike the man of times to come!
Of half that live the butcher and the tomb;
Who, foe to nature, hears the general groan,
Murders their species, and betrays his own.
But just disease to luxury succeeds,   165
And every death its own avenger breeds;
The fury-passions from that blood began,
And turned on man a fiercer savage, man.
    See him from nature rising slow to art!
To copy instinct then was reason's part;   170
Thus then to man the voice of Nature spake—
"Go, from the creatures thy instructions take:
Learn from the birds what food the thickets yield;
Learn from the beasts the physic of the field;
Thy arts of building from the bee receive;   175
Learn of the mole to plough, the worm to weave;
Learn of the little nautilus to sail,
Spread the thin oar, and catch the driving gale.
Here too all forms of social union find,

And hence let reason, late, instruct mankind: 180
Here subterranean works and cities see;
There towns aerial on the waving tree.
Learn each small people's genius, policies,
The ant's republic, and the realm of bees;
How those in common all their wealth bestow,   185
And anarchy without confusion know;
And these forever, though a monarch reign,
Their separate cells and properties maintain.
Mark what unvaried laws preserve each state,
Laws wise as nature and as fixed as fate.   190
In vain thy reason finer webs shall draw,
Entangle justice in her net of law,
And right, too rigid, harden into wrong;
Still for the strong too weak, the weak too strong.
Yet go! and thus o'er all the creatures sway,   195
Thus let the wiser make the rest obey;
And, for those arts mere instinct could afford,
Be crowned as monarchs, or as gods adored."
    V. Great Nature spoke; observant men obeyed;
Cities were built, societies were made: 200
Here rose one little state; another near
Grew by like means, and joined, through love or fear.
Did here the trees with ruddier burdens bend,
And there the streams in purer rills descend?
What war could ravish, commerce could bestow,   205
And he returned a friend, who came a foe.
Converse and love mankind might strongly draw,
When love was liberty, and nature law.
Thus states were formed; the name of king unknown,
Till common interest placed the sway in one.   210
'Twas virtue only (or in arts or arms,
Diffusing blessings, or averting harms)
The same which in a sire the sons obeyed,
A prince the father of a people made.
    VI. Till then, by nature crowned, each patriarch sate,   215
King, priest, and parent of his growing state;
On him, their second Providence, they hung,
Their law his eye, their oracle his tongue.
He from the wondering furrow called the food
Taught to command the fire, control the flood,   220
Draw forth the monsters of the abyss profound,
Or fetch the aerial eagle to the ground.

Till drooping, sickening, dying they began
Whom they revered as God to mourn as man:
Then, looking up from sire to sire, explored   225
One great first father, and that first adored.
Or plain tradition that this all begun,
Conveyed unbroken faith from sire to son;
The worker from the work distinct was known,
And simple reason never sought but one: 230
Ere wit oblique had broke that steady light,
Man, like his Maker, saw that all was right;
To virtue, in the paths of pleasure, trod,
And owned a father when he owned a God.
Love all the faith, and all the allegiance then,   235
For nature knew no right divine in men,
No ill could fear in God; and understood
A sovereign being but a sovereign good.
True faith, true policy, united ran,
This was but love of God, and this of man.   240
    Who first taught souls enslaved, and realms undone,
The enormous faith of many made for one;
That proud exception to all nature's laws,
To invert the world, and counter-work its cause?
Force first made conquest, and that conquest, law;   245
Till superstition taught the tyrant awe,
Then shared the tyranny, then lent it aid,
And gods of conquerors, slaves of subjects made:
She 'midst the lightning's blaze, and thunder's sound,
When rocked the mountains, and when groaned the ground,   250
She taught the weak to bend, the proud to pray,
To power unseen, and mightier far than they:
She from the rending earth and bursting skies
Saw gods descend and fiends infernal rise;
Here fixed the dreadful, there the blessed abodes;   255
Fear made her devils, and weak hope her gods;
Gods partial, changeful, passionate, unjust,
Those attributes were rage, revenge, or lust:
Such as the souls of cowards might conceive,
And, formed like tyrants, tyrants would believe.   260
Zeal then, not charity, became the guide;
And hell was built on spite, and heaven on pride,
Then sacred seemed the ethereal vault no more;
Altars grew marble then, and reeked with gore:
Then first the flamen tasted living food;   265

Next his grim idol smeared with human blood;
With heaven's own thunders shook the world below,
And played the god an engine on his foe.
  So drives self-love, through just and through unjust,
To one man's power, ambition, lucre, lust: 270
The same self-love, in all, becomes the cause
Of what restrains him, government and laws.
For, what one likes if others like as well,
What serves one will, when many wills rebel?
How shall he keep, what, sleeping or awake, 275
A weaker may surprise, a stronger take?
His safety must his liberty restrain;
All join to guard what each desires to gain.
Forced into virtue thus by self-defence,
Even kings learned justice and benevolence; 280
Self-love forsook the path it first pursued,
And found the private in the public good.
  'Twas then the studious head or generous mind,
Follower of God or friend of human kind,
Post or patriot, rose but to restore 285
The faith and moral nature gave before;
Re-lumed her ancient light, not kindled new;
If not God's image, yet his shadow drew:
Taught power's due use to people and to kings
Taught nor to slack, nor strain its tender strings; 290
The less, or greater, sat so justly true,
That touching one must strike the other too;
Till jarring interests of themselves create
The according music of a well-mixed state.
Such is the world's great harmony, that springs 295
From order, union, full consent of things;
Where small and great, where weak and mighty, made
To serve, not suffer, strengthen, not invade—
More powerful each as needful to the rest
And, in proportion as it blesses, blessed— 300
Draw to one point, and to one centre bring
Beast, man, or angel, servant, lord, or king.
  For forms of government let fools contest;
Whate'er is best administered is best:
For modes of faith let graceless zealots fight; 305
His can't be wrong whose life is in the right:
In faith and hope the world will disagree,
But all mankind's concern is charity:

All must be false that thwart this one great end
And all of God, that bless mankind or mend.   310
    Man, like the generous vine, supported lives;
The strength he gains is from the embrace he gives.
On their own axis as the planets run,
Yet make at once their circle round the sun
So two consistent motions act the soul,   315
And one regards itself, and one the whole.
    Thus God and nature linked the general frame,
And bade self-love and social be the same.

Author and Selection Notes

Alexander Pope (1688-1744) was born in London to Catholic parents, and, because of his faith, he was prevented from engaging in political controversy and receiving political rewards. After living in Windsor Forest from 1700 to 1719, he moved to Twickingham, just outside of London, where he became well identified with such Tory writers as Swift, Parnell, and the Earl of Oxford. He became involved in personal and literary controversy, much of which resulted in perhaps his greatest work, *The Dunciad*. Though frail in body and emaciatingly dwarfed, Pope led a vigorous literary and social life.

An Essay on Man was published anonymously in 1733-1734 and was well received not only in England but in other parts of the world. The essay deals with man's relations to other created beings, to his fellows, and to God. The chain of being which was a recognized philosophic dictum of the day becomes a chain of life which binds all things together and declares that "self-love and social be the same."

Questions and Exercises

1. Point out couplets in which you think the author most effectively expresses his ideas concerning man and society.

2. Explain Pope's "chain of love."

3. Pope is the product of the Age of Reason—an age basically optimistic. In Epistle I of *An Essay on Man* he asserts, "Whatever is, is right." Find references from Epistle III which would support this same thesis.

4. How does Pope explain the existence of evil in a world created by a moral God?

5. According to Pope, what caused primitive men to finally band together and form cities?

6. What forms of government and religion does Pope consider best?

7. Theme Topics: Nothing Stands Alone; Man Is *Not* an Island; Instinct and Reason; Whatever Is, Is Right; Man as a Social Being.

ON THE EMIGRATION TO AMERICA
Philip Freneau

To the western woods, and lonely plains,
Palemon from the crowd departs,
Where nature's wildest genius reigns,
To tame the soil, and plant the arts—
What wonders there shall freedom show,   5
What mighty STATES successive grow!

From Europe's proud, despotic shores
Hither the stranger takes his way,
And in our new found world explores
A happier soil, a milder sway,   10
Where no proud despot holds him down
No slaves insult him with a crown.

What charming scenes attract the eye,
On wild Ohio's savage stream!
There Nature reigns, whose works outvie   15
The boldest pattern art can frame;
There ages past have rolled away,
And forests bloomed but to decay.

From these fair plains, these rural seats,
So long concealed, so lately known,   20
The unsocial Indian far retreats,
To make some other clime his own,
When other streams, less pleasing flow,
And darker forests round him grow.

Great Sire of floods! whose varied wave   25
Through climes and countries takes its way,
To whom creating Nature gave
Ten thousand streams to swell thy sway!
No longer shall *they* useless prove,
Nor idly through the forests rove;   30

Nor longer shall your princely flood
From distant lakes be swelled in vain,

Nor longer through a darksome wood
Advance, unnoticed, to the main,
Far other ends, the heavens decree—   35
And commerce plans new freights for thee.

While virtue warms the generous breast,
There heaven-born freedom shall reside,
Nor shall the voice of war molest,
Nor Europe's all-aspiring pride—   40
There Reason shall new laws devise,
And order from confusion rise.

Forsaking kings and regal state,
With all their pomp and fancied bliss,
The traveller owns, convinced though late,   45
No realm so free, so blest as this—
The east is half to slaves consigned,
Where kings and priests enchain the mind.

O come the time, and haste the day.
When man shall man no longer crush,   50
When Reason shall enforce her sway,
Nor these fair regions raise our blush,
Where still the *African* complains,
And mourns his yet unbroken chains.

Far brighter scenes a future age,   55
The muse predicts, these States will hail,
Whose genius may the world engage,
Whose deeds may over death prevail,
And happier systems bring to view,
Than all the eastern sages knew.   60

Author and Selection Notes

Philip Freneau (1752-1832), the son of a New York wine merchant of
French Huguenot descent, was a graduate of Princeton University and
afterward became a sailor. During the Revolution he was captured by
the British and spent some time on a prison ship before being released. In
1791 he became the editor of a radical newspaper in Philadelphia, but in
1798 he took to the sea again. Freneau had very strong feelings about
the new American nation and was ardently sympathetic with the Revolution. His writings reveal that he had no real sympathy with England or
with those in America who sought to assert authority. Freneau was per-

haps the first American man of letters to recognize America as the melting pot of all nations.

Much of his poetry consists of rather reckless satire; however, his "The Indian Burying-Ground" has true beauty and has frequently been compared in motive with Keats' "Ode On A Grecian Urn."

Questions and Exercises

1. Review historically what was happening in Europe and America at the time Freneau wrote the poem. As you read the poem, recall some of the opportunities America offered.

2. To what is the poet referring when he speaks of "A happier soil, a milder sway, / Where no proud despot holds him down"?

3. Explain what you think Freneau means when he speaks of "The unsocial Indian far retreats, / To make some other clime his own, . . ."

4. Give a full interpretation of "The east is half to slaves consigned, / Where kings and priests enchain the mind."

5. The last stanza in the poem reminds one of Burns' "A Man's a Man for A' That." Compare the two poems.

6. Theme Topics: The Man of Independence; The Statue of Liberty; What Do Men Seek? Man's Ultimate Goal; The Retreat of the Indian.

SELF-RELIANCE
Ralph Waldo Emerson

I read the other day some verses written by an eminent painter which were original and not conventional. The soul always hears an admonition in such lines, let the subject be what it may. The sentiment they instil is of more value than any thought they may contain. To believe your own thought, to believe that what is true for you in your private heart is true for all men,—that is genius. Speak your latent conviction, and it shall be the universal sense; for the inmost in due time becomes the outmost, and our first thought is rendered back to us by the trumpets of the Last Judgment. Familiar as the voice of the mind is to each, the highest merit we ascribe to Moses, Plato, and Milton is that they set at naught books and traditions, and spoke not what men, but what *they* thought. A man should learn to detect and watch that gleam of light which flashes across his mind from within, more than the lustre of the firmament of bards and sages. Yet he dismisses without notice his thought, because it is his. In every work of genius we recognize our own rejected thoughts; they come back to us with a certain alienated majesty. Great works of art have no more affecting lesson for us than this. They teach us to abide by our spontaneous impression with good-humored inflexibility then most when the whole cry of voices is on the other side. Else to-morrow a stranger will say with masterly good sense precisely what we have thought and felt all the time, and we shall be forced to take with shame our own opinion from another.

There is a time in every man's education when he arrives at the conviction that envy is ignorance; that imitation is suicide; that he must take himself for better or worse as his portion; that though the wide universe is full of good, no kernel of nourishing corn can come to him but through his toil bestowed on that plot of ground which is given to him to till. The power which resides in him is new in nature, and none but he knows what that is which he can do, nor does he know until he has tried. Not for nothing one face, one character, one fact, makes much impression on him, and another none. This sculpture in the memory is not without pre-established harmony. The eye was placed where one ray should fall, that it might testify of that particular ray. We but half express ourselves, and are ashamed of that divine idea which each of us represents. It may be safely trusted as proportionate and of good issues, so it be faithfully imparted, but God will not have his work made manifest by cowards. A man is relieved and gay when he has put his heart into his work and done his best; but what he has said or done otherwise shall give him no peace. It is a deliverance which does not deliver. In the attempt his genius deserts him; no muse befriends; no invention, no hope.

Trust thyself: every heart vibrates to that iron string. Accept the place the divine providence has found for you, the society of your contemporaries, the connection of events. Great men have always done so, and confided themselves childlike to the genius of their age, betraying their perception that the absolutely trustworthy was seated at their heart, working through their hands, predominating in all of their being. And we are now men, and must accept in the highest mind the same transcendent destiny; and not minors and invalids in a protected corner, not cowards fleeing before a revolution, but guides, redeemers and benefactors, obeying the Almighty effort and advancing on Chaos and the Dark.

What pretty oracles nature yields us on this text in the face and behavior of children, babes, and even brutes! That divided and rebel mind, that distrust of a sentiment because our arithmetic has computed the strength and means opposed to our purpose, these have not. Their mind being whole, their eye is as yet uncon-quered, and when we look in their faces we are disconcerted. Infancy conforms to nobody; all conform to it; so that one babe commonly makes four or five out of the adults who prattle and play to it. So God has armed youth and puberty and manhood no less with its piquancy and charm, and made it enviable and gracious and its claims not to be put by, if it will stand by itself. Do not think the youth has no force, because he cannot speak to you and me. Hark! in the next room his voice is sufficiently clear and emphatic. It seems he knows how to speak to his contemporaries. Bashful or bold then, he will know how to make us seniors very unnecessary.

The nonchalance of boys who are sure of a dinner, and would disdain as much as a lord to do or say aught to conciliate one, is the healthy attitude for human nature. A boy is in the parlor what the pit is in the playhouse; independent, irresponsible, looking out from his corner on such people and facts as pass by, he tries and sentences them on their merits, in the swift, summary way of boys, as good, bad, interesting, silly, eloquent, troublesome. He cumbers himself never about consequences, about interests; he gives an independent, genuine verdict. You must court him; he does not court you. But the man is as it were clapped into jail by his consciousness. As soon as he has once acted or spoken with éclat he is a committed person, watched by the sympathy or the hatred of hundreds, whose affections must now enter into his account. There is no Lethe for this. Ah, that he could pass again into his neutrality! Who can thus avoid all pledges and, having observed, observe again from the same unaffected, unbiased, unbribable, un-affrighted innocence,—must always be formidable. He would utter opinions on all passing affairs, which being seen to be not private but necessary, would sink like darts into the ear of men and put them in fear.

These are the voices which we hear in solitude, but they grow faint and inaudible as we enter into the world. Society everywhere is in conspiracy against the manhood of every one of its members. Society is a joint-stock company, in which the members agree, for the better securing of his bread to each shareholder, to surrender the liberty and culture of the eater. The virtue in most request is conformity. Self-reliance is its aversion. It loves not realities and creatures, but names and customs.

Whoso would be a man, must be a nonconformist. He who would gather immortal palms must not be hindered by the name of good-ness, but must explore if it be goodness. Nothing is at last sacred but the integrity of your own mind. Absolve you to yourself, and you shall have the suffrage of the world. I remember an answer which when quite young I was prompted to make to a valued adviser who was wont to importune me with the dear old doctrines of the church. On my saying, "What have I to do with the sacredness of traditions, if I live wholly from within?" my friend suggested,— "But these impulses may be from below, not from above." I replied, "They do not seem to me to be such; but if I am the Devil's child, I will live then from the Devil." No law can be sacred to me but that of my nature. Good and bad are but names very readily transferable to that or this; the only right is what is after my constitution; the only wrong what is against it. A man is to carry himself in the presence of all opposition as if every thing were titular and ephemeral but he. I am ashamed to think how easily we capitulate to badges and names, to large societies and dead institutions. Every decent and well-spoken individual affects and sways me more than is right. I ought to go upright and vital, and speak the rude truth in all ways. If malice and vanity wear the coat of philanthropy, shall that pass? If an angry bigot assumes this bountiful cause of Abolition, and comes to me with his last news from Barbadoes, why should I not say to him, "Go love thy infant; love thy wood-chopper; be good-natured and modest; have that grace; and never varnish your hard, uncharitable ambition with this incredible tenderness for black folk a thousand miles off. Thy love afar is spite at home." Rough and graceless would be such greeting, but truth is handsomer than the affectation of love. Your goodness must have some edge to it,—else it is none. The doctrine of hatred must be preached, as the counteraction of the doctrine of love, when that pules and whines. I shun father and mother and wife and brother when my genius calls me. I would write on the lintels of the door-post, *Whim*. I hope it is somewhat better than whim at last, but we cannot spend the day in explanation. Expect me not to show cause why I seek or why I exclude company. Then again, do not tell me, as a good man did to-day, of my obligation to put all poor men in good situations. Are they *my* poor? I tell thee, thou foolish philanthropist, that I grudge the dollar, the dime, the cent I give to such men as do not belong to me and to whom I do not belong. There is a class of persons to whom by all spiritual affinity I am bought and sold; for them I will go to prison if need be; but your miscellaneous popular charities; the education at college of fools; the building of meetinghouses to the vain end to which many now stand; alms to sots, and the thousandfold Relief Societies; —though I confess with shame I sometimes succumb and give the dollar, it is a wicked dollar, which by and by I shall have the manhood to withhold.

Virtues are, in the popular estimate, rather the exception than the rule. There is the man *and* his virtues. Men do what is called a good action, as some piece of courage or charity, much as they would pay a fine in expiation of daily nonappearance on parade. Their works are done as an apology or extenuation of their living in the world,—as invalids and the insane pay a high board. Their virtues are penances. I do not wish to expiate, but to live. My life is for itself and not for a spectacle. I much prefer that it should be of a lower strain, so it be genuine and equal, than that it should be glittering and unsteady. I wish it to be sound and sweet, and not to need diet and bleeding. I ask primary evidence that you are a man, and refuse this appeal from the man to his actions. I know that for myself it makes no difference whether I do or forbear those actions which are reckoned excellent. I cannot consent to pay for a privilege where I have intrinsic right. Few and mean as my gifts may be, I actually am, and do not need for my own assurance or the assurance of my fellows any secondary testimony.

What I must do is all that concerns me, not what the people think. This rule, equally arduous in actual and in intellectual life, may serve for the whole distinction between greatness and meanness. It is the harder because you will always find those who think they know what is your duty better than you know it. It is easy in the world to live after the world's opinion; it is easy in solitude to live after our own; but the great man is he who in the midst of the crowd keeps with perfect sweetness the independence of solitude.

The objection to conforming to usages that have become dead to you is that it scatters your force. It loses your time and blurs the impression of your character. If you maintain a dead church, contribute to a dead Bible-society, vote with a great party either for the government or against it, spread your table like base housekeepers, —under all these screens I have difficulty to detect the precise man you are: and of course so much force is withdrawn from your proper life. But do your work, and I shall know you. Do your work, and you shall reinforce yourself. A man must consider what a blind-man's-buff is this game of conformity. If I know your sect I anticipate your argument. I hear a preacher announce for his text and topic the expediency of one of the institutions of his church. Do I not know before hand that not possibly can he say a new and spontaneous word? Do I not know that with all this ostentation of examining the grounds of the institution he will do no such thing? Do I not know that he is pledged to himself not to look but at one side, the permitted side, not as a man, but as a parish minister? He is a retained attorney, and these airs of the bench are the emptiest affectation. Well, most men have bound their eyes with one or another handkerchief and attached themselves to some one of these communities of opinion. This conformity makes them not false in a few particulars, authors of a few lies, but false in all particulars. Their every truth is not quite true. Their two is not the real two, their four not the real four; so that every word they say chagrins us and we know not where to begin to set them right. Meantime nature is not slow to equip us in the prison-uniform of the party to which we adhere. We come to wear one cut of face and figure, and acquire by degrees the gentlest asinine expression. There is a mortifying experience in particular, which does not fail to wreak itself also in the general history; I mean "the foolish face of praise,"[1] the forced smile which we put on in company where we do not feel at ease, in answer to conversation which does not interest us. The muscles, not spontaneously moved but moved by a low usurping willfulness, grow tight about the outline of the face, with the most disagreeable sensation.

For noncomformity the world whips you with its displeasure. And therefore a man must know how to estimate a sour face. The by-standers look askance on him in the public street or in the friend's parlor. If this aversion had its origin in contempt and resistance like his own he might well go home with a sad countenance; but the sour faces of the multitude, like their sweet faces, have no deep cause, but are put on and off as the wind blows and a newspaper directs. Yet is the discontent of the multitude more formidable than that of the senate and the college. It is easy enough for a firm man who knows the world to brook the rage of the cultivated classes. Their rage is decorous and prudent, for they are timid, as being very vulnerable themselves. But when to their feminine rage the indignation of the people is added, when the ignorant and the poor are aroused, when the unintelligent brute force that lies at the bottom of society is made to growl and mow, it needs the habit of magnanimity and religion to treat it godlike as a trifle of no concernment.

The other terror that scares us from self-trust is our consistency; a reverence for our past act or word because the eyes of others have no other data for computing our orbit than our past acts, and we are loth to disappoint them.

---

[1] *the foolish . . . praise:* Pope's "Epistle to Dr. Arbuthnot," line 212.

But why should you keep your head over your shoulder? Why drag about this corpse of your memory, lest you contradict somewhat you have stated in this or that public place? Suppose you should contradict yourself; what then? It seems to be a rule of wisdom never to rely on your memory alone, scarcely even in acts of pure memory, but to bring the past for judgment into the thousand-eyed present, and live ever in a new day. In your metaphysics you have denied personality to the Deity, yet when the devout motions of the soul come, yield to them heart and life, though they should clothe God with shape and color. Leave your theory, as Joseph his coat in the hand of the harlot, and flee.[2]

A foolish consistency is the hobgoblin of little minds, adored by little statesmen and philosophers and divines. With consistency a great soul has simply nothing to do. He may as well concern himself with his shadow on the wall. Speak what you think now in hard words and to-morrow speak what to-morrow thinks in hard words again, though it contradict every thing you said to-day.— "Ah, so you shall be sure to be misunderstood." Is it so bad then to be misunderstood? Pythagoras was misunderstood, and Socrates, and Jesus, and Luther, and Copernicus, and Galileo, and Newton, and every pure and wise spirit that ever took flesh. To be great is to be misunderstood.

I suppose no man can violate his nature. All the sallies of his will are rounded in by the law of his being, as the inequalities of Andes and Himmaleh are insignificant in the curve of the sphere. Nor does it matter how you gauge and try him. A character is like an acrostic or Alexandrian stanza;—read it forward, backward, or across, it still spells the same thing. In this pleasing contrite wood-life which God allows me, let me record day by day my honest thought without prospect or retrospect, and, I cannot doubt, it will be found symmetrical, though I mean it not and see it not. My book should smell of pines and resound with the hum of insects. The swallow over my window should interweave that thread or straw he carries in his bill into my web also. We pass for what we are. Character teaches above our wills. Men imagine that they communicate their virtue or vice only by overt actions, and do not see that virtue or vice emit a breath every moment.

There will be an agreement in whatever variety of actions, so they be each honest and natural in their hour. For of one will, the actions will be harmonious, however unlike they seem. These varieties are lost sight of at a little distance, at a little height

[2] *Joseph . . . flee:* Genesis 39:12.

of thought. One tendency unites them all. The voyage of the best ship is a zigzag line of a hundred tacks. See the line from a sufficient distance, and it straightens itself to the average tendency. Your genuine action will explain itself and will explain your other genuine actions. Your conformity explains nothing. Act singly, and what you have already done singly will justify you now. Greatness appeals to the future. If I can be firm enough to-day to do right and scorn eyes, I must have done so much right before as to defend me now. Be it how it will, do right now. Always scorn appearances and you always may. The force of character is cumulative. All the foregone days of virtue work their health into this. What makes the majesty of the heroes of the senate and the field, which so fills the imagination? The consciousness of a train of great days and victories behind. They shed a united light on the advancing actor. He is attended as by a visible escort of angels. That is it which throws thunder into Chatham's voice, and dignity into Washington's port, and America into Adam's eye. Honor is venerable to us because it is no ephemera. It is always ancient virtue. We worship it to-day because it is not of to-day. We love it and pay it homage because it is not a trap for our love and homage, but is self-dependent, self-derived, and therefore of an old immaculate pedigree, even if shown in a young person.

I hope in these days we have heard the last of conformity and consistency. Let the words be gazetted and ridiculous henceforward. Instead of the gong for dinner, let us hear a whistle from the Spartan fife. Let us never bow and apologize more. A great man is coming to eat at my house. I do not wish to please him; I wish that he should wish to please me. I will stand here for humanity, and though I would make it kind, I would make it true. Let us affront and reprimand the smooth mediocrity and squalid contentment of the times, and hurl in the face of custom and trade and office, the fact which is the upshot of all history, that there is a great responsible Thinker and Actor working wherever a man works; that a true man belongs to no other time or place, but is the centre of things. Where he is, there is nature. He measures you and all men and all events. Ordinarily, every body in society reminds us of somewhat else, or of some other person. Character, reality, reminds you of nothing else; it takes place of the whole creation. The man must be so much that he must make all circumstances indifferent. Every true man is a cause, a country, and an age; requires infinite spaces and numbers and time fully to accomplish his design;—and posterity seem to follow his steps as a train of clients. A man Caesar is born, and for ages after we have a Roman Empire. Christ is born, and millions of minds so grow and cleave to his genius that he is confounded with virtue and the possible of man. An institution is the lengthened shadow of one man; as, Monachism, of the Hermit Antony; the Reformation, of Luther; Quakerism, of Fox; Methodism, of Wesley; Abolition, of Clarkson. Scipio, Milton called "the height of Rome"; and all history resolves itself very easily into the biography of a few stout and earnest persons.[3]

Let a man then know his worth, and keep things under his feet. Let him not peep or steal, or skulk up and down with the air of a charity-boy, a bastard, or an interloper in the world which exists for him. But the man in the street, finding no worth in himself which corresponds to the force which built a tower or sculptured a marble god, feels poor when he looks on these. To him a palace, a statue, or a costly book have an alien and forbidding air, much like a gay equipage, and seem to say like that, "Who are you, Sir?" Yet they all are his, suitors for his notice, petitioners to his faculties that they will come out and take possession. The picture waits for my verdict; it is not to command me, but I am to settle its claims to praise. That popular fable of the sot who was picked up dead-drunk in the street, carried to the duke's house, washed and dressed and laid in the duke's bed, and, on his waking, treated with all obsequious ceremony like the duke, and assured that he had been insane, owes its popularity to the fact that it symbolizes so well the state of man, who is in the world a sort of sot, but now and then wakes up, exercises his reason and finds himself a true prince.

Our reading is mendicant and sycophantic. In history our imagination plays us false. Kingdom and lordship, power and estate, are a gaudier vocabulary than private John and Edward in a small house and common day's work; but the things of life are the same to both; the sum total of both is the same. Why all this deference to Alfred and Scanderbeg and Gustavus? Suppose they were virtuous; did they wear out virtue? As great a stake depends on your private act to-day as followed their public and renowned steps. When private men shall act with original views, the lustre will be transferred from the actions of kings to those of gentlemen.

The world has been instructed by its kings, who have so magnetized the eyes of nations. It has been taught by this colossal symbol the mutual reverence that is due from man to man. The joyful loyalty with which men have everywhere suffered the king, the noble, or the great proprietor to walk among them by a law

[3] *all history . . . persons:* Compare Carlyle in *Heroes and Hero-Worship* (1841): "Universal History, the history of what man has accomplished in this world, is at bottom the History of the Great Men who have worked here."

of his own, make his own scale of men and things and reverse theirs, pay for benefits not with money but with honor, and represent the law in his person, was the hieroglyphic by which they obscurely signified their consciousness of their own right and comeliness, the right of every man.

The magnetism which all original action exerts is explained when we inquire the reason of self-trust. Who is the Trustee? What is the aboriginal Self, on which a universal reliance may be grounded? What is the nature and power of that science-baffling star, without parallax, without calculable elements, which shoots a ray of beauty even into trivial and impure actions, if the least mark of independence appear? The inquiry leads us to that source, at once the essence of genius, of virtue, and of life, which we call Spontaneity or Instinct. We denote this primary wisdom as Intuition, whilst all later teachings are tuitions. In that deep force, the last fact behind which analysis cannot go, all things find their common origin. For the sense of being which in calm hours arises, we know not how, in the soul, is not diverse from things, from space, from light, from time, from man, but one with them and proceeds obviously from the same source whence their life and being also proceed. We first share the life by which things exist and afterwards see them as appearances in nature and forget that we have shared their cause. Here is the fountain of action and of thought. Here are the lungs of that inspiration which giveth man wisdom and which cannot be denied without impiety and atheism. We lie in the lap of immense intelligence, which makes us receivers of its truth and organs of its activity. When we discern justice, when we discern truth, we do nothing of ourselves, but allow a passage to its beams. If we ask whence this comes, if we seek to pry into the soul that causes, all philosophy is at fault. Its presence or its absence is all we can affirm. Every man discriminates between the voluntary acts of his mind and his involuntary perceptions, and knows that to his involuntary perceptions a perfect faith is due. He may err in the expression of them, but he knows that these things are so, like day and night, not to be disputed. My wilful actions and acquisitions are but roving;—the idlest reverie, the faintest native emotion, command my curiosity and respect. Thoughtless people contradict as readily the statement of perception as of opinions, or rather much more readily; for they do not distinguish between perception and notion. They fancy that I choose to see this or that thing. But perception is not whimsical, but fatal. If I see a trait, my children will see it after me, and in course of time all mankind,—although it may chance that no one has seen it before me. For my perception of it is as much a fact as the sun.

The relations of the soul to the divine spirit are so pure that it is profane to seek to interpose helps. It must be that when God speaketh he should communicate, not one thing, but all things; should fill the world with his voice; should scatter forth light, nature, time, souls, from the centre of the present thought; and new date and new create the whole. Whenever a mind is simple and receives a divine wisdom, old things pass away,—means, teachers, texts, temples fall; it lives now, and absorbs past and future into the present hour. All things are made sacred by relation to it, —one as much as another. All things are dissolved to their centre by their cause, and in the universal miracle petty and particular miracles disappear. If therefore a man claims to know and speak of God and carries you backward to the phraseology of some old mouldered nation in another country, in another world, believe him not. Is the acorn better than the oak which is its fulness and completion? Is the parent better than the child into whom he has cast his ripened being? Whence then this worship of the past? The centuries are conspirators against the sanity and authority of the soul. Time and space are but physiological colors which the eye makes, but the soul is light: where it is, is day; where it was, is night; and history is an impertinence and an injury if it be any thing more than a cheerful apologue or parable of my being and becoming.

Man is timid and apologetic; he is no longer upright; he dares not say "I think," "I am," but quotes some saint or sage. He is ashamed before the blade of grass or the blowing rose. These roses under my window make no reference to former roses or to better ones; they are for what they are; they exist with God to-day. There is no time to them. There is simply the rose; it is perfect in every moment of its existence. Before a leafbud has burst, its whole life acts; in the full-blown flower there is no more; in the leafless root there is no less. Its nature is satisfied and it satisfies nature in all moments alike. But man postpones or remembers; he does not live in the present, but with reverted eye laments the past, or, heedless of the riches that surround him, stands on tiptoe to foresee the future. He cannot be happy and strong until he too lives with nature in the present, above time.

This should be plain enough. Yet see what strong intellects dare not yet hear God himself unless he speaks the phraseology of I know not what David, or Jeremiah, or Paul. We shall not always set so great a price on a few texts, on a few lives. We are like children who repeat by rote the sentences of grandames and tutors, and, as they grow older, of the men of talents and character they chance to see,—painfully recollecting the exact words they spoke; afterwards, when they come into the point of view which those had who uttered these sayings, they understand them and are willing to let the words go; for at any time they can use words as good when occasion comes. If we live truly, we shall see truly. It is as easy for the strong man to be strong, as it is for the weak to be weak. When we have new perception, we shall gladly disburden the memory of its hoarded treasures as old rubbish. When a man lives with God, his voice shall be as sweet as the murmur of the brook and the rustle of the corn.

And now at last the highest truth on this subject remains unsaid; probably cannot be said; for all that we say is the far-off remembering of the intuition. That thought by what I can now nearest approach to say it, is this. When good is near you, when you have life in yourself, it is not by any known or accustomed way; you shall not discern the footprints of any other; you shall not see the fact of man; you shall not hear any name;—the way, the thought, the good, shall be wholly strange and new. It shall exclude example and experience. You take the way from man, not to man. All persons that ever existed are its forgotten ministers. Fear and hope are alike beneath it. There is somewhat low even in hope. In the hour of vision there is nothing that can be called gratitude, nor properly joy. The soul raised over passion beholds identity and eternal causation, perceives the self-existence of Truth and Right, and calms itself with knowing that all things go well. Vast spaces of nature, the Atlantic Ocean, the South Sea; long intervals of time, years, centuries, are of no account. This which I think and feel underlay every former state of life and circumstances, as it does underlie my present, and what is called life and what is called death.

Life only avails, not the having lived. Power ceases in the instant of repose; it resides in the moment of transition from a past to a new state, in the shooting of the gulf, in the darting to an aim. This one fact the world hates; that the soul *becomes*; for that forever degrades the past, turns all riches to poverty, all reputation to a shame, confounds the saint with the rogue, shoves Jesus and Judas equally aside. Why then do we prate of self-reliance? Inasmuch as the soul is present there will be power not confident but agent. To talk of reliance is a poor external way of speaking. Speak rather of that which relies because it works and is. Who has more obedience than I masters me, though he should not raise his finger. Round him I must revolve by the gravitation of spirits. We fancy it rhetoric when we speak of eminent virtue. We do not yet see that virtue is Height, and that a man or a company of men, plastic and permeable to principles, by the law of nature must over-power and ride all cities, nations, kings, rich men, poets, who are not.

This is the ultimate fact which we so quickly reach on this, as on every topic, the resolution of all into the ever-blessed ONE. Self-existence is the attribute of the Supreme Cause, and it constitutes the measure of good by the degree in which it enters into all lower forms. All things real are so by so much virtue as they contain. Commerce, husbandry, hunting, whaling, war, eloquence, personal weight, are somewhat, and engage my respect as examples of its presence and impure action. I see the same law working in nature for conservation and growth. Power is, in nature, the essential measure of right. Nature suffers nothing to remain in her kingdoms which cannot help itself. The genesis and maturation of a planet, its poise and orbit, the bended tree recovering itself from the strong wind, the vital resources of every animal and vegetable, are demon-strations of the self-sufficing and therefore self-relying soul.

Thus all concentrates: let us not rove; let us sit at home with the cause. Let us stun and astonish the intruding rabble of men and books and institutions by a simple declaration of the divine fact. Bid the invaders take the shoes from off their feet, for God is here within.[4] Let our simplicity judge them, and our docility to our own law demonstrate the poverty of nature and fortune beside our native riches.

But now we are a mob. Man does not stand in awe of man, nor is his genius admonished to stay at home, to put itself in communi-cation with the internal ocean, but it goes abroad to beg a cup of water of the urns of other men. We must go alone. I like the silent church before the service begins, better than any preaching. How far off, how cool, how chaste the persons look, begirt each one with a precinct or sanctuary! So let us always sit. Why should we assume the faults of our friend, or wife, or father, or child, because they sit around our hearth, or are said to have the same blood? All men have my blood and I all men's. Not for that will I adopt their petulance or folly, even to the extent of being ashamed of it. But your isolation must not be mechanical, but spiritual, that is, must be elevation. At times the whole world seems to be in conspiracy to importune you with emphatic trifles. Friend, client, child, sick-ness, fear, want, charity, all knock at once at thy closet door and

[4] *take . . . within:* Compare Exodus 3:5.

say,—"Come out unto us." But keep thy state; come not into their confusion. The power men possess to annoy me I give them by a weak curiosity. No man can come near me but through my act. "What we love that we have, but by desire we bereave ourselves of the love."

If we cannot at once rise to the sanctities of obedience and faith, let us at least resist our temptations; let us enter into the state of war and wake Thor and Woden, courage and constancy, in our Saxon breasts. This is to be done in our smooth times by speaking the truth. Check this lying hospitality and lying affection. Live no longer to the expectation of these deceived and deceiving people with whom we converse. Say to them, "O father, O mother, O wife, O brother, O friend, I have lived with you after appearances hitherto. Henceforward I am the truth's. Be it known unto you that henceforward I obey no law less than the eternal law. I will have no convenants but proximities. I shall endeavor to nourish my parents, to support my family, to be the chaste husband of one wife,—but these relations I must fill after a new and unprecedented way. I appeal from your customs. I must be myself. I cannot break myself any longer for you, or you. If you can love me for what I am, we shall be the happier. If you cannot, I will still seek to deserve that you should. I will not hide my tastes or aversions. I will so trust that what is deep is holy, that I will do strongly before the sun and moon whatever inly rejoices me and the heart appoints. If you are noble, I will love you; if you are not, I will not hurt you and myself in hypocritical attentions. If you are true, but not in the same truth with me, cleave to your companions; I will seek my own. I do this not selfishly but humbly and truly. It is alike your interest, and mine, and all men's, however long we have dwelt in lies, to live in truth. Does this sound harsh to-day? You will soon love what is dictated by your nature as well as mine, and if we follow the truth it will bring us out safe at last."—But so may you give these friends pain. Yes, but I cannot sell my liberty and my power, to save their sensibility. Besides, all persons have their moments of reason, when they look out into the region of absolute truth; then will they justify me and do the same thing.

The populace think that your rejection of popular standards is a rejection of all standard, and mere antinomianism; and the bold sensualist will use the name of philosophy to gild his crimes. But the law of consciousness abides. There are two confessionals, in one or the other of which we must be shriven. You may fulfill your round of duties by clearing yourself in the *direct,* or in the *reflex* way. Consider whether you have satisfied your relations to father, mother, cousin, neighbor, town, cat and dog—whether any of these can upbraid you. But I may also neglect this reflex standard and absolve me to myself. I have my own stern claims and perfect circle. It denies the name of duty to many offices that are called duties. But if I can discharge its debts it enables me to dispense with the popular code. If any one imagines that this law is lax, let him keep its commandment one day.

And truly it demands something godlike in him who has cast off the common motives of humanity and has ventured to trust himself for a taskmaster. High be his heart, faithful his will, clear his sight, that he may in good earnest be doctrine, society, law, to himself, that a simple purpose may be to him as strong as iron necessity is to others!

If any man consider the present aspects of what is called by distinction *society*, he will see the need of these ethics. The sinew and heart of man seem to be drawn out, and we are become timorous, desponding whimperers. We are afraid of truth, afraid of fortune, afraid of death, and afraid of each other. Our age yields no great and perfect persons. We want men and women who shall renovate life and our social state, but we see that most natures are insolvent, cannot satisfy their own wants, have an ambition out of all proportion to their practical force and do lean and beg day and night continually. Our housekeeping is mendicant, our arts, our occupations, our marriages, our religion we have not chosen, but society has chosen for us. We are parlor soldiers. We shun the rugged battle of fate, where strength is born.

If our young men miscarry in their first enterprises they lose all heart. If the young merchant fails, men say he is *ruined*. If the finest genius studies at one of our colleges and is not installed in an office within one year afterwards in the cities or suburbs of Boston or New York, it seems to his friends and to himself that he is right in being disheartened and in complaining the rest of his life. A sturdy lad from New Hampshire or Vermont, who in turn tries all the professions, who *teams it, farms it, peddles,* keeps a school, preaches, edits a newspaper, goes to Congress, buys a township, and so forth, in successive years, and always like a cat falls on his feet, is worth a hundred of these city dolls. He walks abreast with his days and feels no shame in not "studying a profession," for he does not postpone his life, but lives already. He has not one chance, but a hundred chances. Let a Stoic open the resources of man and tell men they are not leaning willows, but can and must detach themselves; that with the exercise of self-trust, new powers shall appear; that a man is the word made flesh,[5] born to shed healing to the nations;[6] that he should be ashamed of our compassion, and that the moment he acts for himself, tossing the laws, the books, idolatries and customs out of the window, we pity him no more but thank and revere him;—and that teacher shall restore the life of man to splendor and make his name dear to all history.

It is easy to see that a greater self-reliance must work a revolution in all the offices and relations of men; in their religion; in their education; in their pursuits; their modes of living; their association; in their property; in their speculative views.

1. In what prayers do men allow themselves! That which they call a holy office is not so much as brave and manly. Prayer looks abroad and asks for some foreign addition to come through some foreign virtue, and loses itself in endless mazes of natural and supernatural, and mediatorial and miraculous. Prayer that craves a particular commodity, anything less than all good, is vicious. Prayer is the contemplation of the facts of life from the highest point of view. It is the soliloquy of a beholding and jubilant soul. It is the spirit of God pronouncing his works good.[7] But prayer as a means to effect a private end is meanness and theft. It supposes dualism and not a unity in nature and consciousness. As soon as the man is at one with God, he will not beg. He will then see prayer in all action. The prayer of the farmer kneeling in his field to weed it, the prayer of the rower kneeling with the stroke of his oar, are true prayers heard throughout nature, though for cheap ends. Caratach, in Fletcher's "Bonduca," when admonished to inquire the mind of the god Audate, replies,—

> "His hidden meaning lies in our endeavors;
> Our valors are our best gods."

Another sort of false prayers are our regrets. Discontent is the want of self-reliance; it is infirmity of will. Regret calamities if you can thereby help the sufferer; if not, attend your own work and already the evil begins to be repaired. Our sympathy is just as base. We come to them who weep foolishly and sit down and cry for company, instead of imparting to them truth and health in rough electric shocks, putting them once more in communication with their own reason. The secret of fortune is joy in our hands. Welcome evermore to gods and men is the self-helping man. For him

[5] *word made flesh:* John 1:14.
[6] *healing . . . nations:* Revelation 22:2.
[7] *God . . . good:* Genesis 1:31.

all doors are flung wide; him all tongues greet, all honors crown, all eyes follow with desire. Our love goes out to him and embraces him because he did not need it. We solicitously and apologetically caress and celebrate him because he held on his way and scorned our disapprobation. The gods love him because men hated him. "To the persevering mortal," said Zoroaster, "the blessed Immortals are swift."

As men's prayers are a disease of the will, so are their creeds a disease of the intellect. They say with those foolish Israelites, "Let not God speak to us, lest we die. Speak thou, speak any man with us, and we will obey." Everywhere I am hindered of meeting God in my brother, because he has shut his own temple doors and recites fables merely of his brother's, or his brother's brother's God. Every new mind is a new classification. If it prove a mind of uncommon activity and power, a Locke, a Lavoisier, a Hutton, a Bentham, a Fourier, it imposes its classification on other men, and lo! a new system. In proportion to the depth of the thought, and so to the number of the objects it touches and brings within reach of the pupil, is his complacency. But chiefly is this apparent in creeds and churches, which are also classifications of some powerful mind acting on the elemental thought of duty and man's relation to the Highest. Such is Calvinism, Quakerism, Swedenborgism. The pupil takes the same delight in subordinating every thing to the new terminology as a girl who has just learned botany in seeing a new earth and new seasons thereby. It will happen for a time that the pupil will find his intellectual power has grown by the study of his master's mind. But in all unbalanced minds the classification is idolized, passes for the end and not for a speedily exhaustible means, so that the walls of the system blend to their eye in the remote horizon with the walls of the universe; the luminaries of heaven seem to them hung on the arch their master built. They cannot imagine how you aliens have any right to see,—how you can see; "It must be somehow that you stole the light from us." They do not yet perceive that light, unsystematic, indomitable, will break into any cabin, even into theirs. Let them chirp awhile and call it their own. If they are honest and do well, presently their neat new pinfold will be too strait and low, will crack, will lean, will rot and vanish, and the immortal light, all young and joyful, million-orbed, million-colored, will beam over the universe as on the first morning.

2. It is for want of self-culture that the superstition of Travelling, whose idols are Italy, England, Egypt, retains its fascination for all educated Americans. They who made England, Italy, or Greece

venerable in the imagination, did so by sticking fast where they were, like an axis of the earth. In manly hours we feel that duty is our place. The soul is no traveller; the wise man stays at home, and when his necessities, his duties, on any occasion call him from his house, or into foreign lands, he is at home still and shall make men sensible by the expression of his countenance that he goes, the missionary of wisdom and virtue, and visits cities and men like a sovereign and not like an interloper or a valet.

I have no churlish objection to the circumnavigation of the globe for the purposes of art, of study, and benevolence, so that the man is first domesticated, or does not go abroad with the hope of finding somewhat greater than he knows. He who travels to be amused, or get somewhat which he does not carry, travels away from himself, and grows old even in youth among old things. In Thebes, in Palmyra, his will and mind have become old and dilapidated as they. He carries ruins to ruins.

Travelling is a fool's paradise. Our first journeys discover to us the indifference of places. At home I dream that at Naples, at Rome, I can be intoxicated with beauty and lose my sadness, I pack my trunk, embrace my friends, embark on the sea and at last wake up, in Naples, and there beside me is the stern fact, the sad self, unrelenting, identical, that I fled from. I seek the Vatican and the palaces. I affect to be intoxicated with sights and suggestions, but I am not intoxicated. My giant goes with me wherever I go.

3. But the rage of travelling is a symptom of a deeper unsoundness affecting the whole intellectual action. The intellect is vagabond, and our system of education fosters restlessness. Our minds travel when our bodies are forced to stay at home. We imitate; and what is imitation but the travelling of the mind? Our houses are built with foreign taste; our shelves are garnished with foreign ornaments; our opinions, our tastes, our faculties lean, and follow the Past and the Distant. The soul created the arts wherever they have flourished. It was in his own mind that the artist sought his model. It was an application of his own thought to the thing to be done and the conditions to be observed. And why need we copy the Doric or the Gothic model? Beauty, convenience, grandeur of thought and quaint expression are as near to us as to any, and if the American artist will study with hope and love the precise thing to be done by him, considering the climate, the soil, the length of the day, the wants of the people, the habit and form of the government, he will create a house in which all these will find themselves fitted, and taste and sentiment will be satisfied also.

Insist on yourself; never imitate. Your own gift you can present every moment with the cumulative force of a whole life's cultivation; but of the adopted talent of another you have only an extemporaneous half possession. That which each can do best, none but his Maker can teach him. No man yet knows what it is, nor can, till that person has exhibited it. Where is the master who could have taught Shakespeare? Where is the master who could have instructed Franklin, or Washington, or Bacon, or Newton? Every great man is a unique. The Scipionism of Scipio is precisely that part he could not borrow. Shakespeare will never be made by the study of Shakespeare. Do that which is assigned to you, and you cannot hope too much or dare too much. There is at this moment for you an utterance brave and grand as that of the colossal chisel of Phidias, or trowel of the Egyptians, or the pen of Moses or Dante, but different from all these. Not possibly will the soul, all rich, all eloquent, with thousand-cloven tongue, deign to repeat itself; but if you can hear what these patriarchs say, surely you can reply to them in the same pitch of voice; for the ear and the tongue are two organs of one nature. Abide in the simple and noble regions of thy life, obey thy heart, and thou shalt reproduce the Foreworld again.

4. As our Religion, our Education, our Art look abroad, so does our spirit of society. All men plume themselves on the improvement of society, and no man improves.

Society never advances. It recedes as fast on one side as it gains on the other. It undergoes continual changes; it is barbarous, it is civilized, it is christianized, it is rich, it is scientific; but this change is not amelioration. For everything that is given something is taken. Society acquires new arts and loses old instincts. What a contrast between the well-clad, reading, writing, thinking American, with a watch, a pencil and a bill of exchange in his pocket, and the naked New Zealander, whose property is a club, a spear, a mat and an undivided twentieth of a shed to sleep under! But compare the health of the two men and you shall see that the white man has lost his aboriginal strength. If the traveller tell us truly, strike the savage with a broad-axe and in a day or two the flesh will unite and heal as if you struck the blow into soft pitch, and the same blow shall send the white to his grave.

The civilized man has built a coach, but has lost the use of his feet. He is supported on crutches, but lacks so much support of muscle. He has a fine Geneva watch, but he fails of the skill to tell the hour by the sun. A Greenwich nautical almanac he has, and so being sure of the information when he wants it, the man in the street does not know a star in the sky. The solstice he does not observe; the equinox he knows as little; and the whole bright calendar of the year is without a dial in his mind. His note-books impair his memory; his libraries overload his wit; the insurance-office increases the number of accidents; and it may be a question whether machinery does not encumber; whether we have not lost by refinement some energy, by a Christianity, entrenched in establishments and forms, some vigor of wild virtue. For every Stoic was a Stoic; but in Christendom where is the Christian?

There is no more deviation in the moral standard than in the standard of height or bulk. No greater men are now than ever were. A singular equality may be observed between the great men of the first and of the last ages; nor can all the science, art, religion, and philosophy of the nineteenth century avail to educate greater men than Plutarch's heroes, three or four and twenty centuries ago. Not in time is the race progressive. Phocion, Socrates, Anaxagoras, Diogenes, are great men, but they leave no class. He who is really of their class will not be called by their name, but will be his own man, and in his turn the founder of a sect. The arts and inventions of each period are only its costume and do not invigorate men. The harm of the improved machinery may compensate its good. Hudson and Behring accomplished so much in their fishing-boats as to astonish Parry and Franklin, whose equipment exhausted the resources of science and art. Galileo, with an opera-glass, discovered a more splendid series of celestial phenomena than any one since. Columbus found the New World in an undecked boat. It is curious to see the periodical disuse and perishing of means and machinery which were introduced with loud laudation a few years or centuries before. The great genius returns to essential man. We reckoned the improvements of the art of war among the triumphs of science, and yet Napoleon conquered Europe by the bivouac, which consisted of falling back on naked valor and disencumbering it of all aids. The Emperor held it impossible to make a perfect army, says Las Casas, "without abolishing our arms, magazines, commissaries and carriages, until, in imitation of the Roman custom, the soldier should receive his supply of corn, grind it in his hand-mill and bake his bread himself."

Society is a wave. The wave moves onward, but the water of which it is composed does not. The same particle does not rise from the valley to the ridge. Its unity is only phenomenal. The persons who make up a nation to-day, next year die, and their experience dies with them.

And so the reliance on Property, including the reliance on governments which protect it, is the want of self-reliance. Men have looked away from themselves and at things so long that they have come to esteem the religious, learned, and civil institutions as guards of property, and they deprecate assaults on these, because they feel them to be assaults on property. They measure their esteem of each other by what each has, and not by what each is. But a cultivated man becomes ashamed of his property, out of new respect for his nature. Especially he hates what he has if he see that it is accidental, —came to him by inheritance, or gift, or crime; then he feels that it is not having; it does not belong to him, has no root in him and merely lies there because no revolution or no robber takes it away. But that which a man is, does always by necessity acquire; and what the man acquires, is living property, which does not wait the beck of rulers, or mobs, or revolutions, or fire, or storm, or bankruptcies, but perpetually renews itself wherever the man breathes. "Thy lot or portion of life," said the Caliph Ali, "is seeking after thee; therefore be at rest from seeking after it." Our dependence on these foreign goods leads us to our lavish respect for numbers. The political parties meet in numerous conventions; the greater the concourse and with each new uproar of announcement, The delegation from Essex! The Democrats from New Hampshire! The Whigs of Maine! the young patriot feels himself stronger than before by a new thousand of eyes and arms. In like manner the reformers summon conventions and vote and resolve in multitude. Not so, O friends! will the God deign to enter and inhabit you, but by a method precisely the reverse. It is only as a man puts off all foreign support and stands alone that I see him to be strong and to prevail. He is weaker by every recruit to his banner. Is not a man better than a town? Ask nothing of men, and, in the endless mutation, thou only firm column must presently appear the upholder of all that surrounds thee. He who knows that power is inborn, that he is weak because he has looked for good out of him and elsewhere, and, so perceiving, throws himself unhesitatingly on his thought, instantly rights himself, stands in the erect position, commands his limbs, works miracles; just as a man who stands on his feet is stronger than a man who stands on his head.

So use all that is called Fortune. Most men gamble with her, and gain all, and lose all, as her wheel rolls. But do thou leave as unlawful these winnings, and deal with Cause and Effect, the chancellors of God. In the Will work and acquire, and thou hast chained the wheel of Chance, and shall sit hereafter out of fear from her rotations. A political victory, a rise of rents, the recovery of our sick or the return of your absent friend, or some other favorable event raises your spirits, and you think good days are preparing for you. Do not believe it. Nothing can bring you peace but yourself. Nothing can bring you peace but the triumph of principles.

Author and Selection Notes

Ralph Waldo Emerson (1803-1882) was born in Boston and educated at the Latin School, Harvard College, and Divinity School. In 1829 he became a Unitarian minister but resigned three years later because of its cramping restraints. By 1836 he was well known as a lecturer and spiritual leader and was in great demand on the lecture platform not only in New England but in other parts of the United States. Emerson was famous during his lifetime, and for some time afterwards, as an inspirer of youth. He has perhaps lost some influence in the twentieth century but his position as a persuasive exponent of idealistic philosophy cannot be negated.

In "Self-Reliance" Emerson contends that every man should be self-reliant because he has infinite resources at his command and also because he is directly inspired by God. Self-reliance, according to Emerson, is God-reliance. Man is great only when he is "inspired by the Divine Soul which also inspires all men."

Questions and Exercises

1. List ten sentences from Emerson's essay which you think are tersely and brilliantly stated. What are the major characteristics of his writing?

2. Look up "transcendentalism" in a good reference book and point out several of Emerson's statements which identify him as a transcendentalist.

3. Give Emerson's definition of a "nonconformist." Do you agree with him that "Who so would be a man, must be a nonconformist"? Is the modern trend in America toward conformity or nonconformity?

4. Compare Emerson's attitude toward greatness with Montaigne's attitude as it is revealed in "Of the Inconvenience of Greatness."

5. What do you think of Emerson's philosophy of living in the present, above time, and speaking the truth at all times? Does modern society adhere to his philosophy?

6. In light of twentieth-century society discuss Emerson's attitude toward traveling in foreign countries, art, education, religion, government, property, and inventions which make life easier for man.

7. Choose one of the subjects in question 6 and expand it into a theme.

A LETTER TO LOUISE COLET

Gustave Flaubert

[Croisset] [24 April 1852] Saturday evening.

*　　*　　*　　*　　*

I haven't answered your sad, discouraged letter sooner because I have been involved in an outburst of work. Day before yesterday I went to bed at five o'clock in the morning and yesterday at three; since last Monday I have neglected everything else and have struggled all week exclusively at my *Bovary*, discouraged at not making any headway. I've now come up to my ball scene which I'll begin on Monday. I hope it will go better. Since last you saw me I've done 25 whole pages (25 pages in six weeks) and they were hard to get rolling—I plan to read them tomorrow to Bouilhet. As for me, I've worked on them so long and changed and revised them so that for the moment I can make neither head nor tail of them; I feel, however, that they will hold up.

You mention your discouragements: if only you could see mine! Sometimes I wonder why my arms don't drop off from sheer fatigue and why my head doesn't turn into insipid gruel. I lead a harsh life emptied of outer joy and have nothing to keep me going but a sort of permanent rage which makes me weep from impotence sometimes, but which is continuous.

I love my work with a frantic and perverted love, like an ascetic; the haircloth scratches my belly. Sometimes when I feel empty, when the right words just won't come to me, when, after scribbling pages and pages, I realize I've not made even one sentence, I collapse on my couch and lie there dazed in a morass of frustration.

I hate myself and accuse myself of a mad pride which forces me to flutter after vain fancies. Then a quarter of an hour later everything changes and my heart pounds with joy. Last Wednesday I had to get up and look for my handkerchief; the tears were streaming down my cheeks. I had moved myself so while writing that I was in ecstasy not only from the idea expressed but also from the sentence which expressed it and the satisfaction at having found it. At least I think all those things were present in my emotion which, after all, was probably more nerves than anything else. There are

Translated by Will L. McLendon.

more elevated emotions of that sort, emotions in which sensitivity plays no part, for they surpass even virtue in moral beauty so independent are they of the personality and human relationships. Sometimes (on my brighter days), in the light of an enthusiasm which made my flesh tremble from the soles of my feet to the roots of my hair, I have caught glimpses of a state of the soul much superior to real life, a state in which glory would have no part and even happiness would be of no consequence. If all the things round about us, instead of forming of themselves a constant conspiracy to stifle us in their mire, could keep us on a healthful diet, who knows but that we might then find means to discover for esthetics what stoicism invented for morality? Greek art was not an art: it was the basic constitution of a people, of a whole race, a nation even. The mountains there had different contours and were made of marble for the sculptors, etc. The time for beauty is passed. Humanity, waiting to come back to it, will have nothing to do with it in the meantime. The further art goes the more scientific it will become, just as science will become more artistic; the two will meet at the top after having gone separate ways at the bottom. No human thought can now foresee under what brilliant psychic suns future works of art will bloom. In the meantime we are in a passageway filled with shadows, we grope about in the darkness. We lack leverage; the earth spins under our feet, we all lack a fulcrum, men of letters and scribblers that we are! What's the use? What need does this chatter fill? Between us and the masses there is no link: too bad for the masses; too bad for us especially. But, since everything has its reasons, and since an individual's fancy appears to me to be as legitimate as the appetite of a million men and capable of occupying as great a place in the world, one must, forgetting things and a humanity which denies us, live for his calling, climb up into his ivory tower and there, like a dancing-girl in her perfumes, remain alone in one's dreams. I sometimes have great frustrations, great emptiness, and doubts which gloat in my face in the midst of my simplest satisfactions. So what! I wouldn't exchange all that for anything, because in my conscience I feel that I am fulfilling my duty, that I am obeying some higher fate, that I am doing right, that I am on the right side.

Author and Selection Notes

Gustave Flaubert (1821-1880), born in Rouen, France, was the son of a physician. He was sent to Paris to study law, but the prospects of a law career were not pleasing. He early associated himself with the literary world of Paris, notably Victor Hugo and his followers. Flaubert seemed to avoid the romantic flood of the age and by instinct became a realist desiring only to contemplate things as they were.

Physically Flaubert "enjoyed" ill health. He frequently had "spells" which were in appearance epileptic. He traveled much in Southern Europe and the Mediterranean world in order to lessen his disorder, and even in France he traveled so constantly that he became very well known in the most out-of-the-way places in Normandy and other sections. After the death of his father in 1840, Flaubert returned to his home near Rouen and lived the remainder of his life. The quietude and rural air seemed most soothing to his high-strung temperament, and it was here that he wrote his most famous novel, *Madame Bovary*.

Questions and Exercises

1. Identify Louise Colet by checking in a good encyclopedia.

2. Do you have an explanation for the slowness with which Flaubert moved in writing his *Bovary?*

3. Can you understand the passions of the writer in regard to his creativeness? Have you ever experienced "exquisite pleasure" after accomplishing some artistic endeavor?

4. Explain Flaubert's statement that "Greek art was not an art; it was the very constitution of an entire people, of an entire race, of the country itself."

5. Do you believe that American art is not an art, but the total constitution of an entire people? Why or why not?

6. Comment on the statement "The time for beauty is over."

7. Write an argument in support of "The more art develops, the more scientific it will be, . . ."

8. Describe the future status of art as viewed by Flaubert.

9. Is it possible in present-day society to be creative and live happily?

10. Do you believe that no bond exists between a writer and his public? If what an artist does is the result of an honest and profound conviction, should he continue such actions even though society disapproves? Write a theme discussing the relationship of the artist to society.

A LETTER TO ERNEST CHEVALIER
Gustave Flaubert

[Paris, July 22, 1842]

What a charming science law is! Really beautiful! And above all, how literary! Damn, what beautiful styles Messieurs Oudot and

Translated by Will L. McLendon.

Ducondray have! And Monsieur Duranton's head: that of a true artist! And his profile: pure Greek! And to think that for the past month I haven't read a line of poetry, heard a note of music, dreamed quietly for even a couple of hours, or lived a minute. Would you believe it, I was so tired of it all the other night that I dreamed about law! I felt ashamed at having dishonored the institution of dreaming so. I'm sweating blood and tears, but if I don't manage to find some Oudot notebooks, the game's up, and I'll be rejected for next year. Yesterday I went to watch some examinations; it's the most advisable thing for me to do, I believe. Soon it will be my turn to put on that filthy harness. I don't give a damn about law so long as there's none against my smoking my pipe and watching the clouds float by in the sky as I lie on my back and half close my eyes. That's all I want. What do I care about becoming powerful, being a great man, a well-known figure in the precinct, in the county or three provinces, a skinny man, a man who suffers from indigestion? Do I have any ambition, like the bootblack who aspires to being a boot-maker, the coachman who longs to be a groom, the servant who yearns to be a master, or the climber who hopes to be decorated and elected alderman, a congressman or even a cabinet member? All that is pretty boring to me and tempts me about as much as a two-bit dinner or a humanitarian speech. But that's what everybody is bent on. And if for no other reason than to achieve some distinction and not follow one's taste, if only for the sake of good form and not out of inclination, it is a good idea these days to step out of the picture and leave all those things to the rabble who are always pushing themselves ahead and running all over the place. Why don't we just stay at home and from the height of our balcony watch the public pass by: and if we sometimes become too bored, well, we'll just spit on their heads and go on chatting calmly as we watch the sun setting on the horizon.

Good night to you.

Author and Selection Notes

See page 364.

Questions and Exercises

1. What do you think provoked the sentiments expressed by Flaubert to his friend, Ernest Chevalier?

2. How would you describe Flaubert? What kind of person do you think he is?

3. Can you explain why he began the study of Law, despising it as he apparently did?

4. What is the meaning of "Soon I too will have to wear that filthy harness"?

5. Speak of Flaubert's ideas on greatness. Compare them with Emerson's ideas in "Self-Reliance" and Montaigne's in "Of the Inconvenience of Greatness."

6. Are there many laws that prohibit you from doing things you would like to do? Discuss.

7. What is it in society that places a square peg in a round hole?

8. How can you account for Flaubert's cynicism in the latter part of the letter?

9. Theme Topics: I Would (Would Not) Enjoy Being a Creative Person; Real Happiness Comes from Within; My Prospective Career and Why I Chose It; The Sensitivity of the Artist.

USELESS MOUTHS

Octave Henri Mirbeau

On the day upon which it became quite certain that old François could no longer work, his wife, who was much younger than he was and very active, with two bright miserly eyes, said to him: "What can you expect, man? It's no good fretting your heart out about it. Everything in this world has to come to an end. You're as old as the hills. You're nearly eighty, and you're twisted like an old elm stump. You must be reasonable. And you'd better rest now."

And that evening she gave him nothing to eat.

When he saw there was no bread and no coffee on the table as there usually was, old François' heart went cold, and in a meek, trembling, beseeching voice he said:

"I'm hungry, wife. I want a piece of bread."

And she replied, calmly:

"You're hungry? You're hungry, are you? That's a pity, my poor old man. I can't do a thing about it. When one doesn't work one has no right to eat. One must earn the bread one eats. Isn't that true? A man who doesn't work is no longer a man. He's nothing at all. He's less use than a stone in a garden. He's worse than a dead fruit-tree against a wall."

"But if I can't work? There! You know quite well," protested the old man, "that I want to work. But I can't: my arms and legs won't let me."

"I'm not reproaching you. But it isn't my fault, is it? One must always be fair. I'm always fair. When you worked, you ate. Now that you don't work any more you can't eat any more. That's what it comes to. There's no answer to that. It's as plain as the nose on your face. Would you keep an old screw in your stable with a full hay-rack and corn in the manger, when he could no longer stand up to his work? Would you?"

"No, of course not!" loyally replied old François, clearly overwhelmed by the pitiless logic of this comparison.

"There, then! You see how it is. You must be reasonable!" And she added, chaffingly:

"If you're hungry, eat your fist: . . . And keep the other for tomorrow!"

The woman bustled about the poorly furnished but scrupulously clean room, getting everything ready for the next day's work—for in the future she would have to do the work of two people—and, so as not to waste time, she gnawed hastily at a piece of brown bread and an unripe apple which she had picked up under one of the trees in the courtyard.

The old man watched her gloomily with his small screwed-up eyes into which, possibly for the first time in his life, tears were starting. And over him, over his poor stiff bones, a great load of misery came in a wave, for he knew that no argument and no plea could move that heart which was as hard and cold as steel. He knew, too, that she would stoically have accepted for herself the ruthless law which she was applying to him, because she was uncompromising, simple and loyal as death itself. And yet he suggested timidly and without any conviction, with a half-hearted little grin on his lips:

"I've got some savings . . . ."

The woman quickly protested:

"Savings? Savings, indeed! Thank you for nothing! You must be out of your mind. If we began touching our savings what would happen to me, tell me that? And our son, for whom we made them, what would he say? No, no! Work and you'll get some bread. Don't work and you won't get any. That's fair. That's how it should be."

"All right," said old François.

And he relapsed into silence, his eyes fixed hungrily on the bare table, which thenceforth would always be bare for him. He felt that it was hard but in the main he felt that it was just, for his primitive soul had never been able to rise from the savage depths of Nature to the luminous concert of Human Egoism and Love.

He rose painfully, muttering, with little groans of pain: "Oh! my back! Oh! my back!" And he passed into the bedroom whose door opened before him like the dark entrance to a tomb.

This terrible moment had come to him as it had formerly come to his father and his mother whom he himself had refused to feed during their last workless days, deeming them to be nothing but impotent arms and useless mouths. He had seen this moment approaching for a long while. As his strength diminished, so the parsimoniously dealt-out helpings at mealtimes had decreased. At first they had cut down his meat on Sundays and Thursdays, then the vegetables on other days. And now the time was come when his bread was to be taken away. He did not complain and got ready to die in silence, without a sound, like a worn-out plant whose dried-up stem and rotten roots can no longer suck up the rich juices of the earth.

He who had never had a dream in his life dreamed that night of his last goat. It was a very old, very gentle goat, white all over, with little black horns and a long beard like those of the stone devils which disported themselves over the church porch. After having for years produced pretty little kids and good milk, her womb had become sterile and her udders ran dry. She cost nothing to feed or for bedding and did no one any harm. Tied to a stake all day, a few yards away from the house she browsed on the gorse bushes on the common land and moved about at the end of her rope, bleating joyously at the people passing along the distant lane. He might have let her die too. But he had cut her throat one morning, because everything which does not produce something, whether it be milk, seed or work, must disappear and die. And he remembered the goat's eyes full of affection and dying reproach when, holding her gripped between his thighs, he had probed with his knife in her bleeding throat. When he woke, with his mind still full of his dream, old François murmured:

"That's fair. A man is a man, just as a goat is a goat. I've nothing to say. It's quite fair."

Old François never once complained or rebelled. He no longer left the bedroom; he no longer left the bed. Lying on his back and his legs straight out and pressed close together, his arms glued to his sides, his mouth opened and his eyes closed, he remained as motionless as though he were dead. In this corpse-like attitude his back no longer ached and he no longer thought of anything, gradually falling into a gentle stupor, a sort of perpetual somnolence which wafted him far from the ambience of his pallet bed, in a sort of large, pale, endless wave through which little red flashes shot and which was dotted with tiny sparks of fire. And a stench rose from his bed as from a dung-hill.

When she went to work next morning, his wife treble-locked the bedroom. When she came back in the evening she said nothing to him, did not even glance at him and lay down near the bed on a straw mattress, on which she fell into a heavy sleep uninterrupted by any dream or waking. And at dawn the following morning she went about her ordinary work with the same care for order and cleanliness as usual.

She spent the Sunday in collecting the old man's rags and mending them. Then she folded them up and put them carefully away in a corner of the cupboard. In the evening she went and fetched the priest to administer the last sacraments to her man, as she felt that his end was near.

"What's the matter with old François?" asked the priest.

"He's got old age," replied the woman in a peremptory voice. "He's got death. It's his turn, poor chap."

The priest anointed the old man's limbs with the holy oils and said a few prayers.

"He thought he was further off it than that," the priest observed, as he left.

"It's his turn," repeated the woman stolidly.

And when she went into the room on the following day she could no longer hear the vague low rattle, the gurgling sound which issued from the old man's nose as from an empty bottle. She felt his forehead, his chest and his hands, and found they were cold.

"He's gone," she said gravely and respectfully, but without any emotion.

Old François' eyelids had opened at the moment of his last agony and had uncovered his dull, sightless eyes. She drew them down quickly with her thumbs, then she looked dreamily at the corpse for a few seconds and thought: "He was a good man, thrifty and brave. He behaved well all his life. He worked well. I'll put a new shirt on him and his wedding suit and a white shroud and then, if his son will allow it, we might buy a grave for ten years, in a cemetery, like a rich man's."

Author and Selection Notes

Octave Henri Mirbeau (1850-1917) was born in Remalard, Normandy, France. His father was a physician. At his death in 1917, Mirbeau's reputation as a writer almost disappeared. During his life he was a colleague of Edmond de Goncourt in the Naturalist Movement. Andre Gide responded to Mirbeau's warm indignations but complained that "the satirical spirit prevents his having any critical sense." Mirbeau made fun of the Parisian aesthetes and did not comply with the demands of the bourgeois. He was a vigorous and audacious publicist and journalist and lost his first job as an art critic by denouncing the academic painters in favor of Manet and Cezanne. In 1908 his play *Le Foyer* created a scandal by attacking the philanthropic subsidies by the rich for the relief of the poor. Some of his great literary portrayals deal with man's inhumanity to man. The short story in this text is a striking example.

Questions and Exercises

1. Can you identify the theme of this short story?
2. Does old François impress you? Is he real? Would you, in his condition, give up life so easily?
3. Can you explain the acceptance of fate as it is illustrated in the story?
4. Is the wife a real person, or a story make-believe? Are her attitudes consistent throughout the story?
5. Is the wife's philosophy "no work, no food" justifiable?
6. Can you account for the appearance of the priest in the story?
7. Do you think old François' son will condone the treatment his father receives, or will he know?
8. What does the last sentence reveal about the wife's feelings for her husband?
9. Do you think "Useless Mouths" a good example of a short story? Is the story one of cruelty or justice? Discuss.
10. Theme Topics: The Plight (or Pleasure) of Old Age; What a Man Soweth, That Shall He Reap; Retribution; Old François' Son; Resistance, a Virtue; My Solution to Old François' Problem; Justice Tempered with Mercy.

THE MOVING AMERICAN

George Wilson Pierson

Each people has its secrets, and its figures of mystery. Of late I have been led to think more and more about one of the most ubiquitous but enigmatic characters of American history. I call him "The Moving American." And the better I get to know him

Copyright 1954 by Yale University Press. Reprinted from *The Yale Review*, Vol. XLIV, September, 1954.

the more secrets he confides, the more answers to the great riddle of our national character.

What are Americans? At this moment Russia may be the great menace, but to the rest of the world we are the unknown quantity, the number-one puzzle. The power of our economy is no longer a secret, but to our cousins in Europe it seems power in the hands of children. Where we boast a practical know-how, they see us as dollar-chasers, materialistic, money-crazy. We take pride in our democracy, but they notice chiefly its shortcomings—our color prejudices, our spectacular divorce rates, our lurid crimes of violence. To a Frenchman all Americans are wealthy; yet culturally we strike him as discouragingly middle-class, crude, vulgar. In particular we are said to lack the attributes of the highest civilization, for compared to the parent societies of Europe ours is and has been an unartistic, anti-intellectual, and astonishingly herd-minded nation. The optimism of America has been unmistakable, and our idealism and generosity are freely acknowledged. Yet in the absence of an appreciation of older cultures our very humanitarianism often seems too naive, too aggressive. Most of all they find us volatile, excitable, unstable, and contradictory. It troubles the world to contemplate a society so mass-minded and conformist in thought yet so undisciplined in action—at the same time so practical but so visionary —so conservative in many ways yet so unpredictable in foreign policy. How deal with such a tangle of contradictions? The images projected are sharp enough: Uncle Shylock and the Presbyterian preacher, Babbitt of Main Street and the Hollywood Goddess of Love, Chicago gangsters, Yankee uplifters, or bespectacled engineers—but how make of such types a family or a national character?

I would suggest that the American character would be clearer if they would add to this rogues' gallery still another portrait: the portrait of The Moving American. Think of the Mayflower or a prairie schooner, a paddle-wheeler or a Stratocruiser. It doesn't matter. For we began as explorers, empire builders, pilgrims and refugees, and we have been moving, moving ever since. In fact we have been and are still today the most mobile people on the face of the earth. Foreign travelers have sensed it. Our census takers have proved it; our poets have made it their song.

The first great tide flowed west. "Westward the Course of Empire takes its way," prophesied Bishop Berkeley. "Westward the Star of Empire takes its way," agreed John Quincy Adams. "They play at leap-frog with their lands," confessed a startled colonial observer. The settlers, reported Governor Dunmore, "acquire no attachment to Place: but wandering about Seems engrated in their Nature; and it is a weakness incident to it, that they Should forever imagine the Lands further off, are Still better than those upon which they have already Settled." "Americans are the Western Pilgrims," wrote the perceiving Crèvecoeur—and from the Revolution to the Civil War all our pocket compasses continued to point west. "Go West, young man, and grow up with the country," advised Horace Greeley. "Ioway—that's where the tall corn grows." We are "a bivouac rather than a nation," trumpeted an observer in the 1860's, "a grand army moving from the Atlantic to the Pacific, and pitching tents by the way." Still in the twentieth century—"America is west and the wind blowing," sings Archibald MacLeish.

How many Americans actually crossed the Mississippi? We cannot count them exactly, for some who were later found in that land "where never is heard a discouraging word" *must* have been born there. Still, as late as 1930 the census figures indicate that three times as many persons who had been born east of the Mississippi were living west of it as had been born west and were now living east: a net drain from the East of five million souls. Reading such figures one is inclined to agree with the historian who declared that "the most persistent theme in American history is the westward march of the American people."

But notice also a second and rival movement: townward, cityward, to the great centers. Competing with the great open spaces were the great closed places, these new magnets called New York, Pittsburgh, Cincinnati, St. Louis, Chicago. As far back as 1790 the little seaboard towns had started to grow at a faster rate than the rest of the country. By 1870 the nation's 150 cities were actually attracting a larger number of newcomers than the rural regions. And by 1930 our population had become predominantly urban. Going to town became the new American definition of success.

But there has also been a third and even greater movement than these two. Without ever reaching the frontier, or landing in Detroit, San Francisco, or New Orleans, Americans have moved and have kept on moving from farm to farm, from state to state, from town to town, back and forth, from job to job, around and around. There is a fever in our blood. We have itching feet. Here today and gone tomorrow. Let's go. 'Scuse our dust. Fill 'er up. Free wheeling. Howdy, stranger.

As early as 1831 Alexis de Tocqueville was stunned by the sheer restlessness of Jacksonian America. After moving to America the German Francis Lieber declared he felt all the time as if tied to the wing of a windmill. He deduced that there were stationary nations and moving nations, and that movement had become the American "historical task." Said the South American statesman, Sarmiento: "If God were suddenly to call the world to judgment He would surprise two-thirds of the American population on the road like ants." Giant hotels became an American phenomenon. Steamboats were floating hotels. After the Civil War came the parlor car and the sleeper. Next the automobile "restated the national principle" —and today there isn't anything Americans won't do on wheels: eat, drink, sleep, or propagate the race. The Americans, says the horrified Frenchman, even "make the love in the automobile." Also a bank deposit. For we have drive-in banks, drive-in restaurants, drive-in theatres, and drive-in churches, to say nothing of some chapels on wheels, and three times as many motels as we had hotels before.

Can this fever be registered on a thermometer? It can. For example, economists tell us that transportation and communications form and have formed a larger fraction of the economy with us than with any other people except nomads and camel-drivers. It is the testimony of the census takers that after the peak of the westward movement some 20 percent of the people were found in states where they had not been born; but today—with the frontier closed and the cities already fairly occupied, that is, at a time when we ought to have been settling down—the proportion of out-of-state origins has risen to nearly 24 percent, and this takes no account of those who went home the year before, or who have removed more than once, or who have moved around in the same state. Again farm ownership and home ownership have been matters of pride and national well-being—but in 1940 it was estimated that the average American farm had been in the same hands for only twelve years. And if an impressive number of us own our own homes these are certainly not where our grandfathers lived, and probably not where we ourselves were born.

. . . Remember when October 1 was moving day? Today all the days of the year hardly suffice for the moves we wish to make. Three hundred and fifty years ago we took to the woods. Today we knock around the world. The habit of moving is in our blood.

But why?

The answer has seemed simple, in fact of negligible importance. For migration, after all, has been merely a means, a neutral connecting link, the empty corridor down which the pilgrim has passed to his goal. I agree that migration did begin as a method—a device —not as an end in itself but as a means to other ends. Yet these ends deserve examination. So, too, does the connecting link.

What ends has migration served, beside the grand conquest of the continent? First, whether we like it or not, we must face the fact that to a certain degree the new world has served as the dumping ground for the old. No sooner had the beachheads been established than England began shipping out her misfits and her undesirables; such undesirables as her heretics and her rebels, such misfits as her criminals and unemployed. Nor did this flow cease with the Revolution. For the backwoods and the whole West then served as refuse dumps for the East. Thus on every frontier were to be found not only gamblers and adventurers but also a shiftless and criminal scum: murderers, highwaymen, and river toughs—what Crèvecoeur called "the most hideous parts of our society." He who had once, as they said, "skipped to America," was soon in the new lingo "gone to Texas"—and presently the vigilantes would be urging him on again. Having skipped town once or twice more, he might land up in the Los Angeles underworld. Migration brought its undesirables.

Migration, in the second place, meant a voluntary movement of escape. As we all know, for many it offered escape from some kind of tyranny: from religious persecution, or military service, or political oppression, or economic discrimination—all of which made such colonies as Pennsylvania, and the great West afterwards, the land of the free and the asylum of the down-trodden. To the oppressed of Europe America has offered one long series of Emancipation Proclamations.

Perhaps on the other hand migration was inspired by the desire to escape from one's own mistakes and failures, from debts one couldn't pay, from a reputation too bad to live down, from an atmosphere that seemed poisoned and hopeless, from obligations one was unwilling to meet. By crossing the Atlantic one might escape one's neighbors—and even oneself. In Virginia past sins would be forgiven—and with a second move even a New England Puritan might be able to leave behind his sense of original sin. So America became also the home of escapists and dreamers and the land of the second chance. In Ohio one could start over, in California find a new faith. Even today not a little interstate migration seems inspired by the state tax collectors, or an unhappy marriage, or the metropolitan police.

Still another motive for flight was dissatisfaction with the progress of Europe, because it was too slow—or because it was too fast. America appealed to radicals and missionaries and utopians and reformers of all stripes, for here one might build a new and better society, and escape the dead hand of the past. The dead hand of the past but its very live grasp, too. For in some ways and to some people old Europe was entirely too lively, too demanding in its intellectual

standards, too powerfully full of improvement or change. On the
frontiers a man might be allowed to stay what he was. The peasants
of the Continent, in an industrializing century, could go either to
the new cities of Europe, or to farms in the new world—and the
short walk in to town often seemed the harder journey. Occupa-
tionally considered, the westward movement was in part a conservative drift: I confess that it was not until I had been teaching
American history for years that I realized that the settlement of
the Mississippi Valley was to a considerable extent manned by
those who were so set in their habits, or so afraid of the new factory
way of life just being introduced from England, that they preferred
to move and move again, rather than give up their old profession
of farming. We Americans have fled the present as well as the past.

But it is as the road to a better future that migration has served
its greatest use. In our lexicon, movement means improvement.
Some of our immigrants may have been the rejects and the fugitives
of Europe, but the vast majority came to our shores, and then leap-
frogged West, and then went to town, and after that moved from
city to city in order to reach a place where the resources were not
all preempted, where the competition was more open, where promotion was easier, where one could *rise* in society and better oneself.
In other words, lateral movement was no good without vertical
movement, too. On the margins of empire, in the frontier areas,
in the sprawling new cities, class barriers broke down, society became atomic, the enterprising and the aggressive could rise.

Especially if you got there first, for the late-comers would have
to pay you for your land, work in your shop, push you upstairs.
Horace Greeley, remember, gave two pieces of advice, not one:
"Go West, young man, *and grow up with the country*." Thus it
was: onward and *upward* with the West! The West was a kind of
elevator. One moved sideways in order to reach that elevator, then
pressed the button for some higher floor. So in the end American
mobility had to be vertical as well as lateral if it was to be judged
a success. If I may enlarge this metaphor, our society has been
filled with escalators, East as well as West, and if enough of them
failed at once there was trouble. What was it made the despair of
the 1930's? The fact that suddenly all the escalators stopped at
once, and for the first time in our history, for "Okie" and factory
hand alike, there was no place to go.

Mobility has been the lubricant in our society: our fluid drive.
It has even crept into our language, occupied our figures of speech.
How is it we speak of success? You've got to be a go-getter if you
expect to get ahead. Your Uncle Dudley's going places. Look out,

I'm on my way! And then with luck we one day hear the magic words that tell us we have "arrived."

It remains to notice still a fourth kind of movement. To a degree we have always moved, but today more than ever, for sheer excitement and pleasure. In these United States the honeymoon is a natural. Travel is packaged. Tourists support a ten-billion dollar industry. And in "Holiday Magazine" we read that last year 72 million Americans (one-half our total population) spent at least a part of their vacation on trips or on the road. In tomorrow's trailer age, it seems, the angry bride won't have to go home to mother; she'll have a home to take with her.

We began by asserting our rights to Life, Liberty, and the Pursuit of Happiness—but as one of our leading historians has remarked, the pursuit of happiness has changed to the happiness of pursuit. In the last war we became the champions of the Four Freedoms: of speech and of religion, from want and fear—but perhaps the greatest American freedom has always been and still is the Freedom to Move. From outcasts to joy-riders. As the saying goes: "We've come a long way."

But has it all been a joyride? I am told that Pascal has an aphorism to the effect that a large part of man's troubles come from his inability to stay in one room. Now whether or not we Americans have gone out of our way to find trouble, it must be admitted that since time immemorial migration has been a dangerous, costly, desperately difficult business. It has been the great eliminator as well as the great promoter. Sociologists call it *selective*. The drive has to be unusually strong or the attachments to the old society very weak for individuals to be able to leave. So not all elements move. The migration is only partial. And there results the one-sided or unbalanced society. Indeed one may go so far as to assert that the trans-Atlantic and trans-continental migrations not only limited American society but twisted the American temperament and gave shape to our whole national character.

Socially the most obvious thing about the English colonizing process was the fact that it brought us a decapitated society. No royalty, no aristocracy, no leisure class. Practically no bishops or judges or scientists or great statesmen made the journey. With insignificant exceptions the highest ranks, the highest professions, the men of the highest learning and the highest crafts and skills all stayed at home. And so did their arts and way of life: their leisure-class culture. Why? Well, the upper classes were already successful at home and could hardly hope to better themselves in a wilderness. And who came instead? A small army of Puritans to whom their austere faith was more important than all the arts and refinements of life. Also a vast swarm out of the lower middle classes to whom the arts of leisure were suspect, and the chance to better themselves economically meant everything. So if American society started and remained materialistic it was not just because of the wealth of this continent but because for three hundred years we drew far less than our share of cultivated folk and far more than our share of materialists out of Europe. The unbalanced society.

If Americans proved themselves astonishingly anti-intellectual, and unmusical and unartistic, it wasn't just because they had to lead a hand-to-mouth existence, and didn't have time, but because, with certain honorable exceptions, our forefathers were people who even before they took ship had paid no attention to the things of the mind and had given mightly small time to the arts. There were exceptions, but I think this generalization will stand. As the generations passed, of course, the new societies struggled to replace the missing elements with the aid of a home-grown trading and planter aristocracy which in the 18th century did begin to patronize the arts. But first the Revolution drove out the Tories, and then the Louisiana Purchase and the Jacksonian revolution pulled the rug of authority out from under the feet of the cultured classes of the seaboard. In effect it has been the ease of escape, the wealth of new occupations, and the rapidity of change which have again and again postponed the establishment of an American aristocracy. Lacking a settled elite with an organic tradition, yet a little uneasy on that account, we have accordingly been driven to borrow, and in the nineteenth century we distinguished ourselves as the greatest style thieves of modern times. Even in the field of building, where we ought to have excelled, we abandoned our Georgian inheritance to rush into one revival movement after another, to keep up with the Joneses. In the field of literature, I believe it was the Bostonians who most effectively exploited the discovery that to borrow books and ideas from Europe was not only elevating in itself but a sure way to get ahead of the Joneses. So if the American tree has been slow to bear fruit, the fault may be in its having too often been topped and transplanted.

Still another great imbalance produced by migration has been in the emotions. As Hansen quotes a German commentator of 1816: "Emigration is a form of suicide because it separates a person from all that life gives except the material wants of simple animal existence." There are those who dispute the point. But in the face of such risks or possibilities who was most likely to go and to make a go of the venture? The pessimists? Hardly. The timid? Not likely, for it became a proverb that "the cowards never started and the weaklings died on the way." The old, the well-balanced, or the skeptical? No. Rather the young and the enthusiastic and the congenitally optimistic. It was above all the suggestible and the wishful thinkers who caught the American fever. Migration was no more rational than man himself. Pioneering, says Lewis Mumford, was the romantic movement in action. And the new land rewarded and perpetuated the type.

Not to be overlooked, also, are certain psychological effects of the moving process. These exiles had to ship light, and on their rough journeys, like as not, they lost still more baggage overboard. The result, intentionally or not, was a tremendous destruction of culture. Yet they could not bring themselves to part with everything they had known. Even the most careless clung to one or two shreds of their past, and the purposeful clung with such purpose that they achieved an intenser faith. On these empty coasts, what they had struggled so hard to save came to seem still more important than it had at home. It expanded into the vacuum of their lives. They would never give it up. Thus our new world communities, so scornful of their inheritance in many ways, became in some particulars quite astonishingly conservative. Watching how the New England Saints tried to build a whole civilization on the Bible, or how the Pennsylvania Germans struggled to preserve their farming and their arts, one suddenly grasps a secret, a key to one of the contradictions that so puzzle our friends in Europe. From their experience, Americans cannot help being in some things completely experimental, in others just the opposite.

Again the repetition of movement, and especially the forming of new communities out of strangers and chance arrivals, without prior knowledge of each other, credentials of status or established reputations, inevitably made these communities more egalitarian than they might otherwise have been. As a friend of mine has observed, our frontier democracy was a democracy of circumstance and mixture as well as of conviction. It followed that after these conglomerations had a chance to sort themselves out a little, things no longer looked quite the same; and out of the wilderness came monopolists, ruling families, and company towns. Perhaps this will help us to understand the later Middle West, in its vagaries and deviations from the equalitarian ideal.

Finally, we should notice the psychological, almost neurotic after-effects of having to journey so much on one's own. The phenomenon has been remarked and brilliantly interpreted. But it will bear repeating that Americans are a lonely crowd, restless, detached, and craving of company. Hence we have become a nation of joiners. With the old family and village units falling apart in our hands we have had to call on our churches and schools, our Elks and Masons and Odd Fellows and Rotary, to take up the slack. (A. M. Schlesinger quotes Will Rogers as saying that "Americans will join anything in town but their own family.") Perhaps this throws light, too, on our penchant for legislating people into morality—for with the restraints of tradition and custom no longer authoritative, don't we have to try to do a good deal, perhaps too much, governing by statute law? Or again one might ask, with personal backgrounds at such a discount, why would Americans not be aggressive? And with moral insecurity universal and perpetual why should anyone be surprised at the almost religious terror with which even the best of us sometimes regard public opinion? Having repudiated the old gods we must somewhere find an authority that is firm.

Europeans should be told that if Americans are the hardest-working people on earth, and play with the same frenzy, and whip through a museum with almost highway speed, it is not only because there is so much more of Calvinism than of humanism, of the working class than the leisure class, in our blood, but because there is something stifling to us in a museum. In all our history we have never learned to sit still. Similarly, if there are fewer regional differences in the whole United States than in any small country in Europe, the explanation is that we have been the most restless people of whom there is reliable record. The American moves with a fine abandon, but the abandoning leaves its mark: on our churches, on our government, on our schools. How better sum up the dilemma of our liberal arts colleges than by recognizing that they have been trying to teach the great classical-Christian tradition to people in flight from Europe and the whole past? Certainly if strangers find us optimistic to the point of wishful thinking, the answer must be that America started as an escape towards the future and it was the young and the hopeful and the romantic who kept coming and were rewarded. Finally, if European statesmen find public opinion in this country unstable, excitable, impatient and dogmatic, we could tell them why. A hundred years ago Dickens made the same charge. "Your inconstancy," said he, "your inconstancy has passed into a proverb."

Yet our inconstancy can be overestimated. Underneath all the turbulence runs a curious consistency. We may be restless but we have got used to change. Expecting the unexpected, we have learned to live with it, too. Startled visitors will sometimes ask why detachment from place has not destroyed all ties, or the ease of self-improvement all classes. Yet status, code, and way of life: all these The Moving American has been learning to carry with him. His telephone line to the past may seem frayed, but his lateral communications have been developing into a fantastic network of intelligence. No society in history has been so stitched together with information. And no citizens have ever been so assaulted by words. To the European, our advertising inevitably comes as a shock. But let him watch a typical commuter as he drives swiftly home at night —past a succession of giant billboards—only half-listening to the insinuating, insistent voice of some high-pressure radio commercial —and it may dawn on the visitor that for a people who have seen so many strange sights and encountered so many miracles, nothing but the exaggeration of advertising will catch the attention. At all events, through this torrent of persuasion the American moves almost unheeding. Before going to bed he may even out of curiosity turn on the news. And on the morrow, after a breakfast of packaged promises, he drives cheerfully back to his work. Like the nomads or the Plains Indians we have become stabilized in our instability.

Author and Selection Notes

George Wilson Pierson (1904-), historian, was born in New York, where he attended St. Bernard's School. He also attended Groton School in Massachusetts and later took his Ph.D. from Yale in 1933. He has been a member of the history faculty at Yale since 1926 and has done considerable writing and study in the fields of American culture, history, and education with some special interest in American mobility and foreign relations. The essay in this text considers the transitory nature of the American.

Questions and Exercises

1. According to Pierson, what part have transatlantic and transcontinental migrations played in giving shape to our national character?

2. The author catalogs the various motives that have accounted for the moving American. Can you think of others?

3. Explain the statement "Lateral movement was no good without vertical movement too."

4. Notice the author's telegraphic sentences in this essay. How effective are they?

5. Theme Topics: America, an Unknown Quantity; My Life on Wheels; A Static Society (Read "Lubberland" again); We Are (Are Not) a Herd-Minded Nation; We Are (Are Not) an Anti-intellectual Nation.

4

CONSTANT CHALLENGE:
MAN AND NATURE

The people march:
Where to? what next?

Carl Sandburg

The advancement of man is in direct proportion to his conquest of nature, to his ability to manipulate for his own comfort and utility his natural environment. Nature was for ancient man primarily the habitation of his deities, who exacted certain obligations and sacrifices to propitiate their wrath or to gain favors. Only through centuries of surviving nature's cataclysmic powers and through a gradual insight into the miracle of its underlying laws, has man at last been able to achieve the partial mastery that has turned nature into a power to be both reverenced and controlled.

In this section, writers explore different aspects of nature, aspects which man has either conquered or hopes to conquer. However, there are others in this group—poets in particular—who will not allow us to forget that nature has sometimes been a god and has always been a source of life and beauty. Their voices call us back to the woods, the fields, the dark coverts, and the hidden pathways.

PSALM 104

David

Bless the Lord, O my soul. O Lord my God, thou art very great;
thou art clothed with honour and majesty:
Who coverest thyself with light as with a garment; who stretchest
out the heavens like a curtain;
Who layeth the beams of his chambers in the waters; who maketh
the clouds his chariot; who walketh upon the wings of the wind;
Who maketh his angels spirits; his ministers a flaming fire;
Who laid the foundations of the earth, that it should not be re-
moved for ever.
Thou coveredst it with the deep as with a garment: the waters
stood above the mountains.
At thy rebuke they fled; at the voice of thy thunder they hasted
away.
They go up by the mountains; they go down by the valleys unto
the place which thou hast founded for them.
Thou hast set a bound that they may not pass over, that they turn
not again to cover the earth.
He sendeth the springs into the valleys, which run among the
hills.
They give drink to every beast of the field: the wild asses quench
their thirst.
By them shall the fowls of the heaven have their habitation, which
sing among the branches.
He watereth the hills from his chambers; the earth is satisfied with
the fruit of thy works.
He causeth the grass to grow for the cattle, and the herb for the
service of man, that he may bring forth fruit out of the earth;
And wine that maketh glad the heart of man, and oil to make his
face to shine, and bread which strengtheneth man's heart.
The trees of the Lord are full of sap: the cedars of Lebanon which
he hath planted;
Where the birds make their nests: as for the stork, the fir trees are
her house.
The high hills are a refuge for the wild goats, and the rocks for
the conies.
He appointed the moon for seasons: the sun knoweth his going
down.

Thou makest darkness, and it is night, wherein all the beasts of the
forest do creep forth.

The young lions roar after their prey, and seek their meat from God.

The sun ariseth; they gather themselves together, and lay them
down in their dens.

Man goeth forth unto his work, and to his labour, until the evening.

O Lord, how manifold are thy works! in wisdom hast thou made
them all: the earth is full of thy riches.

So is this great and wide sea, wherein are things creeping innumerable, both small and great beasts.

There go the ships; there *is* that leviathan, whom thou hast made to
play therein.

These wait all upon thee, that thou mayest give them their meat in
due season.

That thou givest them they gather: thou openest thine hand, they
are filled with good.

Thou hidest thy face, they are troubled; thou takest away their
breath, they die, and return to their dust.

Thou sendest forth thy spirit, they are created; and thou renewest
the face of the earth.

The glory of the Lord shall endure for ever: the Lord shall rejoice
in his works.

He looketh on the earth, and it trembleth; he toucheth the hills,
and they smoke.

I will sing unto the Lord as long as I live; I will sing praise to my
God while I have my being.

My meditation of him shall be sweet: I will be glad in the Lord.

Let the sinners be consumed out of the earth, and let the wicked
be no more. Bless thou the Lord, O my soul. Praise ye the Lord.

Author and Selection Notes

Although the authorship of many of the Psalms is uncertain, Psalm
104 is usually attributed to David, son of Jesse of Bethlehem and youngest
of ten children. As a youth David was anointed by Samuel to be Saul's
successor. He reigned as King of Judah and Israel from about 1013 B.C.
until his death about 973 B.C.

Questions and Exercises

1. Can you suggest why the Psalmist wrote the poem of recognition and
adulation?

2. What impresses you most about this Psalm?

3. There are many figures of speech in the Psalm. Make a list of them and identify their related meanings.

4. Is the Psalmist exalting only God, or is he exalting both God and His creation—nature? Cite passages to prove your point.

5. Cite the passage which you like best and explain why you like it.

6. Write a brief paper exalting nature, using as a subject your reaction to a beautiful morning, or a quiet twilight in spring or winter, a quiet moonlit night in summer, a storm.

THE SCIENCE OF NATURE

Manilius

Stars conscious of our fates and arts divine,
The wondrous work of Heaven's first wise design,
In numerous verse I boldly first inclose;
Too high a subject, and too great for prose.
At what the ancients with a wild amaze   5
And ignorant wonder were content to gaze,
My verse brings down from Heav'n, design'd to show
Celestial secrets to world below:
What yet the Muses groves ne'er heard, I sing,
And bring unusual offerings to their spring.   10
    Rome's Prince and Father, Thou whose wide command
With awful sway is stretcht o'er sea and land,
Who dost deserve that heaven thy love bestow'd,
On thy great father, thou thyself a God,
Now give me courage, make my fancy strong,   15
And yield me vigour for so great a song.
    Nor doth the world this curious search refuse,
It kindly courts the daring of my Muse,
And will be known; whilst you serenely reign,
Instruct our labor, and reward our pain.   20
    Wings raise my feet, I'm pleas'd to mount on high,
Trace all the mazes of the liquid sky,
Their various turnings, and their whirls declare,
And live in the vast regions of the air:
I'll know the stars, which yet alone to gain   25
Is knowledge mean, unequal to the pain;

For doubts resolv'd it no delight affords,
But fills soft empty heads with rattling words:
I'll search the depths, the most remote recess,
And flying nature to confession press; 30
I'll find what sign and constellation rule,
And make the difference 'twixt the wise and fool;
My verse shall sing what various aspect reigns
When kings are doom'd to crowns and slaves to chains.
I'll turn Fate's books, there read proud Parthia's doom; 35
And see the sure eternity of Rome.
    Two temples rais'd with sacred incense shine,
I bow at Nature's and the Muses' shrine;
Both aids I need, for double cares do throng,
And fill my thought; the subject and the song: 40
And whilst I'm bound to verse with orbs immense
The world rolls round me, and distracts my sense;
Vast is my theme, yet unconceiv'd, and brings
Untoward words scarce loos'ned from the things.
    Who first below these wondrous secrets knew? 45
Who stole that knowledge which the World withdrew?
Whose soaring mind those airy mazes trod
And spite of Heaven desir'd to seem a God!
Open the skies, and teach how stars obey,
And run their race as Nature marks the way, 50
Their power and influence, what directs their course
What whirls them round, and what confines their force.
    First Mercury disclos'd these mysteries,
By him we view the inside of the skies,
And know the stars, and now mankind admires 55
The power, not only lustre of their fires:
By him all know how great, how just and wise,
And good is the contriver of the skies;
At whose command the stars in order met,
Who times appointed when to rise and set; 60
That Heaven's great secrets may lie hid no more,
And man instructed gratefully adore.
    Nature disclos'd herself, and from her springs
Pure streams deriv'd o'erflowed the minds of kings,
Kings next to Heaven, who o'er the East did sway, 65
Where swift Euphrates cuts his rapid way,
Where Nile o'erflows, and whence the whirl restores
The day to us, and passing burns the moors.

And next o'er priests, whose constant cares employ'd
In public service did oblige the god,   70
His presence did their holy minds inspire
With sacred flames, and rais'd their fancies higher,
Till by degrees to due perfection wrought
He made himself the object of their thought:
  Such were those wondrous men who first from far   75
Lookt up, and saw fates hanging at each star:
Their thoughts extended did at once comprise
Ten thousand revolutions of the skies,
They markt the influence, and observ'd the power
Of every sign, and every fatal hour;   80
What tempers they bestow'd, what fortunes gave,
And who was doom'd a king, and who was born a slave;
How aspects vary, and their change creates,
Though little, great variety in fates.
  Thus when the stars their mighty round had run,   85
And all were fixt whence first their race begun,
What hints experience did to search impart
They join'd, and observation grew to art;
Thus rules were fram'd, for by example shown
They knew what should be, from what had been done;   90
They saw the stars their constant round maintain,
Perform their course, and then return again;
They on their aspects saw the fates attend,
Their change on their variety depend;
And thence they fixt unalterable laws,   95
Settling the same effect on the same cause.
  Before that time life was an artless state
Of reason void, and thoughtless in debate:
Nature lay hid in deepest night below,
None knew her wonders, and none car'd to know: 100
Upward men look, they saw the circling light,
Pleas'd with the fires, and wond'red at the sight:
The sun, when night came on, withdrawn, they griev'd,
As dead, and joy'd next morn when he reviv'd;
But why the nights grow long or short, the day   105
Is chang'd, and the shades vary with the ray,
Shorter at his approach, and longer grown
At his remove, the causes were unknown:
For wit lay unimprov'd, the desert plains
Were unmanur'd, nor fed the idle swains: 110
Ev'n gold dwelt safe in hills, and none resign'd

Their lives to seas or wishes to the wind;
Confin'd each search, they knew themselves alone,
And thought that only worthy to be known:
But when long time the wretches' thoughts refin'd;   115
When want had set an edge upon their mind;
When men increast, and want did boldly press,
And forc'd them to be witty for redress;
Then various cares their working thoughts employ'd,
And that which each invented all enjoy'd.   120
   Then corn first grew, then fruit enricht the grounds,
And barbarous noise was first confin'd to sounds:
Through seas unknown the sailor then was hurl'd,
And gainfull traffic join'd the distant world;
Then arts of war were found, and arts of peace,   125
For use is always fruitful in increase.
New hints from settled arts experience gains,
Instructs our labor, and rewards our Pains:
Thus into many streams one spring divides,
And through the valleys roll refreshing tides.   130
But these were little things compar'd, they knew
The voice of birds, in entrails fates could view;
Burst snakes with charms, and in a bullock's blood,
See rage appeas'd, or fear an angry God.
They call'd up ghosts, mov'd deepest Hell, the sun   135
Could stop, and force a night upon his noon;
Then make him rise at night, for all submit
To constant industry, and piercing wit.
Nor stopt they here, unwearied industry
Rose bodily up and mounted through the sky,   140
Saw all that could be seen, view'd Nature's laws,
And young effects still lying in their cause.
What wings the lightning, why from watry clouds
The thunder breaks, and roars the wrath of Gods.
What raises storms, what makes the winds to blow,   145
Why summer's hail's more stiff than winter's snow:
What fires earth's entrails, what doth shake the ball,
Why tempest rattle, and why rain doth fall:
All this she view'd, and did their modes explain,
And taught us to admire no more in vain.   150
Heaven was disarm'd, mad whirlwinds rul'd above,
And clouds and vapors thund'red instead of Jove.
   These things explain'd, their hidden causes known,
The mind grew strong, and ventur'd boldly on;

For rais'd so high, from that convenient rise   155
She took her flight, and quickly reacht the skies;
To every constellation shapes and names
Assign'd, and markt them out their proper frames;
Then view'd their course, and saw the orbs were mov'd
As Heaven did guide, and as the world approv'd;   160
That chance was baffled whilst their whirls create
The interchang'd variety of Fate.

Author and Selection Notes

Manilius (probably Marcus), a Roman poet of the latter half of the first century B.C. and the beginning of the first century A.D., wrote a long poem in five books called *Astronomica,* from which "The Science of Nature" is taken. The poem was possibly written in the time of Augustus or Tiberius. The complete work was probably never published, but it reflects great learning and represents the most advanced views on the subject in his time.

Questions and Exercises

1. What do you think the poet intends when he says "I sing, and bring unusual offerings to [the groves of the Muses]"?

2. The poet asks "Who first below these wondrous secrets knew?/Who stole that knowledge which the world withdrew?" Find an answer to Manilius' question by rereading Psalm 104. Discuss the general attitudes of the two writers as far as the world and its creation are concerned.

3. What is Manilius' attitude toward fate? Cite passages to support your answer.

4. According to Manilius, what stages did man go through in attaining knowledge of the world? What caused man to seek knowledge? In Manilius' time, what knowledge did man possess which Manilius felt was of great importance?

5. Theme Topics: Order Is Heaven's First Law; The Art of Foretelling; When I Had My Fortune Told; Nature's Way of Doing Things; My Opinion of Fate.

CHANCE AND CHANGE
Thomas Campion

What if a day, or a month, or a year,
Crown thy delights, with a thousand sweet contentings?

Cannot a chance of a night, or an hour,
Cross thy desires, with as many sad tormentings?
Fortune, honor, beauty, youth,
Are but blossoms dying!
Wanton pleasure, doting love,
Are but shadows flying!
All our joys are but toys,
Idle thoughts deceiving;
None have power of an hour
In their life's bereaving.

Earth's but a point to the world; and a man
Is but a point to the world's compared center!
Shall, then, a point of a point be so vain
As to triumph in a silly point's adventure?
All is hazard that we have!
There is nothing biding!
Days of pleasure are like streams,
Through fair meadows gliding!
Weal and woe, Time doth go!
Time is never turning!
Secret fates guide our states;
Both in mirth and mourning!

Author and Selection Notes

Thomas Campion (1567-1620) was born in London, and as a young man graduated from Cambridge. By training he was a lawyer, by profession a physician, and by instinct a poet. He is unusual in that he achieved recognition as poet, proser, and composer of masques and the music for them; he ranks next to Ben Jonson in diction and gracefulness of touch.

Questions and Exercises

1. Why might the general signs of advancement in the seventeenth century in the fields of science, commerce, and learning have influenced the author of this poem? Refer to a good source book for information concerning the changes in the Renaissance.

2. Why do you think Campion says, "All our joys are but toys,/Idle thoughts deceiving"? Do you agree with Campion?

3. What is meant by "All is hazard that we have"?

4. What does Campion mean by "Secret fates guide our states"? Do you think he really believes this?

5. Does Campion reveal a sense of humor at any point in this poem?

6. Theme Topics: Security in a Constantly Changing World; I Had My Life Planned When Suddenly . . . ; Why I Changed My College Objective; Laws and Institutions Cannot Remain Static in a Changing World; Is There Anything That Is Not Subject to Chance or Change? I Dislike (Like) Change; Do Secret Fates Guide Our States?

VANITAS VANITATUM

John Webster

All of the flowers of the spring
Meet to perfume our burying;
These have but their growing prime,
And man does flourish but his time;
Survey our progress from our birth,—
We are set, we grow, we turn to earth.
Courts adieu, and all delights,
All bewitching appetites!
Sweetest breath and clearest eye
Like perfumes go out and die;
And consequently this is done
As shadows wait upon the sun.
Vain the ambition of kings
Who seek by trophies and dead things
To leave a living name behind,
And weave but nets to catch the wind.

Author and Selection Notes

John Webster (1580?-1625?), an English dramatist, may have at one time been a London tailor. According to Philip Henslowe, an English theater manager, he did have a share in three plays in 1602. He later collaborated with Ford, Marston, and Thomas Dekker, but after 1623 there seems to be no trace of him. The two plays, "tragedies of blood" or "horror tragedies," which he wrote alone, *The Duchess of Malfi* and *The White Devil*, proved him a dramatist of high rank. His power to express and sustain the tragic emotions of pity and fear is revealed in these two tragedies. *The Duchess of Malfi* is of such merit it is destined to stand not far distant from Shakespeare's plays. Webster was not too unlike most of his literary contemporaries; he was a skillful lyrist as well as a tragedian.

Questions and Exercises

1. Does Webster contend that the laws of nature govern man's span of life?

2. Point out any examples of paradox you find in the poem.

3. What is the prevailing tone of the poem?

4. Read the book Ecclesiastes in the Old Testament and compare the sentiments of the Preacher and Webster.

5. Explain the last four lines of the poem.

6. Point out any metaphors or similes you find in the poem.

7. What line in the poem captures your imagination most? Why is the line so effective?

8. Compare the philosophy of this poem with that in Campion's "Chance and Change."

9. Theme Topics: The Vanity of Life; Artificiality in Modern Life; The Vainest Thing I Ever Did; The Advantages of Vanity.

CONTEMPLATIONS
Anne Bradstreet

18

When I behold the heavens as in their prime,
And then the earth, though old, still clad in green,
The stones and trees insensible of time,
Nor age nor wrinkle on their front are seen:
If winter come, and greenness then doth fade,
A spring returns, and they're more youthful made.
But man grows old, lies down, remains where once he's laid.

19

By birth more noble than those creatures all,
Yet seems by nature and by custom cursed—
No sooner born but grief and care make fall
That state obliterate he had at first;
Nor youth, nor strength, nor wisdom spring again,
Nor habitations long their names retain,
But in oblivion to the final day remain.

20

Shall I then praise the heavens, the trees, the earth,
Because their beauty and their strength last longer?

Shall I wish there or never to had birth,
Because they're bigger and their bodies stronger?
Nay, they shall darken, perish, fade, and die,
And when unmade so ever shall they lie:
But man was made for endless immortality.

33

O time, the fatal wreck of mortal things,
That draws oblivion's curtains over kings!
Their sumptuous monuments men know them not,
Their names without a record are forgot,
Their parts, their ports, their pomps, all laid in the dust,
Nor wit, nor gold, nor buildings 'scape time's rust.
But he whose name is graved in the white stone
Shall last and shine when all of these are gone.

Author and Selection Notes

Anne Bradstreet (1612?-1672) was the daughter of Thomas Dudley, who later became governor of the Massachusetts Bay Colony. Although the first American poetess, she was born in England. At sixteen she married Simon Bradstreet, of Lincolnshire, who served under Dudley, steward to the Earl of Lincoln. In 1630 the Bradstreets came to New England and established a farm near the Merrimac River.

In her spare moments and as mother of a large family, Anne Bradstreet composed poetry. In 1647 John Woodbridge, a brother-in-law, took her manuscripts to England and had them published in 1650 under the title, *The Tenth Muse Lately Sprung Up in America,* or *Severall Poems Compiled with Great Variety of Wit and Learning, Full of Delight.*

Until shortly before her death in 1672 Anne Bradstreet continued to write poetry, prose meditations and admonitions. "Contemplations" has been worthily compared to William Cullen Bryant's "Thanatopsis," Sidney Lanier's "Marshes of Glynn," and Edna St. Vincent Millay's "Renascence."

Questions and Exercises

1. Do you agree with Bradstreet that the stones and trees are "insensible of time"? Why or why not?

2. Do the last two lines of the first stanza leave the impression that oblivion is the fate of man on earth?

3. Explain the apparent inconsistency between the last lines of stanza thirty-three and the rest of the poem.

4. Find in Revelation 2:17 what is meant by "the white stone" in line seven of stanza thirty-three.

5. Discuss the emphasis placed on the hereafter in the poem.

6. Write a theme in which you compare the attitudes toward time, change, and death in Bradstreet's "Contemplations," in Campion's "Chance and Change," and in Webster's "Vanitas Vanitatum."

ODE

Joseph Addison

The Spacious Firmament on high,
With all the blue Ethereal Sky,
And Spangled Heav'ns, a Shining Frame,
Their great Original proclaim.
Th' unwearied Sun, from Day to Day,
Does his Creator's Power display,
And publishes to every Land
The work of an Almighty Hand.
Soon as the Evening Shades prevail,
The Moon takes on the wondrous Tale,
And nightly to the list'ning Earth
Repeats the Story of her Birth:
Whilst all the Stars around her burn,
And all the Planets, in their turn,
Confirm the Tidings as they roll,
And spread the truth from Pole to Pole.
What though, in solemn Silence all
Move round the dark terrestial Ball?
What though nor real Voice nor Sound
Amid their radiant Orbs be found?
In Reason's Ear they all rejoice,
And utter forth a glorious Voice,
For ever singing as they shine,
"The Hand that made us is Divine."

Author and Selection Notes

Joseph Addison (1672-1719) was the son of a clergyman in Wiltshire. After attending Charterhouse school where he met Richard Steele, with whom he was to be later associated in literary endeavors, he entered Oxford and won attention by his scholarship and creative ability. Because of his abilities as a writer, he was sought out by one of the two contending political parties. He became one of the most promising Whig men of letters. After the victory of the Duke of Marlborough at Blenheim, Addison's *The Campaign* (1704) brought him new honors and one of the two secretaryships of state.

Addison is remembered chiefly for his essays, many of which appear in the famous *Tatler* and *Spectator* papers written jointly by him and Sir Richard Steele. The quality and ease of Addison's prose are reflected with brilliance in his essays. The beauty of his poetry is evident in the "Ode."

Questions and Exercises

1. What is the one sustaining idea in Addison's "Ode"?

2. Discuss the difference in attitudes revealed in this poem and Campion's "Chance and Change."

3. What sentiments in the poem are similar to those expressed by the ancient Manilius in "The Science of Nature"?

4. Discuss the meaning in lines 15 and 16 of the "Ode."

5. What do you understand by the use of the word "all" at the end of line 17?

6. Is there any significance in the use of the word "dark" in line 18?

7. Addison lived during the Age of Reason. Why do you think he says in line 21, "In Reason's Ear they all rejoice"?

8. Theme Topics: What I Saw When I Looked Up; Universal Peace; How the Beauty of Nature Affects Me; By Chance or by Plan? An Explanation for the Order and Disorder of Nature.

MICHAEL ANGELO'S STUDIO

Count Joseph Arthur de Gobineau

A cold and dark retreat. The night is black. A statue, still almost in the rough, on which falls the light of a little copper lamp, held by Antonio Urbino, the artist's servant. Michael Angelo is occupied in finishing a sort of cardboard helmet with open peak, arranged so as to serve as a receptacle.

. . . . .

Michael Angelo: You see, Urbino? You said I should not succeed! I have succeeded perfectly. Now, give me the lamp.

Urbino: It will not keep upright in that! It will fall and burn your hair. A fine idea of yours!

Reprinted by permission of G. P. Putnam's Sons from *The Renaissance* by Count Arthur de Gobineau, edited by Dr. Oscar Levy.

Michael Angelo: I tell you it will keep upright! Why do you refuse to admit that?

Urbino: It is not I that refuse to admit it, but the lamp will refuse to keep upright.

Michael Angelo: Come, you obstinate creature! give me your lamp, and roll this wire firmly around the base . . . one more turn. . . . Good! Now, I put the lamp inside . . . I fasten the wire here. . . . You see? . . . It will stay.

Urbino: When you move about with that on your head you will set fire to the cardboard.

Michael Angelo: Not at all! The aperture is wide, and the flame has all the room it needs to waver from left to right. It's splendid! I shall now be able to work at night, with lighting effects on the marble which will give the finest results.

Urbino: It would be better if you went to bed. You always have ideas that occur to no one else.

Michael Angelo: It is quite convenient to carry. My head is perfectly at ease. Pass me the hammer and the flat chisel . . . here . . . on the wooden box.

Urbino: I tell you that you would do far better if you went to bed instead of working like a wretched hireling. You know quite well that Her Excellency the Marchioness does not wish you to over exert yourself.

Michael Angelo: Very well, you will go to-morrow to ask after her health, and you will tell her that it is my wife who will not let me go to bed.

Urbino: Your wife? What does that mean?

Michael Angelo: She is here, at my side, looking at me with her beautiful great eyes; she pushes my arm and says to me: "Work, Michael Angelo, work for your glory and mine!" and she shows me a bit of green leaf that she has in her hand—a laurel.

Urbino: These phrases of yours will not prevent you from tiring yourself to death.

Michael Angelo: I have not been so happy for many a long day. It is a black night, and by the gleam of this little lamp I see a world of ideas . . . What may the time be?

Urbino: I think it cannot be far from midnight. You had better go to bed.

Michael Angelo: It is pouring with rain. One can hear the shower smiting the roof and falling on the flagstones of the courtyard like a great river. It has been a fearful storm. Lightnings furrow the shimmering blackness of the windowpane. But behind all this stern uproar, what calm! The distant rumblings of the thunder and its majestic roarings, but no human voice, no false, lying, peevish, imperious or stupidly arrogant voice is raised to vex me! I can create . . . my spirit is free. . . . I am happy! . . . I am wholly in the power of all that is worth my entire devotion, and the hard bosom of the marble opens . . . the living head begins to appear. . . . White, white, it palpitates beneath the chisel that sets free its features one by one. . . . Out of the material they spring . . . they speak. . . . Urbino.

Urbino: Master?

Michael Angelo: You are falling asleep on your footstool. It is you who would do well to go and seek your bed.

Urbino: I cannot. When you sleep, I will sleep—not before.

Michael Angelo: Strange Obstinacy!

Urbino: True, I am no longer young, and it wearies me to stay up, but the Marchioness said to me: "When your master does not go to rest, do not go to rest either, and we shall see if he cares to tax the strength of his old servant."

Michael Angelo: Give me a few minutes more; there is one thing to be finished.

Urbino: A few minutes, but not more. The Marchioness expressly desires . . .

Michael Angelo: Very well then! . . . Tell me a story to keep me awake.

Urbino: I went to-day to your notary.

Michael Angelo: We won't speak of that.

Urbino: He says that the two girls whom you have dowered are quite respectable.

Michael Angelo: I am glad, Urbino. I wish them all happiness; they are lovable children, though very ugly.

Urbino: I also saw your nephew. He came while you were out.

Michael Angelo: Good. . . . If he should happen to come back, tell him to leave me in peace and go about his business.

Urbino: He thinks, and that rightly, that his most pressing business is to thank you for the three thousand crowns which you, who are not rich, have given him.

Michael Angelo: He knows that I love him; he has no need to thank me.

Urbino: Master, the clock strikes . . . an hour after midnight. . . .

Michael Angelo: I have finished . . . but I am mortally hungry. Have you nothing to eat here? Look in the meal-tub.

Urbino: I will go and see. . . . Ah! your house is kept on a poor footing indeed! As soon as you have money, it is given to the first comer.

Michael Angelo: Man needs but little for his body. But all his strength is insufficient to elevate his soul.

Urbino: Here's some bread . . . a trifle hard . . . and a piece of cheese, and even the end of a bottle. . . .

Michael Angelo: Excellent! bring me all that.

(Takes off his cardboard cap, puts the lamp on the bench and eats, standing up, looking at his statue. Loud knocking at the door).

Who can be coming at this hour? Look through the grill.

Urbino: Who is knocking?

A Voice: It is I, Antonio Mini. . . . Open, master! . . . It is I, your pupil! I have important news for you!

Michael Angelo: My pupil, Antonio Mini? Open! Is it bad tidings?

Antonio Mini (entering): Oh, Master, a terrible misfortune!

Michael Angelo: What is the matter? You are quite pale!

Mini: Raphael is dying! No doubt he is dead by now.

Michael Angelo: Raphael! God in Heaven!

Mini: I was in his studio with two of his pupils, Timoteo Viti and Il Garofalo. It was about three o'clock. A servant came to say the master was ill. He had had fever since yesterday evening.

Michael Angelo: Since yesterday? I am not surprised. He was a man of delicate complexion, half woman, half child. He spent too much time at work and far too much at his pleasures. I met him four days ago, making excavations in the Camp Vaccino, and I even remember warning him of digging at this season of the year. You say he is worse?

Mini: If he is not dead now, he will not last out till daybreak. He had himself carried into his studio, and I saw him, yes, I saw him, white as a shroud, half-fainting, his eyes fixed on his picture of the Transfiguration. . . . Near the bed, which had been set up for him in a hurry, stood his friends, Cardinals Bibbiena, Sadoleto and Bembo, and other Signors whom I do not know. . . . At the pillow-side was a Holy Father, crying and wiping his eyes.

Michael Angelo: Urbino, give me my cap and cloak. I must go there! Raphael . . . Raphael . . . dying! My God, is it possible? . . . Quick, let us go!

Urbino: Here, here, master! Give me time to light a lantern; I will light your way.

Michael Angelo: You say there is no help for it? Are you certain?

Have the physicians been sent for? What did they say? What did they do? Let us go!

Mini: There was no lack of physicians; there was the Holy Father's, Messer Jacopo of Brescia, then Messer Gaëtano Marini, and others. All looked very gloomy and shook their heads; their eyes told us that their science could do no more.

Michael Angelo: Come, Urbino, are you ready?

Urbino: Here I am, Master!

Michael Angelo: Walk in front, Quickly!

> (They go out into the street, which is very dark; however, the rain has ceased falling; the clouds, rapidly rolled upon one another by the wind, are torn asunder and show a part of the orb of the moon, which gives a faint light to the houses and the road. A great noise of footsteps is heard).

What is this uproar?

Urbino: We shall know after turning the corner of the lane!

Mini: Forward! Mind that puddle of water, master!

> (He supports Michael Angelo by the arm. Rapidly and confusedly, there passes a numerous company of officers, soldiers, servants and torch-bearers, whose torches throw a red light on the houses; in the midst of this procession, the pontifical litter with curtains drawn).

Michael Angelo (to a chamberlain): What means this, Sir?

Chamberlain: It is the Holy Father returning to the Vatican.

Michael Angelo: Is Raphael . . . ?

A Voice: Raphael is dead, and Michael Angelo alone remains in Italy!

> (The procession passes; Michael Angelo drops on a stone bench. The clouds have parted, and the moon shines in a clear sky).

Michael Angelo: I remain, it is true . . . I alone remain. Last year it was Lionardo . . . now it is Raphael, and all whom we three knew or listened to have long since gone. It is true, I alone remain. There was a time when I should have loved to be the only one, the peerless, the unique, the greatest confidant of the secrets of creative heaven! I imagined that to resemble the sun, in the centre of the universe, without an equal, without a rival, was the most enviable form of happiness. . . . For years I was not fond of Lionardo. . . . I railed at Raphael in the bottom of my heart. . . . I repeated to myself, so as to convince myself, that I rated them low. . . . Yes, there have been days when you, Michael Angelo, were only a poor creature, of short sight and circumscribed vision, apt to censure and misunderstand all that did not resemble you, and—I tell you, because it is true—all that was quite as good as you and perhaps better! Now I have what my heart desired. The stars have gone out in heaven, and here I am alone . . . quite alone . . . and stifled in my isolation! . . . There is still Titian; he is a great genius, a great brain. . . . There is Andrea del Sarto. . . . There is. . . . But, alas! no— great as they are, they are not the peers of Lionardo and of him who lies down there. . . . Ah, Raphael! . . . His beauty, his subtlety, his sweetness, his grace, and, in his talk as in his aspect, what divine honey! . . . all that I have not, all that I cannot reach . . . all that I am not! . . . He whom all loved and who deserved so well to be loved! . . . My God, my God, what is it that comes over me? What is stirring within me and drawing tears from eyes that never tried to weep? Of what am I thinking? Yes, a river of grief is rising and rolling within my bosom; the tears escape my eyelids, stream down my cheeks, fall upon him whom I always abused and shunned, and who was so much better and more loved of heaven than I! She told me so, she . . . Vittoria . . . she always told me so, and I would not agree. . . . But I know it well at bottom, I felt it, and now that the thunder- bolt of death has passed between him and me, now that I re- main here, my feet in the mud of the world, while his noble and charming countenance appears to me in the bosom of God, shining with celestial light, I see how insincere and petty I have been! No . . . no, Titian and the others, however aimable they may be, are not the equals of these two great departed. About them, and about me who remain, the light is waning and re- ceding, the shadows are lengthening. . . . Yes, here I am alone, and the icy breath of the tomb that is opening strikes my face. What will become of the arts? And we, who have hoped so much, desired so much, imagined so much, worked so much, what have we achieved, what shall we bequeath to them that come after us? Not a quarter of what we should have done.

(Covers his face with his hands).

Urbino: Come, Master, you will take cold.

Mini: Give me your arm, and let us go back to your house.

Michael Angelo: Yes, we must preserve our strength and work as long as we are throttled by the chain of life.

Author and Selection Notes

This brief selection written by Count Joseph Arthur de Gobineau (1816-1882) reveals Michelangelo's interests and the intensive passion which he had for his work. Gobineau was a French diplomat, orientalist, and writer. He wrote much on artistic subjects. He also had keen interest in the sociological aspects of the race and was the originator of "Gobinism," which contended that the Teuton race of man was the superior one. This philosophy has since been disregarded.

Michelangelo (Michelangiolo Buronarroti, 1475-1564), one of the most famous of the great Florentine artists of the Renaissance, was the son of poor but respectable gentlefolk who made some claim of kinship to the titled connections of the Counts of Canossa. Michelangelo was born at Caprese and early in life announced his determination to become an artist. At the age of thirteen he became apprentice to the brothers Ghirlandaio. Though his early studies were directed toward painting, Michelangelo was by nature and inclination a sculptor, and under his illustrious patron, Lorenzo de' Medici, he began a career that has not been equalled before or since in sheer magnificence or artistry. His work and interests were extensive, and nothing of challenge or imaginative concept was too trivial for his attention and effort.

Questions and Exercises

1. How effective is the incident that introduces the dialogue?

2. Urbino says that Michael Angelo always has "ideas that occur to no one else." Do you think this statement is significant? Explain.

3. Who is the wife to whom Michael Angelo refers?

4. As you consider the complete dialogue, do you think Michael Angelo's eighth and ninth speeches are in any way foretelling?

5. What do the comments about the two girls and the nephew reveal about Michael Angelo's personality?

6. Interpret Michael Angelo's words "Man needs but little for his body."

7. What effect does the death of Raphael have on Michael Angelo?

8. Consider thoughtfully Michael Angelo's last long speech in this selection; it is a kind of soliloquy. Is there anything of self-revelation or growth in his words?

9. What has the author gained by telling his story in dialogue form?

10. Theme Topics: On Being Great; The Versatility of the Great; Necessity Is the Mother of Invention; Michael Angelo's Headlamp; What Time Means to the Artist.

THE FITCHBURG RAILROAD

Henry David Thoreau

The Fitchburg Railroad touches the pond about a hundred rods south of where I dwell. I usually go to the village along its causeway, and am, as it were, related to society by this link. The men on the freight trains, who go over the whole length of the road, bow to me as to an old acquaintance, they pass me so often, and apparently they take me for an employee; and so I am. I too would fain be a track-repairer somewhere in the orbit of the earth.

The whistle of the locomotive penetrates my woods summer and winter, sounding like the scream of a hawk sailing over some farmer's yard, informing me that many restless city merchants are arriving within the circle of the town, or adventurous country traders from the other side. As they come under one horizon, they shout their warning to get off the track to the other, heard sometimes through the circles of the two towns. Here come your groceries, country; your rations, countrymen! Nor is there any man so independent on his farm that he can say them nay. And here's your pay for them! screams the countryman's whistle; timber like long battering rams going twenty miles an hour against the city's walls, and chairs enough to set all the weary and heavy laden that dwell within them. With huge and lumbering civility the country hands a chair to the city. All the Indian huckleberry hills are stripped, all the cranberry meadows are raked into the city. Up comes the cotton, down goes the woven cloth; up comes the silk, down goes the woolen; up come the books, but down goes the wit that writes them.

When I meet the engine with its train of cars moving off with planetary motion,—or, rather, like a comet, for the beholder knows not if with that velocity and with that direction it will ever revisit this system, since its orbit does not look like a returning curve,—with its steam cloud like a banner streaming behind in golden and silver wreaths, like many a downy cloud which I have seen, high in the heavens, unfolding its masses to the light,—as if this travelling demigod, this cloud compeller, would ere-long take the sunset sky for the livery of his train; When I heard the iron horse make the hills echo with his snort like thunder, shaking the earth with his feet, and breathing fire and smoke from his nostrils (what kind of winged horse or fiery dragon they will put into the new mythology

I don't know), it seems as if the earth had got a race now worthy to inhabit it. If all were as it seems, and men made the elements their servants for noble ends! If the cloud that hangs over the engine were the perspiration of heroic deeds, or as beneficent as that which floats over the farmer's fields, then the elements and Nature herself would cheerfully accompany men on their errands and be their escort.

I watch the passage of the morning cars with the same feeling that I do the rising of the sun, which is hardly more regular. Their train of clouds stretching far behind and rising higher and higher, going to heaven while the cars are going to Boston, conceals the sun for a minute and casts my distant field into the shade, a celestial train besides which the petty train of cars which hugs the earth is but the barb of the spear. The stabler of the iron horse was up early this winter morning by the light of the stars amid the mountains, to fodder and harness his steed. Fire, too, was awakened thus early to put the vital heat in him and get him off. If the enterprise were as innocent as it is early! If the snow lies deep, they strap on his snow-shoes, and with the giant plough plough a furrow from the mountains to the seaboard, in which the cars, like a following drill-barrow, sprinkle all the restless men and floating merchandise in the country for seed. All day the fire-steed flies over the country, stopping only that his master may rest, and I am awakened by his tramp and defiant snort at midnight, when in some remote glen in the woods he fronts the elements incased in ice and snow; and he will reach his stall only with the morning star, to start once more on his travels without rest or slumber. Or perchance, at evening, I hear him in his stable blowing off the superfluous energy of the day, that he may calm his nerves and cool his liver and brain for a few hours of iron slumber. If the enterprise were as heroic and commanding as it is protracted and unwearied!

Far through unfrequented woods on the confines of the town, where once only the hunter penetrated by day, in the darkest night dart these bright saloons without the knowledge of their inhabitants; this moment stopping at some brilliant station-house in town or city, where a social crowd is gathered, the next in the Dismal Swamp, scaring the owl and the fox. The startings and arrivals of the cars are now the epochs in the village day. They go and come with such regularity and precision, and their whistle can be heard so far, that the farmers set their clocks by them, and thus one well-conducted institution regulates a whole country. Have not men improved somewhat in punctuality since the railroad was invented? Do they not talk and think faster in the depot than they did in the stage office?

There is something electrifying in the atmosphere of the former place. I have been astonished at the miracles it has wrought; that some of my neighbors, who, I should have prophesied, once for all, would never get to Boston by so prompt a conveyance, are on hand when the bell rings. To do things "railroad fashion" is now the by-word; and it is worth the while to be warned so often and sincerely by any power to get off its track. There is no stopping to read the riot act, no firing over the heads of the mob, in this case. We have constructed a fate, an *Atropos,* that never turns aside. (Let that be the name of your engine.) Men are advertised that at a certain hour and minute these bolts will be shot toward particular points of the compass; yet it interferes with no man's business, and the children go to school on the other track. We live the steadier for it. We are all educated thus to be sons of Tell. The air is full of invisible bolts. Every path but your own is the path of fate. Keep on your own track, then.

What recommends commerce to me is its enterprise and bravery. It does not clasp its hands and pray to Jupiter. I see these men every day go about their business with more or less courage and content, doing more even than they suspect, and perchance better employed than they could have consciously devised. I am less affected by their heroism who stood up for half an hour in the front lines at Buena Vista, than by the steady and cheerful valor of the men who inhabit the snow-plough for their winter quarters; who have not merely the three o'clock in the morning courage which Bonaparte thought was the rarest, but whose courage does not go to bed so early, who go to sleep only when the storm sleeps or the sinews of their iron steed are frozen. On this morning of the great snow, perchance, which is still raging and chilling men's blood, I hear the muffled tone of their engine bell from out the fog bank and their chilled breath, which announces that the cars *are coming,* without long delay, not-withstanding the veto of a New England northeast snow storm, and I behold the mould-board which is turning down other than daisies and the nests of field-mice, like boulders of the Sierra Nevada, that occupy an outside place in the universe.

Commerce is unexpectedly confident and serene, alert, adventur-ous, and unwearied. It is very natural in its methods withal, far more so than many fantastic enterprises and sentimental experi-ments, and hence its singular success. I am refreshed and expanded when the freight train rattles past me, and I smell the stores which go dispensing their odors all the way from Long Wharf to Lake Champlain, reminding me of foreign parts, of coral reefs, and Indian oceans, and tropical climes, and the extent of the globe. I feel more like a citizen of the world at the sight of the palm-leaf which will cover so many flaxen New England heads the next summer, the Manilla hemp and cocoa-nut husks, the old junk, gunny bags, scrap iron, and rusty nails. This carload of torn sails is more legible and interesting now than if they should be wrought into paper and printed books. Who can write so graphically the history of the storms they have weathered as these rents have done? They are proof-sheets which need no correction. Here goes lumber from the Maine woods, which did not go out to sea in the last freshet, risen four dollars on the thousand because of what did go out or was split up: pine, spruce, cedar,—first, second, third and fourth qualities, so lately all of one quality, to wave over the bear, the moose, and caribou. Next rolls Thomaston lime, a prime lot, which will get far among the hills before it gets slacked. These rags in bales, of all hues and qualities, the lowest condition to which cotton and linen descend, the final results of dress,—of patterns which are no longer cried up, unless it be in Milwaukee, as those splendid articles, English, French, or American prints, ginghams, muslin, etc., gathered from all quarters both of fashion and poverty, going to become paper of one color or a few shades only, on which forsooth will be written tales of real life, high and low, and founded on fact! This closed car smells of salt fish, the strong New England and commercial scent, reminding me of the Grand Banks and the fisheries. Who has not seen a salt fish, thoroughly cured for this world, so that nothing can spoil it, and putting the perseverance of the saints to the blush? with which you may sweep or pave the streets, and split your kindlings, and the teamster shelter himself and his lading against sun, wind, and rain behind it,—and the trader, as a Concord trader once did, hang it up by his door sign when he commences business, until his oldest customer cannot tell surely whether it be animal, vegetable, or mineral, and yet it shall be as pure as a snowflake, and if it be put into a pot and boiled, will come out an excellent dun fish for a Saturday's dinner. Next Spanish hides, with the tail still preserving their twist and the angle of elevation they had when the oxen that wore them were careering over the pampas of the Spanish main,—a type of all obstinacy, and evincing how almost hopeless and incurable are all constitutional vices. I confess that, practically speaking, when I have learned a man's real disposition, I have no hopes of changing it for the better or worse in this state of existence. . . . Here is a hogshead of molasses or of brandy directed to John Smith, Cuttingsville, Vermont, some trader among the Green Mountains, who imports for the farmers near his clearing, and now perchance stands over his bulk-head and thinks of the last arrivals on the coast, how they may affect the price for him, telling his customers this moment, as he has told them twenty times before this morning, that he expects some by the next train of prime quality. It is advertised in the Cuttingsville Times.

While these things go up other things come down. Warned by the whizzing sound, I look up from my book and see some tall pine, hewn on the far northern hills, which has winged its way over the Green Mountains and the Connecticut, shot like an arrow through the township within ten minutes, and scarce another eye beholds it; going

> to be the mast
> Of some great admiral.

And hark! here comes the cattle-train bearing the cattle of a thousand hills, sheepcots, stables, and cow-yards in the air, drovers with their sticks, and shepherd boys in the midst of their flocks, all but the mountain pastures, whirled along like leaves blown from the mountains by the September gales. The air is filled with the bleating of the calves and sheep, and the hustling of oxen, as if a pastoral valley were going by. When the old bell-wether at the head rattles his bell, the mountains do indeed skip like rams and the little hills like lambs. A car-load of drovers, too, in the midst, on a level with their droves now, their vocation gone, but still clinging to their useless sticks as their badge of office. But their dogs, where are they? It is a stampede to them; they are quite thrown out; they have lost the scent. Me-thinks I hear them barking behind the Peterboro' Hills, or panting up the western slope of the Green Mountains. They will not be in at the death. Their vocation, too, is gone. Their fidelity and sagacity are below par now. They will slink back to their kennels in disgrace, or perchance run wild and strike a league with the wolf and the fox. So is your pastoral life whirled past and away. But the bell rings, and I must get off the track and let the cars go by:

> What's the railroad to me?
> I never go to see
> Where it ends.
> It fills a few hollows,
> And makes banks for the swallows,
> It sets the sand a-blowing,
> And the blackberries a-growing,

but I cross it like a cart path in the woods. I will not have my eyes put out and my ears spoiled by its smoke and steam and hissing.

Now that the cars have gone by and all the reckless world with them, and the fishes in the pond no longer feel their rumbling, I am more alone than ever. For the rest of the long afternoon, perhaps, my meditations are interrupted only by the faint rattle of a carriage or team along the distant highway.

Author and Selection Notes

Henry David Thoreau (1817-1862) was born in Concord, Massachusetts. His father tried many occupations but failed at them all. Henry, however, was a happy child because he had the woods and swamps and rivers and ponds of his native town to tramp over. He fished and hunted and learned much about the habits of fowl and small animals. He later refers to his early life as "ecstasy." His first school was the local academy, and at sixteen he was sent off to Harvard. His poverty and robustness of nature seemed to isolate him from his fellow students, but he found refuge in the college library. His habit of reading avidly introduced him to the great world of thought and experience, which had lasting effect upon his receptive mind.

After graduation from Harvard he tried teaching for a while but left in favor of a more independent career. He kept journals and became a friend of Emerson and other eminent writers of his time. The independence of his life and thought is reflected in his works and actions. To enjoy a simple, undisturbed existence is a major part of his creed, which is reflected in "The Fitchburg Railroad," an excerpt from *Walden*.

Questions and Exercises

1. What is your appraisal of Thoreau's account of the Fitchburg Railroad?

2. In several references in the selection, Thoreau discusses the train metaphorically. Point out the different uses and discuss. Are the comparisons apt?

3. There is much satiric humor in the account. Identify several passages.

4. The author speaks of "one well-constructed institution" regulating a whole country. Can you think of a modern regulatory institution?

5. What is meant by the reference "we are all educated thus to be the sons of Tell"?

6. What tribute does Thoreau pay commerce? Do you think he was serious?

7. How had the railroad affected the fashion of Thoreau's day? Explain what is intended by the term "railroad fashion."

8. Theme Topics: A Modern-Day Nuisance; The Overpowering Weight

of Business Today; The Silence of the Country; Technology Is Disrupting
Nature; Man's Order as Opposed to Nature's Order; Can Nature and
Technology Exist Together? Where Technology Will Finally Lead Us.

DOVER BEACH

Matthew Arnold

The sea is calm to-night.
The tide is full, the moon lies fair
Upon the straits;—on the French coast the light
Gleams and is gone; the cliffs of England stand,
Glimmering and vast, out in the tranquil bay.
Come to the window, sweet is the night-air!
Only, from the long line of spray
Where the sea meets the moon-blanched land,
Listen! you hear the grating roar
Of pebbles which the waves draw back, and fling,
At their return, up the high strand,
Begin, and cease; and then again begin,
With tremulous cadence slow; and bring
The eternal note of sadness in.

Sophocles, long ago,
Heard it on the Aegean, and it brought
Into his mind the turbid ebb and flow
Of human misery; we
Find also in the sound a thought,
Hearing it by this distant northern sea.

The Sea of Faith
Was once, too, at the full, and round earth's shore
Lay like the folds of a bright girdle furled;
But now I only hear
Its melancholy, long, withdrawing roar,
Retreating, to the breath
Of the night-wind, down the vast edges drear
And naked shingles of the world.

Ah, love, let us be true
To one another! for the world, which seems

To lie before us like a land of dreams,
So various, so beautiful, so new,
Hath really neither joy, nor love, nor light,
Nor certitude, nor peace, nor help for pain;
And we are here as on a darkling plain,
Swept with confused alarms of struggle and flight,
Where ignorant armies clash by night.

Author and Selection Notes

Matthew Arnold (1822-1888), critic and poet, was born at Laleham several years before his father became headmaster at Rugby. After an early tutorial education he studied at Rugby and later he entered Balliol College, Oxford, where he distinguished himself academically and socially. In 1847 he became secretary to the Marquis of Lansdowne, who secured for him in 1851 the position of inspector of schools. Arnold was appointed professor of poetry at Oxford in 1857, and during the rest of his life he published much of his important prose and poetry.

In his writings Arnold warned his age of an overemphasis on scientific study and thought at the expense of equally important values of conduct and feeling. "Dover Beach," aside from its sheer beauty and imaginative qualities, reflects Arnold's admiration of ancient literature and his constant search for serenity in an age of doubt and skepticism.

Questions and Exercises

1. What is the setting of the poem?

2. Comment upon the effectiveness of the metaphor contained in the poem.

3. Read the poem again and again for the beauty of its language. Notice Arnold's use of rhyme, rhythm, assonance, and alliteration. How are these devices related to the subject matter and mood of the poem?

4. Identify in the nineteenth century and today "ignorant armies" that "clash by night."

5. Why is the use of the word "night" in the last line significant?

6. In Arnold's hostile universe, what is the only thing that offers solace?

7. Theme Topics: What I Value Most; The Sea at Night; What Confuses Me; Dishonesty in Life; Without Faith in Something or Someone, What? The Relationship of Science and Faith; How Valuable Are Human Relationships?

LOCKSLEY HALL

Alfred Tennyson

For I dipt into the future, far as human eye could see,
Saw the Vision of the world, and all the wonders that would be;

Saw the heavens filled with commerce, argosies of magic sails,
Pilots of the purple twilight, dropping down their costly bales;

Heard the heavens fill with shouting, and there rained a ghastly dew
From the nations' airy navies grappling in the central blue;

Far along the world-wide whisper of the south-wind rushing warm,
With the standards of the peoples plunging thro' the thunder storm;

Till the war-drum throbbed no longer, and the battle flags were
    furled
In the Parliament of man, the Federation of the world.

There the common sense of most shall hold a fretful realm in awe,
And the kindly earth shall slumber, lapt in universal law.

So I triumphed, ere my passion sweeping thro' me left me dry,
Left me with the palsied heart, and left me with the jaundiced eye;

Eye, to which all order festers, all things here are out of joint.
Science moves, but slowly, slowly, creeping on from point to point;

Slowly comes a hungry people, as a lion, creeping nigher,
Glares at one that nods and winks behind a slowly-dying fire.

Yet I doubt not thro' the ages one increasing purpose runs,
And the thoughts of men are widened with the process of the suns.

What is that to him that reaps not harvest of his youthful joys,
Tho' the deep heart of existence beat for ever like a boy's?

This is an excerpt from "Locksley Hall."

Knowledge comes, but wisdom lingers, and I linger on the shore,
And the individual withers, and the world is more and more.

Knowledge comes, but wisdom lingers, and he bears a laden breast,
Full of sad experience, moving toward the stillness of his rest.

Author and Selection Notes

Alfred, Lord Tennyson (1809-1892) was born in Somersby, Lincolnshire, where his father was rector. He attended the village school for a short time and then left to continue his education under the tutelage of his father. In 1827 he and his brother Charles published *Poems by Two Brothers*. In 1828 the brothers entered Trinity College, Cambridge.

In 1850 Tennyson married Emily Sellwood, published *In Memoriam*, a work long belabored because of the sudden death of his great friend Arthur Hallam, and was appointed Poet Laureate to succeed Wordsworth. In 1884 he was made a Baron of the Realm by Queen Victoria. He was greatly saddened by the death of his youngest son, Lionel, that same year, and, though he continued to write until his death in 1892, he lamented the passing "of the old reverence and chivalrous feeling in the world."

"Locksley Hall," a dramatic monologue, is meant to represent youth—its good side, its deficiencies and aspirations. The hero, high-minded and impulsive, is disappointed in love and in the ideals of the Victorian Age. He anticipates a new day which will bring back the eagerness of his youth.

Questions and Exercises

1. Check in a good encyclopedia to see what was happening in England at the time this poem was written.

2. What does Tennyson mean by "human eye" in the first stanza?

3. Consider for meaning "the heavens filled with commerce" and the "Pilots of the purple twilight, dropping down their costly bales."

4. Do you think the third stanza foretells World Wars I and II? Comment on this while remembering the date the poem was published.

5. What could be the meaning of "the standards of the peoples plunging thro' the thunder storm"?

6. Could the "Parliament of man" represent the United Nations today?

7. Has the United Nations organization held "a fretful realm in awe"?

8. Why do you think Tennyson says, "Science moves, but slowly, slowly, creeping on from point to point"?

9. What is the "one increasing purpose" that runs through the ages and widens the thoughts of men?

10. Theme Topics: Tennyson and the Space Age; Scientific Foretelling Today; The Voice of the Past; The Relationship of Knowledge and Wisdom.

WHEN I HEARD THE LEARN'D ASTRONOMER
Walt Whitman

When I heard the learn'd astronomer,
When the proofs, the figures, were ranged in columns before me,
When I was shown the charts and the diagrams, to add, divide,
    and measure them,
When I sitting heard the astronomer where he lectured with much
    applause in the lecture-room,
How soon unaccountable I became tired and sick,
Till rising and gliding out I wander'd off by myself,
In the mystical moist night-air, and from time to time,
Look'd up in perfect silence at the stars.

Author and Selection Notes

Walt Whitman (1819-1892), born on Long Island, was the son of a carpenter. He was a self-educated man and followed a variety of occupations in his youth and young manhood. He was connected with the Brooklyn *Daily Eagle* and was its editor in 1846-1848.

One of his most famous works, *Leaves of Grass,* appeared in 1855. During the poet's life time seven other editions appeared with new poems or old poems in revised form.

During the Civil War he served faithfully as a nurse in the Army hospitals in Washington. A wounded brother was one of his patients for a time.

After the war he lived in Camden, New Jersey, but was ill most of the time until his death. He continued to write, however, and his feelings toward America and democracy were strong enough to instill a sense of national unity in him. The effects of his *Leaves of Grass* upon modern literature are recognized even today.

Questions and Exercises

1. How is the contrast intensified by the length of lines 2-4 and lines 5-8?

2. Explain the effectiveness of the use of the word "stars" only once in the poem, at the end.

3. Instead of rhyme or regular meter, what poetic devices does Whitman employ?

4. Theme Topics: Science and Modern Life; The Astronaut and the

Stars; Does Science Destroy the Sense of Beauty and Wonder? Classroom
Lectures Versus First-Hand Observation.

THE BASE OF ALL METAPHYSICS
Walt Whitman

And now gentlemen,
A word I give to remain in your memories and minds,
As base and finalè too for all metaphysics.
(So to the students the old professor,
At the close of his crowded course.)

Having studied the new and antique, the Greek and Germanic
    system,
Kant having studied and stated, Fichte and Schelling and Hegel,
Stated the lore of Plato, and Socrates greater than Plato,
And greater than Socrates sought and stated, Christ divine having
    studied long,
I see reminiscent to-day those Greek and Germanic systems,
See the philosophies all, Christian churches and tenets see,
Yet underneath Socrates clearly see, and underneath Christ the
    divine I see,
The dear love of man for his comrade, the attraction of friend
    to friend,
Of the well-married husband and wife, of children and parents,
Of city for city and land for land.

Author and Selection Notes

See page 413.

Questions and Exercises

1. What is the meaning of the word "metaphysics"?
2. What, according to Whitman, is the one foundation on which the
great philosophies are built?
3. How is the idea in this poem related to another Whitman declaration, "I am the voice of democracy"?
4. Would Whitman see life as "much ado about nothing" if a "Base"
for life were not recognized? Discuss.

5. Discuss the importance of attraction in social relationships and in relation to inanimate objects such as planets and atoms.

6. Theme Topics: Studies Without Direction; Ineffective Living; Seeing Relationships Between Parts; Why Great Thinkers Always Have Many Ideas in Common; Love Makes the World Go Round.

MORE BIRDS OF HAMPTON

Archibald Rutledge

Because of the increasing interest in birds all over America, and because I am most fortunately located for observing them, it should be worth while to record the birds I have observed here on this ancient plantation. Some five hundred acres of my place are in waste rice lands, which are a natural sanctuary for many aquatic species. Two hundred acres are of cleared upland, under cultivation. About twelve hundred acres are in wildwoods. On the place are eighteen natural ponds or lagoons; I have told of making one artificial lake. The marshes, the forest, the fields, the abundant water—all these attract an unusual number and variety of birds.

It is a habit of my life always to be out of the house before daybreak. There are sights and sounds, there is a glory on the world then that it hardly wears at any other time. And I treasure the memories of things seen and heard then.

At daybreak one November day, in the golden heart of a pine forest magic with autumnal colors and fragrances, I was waiting for the possible sight of a wild turkey that a friend had declared he would drive my way as he rode toward me through the woods. What I expected to see was a tall, snakelike neck and a bronzed, broad back come sedulously, glisteningly and silently forward through the broom sedge and the huckleberry bushes. Instead of that I saw a vain but thrilling race—indeed, as extraordinary an affair as a man ever witnesses.

My friend, riding a swift and sure-footed marsh pony, came out of a thicket of young pines about four hundred yards directly in front of me. Between us lay a level stretch of forest, with a few big pines here and there and a soft growth of tawny broom grass on the wildwood floor. Just as he cleared the thicket, the horseman rode up a wild gobbler, which probably had heard him coming for some time and had squatted under some brush. From this shelter he had finally been roused.

What first attracted my attention to the picturesque performance now beginning was the sudden violent start that the horse made in my direction: he came at a wild, driven gallop. Then I saw the great bird above him, superbly beating his way toward me. At the start of this remarkable race the gobbler was thirty feet above the horse and about as many yards ahead. Clearly my friend's game was to try to beat the wild turkey to me and incidentally, perhaps, to prove his pony's speed, about which he had been amiably regaling me with some tall tales.

On came this singular and harmless hurricane. And most thrilling it was to watch. The pony having fully entered into the spirit of the adventure, and the wild gobbler being aware of some sort of strange menace to be escaped only by the most rigorous valor of flight, there was a real race between the two.

The flight of a wild turkey is always impressive, but peculiarly so when, having gathered momentum by beating his powerful wings, he sets his pinions and sails at cyclone speed—head far extended, feet far extended—swift without exerted motion, onrushing silently, a living airplane, sentient, electric.

The length of time that a wild turkey can sail seems to depend chiefly on the original height obtained. Many observations of the flight of this magnificent voyageur of the sky confirm my opinion that a wild turkey, upon taking wing, usually attempts to attain height first of all; then he gives attention to the details of direction and speed.

Because my friend and his pony had been close upon him ere he took wing, this gobbler I was watching was not able, evidently, to waste time in mounting, thinking it discreet immediately to put all the direct distance he could between himself and his pursuer. The turkey therefore was never more than forty feet from the ground.

With the luxurious autumn sunlight glinting iridescently on his bronze feathers, with the tall yellow pines, and the blue sky, and the glimmering, far swamp of treebays and loblollies and sweet myrtles making a perfect and appealing background for the approach of winged majesty, on came the illustrious fugitive, while beneath him, but every moment falling behind, thundered the excited pony. Above me now the great bird gleamed, splendid and swift, gliding high among the clean pine boles on level, dark wings. He passed, the light on him brightening, fading, flaring softly again.

Far through the joyous forest my eye followed him until he was lost in the quiet, mysterious merging of faint sky and golden leaves and that retired, distant loveliness where beats the forest's heart.

A few seconds after the gobbler had disappeared, my friend arrived on his breathless mount. In the race of about a quarter of a mile the turkey had gained, as nearly as I could estimate, about a hundred yards; but his gaining was continuous, so that there was no doubt of the fact that the pony was outclassed. The matter can be reduced to simplicity when we say that a wild turkey can easily fly on the level at sixty miles an hour, which is a speed no horse can maintain—or perhaps even attain. In flights downhill a wild turkey achieves an almost incredible velocity; and though, as a bird, he makes comparatively small use of his wings, when he does perform, the spectacle is memorable. He always makes me think of a modest champion—unwilling to make a show of himself, but superb when once in action. As a means of escape a wild turkey depends on his legs rather than his wings. In this respect he resembles the Mongolian pheasant, which runs great distances before dogs and pursuers.

*   *   *   *   *

One day in the lonely marshes of Tranquillity, in the Santee delta, I was witness to a spectacular contest in speed between a Wilson snipe and a duck hawk. For the game bird this race was, of course, a matter of life and death; and whenever this is the case, any living thing so jeopardized appears to draw on deep reservoirs of energy which ordinarily lie untapped.

I was standing on an old bank with a wild sea of marsh rolling westward in golden waves. It was mid-October, and I was out in the wasteland country to watch the newly arrived autumn migrants: many shore birds there were, and wild ducks, night herons, a few woodcock and many Wilson snipe. It just happened that I had my eye on this last bird, nervously darting toward a tuft of watery sedge, crouching, and then stealing with artful furtiveness to another tuft when, out of the wide-winged sunset, like some beautiful avenging phantom, a peregrine falcon suddenly appeared. The snipe must have perceived that he was the intended victim, and he must have judged that his best, perhaps his only, chance to escape was in flight. With startled, sharp cries he sprang from the morass and was away on his dashing, dodging, enigmatic flight. The breathless pursuit of this fine game bird by the duck hawk I had an excellent chance to watch, for the sky above the marshes was still radiant with an effulgent afterglow.

I took it for granted that the superb peregrine falcon would overtake the frantically darting fugitive, which had not at best a start of more than a hundred feet, and that distance the hawk could cover in a single second. But what the falcon had in celerity the snipe matched in craft. To begin with, the game bird, much to my surprise, instead of dashing off low over the marshes, suddenly towered, as if safety lay in the zenith. The hawk, a veritable corsair of the sky, of course followed, with a velocity so great that, on account of his swerving at high speed, my eye frequently lost him. That he gained on the English snipe is certain, for again and again he struck at his prey; but in the fraction of a second that it took him to deliver his stroke, his quarry had left the appointed place. Moreover the pursuer lost distance every time he rose above his prey and lunged for it.

Clearly in the pearly twilight I could watch this dramatic race, and I saw the end of it. The proud peregrine falcon, after having attempted desperately to achieve his design, suddenly broke off in disgust, disdainfully, like an aristocrat who withdraws from a contest in which he discovers a menial winning. The snipe escaped in the kindly vastness of the glimmering sky, and the duck hawk haughtily beat his way off toward a lodging for the night in the looming pines at the terminal of the huge delta. Despite the fact that the falcon failed to capture this game bird, I believe that when he is really in earnest, the duck hawk is as swift as any other bird.

*   *   *   *   *

Migration is a phenomenon too great and thrilling to be taken as a mere matter of course. When northward through the night goes a clanging chorus of wild geese; when one hears wings and far cries from the upper darkness haunting the purple deeps; when one senses that this is the triumphant van of the irresistible armies of the spring; is not the heart, by these lone and daring trumpeters, summoned to rejoice?

It is during migration that the telephone of the wild is most active. By it lines of communication are kept intact. It makes the host cohere. There are continual cries of guidance, reassurance, and of being reassured. The wild geese are going to Athabaska, perhaps; and all of them are talking about it. The mallards are headed for Hudson Bay; they know the route, but they keep encouraging one another mile after mile. If there is a straggler, they pick him up by radio. The vast and solitary darkness is atingle with vivid and vital communications of these children of nature.

This region is an anteroom of spring. It is a vernal vestibule. Here, while the vast expanse of country to the northward is still blizzard-bound, while the snow lies deep, and the icy, unrelenting wind grieves through bare boughs and over frozen ground spring pauses in her journey up the land as if she would array herself for a bridal. And the joyous companions of spring, her heralds and her minstrels, the migrating birds, here rest from their epic flights in order to don their nuptial plumage, to sing their sweetest songs, and even to select mates for themselves, though their summer homes lie many leagues away.

From afar these singers have gathered: from the pampas of the Argentine, from the dim and humid forest of the Amazon, from aromatic isles asleep beyond Florida and the Gulf of Mexico. But, however remote and however alluring may have been their winter Riviera, the Voice has infallibly and importunately reached them. And there has been universal response; for it is to the heart of life itself that the voice of love is calling.

Another consideration that impresses the beholder of this annual wonder is the certainty and the punctuality with which even the least voyagers arrive. Through the immensity of the night, over trackless wastes the gossamer wings of the ruby-throated humming-bird bear him as safely to his far desired haven as do the mighty pinions of the great wood ibis; the grebe on his pitifully frail wings arrives as surely as does that graceful living airplane, the swallow-tailed kite. The delicate cerulean warbler is on schedule time together with the whistling swan and the wide-winged egret.

Northward are they hastening, but they pause for a few days in the region of my home, filling the lonely woods and the solitary marshes with ecstatic song.

* * * * *

Of all the troubadours that rejoice in heralding the springtime, none is to me more fascinating than the Baltimore oriole. When he sings from a tall green bough of a live oak, his hearty melody floats like a bright blue banner, luring hearts to follow that flag to a land of dreams. Like a blown blossom or a gorgeous autumn leaf he flits from bough to bough, regal in his tawny-and-black bride-groom's dress. On the northward journey the males arrive first, and they depart before the females come. All day these gay-coated cavaliers carol and call, brilliant firebrands burning against the deep emerald of the leafing trees.

To me the bright wonder of the young year arrives with these birds, and I hear in their singing the calm certainty of joy's return. All that wanders and is wild and beautiful in them finds a voice; they are the meaning of the loveliness that glimmers in forest graces.

Author and Selection Notes

Archibald Rutledge (1883-   ), poet, naturalist, essayist, and lecturer, writes with great warmth about his native coastal South Carolina and more specifically, in *Home by the River,* about his ancestral Hampton plantation with its historic and artistic Georgian house, and the storied flora and fauna surrounding it. Rutledge is heir to the plantation, which has been in the family since 1686, and descendant of Edward Rutledge, a signer of the Declaration of Independence. John, his brother, was one of the early governors of South Carolina. The house on the plantation was built in 1730 and has sheltered such notables as the historic British Colonel Banastre Tarleton, General Francis Marion, and George Washington.

Rutledge records with rare simplicity and love his labors at the beginning of the restoration of the old house in 1937 with the help of the descendants of the original slaves. His fascinating observations of the wild life about Hampton are recorded in the selection from "More Birds of Hampton."

Questions and Exercises

1. Why is Hampton plantation so well suited for a bird sanctuary?

2. Do you agree that the world wears a glory of sight and sound just before dawn? Describe your reaction to early morning.

3. Rutledge relates unusual experiences of wild-life on his plantation such as the race between the sure-footed marsh pony and the wild turkey, and the contest between the Wilson snipe and the duck hawk. What is the author's special gift in recounting these experiences?

4. Give your impression of Rutledge now that you have read about his birds at Hampton.

5. Theme Topics: What Bird-Lore Can Teach; The Inspiration of Wild Life; Life on a Plantation; The Secrets of Nature; When I Went Hunting; Living Out-of-Doors; The Voice of Silence.

THE ITALIAN ATTACK ON THE ALEXANDRIA NAVAL BASE

By
Commander Luigi Durand de la Penne, *Italian Navy*
as told to
Captain Virgilio Spigai, *Italian Navy*

The exploits of midget assault craft in World War II provided what is perhaps the brightest chapter in the whole of Italy's Naval Annals. This magnificent effort was devoted primarily to attack by means of slow speed piloted torpedoes nicknamed "pigs" by the Italians. The success of these human torpedoes was almost entirely at the expense of the British Mediterranean Fleet whose ships were attacked in Gibraltar, Suda Bay, Alexandria, Algiers, and elsewhere. Of special interest is the fact that in all cases the British ships were at anchor inside of booms and nets and in harbors under constant surveillance by patrol craft. Despite all British precautions, their losses to the Italian Tenth Light Flotilla reached the staggering total, sunk or damaged, of:

4 warships, aggregate tonnage	75,690
26 merchant ships, aggregate tonnage	176,662
TOTAL TONNAGE	252,352

Commander Luigi Durand de la Penne, Italian Navy, participated in a successful assault on Gibraltar before engaging in this, his greatest exploit—the sinking of HMS Valiant *in Alexandria on 19 December 1941. The following article provides his personal recollections of the events of the memorable occasion as told to his very good friend, Captain Virgilio Spigai, Italian Navy. The success of this attack was attested by Winston Churchill, who commented (April, 1942) to the House of Commons that as a result of de la Penne's attack the British had no battle squadron in the Mediterranean for several months.*

Commander de la Penne's story starts with his departure from Rome on December 12, 1941, headed for the Italian Submarine Base at Leros in the Dodecanese Islands, where his assault group boarded the specially equipped submarine Sciré, *already loaded and equipped for the forthcoming assault on Alexandria. Much arduous training had preceded the final departure of the assault team from Rome. Likewise, the submarine* Sciré *had been specially modified and equipped for her task of transporting the assault craft and crews to the prescribed launching point*

Reprinted by permission from *Proceedings.* Copyright 1956 by United States Naval Institute. The "Author and Selection Notes" are also from *Proceedings.*

*undetected and on schedule. A few words will bring the reader up to the
author's take-off point in Rome.*

*At twilight on December 3, Sciré had sailed from the Italian Submarine
Base at La Spezia in northern Italy under strictest secrecy. Crews of other
submarines at the base were entirely ignorant of her mission. Even her
own crew knew nothing of the details of the contemplated operation. So
tight were the security measures taken that Sciré sailed without human
torpedoes or even operator's clothing or breathing sets. Not until the
submarine had cleared the harbor and darkness had fallen did she make
rendezvous with a lighter carrying three human torpedoes from the
torpedo shop at San Bartolomeo. After loading this equipment in her
special deck tanks, Sciré set course for Lero, where, on the afternoon of
December 12, Commander de la Penne was expected to report on board
with his assault crews, who had been flown from Rome as an added
security measure.*

We left Rome by plane on December 12, 1941. There were three
regular two-man crews and two additional reserve crews, making a
total of ten men in all assigned to carry out the mission of attacking
the British Fleet at Alexandria. Each human torpedo was to be
manned by a commanding officer, seated forward at the controls,
assisted by one diver, seated aft, whose principal responsibility was
to assist in the final and most strenuous part of the enterprise—the
attaching of the warhead to the keel of the enemy warship.

Every branch of the officer corps was represented. I (de la Penne),
the officer in charge of the assault crews, was a line officer. Antonio
Marceglia was a naval engineer; Vincenzo Martellotta was a member of the construction corps. In the reserve crews were Sub-Lieutenant Luigi Feltrinelli, a line officer, and Surgeon Midshipman
Giorgio Spaccarelli, a medical officer. The officers, all trained divers,
were assisted by the following qualified deep-sea divers—Emilio
Bianchi, Mario Marino, Spartaco Schergat, Armando Memoli, and
Luciano Savare.

In addition to being volunteers, all of these officers and ratings
were men of exceptional physique and endurance. Despite gaps left
in our ranks by those who lost their lives, or were taken prisoner
during these actions, a great number of volunteers could be found
right up to the end of the war. To insure the best caliber of officers
and men, volunteers were accepted from all ranks and all branches
of the naval service.

Among the members of the assault crews there was complete
awareness of the difficulties of the impending operation and the
risks about to be undertaken. Nevertheless, a very cheerful spirit
was evident in the group. We knew that we were going to the sub-

marine base at Leros in the Aegean Islands, on the Island of Rhodes, where we would board the submarine *Sciré* and be transported to a point off the harbor defenses at Alexandria where we would don our diving suits, go out on deck and, while the submarine was submerged, launch our "pigs," get astride them, and somehow or other enter the harbor of Alexandria. On arrival in the midst of the British Fleet, and while it was still completely dark, we would have to attach the warhead to the bilge keels of the most important targets. What would happen to us upon completion of the assignment interested us only up to a point. If we were lucky, it might mean imprisonment for the duration of the war; if unlucky, it meant death. Being very young, none of us believed the worst would happen. Perhaps this was because we had been so lucky during our dangerous assaults against the British Fleet at Gibraltar.

The same evening we reached Leros and proceeded to the submarine base where we found the *Sciré* ready and waiting to take us to Alexandria. This submarine was specially equipped to carry human torpedoes. Cylindrical caissons had been mounted on deck from which the torpedoes could be launched submerged.

Obviously to command a submarine of this type an officer of remarkable ability was needed. Such a person was found in Lieutenant Commander Principe Iunio Valerio Borghese, who had twice entered the Bay of Gibraltar, dropping off assault craft without the British being aware of it. At an earlier date some of our submarines had tried similar operations, and two of them, the *Iride* and the *Gondar,* were sunk before reaching Alexandria. The main operative difficulty in the Eastern Mediterranean was the extreme clearness of the waters and the lack of depth close to Alexandria.

The assignment had been accurately worked out. It had been decided that we should move from Leros with the *Sciré* as soon as weather conditions, the moon, air reconnaissance observations, and the naval situation at Alexandria made it seem possible that the expedition could be undertaken against a target commensurate with our risks.

The high morale of the submarine and air personnel stationed at Leros made a favorable impression on us, as well as the beauty of the island itself. We had complete faith in our "chariots," and in the submarine *Sciré*. We also had confidence in Commander Borghese and, of course, in ourselves. Although we did not mention it out loud, we felt certain that luck would be with us this time and that everything would go well. We could not have been more confident.

The most trying thing about these operations is the waiting, but we were favored by Commander Borghese's decision to leave immediately. Hence, after removing the camouflage from the submarine which concealed it from air-reconnaissance, we left Leros on December 14. We had to cross the Eastern Mediterranean submerged and at the same time avoid such obstacles as enemy air-reconnaissance, naval visual reconnaissance, the minefields outside Alexandria, the electric anti-submarine mines and hydrophone signals, and finally radar indicators. It was these radar indicators which had been the reason for our unsuccessful attempt to break through to Malta four months earlier.

But all these difficulties were the submarine commander's worries, not ours. While the submarine advanced slowly and carefully towards its goal, we passed the time as best we could—reading, writing, and drinking enormous quantities of fruit juices. The *Sciré* was perfectly silent, had good air-conditioning, and other characteristics which helped us to endure the journey fairly well in spite of the rough seas which aided Commander Borghese in avoiding the network of vigilance and in bringing the submarine to rest, earlier than anticipated, on the bottom at the point indicated on the chart—45 feet in depth, 1.3 miles north of the lighthouse on the pier west of the commercial port of Alexandria.

Before submerging, the *Sciré* received from Athens reports of the afternoon reconnaissance by the Italian Air Force from the Egec air base. They reported many ships in the harbor of Alexandria, including two battleships of the *Queen Elizabeth* class. Although our enterprise had hardly begun, we felt a quiver of enthusiasm as though the sinkings had already taken place.

Regulations prescribed that the commanding officer of the submarine have full command of the expedition up to the point of launching the assault craft from the submarine. It was his responsibility to select the targets and designate the attackers. His assignments were as follows:

To the chief of the expedition (myself) and chief diver Bianchi, the first battleship; to Lieutenant Marceglia, Naval Engineer, and diver Corporal Schergat, the second battleship. To the third crew, Lieutenant Martellotta, N.S., and chief diver Marino, the following orders were given: "Check if there are any aircraft carriers in port. If no aircraft carrier is present, give up the idea of attacking smaller warships." This order implied that priority was to be given to tankers before cruisers.

Tankers were given priority over cruisers in order to assist us in our secondary objective of setting fire to the fuel oil which would inevitably cover the surface of the water after the explosions. Intelligence had told us there were about ten tankers in the harbor that night, and it is easy to understand what it would have meant to set fire to thousands of barrels of oil floating on the surface of the harbor.

Two reserve crews, under Sub-Lieutenant Feltrinelli and Midshipman Spaccarelli, were given orders to leave the submarine and assist the regular assault crews in taking the craft out of the caissons where they had been stored during the submarine's journey.

While these orders were being given out, we struggled into our assault kits, which consisted of black, special rubber suits which were perfectly air-tight and perspiration proof, and oppressive as the stranglehold of a wrestler. Struggling into these suits in the humidity and heat of the submarine was a very tiring and unpleasant undertaking.

After dressing and putting on our respirators and luminous, waterproof wrist watches, Commander Borghese ordered the *Sciré* to surface. Having given us his customary kick in the pants for luck, one by one we climbed up the vertical ladder in the escape hatch and climbed out into the open air.

The night was beautiful and still, and in the mild weather under the stars, it seemed as though the war were a myth. Unfortunately, this illusion did not last long.

The hatch of the submarine closed and its conning tower soon disappeared under water, leaving us alone as we began our work of taking the craft out of the caissons preparatory to leaving in formation for the entrance to the port.

Our SLC (slow speed torpedo) assault craft units (which we called "pigs" or "chariots") were barely twenty feet long and had an overall height of about 3½ feet. They were powered by electric storage batteries. Fore and aft, and amidships, small buoyancy tanks similar to those on submarines were placed for submerging and surfacing, with electric pumps for trimming. The speed of an SLC was just over two knots, and its cruising radius was ten miles. To maneuver this sea-going automobile, we had to sit astride and work controls very much like those of an aircraft. The instrument panel with its luminous dials was similar to that of a plane. It contained a magnetic compass, a depth gauge, a manometer for registering pressure in the tanks, a voltmeter for the control of the batteries, an ammeter, and a spirit level for reading the angle to the horizontal.

The torpedo was equipped with a warhead which could be detached without interfering with the operation of the craft. This had been done purposely so as to allow the operators to approach a ship, fix the charge in position, and get away. The charge was fitted with a time fuse. In addition, the assault craft itself was fitted with a self-destructive device which could be used when necessary to avoid its falling into the hands of the enemy. Ordinarily in such cases the operator set the self-destructor, locked the controls on full dive, sent the torpedo to the bottom where it destroyed itself, and then swam ashore following the attack.

The craft were tested for a depth of 100 feet and had been adjusted with infinite patience according to the results of exhaustive trials carried out at the La Spezia Naval Base and on the beach of the Royal estate at San Rossore near Pisa. As a result of the trials in combat during the expeditions on Gibraltar and Malta (which cost the life of the assault craft's inventor, Captain Tesseo Tesi, Naval Engineer, and the imprisonment of his collaborator, Lieutenant Elios Toschi) we had confidence in the readiness of our craft.

Each craft was equipped with a full set of tools and instruments and was fitted with compressed air net lifters and net cutters, heavy shears, clamps for the ship's bilge keel (we call them "sergeants"), and a crude sort of a safety line called a "lift" which consisted of a rope tied to the operator and of sufficient length so as to permit him to leave his saddle, rise vertically from the craft, and return.

To attack a ship, one had to execute the following maneuvers:

(1) Approach on the surface with only the operator's head out of water until about 150 feet abeam of the target.

(2) Submerge and approach until the operator could touch the ship's hull with his hands.

(3) Proceed gently, feeling the ship's bottom by hand, until locating the bilge keel on the near side.

(4) Fix a clamp on the bilge keel and secure it to the warhead with a line.

(5) Continue all the way under the ship and secure the second clamp on the opposite bilge keel.

(6) Secure the rope to the second clamp and stretch tightly.

(7) Cast the warhead loose and move it along the line until it was suspended directly below the center line of the ship.

(8) Set the time fuse.

(9) Cast off and proceed to a point well clear of the ship.

The operator then sets the self-destructor and tries to make good his escape. When the charge explodes directly under the ship's keel, it hits the ship in its most vulnerable and least-protected spot.

It should be mentioned that before arriving at a ship, the operator usually had to pass through the boom defenses of the harbor. This he did by approaching along the bottom and lifting the net, or by approaching the net at a point where it could be cut with the compressed-air shears carried for that specific purpose. During both of these operations, he hoped not to set off any explosives which were frequently to be found on the nets. After entering the harbor, the operator still had to proceed undetected to a point within the torpedo nets which were always placed around ships at anchor.

As a result of our experience during many training tests and expeditions, we had learned that the worst obstacle to success was not the enemy's lookout but the extreme cold, which, as time went by, took hold of us in a vice-like grip. Damage to equipment was also a constant and serious hazard. Rips inevitably occurred to the rubber diving suits during work, and permitted the entry of cold water. The respirators, too, might fail for any of a number of reasons. Any one of a number of small hitches of this kind might interrupt an operation which represented many months of preparation. We had spent many months of training in cold water at night to get accustomed to the cold and to the dark. This we found useful only up to a point—beyond which, in cold water operations, the operator had no alternative but to accept the hardship imposed by the cold. Experience had taught us that best results could only be had by using bare hands. Finally, since our oxygen-filled respirators were good only for five or six hours, the whole operation had to be carried out within that limitation.

Here is what happened that memorable night outside the harbor of Alexandria. We were delayed in leaving the submarine because one of the SLC storage cylinder hatches wouldn't open. During this perilous operation, Surgeon Spaccarelli nearly lost his life. As it turned out later, he fainted from oxygen poisoning induced by exertion and fell to the deck of the submarine—fortunately without sliding off into the mud on which the submarine was resting. He remained thus for nearly half an hour, and only by very good fortune was he discovered by his friend, Feltrinelli, who found him and brought him back inside the submarine where he was finally revived.

Our attack group departed about 2100, and the submarine, having finished her role, departed and returned uneventfully to Leros.

Upon launching our "chariots" from the submarine, the three of us proceeded in formation on the surface toward the harbor. I was in the center, Marceglia on my left, Martellotta on the right. During the run in we proceeded without respirators, with our heads out of water. Two hours later we were abreast of Ras El Tin lighthouse, and, to our surprise, arrived there considerably ahead of schedule. We therefore lay to, broke out our emergency rations, and had something to eat. The cold and the fresh air had given us a terrific appetite, and we felt it necessary to eat in order to be in top shape when we neared the targets. Although the light in the lighthouse was out, the weather was so fine that we could see the structure. Everything thus far had progressed as smooth as oil. Then, while we were eating, the lighthouse of Ras El Tin suddenly lighted up. At this time we were only 500 yards from it. So, very cautiously and very slowly, we moved farther away so as not to be seen. I decided to move at once toward the mouth of the harbor, which was some distance away, but of whose location I was now sure. At about midnight we heard—and felt—sharp underwater explosions which painfully constricted our legs, the only part of us under water. We rounded the south jetty by dead reckoning at minimum speed, keeping station on one another and with only the head of the forward pilot of each "chariot" above water.

We now found ourselves before the outer boom defense, which was patrolled by a large motorboat cruising back and forth and dropping occasional depth charges. Between the explosions it was very quiet, and we could hear a few men talking on the pier; in fact, we were so close that we noticed one of them carried a lantern in his hand. The periodic explosion of the depth charges was very annoying to the pilot, whose legs continued to receive the shock of each explosion. But far worse was the effect of these explosions on the number two pilot who, during this period, had put on his respirator and ducked down so as to be completely submerged. He, of course, received the full jolt from each explosion.

Suddenly we saw signal lights showing at the gate of the boom. This meant that ships were about to enter the harbor. I thereupon decided to attempt to run in with the entering ships through the open gate rather than attempt to go under or through the net. We therefore proceeded to a position near an obstruction buoy hard by the gate.

Soon the lights on this buoy were lighted, and I had a glimpse of dark shapes rapidly approaching. This meant the gate was open. As it turned out, the shapes were three large British destroyers. Cautiously, I submerged and moved forward, and as I passed in the gate, the destroyer passed at what seemed like just a few inches over my head. Fortunately the surge from her bow forced me down, where I touched bottom—happy, indeed, to have missed the screws. As soon as I hit the bottom, I put on full speed, entered the harbor with the second destroyer, and then came up to the surface. By this time the third destroyer, which had followed closely behind, had entered, and it created a bow-wave which hurled me against the inner obstruction buoy—fortunately, without serious effects. Since I had now entered the harbor, this small mishap did not worry me.

During this time, I had lost contact with my friends. This had been anticipated in the instructions, and so I made no effort to contact them, but proceeded on toward my target with only my head showing above water. The third destroyer had stopped near me, her crew on deck preparing to anchor. I changed course, passed her astern, and steered over toward the northern inner breakwater and away from the quay so as to avoid the lights from land. En route to my objective, I passed two enemy cruisers moored stern to shore. I passed across their bows and under the stern of the French battleship *Lorraine*, which was moored near enough to the British battleship I was seeking so that as I passed beyond her I at last caught sight of my target.

She was enormous—a 31,000-ton battleship. I was thrilled by the thought that the strength and daring of only two men were to cripple her.

A thousand yards of fairly well lighted water separated us at this time, and across this stretch I slowly made my way with only my head showing at observation level. In this attitude I came up against the torpedo nets which surrounded the ship. I realized that I could not get through this obstruction without breaking surface with my whole assault craft. Dismounting into the water, and joined by my other operator, we pushed the "chariot" between two spherical floats. We simply could not avoid making some noise, but happily no one noticed us. During this operation my diving suit was punctured, and it immediately flooded. The intense cold bit into me with icy fingers.

I was now within 100 feet of the side of the battleship, with no obstruction in front. It was 0200 on December 19, 1941. My present position was the result of six years of study and strenuous training. For a moment it seemed almost insignificant and hardly worth the effort. This fleeting thought departed as I put on my respirator, which I had not used during the approach to the battleship. I submerged to twenty feet and steered by compass on the bearing of the ship's funnel. This, I expected, would put me amidships.

In a few moments I struck against the hull but could not operate the controls to stop my motor because by now my hands were numb with cold. Out of control, my chariot suddenly became heavy and went to the bottom at fifty feet. I left the assault craft and swam up to the surface to check my position. I could see that I was about 45 feet forward of the number one stack. I then submerged, followed my "lift" rope back to the chariot, where I found to my unpleasant surprise that my number two man, Bianchi, was missing and my motor refused to turn over.

Again I returned to the surface, but could find no sign of Bianchi. On board the enemy battleship everything was quiet. On my next trip down I found that a steel cable had wrapped itself tightly around the propeller of my chariot. I realized the motor would never move again, and I thereupon decided the only thing to do was to drag the torpedo along in the mud by main strength until directly beneath the ship. The mud was extremely gooey and cut out all visibility, but I guided my "pig" by the noise of one of the pumps on board the enemy ship.

The frightful effort made me sweat as if I were in a Turkish bath. Sea water seeped into my mask, and I had to drink it to avoid drowning. Although I was submerged in water and was drinking all the time, I had a continuous sensation of terrible thirst. After what must have been about a twenty-minute struggle, I noticed the noise of the pump becoming louder. I rested a moment and managed at last to check my heading by my compass and insure that I was going in the right direction. At the same time, the depth was gradually decreasing, showing that I was slowly approaching the ship's hull.

After about twenty more minutes, with increasingly longer periods of rest, for my strength was fast giving out, I hit the hull of the ship with my head. At last I had arrived! I was nearly exhausted. I checked my bearings, dragged the torpedo under the center line of the ship, attached the warhead and set the fuses. I did not bother to set the clamps tight because by now I had no doubts as to our success. At the appointed time, everything would be blown up as planned—the ship, and the assault craft as well. Since its location on the bottom was so near the hull of the ship, the explosion would destroy both.

I floated up to the surface and took off my respirator. As I was swimming away, someone on the battleship's deck almost over me saw me and ordered me to stop. I paid no attention and kept on swimming until a hail of machine gun bullets induced me to change my mind. I headed for the ship's mooring buoy, where to my great joy I discovered Bianchi. He had been overcome underwater but had revived when afloat, and with great intelligence, so as not to interrupt the operations or give the alarm, had swum slowly over and hid himself behind the mooring buoy. I reported that everything had been accomplished, but at that very moment I nearly lost my own life through stupidity. As the British were shouting at us from the bow of the ship, I thought to go on board by climbing up the anchor chain. But another deadly hail of machine gun fire made me realize that I had better stay where I was. It was now 3:30 in the morning as Bianchi and I perched prudently on the buoy, awaiting developments.

After a while a boat came by to pick me up, and we were taken on board the British battleship. I handed in my identification papers, and at first was treated rather roughly, although not violently. I declined to give any information and smiled inwardly as the officer who made the cross-examination sympathized with me for the failure of our mission. Then we were taken by motor boat to Ras El Tin and questioned in Italian by other officers. Bianchi and I maintained our stubborn silence, although we were told they would find a way to make us talk.

After this we were taken back aboard the battleship and down into the forward hold between the two gun-turrets. The men on guard were kind and generously offered us rum and cigarettes. Still aching with cold after my long immersion, I reflected on my future at this point. What would happen in this deep hold during the explosion? Would we die by drowning, or be blown to bits? Bianchi didn't seem to be worried by this dubious choice and fell asleep. With deep satisfaction I noted that the ribbon on the sailor's cap said HMS *Valiant*. Whatever happened to me, I could feel proud that I had fulfilled my mission to the letter. I had not failed my country.

Meanwhile, time was hurrying on. Day was breaking. This meant only ten minutes were left before the explosion. I asked to be taken to the ship's captain and warned him to give orders to abandon ship and save the personnel, for the ship would be blown up within a few minutes. He still tried to get me to talk, but receiving no reply, he had me sent back to the hold even as the loud speakers gave the orders which I had suggested.

So it was that I was deep down in the hold when the explosion occurred. But destiny, or what you will, did not intend that I should die at that moment.

The blast shook the vessel with extreme violence, the lights went off, and the hold was filled with smoke. But except for a pain in my knee, I was unhurt. The ship rapidly heeled over to port about five degrees and started to rest on the bottom. Groping my way up the ladder and through the open hatch to the upper bridge, I went toward the stern where a number of officers were standing. They were watching the *Queen Elizabeth,* sister ship of the *Valiant,* which was anchored a hundred yards away from us. At that moment she, too, gave a terrific heave and blew up, belching scrap from her funnel and flooding the stern of the *Valiant* with gasoline. Then I knew that the brave efforts of Marceglia and Schergat had also met with entire success!

Once more Bianchi and I were taken down to the hold to see if we could be forced into giving information about possible further explosions, but seeing that it was useless to try to make us talk, they took us back to Ras El Tin, where we became official prisoners of war. That completes the story of my adventures on that memorable evening. But since my story is only part of the mission so spectacularly accomplished, I must outline briefly what happened to the other two crews, my companions in this adventure.

Lieutenant Marceglia had lost contact with the chief of the expedition before reaching the entrance to the harbor defenses. He followed along the fixed part of the harbor net, and then, seeing the red signals lighted and thinking the gates must be open, he slipped in. As he passed, he heard a slight *swoosh* behind him made by the first enemy destroyer; he was overtaken by the second destroyer and then the third. He headed for the breakwater and passed between it and the wooden pier which was brightly illuminated, as unloading operations were in progress there. Having crossed this expanse of light without being discovered, he was able to discern his target surrounded by its torpedo nets. At exactly three o'clock he was in position for attack, 100 feet away from the target—that is, from the funnel of the battleship. Everything was silent on board.

Marceglia had arrived this far with his head out of water and without using his respirator. He then slipped it on and submerged. He and his number two man proceeded by creeping along on the mud, guided by the noise of the machinery on board, and after a few unsuccessful trials they finally found the bilge keel of the enemy ship. Marceglia pumped in air to surface the assault craft which caused it to hit against the battleship's hull noisily, but no alarm was sounded aboard. Having fixed the first "sergeant," Marceglia sent Schergat to search for the second bilge keel. After two attempts, the second "sergeant" was attached. They then detached the warhead of the craft, but at this moment Schergat was paralyzed as a result of the diving. Marceglia continued the work alone and managed to fix the charge exactly under the hull as prescribed, at five feet below the hull. At 0325, having fixed and set the fuse, everything was done and the craft left by creeping on the bottom.

But Schergat was not able to sustain underwater navigation, and Marceglia had to blow the buoyancy tank. The maneuver was somewhat too successful, and the craft broke surface with a rush, amid violent foam. Although from on board the British ship the rays of a searchlight gave a half-hearted scrutiny, our two men were able to get away safely, planting a few incendiary bombs in the harbor on their way. Passing near HMS *Valiant,* they noticed activity on board a boat underway, and they thought that our mission had failed.

It was not quite four-thirty in the morning, but still very dark. The enterprise had been carried out to perfection and without notable incidents. Marceglia and Schergat sank their craft with its self destructive device set and got ashore safely on the beach.

When it was daylight, they managed to avoid the port patrol and made their way to a bar in Alexandria by posing as French sailors. But here an unpleasant surprise awaited them—the money they had was British and did not circulate in Egypt. To change a small amount, they lost precious time and attracted the attention of the police. However, they did get as far as Rosetta, where, ten miles off the coast, the Italian submarine *Saffiro* was waiting for them. But the next day, just as they were about to reach the sea and freedom, they were arrested by the Egyptian police, recognized as Italians, and handed over to the British authorities.

Actually they had been lost by a stupid oversight concerning the question of money, and by their own lack of experience. Perhaps their first step should not have been taken toward the sea, but toward a religious institution where they might have found sanctuary until the search had subsided.

The third assault craft, commanded by Lieutenant Martellotta, also lost contact with the chief of the expedition, and its pilot carried out the mission by himself. He, too, at about thirty minutes after midnight, was nearly rammed by the first British destroyer. He quickly took the same route as Marceglia, but passed down the passage between the two battleships without seeing him.

He soon noticed that there was no enemy aircraft carrier in port, and was disappointed, but went in search of a tanker as per orders received. At last he located a large ship and decided to attack, but when only a few yards away he noticed that it was a cruiser. So, following strict orders, he reluctantly gave up the idea of attack. As he was very near the enemy ship, he decided to navigate alongside, holding himself off with his hands, so as to reach the stern without being seen, and thus get away quietly. During this operation he was nearly discovered while he was under the ship, and he had a hard job keeping his assistant quiet, for Marino could not bear to give up such a wonderful opportunity to attack. At last they neared a large tanker of 16,000 tons, moored in front of the fuel pier. Martellotta was overtaken by violent attacks of vomiting during the last part of the route, and so it was impossible for him to use the respirator. Having reached the rudder of the tanker, he gave the diver orders to attach the charge under the keel anywhere, because it was impossible for one man alone to put the charge in the exact middle of the ship. This was done; however, the results were none the less effective, for at the given time a terrific explosion blew off the entire stern of the tanker. In addition Martellotta had set incendiary charges, but contrary to our expectations they did not ignite the oil spreading over the surface, and the harbor of Alexandria was saved.

Having conscientiously planted all the incendiary bombs, they sank their craft with its self-destructive device set, and were able to land at the harbor coal pier and even get rid of their kit. Unfortunately, they were later caught and arrested while leaving the port, and were taken prisoners.

* * *

In 1946, Sir Charles Morgan, Admiral of the Royal Navy, in command of the *Valiant* in 1941, wished to do Commander de la Penne the honor of pinning on his chest the gold medal *"Valor Militare,"* which had been awarded him by the Italian Government for the mission at Alexandria. The Admiral expressed his and the Royal Navy's admiration for all Italian assault craft crews, who with great personal integrity and heroism had tried to serve their country in the way they felt was best.

We Italians were satisfied to have struck a hard blow at our opponent at Alexandria. Above all we were glad that this result had been obtained without bloodshed to our own people or to the enemy, thus keeping up a code of chivalry that is traditional with Italian assault craft crews.

The Alexandria venture was neither the first nor the last attack made by the Italian assault craft of the Tenth Light Flotilla during World War II, but it was the most successful. At the cost to us of only six men captured, Great Britain was deprived of her last two battleships in the Mediterranean, as well as a large tanker, and her strategic position there was then completely reversed. For the first—and last—time in the course of the war, the Italian Navy achieved superiority and was able to dominate the Mediterranean until other operations again reversed the situation.

Author and Selection Notes

A graduate of the Italian Naval Academy, Leghorn, Captain Spigai was a submarine skipper during the early years of World War II, served in the operations office of the Italian Navy Department, Rome, from 1950 to 1955, and is now the commanding officer of the Italian School of Naval Command. He is the author of numerous articles and several books on naval subjects.

Captain Spigai explains the genesis of this article as follows:

"Several times I have endeavored to persuade Commander Luigi Durand de la Penne to write his own personal account of the great venture by which Italian sea-commandos immobilized the British battleships *Valiant* and *Queen Elizabeth* inside the port of Alexandria. Although the exploits of the sea-commandos have been described in the book *A Hundred Men Against Two Fleets,* as well as in official reports, nevertheless there remains enough unpublished material concerning this historical event to warrant publication of such an article.

"Unfortunately, Commander de la Penne, like most men of action, is a man of few words and not overly fond of writing, hence only by much questioning have I obtained a first-hand account of the extraordinary events which took place that night."

Questions and Exercises

1. This entire selection appeals to one's sense of adventure and achievement. Relate what are to you the most exciting episodes of the account.

2. What degrees of courage and character do you think are required for the duties of a frogman?

3. List the merits of the frogman attack in maritime struggle. What are the disadvantages?

4. Can you recall other instances, war-time or otherwise, in which underwater exploits by frogmen have been highly successful?

5. Discuss the incidents of capture and treatment of the frogmen by the enemy. Were the men treated fairly or not?

6. Theme Topics: Underwater Warfare; The Excitement of Underwater Sports or Hobbies; Modern Science and the Swimmer; Frogman Courage.

SKYSCRAPERS

John Gould Fletcher

What are these, angels or demons,
Or steel and stone?
Soaring, alert,
Striped with diversified windows,
These sweep aloft
And the multitude crane their necks to them:—
Are they angels, or demons,
Or stone?

If the gray sapless people,
Moving along the street, thought them angels,
They too would be beautiful,
Erect and laughing to the sky for joy.
If as demons they feared them,
They would smite with fierce hatred
These brown haughty foreheads:
They would not suffer them to hold the sun in trust.

What are they, then, angels, or demons,
Or stone?
Deaf sightless towers
Unendowed yet with life;
Soaring vast effort
Spent in the sky till it breaks there.
You men of the country
Who shaped these proud visions,
You have yet to find godhead
Not here, but in the human heart.

Author and Selection Notes

John Gould Fletcher (1886-1950) was born in Little Rock, Arkansas. After spending several years in Massachusetts and graduating from Harvard, he moved to England where he lived for fifteen years. He returned to America in 1933 and made his home in Little Rock, his birthplace.

Beginning in 1913 Fletcher published several books of poems, somewhat experimental and only slightly interesting. He early was interested in the "imagist" movement and became one of its leaders. His writings until his death were deeply searching and varied in subject. He chose English themes and French translations. The poem in this text, "Skyscrapers," reflects his attitude toward contemporary life.

Questions and Exercises

1. In Fletcher's poem one gets the idea that skyscrapers are not the ultimate in man's achievement. What might the skyscrapers symbolize?

2. How is the description of modern man as "gray, sapless" compatible with the tone of the poem?

3. When Fletcher says the skyscrapers are "Deaf sightless towers/ Unendowed yet with life," what is he by association saying about the people who built them?

4. Can you explain the skyscrapers as angels? As demons?

5. Explain the poet's meaning of the last two lines of the poem.

6. Write your interpretation of the poem.

THE HOMOGENIZED WORLD

Sidney Walter Dean

Friends of ours, a married pair with daughters of eight and four, accepted an invitation to two months' occupancy of a grandiose country mansion that would otherwise have to be shut up. They found its mammoth refrigerator stocked with a good many containers of cream. The young mother, besides being one to take her maternal responsibilities hard, had had the education of a good chemist, and she said to herself: "Why not let the children watch all this lovely unusable cream being turned into three pounds or so of the best sweet dairy butter, and so pick up some cardinal facts of life in a form that they will never forget?" She explained what was afoot, got the two into a pleasant glow about the impending miracle, and emptied all the containers into one of those little trick churns that are made for just such uses. And then she cranked.

She and the eight-year-old cranked, turn and turn about, for quite a while. The four-year-old developed affairs elsewhere and slid away. Presently her sister lost ambition and drifted off. The two revisited the kitchen at intervals to check up on results, but the intervals lengthened, and so did the faces. The butter would not begin to come—not even for the standard expedient of setting the churn in a pan of warmish water.

The mother found herself getting slightly grim, churning fast and faster and in the end sprouting a blister on her right hand. Maybe it was the blister that finally goaded her into an overlooked thought process. Anyway she fished one of the containers out of the waste and had a look at what was printed on it.

It was homogenized cream.

Homogenization is one of those sharp ideas that cut both ways. It is the sort of idea that the American purveyor, having once glimpsed its possibilities, is never able to get enough of. Having discovered homogenization as a way of making minimum-standard milk seem better than it is, he started applying the process to other commodities with the same hope. Time was when the owner of a good Guernsey or two gloried in cream that could be skimmed off the setting pans in leathery sheets that would not pour and had to be scraped off the skimmer with a knife; at the right temperature it would be butter in a fraction of a minute. Homogenized, it will pour, all right; it will be butter never; and there is certainly nothing about it to glory in. Superiority is traded for convenience; and then we plume ourselves on the convenience as the very definition of superiority.

Lard, I notice, has almost ceased to represent itself as pure leaf; we are growing a generation of cooks that will have to appeal to dictionaries to find out what "leaf lard" ever meant. Most of the commonly available lard now vaunts itself as homogenized; and even as the homogenized cream will not make butter, so the homogenized lard will not make piecrust. That is, it will not make anything definable as piecrust by the canons of accomplished cooks who have inherited their definitions from the horse-and-buggy era that gave me mine. This stricture the modern packer would demolish by retorting that no one expects to make piecrust with lard any more. He is 80 per cent right—and he is stating one of the reasons why a truly Grade A pie is now almost a museum piece. His homogenization of lard is the most efficient way in the world to make his retort 100 per cent right except for the farms that still try out their own.

It has also become fairly hard to run down a pound of peanut

butter not homogenized. When some of us first bought peanut
butter, perhaps as young parents intent on doing the whole duty
of man by school luncheons, we waited for it to be ground out of
dark, medium, or light peanuts freshly roasted, with salt to taste.
The homogenized article of this decade is much smoother. It
spreads ideally at any reasonable temperature. It never separates
or has to be laboriously remixed. Nobody has to do any waiting
for it. It has, in short, every merit that can be put into words,
except one: edibility.

That point of excellence it would be captious, frivolous, almost
un-American to insist on, with huge corporations spending huge
sums to explain to us with patient and benevolent iteration how
much better they have made the homogenized product than anything known before. All such homogenized staples are undoubtedly
with us to stay. For a while they will be put to the expensive
effort of outshouting us few eccentrics who find them degraded
almost beyond use; but presently they will not even have to shout,
for they will have outstayed the last of the carpers. This is the
regulation process whereby the worse proves that it is the better
and, indeed, the best. Let it but hold out for a season, and it will
be the best to be had. Survival is, after all, the unanswerable
argument, and a commodity need not even argue when it has out-
lived the last of us that can bear witness to our own experience of
something better.

Homogenizing things is, of course, a narrowed application of an
idea that is one of the prime operative principles of our day: the
idea of standardization. And "standardization" is one of the subtlest,
trickiest weasel words ever coined. It enters a tacit claim to have
glorified whatever product it is applied to; it asserts that something
has been graded upward toward an ideal of supernal austerity.
What it means in practice is that excellences a little difficult to
attain are tossed overboard for the sake of practical advantages
easy to attain on a quantity-production scale. Whatever is standardized is compromised, and a compromise is always downward in at
least some particulars. What it means in connection with the
products that we eat and the ingredients that we cook with is
the surrender of an inconvenient superiority in return for a convenient uniformity at a lower level.

Consider flour. When I was a boy, what was in the flour barrel
was of hard winter wheat, and it was such as nobody could dupli-
cate nowadays short of growing the wheat and milling the flour
himself. Cake and pastry flour was a radically different affair, made
out of the soft spring wheat; you can get an approximation of

it today in toy sized packages under revolting brand names at premium prices, with some of the better constituents replaced by chemical substitutes. Today the dominant tendency is toward the so-called family or all-purpose flour, purveyed with claims to being as good for bread and rolls as for pies and cakes. Now, a flour that is pretty good for everything is self-evidently some distance from the possible for anything. The cook knows, with today's flour, just about what she is getting and just about what it will do, and for that security she pays with sacrifice of the higher niceties; whereas the housewife of aforetime was chronically moaning that the current barrel was not so good as the previous one, or congratulating herself on having struck an unusually fine supply. It is certain, though unprovable, that the average of the little domestic bread still made is higher than the average of a lifetime ago, thanks to this comparative uniformity, but that the best of former times was at a height well above anything attainable with the flour now to be had. In the interest of better cooking for everybody, we preclude the very best for anybody.

A good many of these modern improvements by compromise have to be philosophically swallowed as foreordained answers to the rapid increase of population, the swarming to cities, the disappearance of kitchens and of storage room, cooking with metered fuels, and other downward-standardizing factors. But is there any reason why we should tolerate improvements that improve nonessentials and destroy essentials? Is it a virtue to applaud size, transportability, and keeping qualities got at the expense of characteristic flavor in a strawberry or a blueberry? Does not jelly made by an addition of pectin that turns it into India rubber, or of sugar that makes it revoltingly sweet, richly earn our contempt and the remark that the fruit should have been used for decent jam in the first place? The general replacement of white sweet corn by yellow is indefensible except as a growers' fad; and when we accept, for white corn meal from millstones, yellow meal ground (and virtually precooked) by high-speed steel machinery, we are accepting sheer gratuitous degradation.

A limit of perversion very hard to exceed—but nevertheless exceeded in the smoke-curing of ham and bacon by chemical injection —is attained in the tricks of plant genetics played on the latter-day tomato in the interest of size, appearance, comparative seedlessness, and the other talking points dearest to quantity distributors. The tomato—so runs the seedman's boast—has been made completely nonacid; that is, largely devoid of tomato taste and of all taste. This signal triumph of plant breeding is comparable to improving the hardness out of a diamond or the humor out of a joke.

Author and Selection Notes

Sidney Walter Dean (1905-1962), an advertising executive, was born in Boston and educated at Yale University, where he earned his A.B. degree in 1926. He held various executive positions in industry, banking, and business. During World War II he was a captain in the United States Air Force, associated with the Office of Strategic Services and Lend-Lease administration. His observations and experiences of American and international life are poignantly reflected in "The Homogenized World."

Questions and Exercises

1. Comment on the author's statement "Superiority is traded for convenience."

2. Advance your arguments for (or against) the homogenization by great corporations of many items we now use in daily life.

3. Do you think standardization makes better a specific product? Discuss.

4. Can you list advantages of standardization in any area of commerce?

5. Discuss the author's statement, "Whatever is standardized is compromised."

6. Discuss the idea that an inconvenient superiority gives way to a convenient uniformity at a lower level.

7. Do you believe that the addition of many chemical substitutes in much of our foodstuff destroys the real value of it? Discuss your opinions.

8. Theme Topics: What Makes an Excellent Chef? Pure Food Laws; The Absence of Real Artists (or Artisans) in Modern Life; The Superiority of the Rolls Royce over Other Motor Cars; A Hand-made Item Versus a Machine-made One.

5

THE URGE TO CREATE: MAN AND THE ARTS

'Tis wise to learn, 'tis God-like to create.
John Godfrey Saxe

The urge to create is as old as man himself. Through his artifacts and primitive cave drawings, ancient man reminds us that he, like his modern counterpart, had the imagination and the impulse to create. Moreover, it is through art—music, painting, sculpture, literature—that man has always given the richest expression to his feelings.

Man has also shown a lively curiosity about the creative process, and through the centuries has attempted to establish standards of judgment by which to interpret or to criticize. These canons bear various names, such as Classicism, Romanticism, Humanism; and man returns to them again and again for his basic beliefs about art and its relation to life. These traditions, as well as the principles of art that underlie them—symmetry of form and design, rhythm, and the like—are reflected in the following selections, and receive attention from a variety of critical viewpoints. Both old and new concepts about the nature of beauty and the meaning of art appear in this section.

POETICS
Aristotle

[THE NATURE OF TRAGEDY]

Tragedy, then, is an imitation of an action that is serious, complete, and of a certain magnitude; in language embellished with each kind of artistic ornament, the several kinds being found in separate parts of the play; in the form of action, not of narrative; through pity and fear effecting the proper purgation of these emotions. By "language embellished," I mean language into which rhythm, "harmony," and song enter. By "the several kinds in separate parts," I mean, that some parts are rendered through the medium of verse alone, others again with the aid of song.

Now as tragic imitation implies persons acting, it necessarily follows, in the first place, that Spectacular equipment will be a part of Tragedy. Next, Song and Diction, for these are the medium of imitation. By "Diction" I mean the mere metrical arrangement of the words: as for "Song," it is a term whose sense every one understands.

Again, Tragedy is the imitation of an action; and an action implies personal agents, who necessarily possess certain distinctive qualities both of character and thought; for it is by these that we qualify actions themselves, and these—thought and character—are the two natural causes from which actions spring, and on actions again all success or failure depends. Hence, the Plot is the imitation of the action:—for by plot I here mean the arrangement of the incidents. By Character I mean that in virtue of which we ascribe certain qualities to the agents. Thought is required wherever a statement is proved, or, it may be, a general truth enunciated. Every Tragedy, therefore, must have six parts, which parts determine its quality— namely, Plot, Character, Diction, Thought, Spectacle, Song. Two of the parts constitute the medium of imitation, one the manner, and three the objects of imitation. And these complete the list. These elements have been employed, we may say, by the poets to a man; in fact, every play contains Spectacular elements as well as Character, Plot, Diction, Song, and Thought.

But most important of all is the structure of the incidents. For Tragedy is an imitation, not of men, but of an action and of life,

From *Aristotle's Theory of Poetry and Fine Art,* Fourth Edition, ed. S. H. Butcher. Copyright 1920 by Macmillan & Co., Ltd.

and life consists in action, and its end is a mode of action, not a quality. Now character determines men's qualities, but it is by their actions that they are happy or the reverse. Dramatic action, therefore, is not with a view to the representation of character: character comes in as subsidiary to the actions. Hence the incidents and the plot are the end of a tragedy; and the end is the chief thing of all. Again, without action there cannot be a tragedy; there may be without character. The tragedies of most of our modern poets fail in the rendering of character; and of poets in general this is often true. It is the same in painting; and here lies the difference between Zeuxis and Polygnotus. Polygnotus delineates character well: the style of Zeuxis is devoid of ethical quality. Again, if you string together a set of speeches expressive of character, and well finished in point of diction and thought, you will not produce the essential tragic effect nearly so well as with a play which, however deficient in these respects, yet has a plot and artistically constructed incidents. Besides which, the most powerful elements of emotional interest in Tragedy —Peripeteia or Reversal of the situation, and Recognition scenes— are parts of the plot. A further proof is, that novices in the art attain to finish of diction and precision of portraiture before they can construct the plot. It is the same with almost all the early poets.

The Plot, then, is the first principle, and, as it were, the soul of a tragedy: Character holds the second place. A similar fact is seen in painting. The most beautiful colours, laid on confusedly, will not give as much pleasure as the chalk outline of a portrait. Thus Tragedy is the imitation of an action, and of the agents mainly with a view to the action.

Third in order is Thought,—that is, the faculty of saying what is possible and pertinent in given circumstances. In the case of oratory, this is the function of the political art and of the art of rhetoric: and so indeed the older poets make their characters speak the language of civic life; the poets of our time, the language of the rhetoricians.

Character is that which reveals moral purpose, showing what kind of things a man chooses or avoids. Speeches, therefore, which do not make this manifest, or in which the speaker does not choose or avoid anything whatever, are not expressive of character. Thought, on the other hand, is found where something is proved to be or not to be, or a general maxim is enunciated.

Fourth among the elements enumerated comes Diction; by which I mean, as has been already said, the expression of the meaning in words; and its essence is the same both in verse and prose.

Of the remaining elements Song holds the chief place among the embellishments.

The Spectacle has, indeed, an emotional attraction of its own, but, of all the parts, it is the least artistic, and connected least with the art of poetry. For the power of Tragedy, we may be sure, is felt even apart from representation and actors. Besides, the production of spectacular effects depends more on the art of the stage machinist than on that of the poet.

[THE MEANING OF PLOT]

These principles being established, let us now discuss the proper structure of the Plot, since this is the first and most important thing in Tragedy.

Now, according to our definition, Tragedy is an imitation of an action that is complete, and whole, and of a certain magnitude; for there may be a whole that is wanting in magnitude. A whole is that which has a beginning, a middle, and an end. A beginning is that which does not itself follow anything by causal necessity, but after which something naturally is or comes to be. An end, on the contrary, is that which itself naturally follows some other thing, either by necessity, or as a rule, but has nothing following it. A middle is that which follows something as some other thing follows it. A well constructed plot, therefore, must neither begin nor end at haphazard, but conform to these principles.

Again, a beautiful object, whether it be a picture of a living organism or any whole composed of parts, must not only have an orderly arrangement of parts, but must also be of a certain magnitude; for beauty depends on magnitude and order. Hence an exceedingly small picture cannot be beautiful; for the view of it is confused, the object being seen in an almost imperceptible moment of time. Nor, again, can one of vast size be beautiful; for as the eye cannot take it all in at once, the unity and sense of the whole is lost for the spectator; as for instance if there were one a thousand miles long. As, therefore, in the case of animate bodies and organisms a certain magnitude is necessary, and a magnitude which may be easily embraced in one view; so in the plot, a certain length is necessary, and a length which can be easily embraced by the memory. The limit of length in relation to dramatic competition and sensuous presentment, is no part of artistic theory. For had it been the rule for a hundred tragedies to compete together, the performance would have been regulated by the water-clock,—as indeed we are told was formerly done. But the limit as fixed by the nature of the drama itself is this:—the greater the length, the more beautiful will the piece be by reason of its size, provided that the whole be perspicuous. And to define the matter roughly, we may say that the proper magnitude is comprised within such limits, that the sequence of events, according to the law of probability or necessity, will admit of a change from bad fortune to good, or from good fortune to bad.

Unity of plot does not, as some persons think, consist in the unity of the hero. For infinitely various are the incidents in one man's life, which cannot be reduced to unity; and so, too, there are many actions of one man out of which we cannot make one action. Hence the error, as it appears, of all poets who have composed a Heracleid, a Theseid, or other poems of the kind. They imagine that as Heracles was one man, the story of Heracles must also be a unity. But Homer, as in all else he is of surpassing merit, here too—whether from art or natural genius—seems to have happily discerned the truth. In composing the Odyssey he did not include all the adventures of Odysseus—such as his wound on Parnassus, or his feigned madness at the mustering of the host—incidents between which there was no necessary or probable connexion: but he made the Odyssey, and likewise the Iliad, to centre round an action that in our sense of the word is one. As therefore, in the other imitative arts, the imitation is one when the object imitated is one, so the plot, being an imitation of an action, must imitate one action and that a whole, the structural union of the parts being such that, if any one of them is displaced or removed, the whole will be disjointed and disturbed. For a thing whose presence or absence makes no visible difference, is not an organic part of the whole.

[THE PARTS OF A PLOT]

The parts of Tragedy which must be treated as elements of the whole, have been already mentioned. We now come to the quantitative parts—the separate parts into which Tragedy is divided—namely, Prologue, Episode, Exode, Choric song; this last being divided into Parode and Stasimon. These are common to all plays: peculiar to some are the songs of actors from the stage and the Commoi.

The Prologue is that entire part of a tragedy which precedes the Parode of the Chorus. The Episode is that entire part of a tragedy which is between complete choric songs. The Exode is that entire part of a tragedy which has no choric song after it. Of the Choric part the Parode is the first undivided utterance of the Chorus: the

Stasimon is a Choric ode without anapaests or trochaic tetrameters: the Commos is a joint lamentation of Chorus and actors.

[THE PERFECT TRAGEDY]

A perfect tragedy should, as we have seen, be arranged not on the simple but on the complex plan. It should, moreover, imitate actions which excite pity and fear, this being the distinctive mark of tragic imitation. It follows plainly, in the first place, that the change of fortune presented must not be the spectacle of a virtuous man brought from prosperity to adversity: for this moves neither pity nor fear; it merely shocks us. Nor, again, that of a bad man passing from adversity to prosperity: for nothing can be more alien to the spirit of Tragedy; it possesses no single tragic quality; it neither satisfies the moral sense, nor calls forth pity or fear. Nor, again, should the downfall of the utter villain be exhibited. A plot of this kind would, doubtless, satisfy the moral sense, but it would inspire neither pity nor fear; for pity is aroused by unmerited misfortune, fear by the misfortune of a man like ourselves. Such an event, therefore, will be neither pitiful nor terrible. There remains, then, the character between these two extremes,—that of a man who is not eminently good and just, yet whose misfortune is brought about not by vice or depravity, but by some error or frailty. He must be one who is highly renowned and prosperous,—a personage like Oedipus, Thyestes, or other illustrious men of such families.

Author and Selection Notes

One of the most seminal minds of all time, Aristotle (384-322 B.C.) made original contributions in almost every field of thought: mathematics, psychology, logic, ethics, rhetoric, metaphysics, and in many of the physical and natural sciences. Aristotle's *Poetics*—perhaps the most famous critical document in literary history—is concerned primarily with the nature of Greek tragedy, though, as its title implies, it discusses other forms of poetry as well, including the lyric and the epic.

Questions and Exercises

1. How would you characterize Aristotle's style? Eloquent? Dry? Dull? Explain your choice.

2. In his definition of the perfect tragedy, Aristotle uses or implies four famous terms: "imitation," "catharsis," "tragic hero," and "tragic flaw." Look these up in a dictionary of literary terms or some other source and summarize your findings in a paragraph.

3. According to Aristotle, what are the six parts of a tragedy? Explain in your own words what these terms mean.

4. Note Aristotle's famous statement relative to tragedy as having a beginning, a middle, and an end. Choose one of the topics in No. 6 below and make an outline for a possible theme in which the Introduction ("beginning"), Body ("middle"), and Conclusion ("end") are clearly indicated.

5. Read "Riders to the Sea" and write a theme showing how it illustrates Aristotle's rules for a tragedy.

6. Theme Topics: A Modern Tragedy I Have Seen; Tragic Drama Has Changed Since Aristotle; My Definition of a Tragedy.

THE HORN

I was an armed warrior, but now
The youthful courtier covers my proud neck
With twisted filigree of gold and silver.
Sometimes I'm kissed by heroes, and again
I woo to battle with my melody   5
Comrades in full accord. At times the courser
Bears me across the border, and again
Over the floods the stallion of the sea
Conveys me radiant with ornaments.
Sometimes a maiden, garlanded with jewels,   10
Brims full my winding bosom, and again
Perforce I lie—hard, headless, solitary
Upon the board. Sometimes, set off with trappings,
In comely guise upon the wall I hang
Where heroes drink. Again, horsed warriors   15
On forays wear me, glorious apparel;
Then, dappled with gold, I must inspire the wind
From some one's bosom. Whilom stately men
I summon to banquetings and wine; sometimes
My voice resounds with freedom to the captive,   20
Flight to the foe. Now find out what I'm called.

Author and Selection Notes

"The Horn" is one of nearly a hundred anonymous riddle poems that have been preserved from the eighth century, the golden age of Old

From *Select Translations from Old English Poetry* by Albert S. Cook and Chauncey B. Tinker, copyright 1926, 1930. Translated by Herbert B. Brougham. Reprinted by permission of the publisher, Harvard University Press.

English verse. Though these reflect to some extent earlier Latin riddles on which they are modeled, they are essentially English in subject matter and attitude, and, like "The Horn," vividly concrete in image and detail.

Questions and Exercises

1. This eighth-century, Old English verse-riddle has been praised for "its continuous spirit of personification and ingenious interweaving of clues." Cite details in the poem illustrating this description. If the title of the riddle had not been given, at what point would you have been able to solve the riddle?

2. Is the type of horn described in this poem a work of art? Support your opinion.

3. Explain: "I was an armed warrior"; "The stallion of the sea"; "Sometimes a maiden, garlanded with jewels, / Brims full my winding bosom."

4. Explain why the poet uses the first person rather than the third person in the poem.

5. Look up the word "soliloquy." Is the word an accurate description of the poem? Why or why not?

6. Explain to your own satisfaction why the author of this riddle chose to put it into verse form rather than into prose.

7. Theme Topics: Art and Artifacts; The Psychology of the Riddle; The Horn in Fact and Fiction; The Horn as a Part of Military Life Today; Riddles Are Still Popular Today; Why Children Enjoy Riddles.

THE COMPLAINT OF CHAUCER TO HIS PURSE
Geoffrey Chaucer

To yow, my purse, and to noon other wight
Complayne I, for ye be my lady dere!
I am so sory, now that ye been lyght;
For certes, but ye make me hevy chere,
Me were as leef be layd upon my bere;
For which unto your mercy thus I crye:
Beth hevy ageyn, or elles mot I dye!

Now voucheth sauf this day, or yt be nyght,
That I of yow the blisful soun may here,
Or see your colour lyk the sonne bryght,
That of yelownesse hadde never pere.
Ye be my lyf, ye be myn hertes stere,

Quene of comfort and of good companye:
Beth hevy ageyn, or elles moote I dye!

Now purse, that ben to me my lyves lyght
And saveour, as doun in this world here,
Out of this toune helpe me thurgh your myght,
Syn that ye wole nat ben my tresorere;
For I am shave as nye as any frere.
But yet I pray unto your curtesye:
Beth hevy agen, or elles moote I dye!

LENVOY DE CHAUCER

O conquerour of Brutes Albyon,
Which that by lyne and free eleccion
Been verray kyng, this song to yow I sende;
And ye, that mowen alle oure harmes amende,
Have mynde upon my supplicacion!

Author and Selection Notes

Although Geoffrey Chaucer (c. 1340-1400) is better known for his *Canterbury Tales*, his minor poems such as this one offer an equal insight on a smaller scale into the humanity, the wit, and the artistry that characterize his work in general. The poem illustrates rather wittily the tradition of literary patronage, under which a writer is supported in whole or part by a king or noble or other wealthy patron of the arts.

Questions and Exercises

1. Is the general tone of this poem serious or humorous? Support your point of view by specific references to the details of the poem.

2. What does Chaucer mean in stanza one by calling his purse "my lady dere"; in stanza two by the phrase "the blisful soun"; in stanza three by the line "For I am shave as nye as any frere"?

3. What seems to be the purpose of the "Envoy" to Chaucer's poem? Explain in a paragraph.

4. What is peculiar about the last line of each of the first three stanzas? How is such a line usually classified?

5. Look up the word "ballade" in a dictionary or literary handbook, and in a paragraph show how Chaucer's poem fits the description of this form of verse.

6. As a college student in dire need of money, whether it be for tuition, food, or the next dance, write a complaint to your purse or wallet and indicate in the envoy that your song is directed to whoever is helping you with college finances.

7. Theme Topics: The Minor Poems of Chaucer; Chaucer as a Literary Artist; Chaucer and His Age; Literary Patronage Today; Should the Government Help Finance Our Young Artists?

ALEXANDER'S FEAST; OR, THE POWER OF MUSIC

A Song in Honor of St. Cecilia's Day

John Dryden

'Twas at the royal feast, for Persia won
By Philip's warlike son:
Aloft in awful state
The godlike hero sate
On his imperial throne;   5
His valiant peers were placed around;
Their brows with roses and with myrtles bound:
(So should desert in arms be crowned.)
The lovely Thais, by his side,
Sate like a blooming Eastern bride,   10
In flower of youth and beauty's pride.
Happy, happy, happy pair!
None but the brave,
None but the brave,
None but the brave deserves the fair.   15

CHORUS

Happy, happy, happy pair!
None but the brave,
None but the brave,
None but the brave deserves the fair.

Timotheus, placed on high   20
Amid the tuneful quire,
With flying fingers touched the lyre:
The trembling notes ascend the sky,
And heavenly joys inspire.
The song began from Jove,   25
Who left his blissful seats above,
(Such is the power of mighty love.)

A dragon's fiery form belied the god:
Sublime on radiant spires he rode,
When he to fair Olympia pressed;   30
And while he sought her snowy breast,
Then round her slender waist he curled,
And stamped an image of himself, a sovereign of the world.
The listening crowd admire the lofty sound,
"A present deity," they shout around;   35
"A present deity," the vaulted roofs rebound:
With ravished ears
The monarch hears,
Assumes the god,
Affects to nod,   40
And seems to shake the spheres.

CHORUS

With ravished ears
The monarch hears,
Assumes the god,
Affects to nod,   45
And seems to shake the spheres.

The praise of Bacchus then the sweet musician sung,
Of Bacchus ever fair, and ever young.
The jolly god in triumph comes;
Sound the trumpets, beat the drums;   50
Flushed with a purple grace
He shows his honest face:
Now give the hautboys breath; he comes, he comes.
Bacchus, ever fair and young,
Drinking joys did first ordain;   55
Bacchus' blessings are a treasure,
Drinking is the soldier's pleasure;
Rich the treasure,
Sweet the pleasure,
Sweet is pleasure after pain.   60

CHORUS

Bacchus' blessings are a treasure,
Drinking is the soldier's pleasure;
Rich the treasure,
Sweet the pleasure,
Sweet is pleasure after pain.   65

Soothed with the sound the king grew vain;
Fought all his battles o'er again;
And thrice he routed all his foes, and thrice he slew the slain.
The master saw the madness rise,
His glowing cheeks, his ardent eyes;   70
And while he heaven and earth defied,
Changed his hand, and checked his pride.
He chose a mournful Muse,
Soft pity to infuse;
He sung Darius great and good,   75
By too severe a fate,
Fallen, fallen, fallen, fallen,
Fallen from his high estate,
And weltering in his blood;
Deserted at his utmost need   80
By those his former bounty fed;
On the bare earth exposed he lies,
With not a friend to close his eyes.

With downcast looks the joyless victor sate,
Revolving in his altered soul   85
The various turns of chance below;
And, now and then, a sigh he stole,
And tears began to flow.

CHORUS

Revolving in his altered soul
The various turns of chance below;
And, now and then, a sigh he stole,   90
And tears began to flow.

The mighty master smiled to see
That love was in the next degree;
'Twas but a kindred sound to move,
For pity melts the mind to love.   95
Softly sweet, in Lydian measures,
Soon he soothed his soul to pleasures.
"War," he sung, "is toil and trouble;
Honor but an empty bubble;   100
Never ending, still beginning,
Fighting still, and still destroying:
If the world be worth thy winning,
Think, O think it worth enjoying:

Lovely Thais sits beside thee, 105
Take the good the gods provide thee."

The many rend the skies with loud applause;
So Love was crowned, but Music won the cause.
The prince, unable to conceal his pain,
Gazed on the fair 110
Who caused his care,
And sighed and looked, sighed and looked,
Sighed and looked, and sighed again;
At length, with love and wine at once oppressed,
The vanquished victor sunk upon her breast. 115

CHORUS

The prince, unable to conceal his pain,
Gazed on the fair
Who caused his care,
And sighed and looked, sighed and looked,
Sighed and looked, and sighed again; 120
At length, with love and wine at once oppressed,
The vanquished victor sunk upon her breast.

Now strike the golden lyre again;
A louder yet, and yet a louder strain.
Break his bands of sleep asunder, 125
And rouse him, like a rattling peal of thunder.
Hark, hark, the horrid sound
Has raised up his head;
As awaked from the dead,
And, amazed, he stares around. 130
"Revenge, revenge!" Timotheus cries;
"See the Furies arise;
See the snakes that they rear,
How they hiss in their hair,
And the sparkles that flash from their eyes? 135
Behold a ghastly band,
Each a torch in his hand!
Those are Grecian ghosts, that in battle were slain,
And unburied remain
Inglorious on the plain. 140
Give the vengeance due
To the valiant crew.
Behold how they toss their torches on high,

How they point to the Persian abodes,
And glittering temples of their hostile gods!"   145
The princes applaud with a furious joy;
And the king seized a flambeau with zeal to destroy;
Thais led the way,
To light him to his prey,
And, like another Helen, fired another Troy.   150

CHORUS

And the king seized a flambeau with zeal to destroy;
Thais led the way,
To light him to his prey,
And, like another Helen, fired another Troy.

Thus long ago,   155
Ere heaving bellows learned to blow,
While organs yet were mute,
Timotheus, to his breathing flute
And sounding lyre,
Could swell the soul to rage, or kindle soft desire.   160
At last divine Cecilia came,
Inventress of the vocal frame;
The sweet enthusiast, from her sacred store,
Enlarged the former narrow bounds,
And added length to solemn sounds,   165
With Nature's mother wit, and arts unknown before.
Let old Timotheus yield the prize,
Or both divide the crown:
He raised a mortal to the skies;
She drew an angel down.   170

GRAND CHORUS

At last divine Cecilia came,
Inventress of the vocal frame;
The sweet enthusiast, from her sacred store
Enlarged the former narrow bounds,
And added length to solemn sounds,   175
With Nature's mother wit, and arts unknown before.
Let old Timotheus yield the prize,
Or both divide the crown:
He raised a mortal to the skies;
She drew an angel down.   180

Author and Selection Notes

This poem was written by John Dryden (1631-1700) for a London music society to celebrate the birth date (November 22) of St. Cecilia, patron saint of music. Critic, political and literary satirist, dramatist, and lyricist, Dryden was literary dictator of an age in which reason and common sense were dominant. Alexander the Great, subject of the poem, defeated Darius, King of Persia, in 330 B.C.

Questions and Exercises

1. Look up the definition of "ode" in a dictionary or handbook of literature and show in detail how this poem illustrates the form. Compare it in its technical aspects with Joseph Addison's "Ode" and with John Keats' "Ode on a Grecian Urn." Which of the three seems to you to be closest to the definition?

2. Describe the basic situation of the poem.

3. Identify the chief characters by listing a few descriptive phrases for each.

4. Look up the following classical names: "Jove," "Olympia," "Bacchus," "Helen," the "Furies"; and the following terms: "the Spheres," "Lydian measures," "hautboy," "flambeau."

5. Explain why Alexander is hailed as "a present deity."

6. Describe each of the various moods which the music of the harpist Timotheus raises in King Alexander.

7. Why does the poet feel that Timotheus should share the crown with St. Cecilia?

8. Compare the situation in this poem with that in the short story "The Portable Phonograph." In what respects does the situation in the story reveal a similar power of art in human affairs? Write a paragraph summarizing your findings.

9. Theme Topics: The Power of Music; Music in Human Experience; The Song I Love Best; The Kind of Music I Enjoy Most.

ON RAPHAEL'S CARTOONS AT HAMPTON-COURT

Richard Steele

Mutum est pictura poema.—Hor.

I have very often lamented and hinted my sorrow in several speculations, that the art of painting is made so little use of to the improvement of our manners. When we consider that it places the action of the person represented in the most agreeable aspect imaginable, that it does not only express the passion or concern as it sits upon him who is drawn, but has under those features the height of the painter's imagination, what strong images of virtue and humanity might we not expect would be instilled into the mind from the labours of the pencil? This is a poetry which would be understood with much less capacity, and less expense of time, than what is taught by writings; but the use of it is generally perverted, and that admirable skill prostituted to the basest and most unworthy ends. Who is the better man for beholding the most beautiful Venus, the best wrought Bacchanal, the images of sleeping Cupids, languishing nymphs, or any of the representations of gods, goddesses, demigods, satyrs, Polyphemes, sphinxes, or fauns? But if the virtues and vices which are sometimes pretended to be represented under such draughts, were given us by the painter in the characters of real life, and the persons of men and women whose actions have rendered them laudable or infamous, we should not see a good history-piece without receiving an instructive lecture. There needs no other proof of this truth, than the testimony of every reasonable creature who has seen the cartoons in her Majesty's gallery at Hampton Court: these are representations of no less actions than those of our blessed Saviour and His apostles. As I now sit and recollect the warm images which the admirable Raphael has raised, it is impossible, even from the faint traces in one's memory of what one has not seen these two years, to be unmoved at the horror and reverence which appears in the whole assembly when the mercenary man fell down dead; at the amazement of the man born blind, when he first receives sight; or at the graceless indignation of the sorcerer, when he is struck blind. The lame, when they first find strength in their feet, stand doubtful of their new vigour. The heavenly apostles appear acting these great things, with a deep sense of the infirmities which they relieve, but no value of themselves who administer to their weakness. They know themselves to be but instruments; and the generous distress they are painted in when divine honours are offered to them, is a representation in the most exquisite degree of the beauty of holiness. When St. Paul is preaching to the Athenians, with what wonderful art are almost all the different tempers of mankind represented in that elegant audience? You see one credulous of all that is said, another wrapped up in deep suspense, another saying there is some reason in what he says, another angry that the Apostle destroys a favourite opinion which he is unwilling to give up, another wholly convinced and holding out his hands in rapture; while the generality attend, and wait for the opinion of those who are of leading characters in the assembly. I will not pretend so much as to mention that chart on which is drawn the appearance of our blessed Lord after His Resurrection. Present authority, late suffering, humility, and majesty, despotic command and divine love, are at once seated in His celestial aspect. The figures of the eleven apostles are all in the same passion of admiration, but discover it differently according to their characters. Peter receives his Master's orders on his knees, with an admiration mixed with a more particular attention; the two next with a more open ecstasy, though still constrained by the awe of the Divine Presence; the beloved disciple, whom I take to be the right of the two first figures, has in his countenance wonder drowned in love; and the last personage, whose back is towards the spectator and his side towards the Presence, one would fancy to be St Thomas, as abashed by the conscience of his former diffidence; which perplexed concern it is possible Raphael thought too hard a task to draw but by this acknowledgment of the difficulty to describe it.

The whole work is an exercise of the highest piety in the painter; and all the touches of a religious mind are expressed in a manner much more forcible than can possibly be performed by the most moving eloquence. These invaluable pieces are very justly in the hands of the greatest and most pious sovereign in the world, and cannot be the frequent object of every one at their own leisure: but as an engraver is to the painter what a printer is to an author, it is worthy her Majesty's name that she has encouraged that noble artist, Monsieur Dorigny, to publish these works of Raphael. We have of this gentleman a piece of the Transfiguration, which is held a work second to none in the world.

Methinks it would be ridiculous in our people of condition, after their large bounties to foreigners of no name or merit, should they overlook this occasion of having, for a trifling subscription, a work which it is impossible for a man of sense to behold, without being warmed with the noblest sentiments that can be inspired by love, admiration, compassion, contempt of this world, and expectation of a better.

It is certainly the greatest honour we can do our country, to distinguish strangers of merit who apply to us with modesty and diffidence, which generally accompanies merit. No opportunity of this kind ought to be neglected; and a modest behaviour should alarm us to examine whether we do not lose something excellent under that disadvantage in the possessor of that quality. My skill in paintings, where one is not directed by the passion of the pictures, is so inconsiderable, that I am in very great perplexity when I offer to speak of any performances of painters of landscapes, buildings, or single figures. This makes me at a loss how to mention the pieces which Mr. Boul exposes to sale by auction on Wednesday next in Chandos Street. But having heard him commended by those who have bought of him heretofore for great integrity in his dealing, and overheard him himself (though a laudable painter) say nothing of his own was fit to come into the room with those he had to sell, I feared I should lose an occasion of serving a man of worth in omitting to speak of his auction.

ADVERTISEMENT.

There is arrived from Italy a Painter who acknowledges himself the greatest person of the age in that art, and is willing to be as renowned in this island as he declares he is in foreign parts.

The Doctor paints the poor for nothing.

T.

Author and Selection Notes

The name of Richard Steele (1672-1729) is inseparably linked with that of Joseph Addison as co-author of *The Spectator*, one of the series of eighteenth-century periodical essays marking the rise of the modern newspaper. In addition to his work as an essayist, Steele edited *The Gazette*, the official publication of the government, and wrote numerous successful comedies for the stage.

Steele's contributions to *The Spectator*, usually signed with an "R" or a "T," frequently show a practical and moral bias, as in this essay. The Monsieur Dorigny mentioned in the essay is Nicola Dorigny, son of a well-known contemporary French painter and teacher, who was at this time offering a proposed series of engravings of the Raphael cartoons to the public by subscription.

Questions and Exercises

1. Do you feel that this essay reflects a practical and moral bias? Cite passages to support your answer.

2. To what use would Steele like to put art? Do you feel that this attitude toward art is a good one? Defend your opinion.

3. Explain the statement "This is a poetry which would be understood with much less capacity, and less expense of time, than what is taught by writings."

4. Identify the following terms: "Bacchanal," "demigod," "satyr," "Polyphemes," "sphinx," "faun."

5. Describe the type of art which the author feels to be unworthy of the artist's efforts.

6. What type of scenes are portrayed in the cartoons in her Majesty's gallery at Hampton Court? List some of the subjects of these paintings.

7. What qualities appear in the representation of Christ after His resurrection? In the representation of the disciples?

8. The essay concludes with an "Advertisement," which apparently refers to the art dealer Philip Boul, who was also a painter in a small way, and whose advertisement of an auction of old Italian paintings and drawings appeared in the same sheets in which Steele's essay was printed and distributed. Are Steele's concluding comments about Boul, and the "Advertisement," meant to be serious or satiric? Defend your point of view.

9. Look up the definition of "essay" in a dictionary of literary terms and list the basic characteristics given; then point out how this selection fits the description.

10. Theme Topics: Teaching Religion Through Art; Art as a Moral Force; Art in Everyday Life; My Favorite Religious Painting; Art for Art's Sake.

ODE ON A GRECIAN URN

John Keats

Thou still unravished bride of quietness,
Thou foster-child of Silence and slow Time,
Sylvan historian, who canst thus express
A flowery tale more sweetly than our rhyme:
What leaf-fringed legend haunts about thy shape
Of deities or mortals, or of both,
In Tempe or the dales of Arcady?
What men or gods are these? What maidens loath?
What mad pursuit? What struggle to escape?
What pipes and timbrels? What wild ecstasy?

Heard melodies are sweet, but those unheard
Are sweeter; therefore, ye soft pipes, play on;
Not to the sensual ear, but, more endeared
Pipe to the spirit ditties of no tone:
Fair youth, beneath the trees, thou canst not leave
Thy song, nor ever can those trees be bare;

Bold Lover, never, never canst thou kiss,
Though winning near the goal—yet, do not grieve;
She cannot fade, though thou hast not thy bliss,
For ever wilt thou love, and she be fair!

Ah, happy, happy boughs! that cannot shed
Your leaves, nor ever bid the Spring adieu;
And, happy melodist, unwearied,
For ever piping songs for ever new.
More happy love! more happy, happy love!
For ever warm and still to be enjoyed,
For ever panting, and for ever young;
All breathing human passion far above,
That leaves a heart high-sorrowful and cloyed,
A burning forehead, and a parching tongue.

Who are these coming to the sacrifice?
To what green altar, O mysterious priest,
Lead'st thou that heifer lowing at the skies,
And all her silken flanks with garlands drest?
What little town by river or sea shore,
Or mountain-built with peaceful citadel,
Is emptied of this folk, this pious morn?
And, little town, thy streets for evermore
Will silent be; and not a soul to tell
Why thou art desolate, can e'er return.

O Attic shape! Fair attitude! with brede
Of marble men and maidens overwrought,
With forest branches and the trodden weed;
Thou, silent form! dost tease us out of thought
As doth eternity: Cold Pastoral!
When old age shall this generation waste,
Thou shalt remain, in midst of other woe
Than ours, a friend to man, to whom thou say'st,
"Beauty is truth, truth beauty,"—that is all
Ye know on earth, and all ye need to know.

Author and Selection Notes

As a poet John Keats (1795-1821) fought both against the early hostile
reception of his work and against the ravages of tuberculosis long enough
to complete such fine poems as the sonnet "On First Looking into Chap-

man's Homer," the verse tale "The Eve of St. Agnes," and the series of
great odes of which the selection in this text is perhaps the most familiar.
The basic philosophy underlying "Ode on a Grecian Urn" is that of
Plato, for whom true reality existed only in a realm of absolute patterns
lying beyond the sensory world.

Questions and Exercises

1. What is Keats' theory about the nature of beauty, and where is it
most specifically stated in the poem?

2. What basically does the Grecian urn symbolize for Keats in the poem?
Write a paragraph.

3. Explain the following phrases: "unravished bride of quietness,"
"foster child of silence and slow time," "Sylvan historian," "Attic Shape,"

4. What does the poet mean by the lines "Heard melodies are sweet, but
those unheard/Are sweeter"?

5. What does the poet mean when he addresses the urn as "Cold
Pastoral"?

6. Explain the lines "Thou, silent form! dost tease us out of thought/As
doth eternity."

7. Compare this ode in form and technique with John Dryden's "Alexander's Feast."

8. Theme Topics: Definitions of Beauty; Our Art Heritage from Greece;
Keats' Concept of Truth and Beauty; Ceramic Art; My Concept of Beauty.

FRANCE IS A BEWITCHING GARDEN
Mark Twain

We have come five hundred miles by rail through the heart of
France. What a bewitching land it is! What a garden! Surely
the leagues of bright green lawns are swept and brushed and
watered every day and their grasses trimmed by the barber. Surely
the hedges are shaped and measured and their symmetry preserved by the most architectural of gardeners. Surely the long,
straight rows of stately poplars that divide the beautiful landscape
like the squares of a checker-board are set with line and plummet,
and their uniform height determined with a spirit level. Surely
the straight, smooth, pure white turnpikes are jack-planed and
sand papered every day. How else are these marvels of symmetry,
cleanliness, and order attained? It is wonderful. There are no unsightly stone walls, and never a fence of any kind. There is no dirt,

From *The Innocents Abroad* by Mark Twain. Reprinted with the permission
of Harper and Row, Publishers, Incorporated.

no decay, no rubbish anywhere—nothing that even hints at untidiness—nothing that ever suggests neglect. All is orderly and beautiful—everything is charming to the eye.

We had such glimpses of the Rhone gliding along between its grassy banks; of cozy cottages buried in flowers and shrubbery; of quaint old red-tiled villages with mossy medieval cathedrals looming out of their midst; of wooded hills with ivy-grown towers and turrets of feudal castles projecting above the foliage; such glimpses of Paradise, it seemed to us, such visions of fabled fairyland!

We knew, then, what the poet meant, when he sang of—

> "—thy corn-fields green, and sunny vines,
> O pleasant land of France!"

And it *is* a pleasant land. No word described it so felicitously as that one. They say there is no word for "home" in the French language. Well, considering that they have the article itself in such an attractive aspect, they ought to manage to get along without the word. Let us not waste too much pity on "homeless" France. I have observed that Frenchmen abroad seldom wholly give up the idea of going back to France some time or other. I am not surprised at it now.

We are not infatuated with these French railway-cars, though. We took first-class passage, not because we wished to attract attention by doing a thing which is uncommon in Europe, but because we could make our journey quicker by so doing. It is hard to make railroading pleasant, in any country. It is too tedious. Stage-coaching is infinitely more delightful. Once I crossed the plains and deserts and mountains of the West, in a stage-coach, from the Missouri line to California, and since then all my pleasure trips must be measured to that rare holiday frolic. Two thousand miles of ceaseless rush and rattle and clatter, by night and by day, and never a weary moment, never a lapse of interest! The first seven hundred miles a level continent, its grassy carpet greener and softer and smoother than any sea, and figured with designs fitted to its magnitude—the shadows of the clouds. Here were no scenes but summer scenes, and no disposition inspired by them but to lie at full length on the mail-sacks, in the grateful breeze, and dreamily smoke the pipe of peace—what other, where all was repose and contentment? In cool mornings, before the sun was fairly up, it was worth a lifetime of city toiling and moiling, to perch in the foretop with the driver and see the six mustangs scamper under the sharp snapping of a whip that never touched them; to scan the blue distances of a world that knew no lords but us; to cleave the wind with uncovered head and feel the sluggish pulses rousing to the spirit of a speed that pretended to the resistless rush of a typhoon! Then thirteen hundred miles of desert solitudes; of limitless panoramas of bewildering perspective; of mimic cities, of pinnacled cathedrals, of massive fortresses, counterfeited in the eternal rocks and splendid with the crimson and gold of the setting sun; of dizzy altitudes among fog-wreathed peaks and never-melting snows, where thunders and lightnings and tempests warred magnificently at our feet and the storm-clouds above swung their shredded banners in our very faces!

But I forgot. I am in elegant France, now, and not scurrying through the great South Pass and Wind River Mountains, among antelopes and buffaloes, and painted Indians on the war-path. It is not meet that I should make too disparaging comparisons between humdrum travel on a railway and that royal summer flight across a continent in a stage-coach. I meant, in the beginning, to say that railway journeying is tedious and tiresome, and so it is—though, at the time, I was thinking particularly of a dismal fifty-hour pilgrimage between New York and St. Louis. Of course our trip through France was not really tedious, because all its scenes and experiences were new and strange; but as Dan says, it had its "discrepancies."

The cars are built in compartments that hold eight persons each. Each compartment is partially subdivided, and so there are two tolerably distinct parties of four in it. Four face the other four. The seats and backs are thickly padded and cushioned, and are very comfortable; you can smoke, if you wish; there are no bothersome peddlers; you are saved the infliction of a multitude of disagreeable fellow-passengers. So far, so well. But then the conductor locks you in when the train starts; there is no water to drink in the car; there is no heating apparatus for night travel; if a drunken rowdy should get in, you could not remove a matter of twenty seats from him, or enter another car; but, above all, if you are worn out and must sleep, you must sit up and do it in naps, with cramped legs and in a torturing misery that leaves you withered and lifeless the next day —for behold, they have not that culmination of all charity and human kindness, a sleeping-car, in all France. I prefer the American system. It has not so many grievous "discrepancies."

In France, all is clockwork, all is order. They make no mistakes. Every third man wears a uniform, and whether he be a marshal of the empire or a brakeman, he is ready and perfectly willing to answer all your questions with tireless politeness, ready to tell you which car to take, yea, and ready to go and put you into it to make sure that you shall not go astray. You cannot pass into the waiting-room of the depot till you have secured your ticket, and you cannot pass from its only exit till the train is at its threshold to receive you. Once on board, the train will not start till your ticket has been examined—till every passenger's ticket has been inspected. This is chiefly for your own good. If by any possibility you have managed to take the wrong train, you will be handed over to a polite official who will take you whither you belong, and bestow you with many an affable bow. Your ticket will be inspected every now and then along the route, and when it is time to change cars you will know it. You are in the hands of officials who zealously study your welfare and your interest, instead of turning their talents to the invention of new methods of discommoding and snubbing you, as is very often the main employment of that exceedingly self-satisfied monarch, the railroad conductor of America.

But the happiest regulation in French railway government, is— thirty minutes to dinner! No five-minute boltings of flabby rolls, muddy coffee, questionable eggs, gutta-percha beef, and pies whose conception and execution are a dark and bloody mystery to all save the cook who created them! No; we sat calmly down—it was in old Dijon, which is so easy to spell and so impossible to pronounce, except when you civilize it and call it Demijohn—and poured out rich Burgundian wines and munched calmly through a long table d'hôte bill of fare, snail patties, delicious fruits and all, then paid the trifle it cost and stepped happily aboard the train again, without once cursing the railroad company. A rare experience, and one to be treasured forever.

They say they do not have accidents on these French roads, and I think it must be true. If I remember rightly, we passed high above wagon-roads or through tunnels under them, but never crossed them on their own level. About every quarter of a mile, it seemed to me, a man came out and held up a club till the train went by, to signify that everything was safe ahead. Switches were changed a mile in advance, by pulling a wire rope that passed along the ground by the rail, from station to station. Signals for the day and signals for the night gave constant and timely notice of the position of switches.

No, they have no railroad accidents to speak of in France. But why? Because when one occurs, *somebody* has to hang for it![1] Not hang, maybe, but be punished at least with such vigor of emphasis as to make negligence a thing to be shuddered at by railroad officials for many a day thereafter. "No blame attached to the officers"—that lying and disaster-breeding verdict so common to our soft-hearted

[1] They go on the principle that it is better that one innocent man should suffer than five hundred.

juries, is seldom rendered in France. If the trouble occurred in the conductor's department, that officer must suffer if his subordinate cannot be proven guilty; if in the engineer's department, and the case be similar, the engineer must answer.

The Old Travelers—those delightful parrots who have "been here before," and know more about the country than Louis Napoleon knows now or ever will know,—tell us these things, and we believe them because they are pleasant things to believe, and because they are plausible and savor of the rigid subjection to law and order which we behold about us everywhere.

But we love the Old Travelers. We love to hear them prate and drivel and lie. We can tell them the moment we see them. They always throw out a few feelers; they never cast themselves adrift till they have sounded every individual and know that he has not traveled. Then they open their throttle-valves, and how they do brag, and sneer, and swell, and soar, and blaspheme the sacred name of Truth! Their central idea, their grand aim, is to subjugate you, keep you down, make you feel insignificant and humble in the blaze of their cosmopolitan glory! They will not let you know anything. They sneer at your most inoffensive suggestions; they laugh unfeelingly at your treasured dreams of foreign lands; they brand the statements of your traveled aunts and uncles as the stupidest absurdities; they deride your most trusted authors and demolish the fair images they have set up for your willing worship with the pitiless ferocity of the fanatic iconoclast! But still I love the Old Travelers. I love them for their witless platitudes; for their supernatural ability to bore; for their delightful asinine vanity; for their luxuriant fertility of imagination; for their startling, their brilliant, their overwhelming mendacity!

By Lyons and the Saône (where we saw the Lady of Lyons and thought little of her comeliness); by Villa Franca, Tonnerre, venerable Sens, Melun, Fontainebleau, and scores of other beautiful cities, we swept, always noting the absence of hog-wallows, broken fences, cow-lots, unpainted houses, and mud, and always noting, as well, the presence of cleanliness, grace, taste in adorning and beautifying, even to the disposition of a tree or the turning of a hedge, the marvel of roads in perfect repair, void of ruts and guiltless of even an inequality of surface—we bowled along, hour after hour, that brilliant summer day, and as nightfall approached we entered a wilderness of odorous flowers and shrubbery, sped through it, and then, excited, delighted, and half persuaded that we were only the sport of a beautiful dream, lo, we stood in magnificent Paris!

What excellent order they kept about that vast depot! There

was no frantic crowding and jostling, no shouting and swearing, and no swaggering intrusion of services by rowdy hackmen. These latter gentry stood outside—stood quietly by their long line of vehicles and said never a word. A kind of hackman-general seemed to have the whole matter of transportation in his hands. He politely received the passengers and ushered them to the kind of conveyance they wanted, and told the driver where to deliver them. There was no "talking back," no dissatisfaction about overcharging, no grumbling about anything. In a little while we were speeding through the streets of Paris, and delightfully recognizing certain names and places with which books had long ago made us familiar. It was like meeting an old friend when we read *"Rue de Rivoli"* on the street corner; we knew the genuine vast palace of the Louvre as well as we knew its picture; when we passed by the Column of July we needed no one to tell us what it was, or to remind us that on its site once stood the grim Bastile, that grave of human hopes and happiness, that dismal prison-house within whose dungeons so many young faces put on the wrinkles of age, so many proud spirits grew humble, so many brave hearts broke.

We secured rooms at the hotel, or rather, we had three beds put into one room, so that we might be together, and then we went out to a restaurant, just after lamp-lighting, and ate a comfortable, satisfactory, lingering dinner. It was a pleasure to eat where everything was so tidy, the food so well cooked, the waiters so polite, and the coming and departing company so mustached, so frisky, so affable, so fearfully and wonderfully Frenchy! All the surroundings were gay and enlivening. Two hundred people sat at little tables on the sidewalk, sipping wine and coffee; the streets were thronged with light vehicles and with joyous pleasure-seekers; there was music in the air, life and action all about us, and a conflagration of gaslight everywhere!

After dinner we felt like seeing such Parisian specialties as we might see without distressing exertion, and so we sauntered through the brilliant streets and looked at the dainty trifles in variety stores and jewelry shops. Occasionally, merely for the pleasure of being cruel, we put unoffending Frenchmen on the rack with questions framed in the incomprehensible jargon of their native language, and while they writhed, we impaled them, we peppered them, we scarified them, with their own vile verbs and participles.

We noticed that in the jewelry stores they had some of the articles marked "gold," and some labeled "imitation." We wondered at this extravagance of honesty, and inquired into the matter. We were informed that inasmuch as most people are not able to tell false gold from the genuine article, the government compels jewelers to have their gold work assayed and stamped officially according to its fineness, and their imitation work duly labeled with the sign of its falsity. They told us the jewelers would not dare to violate this law, and that whatever a stranger bought in one of their stores might be depended upon as being strictly what it was represented to be. Verily, a wonderful land is France!

Then we hunted for a barber shop. From earliest infancy it had been a cherished ambition of mine to be shaved some day in a palatial barber shop of Paris. I wished to recline at full length in a cushioned invalid-chair, with pictures about me, and sumptuous furniture; with frescoed walls and gilded arches above me, and vistas of Corinthian columns stretching far before me, with perfumes of Araby to intoxicate my senses, and the slumbrous drone of distant noises to soothe me to sleep. At the end of an hour I would wake up regretfully and find my face as smooth and as soft as an infant's. Departing, I would lift my hands above that barber's head and say, "Heaven bless you, my son!"

So we searched high and low, for a matter of two hours, but never a barber shop could we see. We saw only wig making establishments, with shocks of dead and repulsive hair bound upon the heads of painted waxen brigands who stared out from glass boxes upon the passer-by, with their stony eyes, and scared him with the ghostly white of their countenances. We shunned these signs for a time, but finally we concluded that the wig-makers must of necessity be the barbers as well, since we could find no single legitimate representative of the fraternity. We entered and asked, and found that it was even so.

I said I wanted to be shaved. The barber inquired where my room was. I said, never mind where my room was, I wanted to be shaved—there, on the spot. The doctor said he would be shaved also. Then there was an excitement among those two barbers! There was a wild consultation, and afterward a hurrying to and fro and a feverish gathering up of razors from obscure places and a ransacking for soap. Next they took us into a little mean, shabby back room; they got two ordinary sitting-room chairs and placed us in them, with our coats on. My old, old dream of bliss vanished into thin air!

I sat bolt upright, silent, sad, and solemn. One of the wig-making villains lathered my face for ten terrible minutes and finished by plastering a mass of suds into my mouth. I expelled the nasty stuff with a strong English expletive and said, "Foreigner, beware!" Then this outlaw strapped his razor on his boot, hovered over me ominously for six fearful seconds, and then swooped down upon me like the genius of destruction. The first rake of his razor loosened the very hide from my face and lifted me out of the chair. I stormed and raved, and the other boys enjoyed it. Their beards are not strong and thick. Let us draw the curtain over this harrowing scene. Suffice it that I submitted, and went through with the cruel infliction of a shave by a French barber; tears of exquisite agony coursed down my cheeks, now and then, but I survived. Then the incipient assassin held a basin of water under my chin and slopped its contents over my face, and into my bosom, and down the back of my neck, with a mean pretense of washing away the soap and blood. He dried my features with a towel, and was going to comb my hair; but I asked to be excused. I said, with withering irony, that it was sufficient to be skinned—I declined to be scalped.

I went away from there with my handkerchief about my face, and never, never, never desired to dream of palatial Parisian barber shops any more. The truth is, as I believe I have since found out, that they have no barber shops worthy of the name in Paris—and no barbers, either, for that matter. The impostor who does duty as a barber brings his pans and napkins and implements of torture to your residence and deliberately skins you in your private apartments. Ah, I have suffered, suffered, suffered, here in Paris, but never mind—the time is coming when I shall have a dark and bloody revenge. Some day a Parisian barber will come to my room to skin me, and from that day forth that barber will never be heard of more.

At eleven o'clock we alighted upon a sign which manifestly referred to billiards. Joy! We had played billiards in the Azores with balls that were not round, and on an ancient table that was very little smoother than a brick pavement—one of those wretched old things with dead cushions, and with patches in the faded cloth and invisible obstructions that made the balls describe the most astonishing and unsuspected angles and perform feats in the way of unlooked-for and almost impossible "scratches," that were perfectly bewildering. We had played at Gibraltar with balls the size of a walnut, on a table like a public square—and in both instances we achieved far more aggravation than amusement. We expected to fare better here, but we were mistaken. The cushions were a good deal higher than the balls, and as the balls had a fashion of always stopping under the cushions, we accomplished very little in the way of caroms. The cushions were hard and unelastic, and the cues were so crooked that in making a shot you had to allow for the curve or you infallibly put the "English" on the wrong side of the ball. Dan was to mark while the doctor and I played. At the end of an hour neither of us had made a count, and so Dan was tired of keeping tally with nothing to tally, and we were heated and angry and disgusted. We paid the heavy bill—about six cents—and said we would call around some time when we had a week to spend, and finish the game.

We adjourned to one of those pretty cafes and took supper and tested the wines of the country, as we had been instructed to do, and found them harmless and unexciting. They might have been exciting, however, if we had chosen to drink a sufficiency of them.

To close our first day in Paris cheerfully and pleasantly, we now sought our grand room in the Grand Hotel du Louvre and climbed into our sumptuous bed, to read and smoke—but alas!

> It was pitiful,
> In a whole city-full,
> Gas we had none.

no gas to read by—nothing but dismal candles. It was a shame. We tried to map our excursions for the morrow; we puzzled over French "Guides to Paris"; we talked disjointedly, in a vain endeavor to make head or tail of the wild chaos of the day's sights and experiences; we subsided to indolent smoking; we gaped and yawned, and stretched—then feebly wondered if we were really and truly in renowned Paris, and drifted drowsily away into that vast mysterious void which men call sleep.

Author and Selection Notes

Mark Twain (Samuel L. Clemens, 1835-1910) is the example par excellence in American literary history of the frontier humorist, though the world-wide acceptance of such books as *Huckleberry Finn, Tom Sawyer, Life on the Mississippi,* and *The Innocents Abroad,* from which the present selection is taken, suggests that his humor has a universal appeal. Written as a series of travel letters to a newspaper about a trip to Europe and the Near East, *The Innocents Abroad* made him both a famous and a wealthy man.

Questions and Exercises

1. This chapter from Twain's *The Innocents Abroad* immediately made him a famous man. List some of the characteristics of this selection which would effect such popularity.

2. What aspects of the scenery impressed Twain as he traveled by rail across France? In what sense was the countryside a bewitching garden?

3. Why does Twain feel that American stage-coaching is "infinitely more delightful" than railroading?

4. How does the scenery of Western America compare, in Twain's estimation, with that of France?

5. Who are the "Old Travelers," and why does Twain seem to dislike them? What is the tone of the passage in which he describes them?

6. In what respects was Twain disappointed in Parisian barber shops? In the public billiard parlor? In his hotel room?

7. Read Chester H. Opal's essay "American Culture Abroad" and answer the following questions against the background it provides: Is Twain a typical example of the American tourist abroad? To what extent does the current American image abroad seem traceable to the actions and attitudes of nineteenth-century travelers? Is Twain's general attitude toward Europe like that of typical twentieth-century American travelers?

8. Write about a recent trip you have taken and give your essay some such title as "A Modern Innocent Takes a Trip" or "A Modern Innocent Abroad." Stress as much as possible not what you actually did but how you felt about the sights you saw and the people you met casually at hotels, restaurants, or pleasure resorts.

9. Theme Topics: Making a Good Impression Abroad; The Pleasures of Traveling; Foreign Attitudes Toward Americans; Travel Is Broadening; Famous Tourist Sites; Typical American Attitudes Toward Foreigners.

FRA LIPPO LIPPI

Robert Browning

I am poor brother Lippo, by your leave!
You need not clap your torches to my face.
Zooks, what's to blame? you think you see a monk!
What, 'tis past midnight, and you go the rounds,
And here you catch me at an alley's end   5
Where sportive ladies leave their doors ajar?
The Carmine's my cloister: hunt it up,
Do,—harry out, if you must show your zeal,
Whatever rat, there, haps on his wrong hole,
And nip each softling of a wee white mouse,   10
Weke, weke, that's crept to keep him company!
Aha, you know your betters! Then, you'll take
Your hand away that's fiddling on my throat,
And please to know me likewise. Who am I?
Why, one, sir, who is lodging with a friend   15

Three streets off—he's a certain . . . how d'ye call?
Master—a . . . Cosimo of the Medici,
I' the house that caps the corner. Boh! you were best!
Remember and tell me, the day you're hanged,
How you affected such a gullet's-gripe!   20
But you, sir, it concerns you that your knaves
Pick up a manner nor discredit you:
Zooks, are we pilchards, that they sweep the streets
And count fair prize what comes into their net?
He's Judas to a tittle, that man is!   25
Just such a face! Why, sir, you make amends.
Lord, I'm not angry! Bid your hangdogs go
Drink out this quarter-florin to the health
Of the munificent House that harbors me
(And many more beside, lads! more beside!)   30
And all's come square again. I'd like his face—
His, elbowing on his comrade in the door
With the pike and lantern,—for the slave that holds
John Baptist's head a-dangle by the hair
With one hand ("Look you, now," as who should say)   35
And his weapon in the other, yet unwiped!
It's not your chance to have a bit of chalk,
A wood-coal or the like? or you should see!
Yes, I'm the painter, since you style me so.
What, brother Lippo's doings, up and down,   40
You know them and they take you? like enough!
I saw the proper twinkle in your eye—
'Tell you, I liked your looks at very first.
Let's sit and set things straight now, hip to haunch.
Here's spring come, and the nights one makes up bands   45
To roam the town and sing out carnival,
And I've been three weeks shut within my mew,
A-painting for the great man, saints and saints
And saints again. I could not paint all night—
Ouf! I leaned out of window for fresh air.   50
There came a hurry of feet and little feet,
A sweep of lute-strings, laughs, and whiffs of song,—
Flower o' the broom,
Take away love, and our earth is a tomb!
Flower o' the quince,   55
I let Lisa go, and what good in life since?
Flower o' the thyme—and so on. Round they went.
Scarce had they turned the corner when a titter

Like the skipping of rabbits by moonlight,—three slim shapes,
And a face that looked up . . . zooks, sir, flesh and blood,   60
That's all I'm made of! Into shreds it went,
Curtain and counterpane and coverlet,
All the bed-furniture—a dozen knots,
There was a ladder! Down I let myself,
Hands and feet, scrambling somehow, and so dropped,   65
And after them. I came up with the fun
Hard by Saint Laurence, hail fellow, well met,—
Flower o' the rose,
If I've been merry, what matter who knows?
And so as I was stealing back again   70
To get to bed and have a bit of sleep
Ere I rise up to-morrow and go work
On Jerome knocking at his poor old breast
With his great round stone to subdue the flesh,
You snap me of the sudden. Ah, I see!   75
Though your eye twinkles still, you shake your head—
Mine's shaved—a monk, you say—the sting's in that!
If Master Cosimo announced himself,
Mum's the word naturally; but a monk!
Come, what am I a beast for? tell us, now!   80
I was a baby when my mother died
And father died and left me in the street.
I starved there, God knows how, a year or two
On fig-skins, melon-parings, rinds and shucks,
Refuse and rubbish. One fine frosty day,   85
My stomach being empty as your hat,
The wind doubled me up and down I went.
Old Aunt Lapaccia trussed me with one hand,
(Its fellow was a stinger as I knew)
And so along the wall, over the bridge,   90
By the straight cut to the convent. Six words there,
While I stood munching my first bread that month:
"So boy, you're minded," quoth the good fat father,
Wiping his own mouth, 'twas refection-time,—
"To quit this very miserable world?   95
Will you renounce" . . . "The mouthful of bread?" thought I;
By no means! Brief, they made a monk of me;
I did renounce the world, its pride and greed,
Palace, farm, villa, shop, and banking-house,
Trash, such as these poor devils of Medici   100
Have given their hearts to—all at eight years old.

Well, sir, I found in time, you may be sure,
'Twas not for nothing—the good bellyful,
The warm serge and the rope that goes all round,
And day-long blessed idleness beside!   105
"Let's see what the urchin's fit for"—that came next.
Not overmuch their way, I must confess.
Such a to-do! They tried me with their books;
Lord, they'd have taught me Latin in pure waste!
Flower o' the clove,   110
All the Latin I construe is "amo," I love!
But, mind you, when a boy starves in the streets
Eight years together, as my fortune was,
Watching folk's faces to know who will fling
The bit of half-stripped grape-bunch he desires,   115
And who will curse or kick him for his pains,—
Which gentleman processional and fine,
Holding a candle to the Sacrament,
Will wink and let him lift a plate and catch
The droppings of the wax to sell again,   120
Or holla for the Eight and have him whipped,—
How say I?—nay, which dog bites, which lets drop
His bone from the heap of offal in the street,—
Why, soul and sense of him grow sharp alike,
He learns the look of things, and none the less   125
For admonition from the hunger-pinch.
I had a store of such remarks, be sure,
Which, after I found leisure, turned to use.
I drew men's faces on my copy-books,
Scrawled them within the antiphonary's marge,   130
Joined legs and arms to the long music-notes,
Found eyes and nose and chin for A's and B's,
And made a string of pictures of the world
Betwixt the ins and outs of verb and noun,
On the wall, the bench, the door. The monks looked black.   135
"Nay," quoth the Prior, "turn him out, d'ye say?
In no wise. Lose a crow and catch a lark.
What if at last we get our man of parts,
We Carmelites, like those Camaldolese
And Preaching Friars, to do our church up fine   140
And put the front on it that ought to be!"
And hereupon he bade me daub away.
Thank you! my head being crammed, the walls a blank,
Never was such prompt disemburdening.

First, every sort of monk, the black and white,   145
I drew them, fat and lean: then, folk at church,
From good old gossips waiting to confess
Their cribs of barrel-droppings, candle-ends,—
To the breathless fellow at the altar-foot,
Fresh from his murder, safe and sitting there   150
With the little children round him in a row
Of admiration, half for his beard and half
For that white anger of his victim's son
Shaking a fist at him with one fierce arm,
Signing himself with the other because of Christ   155
(Whose sad face on the cross sees only this
After the passion of a thousand years)
Till some poor girl, her apron o'er her head,
(Which the intense eyes looked through) came at eve
On tiptoe, said a word, dropped in a loaf,   160
Her pair of earrings and a bunch of flowers
(The brute took growling), prayed, and so was gone.
I painted all, then cried, " 'Tis ask and have;
Choose, for more's ready!"—laid the ladder flat,
And showed my covered bit of cloister-wall.   165
The monks closed in a circle and praised loud
Till checked, taught what to see and not to see,
Being simple bodies,—"That's the very man!
Look at the boy who stoops to pat the dog!
That woman's like the Prior's niece who comes   170
To care about his asthma: it's the life!"
But there my triumph's straw-fire flared and funked;
Their betters took their turn to see and say:
The Prior and the learned pulled a face
And stopped all that in no time. "How? what's here?   175
Quite from the mark of painting, bless us all!
Faces, arms, legs, and bodies like the true
As much as pea and pea! it's devil's-game!
Your business is not to catch men with show,
With homage to the perishable clay,   180
But lift them over it, ignore it all,
Make them forget there's such a thing as flesh.
Your business is to paint the souls of men—
Man's soul, and it's a fire, smoke . . . no, it's not . . .
It's vapor done up like a new-born babe—   185
(In that shape when you die it leaves your mouth)
It's . . . well, what matters talking, it's the soul!

Give us no more of body than shows soul!
Here's Giotto, with his Saint a-praising God,
That sets us praising,—why not stop with him?   190
Why put all thoughts of praise out of our head
With wonder at lines, colors, and what not?
Paint the soul, never mind the legs and arms!
Rub all out, try at it a second time.
Oh, that white smallish female with the breasts,   195
She's just my niece . . . Herodias, I would say,—
Who went and danced and got men's heads cut off!
Have it all out!" Now, is this sense, I ask?
A fine way to paint soul, by painting body
So ill, the eye can't stop there, must go further   200
And can't fare worse! Thus, yellow does for white
When what you put for yellow's simply black,
And any sort of meaning looks intense
When all beside itself means and looks naught.
Why can't a painter lift each foot in turn,   205
Left foot and right foot, go a double step,
Make his flesh liker and his soul more like,
Both in their order? Take the prettiest face,
The Prior's niece . . . patron-saint   is it so pretty
You can't discover if it means hope, fear,   210
Sorrow or joy? won't beauty go with these?
Suppose I've made her eyes all right and blue,
Can't I take breath and try to add life's flash,
And then add soul and heighten them three-fold?
Or say there's beauty with no soul at all—   215
(I never saw it—put the case the same—)
If you get simple beauty and naught else,
You get about the best thing God invents:
That's somewhat: and you'll find the soul you have missed,
Within yourself, when you return him thanks.   220
"Rub all out!" Well, well, there's my life, in short,
And so the thing has gone on ever since.
I'm grown a man no doubt, I've broken bounds:
You should not take a fellow eight years old
And make him swear to never kiss the girls.   225
I'm my own master, paint now as I please—
Having a friend, you see, in the Corner-house!
Lord, it's fast holding by the rings in front—
Those great rings serve more purposes than just
To plant a flag in, or tie up a horse!   230

And yet the old schooling sticks, the old grave eyes
Are peeping o'er my shoulder as I work,
The heads shake still—"It's art's decline, my son!
You're not of the true painters, great and old;
Brother Angelico's the man, you'll find;   235
Brother Lorenzo stands his single peer:
Fag on at flesh, you'll never make the third!"
Flower o' the pine,
You keep your mistr . . . manners, and I'll stick to mine!
I'm not the third, then: bless us, they must know!   240
Don't you think they're the likeliest to know,
They with their Latin? So, I swallow my rage,
Clench my teeth, suck my lips in tight, and paint
To please them—sometimes do and sometimes don't;
For, doing most, there's pretty sure to come   245
A turn, some warm eve finds me at my saints—
A laugh, a cry, the business of the world—
(*Flower o' the peach,*
Death for us all, and his own life for each!)
And my whole soul revolves, the cup runs over,   250
The world and life's too big to pass for a dream,
And I do these wild things in sheer despite,
And play the fooleries you catch me at,
In pure rage! The old mill-horse, out at grass
After hard years, throws up his stiff heels so,   255
Although the miller does not preach to him
The only good of grass is to make chaff.
What would men have? Do they like grass or no—
May they or mayn't they? all I want's the thing
Settled for ever one way. As it is,   260
You tell too many lies and hurt yourself:
You don't like what you only like too much,
You do like what, if given you at your word,
You find abundantly detestable.
For me, I think I speak as I was taught;   265
I always see the garden and God there
A-making man's wife: and, my lesson learned,
The value and significance of flesh,
I can't unlearn ten minutes afterwards.

You understand me: I'm a beast, I know.   270
But see, now—why, I see as certainly
As that the morning-star's about to shine,

What will hap some day. We've a youngster here
Comes to our convent, studies what I do,
Slouches and stares and lets no atom drop: 275
His name is Guidi—he'll not mind the monks—
They call him Hulking Tom, he lets them talk—
He picks my practice up—he'll paint apace,
I hope so—though I never live so long,
I know what's sure to follow. You be judge!   280
You speak no Latin more than I, belike;
However, you're my man, you've seen the world
—The beauty and the wonder and the power,
The shapes of things, their colors, lights and shades,
Changes, surprises,—and God made it all!   285
—For what? Do you feel thankful, ay or no,
For this fair town's face, yonder river's line,
The mountain round it and the sky above,
Much more the figures of man, woman, child,
These are the frame to? What's it all about?   290
To be passed over, despised? or dwelt upon,
Wondered at? oh, this last of course!—you say.
But why not do as well as say,—paint these
Just as they are, careless what comes of it?
God's works—paint any one, and count it crime   295
To let a truth slip. Don't object, "His works
Are here already; nature is complete:
Suppose you reproduce her—(which you can't)
There's no advantage! you must beat her, then."
For, don't you mark? we're made so that we love   300
First when we see them painted, things we have passed
Perhaps a hundred times nor cared to see;
And so they are better, painted—better to us,
Which is the same thing. Art was given for that;
God uses us to help each other so,   305
Lending our minds out. Have you noticed, now,
Your cullion's hanging face? A bit of chalk,
And trust me but you should, though! How much more,
If I drew higher things with the same truth!
That were to take the Prior's pulpit-place,   310
Interpret God to all of you! Oh, oh,
It makes me mad to see what men shall do
And we in our graves! This world's no blot for us,
Nor blank; it means intensely, and means good:
To find its meaning is my meat and drink.   315

"Ay, but you don't so instigate to prayer!"
Strikes in the Prior: "When your meaning's plain
It does not say to folk—remember matins,
Or, mind you fast next Friday!" Why, for this
What need of art at all? A skull and bones,   320
Two bits of stick nailed crosswise, or, what's best,
A bell to chime the hour with, does as well.
I painted a Saint Laurence six months since
At Prato, splashed the fresco in fine style:
"How looks my painting, now the scaffold's down?"   325
I ask a brother: "Hugely," he returns—
"Already not one phiz of your three slaves
Who turn the Deacon off his toasted side,
But's scratched and prodded to our heart's content,
The pious people have so eased their own   330
With coming to say prayers there in a rage:
We get on fast to see the bricks beneath.
Expect another job this time next year,
For pity and religion grow i' the crowd—
Your painting serves its purpose!" Hang the fools!   335

   —That is—you'll not mistake an idle word
Spoke in a huff by a poor monk, God wot,
Tasting the air this spicy night which turns
The unaccustomed head like Chianti wine!
Oh, the church knows! don't misreport me, now!   340
It's natural a poor monk out of bounds
Should have his apt word to excuse himself:
And hearken how I plot to make amends.
I have bethought me: I shall paint a piece
. . . There's for you! Give me six months, then go, see   345
Something in Sant' Ambrogio's! Bless the nuns!
They want a cast o' my office. I shall paint
God in the midst, Madonna and her babe,
Ringed by a bowery, flowery angel-brood,
Lilies and vestments and white faces, sweet   350
As puff on puff of grated orris-root
When ladies crowd to Church at midsummer.
And then i' the front, of course a saint or two—
Saint John, because he saves the Florentines,
Saint Ambrose, who puts down in black and white   355
The convent's friends and gives them a long day,
And Job, I must have him there past mistake,

The man of Uz (and Us without the z,
Painters who need his patience). Well, all these
Secured at their devotion, up shall come   360
Out of a corner when you least expect,
As one by a dark stair into a great light,
Music and talking, who but Lippo! I!—
Mazed, motionless, and moonstruck—I'm the man!
Back I shrink—what is this I see and hear?   365
I, caught up with my monk's-things by mistake,
My old serge gown and rope that goes all round,
I, in this presence, this pure company!
Where's a hole, where's a corner for escape?
Then steps a sweet angelic slip of a thing   370
Forward, puts out a soft palm—"Not so fast!"
—Addresses the celestial presence, "nay—
He made you and devised you, after all,
Though he's none of you! Could Saint John there draw—
His camel-hair make up a painting-brush?   375
We come to brother Lippo for all that,
Iste perfecit opus!" So, all smile—
I shuffle sideways with my blushing face
Under the cover of a hundred wings
Thrown like a spread of kirtles when you're gay   380
And play hot cockles, all the doors being shut,
Till, wholly unexpected, in there pops
The hothead husband! Thus I scuttle off
To some safe bench behind, not letting go
The palm of her, the little lily thing   385
That spoke the good word for me in the nick,
Like the Prior's niece . . . Saint Lucy, I would say.
And so all's saved for me, and for the church
A pretty picture gained. Go, six months hence!
Your hand, sir, and good-by: no lights, no lights!   390
The street's hushed, and I know my own way back,
Don't fear me! There's the gray beginning. Zooks!

Author and Selection Notes

The greatest contribution to English poetry by Robert Browning (1812-1889), one of the chief spokesmen of the ideals and manners of the age of Queen Victoria, is perhaps the dramatic monologue, used with consummate skill in his masterpiece *The Ring and the Book* and in numerous shorter pieces such as "My Last Duchess," "The Bishop Orders His Tomb," and the present selection. "Fra Lippo Lippi" records an imaginary moment in the life of a painter-monk as he explains to the captain of the city watch his presence in the streets in the late hours of the night.

Questions and Exercises

1. Outline the situation leading up to Fra Lippo's long speech to the captain of the watch. Recount his early life and explain how be became a monk.

2. As in some other poems which he wrote about painting, Browning in this poem expresses a specific theory about art. In a sentence or so state what you feel his theory is.

3. What criticism was brought against Fra Lippo's first painting?

4. Explain the sentence, "Paint the soul, never mind the legs and arms."

5. Summarize Fra Lippo's own defense of his style of painting.

6. Describe in some detail the picture that Fra Lippo is planning to paint, which he suggests to the captain may be seen "some six months hence."

7. Look up in an encyclopedia or handbook of literature the definition of "dramatic monologue"; then show how Browning's poem fits the characteristics listed.

8. Read Richard Steele's essay "On Raphael's Cartoons at Hampton-Court." Would Fra Lippo agree with Steele's ideas about the function of art? Defend your view.

9. Write definitions of each of the following words: "cloister," "pilchard," "urchin," "processional," "antiphonary," "funked," "fresco."

10. Theme Topics: Art Should Not Be Didactic; Browning's Use of the Dramatic Monologue; Art in the Service of Religion; Trends in Religious Art Today.

PIED BEAUTY
Gerard Manley Hopkins

Glory be to God for dappled things—
For skies as couple-colored as a brinded cow;
For rose-moles all in stipple upon trout that swim;
Fresh-firecoal chestnut-falls; finches' wings;
Landscape plotted and pieced—fold, fallow, and plow;
And all trades, their gear and tackle and trim.

All things counter, original, spare, strange;
Whatever is fickle, freckled (who knows how?)
With swift, slow; sweet, sour; adazzle, dim;
He fathers-forth whose beauty is past change:
Praise Him.

Author and Selection Notes

The work of the Victorian poet-priest Gerard Manley Hopkins (1844-1889) was delayed publication until thirty years after his death when his friend Robert Bridges published *Poems by Gerard Manley Hopkins* in 1918. Hopkins was an intensely spiritual and religious poet. His verse shows great originality in form and manner, anticipating in many ways the density and experimentalism of modern poetry.

Questions and Exercises

1. Explain what Gerard Manley Hopkins means by his title "Pied Beauty."

2. What sort of beauty, in contrast, is associated with God, who "fathers-forth" the world of pied beauty? Explain.

3. What does Hopkins mean by "All things counter, original, spare, strange"? Can you think of a word which sums them all up?

4. Structurally this poem falls into two parts. Show where the first part ends and the second begins. Does this make the poem a sonnet? Why or why not?

5. List the last words in each line in a column and identify the rhyme scheme.

6. What effect does Hopkins gain, if any, by the very short last line? Support your answer in a brief paragraph.

7. Theme Topics: My Favorite Religious Poem; Great Religious Poems; The Psalms as Religious Poetry; Hopkins' Concept of God; Hopkins' Concept of Beauty; The Importance of Variety.

EUCLID ALONE HAS LOOKED ON BEAUTY BARE

Edna St. Vincent Millay

Euclid alone has looked on Beauty bare.
Let all who prate of Beauty hold their peace,
And lay them prone upon the earth and cease

From *Collected Poems,* Harper & Brothers. Copyright 1923-1951 by Edna St. Vincent Millay and Norma Millay Ellis.

To ponder on themselves, the while they stare
At nothing, intricately drawn nowhere
In shapes of shifting lineage; let geese
Gabble and hiss, but heroes seek release
From dusty bondage into luminous air.

O blinding hour, O holy, terrible day,
When first the shaft into his vision shone
Of light anatomized! Euclid alone
Has looked on Beauty bare. Fortunate they
Who, though once only and then but far away,
Have heard her massive sandal set on stone.

Author and Selection Notes

The first work of Edna St. Vincent Millay (1892-1950) appeared as part of the poetic renascence in American poetry immediately after World War I. Born in Maine, she made her home most of her adult life on a New England farm, leaving it infrequently for travel and lecture tours. Primarily a facile lyricist, with such volumes as *Second April* and *The Harp Weaver and Other Poems,* her chief contribution to American verse is perhaps the sonnet form, which is illustrated by her sonnet sequence *Fatal Interview* and by other fine sonnets scattered throughout her later volumes.

Questions and Exercises

1. The questions "What is beauty?" and "Why is something beautiful?" have often been asked. Edna St. Vincent Millay offers one answer, which is the basic theme of her poem. In a sentence or two state the central idea contained in the poem.

2. Look up "Euclid" in an encyclopedia or biographical dictionary. Explain Millay's statement "Euclid alone has looked on Beauty bare."

3. With regard to beauty, who are those who are like geese that "gabble and hiss," and who are the heroes?

4. What does the poet mean by the phrase "light anatomized"?

5. Compare the attitude toward beauty shown in this poem with that in Keats' "Ode on a Grecian Urn" and Hopkins' "Pied Beauty."

6. Look up the verse form of the sonnet and analyze this poem in terms of rhyme scheme and formal development.

7. Theme Topics: "Beauty Bare"—The Power of Form in Art; Should Beauty Be Functional? Millay's Concept of Beauty; The Classical Notion of Art; Beauty Is Its Own Excuse for Being.

ARS POETICA

Archibald MacLeish

A poem should be palpable and mute
As a globed fruit

Dumb
As old medallions to the thumb

Silent as the sleeve-worn stone
Of casement ledges where the moss has grown—

A poem should be wordless
As the flight of birds

*

A poem should be motionless in time
As the moon climbs

Leaving, as the moon releases
Twig by twig the night-entangled trees,

Leaving, as the moon behind the winter leaves,
Memory by memory the mind—

A poem should be motionless in time
As the moon climbs

*

A poem should be equal to:
Not true

For all the history of grief
An empty doorway and a maple leaf

For love
The leaning grasses and two lights above the sea—

From *Collected Poems: 1917-1952*, by Archibald MacLeish, Houghton Mifflin Company, 1952. Reprinted by permission of the publisher.

A poem should not mean
But be.

Author and Selection Notes

Reared in the Middle West, Archibald MacLeish (1892-   ) has spent most of his adult life in the East, filling such varied positions as editor of *Fortune Magazine,* Librarian of the Library of Congress, and Boylston Professor of Rhetoric and Oratory at Harvard University. MacLeish's poetic career was climaxed by *Collected Poems: 1917-1952,* which received three national prizes: the Pulitzer, the Bollinger, and the National Book Award. "Ars Poetica" reveals a distinctly modern concept of the meaning of a poem.

Questions and Exercises

1. To what objects does the poet compare a poem in the first stanza? What does he mean by saying that a poem should be wordless as a "flight of birds"?

2. Clarify the difficulties of syntax in stanzas two and three by writing a prose paraphrase of each.

3. The last two lines in each stanza climax the meaning of each stanza. In a paragraph or two show how, taken all together, they summarize the central idea of the whole poem.

4. Give the rhyme scheme of this poem. Are the rhyme irregularities the result of the poet's inability to achieve true rhymes, or are they deliberate on his part? If deliberate, what is gained by such irregularity?

5. Look up the words "figure of speech" and "connotation" in a literary dictionary or handbook and point out several examples in the poem of each.

6. Theme Topics: My Definition of a Poem; What Poetry Means to Me; Imagery in Poetry; The Purpose of Poetry.

THE PORTABLE PHONOGRAPH

Walter Van Tilburg Clark

The red sunset, with narrow, black cloud strips like threats across it, lay on the curved horizon of the prairie. The air was still and cold, and in it settled the mute darkness and greater cold of night. High in the air there was wind, for through the veil of the dusk the clouds could be seen gliding rapidly south and changing shapes. A queer sensation of torment, of two-sided, unpredictable nature, arose from the stillness of the earth air beneath the violence of the upper air. Out of the sunset, through the dead, matted grass and isolated weed stalks of the prairie, crept the narrow and deeply rutted remains of a road. In the road, in places, there were crusts of shallow, brittle ice. There were little islands of an old oiled pavement in the road too, but most of it was mud, now frozen rigid. The frozen mud still bore the toothed impress of great tanks, and a wanderer on the neighboring undulations might have stumbled, in this light, into large, partially filled-in and weed-grown cavities, their banks channelled and beginning to spread into badlands. These pits were such as might have been made by falling meteors, but they were not. They were the scars of gigantic bombs, their rawness already made a little natural by rain, seed, and time. Along the road, there were rakish remnants of fence. There was also, just visible, one portion of tangled and multiple barbed wire still erect, behind which was a shelving ditch with small caves, now very quiet and empty, at intervals in its back wall. Otherwise there was no structure or remnant of a structure visible over the dome of the darkling earth, but only, in sheltered hollows, the darker shadows of young trees trying again.

Under the wuthering arch of the high wind a V of wild geese fled south. The rush of their pinions sounded briefly, and the faint, plaintive notes of their expeditionary talk. Then they left a still greater vacancy. There was the smell and expectation of snow, as there is likely to be when the wild geese fly south. From the remote distance, towards the red sky, came faintly the protracted howl and quick yap-yap of a prairie wolf.

North of the road, perhaps a hundred yards, lay the parallel and deeply intrenched course of a small creek, lined with leafless alders and willows. The creek was already silent under ice. Into the bank above it was dug a sort of cell, with a single opening, like the mouth of a mine tunnel. Within the cell there was a little red of fire, which showed dully through the opening, like a reflection or a deception of the imagination. The light came from the chary burning of four blocks of poorly aged peat, which gave off a petty warmth and much acrid smoke. But the precious remnants of wood, old fence posts and timbers from the long-deserted dugouts, had to be saved for the real cold, for the time when a man's breath blew white, the moisture in his nostrils stiffened at once when he stepped out, and the expansive blizzards paraded for days over the vast open, swirling and settling and thickening, till the dawn of the cleared day when the sky was thin blue-green and the terrible cold, in which a man could not live for three hours unwarmed, lay over the uniformly drifted swell of the plain.

Around the smoldering peat, four men were seated cross-legged. Behind them, traversed by their shadows, was the earth bench, with two old and dirty army blankets, where the owner of the cell slept. In a niche in the opposite wall were a few tin utensils which caught the glint of the coals. The host was rewrapping in a piece of daubed burlap four fine, leather-bound books. He worked slowly and very carefully, and at last tied the bundle securely with a piece of grass-woven cord. The other three looked intently upon the process, as if a great significance lay in it. As the host tied the cord, he spoke. He was an old man, his long, matted beard and hair gray to nearly white. The shadows made his brows and cheekbones appear gnarled, his eyes and cheeks deeply sunken. His big hands, rough with frost and swollen by rheumatism, were awkward but gentle at their task. He was like a prehistoric priest performing a fateful ceremonial rite. Also his voice had in it a suitable quality of deep, reverent despair, yet perhaps at the moment a sharpness of selfish satisfaction.

"When I perceived what was happening," he said, "I told myself, 'It is the end. I cannot take much; I will take these.'

"Perhaps I was impractical," he continued. "But for myself, I do not regret, and what do we know of those who will come after us? We are the doddering remnant of a race of mechanical fools. I have saved what I love; the soul of what was good in us is here; perhaps the new ones will make a strong enough beginning not to fall behind when they become clever."

He rose with slow pain and placed the wrapped volumes in the niche with his utensils. The others watched him with the same ritualistic gaze.

"Shakespeare, the Bible, *Moby Dick, The Divine Comedy,*" one of them said softly. "You might have done worse, much worse."

"You will have a little soul left until you die," said another harshly. "That is more than is true of us. My brain becomes thick, like my hands." He held the big, battered hands, with their black nails, in the glow to be seen.

"I want paper to write on," he said. "And there is none."

The fourth man said nothing. He sat in the shadow farthest from the fire, and sometimes his body jerked in its rags from the cold. Although he was still young, he was sick and coughed often. Writing implied a greater future than he now felt able to consider.

The old man seated himself laboriously, and reached out, groaning at the movement, to put another block of peat on the fire. With bowed heads and averted eyes, his three guests acknowledged his magnanimity.

"We thank you, Doctor Jenkins, for the reading," said the man who had named the books.

They seemed then to be waiting for something. Doctor Jenkins understood, but was loath to comply. In an ordinary moment he would have said nothing. But the words of *The Tempest*, which he had been reading, and the religious attention of the three made this an unusual occasion.

"You wish to hear the phonograph," he said grudgingly.

The two middle-aged men stared into the fire, unable to formulate and expose the enormity of their desire.

The young man, however, said anxiously, between suppressed coughs, "Oh, please," like an excited child.

The old man rose again in his difficult way, and went to the back of the cell. He returned and placed tenderly upon the packed floor, where the firelight might fall upon it, an old portable phonograph in a black case. He smoothed the top with his hands, and then opened it. The lovely green-felt-covered disk became visible.

"I have been using thorns as needles," he said. "But tonight, because we have a musician among us"—he bent his head to the young man, almost invisible in the shadow—"I will use a steel needle. There are only three left."

The two middle-aged men stared at him in speechless adoration. The one with the big hands, who wanted to write, moved his lips, but the whisper was not audible.

"Oh, don't!" cried the young man, as if he were hurt. "The thorns will do beautifully."

"No," the old man said. "I have become accustomed to the thorns, but they are not really good. For you, my young friend, we will have good music tonight."

"After all," he added generously, and beginning to wind the phonograph, which creaked, "they can't last forever."

"No, nor we," the man who needed to write said harshly. "The needle, by all means."

"Oh, thanks," said the young man. "Thanks," he said again in a low, excited voice, and then stifled his coughing with a bowed head.

"The records, though," said the old man when he had finished winding, "are a different matter. Already they are very worn. I do not play them more than once a week. One, once a week, that is what I allow myself.

"More than a week I cannot stand it; not to hear them," he apologized.

"No, how could you?" cried the young man. "And with them here like this."

"A man can stand anything," said the man who wanted to write, in his harsh, antagonistic voice.

"Please, the music," said the young man.

"Only the one," said the old man. "In the long run, we will remember more that way."

He had a dozen records with luxuriant gold and red seals. Even in that light the others could see that the threads of the records were becoming worn. Slowly he read out the titles and the tremendous dead names of the composers and the artists and the orchestras. The three worked upon the names in their minds, carefully. It was difficult to select from such a wealth what they would at once most like to remember. Finally, the man who wanted to write named Gershwin's "New York."

"Oh, no," cried the sick young man, and then could say nothing more because he had to cough. The others understood him, and the harsh man withdrew his selection and waited for the musician to choose.

The musician begged Doctor Jenkins to read the titles again, very slowly, so that he could remember the sounds. While they were read, he lay back against the wall, his eyes closed, his thin, horny hand pulling at his light beard, and listened to the voices and the orchestras and the single instruments in his mind.

When the reading was done he spoke despairingly. "I have forgotten," he complained; "I cannot hear them clearly.

"There are things missing," he explained.

"I know," said Doctor Jenkins. "I thought that I knew all of Shelley by heart. I should have brought Shelley."

"That's more soul than we can use," said the harsh man. "*Moby Dick* is better.

"By God, we can understand that," he emphasized.

The Doctor nodded.

"Still," said the man who had admired the books, "we need the absolute if we are to keep a grasp on anything.

"Anything but these sticks and peat clods and rabbit snares," he said bitterly.

"Shelley desired an ultimate absolute," said the harsh man. "It's too much," he said. "It's no good; no earthly good."

The musician selected a Debussy nocturne. The others considered and approved. They rose to their knees to watch the Doctor prepare for the playing, so that they appeared to be actually in an attitude of worship. The peat glow showed the thinness of their bearded faces, and the deep lines in them, and revealed the condition of their garments. The other two continued to kneel as the old man carefully lowered the needle onto the spinning disk, but the musician suddenly drew back against the wall again, with his knees up, and buried his face in his hands.

At the first notes of the piano the listeners were startled. They stared at each other. Even the musician lifted his head in amazement, but then quickly bowed it again, strainingly, as if he were suffering from a pain he might not be able to endure. They were all listening deeply, without movement. The wet, blue green notes tinkled forth from the old machine, and were individual, delectable presences in the cell. The individual, delectable presences swept into a sudden tide of unbearably beautiful dissonance, and then continued fully the swelling and ebbing of that tide, the dissonant inpourings, and the resolutions, and the diminishments, and the little, quiet wavelets of interlude lapping between. Every sound was piercing and singularly sweet. In all the men except the musician, there occurred rapid sequences of tragically heightened recollection. He heard nothing but what was there. At the final, whispering disappearance, but moving quietly so that the others would not hear him and look at him, he let his head fall back in agony, as if it were drawn there by the hair, and clenched the fingers of one hand over his teeth. He sat that way while the others were silent, and until they began to breathe again normally. His drawn-up legs were trembling violently.

Quickly Doctor Jenkins lifted the needle off, to save it and not to spoil the recollection with scraping. When he had stopped the whirling of the sacred disk, he courteously left the phonograph open and by the fire, in sight.

The others, however, understood. The musician rose last, but then abruptly, and went quickly out at the door without saying anything. The others stopped at the door and gave their thanks in low voices. The Doctor nodded magnificently.

"Come again," he invited, "in a week. We will have the 'New York.'"

When the two had gone together, out towards the rimed road, he stood in the entrance, peering and listening. At first, there was only the resonant boom of the wind overhead, and then far over the dome of the dead, dark plain, the wolf cry lamenting.

In the rifts of clouds the Doctor saw four stars flying. It impressed the Doctor that one of them had just been obscured by the beginning of a flying cloud at the very moment he heard what he had been listening for, a sound of suppressed coughing. It was not nearby, however. He believed that down against the pale alders he could see the moving shadow.

With nervous hands he lowered the piece of canvas which served as his door, and pegged it at the bottom. Then quickly and quietly, looking at the piece of canvas frequently, he slipped the records into the case, snapped the lid shut, and carried the phonograph to his couch. There, pausing often to stare at the canvas and listen, he dug earth from the wall and disclosed a piece of board. Behind this there was a deep hole in the wall, into which he put the phonograph. After a moment's consideration, he went over and reached down his bundle of books and inserted it also. Then, guardedly, he once more sealed up the hole with the board and the earth. He also changed his blankets, and the grass-stuffed sack which served as a pillow, so that he could lie facing the entrance. After carefully placing two more blocks of peat upon the fire, he stood for a long time watching the stretched canvas, but it seemed to billow naturally with the first gusts of a lowering wind. At last he prayed, and got in under his blankets, and closed his smoke-smarting eyes. On the inside of the bed, next the wall, he could feel with his hand the comfortable piece of lead pipe.

Author and Selection Notes

Though born in Maine, Walter Van Tilburg Clark (1909-   ) was reared in the West, the setting of several of his best-known works, including *The Oxbow Incident* and *The Track of the Cat*. Clark combines two abiding interests—writing and teaching. He at present teaches English at San Francisco State College. Clark's much anthologized "The Portable Phonograph" celebrates the vital role of art in the affairs of men, even in a destroyed world.

Questions and Exercises

1. What specific types of art are represented in the story, and what effect do they have on each of the characters?

2. What is the basic situation suggested by the opening description? How does the author control the tone of the story from the very beginning?

3. Explain why each of the books the professor brought with him is significant.

4. Why does the musician object to the writer's choice of a piece to be played upon the portable phonograph?

5. What effect does the music have on each of the three visitors? On the group as a whole?

6. Explain why the doctor listens so intently to the cough of the musician. What do the four stars mentioned in the last part of the story symbolize?

7. Why does the doctor keep the lead pipe so close by his side?

8. Write a paragraph or so explaining the part which music and literature play in preserving in the minds of these men the lost patterns of their civilization.

9. Give the definitions of the following words as used in your text: "wuthering," "chary," "peat," "loath," "delectable," "dissonance."

10. Does the author characterize the men in the story primarily in terms of description or in terms of action and reaction? Illustrate by reference to the details of the story.

11. Outline the events of the story under three headings: Beginning (situation), Middle (complication), and Ending (resolution).

12. Theme Topics: The Place of Art in Civilization; Atomic Energy— Man's Destruction or Man's Salvation? After the H-Bomb, What? Art, Man's Rampart, and His Only One; What Art Means to Me.

ANNA PAVLOVA

Agnes De Mille

Anna Pavlova! My life stops as I write that name. Across the daily preoccupation of lessons, lunch boxes, tooth brushings, and quarrelings with Margaret flashed this bright, unworldly experience and burned in a single afternoon a path over which I could never retrace my steps. I had witnessed the power of beauty, and in some chamber of my heart I lost forever my irresponsibility. I was as clearly marked as though she had looked me in the face and called my name. For generations my father's family had loved and served the theater. All my life I had seen actors and actresses and had heard theater jargon at the dinner table and business talk of box-office grosses. I had thrilled at Father's projects and watched fascinated his picturesque occupations. I took a proprietary pride in the profitable and hasty growth of "The Industry." But nothing

From *Dance to the Piper*, copyright 1951, 1952, by Agnes De Mille, published by Little, Brown and Company. Also published by *The Atlantic Monthly*, Vol. 188, October, 1951. Reprinted by permission of Little, Brown and Company.

in his world or my uncle's prepared me for theater as I saw it that Saturday afternoon.

Since that day I have gained some knowledge in my trade and I recognize that her technique was limited; that her arabesques were not as pure or classically correct as Markova's, that her jumps and *batterie* were paltry, her turns not to be compared in strength and number with the strenuous durability of Baronova or Toumanova. I know that her scenery was designed by second-rate artists, her music was on a level with restaurant orchestrations, her company definitely inferior to all the standards we insist on today, and her choreography mostly hack. And yet I say she was in her person the quintessence of theatrical excitement.

As her little bird body revealed itself on the scene, either immobile in trembling mystery or tense in the incredible arc which was her lift, her instep stretched ahead in an arch never before seen, the tiny bones of her hands in ceaseless vibration, her face radiant, diamonds glittering under her dark hair, her little waist encased in silk, the great tutu balancing, quickening and flashing over her beating, flashing, quivering legs, every man and woman sat forward, every pulse quickened. She never appeared to rest static, some part of her trembled, vibrated, beat like a heart. Before our dazzled eyes, she flashed with the sudden sweetness of a hummingbird in action too quick for understanding by our gross utilitarian standards, in action sensed rather than seen. The movie cameras of her day could not record her allegro. Her feet and hands photographed as a blur.

Bright little bird bones, delicate bird sinews! She was all fire and steel wire. There was not an ounce of spare flesh on her skeleton, and the life force used her body until she died of the fever of moving, gasping for breath, much too young.

She was small, about five feet. She wore a size one and a half slipper, but her feet and hands were large in proportion to her height. Her hand could cover her whole face. Her trunk was small and stripped of all anatomy but the ciphers of adolescence, her arms and legs relatively long, the neck extraordinarily long and mobile. All her gestures were liquid and possessed of an inner rhythm that flowed to inevitable completion with the finality of architecture or music. Her arms seemed to lift not from the elbow or the arm socket, but from the base of the spine. Her legs seemed to function from the waist. When she bent her head her whole spine moved and the motion was completed the length of the arm through the elongation of her slender hand and the quivering reaching fingers. Without in any way being sensual—

being, in fact, almost sexless—she suggested all exhilaration, gaiety, and delight. She jumped, and we broke bonds with reality. We flew. We hung over the earth, spread in the air as we do in dreams, our hands turning in the air as in water—the strong forth-right taut plunging leg balanced on the poised arc of the foot, the other leg stretched to the horizon like the wing of a bird. We lay balancing, quivering, turning, and all things were possible, even to us, the ordinary people.

I have seen two dancers as great or greater since, Alicia Markova and Margot Fonteyn, and many other women who have kicked higher, balanced longer, or turned faster. These are poor substitutes for passion. In spite of her flimsy dances, the bald and blatant virtuosity, there was an intoxicated rapture, a focus of energy, Dionysian in its physical intensity, that I have never seen equaled by a performer in any theater of the world. Also she was the *first* of the truly great in our experience.

I sat with the blood beating in my throat. As I walked into the bright glare of the afternoon, my head ached and I could scarcely swallow. I didn't wish to cry. I certainly couldn't speak. I sat in a daze in the car, oblivious to the grownups' ceaseless prattle. At home I climbed the stairs slowly to my bedroom and, shutting myself in, placed both hands on the brass rail at the foot of my bed; then, rising laboriously to the tips of my white buttoned shoes, I stumped the width of the bed and back again. My toes throbbed with pain, my knees shook, my legs quivered with weakness. I repeated the exercise. The blessed, relieving tears stuck at last on my lashes. Only by hurting my feet could I ease the pain in my throat.

It is a source of sadness to me that few of our contemporary ballet dancers ever saw Anna Pavlova. At the time of which I write, her name was synonymous with the art—Pavlova, the Incomparable, was an internationally known slogan. She was as famous as Caruso and her position as unique. No one today approaches her power over the popular imagination. She half-hypnotized audiences, partaking almost of the nature of a divinity.

My life was wholly altered by her—so I wonder, casting about in vain for similar dazzling influences, what first drove Kaye, Alonso, Fonteyn, Toumanova, and Helpmann to the *barre*.

She danced *The Dying Swan*. Everyone has danced *The Swan*. What was it? A series of *pas de bourrées* around and around the stage with flutterings and undulations of the arms interspersed with broken staggers until the final collapse and folding away. Nothing else. Fokine composed it in half an hour for a charity performance, and it is probably the most famous solo in the history of dancing. When she trembled onto the stage it was a death agony, the voice in the dark, the final anonymous cry against annihilation. And when she lay doubled up and the last shudder passed through feathers and broken bones, drawing as an after-beat when all was finished the shivering inert hand across her face in a gesture of final decency, everyone sat stricken. Death was upon each of us.

Death came to Anna Pavlova in 1931, when she was fifty. She had not stopped touring for a single season. Her knees ·had sustained some damage, but she would not rest, and she was in a state of exhaustion when the train that was carrying her to Holland was wrecked. She ran out into the snow in her night-gown and insisted on helping the wounded. When she reached The Hague she had double pneumonia. Her last words were: "Get the *Swan* dress ready."

Standing on Ninth Avenue under the El, I saw the headlines on the front page of the New York *Times*. It did not seem possible. She was in essence the denial of death. My own life was rooted to her in a deep spiritual sense, and had been during the whole of my growing up. It mattered not that I had only spoken to her once and that my work lay in a different direction. She was the vision and the impulse and the goal.

Pavlova's ashes were laid in the Golder's Green cemetery near her home, Ivy House, Hampstead Heath. All the glory of the last great Imperial days stood by. Karsavina was there, Lopokova, Massine.

But also in New York, in Los Angeles, in Paris, Berlin, Rome, San Francisco, wherever there was a Russian Orthodox Church, the dancers gathered, those that knew her and many more that didn't. I went in New York and all the dancers of the city were there. My mother came. She said she wished to, that she owed her a debt of many hours of joy. We stood. The Russians held lighted candles; the choir chanted with a high tonal insistency that wore down like rain on rock. The priest passed in and out of his painted, holy screens. A friend leaned to me. "They are singing," she whispered. "Receive the soul of Anna. Cherish our Anna. Bless and protect Anna." But I put my handkerchief to my mouth and heard the drums and the beating of feet and the cries she gave as she leaped. At the conclusion of the service Fokine, as senior friend, colleague, and Russian, received our condolences. He knew very few of us. We walked up silently, strangers, and shook his hand.

His wife, Vera Fokina, in black from head to foot with sweeping veils, stood beside him.

We went out into the day. Wherever Pavlova had passed, hearts changed, flames sprang in the grass, and the girls ran out to a strange, wild, ancient dedication.

Author and Selection Notes

Professional dancer and choreographer for such well-known musicals as *Oklahoma!* and *Gentlemen Prefer Blondes,* Agnes De Mille (1905-   ) has given numerous dance recitals both in this country and abroad and directed her own Dance Theatre. Her acknowledgement of the great influence which Anna Pavlova, one of the supreme ballerinas of the world, had upon her as a child is vividly recorded in her autobiography *Dance to the Piper,* from which the present selection is taken.

Questions and Exercises

1. What, according to the author, made Pavlova great despite the deficiencies in her art form?

2. In reading this selection, do you begin to feel that Agnes De Mille has the same quality as a writer, and perhaps also as a dancer, which made Pavlova great? Explain.

3. Describe Pavlova's interpretation of the dying swan.

4. What caused Pavlova's death, and how were her actions characteristic of her?

5. How does the author reveal her reactions to Pavlova's dance and to her death? Does she make direct statements about her reactions, or does she reveal her reactions indirectly? Discuss.

6. Theme Topics: A Famous Performer I Have Known; The Ballet as an Art Form; The Person Who Inspired My Choice of Career; The Greatest Performance I Have Ever Seen; From Ballet to the Twist.

NOTES ON OPERA AS "BASIC THEATRE"

Gian-Carlo Menotti

To criticize a theatre piece as too theatrical is as senseless as to criticize a piece of music for being too musical. There is only one kind of bad theatre: When the author's imagination steps outside the very area of illusion he has created. But as long as the dramatist

From *The New York Times Magazine,* January 2, 1955, Sec. 6. Reprinted by permission of the publisher and Gian-Carlo Menotti.

creates within that area, almost no action on the stage is too violent or implausible. As a matter of fact, the skill of the dramatist is almost measurable by his ability to make even the most daring and unpredictable seem inevitable. After all, what could be more theatrical than the last entrance of Oedipus or the death of Hamlet or the insanity of Oswald in "Ghosts"?

The important thing is that behind these apparent excesses of action, the author is able to maintain that significant symbolism which is the very essence of dramatic illusion. In the words of Goethe: "When all is said and done, nothing suits the theatre except what also makes a symbolic appeal to the eyes. A significant action suggesting a more significant one." Modern dramatists are much too timid about "theatre," and such timidity is fatal to an opera composer, for music intensifies feeling so quickly that, unless a situation is symbolically strong enough to bear this intensity, it becomes ludicrous by contrast.

* * * * *

Nothing in the theatre can be as exciting as the amazing quickness with which music can express a situation or describe a mood. Whereas, in the prose theatre, it often requires many words to establish a single effect, in an opera one note on the horn will illuminate the audience. It is this very power of music to express feelings so much more quickly than words which makes libretti, when read out of the musical context, appear rather brutal and unconvincing.

* * * * *

Opera is the very basis of theatre. In all civilizations, people sang their dramas before they spoke them. I am convinced that the prose theatre is an offspring of these earlier musico-dramatic forms and not vice versa. The need for music accompanying dramatic action is still so strongly felt that in our most popular dramatic form, the cinema, background music is used to underline even the most prosaic and realistic situations.

* * * * *

It is unfair to accuse opera of being an old-fashioned and ungainly dramatic form. Actually, what people put forth as examples is largely the operatic output of the nineteenth century. Considering the length of time that has gone by since then, it is quite amazing what life there still is in those old pieces. How many plays of that same period have survived this test as well? Wouldn't most of us prefer hearing a Verdi opera to sitting through a Victor Hugo play?

I may even venture to say that many of the so-called "great plays" of this century will be forgotten when dear old "Traviata" is still holding the boards. All of this cannot be explained away simply by condemning as foolish or gullible millions of music lovers.

*   *   *   *   *

There is no such thing as a good or bad libretto per se. A good libretto is nothing but one which inspires a composer to write good music. "Goetterdaemmerung" would have been a bad libretto indeed for Puccini, and I can imagine nothing more disastrous than Wagner's deciding to set "Madama Butterfly" to music.

*   *   *   *   *

Too many people think that only exotic subjects from the past are suitable for an opera. That is nothing but a romantic inheritance from the last century. Just as modern poets have been moved to examine and interpret the uniquely contemporary life, there is no reason why the composer should not do the same.

That is not to say that modern opera must have a contemporary subject. As Lorca, Eliot or Dylan Thomas have found inspiration in sources as varied as folklore, remote historical events or newspaper headlines, so should the composer permit himself that same freedom.

*   *   *   *   *

Although the accusation that opera is unrealistic is an indiscriminate one, I have been assailed with it too often not to wish to dispose of it now. If by realistic people mean a literal duplication of life, what art can be called truly realistic? Literal photographic techniques are, as far as I am concerned, the very negation of art.

But it is curious how most people, once they accept the conventional limitations of an art form, are unconscious of its unrealistic pattern. I have been asked again and again why characters should sing instead of talk. Why, then, should they dance instead of speak? Or why, as in a Shakespearean play, should people express themselves in pentameter instead of ordinary speech?

Even the cinema, which is generally upheld as the very essence of realistic art, has imposed upon an audience unaware of it the most extraordinarily unrealistic conventions. Huge faces, fifty times the size of normal ones, are flashed at us without alarming us in the slightest. Hundred-piece orchestras, supposedly hidden behind the sofa, spin out sugary melodies while Van Johnson kisses Jennifer Jones in the living room, and in the flick of an eyelash we are transported, without the slightest explanation, from Ma's kitchen to the very top of K-2.

*   *   *   *   *

One may ask why, if opera is a valid and vital form, it hasn't stimulated more successful contemporary contributions to the theatre. Most modern composers blame their failures on the libretti, but I am afraid that the fault more often lies with the music. Opera is, after all, essentially music, and such is the ennobling or transfiguring power of music that we have numerous examples of what safely could be labeled awkward plays transformed into inspiring operas.

We have, however, no single example of a successful opera whose main strength is in the libretto. I have often been accused of writing good libretti and mediocre music, but I maintain that my libretti become alive or illuminated only through my music. Let anyone read one of my texts divorced from its musical setting to discover the truth of what I say. My operas are either good or bad; but if their libretti seem alive or powerful in performance, then the music must share in this distinction.

*   *   *   *   *

One of the reasons for the failure of so much contemporary opera is that its music lacks immediacy of communication. Theatre music must make its point and communicate its emotion at the same moment the action develops. It cannot wait to be understood until after the curtain comes down. Mozart understood this, and there is a noticeable difference in immediacy between some of his symphonic or chamber music styles on the one hand and his operatic style on the other. Many contemporary composers seem to fear clarity and directness, perhaps because they are afraid of becoming obvious. To quote Goethe again: "We must not disdain what is immediately visible and sensuous. Otherwise we shall be sailing without ballast."

*   *   *   *   *

A great deal of nonsense has been said and written about opera in English and many are the people who still believe that most foreign languages are better suited to music than English is. But I maintain that every language is, potentially, equally musical, and it is up to the composer to absorb and illuminate this language in his music.

The marriage of words and music should be a symbolic relationship, that is, one of interdependence and mutual nourishment. Obviously, each language creates its own kind of inseparable musical setting. To people who maintain that Italian is an ideal language for opera, let them hear "Goetterdaemmerung" sung in Italian, as is customary in Italy.

Great English composers have proven in the past (Purcell, for example, or the English madrigalist) how singable English can be. (This, even though George Bernard Shaw stated rather sadly that the English have an unrequited love for music.) And there is no doubt that the Negro today has set the American vernacular with an irresistible charm. What other language could convey such melancholy ecstasy as the Negro spiritual?

*   *   *   *   *

This brings us to the problem of translation. Should an opera be translated? There is no doubt that many musical values are lost no matter how good the translation may be. It was very shocking for me to hear "The Consul" translated even into Italian, which is my native language. Nevertheless, I insist that an opera must be dramatically understandable to its audience, and if some musical subtleties are lost in translation, there is still much more that has been gained, dramatically.

Although purists writhe in horror at the mere mention of translating operatic masterpieces into foreign languages, is it not quite significant that in so far as I know, no great operatic composer has ever objected to his operas being translated into other languages? And very often, as in the case of Debussy and Strauss, they have themselves contributed to the translation. Poetry, too, is essentially untranslatable, but, as in Shakespeare, for example, the singularity and universality of his genius have survived even the most approximate translation.

Author and Selection Notes

Born in Cadegliano, Italy, Gian-Carlo Menotti (1911-   ) has lived his adult life in the United States. Since his graduation from Curtis Institute of Music, where he now teaches, he has written several operas which have been performed both in America and Europe, among them *Amelia Goes to the Ball, The Old Maid and the Thief,* and *The Island God.* The present selection, as its title suggests, consists of a series of notes in which the author answers some of the basic questions frequently asked about opera.

Questions and Exercises

1. List the main topics discussed in this essay. Are the asterisks which separate the "notes" placed at the most logical points?

2. Explain "that significant symbolism which is the very essence of dramatic illusion."

3. How does the author answer the criticism that opera today does not stimulate successful contributions to the theater?

4. What is the author's feeling about translating operas from their original language into English for American audiences? Write a paragraph giving your own opinion on this subject.

5. Do you feel that Menotti's arguments in this article are sound? Why or why not?

6. Theme Topics: Foreign Opera Should Be Presented in English; Opera Is Here to Stay; Opera Should Be Modernized; The Metropolitan Opera House—Symbol of American Culture? My Opinion of Opera; My Favorite Medium of the Theater (opera, films, or stage plays).

THE OLYMPIAN COWBOY
Harry Schein

When middle-brow people want to express their utter contempt for films, they often cite the "Western" as typical of the idiocy they wish to deprecate. Actually, the Western is the backbone, not the tail, of the art of the film.

The Western, for that matter, is much more than a film. It offers us the opportunity to experience the creation of folklore, to see how it grows and takes form. The roots of the mythology of Europe and the Far East are hidden in the past, and today can be only imperfectly reconstructed. But the white man's America is no older than the Gutenberg Bible. It attained economic independence and, therewith, cultural independence about the time the novel achieved its artistic and popular success. It is no accident that James Fenimore Cooper's work stands as America's first significant contribution to literature. It is just as natural that the film, at its very beginning, seized upon the Western motif. In the life span of less than one generation, it has developed from an apparently innocent, meaningless form into a rigidly patterned and conventional mythology, into one body of young America's folklore.

Reprinted by permission of author and publisher as it appeared in *The American Scholar*, Summer, 1955, Vol. XXIV.

Of course, most of the Westerns of silent films were substantially sideshows performed by puppets. But somewhere between William S. Hart and Hopalong Cassidy, a change occurred. The simple, upright and faithful cowboy became more and more decked out with silver spurs and guitars; he sang much and drank little; he never worried about women even while protecting them. Almost imperceptibly he was changing into an omnipotent father symbol whose young attendants consistently avoided heterosexual and other traps of an unmanly nature.

The child is father to the man. The Western of the days of the silent film already contained the material and the tendencies which, little by little, as the element of sound consolidated the form of the film, were deepened and rigidified. Folklore demands a rigid form. If one is to feel the power of the gods, repetition is required. It is precisely the rigid form of the Western which gives the contents mythological weight and significance. This requires a ritualistic handling, with a rigid cast of characters similar to that of the *commedia dell'arte* and a strict orthodoxy like that of the Japanese Kabuki Theater.

Several years ago, when the Swedish state film censorship bureau wished to demonstrate the justification for its existence by showing what erotic and brutal shocks we escaped because of the intervention of the censor, it was found that these consisted to a great extent of saloon fights in the Westerns. The similarities among these fights, taken from perhaps ten different films, were astounding: the same bar counter, the same supernumeraries, the same groupings, the same chorography in the fights themselves. And when the Czech puppet-film director, Iri Trnka, decided to produce a satire on American films, it was natural that he chose the Western. It was simple enough to use puppets instead of human beings to make the rigid form and strict convention appear grotesque.

The movement in a stereotype is as obvious as the ticking of a clock in an otherwise absolute silence. The postwar shifts in perspective which the Western underwent did not disturb the mythological stability, but gave it a profound meaning aside from its aesthetic value. The genre has produced several good and many bad films, but even the stuttering priest can speak about God. Naturally, the Western does not lack aesthetic interest. Even in its role of nursery for American film directors it has a certain aesthetic significance. Moreover, the rigid form requires speed, action and movement, and, in propitious circumstances, can contribute to a dramatic conclusion. In addition, it creates an enormous demand for freshness within the limitations of the stereotype, an aesthetic stimulus as good as any.

Also characteristic of the Western is the public's relationship to it. The desire to experience the same thing time after time implies on the part of the public a ritualistic passivity similar to that which one finds in a congregation at divine service. It cannot be curiosity which drives the public to the Western; there is no wish for something different and unfamiliar, but a need for something old and well known. One can scarcely talk about escape from reality in the usual sense; it is a hypnotic condition rather than a complicated process of identification. The Western has the same bewitching strength as an incantation: the magic of repetition.

THE HERO AND WOMEN

In the center stands the hero. He is always alone in the little community. He often lacks family and, not infrequently, is one of those exceptional human beings who seem never to have had a mother. Opposed to him are the bandits (there are always several) and their leader, an older, rich, often to all appearances respectable man in league with corrupt political bosses. The bandit, too, usually lacks a wife and only now and then does he have an unfortunate daughter. Finally, there is the little community itself—respectable, timid and neutral in action.

The action often takes place in the period immediately after the Civil War. In such cases, the hero is often a Southern officer and his opponents are Northerners. The struggle between these two elements is an epilogue to the war, often with a reversed outcome. Uncle Sam is like a father figure, powerful and hateful, but at the same time filled with guilt feelings toward the ravished Southerners. Although the Western apparently takes revenge for the defeat of the South, the revenge is still illusory, a rebellious gesture which culminates in loyal submission and father-identification.

The hero is surrounded by a good woman and several bad saloon girls, who later either sing about love or dance the cancan. The good woman is usually a blonde and a specialist in making apple pie. The bad women are the kind one goes to bed with. Although the beds rarely appear in Western interiors, there is reason to assume that the saloon ladies are supposed to suggest those prostitutes who, during the enormous woman shortage of the eighteen-hundreds, were imported into the West and, through their kind actions, saw to it that not all the men shot one another to death. Of course, in more advanced films, the typical mixed-figure appears: an apparently bad woman who seems to be on the side of the bandits but who gradually shows herself to be innocent and finally helpful in their destruction.

The hero's relationship to women is very subtle. He shields them without actually being involved. In more and more Westerns a direct enmity toward women is displayed. Sadism is directed most often toward the bad women, but now and then even toward the mixed-type. "Duel in the Sun" offers the best example of this. Often a triangle drama appears (a woman and two men) which ends with the men becoming good friends and arriving at the realization that the woman is not worth having. In "The Outlaw," the young man, after prolonged abuse, humiliates the woman by choosing, in a tossup between her and a fine horse, the horse. In a priceless homosexual castration fantasy, the father figure of the film shoots off the ear lobes of the young man when he dares to defend himself. The pistol in Westerns is by now accepted as a phallic symbol.

In a series of films, the weapon stands in the center of the action —a bowie knife, a Winchester rifle, a Colt revolver. He who owns the weapon is unconquerable. The good men are the rightful owners from whom the bad men are trying to steal potency. To own the weapon is much more important than to own the woman. It is important how one draws the weapon. Bad men draw it too often but too slowly. Like Casanova, they shoot in all directions without finding their mark. The hero, who defends family and home—as an institution—draws his weapon quickly. He shoots seldom, but never misses. As protector of the community, he cannot afford to be promiscuous. There must be an outcome of the shooting. A strong man is able to fire six shots without reloading.

So much for the rigid Western pattern, familiar even to the more occasional moviegoers. It may be of interest to determine what variations this pattern displays and particularly those tendencies that have been most pronounced since World War II. The question, in other words, is this. Is there a relation between America's politically dominant situation in the postwar period and a new arrangement of luminaries in its mythology?

THE THREE MODERN VARIANTS

Accepting the usual risks of generalization, one may speak of three basic elements in the Western: the symbolic, the psychological and the moral. If one bears in mind the fact that the Western is usually a mixture of these elements, it will not be too gross a simplification to discuss each of these factors separately.

It is said that Chaplin never had any inkling of his profundity until he began to read what various intellectuals wrote about him. Then he himself became intellectual. That is, of course, sheer nonsense. If, however, this kind of reasoning is applied to the symbolism of the Western, it probably has a certain correctness. In other words, the Western seems to have become conscious of its symbolic purport and, as a result of this consciousness, has become quite dreadfully symbolic.

That unconscious enmity toward women, formerly expressed more indirectly, with lip service paid to chivalry while actions denoted inner indifference (placing on a pedestal always implies humiliation), now finds stronger and more direct expression. The hatred of women has become so obvious that it must give rise to speculation. Their ill-treatment in a physical and often purely sadistic sense is an increasingly common element not only in the Western but also in other American films such as "Gilda." "Winchester 73" is an outstanding example. "Colt 45" is a symbolic parody of this motif. Not only must the pistol be regarded from a symbolic point of view—it goes off with a louder bang than the rifle—but the villain in the film has a favorite position, teetering on a chair, half-sprawling, with his hands on his hips and the pistol profile following a naturalistic line. Even if this conscious smuggling in of symbols never can take in an artistically interested customs officer, it indicates an ambition to make more than a classical spectacle of the Western.

This ambition is made even clearer through the psychological element. Though Westerns are undoubtedly unpsychological for the most part, they have a predilection for dealing with the psychology of the villain. Even this is refreshing to an eye that yearns for some gray oases in the black and white desert.

Through trying to clarify the villain's behavior, the films muster a certain sympathy for him. He becomes a product of unfortunate circumstances, orphaned at an early age and brought up in a loveless milieu. He has, as a rule, suffered injustice and seeks revenge in a certain criminal but, in the deepest sense, forgivable way. Often, as stated before, he is a Southern officer whose home was devastated. The villain, of course, must die, but as a rule he dies happy, in a redeeming self-sacrifice through which the blessedness of the final kiss acquires a charmingly melancholy background.

These psychological efforts can give rise to important thematic rearrangements. A few years ago two films were made about Jesse James—a legendary Western figure who is well on the way to becoming America's Robin Hood. In one of these films, "The Great Missouri Raid," the James brothers are formidable enemies, but chivalrous supermen of steel, dutiful toward their mother. They are, of course, Southerners, and their enemy is a Northern general modeled after a hateful Gestapo type. The film is very well made, and belongs to the classical Western pattern. The other film, "I Shot Jesse James," seems more unpretentious. It concerns a man who shot his best—and oldest—friend in the back in order to obtain amnesty for himself and be able to marry a saloon girl (cf. Freud). The victim is the bandit sought by the law, the murderer the one who is protected by the law. The psychological complications caused by this rearrangement of boundaries between the territory of the villain and the hero are dealt with in two sections. The murderer is certainly free, but he is detested by public opinion. Even the girl is unkind enough not to trouble herself about him after the treachery which has been committed for her sake. The murderer, desiring to defy public opinion, accepts an offer from a traveling theatrical troupe to appear on the stage and show how he shot James in the back. In another part of the film, he forces a singer to render the ballad of the murder of Jesse James. Thus, as his crime is repeated again and again, the murderer returns to the mental scene of the crime and suffers an inner decay which leads to a new crime, this time unprotected by the law.

"I Shot Jesse James" is not the only Western which sets friend against friend. Very often the motif is family; now and then brother stands against brother, father against son. As a rule it is a woman who divides them. Something like Biblically elemental conflicts are deftly extracted from, or themselves extract, a taken moral stand. When form and conclusion are rigid, a fundamental moral problem can have some of the simple, primeval strength of the drama of fate, and thus prevent the repetitions from becoming mechanical.

These moral conflicts are undoubtedly the most interesting elements in the modern Western. They are evident in "The Gunfighter," a very fine film with far from ordinary psychological creativity, and in "High Noon," until now the genre's most outstanding artistic success.

"The Gunfighter" deals with a middle-aged and unglamorized gunman. No one in the entire West can handle a gun as he does. He is, therefore, challenged by all the young fighting cocks who wish to take over his reputation for being invincible. He is forced to kill them in self-defense. He flees from his home, but his reputation is swifter than his flight; he is always recognized and the killing is repeated time after time. Though he is fed up to the gills with it, there is always someone who will not leave him in peace. Finally there comes a man who draws the gun a fraction of a second more quickly than he. The gunfighter dies with what is almost relief, but at the same time he is filled with pity for his murderer: now it is *his* turn to take over this reputation as the foremost gunman of the West, his fate to kill and never to be able to flee from killing until he himself is killed.

The Western's moral problem revolves around the Fifth Commandment. One can understand that a country traditionally pacifist but suddenly transformed into the strongest military power in the history of the world must begin to consider how, with good conscience, it can take life. In somewhat awkward situations it is always good to take shelter behind the lofty example of the mythological gods.

I see "High Noon" as having an urgent political message. The little community seems to be crippled with fear before the approaching villains; seems to be timid, neutral and half-hearted, like the United Nations before the Soviet Union, China and North Korea; moral courage is apparent only in the very American sheriff. He is newly married; he wants to have peace and quiet. But duty and the sense of justice come first, in spite of the fact that he must suddenly stand completely alone. Even his wife, who is a Quaker and opposed on principle to killing, wishes to leave him, and only at the last moment does she understand that her duty to justice is greater than her duty to God. The point is, of course, that pacifism is certainly a good thing, but that war in certain situations can be both moral and unavoidable.

"High Noon," artistically, is the most convincing and, likewise, certainly the most honest explanation of American foreign policy. The mythological gods of the Western, who used to shoot unconcernedly, without any moral complications worth mentioning, are now grappling with moral problems and an ethical melancholy which could be called existentialist if they were not shared by Mr. Dulles.

THE SUFFERING GOD

This conscious symbolism, these psychological ambitions and moral statements of account give both color and relief to the mythological substratum. The anchorage in realism, for example, in the historical characters like Billy the Kid and Jesse James, or in the more and more ambitious and thoroughly worked out descriptions of milieux, contribute toward the creation of an impressive space before the footlights of the mythological scene. The native strength and possibilities of the Western are developed in the counterplay between American film production and American film critics. As witness thereof, take that farfetched but characteristic comparison between "High Noon" and "That Old Game about

Everyman" of which Howard A. Burton is guilty in a recent number
of *The Quarterly of Film, Radio, and Television*. His puzzle certainly does not fit together, but one still discerns an Olympian
landscape-model, the Rocky Mountains—saturated with divine morality. Even satires on the Western, such as Bob Hope's "The Pale-
face," indicate a growing consciousness of the genre's true function.

An awareness of the mythological element is thus found not only
among talentless writers, but also among talented directors like
George Stevens. According to a statement in the English film magazine *Sight and Sound,* he is reported to have expressed his desire to
"enlarge" the Western legend and to have said that the pioneers
presented in the Western fill the same role for the Americans as
King Arthur and his knights hold in English mythology. In Stevens'
film "Shane," that ambition is entirely realized. As a matter of fact,
the film incorporates the complete historical development of the
Western, including the protest against the father and the identification with the father. It is, to be sure, an imperfect attempt—but still
an attempt—at synthesis of the classical pattern, enriched with the
three modern variations: symbolic, psychological, moral.

A large and fertile valley in the West is ruled by a powerful and
greedy cattleman. With the help of his myrmidons, he carries on a
private war of attrition against a handful of farmers who are struggling to bring the grazing lands under cultivation. To one of these
small farms, Shane comes, dressed in romantic garb of leather,
cartridge belt and gun. He takes a job there, becomes good friends
with the farmer, his wife and their twelve-year-old boy, Joey. Shane
has a mysterious past; he has been a gunman who now is trying to
begin a new and peaceful life. He manages, for the longest time, to
avoid being provoked by the cattleman's hirelings, but the terror of
the farmers becomes unbearable. When one of them is shot down
by an imported murderer, the others are willing to give up and
move away. No one dares to meet terror with terror. Then Shane
takes off his blue work-clothes and puts on his old leather outfit. He
gets out the gun which he hoped he had laid down forever, rides
forth to the saloon and kills the murderer. He has tried to begin a
new life, but he has not succeeded. He has killed again and must
ride away to the unknown from which he came.

"Shane" cannot, from an artistic point of view, be compared with
"High Noon," possibly because it has not an equally emphasized
main point. It deals, as a matter of fact, with two motifs: Shane and
the little family, and Shane and the community versus the dictatorial
cattleman and his band. But the film is obviously strongly influenced
by "High Noon." The tempo is equally slow and heavy with fate,

the portrayal of the milieu equally penetrating. The action is one unbroken loading of a charge up to the climax. This is unusual for a Western, with its generally very rapid changes of scene.

Like the gunman in "The Gunfighter," Shane is the man marked by fate, he whom the gods set out to kill. The distance between him and Mr. Babbitt, the farmer, and the small-town dweller in "High Noon" is as great as the distance between Brooklyn and Korea. Only the woman lacks perception of the hovering air of fatefulness. She sees only what she can touch. Between Shane and her the atmosphere is tense with fear and eroticism, but only her husband can give her security.

The really original element in "Shane" is the relationship between Shane and the little boy, Joey. Joey cherishes a boundless, completely hysterical admiration for Shane, for his skill with the pistol. He himself is still not permitted to play with loaded weapons, but they occupy his imagination. He smacks his lips to imitate the sound of shooting; he catches sight of game without being able to press after it; he shoots imaginary enemies with imaginary bullets. His confidence in Shane is upset a trifle when Shane knocks his father unconscious. However, when the boy understands that Shane has not robbed his father of life, but only of potency (Shane wants to prevent him, less experienced in the art of shooting, from risking his life, and takes away his pistol), the boy identifies himself completely with Shane. He follows him to the saloon, witnesses the battle, and afterwards takes leave of Shane, prepared to become his heir.

Shane, more than any other Western hero, is a mythological figure. This is partly because the film sees him so much through the eyes of Joey, looking upward. Shane's entry is as godlike as his exit; it is a higher being who comes, driven by fate-impregnated compulsion, to fulfill his mission. Shane is more than Robin Hood, more than Cinderella's prince. He is a suffering god, whose noble and bitter fate it is to sacrifice himself for others.

"Shane" is distinguished by a realism seldom worked out so thoroughly in Westerns. The film takes the time to portray the people in the valley, their everyday lives, their little festivities. A series of impressionistically bold details gives the production a sensitive and fine-grained texture. Its world is familiar and close to reality. Only Shane is alien. He is not Zeus, who, disguised as a human being, visits the earth to cavort with its women, but an American saint, the cowboy who died in the Civil War and sits at God's right hand. He is a leather-bound angel with a gun, a mythological Boy Scout, always ready to keep the hands of true believers and the community unsullied by blood.

A BLOODY FUTURE

As a rule, of course, it is meaningless to discuss the degree of individual vision behind a work of art or a film with a mythological purport. Mythology rests on a collective foundation which also includes the creative artist.

When creative vision is expressed in the form of satire, it has quite obviously freed itself from the mythological substratum, but at the same time it strengthens the existence of that substratum— a puppet show which does not concern itself with the obvious is a paradox. As far as the Western is concerned, Bob Hope and the Marx Brothers demonstrate a blasphemous emancipation. Large sections of the American public, through television's mechanization of the Western, have become surfeited with the genre. Since "Shane" is neither mechanical nor satirical, it ought to be reckoned as the first offspring, and, through Stevens' statement, the first "documented" offspring of the new vision.

The question remains: Is this newly awakened mythological vision going to sabotage mythology itself by dispelling the cloud which carefully used to conceal the summit of Olympus? It is not altogether certain, since vision in and of itself does not preclude piety. Probably, however, these films are going to have a more and more strongly motivated central idea, whereby the distance between the hero of the Western and the rest of its cast is going to increase in proportion to the square of its consciousness. Most interesting, though, will be the future attempts to cram more and more current morality into the mythological pattern. When Shane's little Joey grows up and gets ammunition, he is not going to lack a target worth shooting at.

Author and Selection Notes

A chemist and president of a Swedish engineering firm, Harry Schein (1924-   ) is also film editor for *BLM*, an important Scandinavian literary magazine. Having been intensely interested in movies all his life (as a boy of thirteen he was once arrested for breaking into a theater to see "Frankenstein," presented in Sweden to adult audiences only), he brings to his analysis of Western movies much experience and an acute appraisal.

Questions and Exercises

1. What does the author mean by the statement, "The Western is the backbone, not the tail, of the art of the film"?

2. Look up the meaning of the term "folklore" and explain how the Western offers the opportunity to see how folklore is created, the opportunity "to see how it grows and takes form."

3. List the characteristics of the modern Western which Mr. Schein traces in section one of his article.

4. Explain the relationship, as the author sees it, between the hero in the typical Western and women.

5. Explain and illustrate the three movie formulas designated by the author as "three modern variants."

6. Using the headings of the essay as your major topics, make an outline of the essay.

7. What political message according to Schein is revealed in "The Gunfighters"? In "High Noon"?

8. What is visualized by this author for the Western's future?

9. Why is the movie usually listed as one of the "popular arts"?

10. Theme Topics: The Movie as a Mirror of American Life; Hollywood and American Morality; The Qualities That Make a Good Western; The Image of America Exported in American Movies; Movies That Have Influenced My Life; The Late, Late Show.

AMERICAN CULTURE ABROAD

Chester H. Opal

Every cultural and public affairs officer who has served in Europe under the United States information program has been exposed to the stereotype of America as a land of advanced technical civilization and retarded spiritual growth. Indeed, the fact that these notions so consistently fall together in some European minds suggests that the inescapability of the first characteristic contributes to the inevitable ascription of the second.

The problem has been of serious concern to our policy planners. An attempt to meet it in one of its aspects has been made in the field of religious information and in the quite justified emphasis on spiritual values found in the pronouncements of the nation's chief spokesmen. Yet it is a sad truth that even if we convinced others that Americans are the most pious folk in the world we should have advanced almost nothing to weaken the argument that we are cultural barbarians. If, for example, we sought to prove that the highest Christian principles guide our industrial and business life, most Europeans who are critical of our culture would find this beside the point and ask what connection the things of the spirit have with the creation and distribution of material goods. What about our arts? they ask. What about our manners? What, they would insist, about our *Kultur*?

Our critics have pre-empted certain very limited areas of life and expression; it assumes the name of Culture. It is not the total view of the anthropologist, who unites in the concept of culture the whole range from totem to tool to wall painting to string quartet. Acceptance of so narrow a definition of culture has brought a measurement of bafflement to those charged with stimulating an appreciation of American culture abroad. It has been difficult to determine precisely where to take hold of the problem, *or even to state why the matter should be of concern at all.*

For example, an American ballet troupe travels to Europe and performs, among other items, an American ballet on an American subject—"Fall River Legend," the story of Lizzie Borden. But what do the European critics discuss the following day? This superb demonstration of art? Only fleetingly. They dwell instead on the America reflected in the ballet; they emphasize the horror of this American parricide. How does one meet criticism of this kind? Another example: If we present three chief American novelists, our critics usually say of Faulkner that his theme is incest, of Hemingway that he writes of the tired self-pitying American who is amorous but lives eunuched by the causes for which he has so monosyllabically fought, of Steinbeck that he is sentimental and writes paganistically of the impoverished Okie and the comic half-breed; and the picture which is flung back at us is of America, a prurient eunuch sitting in a broken-down Ford truck on Highway 66, spitting tobacco juice and fondly dwelling on memories of incest.

What happens here is that the critics shift the ground from a consideration of American books as works of art to a consideration of the picture of America projected in the books. *The art that controls the portrayal is conveniently discounted.* We may well ask why this is so—ask not only why the critics find so little Culture in America but also why they appear so determined to find no more.

It may be well to set forth a few general propositions on which it would be helpful to secure agreement before a program to meet the problem is planned. First of all, it is futile to discuss the superiority of one culture *qua* culture over another contemporaneous culture. (If one is lucky and sufficiently dishonest, one may at most convince oneself.) Furthermore, no element of culture abstracted from the total setting can be employed legitimately as a ground for judgment about the cultural setting as a whole.

Americans have an unwholesome sense of inferiority in the presence of older cultures. This compels them, on the one hand, to adopt criteria of judgment which prejudice unfavorably their estimate of their own cultural level, or, on the other hand, to assert their own values in aggressive accents which can only alienate other peoples.

Culture follows power and resists domination; or, to put it another way and more within the spirit of a thesis of Santayana's, where culture accepts and enforces leadership and control, it defines them as legitimate power, while leadership and control that are grafted on culture and draw no sustenance from it are defined as domination. The resistance of certain groups in Europe to alignment with the United States, when they honestly hold that America is culturally unworthy to lead them, is a reflection of this sense of domination by something alien to themselves. We cannot deliberately and significantly modify this feeling by talking about our common culture. We can best modify it by developing, through shared actions, a sense of shared destiny.

Our position of leadership tends to make some Europeans denigrate those things which make for our ascendancy. This is almost always done on cultural—spiritual—grounds. Many Europeans are embarrassed by the robustness of American society and by the impact of our energy on their life. It is only natural that the more material aspects of our civilization are highlighted in their eyes. They are forced to redress the balance in another realm, in order to salvage their pride. Although this makes total acceptance of ourselves into the European family virtually impossible, we must not condemn our critics too harshly, since to do so is to state in effect that what we offer is superior to what they have, only they are too blind to see it—and this is to commit the same intellectual sin for which we are condemning them in the first place. If we sincerely honor the integrity of other men, we will not assault their legitimate pride.

When we find that retreat into pride is weakening the ability of Europeans to accomplish on the social and economic levels what is necessary to the achievement of our shared objectives, we must seek more intensively to stimulate activity on the social and economic levels and not seek to meet the critic in his own camp. For our primary objective is not to achieve recognition as cultural equals, but rather to strengthen those engines of foreign society which will advance the aims of our joint policy. Anything else is a sideshow distracting attention from the main tent.

European peoples who live under Soviet domination and look to us as their potential liberators provide us with a useful lesson: they do not care, for example, about the level of artistic expression in America. It is true that the Eastern and Central European intellectuals have a rather low estimate of it; but this in no way affects their total allegiance, for, when all hands are down, they will admit that although France, for example, has a "higher" culture than the United States, the latter is a "greater" nation and friendly to boot. They may not know precisely how to define this greatness, but no one who has spent any time in that section of Europe can doubt that they believe in it. What this means in effect is that history has forced the intellectual in the satellite states to give a primary status to some transcendent value other than those isolated and used by the intellectuals of the West to belabor America. This is noteworthy when we realize that the choice not even for the Eastern European is one of physical life or death; if the latter were the case, we may be sure the peoples of that region are resourceful enough to manage to stay alive under Communist tyranny. It is what in their eyes makes life worth living that lies at the bottom of this choice between East and West. *And that is nothing more or less than a choice between cultures*; which is the same as saying, *they prefer their own.*

Even if he holds that America lies outside the European cultural stream, the Eastern European attests to a belief of prime importance to us—namely, that he does not see his culture imperiled by the leadership of the United States. America, in short, does not abuse its strength. Those of us who feel uneasy about America's present role in the world may well remind ourselves that there does exist this reputation for benignity, and that it refers to the heart of any culture—the way man treats man.

Needless to say, more sophisticated Europeans see in this quality a proof of our immaturity and naïveté: only a child or a fool would dare practice the social virtues on the international plane. George Kennan in his two books on American foreign policy appears to call this aspect of the American tradition into question. His criticism resolves itself essentially into warning that exclusive reliance on this private ethic as a guide in the conduct of foreign affairs has led and may continue to lead us into adventures of the most tragic kind. Unfortunately, despite what Kennan and, most recently, Walter Lippmann, have been saying, we cannot renounce this tendency to moralize our way into and out of involvement in the affairs of other nations. The whole matter would lend itself to easy solution if we did not have to explain to ourselves the bases of our action in the international arena. We have to give ourselves the same reasons we give others, and we have to give others those explanations which, *pace* Kennan, we ourselves are capable of believing. Our morality, whether practiced at home or abroad, is a datum of culture. If the sophisticated European finds our ethics naïve, we must be clear in our minds whether it is more important for us to be thought of as not naïve than for us to be ethical. In assessing the validity of any aspect of the stereotype which confronts us abroad, some such equation may be useful in providing a clearer perspective. For the real danger in this area of relations is that we do harm to ourselves either by conceding the point or fighting it. We must remain true to our values, and recognize that they *are* ours and only coincidentally another's, if we are to behave in a manner consistent with our nature. To do otherwise may be to lay ourselves open to the danger of publicly espousing values which our very habits betray.

It may be well to ask, what is the nature of the stereotype, and who holds it?

The stereotype takes many forms. We are materialistic. We prize mediocrity. Our arts are unoriginal or inconsequential and usually both. We are ground down into automatons by the machinery of society. There is a homogeneous tastelessness about the American scene. We are loud, uncouth. We are immature. Etc.

Intellectuals of all shades of political opinion are, naturally, most outspoken in projecting this conception of America. The "culture" to which the intellectual refers is something that is, to begin with, the province of the elite. The peasant seldom if ever meditates on whether or not he himself has a "spiritual" or "materialistic" bent; and it is a matter of little moment to him whether we are materialistic or not. If he is interested in us it is more out of concern for how we shall help him live and eat than out of concern over whether we carry great original works of art in our cargo ships. On the spiritual side, it is enough for him if he knows we both believe in the same God; but we can exaggerate the importance even of this.

As for the intellectual, when he dwells on our spiritual poverty, it may be because he needs to temporize before joining his destiny with ours: acceptance is a kind of giving in, a surrender to the flood, and he is understandably sensitive to the dangers of engulfment. His culture is perhaps the last thing he can call his own, and even if we believe he exaggerates its profundity and our superficiality, we shall concern ourselves with it only when and where it is holding up what one of our recent Undersecretaries of State has called "the work of the world." We may be sure that in no event can the intellectual abroad be very happy about surrendering a portion of his autonomy or leadership to a foreign people. He has traditionally played a dominant role in guiding the affairs of his country: it is an affront to his pride to tell him, as some have, that today he is virtually impotent without American support.

In determining the political significance of the stereotype we would be wise to establish first of all the locus of effective public opinion, and then to ascertain what concept of culture these groups hold and how controlling an element it is in the evaluation of individuals, groups, or nations, insofar as it affects basic political loyalties; what image do they have of America in these terms; and, finally, how was this image derived. In connection with this last question, it would be necessary to establish which elements have gone into the image-formation from the outside and which are projections from inner psychological states operating to transmute received information.

When the problem is approached systematically, one finds startling revelations. Five years ago International Public Opinion Research, Inc., conducted a study in Europe for the Voice of America. The IPOR group found that the majority of Germans believed that next to Germany, the United States was the most advanced in the arts of any country in the world; while France stood far behind and Italy, strangely enough, was high on no German's list. England and the Soviet Union were far below the others, and on a par with each other besides. In Austria, on the other hand, Germany and Italy were only slightly below Austria itself, and the United States was close behind; while France and Russia did not collect a single percentage point. Most Frenchmen found Americans loud, spoiled, and materialistic, and were the only people (among Italy, Sweden, Germany, Austria, and France) not to find Americans predominantly "friendly." In a study of the French self-image, it was found that the French considered themselves friendly and sentimental in equal degree, and much more so than cultured; indeed, more thought themselves noisy than thought themselves cultured. Fifty percent of the French found the British "cold," and no other characteristic received so high a selection on any of the tests.

It is the writer's belief that we have exaggerated the significance of the stereotype. While he would not deny that it can affect our ability to convince Europeans that we are deserving of leadership, he would point out that history, of which the intellectuals have been no less the agents than the victims, has thrust this leadership upon us. The best we can do is to wield it wisely and justly and seek to inspire belief in our goodness and wisdom, without making our leadership the subject of our information materials.

This is not to say that American culture, even within the narrow field circumscribed by our critics, should not have a place in our overseas information program. The arts are as important a segment of our life as technology, and in fact there is a marriage between the two, as the industrial arts demonstrate at every turn.

Meanwhile, as he prepares to inform foreign audiences concerning the nature and development of the fine arts in America, the American, as an official or as an exchange student or teacher, finds himself confronted with a background which can be at best only sketchily suggested here.

Music: American music labors overseas under a special burden. Our most effective music is strongly influenced by jazz rhythms, and jazz, precisely because the masses have taken to it in Europe, prejudices the cultured elite against anything affected by it. Because the rhythms are so familiar and recognizable, orchestral works grounded on them are accepted for the most part as sterile tricks of orchestration. (As if the minuet of Mozart or a waltz or mazurka by Chopin could be condemned for being dance music.) That jazz may be the rhythmic category under which our composers experience and externalize their creativity, and that this may be its natural and national mode, enters the minds of foreign critics (as of American) only as further justification for wholesale condemnation. And all this in despite of the receptivity European composers themselves have shown to jazz influences. The fact that the rhythmic components of jazz come largely from the African Negro tends to "prove" that the barbaric, the primitive, dominates the American spirit—a racist theory at best and one hardly consonant, one would think, with that bent of mind which so quickly condemns this nation for the practice of racial discrimination.

Painting: Twentieth-century American art has gone to school in Europe. Where, lately, it has differed from European art it has been not in the techniques employed, but rather, for the most part, in the subject matter explored. Americans too long imitated inner states as well as outward forms represented in European art. That almost morbid inburrowing preoccupation with the self which dictated new techniques to mirror disintegration, and the contrary attempt to take from outer reality its terror by reducing it to abstract, non-representational geometry which could be manipulated to suit the whim, were expressions of the European spirit and could not but be foreign to the more outgoing American temperament. American artists have in recent decades posited, implicitly at least, criteria of judgment that demand evidence both of sanity and health in the artist and of a recognizable inner world. This is not solely because the American public is revolted by evidence of mental disorder, nor because in its easy optimism the public prefers to blind itself to the dark tides that move under the surface glitter of our lives; rather it is because that has been taken into account which has determined the great art of the past—namely, the exploration of, and search for, symbols and images around which are mobilized the sentiments of the generality of mankind in any region or society. Leonardo's notebooks abound in evidence of his neurosis, and we may be sure the neurosis controlled his hand; but Leonardo's neurosis is not the subject of his art. Lacking world-symbols at a time marked by a profound dissolution of spiritual values and a general failure of communication of man with man, the American has sometimes taken recourse in a parochialism which frequently has the aspect of blatant nationalism. The search in American art has been at root semantic; hence the regional and even nationalistic flavor of so many of its products. The life they represent is America, its history, its folklore, its cities, its towns, its landscapes, its people. On both counts the old prejudices of Europe are against them, for, as the techniques are not deemed particularly original, so the American civilization they project is usually condemned as being a mechanistic dehumanization of man.

Literature: Thanks in no small measure to the Swedish Academy, American writing has had a fairly favorable reception abroad. Its influence has been deep. Nevertheless, American writers are usually considered shallow, and as reflecting a general shallowness in American intellectual life. It is, of course, a notorious fact that American writers do not play openly with Big Ideas. No one, in an American novel, sits in a mountain sanitarium at Davos and riddles the problems of Western civilization; Thomas Mann's Settembrini becomes, in American prose, an immigrant fruit peddler at the Fulton market. An idea as such can easily serve as a protagonist in Europe, where nations and sects and ethnic groups have gone to war over all manner of idea and ideology. (One thinks of the many who died over the question of the consubstantiality or transubstantiality of Christ, the quarrel over one Greek *O*, as Gibbon calls it; of the solemn holy butcheries of Torquemada's autos-da-fé; of Bruno burning at the stake and Galileo on his knees; and of the assassin kindness Calvin showed to Servetus.) Whole chapters of Tolstoy and Mann can be devoted to a discussion of freemasonry, Dostoyevsky can build a religious epic around the idea of the third Rome, and in France, Péguy, Bernanos, Bloy, and Mauriac can dramatize Roman Catholic thought and Catholic action which are most poignant when they are closest to atheism. The ideas which have or have had national and sometimes fatal personal meaning to an European, and hence inspire an emotional posture at the merest suggestion of them, do not have the same dramatic potentialities for American writers. It would, however, require a separate paper to present the positive qualities of American writing—its dedication to the treatment of problems as against ideas, for example.

Architecture: Architecture is a social art; just how social it is, even when it adapts itself, as in a dwelling, to the personality of the individual owner is elaborately and eloquently set forth in the writings of Frank Lloyd Wright. The Broadacres Plan which Wright has presented takes account of the personality or character. It is, in fact, the impulse to serve and express character, the humanness of man, that compelled Wright to advance it; but it is a city that he creates. Unfortunately, however, it is the American skyscraper that has become the nation's symbol abroad and has served to confirm in the minds of others our preoccupation with size, numbers, and our alleged submersion of the individual. Yet it is in our recent thinking, planning, and creation in the architectural field that America's unique lesson for other peoples lies.

Wright, in describing organic architecture as the architecture of democracy, suggests to the present writer that the approach which might best be adopted in planning an American information program abroad would be prompted by a consideration of American culture as *integral* or *organic* culture. This would imply a refusal to isolate any element of culture from its setting, and an insistence that where one item of culture becomes the subject of discourse it be treated in such a manner as to suggest the existence and character of the setting. This approach, it is true, will not inevitably win for particular cultural expressions assessment as "superior" or "advanced," but it has the merit of suggesting to non-Americans that understanding of America is a prerequisite of judgment on any specific cultural act. This at once compels sociological and political analysis, and if we should achieve no more than this through our information materials, we shall perhaps have accomplished enough. Such analysis calls so many sets of values into play—social, practical, political, aesthetic, scientific—that we shall at least have escaped the tyranny of the narrow point of view.

It is possible that only as we persuade the world to accept or understand principles of the order of Wright's shall we win for ourselves the only kind of understanding we really desire from others. The heart of American civilization, its drift and its goal, appears to the present writer at least suggested in Wright's philosophy. Technicism informed with humanism; the social fact as the expression and not the suppression of the individual; spiritual impulse and need fulfilling themselves in a building as surely as they ever did in a Gothic cathedral; the centrality of man in any plan; order and stability *and* adventure; the variousness of our land and the accommodation to it—these. It is perhaps not too preposterous to suggest that the basic problems of society and human freedom run together into this one problem of architecture and community planning; for certainly it must be how we organize and use the material world about us that sets the stamp on our civilization and shows the spirit within.

But how effective can any official overseas information program be, it is often asked, if Hollywood maintains its uninhibited sway over the minds of the masses throughout the free world?

This, the writer submits, is usually an unexamined question, and it may be well to close this paper with a discussion of Hollywood films. There has been a great deal of agitation among us about Hollywood movies and their role in muddying the palette from which the picture of America is being painted abroad. It is fashionable for Americans to damn our movies as severely as do some critics overseas. So far have we ourselves gone in this direction that we accord the highest honors to such hybrid hothouse blooms as Olivier's "Henry V," and, looking through the puritanic haze that forms the moral atmosphere of this nation, see high art in the risqué bedroom dramas of Europe.

One is at a loss to determine whom to believe, the critics or the masses. A good movie like "Bicycle Thief," an anxiety dream from beginning to end, was disavowed in its own country, where the masses preferred the antics of Toto and crowded to enjoy the latest importation from America; the critics could see little virtue in it until it began to win national glory and dollars abroad. On the other hand, the Italian critics were enthusiastic about "The Difficult Years," which showed how a charmingly simple man could become a member of the Black Shirts through force of circumstance, as if Fascism had roots in nothing but the gentle befuddled tolerance of humble folk.

We must acknowledge that Hollywood produces films in blithe ignorance of State Department policy. We cannot expect Hollywood deliberately to undertake our propaganda battle overseas. Hollywood is big business. As Robert Briffault once remarked, a banker can be philanthropic, a bank cannot. But are we sure that all this is to the bad? It has been estimated that over 300,000,000 persons go to movies throughout the world each week. Of these, over 200,000,000 see American films. The range in subject and in artistic merit of these American films overseas is almost as broad as we find it in this country; in fact, the range of exported films is narrower only because the worst films are excluded, not the best. (Films of disguised pornography, parading as lessons on the sins of adolescent sex, hoodlumism, and dope addiction, which figure in triple feature presentations for Saturday midnight crowds in larger cities, are not on our export lists.)

In the satellite world the writer found that theatres showing American films were forever jammed, despite the exhortations of the yoked press, while movie houses showing much-publicized Russian films were almost empty and those who attended were usually creatures moved by indentured enthusiasm. In free Europe the picture is fraught with contradictions, and we are often damned and blessed for the same things. But American films are an expression of American culture. Whatever else we may say about them, they reflect our basic values. If there is some hypocrisy in and about our films, it is because there is hypocrisy in us; but this hypocrisy, again, is in large degree a refusal to admit the disparity between our ideals and our actions, or, to put it another way, a refusal to give up our ideals simply because our actions fail to conform.

Without introducing an overly acid note of irony, one may say that Hollywood dramatizes our naïveté, our lack of sophistication. Good triumphs in our films; crime does not pay; the honest man wins the maiden; a deed of kindness is rewarded, sometimes in kind, sometimes in pure ego-satisfaction; citizens help each other; the brave man conquers the wilderness; men find attractive women attractive. . . . Perhaps our values are crudely Manichean; perhaps we do not explore enough gradations of guilt and responsibility. But let us be sure that when others explore the fine shadings of guilt and innocence they are not (as in "The Difficult Years") doing so in order perhaps to absolve themselves of sin and to clear their consciences, which are sore troubled indeed after two world wars. The beautiful realism of French films in the 'thirties, which, according to Roger Manvell, deepened the structure and tone of the film art, was employed to express the *malaise* of France. Our realism, which was no less effective as art, dealt with social issues honestly and, just as honestly, contained an optimistic note. We faced the issues, and, as it turned out, solved some of them. In the light of the parlous conditions that then prevailed it was "realistic" for the French to be pessimistic, and "naïve" for us to be optimistic. But were we really so naïve? Have we had no right to optimism in view of our history?

This is not an argument for complacency. That a good deal of trash has been exported cannot be denied,—nor that just as abominable stuff and worse is produced abroad. This is an argument against exaggeration of the alleged ill effect of our films overseas.

A generation of Europeans have grown up to American films. Our films have given Europe the idea of American space, of the great frontier, of pioneering (spatial and mental), of building new worlds, of vertical social mobility, of our wealth, our application of human resources to the use of natural wealth, our social problems (have many problems really been avoided in our films?) and how we go about solving them in a democracy, our folklore, our music, our basic pieties, our gift for colorful neologisms, our talent for largeness and generosity. The ellipses in our speech and modes of behavior present no problems to Europeans: the masses, at least, feel comfortable in the presence of Americans. *We are probably the only people in the world that other people believe they know better than we know ourselves.*

The unconscious influence of American movies has been profound. It may be charted in the many imitations of American habit, dress, play and in the social and economic aspirations we find almost everywhere in Europe. American movies, having expressed the values of the American people which in turn have given this nation its revolutionary authenticity, cannot but foster something equally creative abroad. It is this quality of our films that provokes so much defensive criticism from critics of the Right and Left, who find creativity a threat to the rigid values that guide their thinking. If our films are really dangerous to Europe from our point of view, it may well be because they inspire dreams and desires which deepen the popular frustrations on which the demagogue rides to power. But neither American nor European leaders have accepted the thesis that Europe has reached the limit of its resources and its capacity to advance.

American films, like all other expressions of our cultural life, may be said to reflect one cardinal virtue, and that is that America is a process, not a thing. One must live, as Augustine said, according to the creator and not according to the created thing.

If Europe and the rest of humanity is to know us, let it be as we really are. Any attempt to tamper with the truth in order to give our virtues greater prominence than they deserve will make us out to be more virtuous than we are, and this can lead only to false expectations by others and to inevitable betrayals by us of their trust.

Author and Selection Notes

The traditional attitude of Europeans toward Americans gets a new look in this essay by Chester H. Opal (1918-   ), American newspaper reporter and writer, and, since World War II, foreign service and public affairs officer for the Department of State. Having been stationed in numerous European cities since the war, and also having been a director of the Voice of America, Opal writes authoritatively about European and American cultural relations.

Questions and Exercises

1. Why is a reappraisal of the attitude of Europeans toward Americans especially necessary since World War II with its influx of servicemen into every nook and corner of the globe?

2. Opal's introductory paragraphs suggest one of his main concerns in the essay. What is it?

3. Go carefully through the essay and mark all the transitional phrases, sentences, or paragraphs. If your instructor asks you to write a theme on one of the topics below, use similar transitional sentences or paragraphs to indicate your basic organization to your reader.

4. Give the definitions of the following words used in your text and write a paragraph or short theme using as many of them as possible: "prurient," "denigrate," "transcendent," "mediocrity," "blatant," "ideology."

5. Read Marshall W. Stearns' "Is Jazz Good Propaganda?" Do you feel that jazz is a good example of American culture to be shipped abroad? Defend your point of view.

6. According to Opal, why are some Europeans so critical of American culture? Do you agree with him?

7. What is your opinion of the stereotyped image which Opal says Europeans have of America? Are the Europeans correct?

8. State your opinion of the European attitude toward American music, art, literature, architecture, and movies.

9. Theme Topics: European Attitudes Toward America; American Attitudes Toward Europe; My Community as an Example of American Culture; My Definition of Culture; The Success of the Voice of America.

IS JAZZ GOOD PROPAGANDA?

The Dizzy Gillespie Tour

Marshall W. Stearns

During the past few years the number of jazzbands touring abroad has swollen mightily while stories of their incredible success have

From *Saturday Review*, July 14, 1956, by Marshall W. Stearns. Reprinted by permission of *Saturday Review*.

multiplied. Louis Armstrong, Stan Kenton, Lionel Hampton, Woody Herman, Count Basie, Jazz at the Philharmonic, and many others have racked up impressive scores. The demand is great and the profit considerable. But early last spring, through the International Exchange Program which is run by ANTA (American National Theatre and Academy), the State Department helped to send a jazzband abroad without thought of profit and to countries where no jazzband has ever played. The tour, which covered eight Middle Eastern and Balkan countries, lasted from approximately the middle of March to the middle of May, and I went along as a sort of combined artistic adviser, bandboy, and lecturer on jazz.

The idea was simply to make new friends for the United States, especially in those critical nations which Russia, at enormous expense, is flooding with free but strictly supervised talent. The American approach was different—a sort of do-it-yourself plan with emphasis upon free enterprise. The band did its own booking, with the help of the American Embassies and the United States Information Service, and the Government more or less guaranteed it against loss. The band was paid a reasonable minimum, no matter how financially successful the concerts might be, and no more. It was a sparkling new idea in the jazz world, and it worked out famously.

After careful consideration the musicians for the modern-styled Gillespie band were selected from those available. The group rehearsed for a month in New York a program which illustrated the history of jazz as well as the latest experimental music. They played Abadan, Dacca, Karachi, Beirut, Damascus, Aleppo, Ankara, Istanbul, Zagreb, Belgrade, and Athens. In some places the people had never heard of jazz—let alone Louis Armstrong ("Then I *knew* I had to work," moaned Gillespie), but the music was received with wild enthusiasm and the musicians were treated like heroes.

Why? On the surface, everybody—even the old folks—seemed to *want* to love jazz, even before they heard it. They definitely associated jazz with the cheerful, informal, and generous side of American life and they were bowled over by its spontaneity and vitality. The stereotype notion that jazz is lowbrow never got in the way of their enjoyment. On the contrary, the folk origins of jazz were considered a high recommendation. "Jazz is fun," they said admiringly, and even respectable middle-aged citizens were transformed into rabid jazz fans in the course of one concert.

Beneath the surface, we bumped into more complicated reasons for this love of jazz. Our stay in Yugoslavia, where the Communist government has only recently permitted jazz, furnished the most illuminating evidence. In Belgrade and Zagreb we found some of the best jazzmen and most devoted fans. They knew the birthplace, age, and recordings of every member of the band—but they begged desperately for more recordings. A process involving several consecutive stages seemed to be at work: Yugoslav jazz musicians had been trying to leave the country for the United States—a dangerous move in their country—for many years; the jazz fans had been applying for American visas when we arrived. And the newly converted fans—young and old—were beginning to think the same way. Their admiration for the United States was unbounded.

What made them think this way? The concerts were a resounding success. In Zagreb, the militia dumped members of the audience back into their seats when they tried to jump up on the stage during the concert, and they formed a cordon across the stage at the end of every performance to let the musicians escape from the admiring crowds. Even the militia seemed to enjoy the music. But one repeated observation by our most devoted fans furnished a clue: "You are all so unorganized," they said, "until the band begins to play."

Other episodes helped to fill in the picture. A minor incident occurred in Zagreb, where a member of the band toasted his local colleagues a little too thoroughly. The press might have used it to discredit the band, but when a well-known native journalist was asked if he would print the story, he replied, "Don't worry, after last night's concert I am a jazz fan first and a newspaperman second." He didn't bother to mention how his government might feel. That night a lady from a fine old family staged a jam session for some members of the band. "The local musicians got down on their knees and salaamed," says Ermet Perry. When the party broke up at dawn, Yugoslav jazzmen serenaded the Americans as they straggled back to their hotel. "What this country needs," the lady was heard to observe, "is fewer ambassadors and more jam sessions."

After some negotiations, the first lecture on jazz to be heard in the sacrosanct halls of the famous Zagreb Music Conservatory was arranged. An audience of fifty students and faculty members concentrated on every word—translated by an interpreter—with an intensity that was frightening. In the following discussion, the group agreed that jazz symbolized an element of unconscious protest which cut through the pretenses of tradition and authority. It spoke directly and truly of real life. Such honest discussion in a country known to be infested with secert police must have taken real courage and conviction. When we were leaving, trumpeter-arranger Quincy Jones remarked casually to a local musician that he hoped to see him someday in New York. The man burst into tears. "It is my dearest wish," he said, "but I haven't a chance."

Did the Gillespie tour create good will? There was no conscious attempt to do so. The musicians just had "a mighty fine time" being themselves and making friends with everyone who seemed interested. In Abadan, bandboy Marion Frazer, who is a disc-jockey back home, gave away two suits to a needy native. Later he didn't have a dark suit to wear to the dinner parties. Clarinetist Jimmy Powell found a local musician who had been using the same clarinet reed for a year. "I laid a couple of reeds on him and he almost cried," Powell recalls cheerfully, although he ran out of reeds himself in Athens. Quincy Jones bought a complete outfit for a sailor in the Pakistan Navy. "Why, he only got $1.50 a month," said Jones.

In Dacca, where there are no juke-boxes and few radios, the audiences didn't know how they were supposed to express their delight. They sat wide-eyed on the edge of their chairs at the first concert, and applauded politely as if the noise might interfere with the strange and wonderful music. By the third concert, however, they were participating fully—clapping on the right beat, yelling, and whistling like any college crowd at home.

At the Shahbaugh Hotel, Gillespie set off a near riot by taking a flute-playing snake-charmer to his room for a duet. The management was flustered but Dizzy remained unmoved: "The man's a musician, isn't he?" You could hear the bellboys spreading the news outside the hotel. In Ankara, Gillespie produced another crisis. At an outdoor concert, sponsored by the Turkish-American society, he noticed that a horde of ragamuffins had gathered outside the walls to hear him. Every now and then a youngster would sneak over, only to be thrown back by a cop. Dizzy forthwith announced that he would rather not perform unless everybody was admitted: "I came here to play for *all* the people." But the refreshments, he was told, were insufficient. Dizzy wasn't hungry. So the kids were admitted; the refreshments disappeared, and Gillespie played far into the night.

The impact went deep. In Karachi, Mrs. Lorraine Gillespie, who spent much of her time in the hotel room taking care of correspondence, gained the confidence of the chambermaid. The chambermaid had been hammered with tales of the terrible fate of dark-skinned people in the United States. She would bare her own arm, compare it with the similar shade of Mrs. Gillespie's, and jump back in wonder. "Are you ordered to come here and play? Do they really pay you? Is the trombone soloist, Melba Liston, really a woman or a man dressed like a woman? Are those white men in the orchestra or do they cover their faces with chalk?" To the chambermaid, the jazzmen seemed like a gang of wealthy and eccentric capitalists and her conversion to capitalism was complete. The musicians hardly realized the close scrutiny they were receiving.

The austere Conservatory of Music in Ankara—a topnotch incubator of great Turkish musicians—was approached about a lecture on jazz. The Dean replied hesitantly that he would rather have the lecture given somewhere else because his students spent too much time with jazz anyway. So a well-received lecture was given in the Political Science auditorium. That evening, however, the Dean went to the Gillespie concert. The next morning he phoned excitedly and begged for a lecture. "This is wonderful modern music," he said. Anyone who knew anything about jazz would have been an overwhelming success on that occasion, for the students were ecstatic and they insisted upon a five-minute standing ovation.

Later, in Istanbul, the musicians noticed a pretty girl who attended every concert and sat in the front row. She turned out to be a famous ballerina who swore that she had sold her slippers in order to pay for the tickets. "This music can even make dance the seats in the hall," she said excitedly. An elderly Turk in charge of lighting backstage memorized the band numbers and was soon conducting the orchestra from the wings. He brought two bottles of Turkish cognac with him every night—with a vile concoction called Kola-Koka for a chaser—and wound up manipulating the lights and conducting from a sitting position. He referred to the orchestra as "his band."

The only thing that might be called trouble came from American tourists. Americans abroad seem to consider themselves automatic authorities on jazz by right of birth, and they would take it upon themselves to tell Gillespie either that he wasn't playing jazz or to request some tune such as "Deep in the Heart of Texas." Gillespie was patient and continued to astonish the members of his own band with new variations on his own tunes. At that, the band educated a few Americans. One wealthy dowager from Arizona, staying at the Hilton Hotel in Istanbul, was gently persuaded by one of the musicians with whom she had fraternized to attend a dinner dance. By midnight she was stationed in front of the band. "If I had been at home and not terribly upset in this foreign country," she boasted, "I never would have discovered jazz!"

The acid test of jazz as an ambassador of good-will came in Athens. We arrived just after the rioting, and anti-American feeling was real and intense. Although the band had been booked months in advance, newspaper editorials asked why the United States was sending jazzbands to Greece when they needed arms against Britain. The USIS office had been stoned and there was a rumor that the Greek government had suggested that the Gillespie tour might be postponed. New arrangements for rooms and transportation were impossible and the band flew into town to play a scheduled matinee for students only. They were the people, we were told, who had hurled the rocks.

The success of the concert was unbelievable. The Greek students danced in the aisles with the local gendarmes who were there to preserve order. They drowned out the large and powerful band, playing fortissimo, with a solid wall of applause. They chanted "Dizzy, Dizzy, Dizzy" over and over again. After the concert, they carried Gillespie home on their shoulders. Traffic was stalled for a half hour and several blocks. Even the traffic cops danced in the streets. It was like a Greek Mardi Gras. GREEK STUDENTS LAY DOWN ROCKS AND ROLL WITH DIZ ran the headlines.

Backstage, members of the Russian Folk Dance troupe, which alternated with us at the same theatre, were jitterbugging quietly, deadpan. We were told that they could not speak to anyone without permission and that their director locked them up every night. On the afternoon of the second concert, however, they came and sat in two rows near the front. During intermission, after the band had finished illustrating the history of jazz, several of them came backstage. They wanted to shake hands.

The spokesman for the group played accordion and looked just like a movie version of a commissar: chunky, determined, and grumpy. He let us know that the Gillespie band has "collossal technique and ensemble precision" but his expression told us that this was not enough. He wanted more "piano," meaning less volume, and more melody—in fact, the music lacked "sentimentality." Then he went back to his seat for the second half of the program when the band played its modern compositions. Gillespie even inserted some improvised phrases from "Ochy Chornia" in honor of the occasion.

The next time I saw the commissar he was rushing backstage at the end of the concert. I arrived in time to see him bow low from the waist, blow Gillespie a kiss, and speak his first word in English: "Master!" Then came a barrage of questions: "How high does Dizzy go?" He was thunder-struck when I diagrammed A-flat above high C. Impossible. "Was the phrase from 'Ochy Chornia' written out for Gillespie and was he commanded to play it?" He wouldn't believe me when I said no and pointed to my forehead to indicate that Gillespie had improvised it. When I added that the band would love to play in Moscow, he said that it would be a great success and clapped his hands to show me what would happen. At that point the frowns of his colleagues silenced him.

What are the lessons to be drawn from the Gillespie tour? There is the old one, of course, that many people in many lands and for many reasons enjoy jazz tremendously. But that is not all. People said to me, "We are sick to death of propaganda about democracy —we want deeds and people, not words and theories. We are convinced that you have many bathtubs, skyscrapers, and automobiles, but we have real doubts about your culture. Send us true examples."

At this point in the conversation, the American-of-good-will speaks anxiously about American opera, painting, theatre, symphony, poetry, sculpture, and the novel. Great as they are, however, these arts were born in Europe and Europeans judge them by their own high standards. In a very real sense they are partly derivative and sometimes competing arts, not new contributions to the culture of the world.

It has never dawned upon Americans that many people in foreign lands consider jazz a new and impressive contribution to culture. It is the old story of finding the bluebird in your own garden. Thus, the concrete example of one good jazzband may communicate more of the sincerity, joy, and vigor of the American way of life than several other American creations inspired by Europe. Jazz was born and grew up in the United States and nowhere else. As a European composer remarked to me: "Jazz is one of America's best-loved *artistic* exports."

Author and Selection Notes

Born in Massachusetts and educated at Harvard and Yale, Marshall W. Stearns (1908-   ) has taught literature and music at various institutions of higher learning. Author of a history of American jazz music entitled *The Story of Jazz*, Stearns is eminently qualified to write about this music form as a propaganda medium abroad.

Questions and Exercises

1. Jazz has often been cited, along with Negro spirituals, as perhaps America's most abiding contribution to the realm of world music. What statements in this essay seem to prove or disprove this?

2. Is the question "Is Jazz Good Propaganda?" answered in the affirmative or negative by this article? Support your point of view in a paragraph.

3. How did the American approach to the problem of making new friends differ from the Russian approach?

4. Why does the author say, ". . . everybody—even the old folks—seemed to *want* to love jazz. . . ."? How does he answer the question "What are the lessons to be drawn from the Gillespie tour?"

5. Describe how Dizzy Gillespie's band met "the acid test of jazz as an ambassador of good-will" in Athens.

6. Do you feel that jazz is a good example of American culture to be shipped abroad?

7. Compare the attitude toward jazz in this essay with that in Opal's "American Culture Abroad."

8. If you were to divide this essay into three parts—into the introduction, main discussion, and significant conclusions to be drawn—where would you make the divisions?

9. Theme Topics: Is Jazz Music? Dance Jazz and Symphonic Jazz; Varieties of American Jazz; Jazz Is (Is Not) Good Propaganda; Exporting American Culture; The Voice of America.

MAIN CURRENTS OF AMERICAN THOUGHT
Irwin Shaw

"FLACKER: All right now, Kid, now you'd better talk," Andrew Draper dictated. "Business: sound of the door closing, the slow turning of the key in the lock. Buddy: You're never going to get me to talk, Flacker. Business: sound of a slap. Flacker: Maybe that'll make you think different, Kid. Where is Jerry Carmichael? Buddy (laughing): Wouldn't you like to know, Flacker? Flacker: Yeah. (Slowly, with great threatening in his voice) And I'm going to find out. One way or another. See? Business: siren fades in, louder, then fades out. Announcer: Will Buddy talk? Will Flacker force him to disclose the whereabouts of the rescued son of the Railroad King? Will Dusty Blades reach him in time? Tune in Monday at the same time etcetera etcetera—"

Andrew dropped onto the couch and put his feet up. He stretched and sighed as he watched his secretary finish scratching the dictation down in her shorthand notebook. "There's another thirty bucks," he said. "Is it the right length?"

"Uh huh," she said. "Eleven and a half pages. This is a very good one, Andy."

"Yeah," Andrew said, closing his eyes. "Put it next to *Moby Dick* on your library shelf."

"It's very exciting," she said, standing up. "I don't know what they're complaining about."

"You're a lovely girl, Lenore." Andrew put his hands over his eyes and rubbed around and around.

"Tomorrow? At ten o'clock?"

"At ten o'clock. Dig me out of the arms of sleep. We shall leave Dusty Blades to his fate for this week and go on with the further adventures of Ronnie Cook and his friends, forty dollars a script. I always enjoy writing 'Ronnie Cook' much better than 'Dusty Blades.' See what ten dollars does to a man." He opened his eyes and watched Lenore putting her hat on in the mirror. When he squinted, she was not so plain-looking. He felt very sorry for Lenore, plain as sand, with her flat-colored face and her hair pulled down like a rope, and never a man to her name. She was putting on a red hat with a kind of ladder arrangement up one side. It looked very funny and sad on her. Andrew realized that it was a new hat. "That's a mighty fine hat," he said.

"I thought a long time before I bought this hat," Lenore said, flushing because he'd noticed it.

"Har*riet!*" the French governess next door screamed, in the alley outside, at the next door's little girl. "Harriet, get away from there this minute."

Andrew turned over on his stomach on the couch and put a pillow over his head. "Have you got any ideas for 'Ronnie Cook and His Friends' for tomorrow?" he asked.

"No. Have you?"

"No."

"You'll get them by tomorrow," she said. "You always do."

"Yeah," said Andrew. "God-damn Ronnie Cook and his god-damn friends."

"You need a vacation," Lenore said. "Goodbye. Get a good night's sleep."

"Anything you say."

Andrew watched her with one eye as she went off the porch on which he worked and through the living room and dining room toward the stairs. Then he closed his eyes and tried to sleep. The sun came in through the open windows, and the curtains blew softly over his head, and the sun was warm and comforting on his closed eyes. Across the street, on the public athletic field, four boys were shagging flies. There would be the neat, pleasant crack of the bat and a long time later the smack of the ball in the fielder's glove. The tall trees outside, as old as Brooklyn, rustled from time to time as little spurts of wind swept across the baseball field.

"Har*riet!*" the governess called. "Stop that or I will make you stand by yourself in the corner all afternoon! Harriet! I demand you to stop!"

The little girl cried, "Mamma! Mamma! Mamma, she's going to hit me!"

The little girl hated the governess and the governess hated the little girl and they continually reported each other to the little girl's mother.

"You are a little liar!" the governess screamed. "You will grow up and you will be a liar all your life. There is no hope for you."

"Mamma!" wailed the little girl.

They went inside the house and it was quiet again.

"Charlie," one of the boys yelled, "hit it to me, Charlie!"

The telephone rang four times, and then Andrew heard his mother talking into it.

"It's a man from the bank," she called to him. "He wants to talk to you."

"You should've told him I wasn't home," Andrew said.

"But you are home," his mother said. "How was I to know that—"

"You're right." Andrew swung his legs over the side of the couch and sat up. "You're perfectly right." He went into the dining room to the telephone.

"You're a hundred and eleven dollars overdrawn," said the man at the bank.

Andrew squinted at his mother, sitting across the room on a straight chair with her arms folded in her lap, her head turned just a little, so as not to miss anything.

"I thought I had about four hundred dollars in the bank," Andrew said into the phone.

"You're a hundred and eleven dollars overdrawn."

Andrew sighed. "I'll check it." He hung up.

"What's the matter?" his mother asked.

"I'm a hundred and eleven dollars overdrawn," he said.

"That's shameful," his mother said. "You ought to be more methodical."

Andrew started back to the porch.

"You're awfully careless," his mother said, following him. "You really ought to keep track of your money."

"Yes." Andrew sat down on the couch.

"Give me a kiss," his mother said.

"Why?"

"No particular reason." She laughed.

"O.K." He kissed her and she held him for a moment. He lay back on the couch. She ran her finger under his eye.

"You've got rings under your eyes," she said.

"That's right."

She kissed him again and went away.

He closed his eyes. From the rear of the house came the sound of the vacuum cleaner. He got up and went to his mother's bedroom. She was down on one knee and bent over, running the machine back and forth under the bed.

"Hey!" Andrew yelled. "Hey, Mom!"

She turned off the machine and looked up at him. "What's the matter?"

"I'm trying to sleep," he said.

"Well, why don't you sleep?"

"The vacuum cleaner. It's shaking the house."

His mother stood up, her face setting into stern lines. "I can't use it while you're working. I can't use it while you're reading. I can't use it until ten o'clock in the morning because you're sleeping." She started the machine. "When am I supposed to clean the house?" she called over the noise of the cleaner. "Why don't you sleep at night, like everybody else?" And she put her head down low and vigorously ran the machine back and forth.

Andrew watched her for a moment. Then he went out of the room, closing the door behind him.

The telephone was ringing again, and he picked it up and said, "Hello."

"Ahndrew?" his agent's voice asked. His agent was from Brooklyn, too, but he had a very broad "a," with which he impressed actors and sponsors.

"Yes, this is Ahndrew." Andrew always made this straight-faced little joke with his agent, but the agent never seemed to catch on. "The 'Dusty Blades' scripts are all through. You'll get them tomorrow."

"I called about something else, Ahndrew. The complaints're piling up on the 'Blades' scripts. They're as slow as gum. Nothing ever happens. Ahndrew, you're not writing for the *Atlantic Monthly*."

"I know I'm not writing for the *Atlantic Monthly*."

"I think you've rather ran out of material," his agent said

lightly, soothingly. "I think perhaps you ought to take a little vacation from the 'Blades' scripts."

"Go to hell, Herman!" Andrew said, knowing that his agent had found somebody to do the scripts more cheaply for him.

"That's hardly the way to talk, Ahndrew," Herman said. "After all, I have to stand in the studio and listen to the complaints."

"Sad, Herman," Andrew said. "That's a sad picture," and hung up.

He rubbed the back of his neck reflectively, feeling the little lump behind his ear. Then he went into his own room and sat at his desk, looking blankly at the notes for his play, which lay to one side, neatly piled, growing older. He took out his check-book and his last months vouchers and arranged them in front of him.

"One hundred and eleven dollars," he murmured as he checked back and added and subtracted, his eyes smarting from the strain, his hands shaking a little because the vacuum cleaner was still going in his mother's room. Out on the athletic field more boys had arrived and formed an infield and were throwing the ball around the bases and yelling at each other.

Dr. Chalmers, seventy-five dollars. That was for his mother and her stomach.

Eighty dollars rent. The roof over his head equaled two "Ronnie Cook and His Friends." Five thousand words for rent.

Buddy was in the hands of Flacker. Flacker could torture him for six pages. Then Dusty Blades could be speeding to the rescue with Sam, by boat, and the boat could spring a leak, because the driver was in Flacker's pay, and there could be a fight for the next six pages. The driver could have a gun. It could be used, Andrew decided, but it wouldn't be liked, because he'd written at least four like it already.

Furniture, a hundred and thirty-seven dollars. His mother had always wanted a good dining-room table. She didn't have a maid, she said, so he ought to get her a dining-room table. How many words for a dining-room table?

"Come on, baby, make it two!" the second baseman out on the field was yelling. "Double 'em up!"

When Andrew was still in college he used to go out on a Saturday at ten o'clock in the morning and shag flies and jump around the infield and run and run all day, playing in pickup games until it got too dark to see. He was always tired now, and even when he played tennis he didn't move his feet right, because he was tired, and hit flatfooted and wild.

Spain, one hundred dollars. Oh, Lord!

A hundred and fifty to his father, to make up the deficit in his payroll. His father had nine people on his payroll, making little tin gadgets that he tried to sell to the dime stores, and at the end of very month Andrew had to meet the payroll. His father always gravely made out a note to him.

Flacker is about to kill Buddy out of anger and desperation. In bursts Dusty, alone. Sam is hurt. On the way to the hospital. Buddy is spirited away a moment before Dusty arrives. Flacker very smooth and oily. Confrontation. "Where is Buddy, Flacker?" "You mean the little lad?" "I mean the little lad, Flacker!" . . .

Fifty dollars to Dorothy's piano teacher. His sister, Dorothy. Another plain girl. She might as well learn how to play the piano. Then one day they'd come to him and say, "Dorothy is ready for her début. All we're asking you to do is rent Town Hall for a Wednesday evening. Just advance the money." She'd never get married. She was too smart for the men who would want her and too plain for the men she'd want herself. She bought her dresses in Saks. He would have to support, for life, a sister who would only buy her dresses in Saks and paid her piano teacher fifty dollars a month every month. She was only twenty-four. She would have a normal life expectancy of at least forty years. Twelve times forty, plus dresses at Saks and Town Hall from time to time. . . .

His father's teeth, ninety dollars. The money it cost to keep a man going in his losing fight against age.

The automobile, nine hundred dollars. A nine-hundred-dollar check looked very austere and impressive, like a penal institution. He was going to go off in the automobile, find a place in the mountains, write a play. Only he could never get himself far enough ahead on "Dusty Blades" and "Ronnie Cook and His Friends." Twenty thousand words a week, each week, recurring like Sunday on the calendar. How many words was *Hamlet?* Thirty, thirty-five thousand?

Twenty-three dollars to Best's. That was Martha's sweater for her birthday. "Either you say yes or no," Martha had said last Saturday night. "I want to get married and I've waited long enough." If he got married, he would pay rent in two places, light, gas, telephone.

Flacker played with something in his pocket. Dusty's hand shoots out, grabs Flacker's wrist, pulls his hand out. Buddy's little penknife, which Dusty had given him for a birthday present, is in Flacker's hand. "Flacker, tell me where Buddy Jones is or I'll kill you with my bare hands." A gong rings. Flacker has stepped on an alarm. Doors open and the room fills with his henchmen. . . .

Twenty dollars to Macy's for books. Parrington's *Main Currents of American Thought.* How does Dusty Blades fit into the *Main Currents of American Thought?*

Ten dollars to Dr. Faber. "I don't sleep at night, Doctor. Can you help me?"

"Do you drink coffee, Mr. Draper?"

"I drink one cup of coffee in the morning. That's all."

Pills, to be taken before retiring. Ten dollars.

If he married, he would take an apartment downtown, because it would be silly to live in Brooklyn this way, and he would buy furniture, four rooms full of furniture, beds, chairs, dishrags, relatives. Martha's family was poor and getting no younger and finally there would be three families, with rent and clothes and doctors and funerals.

Andrew got up and opened the closet door. Inside, stacked in files, were the scripts he had written in the last four years. They stretched from one wall of the wide closet across to the other—a million words. Four years.

Next script. The henchmen close in on Dusty. He hears Buddy screaming in the next room. . . .

How many years more?

The vacuum cleaner roared.

Martha was Jewish. That meant he'd have to lie his way into some hotels if he took her to them at all and he never could escape from one particular meanness of the world around him.

He sat down at his desk. One hundred dollars again to Spain. Barcelona had fallen and the long, dusty lines had beaten their way to the French border with the planes over them. And out of a sense of guilt at not being on a dusty road himself, bloody-footed and in fear of death, he had given a second hundred dollars, feeling at the same time that it was too much and nothing he ever gave could be enough. Three and a third "The Adventures of Dusty Blades" to the dead and dying of Spain.

The world loads you day by day with new burdens that increase on your shoulders. Lift a pound and you find you're carrying a ton. "Marry me," she says, "marry me." Then what does Dusty do? What the hell can he do that he hasn't done before? For five afternoons a week now, for a year, Dusty has been in Flacker's hands, or the hands of somebody else who is Flacker but has another name, and each time he has escaped, but now how?

The vacuum cleaner roared in the hallway outside his room.

"Mom!" he yelled. "Please turn that thing off!"

"What did you say?" his mother called.

"Nothing."

He added up the bank balances. His figures showed that he was four hundred and twelve dollars overdrawn instead of one hundred and eleven dollars, as the bank said. He didn't feel like adding the figures over. He put the vouchers and the bank's sheet into an envelope for his income-tax returns.

"Hit it out, Charlie!" a boy called on the field. "Make it a fast one!"

Andrew felt suddenly like going out and playing with them. He changed his clothes and put on a pair of old spiked shoes that were lying in back of the closet. His old pants were tight on him. Fat. If he ever let go, if anything happened and he couldn't exercise, he'd get as big as a house. Maybe Dusty has a knife in a holster up his sleeve. How plant that? The rent, the food, the piano teacher, the people at Saks who sold his sister dresses, the nimble girls who painted the tin gadgets in his father's shop, the teeth in his father's mouth, the doctors, the doctors, all living on the words that would have to come out of his head. . . . See here, Flacker, I know what you're up to. Business: Sound of a shot. A groan. Hurry, before the train gets to the crossing! Look! He's gaining on us! Hurry! Will he make it? Will Dusty Blades head off the desperate gang of counterfeiters and murderers in the race for the yacht? Will I be able to keep it up? Andrew asked himself. The years, the years ahead. . . . He would grow fat and the lines would become permanent under his eyes and he'd drink too much and pay more to the doctors because death was nearer and there was no stop, no vacation from life, because in no year could he say, "I want to sit this one out. Kindly excuse me."

His mother opened the door. "Martha's on the phone."

Andrew clattered out in his spiked shoes, holding the old, torn fielder's glove. He closed the door to the dining room to show his mother this was going to be a private conversation.

"Hello," he said. "Yes." He listened gravely. "No," he said. "I guess not. Goodbye. Good luck, Martha." He stood looking at the phone after he had put it down. His mother came in and he picked up his glove and started down the steps.

"Andrew," she said, "could you spare fifty dollars?"

"Oh, God!"

"It's for Dorothy. She's going to a party, a very important party—"

"Do the invitations cost fifty dollars apiece?" Andrew kicked

the top step and a little piece of dried mud fell off one of the
spiked shoes.

"No, Andrew. It's for a dress. She can't go without a new dress,
she says. There's a man there she's after."

"She won't get him, dress or no dress," Andrew said. "Your
daughter's a very plain girl."

"I know," his mother said. Her hands waved a little, helpless
and sad. "But it's better if she at least does the best she can. I feel
so sorry for her, Andrew."

"Everybody comes to me!" Andrew yelled, his voice suddenly
high. "Nobody leaves me alone! Not for a minute!"

He was crying now and he turned to hide it from his mother.
She looked at him, surprised, shaking her head. She put her arms
around him. "Just do what you want to do, Andrew, that's all.
Don't do anything you don't want to do."

"Yeah," Andrew said. "Yeah. I'm sorry. I'll give you the money.
I'm sorry I yelled at you."

"Don't give it to me if you don't want to, Andrew."

He laughed a little. "I want to, Mom, I want to."

He patted her shoulder and went down toward the baseball
field, leaving her standing there, puzzled, at the top of the steps.

The sun and the breeze felt good to him on the baseball field
and he forgot for an hour, but he moved slowly. His arm hurt at
the shoulder when he threw, and the boy playing second base
called him "Mister," which he wouldn't have done even last year,
when Andrew was twenty-four.

Author and Selection Notes

Though Irwin Shaw (1913-   ), a native of Brooklyn, has tried his
hand at drama and the novel form, he is best known for his short stories,
collected in such volumes as *Welcome to the City, Act of Faith,* and his
most recent collection *Mixed Company.* The heroes of Shaw's tales, as in
the selection in this text, often find themselves face to face with the common economic problems of a realistic world.

Questions and Exercises

1. Compare this story with "The Complaint of Chaucer to His Purse."
How does each selection attempt to solve the problem of the literary artist
and his livelihood?

2. Which of the following words most adequately describe the tone of
this story and why: "pathetic," "tragic," "realistic," "satiric"?

3. Is the title "Main Currents of American Thought" merely a provoca-

tive label to catch the attention of a prospective reader, or does it suggest some significant insight into the meaning of the story? Defend your point of view.

4. In a sentence or two show the relation of each of the following characters to Andrew: Lenore, Mrs. Draper, Dorothy, Martha, Herman.

5. Would you classify the plot of this story as a problem or a conflict? Explain in a paragraph.

6. List the checks which have caused Andrew to be overdrawn at the bank and state what each reveals about his situation or his relation to his family and friends.

7. What preparation has Andrew made to write the quality play of which he has dreamed?

8. What does the boy's calling Andrew "Mister" suggest about Andrew?

9. Theme Topics: The Profession of Writing; Writers Must Eat; The Literary Artist Today; The Proper Atmosphere for a Writer; What Makes a Person Want to Be a Writer?

6

NOT BY BREAD ALONE: MAN AND THE SPIRIT

Man shall not live by bread alone.
Jesus

Since the beginning of civilization, man has been faced with the conflict between material and spiritual values. He has come to recognize the transience of the material and the ultimate worth of the spiritual. Indeed, it is his concern with the intangible values of the spirit that identifies man as man.

This section concerns man's speculation on such grave matters as the meaning of truth, the purpose of life, and the relationship between man and God. The simple, felicitous moments of life are here too: the use of leisure, the delightful expectancies of holiday time, the quiet happiness invested in giving and receiving—in short, the values which we store up against those hours when, as Wordsworth declares, "the world is too much with us."

THE BOOK OF RUTH

Now it came to pass in the days when the judges ruled, that there was a famine in the land. And a certain man of Bethlehem-judah went to sojourn in the country of Moab, he, and his wife, and his two sons.

And the name of the man was Elimelech, and the name of his wife Naomi, and the name of his two sons Mahlon and Chilion, Ephrathites of Bethlehem-judah. And they came into the country of Moab, and continued there.

And Elimelech Naomi's husband died; and she was left, and her two sons.

And they took them wives of the women of Moab; the name of the one was Orpah, and the name of the other Ruth: and they dwelled there about ten years.

And Mahlon and Chilion died also both of them; and the woman was left of her two sons and her husband.

Then she arose with her daughters-in-law, that she might return from the country of Moab; for she had heard in the country of Moab how that the Lord had visited his people in giving them bread.

Wherefore she went forth out of the place where she was, and her two daughters-in-law with her; and they went on the way to return unto the land of Judah.

And Naomi said unto her two daughters-in-law, Go, return each to her mother's house: the Lord deal kindly with you, as ye have dealt with the dead, and with me.

The Lord grant ye that you may find rest, each of you in the house of her husband. Then she kissed them; and they lifted up their voice, and wept.

And they said unto her, Surely we will return with thee unto thy people.

And Naomi said, Turn again, my daughters: why will ye go with me? are there yet any more sons in my womb, that they may be your husbands?

Turn again, my daughters, go your way; for I am too old to have an husband. If I should say, I have hope, if I should have an husband also to night, and should also bear sons;

Would ye tarry for them till they were grown? would ye stay for them from having husbands? nay, my daughters; for it grieveth me much for your sakes that the hand of the Lord is gone out against me.

And they lifted up their voice, and wept again: and Orpah kissed her mother-in-law; but Ruth clave unto her.

And she said, Behold, thy sister-in-law is gone back unto her people, and unto her gods: return thou after thy sister-in-law.

And Ruth said, Intreat me not to leave thee, or to return from following after thee: for whither thou goest, I will go: and where thou lodgest, I will lodge: thy people shall be my people, and thy God my God:

Where thou diest, will I die, and there will I be buried: the Lord do so to me, and more also, if ought but death part thee and me.

When she saw that she was steadfastly minded to go with her, then she left speaking unto her.

So they two went until they came to Bethlehem. And it came to pass, when they were come to Bethlehem, that all the city was moved about them, and they said, Is this Naomi?

And she said unto them, Call me not Naomi, call me Mara: for the Almighty hath dealt very bitterly with me.

I went out full, and the Lord hath brought me home again empty: why then call ye me Naomi, seeing the Lord hath testified against me, and the Almighty hath afflicted me?

So Naomi returned, and Ruth the Moabitess, her daughter-in-law, with her, which returned out of the country of Moab: and they came to Bethlehem in the beginning of barley harvest.

And Naomi had a kinsman of her husband's, a mighty man of wealth, of the family of Elimelech; and his name was Boaz.

And Ruth the Moabitess said unto Naomi, Let me now go to the field, and glean ears of corn after him in whose sight I shall find grace. And she said unto her, Go, my daughter.

And she went, and came, and gleaned in the field after the reapers: and her hap was to light on a part of the field belonging unto Boaz, who was of the kindred of Elimelech.

And, behold, Boaz came from Bethlehem, and said unto the reapers, The Lord be with you. And they answered him, The Lord bless thee.

Then said Boaz unto his servant that was set over the reapers, Whose damsel is this?

And the servant that was set over the reapers answered and said, It is the Moabitish damsel that came back with Naomi out of the country of Moab:

And she said, I pray you, let me glean and gather after the reapers among the sheaves: so she came, and hath continued even from the morning until now, that she tarried a little in the house.

Then said Boaz unto Ruth, Hearest thou not, my daughter? Go not to glean in another field, neither go from hence, but abide here fast by my maidens:

Let thine eyes be on the field that they do reap, and go thou after them: have I not charged the young men that they shall not touch thee? and when thou art athirst, go unto the vessels, and drink of that which the young men have drawn.

Then she fell on her face, and bowed herself to the ground, and said unto him, Why have I found grace in thine eyes, that thou shouldest take knowledge of me, seeing I am a stranger?

And Boaz answered and said unto her, It hath fully been shewed me, all that thou hast done unto thy mother-in-law since the death of thine husband: and how thou hast left thy father and thy mother, and the land of thy nativity, and art come unto a people which thou knewest not heretofore.

The Lord recompense thy work, and a full reward be given thee of the Lord God of Israel, under whose wings thou art come to trust.

Then she said, Let me find favour in thy sight, my lord; for that thou hast comforted me, and for that thou hast spoken friendly unto thine handmaid, though I be not like unto one of thine handmaidens.

And Boaz said unto her, At mealtime come thou hither, and eat of the bread, and dip thy morsel in the vinegar. And she sat beside the reapers: and he reached her parched corn, and she did eat, and was sufficed, and left.

And when she was risen up to glean, Boaz commanded his young men, saying, Let her glean even among the sheaves, and reproach her not:

And let fall also some of the handfuls of purpose for her, and leave them, that she may glean them, and rebuke her not.

So she gleaned in the field until even, and beat out that she had gleaned: and it was about an ephah of barley.

And she took it up, and went into the city: and her mother-in-law saw what she had gleaned: and she brought forth, and gave to her that she had reserved after she was sufficed.

And her mother-in-law said unto her, Where hast thou gleaned to day? and where wroughtest thou? blessed be he that did take knowledge of thee. And she shewed her mother-in-law with whom she had wrought, and said, The man's name with whom I wrought to day is Boaz.

And Naomi said unto her daughter-in-law, Blessed be he of the Lord, who hath not left off his kindness to the living and to the dead. And Naomi said unto her, The man is near of kin unto us, one of our next kinsmen.

And Ruth the Moabitess said, He said unto me also, Thou shalt keep fast by my young men, until they have ended all my harvest.

And Naomi said unto Ruth her daughter-in-law, It is good, my daughter, that thou go out with his maidens, that they meet thee not in any other field.

So she kept fast by the maidens of Boaz to glean unto the end of barley harvest and of wheat harvest; and dwelt with her mother-in-law.

Then Naomi her mother-in-law said unto her, My daughter, shall I not seek rest for thee, that it may be well with thee?

And now is not Boaz of our kindred, with whose maidens thou wast? Behold, he winnoweth barley to night in the threshingfloor.

Wash thyself therefore, and anoint thee, and put thy raiment upon thee, and get thee down to the floor: but make not thyself known unto the man, until he shall have done eating and drinking.

And it shall be, when he lieth down, that thou shalt mark the place where he shall lie, and thou shalt go in, and uncover his feet, and lay thee down; and he will tell thee what thou shalt do.

And she said unto her, All that thou sayest unto me I will do.

And she went down unto the floor, and did according to all that her mother-in-law bade her.

And when Boaz had eaten and drunk, and his heart was merry, he went to lie down at the end of the heap of corn: and she came softly, and uncovered his feet, and laid her down.

And it came to pass at midnight, that the man was afraid, and turned himself: and, behold, a woman lay at his feet.

And he said, Who art thou? And she answered, I am Ruth thine handmaid: spread therefore thy skirt over thine handmaid; for thou art a near kinsman.

And he said, Blessed be thou of the Lord, my daughter: for thou hast shewed more kindness in the latter end than at the beginning, inasmuch as thou followedst not young men, whether poor or rich.

And now, my daughter, fear not; I will do to thee all that thou requirest: for all the city of my people doth know that thou art a virtuous woman.

And now it is true that I am thy near kinsman: howbeit there is a kinsman nearer than I.

Tarry this night, and it shall be in the morning, that if he will perform unto thee the part of a kinsman, well; let him do the kinsman's part: but if he will not do the part of a kinsman to thee, then will I do the part of a kinsman to thee, as the Lord liveth: lie down until the morning.

And she lay at his feet until the morning: and she rose up before one could know another. And he said, Let it not be known that a woman came into the floor.

Also he said, Bring the vail that thou hast upon thee, and hold it. And when she held it, he measured six measures of barley, and laid it on her: and she went into the city.

And when she came to her mother-in-law, she said, Who art thou, my daughter? And she told her all that the man had done to her.

And she said, These six measures of barley gave he me; for he said to me, Go not empty unto thy mother-in-law.

Then said she, Sit still, my daughter, until thou know how the matter will fall: for the man will not be in rest, until he have finished the thing this day.

Then went Boaz up to the gate, and sat him down there: and, behold, the kinsman of whom Boaz spake came by; unto whom he said, Ho, such a one! turn aside, sit down here. And he turned aside, and sat down.

And he took ten men of the elders of the city, and said, Sit ye down here. And they sat down.

And he said unto the kinsman, Naomi, that is come again out of the country of Moab, selleth a parcel of land, which was our brother Elimelech's:

And I thought to advertise thee, saying, Buy it before the inhabitants, and before the elders of my people. If thou wilt redeem it, redeem it: but if thou wilt not redeem it, then tell me, that I may know: for there is none to redeem it beside thee; and I am after thee. And he said, I will redeem it.

Then said Boaz, What day thou buyest the field of the hand of Naomi, thou must buy it also of Ruth the Moabitess, the wife of the dead, to raise up the name of the dead upon his inheritance.

And the kinsman said, I cannot redeem it for myself, lest I mar mine own inheritance: redeem thou my right to thyself; for I cannot redeem it.

Now this was the manner in former time in Israel concerning redeeming and concerning changing, for to confirm all things; a man plucked off his shoe, and gave it to his neighbour: and this was a testimony in Israel.

Therefore the kinsman said unto Boaz, Buy it for thee. So he drew off his shoe.

And Boaz said unto the elders, and unto all the people, Ye are witnesses this day, that I have bought all that was Elimelech's, and all that was Chilion's and Mahlon's, of the hand of Naomi.

Moreover Ruth the Moabitess, the wife of Mahlon, have I purchased to be my wife, to raise up the name of the dead upon his inheritance, that the name of the dead be not cut off from among his brethren, and from the gate of his place: ye are witnesses this day.

And all the people that were in the gate, and the elders, said, We are witnesses. The Lord make the woman that is come into thine house like Rachel and like Leah, which two did build the house of Israel: and do thou worthily in Ephratah, and be famous in Bethlehem:

And let thy house be like the house of Pharez, whom Tamar bare unto Judah, of the seed which the Lord shall give thee of this young woman.

So Boaz took Ruth, and she was his wife: and when he went in unto her, the Lord gave her conception, and she bare a son.

And the women said unto Naomi, Blessed be the Lord, which hath not left thee this day without a kinsman, that his name may be famous in Israel.

And he shall be unto thee a restorer of thy life, and a nourisher of thine old age: for thy daughter-in law, which loveth thee, which is better to thee than seven sons, hath born him.

And Naomi took the child, and laid it in her bosom, and became nurse unto it.

And the women her neighbours gave it a name, saying, There is a son born to Naomi; and they called his name Obed: he is the father of Jesse, the father of David.

Author and Selection Notes

The story of Ruth, written about 450 B.C., but reflecting the times of the Judges some six or seven hundred years earlier, is world-renowned for its poignancy and charm. This ancient short story of the Moabite maiden who chose for love to follow her Jewish mother-in-law, Naomi, and who became an ancestor of the great Hebrew king David, was written, Bible scholars feel, as a plea for greater toleration of foreign marriages and as a protest against exclusive nationalism.

Questions and Exercises

1. Show how in plot and style this tale resembles a modern short story.
2. Study the punctuation, capitalization, and syntax used in this selection and compare it with that of the twentieth century. What does the comparison reveal about the nature of our language?
3. Why does Naomi say when she returns to her native land: "Do not call me Naomi, call me Mara"? (Look up the meaning of these proper names in a good, unabridged dictionary.)
4. Describe the ceremonial practice involved in the redeeming of the

"parcel of land" being sold by Naomi. List other, similar special customs appearing in the story.

5. Theme Topics: Social Customs in The Book of Ruth; Great Love Stories in the Bible; The Character of Ruth; The Significance of Family and Clan Units in Biblical History.

HERACLITUS

Callimachus

They told me, Heraclitus, they told me you were dead;
They brought me bitter news to hear and bitter tears to shed.
I wept as I remembered how often you and I
Had tired the sun with talking and sent him down the sky.
And now that thou art lying, my dear old Carian guest,
A handful of gray ashes, long, long ago at rest,
Still are thy pleasant voices, thy nightingales, awake;
For Death, he taketh all away, but them he cannot take.

Author and Selection Notes

Callimachus (c. 310-235 B.C.), a native of Cyrene in north Africa, became a poet, a schoolmaster, and a librarian in the great library at Alexandria. A number of his poems, including the present one, are included in *The Greek Anthology,* an anthology of 4500 Greek poems compiled in the tenth century and representing over a thousand years of Greek verse from some three hundred poets.

Questions and Exercises

1. Callimachus addresses his dead friend Heraclitus in a poignant epitaph. What aspects of their friendship does Callimachus cherish most?

2. Look up a description of *The Greek Anthology* in an encyclopedia or history of world literature, or—better still—secure a copy from the library in which to browse. In what respects is Callimachus' poem typical of many of the poems in the *Anthology*?

3. Why is Heraclitus spoken of as Callimachus' "Carian" guest? Look up the word "Carian" in an encyclopedia or dictionary of literary allusions.

4. Explain why death, which takes all away, cannot take Heraclitus' nightingales. (Refer to an encyclopedia for the story of Philomela.)

5. Look up the term "elegy" in a dictionary or literary handbook. Would you classify this poem as an elegy? Explain.

6. Theme Topics: *The Greek Anthology;* Famous Friendships; The Meaning of Friendship; Character Sketch of a Friend; The Loss of a Friend.

FIRST CORINTHIANS 13

St. Paul

Though I speak with the tongues of men and of angels, and have not charity, I am become as sounding brass, or a tinkling cymbal. And though I have the gift of prophecy, and understand all mysteries, and all knowledge; and though I have all faith, so that I could remove mountains, and have not charity, I am nothing. And though I bestow all my goods to feed the poor, and though I give my body to be burned, and have not charity, it profiteth me nothing.

Charity suffereth long, and is kind; charity envieth not; charity vaunteth not itself, is not puffed up, doth not behave itself unseemly, seeketh not her own, is not easily provoked, thinketh no evil; rejoiceth not in iniquity, but rejoiceth in the truth; beareth all things, believeth all things, hopeth all things, endureth all things.

Charity never faileth; but whether there be prophecies, they shall fail; whether there be tongues, they shall cease; whether there be knowledge, it shall vanish away. For we know in part, and we prophesy in part. But when that which is perfect is come, then that which is in part shall be done away.

When I was a child, I spake as a child, I understood as a child, I thought as a child: but when I became a man, I put away childish things. For now we see through a glass, darkly; but then face to face: now I know in part; but then shall I know even as also I am known.

And now abideth faith, hope, charity, these three; but the greatest of these is charity.

Author and Selection Notes

St. Paul's extensive missionary activities throughout Asia Minor and the Roman world, until his death about 67 A.D., and his superlative pastoral and theological writings made him a monumental force in the establishment and spread of early Christianity. Paul's letter to the church located in the Grecian city of Corinth is a striking example of his concern, even after his departure to other missionary fields, for the individual churches which he had founded or ministered to as an apostle to the Gentile world. Although First Corinthians is concerned primarily with certain problems of Christian doctrine and practice, it frequently rises, as in the present selection, to eloquent emotional peaks.

Questions and Exercises

1. St. Paul's passage on love (or "charity," as the King James Version translates the word) is one of the most cherished in the Bible. What sort of love does Paul have in mind in this selection?

2. Examine this same passage in the American Standard Version of the Bible. In a short theme point out what you feel to be the chief differences in the two versions.

3. Make a topic outline of the passage; list the characteristics of love under three or four major headings.

4. On what grounds does St. Paul feel that charity is more perfect, or more sure, than "prophecies," "tongues," "knowledge"? Explain in a paragraph.

5. Explain the phrase "see through a glass, darkly."

6. Try defining the words "faith" and "hope" without referring to a dictionary. Write a paragraph in which you include illustrations from your own or from other people's experiences and, afterward, check the meaning you have developed with that contained in a dictionary.

7. Theme Topics: Paul's Concept of Love; The Meaning of Christian Love; Man's Humanity to Man; "These Three"—a Comparison; Love Conquers All.

THE PARABLE OF THE SPARROW

The Venerable Bede

The king, hearing these words, answered, that he was both willing and bound to receive the faith which he taught; but that he would confer about it with his principal friends and counsellors, to the end that if they also were of his opinion, they might all together be cleansed in Christ the Fountain of Life. Paulinus consenting, the king did as he said; for, holding a council with the wise men, he asked of every one in particular what he thought of the new doctrine, and the new worship that was preached? To which the chief of his own priests, Coifi, immediately answered, "O king, consider what this is which is now preached to us; for I verily declare to you, that the religion which we have hitherto professed has, as far as I can learn, no virtue in it. For none of your people has applied himself more diligently to the worship of our gods than I; and yet there are many who receive greater favours from you, and are more preferred than I, and are more prosperous in all their undertakings. Now if the gods were good for any thing, they would rather forward me, who have been more careful to serve them. It remains, therefore, that if upon examination you find those new doctrines, which are now preached to us, better and more efficacious, we immediately receive them without any delay."

Another of the king's chief men, approving of his words and exhortations, presently added: "The present life of man, O king, seems to me, in comparison of that time which is unknown to us, like to the swift flight of a sparrow through the room wherein you sit at supper in winter, with your commanders and ministers, and a good fire in the midst, whilst the storms of rain and snow prevail abroad; the sparrow, I say, flying in at one door, and immediately out at another, whilst he is within, is safe from the wintry storm; but after a short space of fair weather, he immediately vanishes out of your sight, into the dark winter from which he had emerged. So this life of man appears for a short space, but of what went before, or what is to follow, we are utterly ignorant. If, therefore, this new doctrine contains something more certain, it seems justly to deserve to be followed." The other elders and king's counsellors, by Divine inspiration, spoke to the same effect.

Author and Selection Notes

In the midst of the dramatic story by the Venerable Bede (673-735) of the conversion in 633 of Anglo-Saxon Northumbria, appears the parable of the sparrow. Old English religious belief prior to Christianity was intensely pagan, including worship of gods representing the forces of nature —Woden, Thor, Frea—and ceremonies which possibly included human sacrifice. Of Bede's voluminous writings, which include grammatical and critical handbooks, scientific treatises, saints' lives, and homilies, none compares in importance to his monumental *Ecclesiastical History of the English People.*

Questions and Exercises

1. Look up the word "parable" in a dictionary or Biblical handbook and show in some detail how the story about the sparrow illustrates this form of literature.

2. What is the argument of Coifi, the chief of the King's priests, for accepting the new doctrine of Christianity?

3. Compare Coifi's argument with the argument contained in the parable. Which is more valid spiritually? Defend your point of view.

4. How would you characterize Bede's narrative style?

5. Compare this selection with St. Paul's First Corinthians 13. What basic aspect of religion is revealed by each? Write a paragraph.

6. Theme Topics: Taking Religion Seriously; The Ideal Religion—as I See It; Religion's Answer to Life's Problems.

SONNET 29

William Shakespeare

When, in disgrace with fortune and men's eyes,
I all alone beweep my outcast state,
And trouble deaf heaven with my bootless cries,
And look upon myself, and curse my fate,
Wishing me like to one more rich in hope,
Featured like him, like him with friends possessed,
Desiring this man's art and that man's scope,
With what I most enjoy contented least;
Yet in these thoughts myself almost despising,
Haply I think on thee,—and then my state,
Like to the lark at break of day arising
From sullen earth, sings hymns at heaven's gate;
For thy sweet love remembered such wealth brings
That then I scorn to change my state with kings.

Author and Selection Notes

The sonnets of William Shakespeare (1564-1616) rank with the world's most magnificent expressions of love and friendship. Shakespeare's sonnet sequence contains one hundred and fifty-four sonnets, the majority of them addressed to a young man of noble rank and great personal beauty and the remainder to a "dark lady," who, one may judge, was disdainful. Whether the sonnets are actually autobiographical or not need not bother the reader of the above sonnet, which illustrates a universal emotion.

Questions and Exercises

1. Is this sonnet addressed to a beloved woman or a beloved friend? Support your opinion by reference to specific statements in the poem.

2. Explain what is meant by the following phrases: "in disgrace with

fortune and men's eyes"; "bootless cries"; "This man's art and that man's scope."

3. Explain the figure of speech given in lines 11 and 12.

4. At what point in the poem does the mood change from despair to hope?

5. Consult a literary handbook for a discussion of the sonnet form and list the characteristics of the English (Shakespearean) and Italian (Petrarchan) forms. Read Wordsworth's sonnet "The World Is Too Much with Us" and write a theme showing how Shakespeare's and Wordsworth's poems fit the sonnet scheme.

6. Theme Topics: The Sonnet Form in English; The Imperishableness of Friendship; The Psychology of Despair and Joy; A Description of a True Friend; Why Friends Are Important.

DEATH, BE NOT PROUD
John Donne

Death, be not proud, though some have called thee
Mighty and dreadful, for thou art not so;
For those whom thou think'st thou dost overthrow
Die not, poor Death; nor yet canst thou kill me.
From Rest and Sleep, which but thy pictures be,
Much pleasure, then from thee much more must flow;
And soonest our best men with thee do go,
Rest of their bones and souls' delivery!
Thou art slave to fate, chance, kings, and desperate men,
And dost with poison, war, and sickness dwell;
And poppy or charms can make us sleep as well
And better than thy stroke. Why swell'st thou then?
One short sleep past, we wake eternally,
And Death shall be no more: Death, thou shalt die!

Author and Selection Notes

For many years Dean of St. Paul's Cathedral in London and perhaps the most brilliant preacher of his age, John Donne (1572-1631) wrote both secular and spiritual lyrics. His poems, generally, reflect the fantastic imagery and the intellectual subtleties of the seventeenth-century metaphysical poets. "Death, Be Not Proud" appears as one of a group of religious sonnets entitled *Holy Sonnets*.

Questions and Exercises

1. Consult a literary handbook for a discussion of metaphysical poetry. Would you classify this poem as a metaphysical poem? If so, explain why.

2. Compare this sonnet in form and rhyme scheme with Shakespeare's "Sonnet 29" and Wordsworth's "The World Is Too Much with Us."

3. State in a sentence or two the general theme of the sonnet.

4. Explain in your own words how Death is "slave to fate, chance, kings, and desperate men."

5. Read "The Jilting of Granny Weatherall." Is the attitude of this selection toward death the same or different? Defend your point of view.

6. Theme Topics: The Meaning of Death; Even Death Shall Die: an Explication of "Death, Be Not Proud"; Is Death the End of the Soul? The Bible's Teaching on Death.

THE WORLD IS TOO MUCH WITH US
William Wordsworth

The world is too much with us; late and soon,
Getting and spending, we lay waste our powers:
Little we see in Nature that is ours;
We have given our hearts away, a sordid boon!
The Sea that bares her bosom to the moon;
The winds that will be howling at all hours
And are up-gathered now like sleeping flowers;
For this, for every thing, we are out of tune;
It moves us not.—Great God! I'd rather be
A Pagan suckled in a creed outworn,—
So might I, standing on this pleasant lea,
Have glimpses that would make me less forlorn;
Have sight of Proteus rising from the sea;
Or hear old Triton blow his wreathed horn.

Author and Selection Notes

William Wordsworth (1770-1850) illustrates in his verse many of the characteristics of the Romantic Movement in English literature—for example, an emphasis on nature, as in the present sonnet, and an escape from the tyranny of eighteenth-century diction and the heroic couplet. His *Lyrical Ballads,* written with Samuel Taylor Coleridge, has often been cited as marking the beginning of the movement. Wordsworth's collected poems include approximately five hundred sonnets, some of which are among his finest poems.

Questions and Exercises

1. This sonnet has been characterized as a protest against materialistic industrialism. Show how this is true by citing details of the poem.

2. The rhyme scheme and general development of this poem suggest the sonnet form. Should this be classified as the Italian or the English form of the sonnet? (Checking the description of the Italian and English forms of the sonnet in a handbook of literature may prove helpful in making your decision.)

3. Compare this poem with Robert Frost's "Stopping by Woods on a Snowy Evening." Are these poems similar in theme? Support your point of view.

4. There are several figures of speech in the poem, either stated or implied. Cite and classify them as simile, metaphor, personification, etc.

5. Give the definitions of the words "boon," "lea," "Proteus," and "Triton."

6. Write a theme of two or three pages in which you show how the message of this poem is applicable to our own times; or you may wish to show how it is not true of our age.

7. Theme Topics: Spiritual Values for a Materialistic Age; The Solace of Solitude; With This Sonnet Wordsworth Unlocked His Heart; Materialism Versus Spiritual Values.

OLD CHINA

Charles Lamb

I have an almost feminine partiality for old china. When I go to see any great house, I inquire for the china-closet, and next for the picture gallery. I cannot defend the order of preference, but by saying that we have all some taste or other, of too ancient a date to admit of our remembering distinctly that it was an acquired one. I can call to mind the first play, and the first exhibition, that I was taken to; but I am not conscious of a time when china jars and saucers were introduced into my imagination.

I had no repugnance then—why should I now have?—to those little, lawless, azure-tinctured grotesques, that under the notion of men and women, float about, uncircumscribed by any element, in that world before perspective—a china tea-cup.

I like to see my old friends—whom distance cannot diminish—figuring up in the air (so they appear to our optics), yet on *terra firma* still—for so we must in courtesy interpret that speck of deeper blue,—which the decorous artist, to prevent absurdity, had made to spring up beneath their sandals.

I love the men with women's faces, and the women, if possible, with still more womanish expressions.

Here is a young and courtly Mandarin, handing tea to a lady from a salver—two miles off. See how distance seems to set off respect! And here the same lady, or another—for likeness is identity on tea-cups—is stepping into a little fairy boat, moored on the hither side of this calm garden river, with a dainty mincing foot, which in a right angle of incidence (as angles go in our world) must infallibly land her in the midst of a flowery mead—a furlong off on the other side of the same strange stream!

Farther on—if far or near can be predicated of their world—see horses, trees, pagodas, dancing the hays.

Here—a cow and rabbit couchant, and coextensive—so objects show, seen through the lucid atmosphere of fine Cathay.

I was pointing out to my cousin last evening, over our Hyson (which we are old-fashioned enough to drink unmixed still of an afternoon), some of these *speciosa miracula* upon a set of extraordinary old blue china (a recent purchase) which we were now for the first time using; and could not help remarking, how favourable circumstances had been to us of late years, that we could afford to please the eye sometimes with trifles of this sort—when a passing sentiment seemed to overshade the brows of my companion. I am quick at detecting these summer clouds in Bridget.

"I wish the good old times would come again," she said, "when we were not quite so rich. I do not mean, that I want to be poor; but there was a middle state"—so she was pleased to ramble on,—"in which I am sure we were a great deal happier. A purchase is but a purchase, now that you have money enough and to spare. Formerly it used to be a triumph. When we coveted a cheap luxury (and, O! how much ado I had to get you to consent in those times!)—we were used to have a debate two or three days before, and to weigh the *for* and *against,* and think what we might spare it out of, and what saving we could hit upon, that should be an equivalent. A thing was worth buying then, when we felt the money that we paid for it.

"Do you remember the brown suit, which you made to hang upon you, till all your friends cried shame upon you, it grew so threadbare—and all because of that folio Beaumont and Fletcher, which you dragged home late at night from Barker's in Covent Garden?

Do you remember how we eyed it for weeks before we could make up our minds to the purchase, and had not come to a determination till it was near ten o'clock of the Saturday night, when you set off from Islington, fearing you should be too late—and when the old bookseller with some grumbling opened his shop, and by the twinkling taper (for he was setting bedwards) lighted out the relic from his dusty treasures—and when you lugged it home, wishing it were twice as cumbersome—and when you presented it to me—and when we were exploring the perfectness of it (*collating*, you called it)—and while I was repairing some of the loose leaves with paste, which your impatience would not suffer to be left till daybreak—was there no pleasure in being a poor man? or can those neat black clothes which you wear now, and are so careful to keep brushed, since we have become rich and finical, give you half the honest vanity with which you flaunted it about in that overworn suit—your old corbeau—for four or five weeks longer than you should have done, to pacify your conscience for the mighty sum of fifteen—or sixteen shillings was it?—a great affair we thought it then—which you had lavished on the old folio. Now you can afford to buy any book that pleases you, but I do not see that you ever bring me home any nice old purchases now.

"When you came home with twenty apologies for laying out a less number of shillings upon that print after Lionardo, which we christened the 'Lady Blanch'; when you looked at the purchase, and thought of the money—and thought of the money, and looked again at the picture— was there no pleasure in being a poor man? Now, you have nothing to do but to walk into Colnaghi's, and buy a wilderness of Lionardos. Yet do you?

"Then, do you remember our pleasant walks to Enfield, and Potter's Bar, and Waltham, when we had a holyday—holydays, and all other fun, are gone now we are rich—and the little hand-basket in which I used to deposit our day's fare of savoury cold lamb and salad—and how you would pry about at noon-tide for some decent house, where we might go in and produce our store—only paying for the ale that you must call for—and speculate upon the looks of the landlady, and whether she was likely to allow us a table-cloth—and wish for such another honest hostess as Izaak Walton has described many a one on the pleasant banks of the Lea, when he went a-fishing—and sometimes they would prove obliging enough, and sometimes they would look grudgingly upon us—but we had cheerful looks still for one another, and would eat our plain food savourily, scarcely grudging Piscator his Trout Hall? Now—when we go out a day's pleasuring, which is seldom, moreover, we *ride* part of the way—and go into a fine inn, and order the best of dinners, never debating the expense—which, after all, never has half the relish of those chance country snaps, when we were at the mercy of uncertain usage, and a precarious welcome.

"You are too proud to see a play anywhere now but in the pit. Do you remember where it was we used to sit, when we saw the Battle of Hexham, and the Surrender of Calais, and Bannister and Mrs. Bland in the Children in the Wood—when we squeezed out our shillings apiece to sit three or four times in a season in the one-shilling gallery—where you felt all the time that you ought not to have brought me—and more strongly I felt obligation to you for having brought me—and the pleasure was the better for a little shame—and when the curtain drew up, what cared we for our place in the house, or what mattered it where we were sitting, when our thoughts were with Rosalind in Arden, or with Viola at the Court of Illyria. You used to say that the Gallery was the best place of all for enjoying a play socially—that the relish of such exhibitions must be in proportion to the infrequency of going—that the company we met there, not being in general readers of plays, were obliged to attend the more, and did attend, to what was going on, on the stage—because a word lost would have been a chasm, which it was impossible for them to fill up. With such reflections we consoled our pride then—and I appeal to you whether, as a woman, I met generally with less attention and accommodation than I have done since in more expensive situations in the house? The getting in indeed, and the crowding up those inconvenient staircases, was bad enough,—but there was still a law of civility to woman recognised to quite as great an extent as we ever found in the other passages—and how a little difficulty overcome heightened the snug seat and the play, afterwards! Now we can only pay our money and walk in. You cannot see, you say, in the galleries now. I am sure we saw, and heard too, well enough then—but sight, and all, I think, is gone with our poverty.

"There was pleasure in eating strawberries, before they became quite common—in the first dish of peas, while they were yet dear— to have them for a nice supper, a treat. What treat can we have now? If we were to treat ourselves now—that is, to have dainties a little above our means, it would be selfish and wicked. It is the very little more that we allow ourselves beyond what the actual poor can get at, that makes what I call a treat—when two people living together, as we have done, now and then indulge themselves in a cheap luxury, which both like; while each apologises, and is

willing to take both halves of the blame to his single share. I see
no harm in people making much of themselves, in that sense of
the word. It may give them a hint how to make much of others.
But now—what I mean by the word—we never do make much of
ourselves. None but the poor can do it. I do not mean the veriest
poor of all, but persons as we were, just above poverty.

"I know what you were going to say, that it is mighty pleasant
at the end of the year to make all meet,—and much ado we used
to have every Thirty-first Night of December to account for our
exceedings—many a long face did you make over your puzzled
accounts, and in contriving to make it out how we had spent so
much—or that we had not spent so much—or that it was impossible we should spend so much next year—and still we found our
slender capital decreasing—but then, betwixt ways, and projects,
and compromises of one sort or another, and talk of curtailing
this charge, and doing without that for the future—and the hope
that youth brings, and laughing spirits (in which you were never
poor till now), we pocketed up our loss, and in conclusion, with
'lusty brimmers' (as you used to quote it out of *hearty cheerful
Mr. Cotton*, as you called him), we used to welcome in 'the coming
guest.' Now we have no reckoning at all at the end of the old year
—no flattering promises about the new year doing better for us."

Bridget is so sparing of her speech on most occasions, that when
she gets into a rhetorical vein, I am careful how I interrupt it. I
could not help, however, smiling at the phantom of wealth which
her dear imagination had conjured up out of a clear income of
poor——hundred pounds a year. "It is true we were happier when
we were poor but we were also younger, my cousin. I am afraid
we must put up with the excess, for if we were to shake the super-
flux into the sea, we should not much mend ourselves. That we had
much to struggle with, as we grew up together, we have reason to
be most thankful. It strengthened and knit our compact closer. We
could never have been what we have been to each other, if we
had always had the sufficiency which you now complain of. The
resisting power—those natural dilations of the youthful spirit,
which circumstances cannot straiten—with us are long since passed
away. Competence to age is supplementary youth, a sorry supplement indeed, but I fear the best that is to be had. We must ride
where we formerly walked: live better and lie softer—and shall be
wise to do so—than we had means to do in those good old days
you speak of. Yet could those days return—could you and I once
more walk our thirty miles a day—could Bannister and Mrs.
Bland again be young, and you and I be young to see them—

could the good old one-shilling gallery days return—they are dreams, my cousin, now—but could you and I at this moment, instead of this quiet argument, by our well-carpeted fireside, sitting on this luxurious sofa—be once more struggling up those inconvenient staircases, pushed about, and squeezed, and elbowed by the poorest rabble of poor gallery scramblers—could I once more hear those anxious shrieks of yours—and the delicious *Thank God, we are safe,* which always followed when the topmost stair, conquered, let in the first light of the whole cheerful theatre down beneath us— I know not the fathom line that ever touched a descent so deep as I would be willing to bury more wealth in than Croesus had, or the great Jew R—— is supposed to have, to purchase it. And now do just look at that merry little Chinese waiter holding an umbrella, big enough for a bed-tester, over the head of that pretty insipid half Madonna-ish chit of a lady in that very blue summer-house."

Author and Selection Notes

Although Charles Lamb (1775-1834) tried writing in several forms, his chief literary fame rests upon his familiar essays, published under his pen name "Elia." The selection in this text is typical, in its charm and subject matter, of the essays contained in *Elia. Essays Which Have Appeared under that Signature in the London Magazine* and *The Last Essays of Elia.* The Bridget of "Old China" is Lamb's sister Mary.

Questions and Exercises

1. The characteristics of the "familiar essay" have been described as novelty of theme and freshness of form; graceful style and rambling structure; incomplete or tentative treatment of subject; reverie or associative logic; emotional unity rather than logical unity. Write a paragraph showing how "Old China" fulfills or fails to fulfill these requirements.

2. Does Lamb's use of the Latin terms *terra firma* and *speciosa miracula,* in your opinion, add or detract from the essay? Defend your view.

3. Summarize the arguments given by Bridget for wishing that the "good old times would come again."

4. What is the author's basic answer to her?

5. Why does Lamb use so many dashes as punctuation marks? Do they seem appropriate in view of the general style of the essay?

6. After reading Richard Steele's essay, "On Raphael's Cartoons at Hampton-Court," write a brief theme designating similarities of organization and tone.

7. Explain the phrase "in that world before perspective" and show how it is related to Lamb's general attitude toward old china.

8. Theme Topics: My First Love in Art; Fine China as a Hobby; Art Is (Is Not) Worth the Price; Writing the Personal Essay; Charles Lamb as a Literary Stylist.

THE REVOLT OF MOTHER
Mary E. Wilkins Freeman

"Father!"

"What is it?"

"What are them men diggin' over there in the field for?"

There was a sudden dropping and enlarging of the lower part of the old man's face, as if some heavy weight had settled therein; he shut his mouth tight, and went on harnessing the great bay mare. He hustled the collar on to her neck with a jerk.

"Father!"

The old man slapped the saddle upon the mare's back.

"Look here, father, I want to know what them men are diggin' over in the field for, an' I'm goin' to know."

"I wish you'd go into the house, mother, an' 'tend to your own affairs," the old man said then. He ran his words together, and his speech was almost as inarticulate as a growl.

But the woman understood; it was her most native tongue. "I ain't goin' into the house till you tell me what them men are doin' over there in the field," said she.

Then she stood waiting. She was a small woman, short and straight-waisted like a child in her brown cotton gown. Her forehead was mild and benevolent between the smooth curves of grey hair; there were meek downward lines about her nose and mouth; but her eyes, fixed upon the old man, looked as if the meekness had been the result of her own will, never the will of another.

They were in the barn, standing before the wide open doors. The spring air, full of the smell of growing grass and unseen blossoms, came in their faces. The deep yard in front was littered with farm wagons and piles of wood; on the edges, close to the fence and the house, the grass was a vivid green, and there were some dandelions.

The old man glanced doggedly at his wife as he tightened the last buckles on the harness. She looked as immovable to him as one of the rocks in his pasture-land, bound to the earth with generations of blackberry vines. He slapped the reins over the horse, and started forth from the barn.

"Father!" said she.

The old man pulled up. "What is it?"

"I want to know what them men are diggin' over there in that field for."

"They're diggin' a cellar, I s'pose, if you've got to know."

"A cellar for what?"

"A barn."

"A barn? You ain't goin' to build a barn over there where we was goin' to have a house, father?"

The old man said not another word. He hurried the horse into the farm wagon, and clattered out of the yard, jouncing as sturdily on his seat as a boy.

The woman stood a moment looking after him, then she went out of the barn across the corner of the yard to the house. The house, standing at right angles with the great barn and a long reach of sheds and out-buildings, was infinitesimal compared with them. It was scarcely as commodious for people as the little boxes under the barn eaves were for doves.

A pretty girl's face, pink and delicate as a flower, was looking out of one of the house windows. She was watching three men who were digging over in the field which bounded the yard near the road line. She turned quietly when the woman entered.

"What are they digging for, mother?" said she. "Did he tell you?"

"They're diggin' for—a cellar for a new barn."

"Oh, mother, he ain't going to build another barn?"

"That's what he says."

A boy stood before the kitchen glass combing his hair. He combed slowly and painstakingly, arranging his brown hair in a smooth hillock over his forehead. He did not seem to pay any attention to the conversation.

"Sammy, did you know father was going to build a new barn?" asked the girl.

The boy combed assiduously.

"Sammy!"

He turned, and showed a face like his father's under his smooth crest of hair. "Yes, I s'pose I did," he said, reluctantly.

"How long have you known it?" asked his mother.

"'Bout three months, I guess."

"Why didn't you tell of it?"

"Didn't think 'twould do no good."

"I don't see what father wants another barn for," said the girl, in her sweet, slow voice. She turned again to the window, and stared

out at the digging men in the field. Her tender, sweet face was full of
a gentle distress. Her forehead was as bald and as innocent as a
baby's, with the light hair strained back from it in a row of curl
papers. She was quite large, but her soft curves did not look as if
they covered muscles.

Her mother looked sternly at the boy. "Is he goin' to buy more
cows?" said she.

The boy did not reply; he was tying his shoes.

"Sammy, I want you to tell me if he's goin' to buy more cows."

"I s'pose he is."

"How many?"

"Four, I guess."

His mother said nothing more. She went into the pantry, and
there was a clatter of dishes. The boy got his cap from a nail behind the door, took an old arithmetic from the shelf, and started
for school. He was lightly built, but clumsy. He went out of the
yard with a curious spring in the hips, that made his loose home-
made jacket tilt up in the rear.

The girl went to the sink, and began to wash the dishes that
were piled up there. Her mother came promptly out of the pantry,
and shoved her aside. "You wipe 'em," said she, "I'll wash. There's
a good many this mornin'."

The mother plunged her hands vigorously into the water, the
girl wiped the plates slowly and dreamily. "Mother," said she,
"don't you think it's too bad father's going to build that new barn,
much as we need a decent house to live in?"

Her mother scrubbed a dish fiercely. "You ain't found out yet
we're women-folks, Nanny Penn," said she. "You ain't seen enough
of men-folks yet to. One of these days you'll find it out, an' then
you'll know that, we know only what men-folks think we do, so far
as any use of it goes, an' how we'd ought to reckon men-folks in
with Providence, an' not complain of what they do any more than
we do of the weather."

"I don't care; I don't believe George is anything like that, any-
how," said Nanny. Her delicate face flushed pink, her lips pouted
softly, as if she were going to cry.

"You wait an' see. I guess George Eastman ain't no better than
other men. You hadn't ought to judge father, though. He can't help
it, 'cause he don't look at things jest the way we do. An' we've been
pretty comfortable here, after all. The roof don't leak—ain't never
but once—that's one thing. Father's kept it shingled right up."

"I do wish we had a parlor."

"I guess it won't hurt George Eastman any to come to see you in a nice clean kitchen. I guess a good many girls don't have as good a place as this. Nobody's ever heard me complain."

"I ain't complained either, mother."

"Well, I don't think you'd better, a good father an' a good home as you've got. S'pose your father made you go out an' work for your livin'? Lots of girls have to that ain't no stronger an' better able to than you be."

Sarah Penn washed the frying pan with a conclusive air. She scrubbed the outside of it as faithfully as the inside. She was a masterly keeper of her box of a house. Her one living room never seemed to have in it any of the dust that the friction of life with inanimate matter produces. She swept, and there seemed to be no dirt to go before the broom; she cleaned, and one could see no difference. She was like an artist; so perfect that he apparently has no art. Today she got out a mixing bowl and a board, and rolled some pies, and there was no more flour upon her than there was upon her daughter who was doing finer work. Nanny was to be married in the fall, and she was sewing on some white cambric and embroidery. She sewed industriously while her mother cooked; her soft, milk-white hands and wrists showed whiter than her delicate work.

"We must have the stove moved out in the shed before long," said Mrs. Penn. "Talk about not havin' things, it's been a real blessin' to be able to put a stove up in that shed in hot weather. Father did one good thing when he fixed that stove-pipe out there."

Sarah Penn's face as she rolled her pies had that expression of meek vigor which might have characterized one of the New Testament saints. She was making mince pies. Her husband, Adoniram Penn, liked them better than any other kind. She baked twice a week. Adoniram often liked a piece of pie between meals. She hurried this morning. It had been later than usual when she began, and she wanted to have a pie baked for dinner. However deep a resentment she might be forced to hold against her husband, she would never fail in sedulous attention to his wants.

Nobility of character manifests itself at loop-holes when it is not provided with large doors. Sarah Penn's showed itself today in flaky dishes of pastry. So she made pies faithfully, while across the table she could see, when she glanced up from her work, the sight that rankled in her patient and steadfast soul—the digging of the cellar of the new barn in the place where Adoniram forty years ago had promised her their new house should stand.

The pies were done for dinner. Adoniram and Sammy were

home a few minutes after twelve o'clock. The dinner was eaten with serious haste. There was never much conversation at the table in the Penn family. Adoniram asked a blessing, and they ate promptly, then rose up and went about their work.

Sammy went back to school, taking soft, sly lopes out of the yard like a rabbit. He wanted a game of marbles before school, and feared his father would give him some chores to do. Adoniram hastened to the door and called after him, but he was out of sight.

"I don't see what you let him go for, mother," said he. "I wanted him to help me unload that wood."

Adoniram went to work out in the yard, unloading wood from the wagon. Sarah put away the dinner dishes, while Nanny took down her curl-papers and changed her dress. She was going down to the store to buy some more embroidery and thread.

When Nanny was gone, Mrs. Penn went to the door. "Father!" she called.

"Well, what is it!"

"I want to see you jest a minute, father."

"I can't leave this wood nohow. I've got to git it unloaded an' go for a load of gravel afore two o'clock. Sammy had ought to help me. You hadn't ought to let him go to school so early."

"I want to see you jest a minute."

"I tell ye I can't, nohow, mother."

"Father, you come here." Sarah Penn stood in the door like a queen; she held her head as if it bore a crown; there was that patience which makes authority royal in her voice. Adoniram went.

Mrs. Penn led the way into the kitchen, and pointed to a chair. "Sit down, father," said she; "I've got somethin' I want to say to you."

He sat down heavily; his face was quite stolid, but he looked at her with restive eyes. "Well, what is it, mother?"

"I want to know what you're buildin' that new barn for, father?"

"I tell ye I ain't got nothin' to say about it, mother; an' I ain't goin' to say nothin'."

"Be you goin' to buy more cows?"

Adoniram did not reply; he shut his mouth tight.

"I know you be, as well as I want to. Now, father, look here"—Sarah Penn had not sat down; she stood before her husband in the humble fashion of a Scripture woman—"I'm goin' to talk real plain to you; I never have since I married you, but I'm goin' to now. I ain't never complained, and I ain't goin' to complain now, but I'm goin' to talk plain. You see this room here, father; you look at it well. You see there ain't no carpet on the floor, an' you see the paper is all dirty, an' droppin' off the walls. We ain't had no new paper on it for ten year, an' then I put it on myself, and it didn't cost but ninepence a roll. You see this room, father; it's all the one I've had to work in an' eat in an' sit in sence we was married. There ain't another woman in the whole town whose husband ain't got half the means you have but what's got better. It's all the room Nanny's got to have her company in; an' there ain't one of her mates but what's got better, an' their fathers not so able as hers is. It's all the room she'll have to be married in. What would you have thought, father, if we had had our weddin' in a room no better than this? I was married in my mother's parlor, with a carpet on the floor, an' stuffed furniture, and a mahogany card-table. An' this is all the room my daughter will have to be married in. Look here, father!"

Sarah Penn went across the room as though it were a tragic stage. She flung open a door and disclosed a tiny bedroom, only large enough for a bed and a bureau, with a path between. "There, father," said she—"there's all the room I've had to sleep in forty year. All my children was born there—the two that died, an' the two that's livin'. I was sick with a fever there."

She stepped to another door and opened it. It led into a small, ill-lighted pantry. "Here," said she, "is all the buttery I've got— every place I've got for my dishes, to set away my victuals in, an' to keep my milk-pans in. Father, I've been takin' care of the milk of six cows in this place, an' now you're goin' to build a new barn, an' keep more cows, an' give me more to do in it."

She threw open another door. A narrow crooked flight of stairs wound upward from it. "There, father," said she, "I want you to look at the stairs that go up to them two unfinished chambers that are all the places our son an' daughter have had to sleep in all their lives. There ain't a prettier girl in town nor a more ladylike one than Nanny, an' that's the place she has to sleep in. It ain't so good as your horse's stall; it ain't so warm and tight."

Sarah Penn went back and stood before her husband. "Now, father," said she, "I want to know if you think you're doin' right an' accordin' to what you profess. Here, when we was married, forty years ago, you promised me faithful that we should have a new house built in that lot over in the field before the year was out. You said you had money enough, an' you wouldn't ask me to live in no such place as this. It is forty year now, an' you've been makin' more money, an' I've been savin' of it for you ever since, an' you ain't built no house yet. You've built sheds an' cow-houses an' one new barn, an' now you're goin' to build another. Father, I want to know if you think it's right. You're lodgin' your dumb beasts better than you are your own flesh and blood. I want to know if you think it's right."

"I ain't got nothin' to say."

"You can't say nothin' without ownin' it ain't right, father. An' there's another thing—I ain't complained; I've got along forty year, an' I suppose I should forty more, if it wa'n't for that—if we don't have another house. Nanny, she can't live with us after she's married. She'll have to go somewhere else to live away from us, an' it don't seem as if I could have it so, noways, father. She wa'n't ever strong. She's got considerable color, but there wa'n't never any backbone to her. I've always took the heft of everything off her, an' she ain't fit to keep house an' do everything herself. She'll be all worn out inside of a year. Think of her doin' all the washin' an' ironin' an' bakin' with them soft white hands an' arms, an' sweepin'! I can't have it so, noways, father."

Mrs. Penn's face was burning; her mild eyes gleamed. She had pleaded her little cause like a Webster; she had ranged from severity to pathos; but her opponent employed that obstinate silence which makes eloquence futile with mocking echoes. Adoniram arose clumsily.

"Father, ain't you got nothin' to say?" said Mrs. Penn.

"I've got to go off after that load of gravel. I can't stan' here talkin' all day."

"Father, won't you think it over, an' have a house built there, instead of a barn."

"I ain't got nothin' to say."

Adoniram shuffled out. Mrs. Penn went into her bedroom. When she came out, her eyes were red. She had a roll of unbleached cotton cloth. She spread it out on the kitchen table, and began cutting out some shirts for her husband. The men over in the field had a team to help them this afternoon; she could hear their halloos. She had a scanty pattern for the shirts; she had to plan and piece the sleeves. Nanny came home with her embroidery, and sat down with her needlework. She had taken down her curl-papers, and there was a soft roll of fair hair like an aureole over her forehead; her face was as delicately fine and clear as porcelain. Suddenly she looked up, and the tender red flamed all over her face and neck. "Mother," said she.

"What say?"

"I've been thinking—I don't see how we're goin' to have any —wedding in this room. I'd be ashamed to have his folks come if we didn't have anybody else."

"Mebbe we can have some new paper before then; I can put it on. I guess you won't have no call to be ashamed of your belongin's."

"We might have the wedding in the new barn," said Nanny, with gentle pettishness. "Why, mother, what makes you look so?"

Mrs. Penn had started, and was staring at her with a curious expression. She turned again to her work, and spread out a pattern carefully on the cloth. "Nothin'," said she.

Presently Adoniram clattered out of the yard in his two wheeled dump cart, standing as proudly upright as a Roman charioteer. Mrs. Penn opened the door and stood there a minute looking out; the halloos of the men sounded louder.

It seemed to her all through the spring months that she heard nothing but the halloos and the noises of the saws and hammers. The new barn grew fast. It was a fine edifice for this little village. Men came on pleasant Sundays, in their meeting suits and clean shirt bosoms, and stood around it admiringly. Mrs. Penn did not speak of it, and Adoniram did not mention it to her, although, sometimes, upon a return from inspecting it, he bore himself with injured dignity.

"It's a strange thing how your mother feels about the new barn," he said, confidentially, to Sammy one day.

Sammy only grunted after an odd fashion for a boy; he had learned it from his father.

The barn was all completed ready for use by the third week of July. Adoniram had planned to move his stock in on Wednesday; on Tuesday he received a letter which changed his plans. He came in with it early in the morning. "Sammy's been to the postoffice," said he, "and I've got a letter from Hiram." Hiram was Mrs. Penn's brother, who lived in Vermont.

"Well," said Mrs. Penn, "what does he say about the folks?"

"I guess they're all right. He says he thinks if I come up country right off there's a chance to buy jest the kind of a horse I want." He stared reflectively out of the window at the new barn.

Mrs. Penn was making pies. She went on clapping the rolling pin into the crust, although she was very pale, and her heart beat loudly.

"I dun' know but what I'd better go," said Adoniram. "I hate to go off jest now, right in the midst of hayin', but the ten-acre lot's cut, an' I guess Rufus an' the others can git along without me three or four days. I can't get a horse round here to suit me, nohow, an' I've got to have another for all that wood-haulin' in the fall. I told Hiram to watch out, an' if he got wind of a good horse to let me know. I guess I'd better go."

"I'll get out your clean shirt an' collar," said Mrs. Penn calmly.

She laid out Adoniram's Sunday suit and his clean clothes on the bed in the little bedroom. She got his shaving water and razor ready. At last she buttoned on his collar and fastened his black cravat.

Adoniram never wore his collar and cravat except on extra occasions. He held his head high, with a rasped dignity. When he was all ready, with his coat and hat brushed, and a lunch of pie and cheese in a paper bag, he hesitated on the threshold of the door. He looked at his wife and his manner was defiantly apologetic. "*If* them cows come today, Sammy can drive 'em into the new barn," said he; "an' when they bring the hay up, they can pitch it in there."

"Well," replied Mrs. Penn.

Adoniram set his shaven face ahead and started. When he had cleared the doorstep, he turned and looked back with a kind of nervous solemnity. "I shall be back by Saturday if nothin' happens," said he.

"Do be careful, father," returned his wife.

She stood in the door with Nanny at her elbow and watched him out of sight. Her eyes had a strange, doubtful expression in them; her peaceful forehead was contracted. She went in, and about her baking again. Nanny sat sewing. Her wedding-day was drawing nearer, and she was getting pale and thin with her steady sewing. Her mother kept glancing at her.

"Have you got that pain in your side this mornin'?" she asked.

"A little."

Mrs. Penn's face, as she worked, changed, her perplexed forehead smoothed, her eyes were steady, her lips firmly set. She formed a maxim for herself, although incoherently, with her unlettered thoughts. "Unsolicited opportunities are the guide-posts of the Lord to the new roads of life," she repeated in effect, and she made up her mind to her course of action.

"S'posin' I *had* wrote to Hiram," she muttered once, when she was in the pantry—"s'posin' I had wrote, an' asked him if he knew of any horse? But I didn't, an' father's goin' wa'n't none of my doin'. It looks like a providence." Her voice rang out quite loud at the last.

"What are you talkin' about, mother?" called Nanny.

"Nothin'."

Mrs. Penn hurried her baking; at eleven o'clock it was all done. The load of hay from the west field came slowly down the cart track, and drew up at the new barn. Mrs. Penn ran out. "Stop!" she screamed—"stop!"

The men stopped and looked; Sammy up-reared from the top of the load and stared at his mother.

"Stop!" she cried out again. "Don't you put the hay in that barn; put it in the old one."

"Why, he said to put it in here," returned one of the haymakers, wonderingly. He was a young man, a neighbor's son, whom Adoniram hired by the year to help on the farm.

"Don't you put the hay in the new barn; there's room enough in the old one, ain't there?" said Mrs. Penn.

"Room enough," returned the hired man, in his thick, rustic tones. "Didn't need the new barn, nohow, far as room's concerned. Well, I s'pose he changed his mind." He took hold of the horses' bridles.

Mrs. Penn went back to the house. Soon the kitchen windows were darkened, and a fragrance like warm honey came into the room.

Nanny laid down her work. "I thought father wanted them to put the hay into the new barn?" she said wonderingly.

"It's all right," replied her mother.

Sammy slid down from the load of hay, and came in to see if dinner was ready.

"I ain't goin' to get a regular dinner today, as long as father's gone," said his mother. "I've let the fire go out. You can have some bread an' milk an' pie. I thought we could get along." She set out some bowls of milk, some bread, and a pie on the kitchen table. "You'd better eat your dinner now," said she. "You might jest as well get through with it. I want you to help me afterward."

Nanny and Sammy stared at each other. There was something strange in their mother's manner. Mrs. Penn did not eat anything herself. She went into the pantry, and they heard her moving dishes while they ate. Presently she came out with a pile of plates. She got the clothes basket out of the shed, and packed them into it. She brought out cups and saucers, and put them in with the plates.

"What are you goin' to do, mother?" inquired Nanny, in a timid voice. A sense of something unusual made her tremble, as if it were a ghost. Sammy rolled his eyes over his pie.

"You'll see what I'm goin' to do," replied Mrs. Penn. "If you're through, Nanny, I want you to go upstairs an' pack up your things; an' I want you, Sammy, to help me take down the bed in the bedroom."

"Oh, mother, what for?" gasped Nanny.

"You'll see."

During the next few hours a feat was performed by this simple, pious New England mother which was equal in its way to Wolfe's storming of the Heights of Abraham. It took no more genius and audacity of bravery for Wolfe to cheer his wondering soldiers up those steep precipices, under the sleeping eyes of the enemy, than for Sarah Penn, at the head of her children, to move all their little household goods into the new barn while her husband was away.

Nanny and Sammy followed their mother's instructions without a murmur; indeed, they were overawed. There is a certain uncanny and superhuman quality about all such purely original undertakings as their mother's was to them. Nanny went back and forth with her light loads, and Sammy tugged with sober energy.

At five o'clock in the afternoon the little house in which the Penns had lived for forty years had emptied itself into the new barn.

Every builder builds somewhat for unknown purposes, and is in a measure a prophet. The architect of Adoniram Penn's barn, while he designed it for the comfort of four-footed animals had planned better than he knew for the comfort of humans. Sarah Penn saw at a glance its possibilities. Those great box-stalls, with quilts hung before them, would make better bedrooms than the one she had occupied for forty years, and there was a tight carriage room. The harness room, with its chimney and shelves, would make a kitchen of her dreams. The great middle space would make a parlor, by and by, fit for a palace. Upstairs, there was as much room as down. With partitions and windows, what a house would there be! Sarah looked at the row of stanchions before the allotted space for cows, and reflected that she would have her front entry there.

At six o'clock the stove was set up in the harness-room, the kettle was boiling, and the table was set for tea. It looked almost as home-like as the abandoned house across the yard had ever done. The young hired man milked, and Sarah directed him calmly to bring the milk to the new barn. He came, gaping, dropping little blots of foam from the brimming pails on the grass. Before the next morning he had spread all over the little village the story of Adoniram Penn's wife moving into the new barn. Men assembled in the store and talked it over, women with shawls over their heads scuttled into each other's houses before their work was done. Any deviation from the ordinary course of life in this quiet town was enough to stop all progress in it. Everybody paused to look at the staid, independent figure on the side track. There was a difference of opinion in regard to her. Some held her to be insane; some, of a lawless and rebellious spirit.

Friday the minister went to see her. It was in the forenoon, and she was at the barn door shelling peas for dinner. She looked up and returned his salutation with dignity; then she went on with her work. She did not invite him in. The saintly expression of her face remained fixed, but there was an angry flush over it.

The minister stood awkwardly before her, and talked. She handled the peas as if they were bullets. At last, she looked up, and her eyes showed the spirit that her meek front had covered up for a lifetime.

"There ain't no use talkin', Mr. Hersey," said she. "I've thought it all over an' over, an' I believe I'm doin' what's right. I've made it the subject of prayer, an' it's betwixt me an' the Lord an' Adoniram. There ain't no call for nobody else to worry about it."

"Well, of course, if you have brought it to the Lord in prayer, and feel satisfied that you are doing right, Mrs. Penn," said the minister, helplessly. His thin, grey-bearded face was pathetic. He was a sickly man; his youthful confidence had cooled; he had to scourge himself up to some of his pastoral duties as relentlessly as a Catholic ascetic, and then he was prostrated by the smart.

"I think it's right jest as much as I think it was right for our forefathers to come over from the old country 'cause they didn't have what belonged to 'em," said Mrs. Penn. She arose. The barn threshold might have been Plymouth Rock from her bearing. "I don't doubt you mean well, Mr. Hersey," said she, "but there are things people hadn't ought to interfere with. I've been a member of the church for over forty years. I've got my own mind an' my own feet, an' I'm goin' to think my own thoughts an' go my own ways, an' nobody but the Lord is goin' to dictate to me unless I've a mind to have him. Won't you come in and set down? How is Mis' Hersey?"

"She is well, I thank you," replied the minister. He added some more perplexed apologetic remarks; then he retreated.

He could expound the intricacies of every character study in the Scriptures; he was competent to grasp the Pilgrim Fathers and all historical innovators; but Sarah Penn was beyond him. He could deal with primal cases, but parallel ones worsted him. But after all, it was aside from his province, he wondered more how Adoniram Penn would deal with his wife than how the Lord would. Everybody shared the wonder. When Adoniram's four new cows arrived, Sarah ordered three to be put in the old barn, the other in the house shed where the cooking stove had stood. That added to the excite-ment. It was whispered that all four cows were domiciled in the house.

Toward sunset on Saturday, when Adoniram was expected home, there was a knot of men in the road near the new barn. The hired man had milked, but he still hung around the premises. Sarah Penn had supper all ready. There were brown bread and baked beans and a custard pie; it was the supper that Adoniram loved on a Saturday night. She had on a clean calico, and she bore herself imperturbably. Nanny and Sammy kept close at her heels. Their eyes were large, and Nanny was full of nervous tremors. Still, there was to them more pleasant excitement than anything else. An in-born confidence in their mother over their father asserted itself.

Sammy looked out of the harness-room window. "There he is," he announced in an awed whisper. He and Nanny peeped around the casing. Mrs. Penn kept on about her work. The children watched Adoniram leave the new horse standing in the drive while he went to the house door. It was fastened. Then he went around to the shed. That door was seldom locked, even when the family was away. The thought how her father would be confronted by the cow flashed upon Nanny. There was a hysterical sob in her throat. Adoniram emerged from the shed and stood looking around in a dazed fashion. His lips moved; he was saying something, but they could not hear what it was. The hired man was peeping around a corner of the old barn, but nobody saw him.

Adoniram took the new horse by the bridle and led him across the yard to the new barn. Nanny and Sammy slunk close to their mother. The barn doors rolled back, and there stood Adoniram, with the long mild face of the Canadian farm horse looking over his shoulder.

Nanny kept behind her mother, but Sammy stepped suddenly forward, and stood in front of her.

Adoniram stared at the group. "What on airth you all down here for?" said he. "What's the matter over to the house?"

"We've come here to live, father," said Sammy. His shrill voice quavered out bravely.

"What"—Adoniram sniffed—"what is it smells like cookin'?" said he. He stepped forward and looked in the open door of the harness-room. Then he turned to his wife. His old bristling face was pale and frightened. "What on airth does this mean, mother?" he gasped.

"You come in here, father," said Sarah. She led the way into the harness room and shut the door. "Now, father," said she, "you needn't be scared. I ain't crazy. There ain't nothin' to be upset over. But we've come here to live, an' we're goin' to live here. We've got just as good a right here as new horses an' cows. The house wa'n't fit for us to live in any longer, an' I made up my mind I wa'n't goin' to stay there. I've done my duty by you forty year, an' I'm goin' to do it now, but I'm goin' to live here. You've got to put in some windows and partitions; an' you'll have to buy some furniture."

"Why, mother!" the old man gasped.

"You'd better take your coat off an' get washed—there's the wash-basin—an' then we'll have supper."

"Why, mother!"

Sammy went past the window, leading the new horse to the old barn. The old man saw him, and shook his head speechlessly. He tried to take off his coat, but his arms seemed to lack the power. His wife helped him. She poured some water into the tin basin, and put in a piece of soap. She got the comb and brush, and smoothed his thin grey hair after he had washed. Then she put the beans, hot bread, and tea on the table. Sammy came in and the family drew up. Adoniram sat looking dazedly at his plate and they waited.

"Ain't you goin' to ask a blessin', father?" said Sarah.

And the old man bent his head and mumbled.

All through the meal he stopped eating at intervals, and stared furtively at his wife; but he ate well. The home food tasted good to him, and his old frame was too sturdily healthy to be affected by his mind. But after supper he went out, and sat down on the step of the smaller door at the right of the barn, through which he had meant his Jerseys to pass in stately file, but which Sarah designed for her front house door, and he leaned his head on his hands.

After the supper dishes were cleared away and the milk pans washed, Sarah went out to him. The twilight was deepening. There was a clear green glow in the sky. Before them stretched the smooth level of field; in the distance was a cluster of haystacks like the huts of a village; the air was very cool and calm and sweet. The landscape might have been an ideal one of peace.

Sarah bent over and touched her husband on one of his thin, sinewy shoulders. "Father!"

The old man's shoulders heaved; he was weeping.

"Why, don't do so, father," said Sarah.

"I'll—put up the—partitions, an'—everything you—want, mother."

Sarah put her apron up to her face; she was overcome by her own triumph.

Adoniram was like a fortress whose walls had no active resistance, and went down the instant the right besieging tools were used. "Why, mother," he said hoarsely, "I hadn't no idee you was so set on't as all this comes to."

Author and Selection Notes

The village of Randolph, Massachusetts, where Mary E. Wilkins Freeman (1852-1930) was born, and where she lived for many years, and the countryside around it, have furnished both material and locale for much of her fiction. Collected in *A Humble Romance and Other Stories, People of Our Neighborhood,* and *A New England Nun and Other Stories,* from which the present selection is taken, many of her tales reflect the same emphasis upon regional life patterns that characterizes the local-color fiction of the last quarter of the nineteenth century.

Questions and Exercises

1. Point out what you feel to be distinctive regional characteristics in this story in terms of setting, dialogue, customs.

2. Write a page character sketch of Mrs. Penn, showing how the author enables her to become individualized though represented as a typical New England farm wife of the last century.

3. Characterize briefly her husband and children. Which of the three seems most fully delineated?

4. On what grounds does Mrs. Penn, early in the story, defend her husband to her daughter?

5. How is Mrs. Penn's great concern for her daughter related to the matter of the new barn?

6. Explain: "Nobility of character manifests itself at loop-holes when it is not provided with large doors"; "Unsolicited opportunities are the guide-posts of the Lord to the new roads of life."

7. Read Irwin Shaw's "Main Currents of American Thought" and write a brief essay comparing the plots and characterization in the two stories.

8. At what point in the story does Mrs. Penn conceive of the idea of moving into the new barn and making it their home?

9. Theme Topics: "The Revolt of Mother" as Local-Color Fiction; The Position of Women in Nineteenth-Century American Society; Home, Sweet Home"; The Rights of Women in a Free Society.

RIDERS TO THE SEA

A Play in One Act

John M. Synge

PERSONS IN THE PLAY

First performed at the Molesworth Hall, Dublin,

February 25, 1904.

MAURYA *(an old woman)*	Honor Lavelle
BARTLEY *(her son)*	W. G. Fay
CATHLEEN *(her daughter)*	Sarah Allgood
NORA *(a younger daughter)*	Emma Vernon
MEN and WOMEN	

SCENE. *An Island off the West of Ireland.*
(Cottage kitchen, with nets, oil-skins, spinning wheel, some new boards standing by the wall, etc. CATHLEEN, *a girl of about twenty, finishes kneading cake, and puts it down in the pot-oven by the fire; then wipes her hands, and begins to spin at the wheel.*
NORA, *a young girl, puts her head in at the door.)*
NORA *(in a low voice).* Where is she?
CATHLEEN. She's lying down, God help her, and may be sleeping, if she's able.
[NORA *comes in softly, and takes a bundle from under her shawl.*]
CATHLEEN *(spinning the wheel rapidly).* What is it you have?
NORA. The young priest is after bringing them. It's a shirt and a plain stocking were got off a drowned man in Donegal.
[CATHLEEN *stops her wheel with a sudden movement, and leans out to listen.*]
NORA. We're to find out if it's Michael's they are, some time herself will be down looking by the sea.
CATHLEEN. How would they be Michael's, Nora. How would he go the length of that way to the far north?
NORA. The young priest says he's known the like of it. "If it's Michael's they are," says he, "you can tell herself he's got a clean burial by the grace of God, and if they're not his, let no one say a word about them, for she'll be getting her death," says he, "with crying and lamenting."
[*The door which* NORA *half closed is blown open by a gust of wind.*]

From *The Complete Works of John M. Synge.* Random House, 1935.

CATHLEEN (*looking out anxiously*). Did you ask him would he stop Bartley going this day with the horses to the Galway fair?

NORA. "I won't stop him," says he, "but let you not be afraid. Herself does be saying prayers half through the night, and the Almighty God won't leave her destitute," says he, "with no son living."

CATHLEEN. Is the sea bad by the white rocks, Nora?

NORA. Middling bad, God help us. There's a great roaring in the west, and it's worse it'll be getting when the tide's turned to the wind.

[*She goes over to the table with the bundle.*] Shall I open it now?

CATHLEEN. Maybe she'd wake up on us, and come in before we'd done. (*Coming to the table.*) It's a long time we'll be, and the two of us crying.

NORA (*goes to the inner door and listens*). She's moving about on the bed. She'll be coming in a minute.

CATHLEEN. Give me the ladder, and I'll put them up in the turf-loft, the way she won't know of them at all, and maybe when the tide turns she'll be going down to see would he be floating from the east.

[*They put the ladder against the gable of the chimney;* CATHLEEN *goes up a few steps and hides the bundle in the turf-loft.* MAURYA *comes from the inner room.*]

MAURYA (*looking up at* CATHLEEN *and speaking querulously*). Isn't it turf enough you have for this day and evening?

CATHLEEN. There's a cake baking at the fire for a short space (*throwing down the turf*) and Bartley will want it when the tide turns if he goes to Connemara.

[NORA *picks up the turf and puts it round the pot-oven.*]

MAURYA (*sitting down on a stool at the fire*). He won't go this day with the wind rising from the south and west. He won't go this day, for the young priest will stop him surely.

NORA. He'll not stop him, mother, and I heard Eamon Simon and Stephen Pheety and Colum Shawn saying he would go.

MAURYA. Where is he itself?

NORA. He went down to see would there be another boat sailing in the week, and I'm thinking it won't be long till he's here now, for the tide's turning at the green head, and the hooker's tacking from the east.

CATHLEEN. I hear some one passing the big stones.

NORA (*looking out*). He's coming now, and he's in a hurry.

BARTLEY (*comes in and looks round the room. Speaking sadly and quietly*). Where is the bit of new rope, Cathleen, was bought in Connemara?

CATHLEEN (*coming down*). Give it to him, Nora; it's on a nail by the white boards. I hung it up this morning, for the pig with the black feet was eating it.

NORA (*giving him a rope*). Is that it, Bartley?

MAURYA. You'd do right to leave that rope, Bartley, hanging by the boards. (BARTLEY *takes the rope*.) It will be wanting in this place, I'm telling you, if Michael is washed up to-morrow morning, or the next morning, or any morning in the week, for it's a deep grave we'll make him by the grace of God.

BARTLEY (*beginning to work with the rope*). I've no halter the way I can ride down on the mare, and I must go now quickly. This is the one boat going for two weeks or beyond it, and the fair will be a good fair for horses I heard them saying below.

MAURYA. It's a hard thing they'll be saying below if the body is washed up and there's no man in it to make the coffin, and I after giving a big price for the finest white boards you'd find in Connemara.

[*She looks round at the boards.*]

BARTLEY. How would it be washed up, and we after looking each day for nine days, and a strong wind blowing a while back from the west and south?

MAURYA. If it wasn't found itself, that wind is raising the sea, and there was a star up against the moon, and it rising in the night. If it was a hundred horses, or a thousand horses you had itself, what is the price of a thousand horses against a son where there is one son only?

BARTLEY (*working at the halter, to* CATHLEEN). Let you go down each day, and see the sheep aren't jumping in on the rye, and if the jobber comes you can sell the pig with the black feet if there is a good price going.

MAURYA. How would the like of her get a good price for a pig?

BARTLEY (*to* CATHLEEN). If the west wind holds with the last bit of the moon let you and Nora get up weed enough for another cock for the kelp. It's hard set we'll be from this day with no one in it but one man to work.

MAURYA. It's hard set we'll be surely the day you're drownd'd with the rest. What way will I live and the girls with me, and I an old woman looking for the grave?

[BARTLEY *lays down the halter, takes off his old coat, and puts on a newer one of the same flannel.*]

BARTLEY (*to* NORA). Is she coming to the pier?

NORA (*looking out*). She's passing the green head and letting fall her sails.

BARTLEY (*getting his purse and tobacco*). I'll have half an hour to go down, and you'll see me coming again in two days, or in three days, or maybe in four days if the wind is bad.

MAURYA (*turning round to the fire, and putting her shawl over her head*). Isn't it a hard and cruel man won't hear a word from an old woman, and she holding him from the sea?

CATHLEEN. It's the life of a young man to be going on the sea, and who would listen to an old woman with one thing and she saying it over?

BARTLEY (*taking the halter*). I must go now quickly. I'll ride down on the red mare, and the gray pony'll run behind me. . . . The blessing of God on you.

[*He goes out.*]

MAURYA (*crying out as he is in the door*). He's gone now, God spare us, and we'll not see him again. He's gone now, and when the black night is falling I'll have no son left me in the world.

CATHLEEN. Why wouldn't you give him your blessing and he looking round in the door? Isn't it sorrow enough is on every one in this house without your sending him out with an unlucky word behind him, and a hard word in his ear?

[MAURYA *takes up the tongs and begins raking the fire aimlessly without looking round.*]

NORA (*turning towards her*). You're taking away the turf from the cake.

CATHLEEN (*crying out*). The Son of God forgive us, Nora, we're after forgetting his bit of bread.

[*She comes over to the fire.*]

NORA. And it's destroyed he'll be going till dark night, and he after eating nothing since the sun went up.

CATHLEEN (*turning the cake out of the oven*). It's destroyed he'll be, surely. There's no sense left on any person in a house where an old woman will be talking for ever.

[MAURYA *sways herself on her stool.*]

CATHLEEN (*cutting off some of the bread and rolling it in a cloth; to* MAURYA). Let you go down now to the spring well and give him this and he passing. You'll see him then and the dark word will be broken, and you can say "God speed you," the way he'll be easy in his mind.

MAURYA (*taking the bread*). Will I be in it as soon as himself?

CATHLEEN. If you go now quickly.

MAURYA (*standing up unsteadily*). It's hard set I am to walk.

CATHLEEN (*looking at her anxiously*). Give her the stick, Nora, or maybe she'll slip on the big stones.

NORA. What stick?

CATHLEEN. The stick Michael brought from Connemara.

MAURYA (*taking a stick* NORA *gives her*). In the big world the old people do be leaving things after them for their sons and children, but in this place it is the young men do be leaving things behind for them that do be old.

[*She goes out slowly.* NORA *goes over to the ladder.*]

CATHLEEN. Wait, Nora, maybe she'd turn back quickly. She's that sorry, God help her, you wouldn't know the thing she'd do.

NORA. Is she gone round by the bush?

CATHLEEN (*looking out*). She's gone now. Throw it down quickly, for the Lord knows when she'll be out of it again.

NORA (*getting the bundle from the loft*). The young priest said he'd be passing to-morrow, and we might go down and speak to him below if it's Michael's they are surely.

CATHLEEN (*taking the bundle*). Did he say what way they were found?

NORA (*coming down*). "There were two men," says he, "and they rowing round with poteen before the cocks crowed, and the oar of one of them caught the body, and they passing the black cliffs of the north."

CATHLEEN (*trying to open the bundle*). Give me a knife, Nora, the string's perished with the salt water, and there's a black knot on it you wouldn't loosen in a week.

NORA (*giving her a knife*). I've heard tell it was a long way to Donegal.

CATHLEEN (*cutting the string*). It is surely. There was a man in here a while ago—the man sold us that knife—and he said if you set off walking from the rocks beyond, it would be seven days you'd be in Donegal.

NORA. And what time would a man take, and he floating?

[CATHLEEN *opens the bundle and takes out a bit of a stocking. They look at them eagerly.*]

CATHLEEN (*in a low voice*). The Lord spare us, Nora! isn't it a queer hard thing to say if it's his they are surely?

NORA. I'll get his shirt off the hook the way we can put the one flannel on the other. (*She looks through some clothes hanging in the corner.*) It's not with them, Cathleen, and where will it be?

CATHLEEN. I'm thinking Bartley put it on him in the morning, for his own shirt was heavy with the salt in it (*pointing to the cor-*

ner). There's a bit of a sleeve was of the same stuff. Give me that and it will do.

[NORA *brings it to her and they compare the flannel.*]

CATHLEEN. It's the same stuff, Nora; but if it is itself aren't there great rolls of it in the shops of Galway, and isn't it many another man may have a shirt of it as well as Michael himself?

NORA (*who has taken up the stocking and counted the stitches, crying out*). It's Michael, Cathleen, it's Michael; God spare his soul, and what will herself say when she hears this story, and Bartley on the sea?

CATHLEEN (*taking the stocking*). It's a plain stocking.

NORA. It's the second one of the third pair I knitted, and I put up three score stitches, and I dropped four of them.

CATHLEEN (*counts the stitches*). It's that number is in it (*crying out*). Ah, Nora, isn't it a bitter thing to think of him floating that way to the far north, and no one to keen him but the black hags that do be flying on the sea?

NORA (*swinging herself round, and throwing out her arms on the clothes*). And isn't it a pitiful thing when there is nothing left of a man who was a great rower and fisher, but a bit of an old shirt and a plain stocking?

CATHLEEN (*after an instant*). Tell me is herself coming, Nora? I hear a little sound on the path.

NORA (*looking out*). She is, Cathleen. She's coming up to the door.

CATHLEEN. Put these things away before she'll come in. Maybe it's easier she'll be after giving her blessing to Bartley, and we won't let on we've heard anything the time he's on the sea.

NORA (*helping* CATHLEEN *to close the bundle*). We'll put them here in the corner.

[*They put them into a hole in the chimney corner.* CATHLEEN *goes back to the spinning-wheel.*]

NORA. Will she see it was crying I was?

CATHLEEN. Keep your back to the door the way the light'll not be on you.

[NORA *sits down at the chimney corner, with her back to the door.* MAURYA *comes in very slowly, without looking at the girls, and goes over to her stool at the other side of the fire. The cloth with the bread is still in her hand. The girls look at each other, and* NORA *points to the bundle of bread.*]

CATHLEEN (*after spinning for a moment*). You didn't give him his bit of bread?

[MAURYA *begins to keen softly, without turning round.*]

CATHLEEN. Did you see him riding down?

[MAURYA *goes on keening.*]

CATHLEEN (*a little impatiently*). God forgive you; isn't it a better thing to raise your voice and tell what you seen, than to be making lamentation for a thing that's done? Did you see Bartley, I'm saying to you.

MAURYA (*with a weak voice*). My heart's broken from this day.

CATHLEEN (*as before*). Did you see Bartley?

MAURYA. I seen the fearfulest thing.

CATHLEEN (*leaves her wheel and looks out*). God forgive you; he's riding the mare now over the green head, and the gray pony behind him.

MAURYA (*starts, so that her shawl falls back from her head and shows her white tossed hair. With a frightened voice*). The gray pony behind him.

CATHLEEN (*coming to the fire*). What is it ails you, at all?

MAURYA (*speaking very slowly*). I've seen the fearfulest thing any person has seen, since the day Bride Dara seen the dead man with the child in his arms.

CATHLEEN AND NORA. Uah!

[*They crouch down in front of the old woman at the fire.*]

NORA. Tell us what it is you seen.

MAURYA. I went down to the spring well, and I stood there saying a prayer to myself. Then Bartley came along, and he riding on the red mare with the gray pony behind him. (*She puts up her hands, as if to hide something from her eyes.*) The Son of God spare us, Nora!

CATHLEEN. What is it you seen.

MAURYA. I seen Michael himself.

CATHLEEN (*speaking softly*). You did not, mother. It wasn't Michael you seen, for his body is after being found in the far north, and he's got a clean burial by the grace of God.

MAURYA (*a little defiantly*). I'm after seeing him this day, and he riding and galloping. Bartley came first on the red mare; and I tried to say "God speed you," but something choked the words in my throat. He went by quickly; and "the blessing of God on you," says he, and I could say nothing. I looked up then, and I crying, at the gray pony, and there was Michael upon it—with fine clothes on him, and new shoes on his feet.

CATHLEEN (*begins to keen*). It's destroyed we are from this day. It's destroyed, surely.

NORA. Didn't the young priest say the Almighty God wouldn't leave her destitute with no son living?

MAURYA (*in a low voice, but clearly*). It's little the like of him knows of the sea. . . . Bartley will be lost now, and let you call in Eamon and make me a good coffin out of the white boards, for I won't live after them. I've had a husband, and a husband's father, and six sons in this house—six fine men, though it was a hard birth I had with every one of them and they coming to the world—and some of them were found and some of them were not found, but they're gone now the lot of them. . . . There were Stephen, and Shawn, were lost in the great wind, and found after in the Bay of Gregory of the Golden Mouth, and carried up the two of them on the one plank, and in by that door.

[*She pauses for a moment, the girls start as if they heard something through the door that is half open behind them.*]

NORA (*in a whisper*). Did you hear that, Cathleen? Did you hear a noise in the north-east?

CATHLEEN (*in a whisper*). There's some one after crying out by the seashore.

MAURYA (*continues without hearing anything*). There was Sheamus and his father, and his own father again, were lost in a dark night, and not a stick or sign was seen of them when the sun went up. There was Patch after was drowned out of a curagh that turned over. I was sitting here with Bartley, and he a baby, lying on my two knees, and I seen two women, and three women, and four women coming in, and they crossing themselves, and not saying a word. I looked out then, and there were men coming after them, and they holding a thing in the half of a red sail, and water dripping out of it—it was a dry day, Nora—and leaving a track to the door. [*She pauses again with her hand stretched out towards the door. It opens softly and* OLD WOMEN *begin to come in, crossing themselves on the threshold, and kneeling down in front of the stage with red petticoats over their heads.*]

MAURYA (*half in a dream, to* CATHLEEN). Is it Patch, or Michael, or what is it at all?

CATHLEEN. Michael is after being found in the far north, and when he is found there how could he be here in this place?

MAURYA. There does be a power of young men floating round in the sea, and what way would they know if it was Michael they had, or another man like him, for when a man is nine days in the sea, and the wind blowing, it's hard set his own mother would be to say what man was it.

CATHLEEN. It's Michael, God spare him, for they're after sending us a bit of his clothes from the far north.

[*She reaches out and hands* MAURYA *the clothes that belonged to Michael.* MAURYA *stands up slowly and takes them in her hands.* NORA *looks out.*]

NORA. They're carrying a thing among them and there's water dripping out of it and leaving a track by the big stones.

CATHLEEN (*in a whisper to the* WOMEN *who have come in*). Is it Bartley it is?

ONE OF THE WOMEN. It is surely, God rest his soul.

[*Two younger* WOMEN *come in and pull out the table. Then* MEN *carry in the body of* BARTLEY, *laid on a plank, with a bit of a sail over it, and lay it on the table.*]

CATHLEEN (*to the* WOMEN, *as they are doing so*). What way was he drowned?

ONE OF THE WOMEN. The gray pony knocked him into the sea, and he was washed out where there is a great surf on the white rocks. [MAURYA *has gone over and knelt down at the head of the table. The* WOMEN *are keening softly and swaying themselves with a slow movement.* CATHLEEN *and* NORA *kneel at the other end of the table. The* MEN *kneel near the door.*]

MAURYA (*raising her head and speaking as if she did not see the people around her*). They're all gone now, and there isn't anything more the sea can do to me. . . . I'll have no call now to be up crying and praying when the wind breaks from the south, and you can hear the surf is in the east, and the surf is in the west, making a great stir with the two noises, and they hitting one on the other. I'll have no call now to be going down and getting Holy Water in the dark nights after Samhain, and I won't care what way the sea is when the other women will be keening. (*To* NORA.) Give me the Holy Water, Nora, there's a small sup still on the dresser. [NORA *gives it to her.*]

MAURYA (*drops Michael's clothes across* BARTLEY's *feet, and sprinkles the Holy Water over him*). It isn't that I haven't prayed for you, Bartley, to the Almighty God. It isn't that I haven't said prayers in the dark night till you wouldn't know what I'd be saying; but it's a great rest I'll have now, and it's time surely. It's a great rest I'll have now, and great sleeping in the long nights after Samhain, if it's only a bit of wet flour we do have to eat, and maybe a fish that would be stinking.

[*She kneels down again, crossing herself, and saying prayers under her breath.*]

CATHLEEN (*to an* OLD MAN). Maybe yourself and Eamon would

make a coffin when the sun rises. We have fine white boards herself bought, God help her, thinking Michael would be found, and I have a new cake you can eat while you'll be working.

THE OLD MAN (*looking at the boards*). Are there nails with them?

CATHLEEN. There are not, Colum; we didn't think of the nails.

ANOTHER MAN. It's a great wonder she wouldn't think of the nails, and all the coffins she's seen made already.

CATHLEEN. It's getting old she is, and broken.

[MAURYA *stands up again very slowly and spreads out the pieces of Michael's clothes beside the body, sprinkling them with the last of the Holy Water.*]

NORA (*in a whisper to* CATHLEEN). She's quiet now and easy; but the day Michael was drowned you could hear her crying out from this to the spring well. It's fonder she was of Michael, and would any one have thought that?

CATHLEEN (*slowly and clearly*). An old woman will be soon tired with anything she will do, and isn't it nine days herself is after crying and keening, and making great sorrow in the house?

MAURYA (*puts the empty cup mouth downwards on the table, and lays her hands together on* BARTLEY'S *feet*). They're all together this time, and the end is come. May the Almighty God have mercy on Bartley's soul, and on Michael's soul, and on the souls of Sheamus and Patch, and Stephen and Shawn (*bending her head*); and may He have mercy on my soul, Nora, and on the soul of every one is left living in the world.

[*She pauses, and the keen rises a little more loudly from the* WOMEN, *then sinks away.*]

MAURYA (*continuing*). Michael has a clean burial in the far north, by the grace of the Almighty God. Bartley will have a fine coffin out of the white boards, and a deep grave surely. What more can we want than that? No man at all can be living for ever, and we must be satisfied.

[*She kneels down again and the curtain falls slowly.*]

Author and Selection Notes

Though the dramatic promise of John M. Synge (1871-1909) was cut off by his early death, he completed several dramas based upon the Irish peasantry of the Aran Islands in the west of Ireland, among them *The Well of the Saints, The Playboy of the Western World,* and the present play, which depicts the struggle of the Irish fisher folk with the sea, which is both their livelihood and—frequently—their doom.

Questions and Exercises

1. This one-act play is sometimes classified as a form of "folk drama." Look up the term in a handbook of literary terms and point out those characteristics which lend support to this classification.

2. What does the title mean and what does it suggest about the pattern of life of the people represented in the play?

3. Some of the following words have special meanings. Look them up and jot down the definitions: "turf," "keen," "hooker," "jobber," "poteen."

4. On the basis of details given in the play, identify the general locale which furnishes its setting.

5. List the characters of the play in a column and write a thumbnail characterization of each.

6. What does Maurya's vision of Michael on the gray horse have to do with Bartley's death?

7. What experiences with death has Maurya had prior to the death of Bartley? Why does Bartley's death seem to give her a sense of relief?

8. In a paragraph or two point out the peculiarities of expression which suggest that the language of the play is in a distinct dialect.

9. Theme Topics: Dramatic Possibilities of the One-Act Play; The Dramatic Career of John M. Synge; Folkways of the Irish Sea Coast; Maurya—a Tragic Figure; Maurya's Answer to the Evils of Life; Maurya and Fate.

STOPPING BY WOODS ON A SNOWY EVENING
Robert Frost

Whose woods these are I think I know.
His house is in the village though;
He will not see me stopping here
To watch his woods fill up with snow.

My little horse must think it queer
To stop without a farmhouse near
Between the woods and frozen lake
The darkest evening of the year.

From *Complete Poems of Robert Frost*. Copyright 1923, 1949 by Holt, Rinehart and Winston, Inc. Copyright 1942 by Robert Frost. Copyright renewed 1951 by Robert Frost. Reprinted by permission of Holt, Rinehart and Winston, Inc.

He gives his harness bells a shake
To ask if there is some mistake.
The only other sound's the sweep
Of easy wind and downy flake.

The woods are lovely, dark and deep,
But I have promises to keep,
And miles to go before I sleep,
And miles to go before I sleep.

Author and Selection Notes

The work of Robert Frost (1874-1963) is intensely imbued with the flavor, the wisdom, and the folkways of rural New England, which was his home most of his life; though frequently the local truths which he discovered in rural surroundings turned out to be universal as well. Frost's works include *A Boy's Will, West-Running Brook, A Witness Tree,* and two philosophical plays, *Masque of Reason* and *A Masque of Mercy.* The emotional truths and simplicity of style and subject matter in this picture of a man stopping by a wayside woods to watch the falling snow are typical of much of Frost's poetry.

Questions and Exercises

1. What details in this poem suggest a strong sense of responsibility and practical consideration?

2. What contrasting points of view seem to be presented in the poem? Write a paragraph supporting your position on the matter.

3. Why does the horse think it queer to stop without a farmhouse near?

4. Explain why the impression we get of the snowy woods, described as "dark" and "deep," is a pleasant one rather than an unpleasant one.

5. What is particularly noticeable about the rhyme scheme of this poem, and what relation does it have to the repetition of the last two lines?

6. Does this poem give us merely a literal picture of the snowy scene, or is it to be taken symbolically? (Look up the word "symbol.") Write a short theme defending your answer.

7. Theme Topics: Frost as a Poet of Rural Life; Symbolism and Poetry; The Function of Beauty in Men's Lives; The Descriptive Lyric; Making the Right Choice.

I THINK CONTINUALLY OF THOSE WHO WERE TRULY GREAT

Stephen Spender

I think continually of those who were truly great.
Who, from the womb, remembered the soul's history
Through corridors of light where the hours are suns,
Endless and singing. Whose lovely ambition
Was that their lips, still touched with fire,
Should tell of the spirit clothed from head to foot in song.
And who hoarded from the spring branches
The desires falling across their bodies like blossoms.

What is precious is never to forget
The delight of the blood drawn from ageless springs
Breaking through rocks in worlds before our earth;
Never to deny its pleasure in the simple morning light,
Nor its grave evening demand for love;
Never to allow gradually the traffic to smother
With noise and fog the flowering of the spirit.

Near the snow, near the sun, in the highest fields
See how these names are fêted by the waving grass,
And by the streamers of white cloud,
And whispers of wind in the listening sky;
The names of those who in their lives fought for life,
Who wore at their hearts the fire's center.
Born of the sun they traveled a short while towards the sun,
And left the vivid air signed with their honor.

Author and Selection Notes

The early work of Stephen Spender (1909-   ) is associated with left-wing political verse of the 1930's, when he first gained recognition as a poet. The present poem is more representative of his later work, in which he has turned from social criticism to more personal subjects. Educated at University College, Oxford, Spender has supported himself mainly by writing and editorial work. Recently he has lived in the United States, where he teaches and lectures. Spender's *Collected Poems* appeared in 1955.

Questions and Exercises

1. In this poem Stepehen Spender expresses his concept of true greatness. State in your own words what you feel this concept is. Note especially stanza one and the last four lines of the poem.

2. List the aspects of true greatness given in stanza two and explain them.

3. Compare the idea contained in the last two lines of stanza two with the central theme of Wordsworth's sonnet "The World Is Too Much with Us." In what respects are the two concepts alike?

4. How, in the last stanza, are the names of the truly great said to be feted?

5. Classify the verse form of the poem by indicating characteristic technical features. Is the poem in blank verse or free verse? Defend your position.

6. Find and classify all the figures of speech in the poem.

7. Theme Topics: The Meaning of True Greatness; A Great Man I Have Known; Great Men as Models; An Unforgettable Character; The Rewards of Greatness.

THE JILTING OF GRANNY WEATHERALL

Katherine Anne Porter

She flicked her wrist neatly out of Doctor Harry's pudgy careful fingers and pulled the sheet up to her chin. The brat ought to be in knee breeches. Doctoring around the country with spectacles on his nose! "Get along now, take your school-books and go. There's nothing wrong with me."

Doctor Harry spread a warm paw like a cushion on her forehead where the forked green vein danced and made her eyelids twitch. "Now, now, be a good girl, and we'll have you up in no time."

"That's no way to speak to a woman nearly eighty years old just because she's down. I'd have you respect your elders, young man."

"Well, Missy, excuse me." Doctor Harry patted her cheek. "But I've got to warn you, haven't I? You're a marvel, but you must be careful or you're going to be good and sorry."

"Don't tell me what I'm going to be. I'm on my feet now, morally speaking. It's Cornelia. I had to go to bed to get rid of her."

Her bones felt loose, and floated around in her skin, and Doctor Harry floated like a balloon around the foot of the bed. He floated and pulled down his waistcoat and swung his glasses on a cord. "Well, stay where you are, it certainly can't hurt you."

"Get along and doctor your sick," said Granny Weatherall. "Leave a well woman alone. I'll call for you when I want you. . . . Where were you forty years ago when I pulled through milk-leg and double pneumonia? You weren't even born. Don't let Cornelia lead you on," she shouted, because Doctor Harry appeared to float up to the ceiling and out. "I pay my own bills, and I don't throw my money away on nonsense!"

She meant to wave good-by, but it was too much trouble. Her eyes closed of themselves, it was like a dark curtain drawn around the bed. The pillow rose and floated under her, pleasant as a hammock in a light wind. She listened to the leaves rustling outside the window. No, somebody was swishing newspapers: no, Cornelia and Doctor Harry were whispering together. She leaped broad awake, thinking they whispered in her ear.

"She was never like this, *never* like this!" "Well, what can we expect?" "Yes, eighty years old. . . ."

Well, and what if she was? She still had ears. It was like Cornelia to whisper around doors. She always kept things secret in such a public way. She was always being tactful and kind. Cornelia was dutiful; that was the trouble with her. Dutiful and good: "So good and dutiful," said Granny, "that I'd like to spank her." She saw herself spanking Cornelia and making a fine job of it.

"What'd you say, Mother?"

Granny felt her face tying up in hard knots.

"Can't a body think, I'd like to know?"

"I thought you might want something."

"I do. I want a lot of things. First off, go away and don't whisper."

She lay and drowsed, hoping in her sleep that the children would keep out and let her rest a minute. It had been a long day. Not that she was tired. It was always pleasant to snatch a minute now and then. There was always so much to be done, let me see: to-morrow.

Tomorrow was far away and there was nothing to trouble about. Things were finished some how when the time came; thank God there was always a little margin over for peace: then a person could spread out the plan of life and tuck in the edges orderly. It was good to have everything clean and folded away, with the hair brushes and tonic bottles sitting straight on the white embroidered linen: the day started without fuss and the pantry shelves laid out with rows of jelly glasses and brown jugs and white stone-china jars with blue whirligigs and words painted on them: coffee, tea, sugar, ginger, cinnamon, allspice: and the bronze clock with the lion on top nicely dusted off. The dust that lion could collect in twenty-four hours! The box in the attic with all those letters tied up, well, she'd have to go through that tomorrow. All those letters— George's letters and John's letters and her letters to them both— lying around for the children to find afterwards made her uneasy. Yes, that would be tomorrow's business. No use to let them know how silly she had been once.

While she was rummaging around she found death in her mind and it felt clammy and unfamiliar. She had spent so much time preparing for death there was no need for bringing it up again. Let it take care of itself now. When she was sixty she had felt very old, finished, and went around making farewell trips to see her children and grandchildren, with a secret in her mind: This is the very last of your mother, children! Then she made her will and came down with a long fever. That was all just a notion like a lot of other things, but it was lucky too, for she had once for all got over the idea of dying for a long time. Now she couldn't be worried. She hoped she had better sense now. Her father had lived to be one hundred and two years old and had drunk a noggin of strong hot toddy on his last birthday. He told the reporters it was his daily habit, and he owed his long life to that. He had made quite a scandal and was very pleased about it. She believed she'd just plague Cornelia a little.

"Cornelia! Cornelia!" No footsteps, but a sudden hand on her cheek. "Bless you, where have you been?"

"Here, Mother."

"Well, Cornelia, I want a noggin of hot toddy."

"Are you cold, darling?"

"I'm chilly, Cornelia. Lying in bed stops the circulation. I must have told you that a thousand times."

Well, she could just hear Cornelia telling her husband that Mother was getting a little childish and they'd have to humor her. The thing that most annoyed her was that Cornelia thought she was deaf, dumb, and blind. Little hasty glances and tiny gestures tossed around her and over her head saying, "Don't cross her, let her have her way, she's eighty years old," and she sitting there as if she lived in a thin glass cage. Sometimes Granny almost made up her mind to pack up and move back to her own house where nobody could remind her every minute that she was old. Wait, wait, Cornelia, till your own children whisper behind your back!

In her day she had kept a better house and had got more work done. She wasn't too old yet for Lydia to be driving eighty miles for advice when one of the children jumped the track, and Jimmy still dropped in and talked things over: "Now, Mammy, you've a good business head, I want to know what you think of this?" . . . Old? Cornelia couldn't change the furniture around without asking. Little things, little things! They had been so sweet when they were little. Granny wished the old days were back again with the children young and everything to be done over. It had been a hard pull, but not too much for her. When she thought of all the food she had cooked, and all the clothes she had cut and sewed, and all the gardens she had made—well, the children showed it. There they were, made out of her, and they couldn't get away from that. Sometimes she wanted to see John again and point to them and say, Well, I didn't do so badly, did I? But that would have to wait. That was for tomorrow. She used to think of him as a man, but now all the children were older than their father, and he would be a child beside her if she saw him now. It seemed strange and there was something wrong in the idea. Why, he couldn't possibly recognize her. She had fenced in a hundred acres once, digging the post holes herself and clamping the wires with just a Negro boy to help. That changed a woman. John would be looking for a young woman with the peaked Spanish comb in her hair and the painted fan. Digging post holes changed a woman. Riding country roads in the winter when women had their babies was another thing: sitting up nights with sick horses and sick Negroes and sick children and hardly ever losing one. John, I hardly ever lost one of them! John would see that in a minute, that would be something he could understand, she wouldn't have to explain anything!

It made her feel like rolling up her sleeves and putting the whole place to rights again. No matter if Cornelia was determined to be everywhere at once, there were a great many things left undone on this place. She would start tomorrow and do them. It was good to be strong enough for everything, even if all you made melted and changed and slipped under your hands, so that by the time you finished you almost forgot what you were working for. What was it I set out to do? she asked herself intently, but she could not remember. A fog rose over the valley, she saw it marching across the creek swallowing the trees and moving up the hill like an army of ghosts. Soon it would be at the near edge of the orchard, and then it was time to go in and light the lamps. Come in, children, don't stay out in the night air.

Lighting the lamps had been beautiful. The children huddled up to her and breathed like little calves waiting at the bars in the twilight. Their eyes followed the match and watched the flame rise and settle in a blue curve, then they moved away from her. The lamp was lit, they didn't have to be scared and hang on to mother any more. Never, never, never more. God, for all my life I thank Thee. Without Thee, my God, I could never have done it. Hail, Mary, full of grace.

I want you to pick all the fruit this year and see that nothing is wasted. There's always someone who can use it. Don't let good things rot for want of using. You waste life when you waste good food. Don't let things get lost. It's bitter to lose things. Now, don't let me get to thinking, not when I am tired and taking a little nap before supper. . . .

The pillow rose about her shoulders and pressed against her heart and the memory was being squeezed out of it: oh, push down the pillow, somebody: it would smother her if she tried to hold it. Such a fresh breeze blowing and such a green day with no threats in it. But he had not come, just the same. What does a woman do when she has put on the white veil and set out the white cake for a man and he doesn't come? She tried to remember. No, I swear he never harmed me but in that. He never harmed me but in that . . . and what if he did? There was the day, the day, but a whirl of dark smoke rose and covered it, crept up and over into the bright field where everything was planted so carefully in orderly rows. That was hell, she knew hell when she saw it. For sixty years she had prayed against remembering him and against losing her soul in the deep pit of hell, and now the two things were mingled in one and the thought of him was a smoky cloud from hell that moved and crept in her head when she had just got rid of Doctor Harry and was trying to rest a minute. Wounded vanity, Ellen, said a sharp voice in the top of her mind. Don't let your wounded vanity get the upper hand of you. Plenty of girls get jilted. You were jilted, weren't you? Then stand up to it. Her eyelids wavered and let in streamers of blue-gray light like tissue paper over her eyes. She must get up and pull the shades down or she'd never sleep. She was in bed again and the shades were not down. How could that happen? Better turn over, hide from the light, sleeping in the light gave you nightmares. "Mother, how do you feel now?" and a stinging wetness on her forehead. But I don't like having my face washed in cold water!

Hapsy? George? Lydia? Jimmy? No, Cornelia, and her features were swollen and full of little puddles. "They're coming, darling, they'll all be here soon." Go wash your face, child, you look funny.

Instead of obeying, Cornelia knelt down and put her head on the pillow. She seemed to be talking but there was no sound. "Well, are you tongue-tied? Whose birthday is it? Are you going to give a party?"

Cornelia's mouth moved urgently in strange shapes. "Don't do that, you bother me, daughter."

"Oh, no, Mother. Oh, no. . . ."

Nonsense. It was strange about children. They disputed your every word. "No what, Cornelia?"

"Here's Doctor Harry."

"I won't see that boy again. He just left five minutes ago."

"That was this morning, Mother. It's night now. Here's the nurse."

"This is Doctor Harry, Mrs. Weatherall. I never saw you look so young and happy!"

"Ah, I'll never be young again—but I'd be happy if they'd let me lie in peace and get rested."

She thought she spoke up loudly, but no one answered. A warm weight on her forehead, a warm bracelet on her wrist, and a breeze went on whispering, trying to tell her something. A shuffle of leaves in the everlasting hand of God, He blew on them and they danced and rattled. "Mother, don't mind, we're going to give you a little hypodermic." "Look here, daughter, how do ants get in this bed? I saw sugar ants yesterday." Did you send for Hapsy too?

It was Hapsy she really wanted. She had to go a long way back through a great many rooms to find Hapsy standing with a baby on her arm. She seemed to herself to be Hapsy also, and the baby on Hapsy's arm was Hapsy and himself and herself, all at once, and there was no surprise in the meeting. Then Hapsy melted from within and turned flimsy as gray gauze and the baby was a gauzy shadow, and Hapsy came up close and said, "I thought you'd never come," and looked at her very searchingly and said, "You haven't changed a bit!" They leaned forward to kiss, when Cornelia began whispering from a long way off, "Oh, is there anything you want to tell me? Is there anything I can do for you?"

Yes, she had changed her mind after sixty years and she would like to see George. I want you to find George. Find him and be sure to tell him I forgot him. I want him to know I had my husband just the same and my children and my house like any other woman. A good house too and a good husband that I loved and fine children out of him. Better than I hoped for even. Tell him I was given back everything he took away and more. Oh, no, oh, God, no, there was something else besides the house and the man and the children. Oh, surely they were not all? What was it? Something not given back. . . . Her breath crowded down under her ribs and grew into a monstrous frightening shape with cutting edges; it bored up into her head, and the agony was unbelievable: Yes, John, get the Doctor now, no more talk, my time has come.

When this one was born it should be the last. The last. It should have been born first, for it was the one she had truly wanted. Everything came in good time. Nothing left out, left over. She was strong, in three days she would be as well as ever. Better. A woman needed milk in her to have her full health.

"Mother, do you hear me?"

"I've been telling you—"

"Mother, Father Connolly's here."

"I went to Holy Communion only last week. Tell him I'm not so sinful as all that."

"Father just wants to speak to you."

He could speak as much as he pleased. It was like him to drop in and inquire about her soul as if it were a teething baby, and then stay on for a cup of tea and a round of cards and gossip. He always had a funny story of some sort, usually about an Irishman who made his little mistakes and confessed them, and the point lay in some absurd thing he would blurt out in the confessional showing his struggles between native piety and original sin. Granny felt easy about her soul. Cornelia, where are your manners? Give Father Connolly a chair. She had her secret comfortable understanding with a few favorite saints who cleared a straight road to God for her. All as surely signed and sealed as the papers for the new Forty Acres. Forever . . . heirs and assigns forever. Since the day the wedding cake was not cut, but thrown out and wasted. The whole bottom dropped out of the world, and there she was blind and sweating with nothing under her feet and the walls falling away. His hand had caught her under the breast, she had not fallen, there was the freshly polished floor with the green rug on it, just as before. He had cursed like a sailor's parrot and said, "I'll kill him for you." Don't lay a hand on him, for my sake leave something to God. "Now, Ellen, you must believe what I tell you. . . ."

So there was nothing, nothing to worry about any more, except sometimes in the night one of the children screamed in a nightmare, and they both hustled out shaking and hunting for the matches and calling, "There, wait a minute, here we are!" John, get the doctor now, Hapsy's time has come. But there was Hapsy standing by the bed in a white cap. "Cornelia, tell Hapsy to take off her cap. I can't see her plain."

Her eyes opened very wide and the room stood out like a picture she had seen somewhere. Dark colors with the shadows rising toward the ceiling in long angles. The tall black dresser gleamed with nothing on it but John's picture, enlarged from a little one, with John's eyes very black when they should have been blue. You never saw him, so how do you know how he looked? But the man insisted the copy was perfect, it was very rich and handsome. For a picture, yes, but it's not my husband. The table by the bed had a linen cover and a candle and a crucifix. The light was blue from Cornelia's silk lampshades. No sort of light at all, just frippery. You had to live forty years with kerosene lamps to appreciate honest electricty. She felt very strong and she saw Doctor Harry with a rosy nimbus around him.

"You look like a saint, Doctor Harry, and I vow that's as near as you'll ever come to it."

"She's saying something."

"I heard you, Cornelia. What's all this carrying-on?"

"Father Connolly's saying—"

Cornelia's voice staggered and bumped like a cart in a bad road. It rounded corners and turned back again and arrived nowhere. Granny stepped up in the cart very lightly and reached for the reins, but a man sat beside her and she knew him by his hands, driving the cart. She did not look in his face, for she knew without seeing, but looked instead down the road where the trees leaned over and bowed to each other and a thousand birds were singing a Mass. She felt like singing too, but she put her hand in the bosom of her dress and pulled out a rosary, and Father Connolly murmured Latin in a very solemn voice and tickled her feet. My God, will you stop that nonsense? I'm a married woman. What if he did run away and leave me to face the priest by myself? I found another a whole world better. I wouldn't have exchanged my husband for anybody except St. Michael himself, and you may tell him that for me with a thank you in the bargain.

Light flashed on her closed eyelids, and a deep roaring shook her. Cornelia, is that lightning? I hear thunder. There's going to be a storm. Close all the windows. Call the children in. . . . "Mother, here we are, all of us." "Is that you, Hapsy?" "Oh, no, I'm Lydia. We drove as fast as we could." Their faces drifted above her, drifted away. The rosary fell out of her hands and Lydia put it back. Jimmy tried to help, their hands fumbled together, and Granny closed two fingers around Jimmy's thumb. Beads wouldn't do, it must be something alive. She was so amazed her thoughts ran round and round. So, my dear Lord, this is my death and I wasn't even thinking about it. My children have come to see me die. But I can't, it's not time. Oh, I always hated surprises. I wanted to give Cornelia the amethyst set—Cornelia, you're to have the amethyst set, but Hapsy's to wear it when she wants, and, Doctor Harry, do shut up. Nobody sent for you. Oh, my dear Lord, do wait a minute. I meant to do something about the Forty Acres, Jimmy doesn't need it and Lydia will later on, with that worthless husband of hers. I meant to finish the altar cloth and send six bottles of wine to Sister Borgia for her dyspepsia. I want to send six bottles of wine to Sister Borgia, Father Connolly, now don't let me forget.

Cornelia's voice made short turns and tilted over and crashed. "Oh, Mother, oh, Mother, oh, Mother. . . ."

"I'm not going, Cornelia. I'm taken by surprise. I can't go."

You'll see Hapsy again. What about her? "I thought you'd never come." Granny made a long journey outward, looking for Hapsy. What if I don't find her? What then? Her heart sank down and down, there was no bottom to death, she couldn't come to the end of it. The blue light from Cornelia's lampshade drew into a tiny point in the center of her brain, it flickered and winked like an eye, quietly it fluttered and dwindled. Granny lay curled down within herself, amazed and watchful, staring at the point of light that was herself; her body was now only a deeper mass of shadow in an endless darkness and this darkness would curl around the light and swallow it up. God, give a sign!

For the second time there was no sign. Again no bridegroom and the priest in the house. She could not remember any other sorrow because this grief wiped them all away. Oh, no, there's nothing more cruel than this—I'll never forgive it. She stretched herself with a deep breath and blew out the light.

Author and Selection Notes

The fiction of Katherine Anne Porter (1894-   ) is notable for its exquisite style and penetrating psychological analysis; and such collections of her stories as *Flowering Judas, Noon Wine, Hacienda, The Leaning Tower,* and her latest novel *Ship of Fools,* have brought her numerous awards and honors. Although, as in the present story, the scenes of her tales vary widely, she frequently returns to her native Southwest, and to Mexico, for her locales. Miss Porter now makes her home in New York.

Questions and Exercises

1. The fiction of Katherine Anne Porter has been characterized as revealing an "interplay of the humorous and the serious." Show how this characterization is true of the present story.

2. Look up the words "plot" and "characterization" in a handbook of literary terms and analyze the plot in a paragraph or so; also write a page character sketch of Granny.

3. Point out details in the first several paragraphs which suggest that Granny is on the verge of death.

4. Why does Granny feel that there is no need for her to bring up in her mind the subject of death?

5. By what means does the author manage to give us a great deal of Granny Weatherall's life history? Sketch in a paragraph the main events or her life.

6. Identify the following characters mentioned or described in the story: Cornelia, John, George, Hapsy, Lydia, Jimmy.

7. List some of the indications of Granny's hallucinations as death approaches.

8. Explain why the child that was born last was the one that Granny wanted most.

9. Explain the last paragraph in the story; is the word "bridegroom" to be taken in a literal sense or a symbolic one; what is the grief that wipes all other sorrows away? Discuss your ideas regarding this last paragraph in a short theme.

10. Read John Donne's sonnet "Death, Be Not Proud." Which selection reveals the more traditional concept of immortality? Support your view in a paragraph.

11. Theme Topics: The Joys and Trials of Family Life; The Role of the Mother in a Family; The Meaning of Plot in Fiction; Death's Ultimate Meaning; The End of Life Is a Beginning.

CHRISTMAS

Armine Von Tempski

Like cadenced *meles*-chants which put an everlasting spell upon you, memories of Christmases on the ranch persist with undying vividness. Contrary to the common belief that seasons in the subtropics are much alike, each season is invested with distinct charac-

From *Born in Paradise*, copyright 1940, by Armine Von Tempski, by permission of Duell, Sloan & Pearce, an affiliate of Meredith Press.

teristics. In autumn, days are so utterly beautiful that you scarcely dare to breathe for fear of shattering the fragile loveliness of earth, water, and sky. In winter, mountains look stronger and more saturated with mystery. Periods of slashing silver rain alternate with days of brilliant sunshine while the atmosphere is impregnated with an electric quality that defies description. Trees look scared and rocks seem on the verge of giving up the spirits lurking in them. *Kona*[1] storms roar up from the equator, convulsing the land for forty-eight to seventy-two hours. First comes a louder note in the surf, then a shouting hurricane followed by clouds black with thunder and heavy with savage rain. When the atmospheric convulsion is over, the ten-thousand-foot volcano of Haleakala is covered with a glittering cape of snow, in contrast to sun soaked, palm-fringed beaches at its feet.

We children used to watch the sea and sky for days before Christmas, praying to God and propitiating *akuas*[2] with *leis*[3] to send a *kona* gale to crown Haleakala with silver. If our prayers and offerings were rewarded by the white beauty of snow on the summit it seemed as if God, the *akuas,* and the mountains were all celebrating the holiday season with us.

With the white cap safely established, we dived wholeheartedly into the exciting preparations which took place on the ranch for a week before Christmas. Days weren't long enough to hold all that there was to do and our activities spilled far over into the nights.

First came the ride up Haleakala with Daddy and two cowboys to choose a sandalwood log to burn Christmas Eve. A short distance below the summit, but miles above the last outpost of common trees, was a small grove overlooked by the men who raped the Hawaiian forests of the precious fragrant wood in the early 1800's. Daddy cherished this grove. It was the last on Maui. Logs were cut only from fallen trees. When a section sufficient to fill the fireplace had been measured and sawed through, it was placed on the pack-horse; then we rode back to the forests below our mountain dairy and wove wreaths of green fragrant *maile*[4] and draped the log with them.

When we got home at sunset, with our garland-draped trophy, the Yule season was formally ushered in. Next morning the ranch had a new bustle, a new activity. The usual work of herds and pastures continued but became of secondary importance. Two heifers,

---

[1] leeward side of the island; name of a leeward wind.
[2] gods.
[3] necklaces of flowers.
[4] a twining shrub with shiny, fragrant leaves.

the fattest and best on the place, were slaughtered and divided equally among the workmen and their families. Pack-trains of horses and mules were dispatched to distant valleys for additional supplies of *poi*[5] and sweet potatoes. Each family must have all it could possibly eat between Christmas and New Year's to make a good *kahuna*[6] and ensure abundance during the coming year. Next came expeditions to the forests and up the mountain for wild hogs, turkeys, and sheep.

While these happenings were going on, matters of breathless interest were in progress about the house. Japanese were concocting *mochi,* a species of rice-cake made only at that time of year. Portuguese were baking great yellow loaves of bread a yard in diameter with whole hard-boiled eggs in them. Ah Sin was mixing plum puddings and Christmas cakes made from recipes three hundred years old which had been handed down in Mother's family. Hawaiina were making *kulolo*[7] and *haupia.*[8]

I used to wish I were half a dozen persons instead of one so I could divide myself equally among the enchanting activities going on around me. Should I watch the Japanese working about a hollowed tree-trunk beating rice-grains to powder-fineness with great flails, smashing up *shoyu* beans and mixing them into a black, smooth paste? It was an adventure to watch them working with white cloths bound about their foreheads to catch the sweat, men and women working in turns, thrashing at glistening white kernels which they kneaded with water into flat cakes like pale, round pieces of soap. When they had been patted into shape, a finger was deftly inserted into the center of each one and a wad of slightly sweet, slightly salty bean paste was poked in and covered over. Great tubs were filled with layers upon layers of the dainties, covered with clean cloths and set away until Christmas and New Year's morning when they would be heated and eaten. After they had been in the oven fifteen minutes they puffed into huge round balls slightly crisp on the outside, like a persimmon, and inside like chewy white rubber.

Or should I go across the gulch, to the Portuguese Camp? There Old Marias were boiling dozens of eggs hard, pounding at mountains of dough, into which they broke other dozens of eggs, while younger and less expert women stoked the white cone-shaped ovens behind

---

[5] a native Hawaiian food prepared from the taro root pounded to a paste and allowed to ferment.

[6] expert in any profession.

[7] pudding made of coconut and taro or breadfruit.

[8] sweetmeat made by baking coconut and arrowroot.

the houses until they reached the right heat to bake the bread to proper brownness.

If I lingered among the Portuguese, snatches of music and laughter would tempt me to the Hawaiian Camp where large good-natured *wahines*[9] were seated cross-legged on the ground kneading *kulolo* and *haupia*. *Kulolo,* made from sweet potatoes and taro and shredded cocoanut and baked for hours underground, looked like great yellowish-brown plum puddings and was chewy and stiff like caramels. *Haupia,* made from a starchy root mixed with sweetened cocoanut cream, had the consistency of soft jello and tasted like divinity fudge crossed with arrowroot pudding.

If I lingered too long among the Hawaiians, I might miss being allowed to lick the great basin in which Ah Sin was mixing Christmas cake, or might not see him frosting it with almond flavored icing, squeezed through a twisted piece of brown paper with a hole in it.

Enticing smells filled the air. Spurred men rode out and returned with the plunder of forest and mountains. Great gunny sacks, sprouting *maile* vines, which would be twisted into fragrant wreaths, were brought in. Turkeys, hogs, sheep dangled against the heated flanks of pack-animals.

The day before Christmas a small light cart, drawn by six yoke of sturdy oxen, was dispatched up the mountain for the trees. Real pine or spruce. At the seven-thousand-foot level, where frost broke the ground and occasional snow fell, Daddy had planted a grove of evergreens to supply the ranch and special friends with Christmas trees. He called the spot Little America and had a great pride and affection for these strange green friends from colder lands. New seedlings were always taken up to replace the trees which were cut down.

When the wagon was loaded it started home, escorted by riders on horseback. Decorating the family tree, set up in the living room, was a ceremony. Mother supervised proceedings but Dad always mounted the ladder, placed the silver star on the tip with three white angels beneath it, then arranged the Savior in his Manger on the right and the Three Wise Men Bringing Gifts on the left. Then, his part over, he went off and Ah Sin, Mother, and the house-servants took over the rest of the decorating. Glittering ornaments, yards of tinsel, transparent bags of hard candy were hung among the branches. Gifts were stacked around the base; toys for little boy-sans and girl-sans, yards of material for kimonos, yards of calico for *holokus,*[10] bolts of sturdy dungaree for *paniolos*[11] riding breeches,

[9] women.
[10] women's outer garments.
[11] cowboys.

shawls to cover Portuguese heads. Bangles for young girls, necker-chiefs for young bloods. Silly gifts to make Hawaiians yell with mirth, funny gifts to make Japanese chuckle.

The day of Christmas Eve was always unending. The instant breakfast was cleared away, Hawaiians began arriving carrying yards and yards of *maile* wreaths to drape doors and windows, rafters and fireplace. Bowls of fruit and candy were set out, the fire laid and the sandalwood log placed carefully upon it. Suddenly the house, the ranch, the whole world smelled of Christmas.

All afternoon the ranch hands came and went, adding their presents to those already stacked for yards about the base of the tree: bunches of bananas swathed in garlands; lengths of black Portuguese sausage, like policeman's clubs; brown paper packages tied with red string and decked with flowers. We knew the light packages were egg-bread, the heavy ones *mochi* or *kulolo*.

Then *leis* which Hawaiian girls had been weaving for the past twenty-four hours began arriving. *Leis* for each member of the family, for noted visitors, for old friends. Special red carnation *leis*, like fluffy red feather boas, were hung in the trees, giving the already heady Christmas smell which filled the house its final fillip.

As the afternoon waned, wonderful odors began emanating from the kitchen: plum puddings boiling rowdily, turkeys and pheasants roasting. Behind the Beef House, hidden by clumps of oleanders and graceful bamboos, men were preparing an earth oven for the hogs which would be roasted for the *luau* held on Christmas Day.

As evening drew closer I could hardly stay inside my skin. All the joy, excitement, and beauty of the world seemed centered in our house. Distant islands, pastures, and cane fields seemed to inch closer, as if the soil under our house was a magnetized spot drawing the rest of the earth toward it.

Steadily the atmosphere of wonder-in-waiting mounted toward its climax. Dinner, set for thirty or more people, was only another rung up the ladder of thrills when Christmas would really begin. The gleam of fine damask, light shed from heavy silver candle-stick, mammoth turkeys, flanked by pheasants, blazing plum-puddings, goblets of wine hurried the evening toward the moment my soul craved.

My ears strained toward the dark waiting garden. On Maui and other outlying islands, Christmas was carried in on horseback and the jingle of *paniolos'* spurs replaced the imagined tinkle of Santa's sleighbells, as cowboy serenaders rode from ranch to ranch filling an already overflowing occasion with more beauty and glamor.

Behind the merriment of guests seated around our table my

ears strained for the sound of horses' hoofs, and men's joyous voices singing. Yes . . . no . . . there they were. Off in the distance, coming down the road.

Then came the moment I loved beyond everything, that brought Christmas to life in a leap: the shouting *Kilo-kilo o Haleakala hula*[12] bursting from strong brown throats and big brown guitars, blending into a joyful symphony that seemed to well up from the depths of the earth. Our *paniolos* had come, mounted on their best horses, decked with *leis,* to serenade us with the great *hula,* telling of their love and allegiance to the mountain of Haleakala and to the island of Maui, on which we all lived, and which blended our lives into a whole. Behind them, on foot, came their wives, children, and relatives. We were one: a great funny family made up of all nationalities.

Daddy went out to greet them. Chairs were thrust back, guests, men in formal black and white, women in evening dress, swarmed into the eighty foot veranda fronting the lawn. When the last stirring line of the *hula* died away, Daddy shouted, "Aloha my love to you! Merry Christmas." And was answered with the same words.

Men dismounted, tied their horses to the trees, and came in hugging musical instruments to their broad breasts. Sitting on *puunes*[13]—couches—in corners of the room they struck up a new song. Their women, carrying the newest, littlest babies, came up the steps. Japanese mama-sans hoisting sons or daughters into more comfortable positions on their backs. Hawaiian *wahines* cuddling infants against their ample breasts. Hordes of children. Portuguese Marias looking out from under shawls wrapped about their heads. Scrubbed Japanese men holding their first born sons by the hand.

Every available chair was filled, couches were jammed, and the overflow sat cross-legged on the floor. Ah Sin, his mummy-face cracked by a grin, lighted the tree with a candle tied to the end of a slender bamboo pole. When the tree was a blaze of quivering light, Dad went to the piano and struck the opening chords of "Little Town of Bethlehem." With the simultaneous singing of the words by all nationalities, light brighter and stronger than that shed by candles, or sent up by the sandalwood fire, filled the room and stayed there until dawn.

When the last verse was finished the distribution of presents began, interspersed by jokes, speeches, *hulas,* and ancient chants

[12] hula of the star-gazer of the House of the Sun.
[13] movable couches.

sung by the *paniolos*. Babies too small to participate actively in the gaiety were parked on beds, children played with new toys or rolled oranges and apples across the floor. Busy mothers abandoned themselves to the fun. Staid Japanese women and their stolid husbands danced Japanese dances. Portuguese gave jerky imitations of *hulas* which evoked shouts of glee from the Hawaiians.

Daddy went onto the floor, his erect, military figure suddenly fluid as a Polynesian's while he went through intricate *hula* steps learned when he was a gay young blade in the days of the Monarchy. Shy young girls, sumptuous *wahines* uttering cascades of smothered chuckles, danced with American and English ranch owners or sugar planters. Visiting celebrities became infected with the spirit of the evening. *Paniolos* gravely asked lovely white ladies for the "honor of a dance."

House-servants made unending rounds with cups of claret punch, cake, fruit, and candy, eating as they went. The evening mounted and mounted. . . . Then once again the night caught its breath. More hoofs approaching, more ringing spurs and singing voices. The first group of visiting serenaders from another ranch were coming in to swell the ever-increasing richness of the evening. Our men determined not to be outdone. Daddy out to welcome the newcomers. Horses being tied up. Men stamping in. More shouts of "Aloha[14]—Merry Christmas!" Then competitive singing.

Supposedly these wandering troupes of Christmas musicians, mounted on their top horses, spent the night riding from estate to estate. But the ones who came to serenade Dad, either made the rounds early, or did not bother to go on. Why move when the ultimate in fun had been attained?

Wild with happiness I dashed around, spoke briefly to people, went to the door to gaze on the glittering snow-cap of Haleakala looming against legions of stars. The night mounted steadily to a peak. Children dozed and played alternately. Adults sang, ate, chatted, or paused to nurse a child. Gifts were re-examined and gloated over. More troupes of singers arrived, contributing their particular numbers, then joining in the songs being sung by erstwhile rival bands of serenaders. All differences of race, sex, age, and station were obliterated. Something radiant and tangible had come to earth.

When dawn began breaking, slowly and sacredly, behind the vast blue dome of Haleakala, everyone began dispersing, calling

---

[14] term of greeting or farewell.

over their shoulders, "Aloha—my love to you!—Merry Christmas!" then adding, as an afterthought, "See you at the *luau!*"[15]

And the Day of Days, the Birthday of Birthdays, was ushered in by singing horsemen riding off into the light pouring its splendor out of the east.

Author and Selection Notes

Daughter of a Polish father and an English mother, Armine Von Tempski (1899-   ) was born on a large cattle ranch in Maui, one of the Hawaiian Islands. *Born in Paradise,* from which the present selection is taken, is a charming reminiscence of the author's childhood. A member of The Author's League of America, she has written other books about the Islands, including *Ripe Breadfruit, Hula,* and *Hawaiian Harvest.*

Questions and Exercises

1. Outline this selection and analyze its organization.

2. Write a short theme comparing the Christmas celebration described in this selection with your own Christmas celebration.

3. Does the celebration depicted here seem appropriate for celebrating the birth of Christ? Why or why not?

4. How would you classify this selection: biography, essay, simple narrative? Support your opinion in a paragraph.

5. Point out the features which best characterize the author's style of writing. How does the author gain variety in sentence structure?

6. Theme Topics: My Most Unusual Christmas; Memories of Christmas; A Christmas Overseas; The Christmas Dream of Peace on Earth.

VALE FROM CARTHAGE

(Spring, 1944)

Peter Viereck

I, now at Carthage. He, shot dead at Rome.
Shipmates last May. "And what if one of us,"
I asked last May, in fun, in gentleness,
"Wears doom, like dungarees, and doesn't know?"
He laughed, "Not see Times Square again?" The foam

[15] leaf of the taro plant; modern term for a feast.

From *Terror and Decorum,* by Peter Viereck, Charles Scribner's Sons, 1948. Reprinted by permission of the author.

Feathering across that deck a year ago,
Swept those five words—like seeds—beyond the seas
Into his future. There they grew like trees;
And as he passed them there next spring, they laid
Upon his road of fire their sudden shade.
Though he had always scraped his mess-kit pure
And scrubbed redeemingly his barracks floor,
Though all his buttons glowed their ritual-hymn
Like cloudless moons to intercede for him,
No furlough fluttered from the sky. He will
Not see Times Square—he will not see—he will
Not see Times
              change; at Carthage (while my friend,
Living those words at Rome, screamed in the end)
I saw an ancient Roman's tomb and read
"Vale" in stone. Here two wars mix their dead:
Roman, my shipmate's dream walks hand in hand
With yours tonight ("New York again" and "Rome"),
Like widowed sisters bearing water home
On tired heads through hot Tunisian sand
In good cool urns, and says, "I understand."
Roman, you'll see your Forum Square no more;
What's left but this to say of any war?

Author and Selection Notes

In much modern war poetry which stresses the horrors and the useless waste of modern total war, the traditional elegiac note is still represented, as in the present poem. Born in New York and educated at Harvard, Peter Viereck (1916-   ) served in the African and Italian campaigns in World War II and returned to the United States to teach at Harvard and other institutions. His volume of verse, *Terror and Decorum,* won the Pulitzer Prize in 1949.

Questions and Exercises

1. This poem comes from the experience of Peter Viereck as an American soldier in World War II. What aspects of modern warfare are reflected in the poem? Write a paragraph.

2. What does the word *Vale* in the title mean? Why is the Latin appropriate here?

3. Read the poem "Heraclitus." Name the qualities of friendship that seem most alike in these two poems and write a brief theme analyzing the poems as examples of the "elegy."

4. What do such words as "dungarees," "mess-kit," "barracks," and "furlough" add to the poem? If you feel they are appropriate words, explain why in a paragraph.

5. Why does the poet compare the words of his friend to seeds?

6. Explain why the poet addresses the dead Roman soldier in the concluding lines of the poem.

7. Why does the poet compare the dreams of his friend and of the Roman soldier to "widowed sisters" bearing water home through "hot Tunisian sands"?

8. State in your own words the concept of war that is implicit in the last two lines of the poem.

9. Explain why the poem is divided into two parts. What effect does the division have in relation to tone and meaning?

10. Theme Topics: Poetry of War; The Nature of the Elegy; Famous War Heroes of the Twentieth Century; "War Is Hell"; My Favorite War Poem.

HEAVY, HEAVY, WHAT HANGS OVER?
Bernard DeVoto

A standard model of the American novel, f. o. b. Bucks County, Pa., tells the life story of Richard Grimm, manufacturer of doohickeys and miniature tycoon. To the development of Grimm Products, Inc., he devotes the passion of a lover, the imagination of a poet, the wisdom of a sage, and the strategy of a general staff. At last, quoting Browning on the last of life for which the first was made, he retires to enjoy the leisure he has earned and to do all the things he has always looked forward to. He finds that they are empty frauds, that nothing really gives him any satisfaction, and that the last of life lacks meaning. So he dies.

This is intended to be satire but it comes out tragedy. Also it is true enough often enough to be a disquieting comment on our culture.

Europeans have made a cliché of saying that nothing is so sad as the sight of Americans having a good time. They see us in special but revealing circumstances, making a job of what is supposed to be a pleasure trip, exercising our native resolution, doggedness, and grit. The qualities were indispensable to creating

Reprinted by permission of Mrs. Bernard DeVoto, owner of copyright, and by special permission from *Holiday* (Philadelphia: Curtis Publishing Company, March, 1956).

the standard of living that enables the American to make his tour, but they are a formidable handicap while he is making it. They professionalize his pleasure, put it on a sound business basis, make an investment of it. It has got to show a profit—pay off in self-improvement, culture, *savoir-faire,* small talk about restaurants and exchange rates. There must be no red ink representing lost time or wasted effort. Are we investing for safety of principal, for income, or long-term appreciation? Program this trip accordingly— budget it, it's costing plenty, isn't it?

One infers a kind of point system in which the Tower of London, say, counts fifteen, the changing of the Guard ten, and Stonehenge five. The tourist is playing against bogey. Or he is making a judicious determination of par. Given total length of tour, how many days shall the work-sheet allot to Paris? How many hours to Montmartre, the Invalides, Sainte-Chapelle, Fontainbleau? What are permissible alternatives? Should he play it with a number-four iron or should he sell out at the market and get into something else? And don't think the metaphor is mixed, for the tourist is likely to play golf so that it will show a return, too, he hopes.

There may be a vagrant thought that, given an afternoon in Paris, he would have a fine time simply sitting at a sidewalk table and watching the girls' skirts blow, or drifting down the Seine while getting mildly buzzed on bad beer and watching the light change. But if he is on a conducted tour he won't get a chance, for there are stern obligations to be met. If he is on his own he won't dare to, for he hasn't seen the Mona Lisa yet and so is still in the red. Besides, the idea of a free afternoon is a dangerous thought.

We begin to sniff certain anxieties. They affect the most popular of American vacations, the automobile tour. I eagerly admit that it is my most dependable source of pleasure and I indulge my liking for it whenever I can afford, and all too often when I can't. I am therefore often in contact with fellow Americans who are making desperately hard labor of what they undertook for fun. They exhibit the indomitability I have described and they tend to be strained, harried, and tired out. So they are fretful, querulous, bad-mannered, childish, and in a hell of a hurry. Having succeeded in getting a headlock on pleasure, they have gone on to choke it to death.

Watch the arrivals at any famous scenic point, say one of the overlooks on the edge of the Canyon of the Yellowstone River in Yellowstone Park. A car pulls into the parking space, a family piles out of it at the double, and everyone lines up along the edge.

They perform the ceremonial rite of littering the place with Kleenex (known as the national park flower) and chewing-gum wrappers. Pop takes a color shot that with luck will have both Mom and the Lower Falls in it, or runs off some footage of Junior leaning over the railing to see if he can spit into the river. Having thus made sure that he will have something to prove they have seen the Canyon, he puts the camera back in the case and looks at his watch. Got it in eight minutes, by God!—and they are off with a squeal of tires to Old Faithful. If they get there five minutes after an eruption they will be miserable, for here is an enforced wait of fifty-five minutes with absolutely nothing to do.

If they can cut it a little finer, understand, then maybe they can get away from Yellowstone a day sooner than the schedule calls for. If so, then maybe they will be able to restore the Columbia Gorge to their itinerary.

One has a vision of the family sedan streaking into Montana at seventy-five miles an hour, diving through the Bitterroots, hurtling past Flathead Lake, skidding into the distant prospect of Mount Hood. Oh, fleet chariot, conquering distance, annihilating space, by the miracle of technology laying a whole continent at the feet of a fortunate people, so that one more notch can be carved in the traveler's gunstock. Or with the favor of providence two notches, for if we get through the Gorge betimes and crowd ourselves, maybe we can go home by way of the Redwood Highway.

What has been accomplished at the Canyon of the Yellowstone, the Columbia Gorge, or the Redwood Highway? Even the tourist's claim that he has seen them is fraudulent, for he has only glanced at them. He is barely telling the truth when he claims that he has been there, for he was in process of getting somewhere else. He may have strung another celebrated name on his rosary but he has had no experience of the place. He has not even acquired a visual image of it except what will show behind Mom's blowing hair in the Kodachrome. (How often, looking at your friends' slides, have you found them unable to identify the subject?) Nothing has given significance to the countryside his winged chariot has taken him across. He has some statistics: miles, gallons, daily average, national parks, historic sites, and a table that analyzes costs per day. He will soon get over his physical fatigue, his spiritual fatigue may last longer; but don't the Americans play just as hard as they work?

This compulsion to keep on the move may provide welcome protections against the anxieties I have diagnosed. What would happen to this obsessed man if he were to linger on somewhere long enough to open the possibility of perceiving and understanding? Evidently something that scares him. As at Old Faithful there might be nothing to do, as in Paris a free afternoon might be dangerous. This is what Richard Grimm died of, and we may recall the gentleman who consulted a psychiatrist because he couldn't break the habit of talking to himself. After subjecting him to a careful study, the psychiatrist reported that he was normal enough and bade him go home and forget it—talking to himself was an innocent eccentricity that harmed no one. "But, Doctor," the appalled patient said, "I'm such a bore." What killed the manufacturer and what keeps the tourist trying to get a varsity letter for total mileage is emptiness and incapacity, inability to fill a pause in the day's occupations with anything worth doing, justified fear of leisure time. The radio and television industries are grounded on the assumption that the American people are so poor in personal resources that they must have entertainment available at the turn of a switch twenty-four hours a day.

Our history has a hold on us that we have found hard to break. For one thing we got rid of aristocracies, didn't we?; of the contemptible parasites known as the Leisure Class who devoted themselves to pleasurable and unprofitable occupations? For another, subduing the continent was touch and go; our ancestors had to work from dawn to dusk and the real reason for keeping the Sabbath holy was to get back enough strength to make an early start on Monday. It followed that work was virtue and idleness was sin. It followed further that profits and sound business procedure were an outward and visible sign of an inner and spiritual grace. Conversely, anyone not practicing virtue diligently, and visibly, was a set-up for Satan.

When a neighbor elects to go fishing on a fine summer day and you shoulder a scythe and trudge off to cut the grass in the high mowing, it is comforting to know that he is headed straight to hell and the town poor farm. He has a jug of corn along and you reflect that if any of it is left when he gets back he will spend the evening sharing it with other sinners singing bawdy songs, and chasing off with them to find some loose women. Taxing you to support him on the poor farm is unjust but your tax bill is a certificate of righteousness for all other righteous men to see.

The trouble with this puritanism of labor is not only how it stigmatizes the inoffensive grasshopper but how it affects the ant. When the hay is in there comes another fine morning and you go fishing. But this is yielding to sin, and a sense of guilt keeps you from enjoying the trout stream. Like the motorist you feel uneasy and like Richard Grimm you find the sport unsatisfying. How to handle this nagging self-accusation? That's easy: professionalize fishing. Methodize and systematize it and provide yourself with an efficient production line, including wind-gauge and stream-thermometer. Then fish the daylights out of the Miramichi, the Batten Kill, and any other you can add to your rosary—drive across the continent, so to speak, in four and a half days—and strive to show a credit balance in cups and record catches. Nobody can say that you have been unbusinesslike about it or accuse you of light-mindedness.

Like all suspicions, this one widens out to create guilt by association. It has taken the righteous a long time to lose the conviction that listening to a fiddle was flirting with temptation and playing one positively disreputable. To the upright man, the proprietor of a filling station or a vice-president in charge of sales, the intellectual has seemed a weakling and the artist a sissy if not indeed a pansy. Singers, painters, and sculptors, actors, dancers, writers—clearly they were not participating in the world's work. Worse, others took time off to derive pleasure from their activities. Worse still, these derelict ants actually paid the grasshoppers money that could otherwise have been banked, and thus in a highly illegitimate way seemed to be legitimatizing them. The solution of this dilemma was to consign the frivolities to the womenfolk, to one's wife and daughters—if there's going to be any subversion around this house, the whole world can see that I'm clean. . . . It may well be that President Eisenhower and Sir Winston Churchill, who like to paint pictures, have done more to liberate the hard-working American male to the satisfactions of the arts than all the museums in our history.

Ascribe some more of our incapacity for leisure to the educational system. It has increased our will to professionalize, to specialize, even our sports and games, leaving us incurious about any intellectual or sensuous experience that a specialist cannot put to use. In differing degrees, we are all born with the same senses and potentialities. When the child who has enjoyed finger painting in kindergarten grows up, nothing has happened to deny him the same satisfaction that the President gets at an easel—nothing except that the faculty was allowed to atrophy from disuse. In kindergarten he also enjoyed dancing and singing and learned to pick out tunes on a block flute, but as he went on to school and college, he learned that nothing was worth learning unless it advanced his specialization. We regard ourselves as the Romans of the modern world, unrivaled in the construction of sewage systems. We would be better off if we turned our backs on the Romans and became Renaissance Man. If we ran less to specialization and more to versatility. If fewer of us were pros and more of us were amateurs.

I have noted that Richard Grimm lavishes ingenuity, passion, wisdom, and imagination on the conduct of his firm. The trouble is that he has no other outlet for passion, imagination, and the rest; and no absorption, curiosity or skill that will turn back the boredom which begins to close in on him when he leaves the office. Oh, he plays golf, bridge, and poker—plays them as if a penalty clause were about to be invoked against him—and he has a number of shotguns that cost as much as chronometers. By at least that much he is more civilized than his father. The old man thought doohickeys every waking moment except when begetting children, and probably begot them because he anticipated a need for more sub-managers at the mill. But look at Richard's counterpart in England, where the mill's product is called a widget.

Don't think that the manufacturer of widgets it not a specialist: a grateful government has knighted him for helping to build up the dollar balance and Congress has had to raise the tariff to protect the domestic article. Sir Richard is a good gun, too, and has invented a system of bridge conventions that bears his name. But that is only a beginning. At his country house he has an astronomical observatory where he has done such sound work that the Royal Observatory calls on him whenever it sets up group measurements or counts. (He may have ground his own lenses or polished his own mirrors.) He is secretary of an association that studies Roman antiquities in Britain and he has published several papers announcing theories of his own. It is not surprising to learn that he has written a book on hunting (or photographing) wildebeest, but who would have expected a businessman to have written *Lichens of the Hebrides,* a standard work? Also he is "R.D.," a regular entrant in competitions in the *Spectator* and other weeklies that to an American are the last intelligible segment of British culture.

This combination of purely personal interests pursued to no end but themselves is fictitious but representative. Make it meteorology or oceanography instead of astronomy, moths or molluscs instead of lichens, liturgy or heraldry instead of Roman antiquities, and choose at random among the history of steam power, the study of Syracusan inscriptions, the culture of hyacinths, playing the virginals, and the writing of light verse or monographs on arithmetical primes. Among British businessmen, civil servants, or

M.P.'s you may at any moment encounter an accomplished amateur of any half dozen of these or similar pursuits. Such men do not throng American directors' rooms. And when I once went through the *Congressional Directory* to see how many writers of books there were on the Hill I found nothing to interest the Authors' League.

Or take the man who writes under the pseudonym John Crompton. He left Manchester University to be a trooper in the Rhodesian Mounted Police, and naturally became a hunter of big game. After six years in Africa he went to China for a business firm and traveled widely there for thirteen years as a kind of fiscal agent. During the war he was in the R.A.F., in charge of "flying control" in Iceland. I mention Mr. Crompton because of a sentence in the biographical material he sent to his publishers. He says that when he was in Rhodesia he became interested in insects and never tired of watching them—"so while my fellow troopers were complaining of the monotony of life I myself never had a dull moment." In his leisure time he became a naturalist, and since the war he has written three fascinating volumes of natural history in the tradition of Fabre but quite unlike him, *The Life of the Spider, Ways of the Ant,* and *The Hunting Wasp.* They are authoritative—and amateur. How likely a development is this in American terms? The man has been, so to speak, a state cop and a C.P.A.

Trooper Crompton found outside his barracks so much to be seen and learned that he "never had a dull moment." Compared with him, Richard Grimm and the compulsive motorist seem defective or stunted. They have cultivated no appetites except for food and drink, and probably have not cultivated them very much. Apart from making a living, they have found no zest. Except in relation to their jobs, their minds are color-blind, tone-deaf, and mute. Inborn faculties whose use would create gusto and delight have fossilized. They are unskilled, they are incurious, they have no passion for learning or understanding. No wonder they are bored—and bores. No wonder that leisure scares them.

They are going to be scared worse. Their industriousness—plus the richest natural resources in the world—have provided Americans with steadily increasing leisure. The seventy-two-hour work week has become the forty-hour week; the grasshopper who sings the summer away is now assured a two-week vacation as his natural right. Presently it will be a month, or two months, and the forty-hour week will shrink to some now unpredictable fraction. Having endowed everyone with leisure by substituting machines for muscles, we are now fashioning machines to operate the machines, which is what automation means. Tough luck if they intensify our neuroses and increase our unhappiness.

And yet.

There comes a moment when banging a tennis ball merely to discharge one's hostility ceases to be enough. There comes another moment when one requires more of a tennis match than winning to compensate for that impotent silence when the boss has bawled one out. At this point in any sport an amateur can be born, and amateurs seem to be appearing in ever-larger numbers as the popularity of spectator sports declines. The significance of the amateur is that his sport is to no end but itself. It is pursued solely for an enjoyment beyond which there is no end except excellence. However slight the excellence, however limited his capacity to refine or increase it, the amateur's reward is that he has done what he can, without usefulness or practical gain.

No doubt the spread of home workshops begins in the simple fact that we want things done in our homes that we cannot afford to have done for us. No doubt much of it continues as mere love of gadgetry. No doubt most of us who begin as duffers, and pretty comic ones, are destined to progress but slightly. But here, too, the pursuit of excellence is manifest. The industrialization that has made our standard of living possible has also come close to destroying the handicrafts. In the course of laying their own floors and repairing their own cornices people are rediscovering craftsmanship. You cannot train or inspire a machine to improve the quality of its product; you can only design an improved machine. But the human personality includes what Thorstein Veblen called the instinct of workmanship, the instinct to do a job as perfectly as it can be done, granted the properties of the material and the limitations of the workman. Many a home craftsman has found a fulfillment the very existence of which he had been ignorant. He has discovered the pleasure of skill that is exercised for its own sake—and a need to possess skill. He may never become an expert, but he will be as expert as it is in him to be. And he is more than he was, for he did not know that it was in him at all.

There is fulfillment in doing the thing well, but there is an even more basic one simply in doing it—in finding expression for a creativeness that hitherto has been frustrated. So the handicrafts neighbor with the arts. However badly a man may paint a landscape, play a fugue, or sing bass in a quartet, he has crossed the boundary into a domain of satisfaction and self-realization from which those who cannot do what he does are excluded. The richness he finds there is everyone's birthright, but most of us forfeit it without ever understanding that it exists.

Moreover, to be a little of an artist is to acquire new dimensions of personality. The amateur painter's experience opens all paintings to him as experience, which the rest of us know only by hearsay. And it creates for him a wholly new absorption in the colors, shapes, and designs of the physical world. Similarly radio, till television the most vacuous of human enterprises, has done our national life a service that may well outweigh all its disservices. In a single generation it has given the American people a wider experience of music, a more discriminating understanding of it, and therefore a vastly greater ability to enjoy it. A generation ago most Americans were musical illiterates; today many of them are initiates at the age of twelve and connoisseurs and sophisticates at sixteen.

Beyond such matters is an infinity of ways in which knowledge and understanding can be pursued to no end but the satisfaction of knowing and understanding. It is the dreariest commonplace that we all live far below our capacity, with most of our faculties used less fully than they might be and many of them never used at all.

It is equally a commonplace that there are many easily learnable alphabets which will enable us to read aspects of nature, mankind, society, and ourselves that have been like books printed in languages we do not understand. On this instrument called personality most of us play but few and simple tunes, yet like Hamlet's pipe it is capable of most eloquent music.

The facility with which we have converted our natural resources to wealth is the astonishment of the world, but there is little admiration of our success in enriching our personal resources. Now that an even greater freedom from labor seems assured, it would be a gross farce if we should find ourselves unable to use it. We must use our new freedom without thought of financial gain, bringing to our leisure pursuits curiosity and passion, and the amateur spirit we have so long distrusted. If we do we will be more civilized; but what counts is that we will be neither bores nor bored.

Author and Selection Notes

Born in Utah and educated at Harvard, Bernard DeVoto (1897-1955) taught and lectured at numerous institutions, including his alma mater.

His wide writing interests include history, literary criticism, and books on professional writing, representative titles being *The Year of Decision, Across the Wide Missouri, Mark Twain's America,* and *The World of Fiction.* His later career included editorial posts on *The Saturday Review of Literature* and *Harper's Magazine.*

Questions and Exercises

1. The author offers both a criticism of American life and an answer to the problem he raises. Using these points of view as your main headings, outline the essay.

2. What is the significance of the title? Do you know the source of the title?

3. Analyze and evaluate DeVoto's method of beginning his essay: tell what effect the first paragraph has on the reader.

4. Explain the following statement concerning the opening paragraph: "This is intended to be satire but it comes out tragedy."

5. Summarize the chief characteristics of the American tourist abroad and at home. Compare this picture with that of the tourist in Mark Twain's account in "France Is a Bewitching Garden."

6. Explain the following phrases within the context in which each appears: "kleenex (known as the national park flower)"; "one more notch can be carved in the traveler's gunstock"; "compulsive motorist"; "the instinct of workmanship"; "dimensions of personality"; "love of gadgetry."

7. In a paragraph or so show how the following description presents the basic premise of the first part of the essay: "emptiness and incapacity, inability to fill a pause in the day's occupation with anything worth doing, justified fear of leisure time."

8. Explain, quoting from the essay if you wish, the phrase "this puritanism of labor."

9. In what respects does Richard Grimm's counterpart in England differ from him?

10. "Having endowed everyone with leisure by substituting machines for muscles, we are now fashioning machines to operate the machines." What effect, in your estimation, will this have on Americans in the future?

11. What, according to the author, is "the amateur's reward"?

12. What principal values does the author see in the popular "do-it-yourself" fad?

13. Theme Topics: Do-It-Yourself Gadgetry; My Favorite Hobby; It Does Not Pay to Do It Yourself; Americans Don't Know How to Use Leisure; Making Good Use of Leisure; Handicraft Versus Machine-Made Products.

THE STOCKHOLM ADDRESS
William Faulkner

I feel that this award was not made to me as a man but to my work—a life's work in the agony and sweat of the human spirit, not for glory and least of all for profit, but to create out of the materials of the human spirit something which did not exist before. So this award is only mine in trust. It will not be difficult to find a dedication for the money part of it commensurate with the purpose and significance of its origin. But I would like to do the same with the acclaim too, by using this moment as a pinnacle from which I might be listened to by the young men and women already dedicated to the same anguish and travail, among whom is already that one who will some day stand here where I am standing.

Our tragedy today is a general and universal physical fear so long sustained by now that we can even bear it. There are no longer problems of the spirit. There is only the question: When will I be blown up? Because of this, the young man or woman writing today has forgotten the problems of the human heart in conflict with itself which alone can make good writing because only that is worth writing about, worth the agony and the sweat.

He must learn them again. He must teach himself that the basest of all things is to be afraid; and, teaching himself that, forget it forever, leaving no room in his workshop for anything but the old verities and truths of the heart, the old universal truths lacking which any story is ephemeral and doomed—love and honor and pity and pride and compassion and sacrifice. Until he does so, he labors under a curse. He writes not of love but of lust, of defeats in which nobody loses anything of value, of victories without hope and, worst of all, without pity or compassion. His griefs grieve on no universal bones, leaving no scars. He writes not of the heart but of the glands.

Until he relearns these things, he will write as though he stood alone and watched the end of man. I decline to accept the end of man. It is easy enough to say that man is immortal simply because he will endure; that when the last ding-dong of doom has clanged and faded from the last worthless rock hanging tideless in the last red and dying evening, that even then there will still be one more sound: that of his puny inexhaustible voice, still talking. I refuse to accept this. I believe that man will not merely endure: he will prevail. He is immortal, not because he alone among creatures has an inexhaustible voice but because he has a soul, a spirit capable of compassion and sacrifice and endurance. The poet's, the writer's, duty is to write about these things. It is his privilege to help man endure by lifting his heart, by reminding him of the courage and honor and hope and pride and compassion and pity and sacrifice which have been the glory of his past. The poet's voice need not merely be the record of man, it can be one of the props, the pillars to help him endure and prevail.

Author and Selection Notes

The speech of William Faulkner (1897-1962) accepting the Nobel Prize for Literature for 1950 represents an important reaffirmation of fundamental human values in a century of depressions, political unrest, and war both hot and cold. This same concern with the "verities and truths of the human heart" permeates his fictional studies of Southern life in his native Mississippi, including such volumes as *Go Down, Moses, The Sound and the Fury,* and *As I Lay Dying.*

Questions and Exercises

1. For what purpose does Faulkner wish to use the "acclaim" represented in his receiving of the Nobel Prize for Literature?

2. What, according to Faulkner, is the tragedy of contemporary civilization? What is his proposed remedy?

3. Is Faulkner in his address attempting to inform or persuade? Support your answer by specific references to general tone, word usage, imagery, sentence structure.

4. State in some detail the basis in the concluding paragraph of the address for Faulkner's optimism concerning man's fate in the universe.

5. In the closing paragraph Faulkner uses two words: "endure" and "prevail." How, basically, in Faulkner's usage do these words differ?

6. Look up the meanings of the following words: "love," "honor," "pity," "pride," "compassion," "sacrifice." Are these words more important for their connotative or for their literal meanings? Explain.

7. Explain the following phrases: "the problem of the human heart in conflict with itself"; "he writes not of love but of lust"; "His griefs grieve on no universal bones."

8. Compare this address with Walter Van Tilburg Clark's "The Portable Phonograph." In what ways are they alike in their attitudes toward humanity? Do they differ in any respects?

9. Theme Topics: Man's Destiny in the Universe; The Atomic Bomb—Beginning of the End? The Hope of Humanity; Which Way Civilization? The Indomitable Spirit of Man.